AMERICAN GOVERNMENT
POWER & PURPOSE

CORE FOURTEENTH EDITION

AMERICAN GOVERNMENT
POWER & PURPOSE

Theodore J. Lowi
Cornell University

Benjamin Ginsberg
The Johns Hopkins University

Kenneth A. Shepsle
Harvard University

Stephen Ansolabehere
Harvard University

W.W. NORTON
NEW YORK · LONDON

W. W. Norton & Company has been independent since its founding in 1923, when
William Warder Norton and Mary D. Herter Norton first published lectures delivered
at the People's Institute, the adult education division of New York City's Cooper
Union. The firm soon expanded its program beyond the Institute, publishing books
by celebrated academics from America and abroad. By mid-century, the two major
pillars of Norton's publishing program—trade books and college texts—were firmly
established. In the 1950s, the Norton family transferred control of the company to
its employees, and today—with a staff of four hundred and a comparable number of
trade, college, and professional titles published each year—W. W. Norton & Company
stands as the largest and oldest publishing house owned wholly by its employees.

Editor: Ann Shin
Associate Editor: Emily Stuart
Editorial Assistant: Shannon Jilek
Project Editor: David Bradley
Media Editor: Spencer Richardson-Jones
Associate Media Editor: Michael Jaoui
Media Editorial Assistant: Ariel Eaton
Marketing Manager: Erin Brown
Production Manager: Ben Reynolds
Book Designer: Kiss Me I'm Polish LLC, New York
Design Director: Rubina Yeh
Permissions Manager: Megan Schindel
Composition: GraphicWorld
Manufacturing: Quad/Graphics—Taunton MA

Permission to use copyrighted material is included in the credits section of this book,
which begins on page A55.

ISBN: 978-0-393-28376-1 (pbk.)

W. W. Norton & Company, Inc., 500 Fifth Avenue, New York, N.Y. 10110
www.wwnorton.com

W. W. Norton & Company Ltd., 15 Carlisle Street, London W1D 3BS

1 2 3 4 5 6 7 8 9 0

For Our Families

Angele, Anna, and Jason Lowi
Sandy, Cindy, and Alex Ginsberg
Rise, Nilsa, and Seth Shepsle
Laurie Gould and Rebecca and
    Julia Ansolabehere

Contents

2   Constructing a Government: The Founding and the Constitution   30

3   Federalism and the Separation of Powers   72

5 Civil Rights 144

PART 2 INSTITUTIONS

6 Congress: The First Branch 182

8   The Executive Branch: Bureaucracy in a Democracy   290

9 The Federal Courts   328

PART 3   DEMOCRATIC POLITICS

10   Public Opinion   376

Preface

This book was written for faculty and students who are looking for a little more than just "nuts and bolts" and who are drawn to an analytical perspective. No fact about American government is intrinsically difficult to grasp, and in an open society such as ours, facts abound. The philosophy of a free and open media in the United States makes information about the government that would be suppressed elsewhere readily available. The advent of the Internet and other new communication technologies has further expanded the opportunity to learn about our government. The ubiquity of information in our society is a great virtue. Common knowledge about the government gives our society a vocabulary that is widely shared among its citizens and enables us to communicate effectively with each other about politics. But it is also important to reach beyond that common vocabulary and develop a more sophisticated understanding of politics and government. The sheer quantity of facts in our society can be overwhelming. In a 24/7 news cycle it can be hard to pick out what stories are important and to stay focused on them. Today, moreover, Americans may choose among a variety of news sources, including broadcast, print, and various online formats all clamoring for attention. The single most important task of the teacher of political science is to confront popular ideas and information and to choose from among them the small number of really significant concepts that help us make better sense of the world. This book aims to help instructors and students accomplish this task.

The analytical framework of this book is oriented around five principles that we use to help make sense of politics:

1. All political behavior has a purpose.

2. Institutions structure politics.

3. All politics is collective action.

4. Political outcomes are the products of individual preferences and institutional procedures.

5. How we got here matters.

This Fourteenth Edition continues our endeavor to make *American Government: Power and Purpose* the most authoritative and contemporary introductory text on the market. The approach of the book has not changed. Those who have used this book in the past are familiar with the narrative it presents about American government and politics—the storyline of how the United States government has evolved, how it operates, and the characters involved in the unfolding development of our polity. This book also presents an analytical approach to understanding American politics based on the five principles outlined on the previous page. We are guided by the belief that students of government need an analytical framework for understanding political phenomena—a framework rooted in some of the most important insights the discipline of political science has to offer and that encourages students to draw out the general lessons about collective action and collective decision making.

The major changes in this Fourteenth Edition are intended to combine authoritative, concise coverage of the central topics in American politics with smart pedagogical features designed to get students thinking analytically about quantitative data and current issues. The most significant changes include:

- **More than 15 pages on the 2016 elections, including data figures**, walk students through what happened and why. This edition includes a section devoted to analyzing the 2016 elections in Chapter 11, as well as updated data, examples, and other information throughout the book.

- **New Policy Principle boxes** in every chapter each provide a mini casestudy on how individual preferences and institutional procedures led to a given policy outcome. These new sections make it easy to teach an analytical approach to policy throughout the course.

- **New Timeplot features** use quantitative data to illuminate long-term trends in American politics, such as shifts in party coalitions, the growth of the American electorate, and representation in Congress.

- **Five new Analyzing the Evidence units written by expert researchers** highlight the political science behind the information in the book, while the remaining units have been updated with new data and analysis. Each unit poses an important question from political science and presents evidence that can be used to analyze the question. The five new units are:

  "Constitutional Engineering: How Many Veto Gates?" in Chapter 2 Contributed by Steven L. Taylor, Troy University; and Matthew S. Shugart, University of California, Davis

"Americans' Attitudes Toward Church and State" in Chapter 4
Contributed by David E. Campbell, University of Notre Dame

"Why Congress Can't Make Ends Meet" in Chapter 6
Contributed by David M. Primo, University of Rochester

"Economic Influence on Presidential Elections" in Chapter 11
Contributed by Robert S. Erikson, Columbia University

"Where Do Americans Get News about Politics?" in Chapter 14
Contributed by Rasmus Kleis Nielsen, University of Oxford

For the Fourteenth Edition we have profited greatly from the guidance of many teachers who have used earlier editions and from the suggestions of numerous thoughtful reviewers. We thank them by name in the Acknowledgments. We recognize that there is no single best way to craft an introductory text, and we are grateful for the advice we have received.

Theodore J. Lowi
Benjamin Ginsberg
Kenneth A. Shepsle
Stephen Ansolabehere

Acknowledgments

Our students at Cornell, Johns Hopkins, and Harvard have already been identified as an essential factor in the writing of this book. They have been our most immediate intellectual community, a hospitable one indeed. Another part of our community, perhaps a large suburb, is the discipline of political science itself. Our debt to the scholarship of our colleagues is scientifically measurable, probably to several decimal points, in the footnotes of each chapter. Despite many complaints that the field is too scientific or not scientific enough, political science is alive and well in the United States. Political science has never been at a loss for relevant literature, and without that literature, our job would have been impossible.

We are pleased to acknowledge our debt to the many colleagues who had a direct and active role in criticism and preparation of the manuscript. The First Edition was read and reviewed by Gary Bryner, Brigham Young University; James F. Herndon, Virginia Polytechnic Institute and State University; James W. Riddlesperger, Jr., Texas Christian University; John Schwarz, University of Arizona; Toni-Michelle Travis, George Mason University; and Lois Vietri, University of Maryland. We also want to reiterate our thanks to the four colleagues who allowed us the privilege of testing a trial edition of our book by using it as the major text in their introductory American Government courses: Gary Bryner, Brigham Young University; Allan J. Cigler, University of Kansas; Burnet V. Davis, Albion College; and Erwin A. Jaffe, California State University–Stanislaus.

For second through seventh editions, we relied heavily on the thoughtful manuscript reviews we received from J. Roger Baker, Wittenburg University; Timothy Boylan, Winthrop University; David Canon, University of Wisconsin; Victoria Farrar-Myers, University of Texas at Arlington; John Gilmour, College of William and Mary; Mark Graber, University of Maryland; Russell Hanson, Indiana University; Robert Huckfeldt, University of California–Davis; Mark Joslyn, University of Kansas; William Keech, Carnegie Mellon

University; Donald Kettl, University of Wisconsin; Anne Khademian, University of Wisconsin; Beth Leech, Rutgers University; James Lennertz, Lafayette College; Allan McBride, Grambling State University; William McLauchlan, Purdue University; Grant Neeley, Texas Tech University; Charles Noble, California State University, Long Beach; and Joseph Peek, Jr., Georgia State University.

For the Eighth Edition, we benefited from the comments of Scott Ainsworth, University of Georgia; Thomas Brunell, Northern Arizona University; Daniel Carpenter, Harvard University; Brad Gomez, University of South Carolina; Paul Gronke, Reed College; Marc Hetherington, Bowdoin College; Gregory Huber, Yale University; Robert Lowry, Iowa State University; Anthony Nownes, University of Tennessee; Scott Adler, University of Colorado–Boulder; John Coleman, University of Wisconsin–Madison; Richard Conley, University of Florida; Keith Dougherty, University of Georgia; John Ferejohn, Stanford University; Douglas Harris, Loyola College; Brian Humes, University of Nebraska–Lincoln; Jeffrey Jenkins, Northwestern University; Paul Johnson, University of Kansas; Andrew Polsky, Hunter College–CUNY; Mark Richards, Grand Valley State University; Charles Shipan, University of Iowa; Craig Volden, Ohio State University; and Garry Young, George Washington University.

For the Ninth Edition, we were guided by the comments of John Baughman; Lawrence Baum, Ohio State University; Chris Cooper, Western Carolina State University; Charles Finochiaro, State University of New York–Buffalo; Lisa Garcia-Bellorda, University of California–Irvine; Sandy Gordon, New York University; Steven Greene, North Carolina State University; Richard Herrera, Arizona State University; Ben Highton, University of California–Davis; Trey Hood, University of Georgia; Andy Karch, University of Texas at Austin; Glen Krutz, University of Oklahoma; Paul Labedz, Valencia Community College; Brad Lockerbie, University of Georgia; Wendy Martinek, State University of New York–Binghamton; Nicholas Miller, University of Maryland Baltimore County; Russell Renka, Southeast Missouri State University; Debbie Schildkraut, Tufts University; Charles Shipan, University of Iowa; Chris Shortell, California State University, Northridge; John Sides, University of Texas at Austin; Sean Theriault, University of Texas at Austin; and Lynn Vavreck, University of California, Los Angeles.

For the Tenth Edition, we were grateful for the detailed comments of Christian Grose, Vanderbilt University; Kevin Esterling, University of California–Riverside; Martin Johnson, University of California–Riverside; Scott Meinke, Bucknell University; Jason MacDonald, Kent State University; Alan Wiseman, Ohio State University; Michelle Swers, Georgetown University; William Hixon, Lawrence University; Gregory Koger, University of Miami; and Renan Levine, University of Toronto.

For their advice on the Eleventh Edition, we thank Scott Ainsworth, University of Georgia; Bethany Albertson, University of Washington; Brian Arbour, John Jay College; James Battista, University at Buffalo, State University of New York; Lawrence Becker, California State University, Northridge; Damon Cann, Utah State University; Jamie Carson, University of Georgia;

Suzanne Chod, Pennsylvania State University; Michael Crespin, University of Georgia; Ryan Emenaker, College of the Redwoods; Kevin Esterling, University of California–Riverside; Brad Gomez, Florida State University; Sanford Gordon, New York University; Christian Grose, Vanderbilt University; James Hanley, Adrian College; Ryan Hurl, University of Toronto; Josh Kaplan, University of Notre Dame; Wendy Martinek, Binghamton University; Will Miller, Southeast Missouri State University; Evan Parker-Stephen, Texas A&M University; Melody Rose, Portland State University; Eric Schickler, University of California–Berkeley; John Sides, George Washington University; and Lynn Vavreck, University of California–Los Angeles.

For the Twelfth Edition we looked to comments from John M. Aughenbaugh, Virginia Commonwealth University; Christopher Banks, Kent State University; Michael Berkman, Pennsylvania State University; Cynthia Bowling, Auburn University; Matthew Cahn, California State University, Northridge; Damon Cann, Utah State University; Tom Cioppa, Brookdale Community College; David Damore, University of Nevada, Las Vegas; Kevin Esterling, University of California–Riverside; Jessica Feezell, University of California–Santa Barbara; Charle J. Finocchiaro, University of South Carolina; Rodd Freitag, University of Wisconsin, Eau Claire; Kevin Jefferies, Alvin Community College; Nancy Jimeno, California State University, Fullerton; Gregory Koger, University of Miami; David E. Lewis, Vanderbilt University; Allison M. Martens, University of Louisville; Thomas M. Martin, Eastern Kentucky University; Michael Andrew McLatchy, Clarendon College; Ken Mulligan, Southern Illinois University, Carbondale; Geoffrey D. Peterson, University of Wisconsin, Eau Claire; Jesse Richman, Old Dominion University; Mark C. Rom, Georgetown University; Laura Schneider, Grand Valley State University; Scot Schraufnagel, Northern Illinois University; Ronald P. Seyb, Skidmore College; Martin S. Sheffer, Tidewater Community College; Charles R. Shipan, University of Michigan; Howard A. Smith, Florida Gulf Coast University; Michele Swers, Georgetown University; Charles Tien, Hunter College; Elizabeth Trentanelli, Gulf Coast State College; and Kenneth C. Williams, Michigan State University.

For the Thirteenth Edition we are indebted to: Michael M. Binder, University of North Florida; Stephen Borrelli, The University of Alabama; Dan Cassino, Fairleigh Dickinson University; Jangsup Choi, Texas A&M University–Commerce; Martin Cohen, James Madison University; Jeff Colbert, Elon University; Richard S. Conley, University of Florida; Mark Croatti, American University; David Dulio, Oakland University; Andrew M. Essig, DeSales University; Kathleen Ferraiolo, James Madison University; Emily R. Gill, Bradley University; Brad T. Gomez, Florida State University; Paul N. Goren, University of Minnesota; Thomas Halper, Baruch College; Audrey A. Haynes, University of Georgia; Diane J. Heith, St. John's University; Ronald J. Hrebenar, The University of Utah; Ryan Hurl, University of Toronto Scarborough; Richard Jankowski, SUNY Fredonia; Kevin Jefferies, Alvin Community College; Timothy R. Johnson, University of Minnesota; Kenneth R. Mayer, University of Wisconsin–Madison; Mark McKenzie, Texas Tech University; Fiona Miller, University of Toronto Mississauga; Richard M.

Pious, Barnard College; Tim Reynolds, Alvin Community College; Martin Saiz, California State University, Northridge; Dante Scala, University of New Hampshire; Sean M. Theriault, University of Texas at Austin; J. Alejandro Tirado, Texas Tech University; Terri Towner, Oakland University; Nicholas Valentino, University of Michigan; Harold M. Waller, McGill University; and Jeffrey S. Worsham, West Virginia University.

We also thank the reviewers who advised us on this Fourteenth Edition: Michael E. Aleprete, Westminster College–Community College of Allegheny County; James Binney, Pennsylvania State University; William Blake, Indiana University–Purdue University, Indianapolis; Eric Boyer, Colby-Sawyer College; Chelsie L. M. Bright, Mills College; Scott Englund, University of California–Santa Barbara; Amanda Friesen, Indiana University–Purdue University, Indianapolis; Frank Fuller, Lincoln University; Baogang Guo, Dalton State College; Eric Hanson, State University of New York at Fredonia; Jennifer Haydel, Montgomery College; Tseggai Isaac, Missouri University of Science and Technology; Vicki Jeffries-Bilton, Portland State University; Nicole Kalaf-Hughes, Bowing Green State University; Ervin Kallfa, Hostos Community College of CUNY; Samantha Majic, John Jay College–City University of New York; William McLauchlan, Purdue University; Hong Min Park, University of Wisconsin–Milwaukee; John Patty, Washington University in Saint Louis; John W. Ray, Montana Tech of the University of Montana; Eric Sands, Berry College; and Kathleen Tipler, Wake Forest University.

An important contribution to recent editions was made by the authors of the Analyzing the Evidence units. We are grateful to the authors of the new Analyzing the Evidence units in the Fourteenth Edition, who are named in the Preface. In addition, Jenna Bednar, David E. Campbell, Jeremiah D. Castle, Patrick J. Egan, Sean Gailmard, John C. Green, Geoffrey C. Layman, Beth L. Leech, David Lewis, Andrew D. Martin, Kevin M. Quinn, and Dara Z. Strolovitch contributed to this feature in earlier editions, and much of their work is still reflected in this edition. We also thank Zachary Hodges, who provided valuable assistance in updating the data figures and tables throughout the book.

We would also like to thank our partners at W. W. Norton & Company, who have continued to apply their talents and energy to this textbook. The efforts of Ann Shin, Emily Stuart, Shannon Jilek, David Bradley, Ben Reynolds, Spencer-Richardson-Jones, Michael Jaoui, and Ariel Eaton kept the production of the Fourteenth Edition and its accompanying resources coherent and in focus. We also thank Roby Harrington and Steve Dunn, whose contributions to previous editions remain invaluable.

We are more than happy, however, to absolve all these contributors from any flaws, errors, and misjudgments that this book contains. We wish it could be free of all production errors, grammatical errors, misspellings, misquotes, missed citations, etc. From that standpoint, a book ought to try to be perfect. But substantively we have not tried to write a flawless book; we have not tried to write a book to please everyone. We have again tried to write an effective book, a book that cannot be taken lightly. Our goal was not to make every reader a political scientist. Our goal was to restore politics as a subject of vigorous and enjoyable discourse, releasing it from the bondage of the 30-second sound bite and the 30-page technical briefing. Every person can be knowledgeable because everything about politics is accessible. One does not have to be a philosopher to argue about the requisites of democracy, a lawyer to dispute constitutional interpretations, an economist to debate public policy. We will be very proud if our book contributes in a small way to the restoration of the ancient art of political controversy.

Theodore J. Lowi
Benjamin Ginsberg
Kenneth A. Shepsle
Stephen Ansolabehere

AMERICAN GOVERNMENT
POWER & PURPOSE

1

Five Principles of Politics

American government and politics are extraordinarily complex. The United States has many levels of government: federal, state, county, city, and town—to say nothing of a host of special and regional authorities. Each of these governments operates under its own rules and statutory authority and is related to the others in complex ways. In many nations, regional and local governments are appendages of the national government. This is not true in the United States, where state and local governments possess considerable independence and authority. Each level of government, moreover, consists of an array of departments, agencies, offices, and bureaus, each with its own policies, jurisdiction, and responsibilities and undertaking a variety of sometimes overlapping tasks. At times this complexity gets in the way of effective governance, as in the case of governmental response to emergencies. America's federal, state, and local public safety agencies seldom share information and frequently use incompatible communications equipment, so they often cannot even speak to one another. For example, on September 11, 2001, New York City's police and fire departments could not effectively coordinate their responses to the attack on the World Trade Center because their communications systems were not linked. While communication has improved in the last decade, many security and policy agencies, ranging from the Central Intelligence Agency (CIA) to the Department of Homeland Security (DHS), still possess separate computer operating systems and databases, which inhibits cooperation through sharing.

The complexity of America's government is no accident. Complexity was one element of the Founders' grand constitutional design. The framers of the Constitution hoped that an elaborate division of power among institutions and between the states and the federal government would allow competing interests access to arenas of decision making and a voice in public affairs—while preventing any single group or coalition from monopolizing power. One set of interests might be active in some states, other forces would be influential in the national legislature, and still others might prevail in the executive branch. The dispersion of power and opportunity would allow many groups to achieve at least some of their political goals. In this way, America's political tradition associates complexity with liberty and political opportunity.

But although institutionalization creates many avenues for political action, it also places a burden on citizens who wish to achieve something through political participation. They may be unable to discern where particular policies are actually made, who the decision makers are, and what forms of political participation are most effective. This is one of the paradoxes of political life: In a dictatorship, lines of political authority may be simple, but opportunities to influence the use of power are few; in the United States, political opportunities are plentiful, but how they should be used is far from obvious. Indeed, precisely because the United States' institutional and political arrangements are so complex, many Americans are mystified by government. As we see in Chapter 10, many Americans have difficulty making sense of even the basic features of the Constitution.

If the United States' government seems complex, its politics can be utterly bewildering. Like the nation's governmental structure, its political processes have numerous components. For most Americans, the focal point of politics is the electoral process. As we see in Chapter 11, tens of millions of Americans participate in national, state, and local elections, during which they hear thousands of candidates debate a perplexing array of issues. Candidates inundate the media with promises, charges, and countercharges while pundits and journalists, whom we also discuss in Chapters 10 and 14, add their own clamor to the din.

Politics, however, does not end on Election Day. Long after the voters have spoken, political struggles continue in Congress, the executive branch, and the courts; they embroil political parties, interest groups, and the mass media. In

CORE OF THE ANALYSIS

➡ Five principles of politics can help us think analytically about American government and make sense of the apparent chaos and complexity of the political world. These five principles are

➡ All political behavior has a purpose (rationality principle).

➡ Institutions structure politics (institution principle).

➡ All politics is collective action (collective action principle).

➡ Political outcomes are the products of individual preferences and institutional procedures (policy principle).

➡ How we got here matters (history principle).

some instances, the participants and their goals seem fairly obvious. For example, it is no secret that businesses and upper-income wage earners strongly support tax reduction, farmers support agricultural subsidies, and labor unions oppose increasing the eligibility age for Social Security. Each of these forces has created or joined organized groups to advance its cause. We examine some of these groups in Chapter 13.

In other instances, though, the participants and their goals are not so clear. Sometimes corporate groups hide behind environmental causes to surreptitiously promote their economic interests. Strong environmental requirements make it difficult for prospective competitors to enter their markets. Other times groups claiming to want to help the poor and downtrodden seek only to help themselves. And worse, many government policies are made behind closed doors, away from the light of publicity. Ordinary citizens can hardly be blamed for failing to understand bureaucratic rule making and other obscure techniques of government.

MAKING SENSE OF GOVERNMENT AND POLITICS

Can we find order in the apparent chaos of politics? Yes, and doing so is the purpose of this text. Finding order in the apparent chaos of politics is precisely what political scientists do. The discipline of political science, and especially the study of American politics, seeks to identify patterns in all the noise and maneuvering of everyday political life. This is motivated by two fundamental questions: What do we observe? And why?

The first question makes clear that political science is an *empirical* enterprise: it aims to identify facts and patterns that are true in the world around us. What strategies do candidates use to capture votes? How do legislators decide about how to vote on bills? What groups put pressure on the institutions of government? How do the media report politics? How have courts intervened in regulating political life? These and many other questions have prompted political scientists to observe and ascertain what is true about the political world, and we will take them up in detail in later chapters.

The second question—Why?—is the fundamental concern of science. We not only would like to know that something is true about the world. We also want to know why it is true, which requires us to create a theory of how the world works. And a theory is constructed from basic principles. The remainder of this chapter presents a set of such basic principles to help us navigate the apparent chaos of politics and make sense of what we observe. In this way we not only describe politics, we analyze it.

There is a third type of question that is *normative* rather than empirical or analytical. Normative questions focus on "should" issues—What should the responsibilities of citizenship consist of? How should judges judge and presidents lead? Political science grapples with all three types of questions. In this book we believe that answers to the empirical and analytical help us formulate answers to the normative.

One of the most important goals of this book is to help readers learn to analyze what they observe in American politics.[1] Analysis requires abstracting. For example, in political science, we are not much interested in an analysis that explains *only* why the Republicans gained congressional seats in the 2014 elections. Such explanations are the province of pundits, journalists, and other commentators. Rather, as political scientists, we seek a more general theory of voting choice that we can apply to many particular instances—not just the 2014 elections, but the 2016 elections as well.

In this chapter, we first discuss what we mean by *government* and *politics*. Then we introduce our five principles of politics. These principles are intentionally somewhat abstract, because we want them to apply to a wide range of circumstances. However, we provide concrete illustrations along the way, and in later chapters we apply the principles more extensively to specific features of politics and government in the United States. We conclude with a guide to analyzing evidence, something you will find useful as we examine empirical information throughout the rest of the book.

What Is Government?

Government is the term generally used to describe the formal political arrangements by which a land and its people are ruled. Government is composed of institutions and processes that rulers establish to strengthen and perpetuate their power or control over a land and its inhabitants. A government may be as simple as a tribal council that meets occasionally to advise the chief or as complex as our own vast establishment, with elaborate procedures, laws, governmental bodies, and bureaucracies. This more complex government is sometimes called the *state*, an abstract concept referring to the source of all public authority.

Forms of Government

Governments vary in institutional structure, size, and modes of operation. Two questions are key in determining how governments differ: Who governs? And, how much government control is permitted?

In some nations political authority is vested in a single individual—a king or dictator, for example. This state of affairs is called an **autocracy**. When a small group of landowners, military officers, or wealthy merchants controls most of the governing decisions, the government is an **oligarchy**. If more people participate and the populace has some influence over decision making, the government is tending toward **democracy**.

Governments also vary in terms of how they govern. In the United States and some other nations, governments are severely limited in *what* they are permitted

government

The institutions and procedures through which a land and its people are ruled

autocracy

A form of government in which a single individual rules

oligarchy

A form of government in which a small group of landowners, military officers, or wealthy merchants controls most of the governing decisions

democracy

A system of rule that permits citizens to play a significant part in the governmental process, usually through the selection of key public officials

---

1 For an entire book devoted to the issue of analysis, see Kenneth A. Shepsle, *Analyzing Politics: Rationality, Behavior, and Institutions,* 2nd ed. (New York: Norton, 2010).

constitutional government →

A system of rule—a constitution—that specifies formal and effective limits on the powers of the government

authoritarian government →

A system of rule in which the government recognizes no formal limits but may nevertheless be restrained by the power of other social institutions

totalitarian government →

A system of rule in which the government recognizes no formal limits on its power and seeks to absorb or eliminate other social institutions that might challenge it

politics →

Conflict, struggle, cooperation, and collaboration over the leadership, structure, and policies of government—over who governs and who has power

to control (they are restricted by substantive limits) as well as in *how* they exercise that control (they are restricted by procedural limits). These are called **constitutional** governments. In other nations, the law imposes few real limits on the government, but it is nevertheless kept in check by other political and social institutions that it cannot control but must come to terms with, such as autonomous territories or an organized church. Such governments are called **authoritarian**. In a third, very small group of nations, including the Soviet Union under Joseph Stalin, Nazi Germany, and present-day North Korea, governments not only are free of legal limits but also seek to eliminate organized social groupings that might challenge their authority. These governments attempt to dominate political, economic, and social life and, as a result, are called **totalitarian**.

Politics

The term *politics* broadly refers to conflicts over the character, membership, and policies of any organization to which people belong. As Harold Lasswell, a famous political scientist, once put it, politics is the struggle over "who gets what, when, how."[2] Although politics exists in any organization, in this book **politics** refers to conflicts over the leadership, structure, and policies of governments, that is, over who governs and who has power. But politics also involves collaboration and cooperation. The goal of politics, as we define it, is to have a say in the composition of the government's leadership, how the government is organized, or what its policies will be.

Politics takes many forms. Individuals may run for office, vote, join political parties and movements, contribute money to candidates, lobby public officials, participate in demonstrations, write letters, talk to their friends and neighbors, go to court, and engage in numerous other activities. Some forms of politics aim at gaining power, some at influencing those in power, and others at bringing new people to power and throwing the old leaders out. Those in power use myriad strategies to try to achieve their goals. Power, in short, is a central focus of politics, but not always for its own sake. Power is sought for purposes—to elevate some and remove others, to introduce new policies, and to preserve old ones.

FIVE PRINCIPLES OF POLITICS

Politics possesses an underlying logic that can be understood in terms of five simple principles:

1. All political behavior has a purpose.
2. Institutions structure politics.

2   Harold D. Lasswell, *Politics: Who Gets What, When, How* (1936; repr., New York: Meridian, 1958).

3. All politics is collective action.

4. Political outcomes are the products of individual preferences, institutional procedures, and collective action.

5. How we got here matters.

Some of these principles may seem obvious or abstract. They are useful, however, because they possess a distinct kernel of truth on the one hand, yet on the other hand are sufficiently general to help us understand politics in a variety of settings. Armed with these principles, we can perceive the order underlying the apparent chaos of political events and processes whenever and wherever they take place.

The Rationality Principle: All Political Behavior Has a Purpose

One compelling reason governments do what they do is that they respond to what people want. All people have goals, and their political behavior is guided by these goals. For many citizens, political behavior is as simple and familiar as reading news headlines on Twitter or discussing local political controversies with a neighbor over the back fence. Beyond these basic acts, political behavior broadens to include watching a political debate on television, arguing about politics with a co-worker, signing a petition, or attending a city council meeting. These are explicitly political activities that require some forethought. Political behavior requiring even more effort includes casting a vote in the November election (having first registered in a timely manner), contacting one's legislative representatives about a political issue, contributing time or money to a political campaign, or even running for local office.

Some of these acts require time, effort, financial resources, and resolve, whereas others place small, even insignificant, demands on a person. Nevertheless, all of them are done for specific reasons. They are not random; they are not entirely automatic or mechanical, even the smallest of them; they are purposeful. Sometimes they are engaged in for the sake of entertainment (reading the front page in the morning) or just to be sociable (chatting about politics with a neighbor, co-worker, or family member). At other times, they take on considerable personal importance explicitly because of their political content—because an individual cares about, and wants to influence, an issue, a candidate, a party, or a cause. We will treat all of this political activity as purposeful, as having a goal. Indeed, our attempts to identify the goals of various political activities will help us understand them better.

We've just noted that many of the political activities of ordinary citizens are hard to distinguish from conventional everyday behavior—reading newspapers, watching television news, discussing politics, and so on. For the professional politician, on the other hand—the legislator, executive, judge, party leader, bureau chief, or agency head—nearly every act is explicitly political. The legislator's decision to introduce a particular piece of legislation, give a speech in the legislative chamber, move an amendment to a pending bill, vote for or against that bill, or accept a contribution from a particular group requires her careful attention. There are pitfalls and dangers, and the slightest miscalculation can have huge consequences. Introduce a bill that appears to be too pro-labor in the eyes of your constituents, for example, and before you know it you're charged with being in bed with the unions during the next election campaign. Give a speech against job quotas for minorities, and you risk alienating the minority communities in your state or district. Accept campaign contributions from industries known to pollute, and environmentalists think you are no friend of the earth. Because nearly every move is fraught with risks, legislators make their choices with forethought and calculation. Their actions are, in a word, **instrumental**. Individuals think through the benefits and the costs of a decision, speculate about future effects, and weigh the risks of their decision. Making decisions is all about weighing the probabilities of various events and determining the personal value of the potential outcomes.

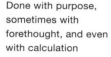

instrumental

Done with purpose, sometimes with forethought, and even with calculation

As examples of instrumental behavior, consider elected officials. Most politicians want to keep their positions or move up to more important positions. They like their jobs for a variety of reasons—salary, privileges, prestige, stepping-stones, and opportunities for accomplishment, to name just a few. So we can understand why politicians do what they do by thinking of their behavior as instrumental, with a goal of keeping their jobs. This is quite straightforward in regard to elected politicians, who often see no further than the next election and think mainly about how to prevail and who can help them win. "Retail" politics involves dealing directly with constituents, as when a politician helps an individual navigate a federal agency or find a misplaced Social Security check. "Wholesale" politics involves appealing to collections of constituents, as when a legislator introduces a bill that would benefit a group that is active in his state or district (say, veterans), secures money for a public building in his hometown, or intervenes in an official proceeding on behalf of an interest group that will, in turn, contribute to the next campaign. Politicians may do these things for ideological reasons. But we institute elections and provide incentives for politicians to help constituents as a means of winning elections, just in case their generosity of spirit and personal ideology are insufficient. Elections and electoral politics are thus premised on instrumental behavior by politicians.

Political scientists explain the behavior of elected politicians by treating the "electoral connection" as the principal motivation.[3] Elected politicians, in this view, base their behavior on the goal of maximizing votes at the next election or maximizing their probability of winning. Of course, politicians seek other things as well—public policy objectives, power within their institution, and ambition for higher office.[4] Primary emphasis on the electoral motivation

---

3 The classic statement of this premise is David R. Mayhew, *Congress: The Electoral Connection* (New Haven, CT: Yale University Press, 1974). Although four decades old, this book remains a source of insight and wisdom.

4 The classic statement of this additional premise is Richard F. Fenno, *Congressmen in Committees* (Boston: Little, Brown, 1973), another book that remains relevant decades after its publication.

is premised on the fact that reelection is a necessary condition for pursuing any of the other objectives.[5]

But what about political actors who are not elected? What do they want? Consider a few examples:

- Agency heads and bureau chiefs, motivated by policy preferences and power, seek to maximize their budgets.

- Legislative committee chairs (who are elected to Congress but appointed to committees) are "turf minded," intent on maximizing their committee's policy jurisdiction and thus its power.

- Voters cast ballots to influence the policies of government, with an eye to their own personal welfare as well as their conception of "what's best for the country."

- Justices, serving lifetime terms, maximize the prospects for their view of constitutional interpretation to prevail.[6]

In each instance, we can postulate motivations that fit the political context. These goals often have a strong element of self-interest, but they may also incorporate "enlightened self-interest," including the welfare of others such as their families, the entire society, or even all of humanity.

The Institution Principle: Institutions Structure Politics

In pursuing political goals, people—especially elected leaders and other government officials—confront certain recurring problems, and they develop standard ways of addressing them. Routinized, structured relations for pursuing goals and addressing recurring problems are what we call institutions. **Institutions** are the rules and procedures that provide incentives for political behavior, thereby shaping politics. Institutions may discourage conflict, encourage coordination, enable bargaining, and thus facilitate decision making, cooperation, and collective action.

Institutions are part script and part scorecard. As scripts, they choreograph political activity. As scorecards, they list the players, their positions, what they

 institutions

The rules and procedures that provide incentives for political behavior, thereby shaping politics

---

5   As Vince Lombardi, the famous coach of the Green Bay Packers football team, once said, "Winning isn't everything; it's the only thing."

6   Most political actors are motivated by self-interest. The motivations or purposes of judges and justices have proved more difficult to ascertain in that they typically enjoy lifetime appointments (and thus are not looking ahead to the next election or occasion for "contract renewal"). For an interesting discussion of judicial motivations by an eminent law professor and incumbent judge, see Richard Posner, "What Do Judges Maximize? (The Same Thing Everybody Else Does)," *Supreme Court Economic Review* 3 (1993): 1–41.

want, what they know when they take actions, what they can do, and when they can do it. As a consequence, institutions *matter*. The U.S. Senate, for example, was one kind of legislative body when its members were selected via election by state legislature; it became quite a different kind of legislative body when its members were popularly elected by a state's voters. To take another example of how institutions matter, affect the power of an incumbent mayor, governor, or president: A prohibition against running for reelection weakens an executive by removing the leverage she might have had if there were the possibility of securing another term in office.

Although the Constitution sets the broad framework for American political institutions, much adaptation takes place as the institutions themselves are bent to the various purposes of strategic political actors. Our focus here will be on the authority that institutions provide politicians for the pursuit of public policies. The discussion covers four broad subjects: jurisdiction, agenda and veto power, decisiveness, and delegation.

Jurisdiction. A critical feature of an institution is the domain over which its members have the authority to make decisions. Political institutions are full of specialized **jurisdictions** over which individuals or subsets of members have authority. One feature of the U.S. Congress, for example, is its "standing committees," whose jurisdictions are carefully defined by law. Most members of Congress become specialists in all aspects of their committees' jurisdiction—and they often seek committee assignments based on the subjects in which they want to specialize. Committee members are granted specific authority within their jurisdiction to set the agenda of the larger parent chamber. For example, proposed legislation related to the military must pass through the Armed Services Committee before the entire House or Senate can vote on it. Thus the politics of the U.S. legislative institution is affected by the way its jurisdiction-specific committees are structured. Similarly, a bureau or agency is established by law, and its jurisdiction—its scope of authority—is firmly fixed. For example, the Food and Drug Administration (FDA) possesses authority to regulate the marketing of pharmaceuticals but is not permitted to regulate products falling outside its jurisdiction.

jurisdiction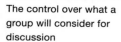

The domain over which an institution or member of an institution has authority

Agenda Power and Veto Power. **Agenda power** describes who determines what will be taken up for consideration in an institution. Those who exercise some form of agenda power are said to engage in gatekeeping. They determine which alternatives may pass through the gate onto the institution's agenda and which alternatives will have the gate slammed in their face. Gatekeeping, in other words, consists of the power to make proposals and the power to block proposals from being made. The ability to keep something off an institution's agenda should not be confused with **veto power**, which is the ability to defeat something even if it does become part of the agenda. In the legislative process, for example, the president has no general gatekeeping authority—he has no agenda power and thus cannot force the legislature to take up a proposal—but does have (limited) veto power. Congress, in contrast, controls its own agenda; its members can place matters on the legislative agenda. Congress

agenda power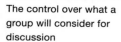

The control over what a group will consider for discussion

veto power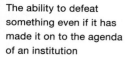

The ability to defeat something even if it has made it on to the agenda of an institution

cannot be prevented from passing a measure, but a presidential veto can prevent a measure from becoming the law of the land. Thus, when it comes to legislation, agenda power is vested in the legislature. Veto power is possessed both by the legislature and the president (the assent of each is required for a bill to become a law). We examine these processes in more detail in Chapters 6 and 7.

Decisiveness. Another crucial feature of an institution is its rules for making decisions. Indeed, laying out the rules for decision making often requires a raft of conditions and qualifications. The more an organization values participation by the broadest range of members, the more it needs those rules: the requirement of participation must be balanced with the need to bring activity to a close so that a decision can be made. This is why it is possible on the floor of a legislature to "move" the previous question, a motion to close the debate and move immediately to a vote.[7] In some legislatures, though, inaction seems to take precedence over action. In the U.S. House of Representatives, for example, a motion to adjourn (and thus not vote on a measure) takes precedence over a motion to move the previous question. In the U.S. Senate, to take another example, a supermajority (60 votes) is required to close debate and move to a vote. **Decisiveness rules** thus specify when votes may be taken, the sequence in which votes may occur, and—most important—how many individuals supporting a motion are sufficient for it to pass.

 decisiveness rules

A specification of when a vote may be taken, the sequence in which votes on amendments occur, and how many supporters determine whether a motion passes or fails

Delegation. A final aspect of institutional authority concerns delegation. Representative democracy is the quintessential instance of **delegation**. Citizens, through voting, delegate the authority to make decisions on their behalf to representatives—chiefly legislators and executives—rather than exercising political authority directly. We can think of our political representatives as our *agents*, just as we may think of professionals and craftspeople (doctors, accountants, plumbers, and so on) as agents whom we hire to act on our behalf. Why would those with authority, whom we will call *principals*, delegate some of their authority to agents? This has to do with decentralization and the division and specialization of labor. The answer is that both principals and agents benefit from it. Principals benefit because they are able to off-load to specialists tasks that they themselves are less capable of performing. Ordinary citizens, for example, are not as versed in the tasks of governance as are professional politicians. Thus by delegating, citizens do not have to be specialists and can focus on other things. This is the rationale for representative democracy. Agents benefit as well, since delegation means there is a demand for their services, which enables them to exercise authority and receive compensation for their efforts.

 delegation

The transmission of authority to some other official or body for the latter's use (though often with the right of review and revision)

Examples of principals and agents abound in politics. Elected officials are agents for citizen-principals. Leaders are agents for their followers. Government bureaus—called *agencies* after all—serve as agents for elected principals in the

---

7   For a general discussion of motions to close debate and get on with the decision, see Henry M. Robert, *Robert's Rules of Order* (1876), items III. 21 and VI. 38. *Robert's Rules* has achieved icon status and now exists in an enormous variety of forms.

executive and legislative branches.[8] Law clerks are agents for the judges who employ them. Lobbyists are agents of special interests. In short, the political world is replete with links between principals and agents.

The relationship between a principal and agent allows the former to delegate to the latter, with gains for both. But there is a dark side to this **principal-agent relationship**. As the eighteenth-century economist Adam Smith noted in *The Wealth of Nations* (1776), economic agents are not motivated by the welfare of their customers to grow vegetables, make shoes, or weave cloth; rather, they do those things out of their own self-interest. Thus a principal must take care when delegating to agents that those agents are properly motivated to serve the principal's interests, either by sharing those interests or by deriving something of value for acting to advance them. The principal will need instruments by which to monitor what her agent is doing and then reward or punish the agent accordingly. Nevertheless, a principal will not eliminate entirely the agent's prospective deviations from her interests. The reason is **transaction costs**. The effort necessary to negotiate and then police every aspect of a principal-agent relationship becomes, at some point, more costly than it is worth. In sum, the upside of delegation consists of the assignment of activities to precisely those agents who possess a comparative advantage in performing them. The downside is the prospective misalignment of the agents' goals with the principals' goals, and thus the possibility of agents marching to the beat of their own drummers. Delegation is a double-edged sword.

Characterizing institutions in terms of jurisdiction, agenda power, veto power, decisiveness, and delegation covers an immense amount of ground. Our purpose here has been to introduce the many ways collectivities arrange their business and routinize it, thereby enabling cooperation and facilitating political bargaining and decision making. A second purpose has been to highlight the potential diversity in institutional arrangements—there are so many ways to do things collectively. This diversity underscores the intelligence of the framers of the U.S. Constitution in the institutional choices they made more than two centuries ago. Finally, we want to make clear that institutions not only make rules for governing but also present strategic opportunities for various political interests, depending on how the institutions are designed. As George Washington Plunkitt, the savvy political boss of Tammany Hall, said of the institutional situations in which he found himself, "I seen my opportunities, and I took 'em."[9]

The Collective Action Principle: All Politics Is Collective Action

Political action is collective: it involves building, combining, mixing, and amalgamating people's individual goals. This sometimes occurs in highly institutionalized settings—a committee, legislature, or bureaucracy, for example.

---

8 Thus elected officials are simultaneously agents of their constituents and principals for bureaucrats to whom they delegate authority to implement policy.

9 In the nineteenth century and well into the twentieth, Tammany Hall was the club that ran New York City's Democratic Party like a machine.

---

principal-agent relationship

The relationship between someone with authority (the principal) and someone to whom he or she delegates the authority (the agent). This relationship may be affected by the fact that each party is motivated by self-interest, yet their interests may not align

transaction costs

The cost of clarifying each aspect of a principal-agent relationship and monitoring it to make sure arrangements are complied with

However, it also occurs in less institutionalized settings—a campaign rally, a get-out-the-vote drive, or a civil rights march. Moreover, collective action can be difficult to orchestrate because the individuals involved often have different goals and preferences. The result is mixed motives for cooperation. Conflict is inevitable; the question is how it can be resolved. The most typical means of resolving collective dilemmas is bargaining among individuals. But when the number of parties involved is too large for face-to-face bargaining, incentives must be provided to get everyone to act collectively.

Informal Bargaining. Political bargaining may be highly formal or entirely informal. We engage in informal bargaining often in our everyday lives. One of this book's authors, for example, has a neighbor with whom he shares a hedge on their property line. First one takes responsibility for trimming the hedge and then the other, alternating from year to year. This arrangement (or bargain) is merely an understanding, not a legally binding agreement, and it was reached amicably and without much fuss or fanfare after a brief conversation. No organized effort—such as hiring lawyers, drafting an agreement, and having it signed, witnessed, notarized, filed at the county courthouse, and so on—was required.

Bargaining in politics can be similarly informal. Whether called horse trading, back-scratching, logrolling, or wheeling and dealing, it has the same flavor as the casual negotiation between neighbors. Deals will be struck depending on the participants' preferences and beliefs. If preferences are incompatible or beliefs inconsistent with one another, then a deal simply may not be possible. If preferences and beliefs are not too far out of line, then there will be a range of possible bargaining outcomes, some advantaging one party, others advantaging other parties. In short, there will be room for a compromise.

In fact, much of politics *is* informal, unstructured bargaining. First, many disputes subjected to bargaining are of sufficiently low impact that establishing formal machinery for dealing with them is not worth the effort. Rules of thumb often develop as a benchmark—such as "split the difference" or "take turns." Second, repetition can contribute to successful cooperation. If a small group engages in bargaining today over one matter and tomorrow over another— as neighbors bargain over draining a swampy meadow one day, fixing a fence another, and trimming a hedge on yet another—then patterns develop. If one party constantly tries to extract maximal advantage, then the others will cease doing business with him or her. If, however, each party "gives a little to get a little," then a pattern of cooperation develops. It is the repetition of similar, mixed-motive occasions that allows this pattern to emerge without formal trappings. Many political circumstances are either amenable to informal rules or are repeated often enough to allow cooperative patterns to emerge.[10]

---

10 For a wonderful description of how ranchers in Shasta County, California, organized their social lives and collective interactions in just this fashion, see Robert C. Ellickson, *Order without Law: How Neighbors Settle Disputes* (Cambridge: Harvard University Press, 1991).

Formal Bargaining. Other bargaining situations are governed by rules. The rules describe such things as who gets to make the first offer, how long the other parties have to consider it, whether other parties can make counteroffers, the method by which they convey assent or rejection, what happens when all (or some decisive subset) of the others accept or reject it, and what happens next if the proposal is rejected. It may be hard to imagine two neighbors deciding how to trim their common hedge under procedures as explicit as these. It makes more sense, however, to imagine a bargaining session over wages and working conditions between labor and management at a large manufacturing plant proceeding in just this manner. The distinction suggests that some parties are more suited to formal proceedings, whereas others get on well enough without them. The same may be said about situations. A husband and wife are likely to divide household chores by informal bargaining, but this same couple would employ a formal procedure if they were dividing household assets in a divorce settlement.

Formal bargaining is often associated with events in official institutions—legislatures, courts, party conventions, administrative and regulatory agencies. In these settings, situations involving mixed motives arise repeatedly. Year in and year out, legislatures pass statutes, approve executive budgets, and oversee the administrative branch of government. Courts administer justice, determine guilt or innocence, resolve differences between disputants, and render interpretive opinions. Party conventions nominate candidates and approve their campaign platforms. Administrative and regulatory agencies implement policy and make rulings about its applicability. All of these are mixed-motive circumstances in which different parties have different goals; thus while gains from cooperation are possible, bargaining failures are also a definite possibility. In general the formal bargaining that takes place through institutions is governed by rules that regularize proceedings both to maximize the prospects of reaching agreement and to guarantee that procedural wheels are already in place each time a similar bargaining problem arises. This is our first application of the institution principle: institutions facilitate (but do not always succeed in producing) collective action.

Collective Dilemmas and Bargaining Failures. Even when gains are possible from collective action—when people share some common objective, for example—it still may not be feasible to arrive at a satisfactory conclusion. Consider two farmers interested in mending a fence that separates their properties. Suppose that Farmer Jones and Farmer Smith each value the mended fence at some positive level, V. Suppose that the total cost (in terms of time or effort) to do this chore is c, a big enough cost to make the job not worth the effort if a farmer had to do it all by himself. For example, if each farmer values the mended fence at $700, but the cost of one of them to repair it on his own is $1,000, the net benefit to one farmer repairing it alone ($700 − $1,000) is less than zero—and thus not an attractive option. If they shared the cost equally, though, their net benefit would each be $V − c/2$, in our example, $700 − $500—a positive net benefit of $200 to both. If one of the farmers, however, could off-load the entire project on his neighbor, then he would not have to bear any of the cost and would still enjoy the mended fence valued by him at V ($700). The situation is displayed in Figure 1.1. Each row gives the options available to Jones

Figure 1.1
A COLLECTIVE DILEMMA

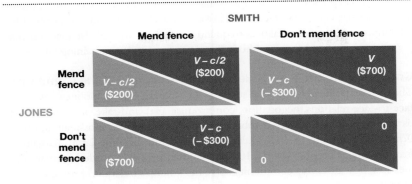

SMITH

		Mend fence	Don't mend fence
JONES	**Mend fence**	$V - c/2$ ($200) / $V - c/2$ ($200)	$V - c$ (−$300) / V ($700)
	Don't mend fence	V ($700) / $V - c$ (−$300)	0 / 0

and each column the options available to Smith. The lower-left entry in each cell is the payoff to Jones if he selects the row option and Smith selects the column option; the upper-right entry in each cell is Smith's payoff. Thus if both choose to mend the fence (the upper-left cell), then they each enjoy a (positive) net benefit of $V - c/2$. If, however, Jones takes on the job but Smith does not—this is the upper-right cell of the figure—then Jones pays the full price and receives $V - c$ (which is negative) and Smith gets the full value, V. The other two cells are filled in according to this logic.

Consider now how Jones might think about this problem. On the one hand, if Smith chooses to mend the fence (left column in the figure), then Jones gets $V - c/2$ if he does too; but he does even better, V, if he lets Smith do the whole job. On the other hand, if Smith chooses not to mend the fence (right column in the figure), then Jones gets $V - c$ if he goes ahead and does the job himself (this is negative) but gets zero if he too does not take up the task. Putting these together, Jones realizes that *no matter what Smith does, Jones is better off not mending the fence.* Following the same logic, Smith will arrive at the same conclusion. So each chooses "don't mend fence," and each gets a payoff of zero, even though both would have been better off if both had chosen "mend the fence."

This is a famous dilemma in social science.[11] It is a dilemma because the two individuals share a common goal—mending the fence—but each person's individual rationality causes both of them to do worse than they needed to. Had they only "suspended" their rationality and contributed to the common objective, then each would have been better served than when both are behaving in a fully rational manner. Even if the two farmers tried to overcome this dilemma, the dilemma persists, as each has a rational temptation to defect from a bargain

---

11 In another context, it is known as the prisoner's dilemma. We encounter it again in Chapter 13 when we discuss interest groups.

in which both agree to mend the fence. Moreover, each is nervous that the other will defect, given the incentives of the situation, and so feels compelled to defect himself.

The broad point of this example is that bargaining, even with common values and objectives, is no guarantee that a positive outcome will occur. We encounter dilemmas and bargaining failures frequently in politics. We will also discover that people have invented some methods that partially mitigate bargaining failures.

Collective Action, Free Riders, Public Goods, and the Commons.

The idea of political bargaining suggests an intimate kind of politics, involving face-to-face relations, negotiation, compromise, give-and-take, and so on. Such bargaining results from the combination of mixed motives and small numbers. When the numbers of individuals or other actors become large, bargaining may no longer be practical. If 100 people own property bordering a swampy meadow, how does this community solve the swamp's mosquito problem? How does the community secure the benefits that arise from cooperation? In short, what happens if a simple face-to-face interaction, possibly amenable to bargaining, now requires coordination among a large number of people?

In the swamp meadow example, everyone shares some common value—eliminating the mosquito habitat—but they may disagree on other matters. Some may want to use pesticides; others may be concerned about the environmental impact. And there are bound to be disagreements over how to pay for the project. A collective action problem arises, as in this example, when there is something to be gained if the group can cooperate and assure one another that no one will get away with bearing less than her fair share of the effort. Face-to-face bargaining, however, is made impractical by sheer numbers. The issue, then, is how to accomplish some common objective among a large number of interested parties.

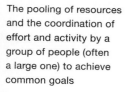

collective action

The pooling of resources and the coordination of effort and activity by a group of people (often a large one) to achieve common goals

Groups of individuals intent on **collective action** ordinarily establish decision-making procedures—relatively formal arrangements by which to resolve differences, coordinate the group to pursue a course of action, and sanction slackers. Workers in a manufacturing plant may attempt to form a union; like-minded citizens may organize a political party. Most groups will also require a leadership structure, which is necessary to deal with a phenomenon known as **free riding**. Imagine that each landowner bordering a swamp wants the area cleared of mosquitoes. If one or a few owners were to clear the swamp alone, their actions would benefit all the other owners as well. The other owners would be free riders, enjoying the benefit of the efforts of a few without contributing themselves. (The same issue faced farmers Smith and Jones in the fence-mending problem described earlier.) It is this prospect of free riding that risks undermining collective action. A leadership structure will have to be in place to enforce punishments to discourage individuals from reneging on the individual contributions required to enable the group to pursue its common goals.

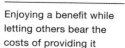

free riding

Enjoying a benefit while letting others bear the costs of providing it

Another way to think about this is to describe a commonly shared goal—say, the mosquito-free meadow—as a public good. A **public good** is a benefit that others cannot be denied from enjoying, once it has been provided. Once the meadow is mosquito free, it will constitute a benefit to *all* the members of

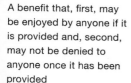

public good

A benefit that, first, may be enjoyed by anyone if it is provided and, second, may not be denied to anyone once it has been provided the group, even those who have not contributed to its provision. More generally, a public good is one that can be "consumed" by individuals without using it up and for which there are no easy means to exclude individuals. A classic example is a lighthouse. Once erected, it aids all ships, and there is no simple way to charge a ship for its use. Likewise, national defense protects taxpayers and tax avoiders alike. Another example is clean air. Once enough people restrict their polluting, the cleansed air may be enjoyed even by those who have not restricted their polluting. Because public goods have these properties, it is easy for some members of a group to free ride on others' efforts. And as a result, it may be difficult to get anyone to provide it in the first place. Collective action is required, and this often requires leaders (or governments) with the capacity to induce all to contribute to its provision.

One of the most notorious collective action problems involves too much of a good thing. Known as the **tragedy of the commons**, this type of problem reveals how unbridled self-interest can have damaging collective consequences. A political party's reputation, for example, can be seen as something that benefits all politicians affiliated with the party. This collective reputation is not irreparably harmed if one legislator in the party pushes her advantage by securing a minor amendment helpful to a special interest in her district. But if lots of party members do it, the party comes to be known as the champion of special interests, and its reputation is tarnished. A pool of resources is not much depleted if someone takes a little of it, but it is if lots of people take from it—a forest is lost a pine tree at a time; the atmosphere is polluted a particle at a time. The party's reputation, the forest, and the atmosphere are all *commons*.[12] The problem to which they are vulnerable is *overgrazing*—a common resource that is irreparably depleted by individual actions.[13]

To summarize, individuals try to accomplish goals not only as individuals but also as members of larger collectivities (families, associations, political parties) and even larger categories (economic classes, ethnic groups, nationalities). The rationality principle covers individual initiative. The collective action principle describes the paradoxes encountered, the obstacles to be overcome, and the incentives necessary for individuals to coordinate their energies, accomplish collective purposes, and secure the dividends of cooperation. Much of politics is about doing this or failing to do this. The institution principle takes this argument to its logical conclusion, focusing on collective activities that are regularized because they are both important and frequently occurring. Institutions do the public's business while relieving communities of having to reinvent collective action each time it is required. Thus we have a rationale for government.

 tragedy of the commons

The idea that a common-access facility, owned by no one because it is available to everyone, will be overused

---

12 The original meaning is of a pasture on which cows graze to the point of damaging the land. A most insightful discussion of "commons problems," of which these are examples, is Elinor Ostrom, *Governing the Commons: The Evolution of Institutions for Collective Action* (New York: Cambridge University Press, 1990).

13 The classic statement is Garrett Hardin, "The Tragedy of the Commons," *Science* 162 (1968): 1243–48.

The Policy Principle: Political Outcomes Are the Products of Individual Preferences and Institutional Procedures

Ultimately, we are interested in the results of politics—the collective decisions that emerge from the political process. A Nebraska farmer, for example, cares about how public laws affect his welfare and that of his family, friends, and neighbors. He cares about how export policies affect the prices his crops and livestock products earn in international markets and how monetary policy influences the cost of fuel, feed, seed, and fertilizer; about the funding of research and development efforts in agriculture and their effect on the quality of the scientific information he obtains; and about the affordability of the state university where he hopes to educate his children. He also cares, eventually, about inheritance laws and their effect on his ability to pass his farm on to his kids without the government taking much of it in estate taxes. As students of American politics, we need to consider the link between individual goals, institutional arrangements, collective action, and policy outcomes. How do all of these leave their marks on policy? What biases and tendencies manifest themselves in public decisions?

The linchpin is the motivations of political actors. As we saw in our discussion of the rationality principle, their ambitions—ideological, personal, electoral, and institutional—provide incentives to craft policies in particular ways. In fact, most policies make sense only as reflections of individual politicians' interests, goals, and beliefs. Examples include

Personal interests:	Congressman X is an enthusiastic supporter of subsidizing home heating oil (but opposes regulation to keep its price down) because some of his friends own heating-oil distributorships.[14]
Electoral ambitions:	Senator Y, a well-known political moderate, has lately been introducing very conservative amendments to bills dealing with the economy to appeal to more conservative financial donors, who might then contribute to her budding presidential campaign.
Institutional ambitions:	Representative Z has promised his vote and given a rousing speech on the House floor supporting a particular amendment because he knows it is near and dear to his party leader. He hopes his support will earn him her endorsement next year for an assignment to the prestigious Appropriations Committee.

---

14 These friends would benefit from people having the financial means to buy home heating oil from a government subsidy, but they would not want the price they charge for the oil restricted.

These examples illustrate how policies reflect both institutional procedures and individual aspirations. The procedures are essentially a series of chutes and ladders that shape, channel, filter, and prune the alternatives from which policy choices are ultimately made. The politicians who populate these institutions are driven both by private objectives and by public purposes, pursuing their private interests while working on behalf of their conception of the public interest.

Because the institutional features of the American political system are complex and policy change requires success at every step, change is often impossibly difficult, meaning the status quo usually prevails. A long list of players must be satisfied with the change, or it won't happen. Most of these politicians will need some form of "compensation" to provide their endorsement and support.

Majorities are usually built by legislators drafting bills in a way that spreads the benefits to enough members to get the requisite number of supporting votes. Derisively, this is called pork-barrel legislation. In fact, most pork-barrel projects that are distributed to build policy majorities are justified as valuable additions to the public good of the various districts. What may be pork to the critic is actual bridges, roads, and post offices.

Elaborate institutional arrangements, complicated policy processes, and intricate political motivations make for a highly combustible mixture. The policies that emerge may be lacking in the neatness that citizens desire, but they are sloppy and slapdash for a reason: the tendency to spread benefits broadly is the result when political ambition comes up against a decentralized political system.

The History Principle: How We Got Here Matters

One more aspect of our analysis is important: we must ask how we have gotten where we are. How did we get the institutions and policies that are in place? By what series of steps? When by choice and when by accident? Every question and problem we confront has a history. History will not tell the same story for every institution. Nevertheless, without history, we have neither a sense of causation nor a full sense of how institutions are related to one another. In explaining why governments do what they do, we must turn to history to see what choices were available to political actors at a given time, what consequences resulted, and what consequences might have flowed from the paths not chosen.

Imagine a tree growing from the bottom of the page. Its trunk grows upward from some root ball at the bottom, dividing into branches that continue upward, further dividing into smaller branches. Imagine a path through this tree, from its bottommost roots to the tip of one of the highest branches at the top of the page. There are many such paths, from the one point at the bottom to many possible points at the top. If this were a time diagram, then the root ball would represent some beginning point and all of the top-branch endings would represent some terminal time. Each path is now a possible history, the delineation of movement from some beginning to some concluding time. Alternative histories, like paths through trees, entail irreversibilities: Once one starts down a historical path, one cannot always retrace one's steps.[15] Some futures are foreclosed by the choices people have already made or, if not literally foreclosed, then made extremely unlikely.

In this sense we explain a current situation at least in part by describing the historical path that led to it. Certain scholars use the term **path dependency** to suggest that some possibilities are more or less likely because of earlier events and choices. Both the status quo and the path from it significantly delimit future possibilities. For example, in the early 1990s, President Bill Clinton formulated the "Don't Ask, Don't Tell" policy for the treatment of gay men and lesbians in the military: the military could not ask about a soldier's sexual orientation, and gay troops could serve so long as they did not reveal their sexual orientation. This move made it virtually impossible to return to the old status quo (in which gay men and lesbians could not serve at all). However, the path chosen by the Clinton administration also made it difficult to propose an even more enlightened policy in which gay troops were not prevented from asserting their identity (a change that did not happen for two decades).

Three factors that help explain why history often matters in political life are rules and procedures, loyalties and alliances, and historically conditioned points of view. As for rules and procedures, choices made during one point in time continue to have consequences for years, decades, or even centuries. For example, the United States' single-member-district plurality voting rules, established in the eighteenth century, continue to shape the nation's party system today.[16] Those voting rules, as we shall see in Chapter 12, help explain why the United States has a two-party system rather than a multiparty system, as found in many other Western democracies. Thus a set of choices made 200 years ago affects party politics today.

A second way in which history often matters in politics is through the persistence of loyalties and alliances. Many of the United States' important political alliances today are products of events from decades ago. For example, Jewish voters are among the Democratic Party's most loyal supporters, consistently giving 80 or 90 percent of their votes to Democratic presidential candidates. Yet on the basis of economic interest, Jews, a generally wealthy social group, might be expected to vote for the Republicans. Moreover, recently the GOP has been a stronger supporter of Israel than the Democrats. Why, then, do Jews overwhelmingly support the Democrats? Part of the answer has to do

path dependency

The idea that certain possibilities are made more or less likely because of earlier decisions—because of the historical path taken

---

15 Clearly with tree climbing this is not literally true, or once we started climbing a tree, we would never get down! So the tree analogy is not perfect here.

16 Single-member districts are arrangements in which one legislator is selected from each district. (Other electoral systems select multiple members from each district.) A plurality voting rule declares that the one legislator selected in a district is the one with the most votes (not necessarily a majority).

with history. In the late nineteenth and early twentieth centuries, Jews suffered considerable discrimination in the United States. In the 1930s, though, under Franklin Delano Roosevelt the Democratic Party was one vehicle through which Jews in America began their climb to the success they enjoy today. This historical experience continues to shape Jewish political identity. Similar historical experiences underlie the political loyalties of African Americans, Cuban Americans, and others.

A third factor explaining why history matters is that past events shape current perspectives. For example, many Americans now in their late 60s and 70s viewed events during the wars in Iraq and Afghanistan through the lens of the Vietnam War, seeing U.S. military involvement in a third world country as likely to lead to a quagmire of costs and casualties. It is interesting that in the 1960s, many older Americans viewed events in Vietnam through the lens of the 1930s, when the Western democracies were slow to resist Adolf Hitler's Germany. Thus to those influenced by the 1930s and World War II, failure to respond strongly to aggression was considered a form of appeasement that would only encourage hostile powers to use force against American interests. Both groups saw the world through perspectives that they had learned from their own histories.

CONCLUSION: PREPARING TO ANALYZE THE AMERICAN POLITICAL SYSTEM

This introductory chapter has set the stage for an analytical treatment of the phenomena that constitute American politics. This analytical approach requires attention to *argument* and *evidence*. To construct an argument about some facet of American politics—Why do incumbent legislators in the House and Senate have so much success in securing reelection? Why does the president dominate media attention?—we can draw on a set of five principles. The linchpin is the rationality principle, emphasizing individual goal seeking as a key explanation for behavioral patterns. But politics is a collective undertaking, and it is often structured by political arrangements, so we also focus on collective action and the institutions in which such action occurs (collective action principle, institution principle). The combination of goal-seeking individuals engaging in collective activity in institutional contexts provides leverage for understanding why governments govern as they do—making laws, passing budgets, implementing policies, rendering judicial judgments (policy principle). But we could not make entire sense of these activities without an appreciation of the broader historical path (history principle). These five principles, then, are tools of analysis. They are also tools of discovery, permitting the interested observer to uncover new ideas about why politics works as it does.

To know if an argument truly contributes to our understanding of the real world, we need to look at evidence. In the study of American politics, much of this evidence takes the form of quantitative data, and much of it is accessible on websites. Making sense of such evidence is what political scientists do. In the Analyzing the Evidence unit beginning on page 24 we provide a brief glimpse of how to go about this task. We hope it helps you think analytically about political information as we move through the rest of the book.

Drawing on the lesson of the history principle, we begin in the remaining chapters of Part 1 by setting the historical stage. Then, with analytical principles and strategies in hand, we can understand what influenced and inspired the Founding generation to create a national government and a federal political system, while preserving individual rights and liberties.

For Further Reading

Bianco, William T. *American Politics: Strategy and Choice.* New York: Norton, 2001.

Crawford, Sue E., and Elinor Ostrom. "A Grammar of Institutions." *American Political Science Review* 89 (1995): 582–600.

Dahl, Robert A. *Who Governs? Democracy and Power in an American City.* New Haven, CT: Yale University Press, 1961.

Downs, Anthony. *An Economic Theory of Democracy.* New York: Harper & Row, 1957.

Ellickson, Robert C. *Order without Law: How Neighbors Settle Disputes.* Cambridge: Harvard University Press, 1991.

Hardin, Garrett. "The Tragedy of the Commons." *Science* 162 (1968): 1243–48.

Kiewiet, D. Roderick, and Mathew McCubbins. *The Logic of Delegation.* Chicago: University of Chicago Press, 1991.

Mayhew, David R. *Congress: The Electoral Connection.* New Haven, CT: Yale University Press, 1974.

Mueller, Dennis. *Public Choice III.* New York: Cambridge, 2003.

North, Douglass A. *Institutions, Institutional Change, and Economic Performance.* New York: Cambridge University Press, 1990.

Olson, Mancur, Jr. *The Logic of Collective Action: Public Goods and the Theory of Groups.* 1965. Reprinted with new preface and appendix. Cambridge: Harvard University Press, 1971.

Riker, William H. *Liberalism against Populism: A Confrontation between the Theory of Democracy and the Theory of Social Choice.* San Francisco: Freeman, 1982.

Shepsle, Kenneth A. *Analyzing Politics: Rationality, Behavior, and Institutions.* 2nd ed. New York: Norton, 2010.

Shepsle, Kenneth A. "Rational Choice Institutionalism." In R. A. W. Rhodes, Sarah A. Binder, and Bert A. Rockman, eds. *The Oxford Handbook of Political Institutions.* New York: Oxford University Press, 2006, pp. 23–39.

How Do Political Scientists Know What They Know?

The five principles introduced in this chapter provide a foundation for understanding and explaining political life. However, to make and test arguments about politics, we need more than just an analytical framework; we also need empirical evidence. Political scientists study facts about politics and analyze and interpret these facts to assess different arguments and claims. Typically, we study data, systematically collecting facts and information, and examining the structure of data to see whether they are consistent, or not, with a given line of thinking.

Consider one of the most basic questions about voting: Why do people vote the way they do? In elections, Americans face two main alternatives in the form of the Democratic Party and the Republican Party. These parties have distinctive policy priorities, notably in the important area of economic policy. Since at least the 1930s, the Democratic Party has favored economic policies that redistribute income to poorer segments of society; Republicans, on the other hand, favor lower taxes and little or no redistribution. It is often argued that people vote according to their economic self-interest: people choose the candidate from the party that maximizes their income. On reflection, however, we can see that other factors may also affect voting decisions, including the candidates' personal qualities, important noneconomic issues, and even candidates' appearance or habits. Which factor best explains vote choice?

Table A Votes Cast for President, 2016

VOTE CAST	NUMBER*
HILLARY CLINTON (Democrat)	65.2 million
DONALD TRUMP (Republican)	62.7 million
Other candidates	8.0 million
Did not vote	101.1 million

*As of December 2, 2016.

What Are Data? Data are systematic measurements or observations that are collected as a source of information about a theoretically defined concept or idea. In our example there is a political behavior that we want to explain, *vote choice*. Vote choice is a general concept, and we can define it before we ever observe an election. The first step in collecting data is to represent the concept that we are interested in as a variable. A variable defines all possible outcomes of a concept that could occur and assigns them a unique label or value. Vote choice, for instance, may take four possible values or outcomes: vote for the Democratic Party candidate, vote for the Republican Party candidate, vote for another party or candidate, or don't vote.

The second step in collecting data is to measure the behavior of interest. This requires the collection of information. Observation of a small set of events can be quite enlightening.

We might, for instance, conduct in-depth interviews with a dozen or so people about how they decided to vote. However, we often require more evidence to support a given claim; a small number of people might not be sufficiently representative.

Censuses and random sample surveys allow social scientists to collect information systematically on a large number of cases. These means of collecting data are staples of social sciences. With a census we observe all individuals in the population at a given moment. Every 10 years, the United States conducts a comprehensive enumeration of all people living in the country, including information on families, education levels, income, race and ethnicity, commuting, housing, and employment. An election is a census, as it is a comprehensive count of all votes cast in a given election. So we can measure a variable such as vote choice by taking count of all electoral votes and nonvotes in the voting-eligible population (Table A).

A survey, on the other hand, consists of a study of a relatively small subset of individuals. We call this subset a sample. We can measure a variable for those individuals in the sample, and extrapolate patterns from the sample to the entire population. One of the most important social science research projects of the second half of the twentieth century is the American National Election Study, or ANES. The ANES is a national survey that has been conducted during every presidential election and most midterm congressional elections since 1948 to gauge how people voted and to understand why. In recent years, the ANES has used a sample of 2,000 Americans to make inferences about the entire voting population of over 100 million. Today, most of the information used by public policy makers, businesses, and academic researchers, including estimates of variables like unemployment and inflation, television and radio ratings, and most demographics of the population, are measured using surveys.

Summarizing Data. Communicating the information in a census or survey requires tools for summarizing data. First, we compute the frequency with which each value of a variable occurs. Frequency may be either the *number of times* that a specific behavior or value of a variable occurs or the percent of the observations in which it occurs.

Second, we construct a graph or statistic that summarizes the frequencies of all values of the variable. The distribution of a variable expresses how often each of the values of the variable occurs. A bar chart displays all possible values of a variable on one axis, usually the horizontal axis; the heights of the bars equal the frequency or *percent* of cases observed for each value (Figure A).

Votes Cast for President, 2016

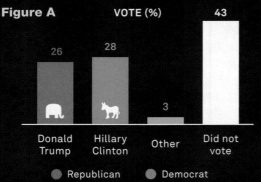

Figure A

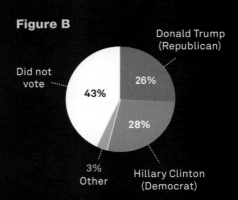

Figure B

Figure C Party Identification, 1952–2016

PERCENTAGE

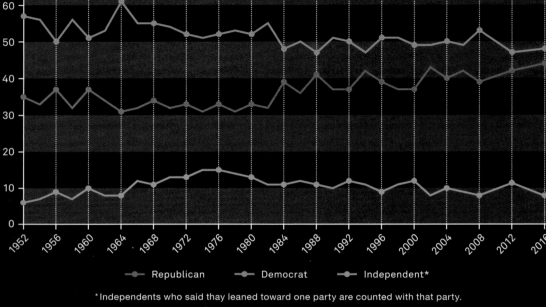

● Republican ● Democrat ● Independent*

*Independents who said thay leaned toward one party are counted with that party.

In a pie chart, the frequency for each value is depicted as a share of the whole (Figure B). A line graph is ofte used to show frequency over time (Figure C).

The distribution of income in the United States offers a somewhat different example. This variabl takes a range of values, from the smallest household income to the largest household income. For ease o presentation, we can organize this variable into categories. In Figure D, the first category is "less tha $10,000," the second category is "$10,000 to $19,999," and so forth up to the top category, "$200,000 o more." All possible income levels are covered in this classification.

Variables such as income can also be characterized with statistics, such as the median or mean. In thi example, the median is the value of household income such that half of all households have incomes belo the value and half have income above it. Fifty percent of all cases have income above the median valu and 50 percent have income below it; thus the median is also called the 50th percentile. The media household income in the United States in 2015 was $56,516, meaning that half of all households hav income below that value and half have income above that amount. The mean is the average value for th variable. In the case of household income, the mean equals the sum of all households' incomes divided b the number of households. Personal income received by households totaled approximately $10 trillion i 2015, and there were 126 million households. So the average household income was $79,263.

Figure D Distribution of Household Income in the United States, 2015

PERCENTAGE OF ALL HOUSEHOLDS

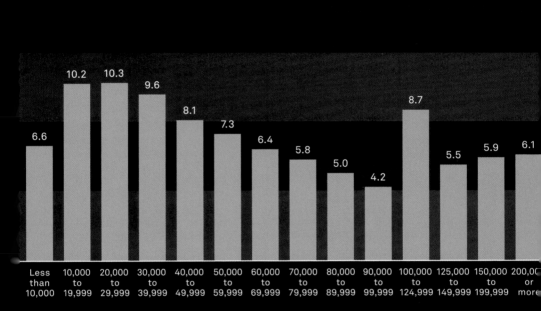

6.6	10.2	10.3	9.6	8.1	7.3	6.4	5.8	5.0	4.2	8.7	5.5	5.9	6.1
Less than 10,000	10,000 to 19,999	20,000 to 29,999	30,000 to 39,999	40,000 to 49,999	50,000 to 59,999	60,000 to 69,999	70,000 to 79,999	80,000 to 89,999	90,000 to 99,999	100,000 to 124,999	125,000 to 149,999	150,000 to 199,999	200,000 or more

HOUSEHOLD INCOME (U.S. DOLLARS)

y do the median and mean differ? In calculating the median, every household is equal. We merely cou
percent above and below a certain income level. The mean value weights households according
incomes; consequently, a household with $200,000 income contributes 10 times as much to t
ulation of the mean as a household with $20,000. If there were only a small difference in income amo
seholds, the mean would be very close to the median. The difference between the median income an
mean income thus provides a way to measure inequality. Only about one-third of households h
me above the mean value of $79,263.

sting Arguments Using Data. Let's return to the idea discussed at the beginning of the sectic
people vote their economic self-interest. Is this claim correct?
To test this idea, we need to formulate a hypothesis. In the social sciences, hypotheses often take t

o test the hypothesis that people vote their economic self-interest, we want to know to what extent votin ecisions match up with individuals' income levels. As stated earlier, in the United States today, th epublican Party generally favors lower income taxes and less income redistribution, and the Democrati arty favors higher income taxes and more income redistribution. We therefore want to know if people i gh-income households vote Republican more often than people in low-income households. The diffe nce we observe in vote choice between high- and low-income groups is considered to be the effect c come on vote choice.

To see whether the effect of income on the vote is indeed large, we can use the data in Table B t xamine the actual voting behavior of different sorts of individuals. The national exit polls in 2016 revea at 41 percent of voters with income less than $30,000 chose the Republican candidate, Donald Trump y comparison, 48 percent of those with income over $100,000 chose Donald Trump. This difference (ercentage points) reveals that income is associated with vote choice, but it is not absolutely determine ve: not every person of high income voted Republican in this election, and not everyone in low-incom oups voted Democrat.

able B Vote by Level of Income

INCOME	🐴 CLINTON	🐘 TRUMP
Under $30,000	53%	41%
$30,000–$49,999	51%	42%
$50,000–$99,999	46%	50%
$100,000 or more	47%	48%

s we explore alternative arguments about what determines vote choice, we can make many differer omparisons—men versus women, college graduates versus high school graduates, and so forth. Ou pal is to find which, if any, of these potential explanations best accounts for the variation in vote choice nroughout this book, we will consider other political outcomes besides voter behavior, such as th upport by members of Congress for different types of legislation and how often the executive succeed passing legislation.

Many times we will look for a relationship or association between two variables to see if the prediction om an argument hold true, and if they do, we take that as evidence supporting the argument. A relationshi association between two variables, sometimes called a correlation, should not be taken to mean that on the variables caused the other to occur. Causation is more difficult to establish. A correlation between tw iriables X (say X is a measure of education) and Y (say Y is a measure of income) is consistent with a theor at education increases one's earning power. From a simple correlation, however, one cannot tell whethe

Social scientists design experiments and carefully controlled comparisons in order to measure causal relationships. Observing simple associations and correlations, though, is not the final step in verifying our arguments, ideas, or theories about how politics works.

Be a Savvy Consumer of Quantitative Data. Beyond the figures and tables in this book, which reflect data from sources that we consider reliable and accurate, you will undoubtedly encounter other data about politics in the news and elsewhere. Before you take such data—and whatever argument they seem to support—at face value, it is worth asking a few questions about how the data were gathered and presented.

➡ What is the source of the data? Is it a respected source like a government office or a major mainstream news organization, which may be relied upon to gather and report data accurately? Or are they from a source that is likely to have a goal other than accurate presentation of the data, like an interest group, a campaign, or an entertainment website?

➡ When were the data collected and how? What is the date (or date range) for the data? Are the data from a census or sample, and how large is the sample?

➡ What is being measured? For example, in a poll showing support for a candidate, is it the percent of all Americans? The percentage of likely voters? The percentage of Democrats or Republicans?

➡ Why are the data presented a certain way? Is this the best way to present these data? Does it distort the data in any way? What relationships and patterns do we observe in the data?

Thinking through the questions above can help you better understand the information in the data figures and tables found throughout this book as well as in other academic writing and in the news. In each of the chapters to follow, you will find an Analyzing the Evidence unit, highlighting arguments and evidence on some of the subjects of that chapter. Many of these sections discuss how political scientists use the basic methodology discussed above to test arguments about American politics.

SOURCES:

Table A "2016 Presidential General Election Results," U.S. Election Atlas, www.uselectionatlas.org/RESULTS/national.php (accessed 11/28/16).

Table B "Election 2016: Exit Polls," *The New York Times*, www.nytimes.com/interactive/2016/11/08/us/politics/election-exit-polls.html (accessed 11/12/16).

Figure C Gallup, "Party Affiliation," www.gallup.com/poll/15370/party-affiliation.aspx (accessed 11/7/16).

Figure D U.S. Census Bureau, Household Income in 2015, www.census.gov/data/tables/time-series/demo/income-poverty/cps-hinc.html (accessed 11/3/16).

2

Constructing a Government: The Founding and the Constitution

To understand the character of the American Founding and the meaning of the American Constitution, we must look beyond myths and rhetoric. Our first principle of politics is that all political behavior has a purpose. The men and women who became revolutionaries were guided by numerous purposes. Most of the nation's Founders, though highly educated, were not political theorists. They were, rather, hardheaded and pragmatic in their commitments and activities. Although their interests differed, they did agree that a relationship of political and economic dependence on a colonial power, one that did not treat them as full-fledged citizens of the empire, was intolerable. The decision to break away from Britain in 1776 and subsequently to fashion institutions of self-governance was the consequence.

Many of those most active in the initial days of the Revolution felt backed into a corner, their decisions forced. For years, the imperial center in London, preoccupied by wars with France that had spread across several continents, had left the colonists to their own devices. These were years of substantial local control and home rule—institutional arrangements that suited merchants, farmers, and planters in the separate colonies. Local control under the mild direction of colonial governors left colonists to tend to their own business for the most part. But suddenly, as the war with France concluded in the 1760s, the British presence became more onerous. This experience incited collective action.

In reaction to English attempts to extract tax revenues to pay for the troops—which were in fact being sent to defend the colonial frontier— protests erupted throughout the colonies against the infamous Stamp Act of 1765. This act required that all printed and legal documents—including newspapers, pamphlets, advertisements, notes and bonds, leases, deeds, and licenses—be printed on official paper stamped and sold by English officials. To show their displeasure with the act, the colonists held mass meetings, participated in parades, and conducted other demonstrations throughout the spring and summer of 1765. In Boston, for example, a stamp agent was hanged and burned in effigy, leading to his resignation. Later the lieutenant governor's home was sacked because of a rumor that he supported the Stamp Act. By November 1765, business was proceeding and newspapers were being published without stamps; in March 1766, Parliament repealed the detested law. Through their protest, the nonimportation agreements that the colonists subsequently adopted, and the Stamp Act Congress that met in October 1765, the colonists took the first steps down a path that ultimately would lead to war and the establishment of a new nation.

This is where we begin our story in the present chapter. We first assess the political backdrop of the American Revolution. From the history principle we can understand how nearly a century of relatively light-handed colonial administration by London produced a set of expectations among the colonists that later British actions unmistakably violated. Then we examine the Constitution that ultimately emerged—after a bumpy experience in self-government just after the Revolution—as the basis for America's government. This document is the quintessential institutional arrangement that structures political relationships, facilitates collective action, and encourages peaceful conflict resolution. We conclude with a reflection on the Founding period by emphasizing a lesson that resonates throughout American history: that politics generally involves struggles among conflicting interests. In 1776, the main conflict was between pro-Revolutionary

CORE OF THE ANALYSIS

 The framers of the Constitution, although guided by underlying values, also had conflicting goals and interests, leading to intensive political bargaining, negotiation, and compromise.

 The first attempt at a new arrangement for self-government relied on institutions that were too weak to achieve collective action on behalf of the nation.

 The conflicting interests of the Founders were eventually accommodated through a complex set of rules and procedures set forth in the Constitution, which divided power among three branches of the federal government and between states and the federal government.

 The Constitution not only provides a framework for government but also often guides the policy process, even to this day.

and anti-Revolutionary forces. In 1787, the major struggle was between the Federalists and the Antifederalists. Today the struggle is between the Democratic and Republican parties, each representing competing economic, social, and sectional interests. Often political ideas are the weapons developed by competing interests to further their own causes. The New England merchants who cried "No taxation without representation" cared more about lower taxes than about expanded representation. Yet today representation is one of the foundations of American democracy.

As we try to understand American politics, we see that institutions matter a good deal. First, the institution principle tells us that institutions shape politics and affect the results of political conflicts—who wins and who loses. Second, the policy principle tells us that institutional procedures (coupled with individual preferences) help determine policy outcomes—what the government can and cannot do. In the United States, no set of institutions is more important than the Constitution. What are the basic rules embodied in the Constitution? What significance have constitutional precepts had for American life? These are key questions addressed in this chapter. Of course, the history principle suggests that the Constitution itself was affected by the events of the colonial and founding periods. So, let us first turn to the events that preceded and shaped America's basic law.

THE FIRST FOUNDING: INTERESTS AND CONFLICTS

Competing ideals often reflect competing interests, and so it was in Revolutionary America. The American Revolution and the Constitution were expressions of a struggle among economic and political forces within the colonies. Five sectors of society had interests that were important in colonial politics: (1) the New England merchants; (2) the southern planters; (3) the "royalists," or holders of royal lands, offices, and patents (licenses to engage in a profession or business activity); (4) shopkeepers, artisans, and laborers; and (5) small farmers. Throughout the eighteenth century, these groups differed over issues of taxation, trade, and commerce. For the most part, however, the southern planters, the New England merchants, and the royal officeholders and patent holders—in other words, the colonial elite—maintained a political alliance that held in check the more radical forces representing shopkeepers, laborers, and small farmers. After 1750, however, by threatening the interests of New England merchants and southern planters, British tax and trade policies split the elite. This split permitted radical forces to expand their political influence and unfurled a chain of events that culminated in the American Revolution.[1]

---

1   The social makeup of colonial America and some of the social conflicts that divided colonial society are discussed in Jackson Turner Main, *The Social Structure of Revolutionary America* (Princeton, NJ: Princeton University Press, 1965).

British Taxes and Colonial Interests

Beginning in the 1750s, debts and other financial problems forced the British government to search for new revenue sources. This search led to the Crown's North American colonies, which paid remarkably little in taxes to the mother country—especially given that the colonies accounted for a sizable portion of its debt owing to (1) the Crown's defense of the colonies during the recent French and Indian War, (2) continuing protection of the colonists from Indian attacks, and (3) protection that the British navy was providing for colonial shipping. Thus during the 1760s, Britain sought to impose new taxes on the colonists.

Like most governments of the period, the British regime had only limited ways to collect revenues. The income tax (which in the twentieth century became the most important source of government revenue) had not yet been developed. In the mid-eighteenth century, governments generally relied on tariffs, duties, and other taxes on commerce, and it was to such taxes, including the Stamp Act, that the British turned during the 1760s. British interests (revenue) and institutions (Parliament and colonial administration) combined to produce a plausible solution to an existing problem, as suggested by the policy principle.[2]

The colonists, accustomed to managing their own affairs, resented this British meddling. Moreover, the Stamp Act and other taxes on commerce, such as the Sugar Act of 1764, heavily affected the two groups whose commercial interests were most extensive: the New England merchants and the southern planters. Because their interests coincided, these two groups engaged in collective action to address the problems. Under the famous slogan "No taxation without representation," the merchants and planters together organized opposition to the new taxes; these groups broke with their royalist allies and turned to their former adversaries—the shopkeepers, small farmers, laborers, and artisans, all of whom had their own grievances against the established colonial government—for help. With the assistance of these groups, the merchants and planters organized demonstrations and boycotts of British goods that ultimately forced the Crown to rescind most of its new taxes. It was in the context of this unrest that a confrontation between colonists and British soldiers in front of the Boston customs house on the night of March 5, 1770, resulted in what came to be known as the Boston Massacre. Nervous British soldiers opened fire on the mob surrounding them, killing five colonists and wounding eight others. News of the event quickly spread throughout the colonies and served to fan anti-British sentiment.

---

2 Parliament also enacted the Proclamation of 1763 as part of the British settlement with the Native Americans. This withdrew the right of colonists to settle lands west of the Allegheny Mountains, preserving them for native populations. Among others, the families of George Washington and Benjamin Franklin had speculated on these lands and thus faced serious financial loss. See Norman Schofield, *Architects of Political Change: Constitutional Quandaries and Social Choice Theory* (New York: Cambridge University Press, 2006), chap. 3. A compact version is found in Norman Schofield, "Evolution of the Constitution," *British Journal of Political Science* 32 (2002): 1–23.

For the merchants and planters, however, the British government's decision to eliminate most of the hated taxes meant a victorious end to their struggle with the mother country. Eager to end the unrest they had helped arouse, they supported the British government's efforts to restore order. Indeed, most respectable Bostonians supported the actions of the British soldiers involved in the Boston Massacre. In their subsequent trial, the soldiers were defended by John Adams, a pillar of Boston society and a future president of the United States. Adams asserted that the soldiers' actions were entirely justified, provoked by a "motley rabble of saucy boys, negroes and mulattoes, Irish teagues and outlandish Jack tars." All but two of the soldiers were acquitted.[3]

Despite the efforts of the British government and the colonial elite, it proved difficult to end the political strife. The more radical forces representing shopkeepers, artisans, laborers, and small farmers continued to agitate for political and social change. Generally representing the middling classes with some education and often an intellectual skill but little political influence, these "radicals" believed that people like themselves were just as fit to govern as members of the colonial elite. Led by individuals such as Samuel Adams, a cousin of John Adams, the radicals asserted that British power supported an unjust political and social structure within the colonies, and they began to advocate an end to British rule.[4]

The British revenue-raising policies backfired so dramatically because colonial resistance was so greatly underestimated. Although the policies seemed sensible before the fact, they later appeared mistaken and were rescinded. The rationality principle requires only that people do the best they can at the time they act. There are bound to be uncertainties that can only imperfectly be taken into account and thus necessitate subsequent adaptation. So the British attempts to raise revenue and then to adapt this strategy because of the resulting unrest were rational, but it proved difficult to undo the damage caused by their initial misreading of the situation.

Organizing resistance to the British authorities required widespread support. Collective action, as noted, may emerge spontaneously in certain circumstances, but the colonists' campaign against the British imperial power required strategic planning, coalition building, bargaining, persuading, compromising, and coordinating—all elements of the give-and-take of politics. Cooperation needed cultivation and encouragement. Leadership was clearly a necessary ingredient.

Political Strife and the Radicalizing of the Colonists

The political strife within the colonies was the background for the events of 1773–74. With the Tea Act of 1773, the British government granted the politically powerful East India Company a monopoly on the export of tea from

3 Quoted in George B. Tindall and David E. Shi, *America: A Narrative History*, 8th ed. (New York: Norton, 2010), p. 202.

4 For a discussion of events leading up to the Revolution, see Charles M. Andrews, *The Colonial Background of the American Revolution: Four Essays in American Colonial History* (New Haven, CT: Yale University Press, 1924).

Britain, eliminating a lucrative trade for colonial merchants. Worse, the East India Company sought to sell the tea directly in the colonies instead of working through the colonial merchants. Because tea was an important commodity in the 1770s, these British actions posed a mortal threat to the New England merchants—who once again called on their radical adversaries for support. The most dramatic result was the Boston Tea Party of 1773, led by Samuel Adams. The protesters were mostly radicals hoping to undermine the British government's authority. (Today's "Tea Party" protesters are generally conservatives opposing taxes and regulation.)

The Boston Tea Party was decisive in American history. The merchants had wanted to force the British government to rescind the Tea Act, but they certainly did not seek independence from Britain. Samuel Adams and the other radicals, however, hoped to provoke the British government to take actions that would alienate its colonial supporters and pave the way for a rebellion. By dumping the East India Company's tea into Boston Harbor, Adams and his followers goaded the British into enacting harsh reprisals: a series of acts that closed the port of Boston to commerce, changed the provincial government of Massachusetts, provided for the removal of accused persons to Britain for trial, and added new restrictions upon movement to the West from the southern colonies—further alienating the southern planters who depended on access to new western lands. These acts of retaliation helped radicalize Americans and move them toward collective resistance to British rule.[5]

This course of action by British politicians looks puzzling in retrospect, but at the time a show of force appeared reasonable. Those who prevailed in Parliament felt the toleration of lawlessness and the making of concessions would only prompt the more radical elements to take additional liberties and demand further concessions. The British, in effect, drew a line in the sand. Their repressive reactions became a clear point around which dissatisfied colonists could rally. Radicals had been agitating for more violent measures to deal with Britain. But ultimately they needed Britain's political repression to create widespread support for independence.[6]

Thus the Boston Tea Party sparked a cycle of disputes that in 1774 resulted in the convening of the First Continental Congress, with delegates attending from all parts of the colonies. The Congress called for a total boycott of British goods and, under the radicals' prodding, began to consider independence from British rule. The eventual result was the Declaration of Independence.

5 For an intriguing take on the role of dense population networks in cities that promoted collective action against the British, see Edward L. Glaeser, "Revolution of Urban Rebels," *Boston Globe*, July 4, 2008, sec. A.

6 For an extensive discussion of how misunderstandings and incorrect beliefs caused the situation to spin out of control, see Jack N. Rakove, Andrew R. Rutten, and Barry R. Weingast, "Ideas, Interest, and Credible Commitments in the American Revolution," 2008, http://ssrn.com/abstract51153515 (accessed 2/3/09).

The Declaration of Independence

In 1776, the Second Continental Congress appointed a committee consisting of Thomas Jefferson of Virginia, Benjamin Franklin of Pennsylvania, Roger Sherman of Connecticut, John Adams of Massachusetts, and Robert Livingston of New York to draft a statement of American independence from British rule. The Declaration of Independence was written by Jefferson, who drew many ideas from the British philosopher John Locke, whose work was widely read in the colonies. Adopted by the Second Continental Congress, the Declaration was an extraordinary document in both philosophical and political terms. Philosophically, the Declaration was remarkable for its assertion (derived from Locke) that certain "unalienable rights"—including life, liberty, and the pursuit of happiness—could not be abridged by governments. In the world of 1776, in which some kings still claimed to rule by divine right, this was a dramatic statement. Politically, the Declaration was remarkable because despite the colonists' widely differing interests, it focused on grievances, aspirations, and principles that might unify the various colonial groups. The Declaration was an attempt to articulate a history and a set of principles that might help forge national unity.[7]

The Declaration of Independence, however, was not a blueprint for governance. Often, scholars call the Declaration a more radical or even libertarian document and the Constitution a more conservative text. Both documents, however, share some common philosophical underpinnings. Both apply Locke's idea that the purpose of government is the protection of life, liberty, and property. The Declaration uses these ideas as justification for overthrowing a monarchical government. The Constitution, in contrast, seeks to create a government that will guarantee the achievement of these goals. Thus America's founding documents share philosophical underpinnings but apply them to different purposes.

The Revolutionary War

In 1775, even before formally declaring their independence, the colonies had begun to fight the British, most notably at Lexington and Concord, Massachusetts, where colonial militias acquitted themselves against trained British soldiers. Nevertheless, the task of defeating Britain, then the world's premier military power, seemed impossible. To maintain their hold on the colonies, the British sent a huge expeditionary force comprising British regulars and German mercenaries along with artillery and equipment. To face this force, the colonists relied on inexperienced and lightly armed militias. To make matters worse, the colonists were hardly united in their opposition to British rule. Many colonists saw themselves as loyal British subjects and refused to take up arms against the king. Thousands, indeed, took up arms *for* the king and joined pro-British militia forces.

---

7   A "biography" of the Declaration is found in Pauline Maier, *American Scripture: Making the Declaration of Independence* (New York: Knopf, 1997).

The war was brutal and bloody with tens of thousands of casualties among the colonists, among British troops, and among the Native Americans who fought on both sides. Eventually the revolutionary armies prevailed mainly because England's cost of fighting a war thousands of miles from home became too great. As colonial militias prevented British forces from acquiring enough food and supplies locally, these had to be brought from Europe at enormous expense. The colonial forces did not have to defeat the British—they needed only to prevent the British from defeating them until Britain's will and ability to fight waned. Thus, with the eventual help of Britain's enemy, France, the colonists fought until Britain had had enough. The war ended with the signing of the Treaty of Paris, which officially granted the 13 American colonies their independence.

The Articles of Confederation

Having declared their independence, the colonies needed to establish a governmental structure—a set of institutions through which to govern. In November 1777, the Continental Congress adopted the **Articles of Confederation and Perpetual Union**—the United States' first written constitution. Although it was not ratified by all the states until 1781, it was the country's operative constitution for almost 12 years, until March 1789.

 Articles of Confederation and Perpetual Union

America's first written constitution; adopted by the Continental Congress in 1777, they were the formal basis for America's national government until 1789, when they were superseded by the Constitution

The Articles of Confederation formed a constitution concerned primarily with limiting the powers of the central government. The central government, first of all, was based entirely in Congress. Because it was not intended to be a powerful government, it was given no executive branch. Execution of its laws was to be left to the individual states. Second, Congress had little power. Its members were not much more than messengers from the state legislatures. They were chosen by the state legislatures, paid out of the state treasuries, and subject to immediate recall by state authorities. In addition, each state, regardless of size, had only a single vote. Furthermore, amendments to the Articles required the unanimous agreement of the 13 states.

Congress was given the power to declare war and make peace, to make treaties and alliances, to coin or borrow money, and to regulate trade with Native Americans. It could also appoint the senior officers of the United States Army. But it could not levy taxes or regulate commerce among the states. Moreover, the army officers it appointed had no army to serve in because the nation's armed forces were composed of the state militias. An especially dysfunctional aspect of the Articles of Confederation was that the central government could not prevent one state from discriminating against other states in the quest for foreign commerce.

In brief, the relationship between Congress and the states under the Articles of Confederation was much like the contemporary relationship between the United Nations and its member states, a relationship in which the states retain virtually all governmental powers. It was properly called a confederation because, as provided under Article II, "each state retains its sovereignty, freedom, and independence, and every power, jurisdiction, and right, which is not by this Confederation expressly delegated to the United States, in Congress assembled." Not only was there no executive but there was also no judicial authority and no other means of enforcing Congress's will. Any enforcement would be done by the states.[8] In essence, each state was an independent nation-state. All told, the Articles of Confederation were an inadequate institutional basis for collective action.

THE SECOND FOUNDING: FROM COMPROMISE TO CONSTITUTION

Institutional arrangements, devised to accomplish collective purposes by creating routines and processes, aren't always well suited to these tasks. The Declaration of Independence and the Articles of Confederation were insufficient to hold the nation together as an independent and effective nation-state. Almost from the moment of armistice with the British in 1783, moves were afoot to reform and strengthen the Articles of Confederation.

International Standing, Economic Difficulties, and Balance of Power

There was a special concern for the country's international position. Competition among the states for foreign commerce allowed the European powers to play the states against one another, creating confusion on both sides of the Atlantic. At one point John Adams, a leader in the struggle for independence, was sent to negotiate a new treaty with the British, one that would cover disputes left over from the war. The British government responded that because the United States under the Articles of Confederation was unable to enforce existing treaties, it would negotiate with each of the 13 states separately. Moreover, absent the protection of the British navy, American shipping—upon which the New England states depended—was easy prey for pirates and predator nations. The government under the Articles could offer no help.

At the same time, well-to-do Americans—in particular the New England merchants and southern planters—were troubled by the influence of populist forces in the Continental Congress and in several state governments. The colonists' victory in the Revolutionary War not only had meant the end of British rule but also had significantly changed the balance of political power within the new states. As a result, one key segment of the colonial elite—the royal land, office, and patent holders—was stripped of its economic and political privileges. In fact, many of these individuals, along with throngs of other colonists who considered themselves loyal British subjects, had left for Canada after the British surrender. And as the pre-Revolutionary elite was weakened, the pre-Revolutionary radicals became controlling forces in several states, where they

8   See Merrill Jensen, *The Articles of Confederation* (Madison: University of Wisconsin Press, 1963).

pursued economic and political policies that struck terror in the pre-Revolutionary political establishment. In Rhode Island, for example, between 1783 and 1785 a legislature dominated by representatives of small farmers, artisans, and shopkeepers had instituted economic policies, including drastic currency inflation, that frightened businessmen and property owners throughout the country. Of course, the central government under the Articles of Confederation was powerless to intervene. Commerce within the states stagnated, and several states borrowed money just to finance their Revolutionary War debts. Americans were facing their first, but not last, debt crisis.

The Annapolis Convention

The continuation of international weakness and domestic economic turmoil led many Americans to consider whether their newly adopted form of government already required revision. After nearly a decade under the Articles, many state leaders accepted an invitation from the Virginia legislature to attend a conference of representatives of all the states. Delegates from five states actually attended. This conference, held in Annapolis, Maryland, in the fall of 1786, was the first step toward the second founding. One positive result was a resolution calling on Congress to send commissioners to Philadelphia at a later time "to devise such further provisions as shall appear to them necessary to render the Constitution of the Federal Government adequate to the exigencies of the Union."[9] This resolution was drafted by Alexander Hamilton, a New York lawyer who had served during the Revolution as George Washington's secretary and who would play a more significant role in framing the Constitution and forming the new government in the 1790s. But the resolution did not necessarily imply any desire to do more than improve and reform the Articles of Confederation.

Shays's Rebellion

It is possible that the Constitutional Convention of 1787 in Philadelphia would never have taken place except for a single event that occurred soon after the Annapolis Convention: Shays's Rebellion. Like the Boston Tea Party, this was a focal event. It concentrated attention, coordinated beliefs, produced widespread fear and apprehension, and thus convinced waverers that something needed fixing. It prompted collective action by providing politicians who felt that the Articles were insufficient with just the ammunition they needed to convince a broader public of these facts.[10]

---

9 Quoted in Samuel Eliot Morison, Henry Steele Commager, and William E. Leuchtenburg, *The Growth of the American Republic*, 6th ed. (New York: Oxford University Press, 1969), I: 244.

10 For an easy-to-read argument that supports this view, see Keith L. Dougherty, *Collective Action under the Articles of Confederation* (New York: Cambridge University Press, 2001).

Daniel Shays, a former army captain, led a mob of farmers in a rebellion against the government of Massachusetts in 1787. Their goal was to prevent foreclosures on their debt-ridden land by keeping the county courts of western Massachusetts from sitting until after the next election. The state militia dispersed the mob, but for several days Shays and his followers terrified the state government by attempting to capture the federal arsenal at Springfield, provoking an appeal to Congress to help restore order. Within a few days, the state government regained control and captured 14 of the rebels (all were eventually pardoned). Later that year, a newly elected Massachusetts legislature granted some of the farmers' demands. Although the incident ended peacefully, its effects lingered and spread.

The episode showed that Congress under the Confederation had been unable to act decisively in a time of crisis. This inadequacy provided critics of the Articles of Confederation with the evidence they needed to push Hamilton's Annapolis resolution through the Congress. Thus the states were asked to send representatives to Philadelphia to discuss constitutional revision. Delegates were eventually sent by every state except Rhode Island.

The Constitutional Convention

In May 1787, 29 of a total of 73 delegates selected by the state governments convened in Philadelphia. Recognizing that political strife, international embarrassment, national weakness, and local rebellion were symptoms of fundamental flaws in the Articles of Confederation, the delegates soon abandoned plans for revision and undertook a second founding instead—an ultimately successful attempt to create a legitimate and effective national system. Americans had learned a good deal from what many saw as the shortcomings of the Articles of Confederation: for example, that executive power was a necessary component of effective government; that without an army or navy the government could not protect its citizens' interests. Demonstrating once again that history matters, Americans' experiences under the Articles helped shape the new Constitution.

A Marriage of Interest and Ideals. For years, scholars have disagreed about the motives of the Founders in Philadelphia. Among the most controversial views is the "economic" interpretation put forward by the historian Charles Beard and his disciples.[11] According to Beard, America's Founders were a collection of securities speculators and property owners whose only aim was personal enrichment. From this perspective, the Constitution's lofty principles were little more than sophisticated masks behind which the most venal interests sought to enrich themselves. Although Beard's arguments are extreme, there is some foundation for them. Northern economic interests feared debtor revolts, while southern planters feared slave revolts. Capital investment and its protection

---

11 Charles A. Beard, *An Economic Interpretation of the Constitution of the United States* (New York: Macmillan, 1913).

were weak under the Articles not only because of potential rebellions but also because of inflated currencies, limited credit markets, and outstanding public debt. Also, manufacturers needed protection from foreign competition, and exporters (primarily of southern cotton) needed the security of safe passage for their cargoes on the high seas.

Contrary to Beard's approach is the view that the Founders were in fact concerned with philosophical and ethical ideas. That indeed, the Founders sought to devise a system of government consistent with the dominant philosophical and moral values of the day.[12]

Lurking in the background was a generalized suspicion of distant central government. As the historian Joseph Ellis observed, this was the "core argument used to discredit the authority of Parliament and the British monarch."[13] But in fact, these interests and ideals belong together: the Founders' interests were reinforced by their principles. The Constitutional Convention was chiefly organized by the New England merchants and the southern planters. Although the delegates did not all hope to profit personally from an increase in the value of their securities, as Beard would have it, they did hope to benefit by breaking the power of their radical foes and establishing a system of government more compatible with their long-term economic and political interests. Thus the framers—in line with the rationality principle—desired a new government capable of promoting commerce and protecting property from radical state legislatures. They also sought to liberate the national government from the power of individual states and sometimes corrupt local politicians. At the same time, they wanted a government that was less susceptible than the existing state and national regimes to populist forces that were hostile to the elite's interests. Both interests and ideals motivated these politicians. The Constitutional Convention was a grand exercise in rationality and collective action.

The Great Compromise. The proponents of a new government fired their opening shot on May 29, 1787, when Edmund Randolph of Virginia offered a resolution that proposed corrections and enlargements in the Articles of Confederation. Not a simple motion, it provided for virtually every aspect of a new government—and it did in fact serve as the framework for what ultimately became the Constitution.[14]

This proposal, known as the Virginia Plan, provided for a system of representation in the national legislature based on the population of each state, the proportion of each state's revenue contribution, or both. (Randolph also

---

12 For an analytical treatment, see Schofield, *Architects of Political Change,* chap. 4.

13 Joseph Ellis, *Founding Brothers: The Revolutionary Generation* (New York: Knopf, 2000), p. 7.

14 There is no verbatim record of the debates, but Madison was present during virtually all of the deliberations and kept full notes on them. Madison's notes, along with the somewhat less complete records kept by several other participants in the convention, are available in a four-volume set. See Max Farrand, ed., *The Records of the Federal Convention of 1787,* rev. ed., 4 vols. (New Haven, CT: Yale University Press, 1966).

Representation in Congress: States' Ranks

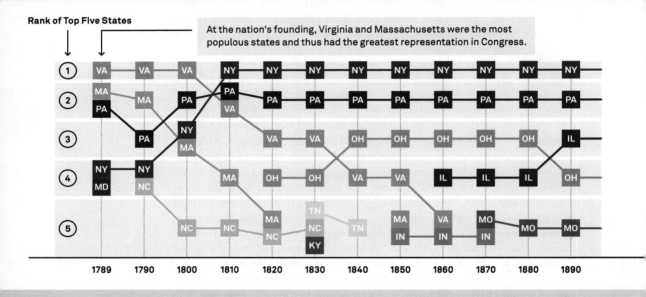

Rank of Top Five States

At the nation's founding, Virginia and Massachusetts were the most populous states and thus had the greatest representation in Congress.

proposed a second branch of the legislature, but it was to be elected by the members of the first branch.) Because the states varied enormously in size and wealth, the Virginia Plan appeared to be heavily biased in favor of the large states, which would have greater representation.

While the convention was debating the Virginia Plan, additional delegates arriving in Philadelphia were beginning to mount opposition to it. Their resolution, introduced by William Paterson of New Jersey and known as the New Jersey Plan, did not oppose the Virginia Plan point for point. Instead, it concentrated on weaknesses in the Articles of Confederation, in the spirit of revision rather than radical replacement of that document. However, their opposition to the Virginia Plan's scheme of representation was sufficient to send its proposals back to the committee to be worked into a common document. In particular, delegates from the less populous states, which included Delaware, New Jersey, Connecticut, and New York, asserted that the more populous states, such as Virginia, Pennsylvania, North Carolina, and Massachusetts, would dominate the new government if representation were to be determined by population. The smaller states argued that each state should be equally represented regardless of its population.

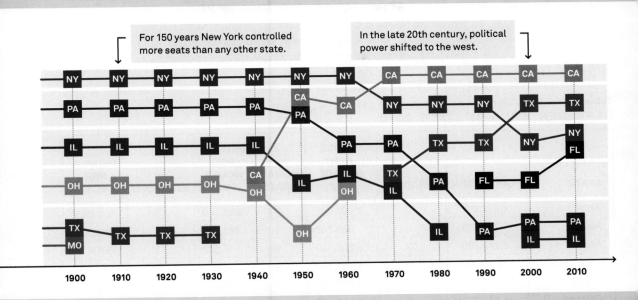

For 150 years New York controlled more seats than any other state.

In the late 20th century, political power shifted to the west.

The issue of representation threatened to wreck the entire constitutional enterprise. Delegates conferred, factions maneuvered, and tempers flared. James Wilson of Pennsylvania told the small-state delegates that if they wanted to disrupt the Union they should go ahead. Gunning Bedford of Delaware declared that the small states might look elsewhere for friends if they were forced. "The large states," he said, "dare not dissolve the confederation. If they do the small ones will find some foreign ally of more honor and good faith, who will take them by the hand and do them justice." These sentiments were widely shared. Convention delegates, acting as agents for the interests of their respective states, bargained and made attempts at persuasion in the rational pursuit of a result they would prefer.

The outcome of this debate was the **Great Compromise**, also known as the Connecticut Compromise. Under its terms, in the first chamber of Congress—the House of Representatives—the members would be apportioned according to the number of inhabitants in each state. This was what delegates from the large states had sought. But in the second chamber—the Senate—each state would have an equal vote regardless of its size; this would address the small states' concerns. The compromise was not immediately satisfactory to all the

 Great Compromise

An agreement reached at the Constitutional Convention of 1787 that gave each state an equal number of senators regardless of its population but linked representation in the House of Representatives to population

delegates. Indeed, two of the most vocal supporters of the small-state faction were so incensed by the concession that their colleagues had made to the large-state forces that they stormed out of the convention. In the end, however, both sides preferred compromise to the breakup of the Union, and the plan was accepted. The framers might have been surprised by the eventual consequences of the Great Compromise. The timeplot on pp. 42–3 shows the top five most represented states in Congress from 1789 to today. As we can see from Table 2.1, the states with the most House seats and Electoral College delegates (Electors) today did not even exist at the time of the nation's founding.

Table 2.1

REPRESENTATION BY STATE, 2010

STATE	POPULATION	SENATORS	PEOPLE PER SENATE SEAT	HOUSE SEATS	PEOPLE PER HOUSE SEAT	ELECTORS	PEOPLE PER ELECTOR
Alabama	4,802,982	2	2,401,491	7	686,140	9	533,665
Alaska	721,523	2	360,762	1	721,523	3	240,508
Arizona	6,412,700	2	3,206,350	9	712,522	11	582,973
Arkansas	2,926,229	2	1,463,115	4	731,557	6	487,705
California	37,341,989	2	18,670,995	53	704,566	55	678,945
Colorado	5,044,930	2	2,522,465	7	720,704	9	560,548
Connecticut	3,581,628	2	1,790,814	5	716,326	7	511,661
Delaware	900,877	2	450,439	1	900,877	3	300,292
Florida	18,900,773	2	9,450,387	27	700,029	29	651,751
Georgia	9,727,566	2	4,863,783	14	694,826	16	607,973
Hawaii	1,366,862	2	683,431	2	683,431	4	341,716
Idaho	1,573,499	2	786,750	2	786,750	4	393,375
Illinois	12,864,380	2	6,432,190	18	714,688	20	643,219
Indiana	6,501,582	2	3,250,791	9	722,398	11	591,053
Iowa	3,053,787	2	1,526,894	4	763,447	6	508,965
Kansas	2,863,813	2	1,431,907	4	715,953	6	477,302
Kentucky	4,350,606	2	2,175,303	6	725,101	8	543,826
Louisiana	4,553,962	2	2,276,981	6	758,994	8	569,245
Maine	1,333,074	2	666,537	2	666,537	4	333,269
Maryland	5,789,929	2	2,894,965	8	723,741	10	578,993
Massachusetts	6,559,644	2	3,279,822	9	728,849	11	596,331
Michigan	9,911,626	2	4,955,813	14	707,973	16	619,477
Minnesota	5,314,879	2	2,657,440	8	664,360	10	531,488
Mississippi	2,978,240	2	1,489,120	4	744,560	6	496,373

Table 2.1

REPRESENTATION BY STATE, 2010—*cont'd*

STATE	POPULATION	SENATORS	PEOPLE PER SENATE SEAT	HOUSE SEATS	PEOPLE PER HOUSE SEAT	ELECTORS	PEOPLE PER ELECTOR
Missouri	6,011,478	2	3,005,739	8	751,435	10	601,148
Montana	994,416	2	497,208	1	994,416	3	331,472
Nebraska	1,831,825	2	915,913	3	610,608	5	366,365
Nevada	2,709,432	2	1,354,716	4	677,358	6	451,572
New Hampshire	1,321,445	2	660,723	2	660,723	4	330,361
New Jersey	8,807,501	2	4,403,751	12	733,958	14	629,107
New Mexico	2,067,273	2	1,033,637	3	689,091	5	413,455
New York	19,421,055	2	9,710,528	27	719,298	29	669,692
North Carolina	9,565,781	2	4,782,891	13	735,829	15	637,719
North Dakota	675,905	2	337,953	1	675,905	3	225,302
Ohio	11,568,495	2	5,784,248	16	723,031	18	642,694
Oklahoma	3,764,882	2	1,882,441	5	752,976	7	537,840
Oregon	3,848,606	2	1,924,303	5	769,721	7	549,801
Pennsylvania	12,734,905	2	6,367,453	18	707,495	20	636,745
Rhode Island	1,055,247	2	527,624	2	527,624	4	263,812
South Carolina	4,645,975	2	2,322,988	7	663,711	9	516,219
South Dakota	819,761	2	409,881	1	819,761	3	273,254
Tennessee	6,375,431	2	3,187,716	9	708,381	11	579,585
Texas	25,268,418	2	12,634,209	36	701,901	38	644,958
Utah	2,770,765	2	1,385,383	4	692,691	6	461,794
Vermont	630,337	2	315,169	1	630,337	3	210,112
Virginia	8,037,736	2	4,018,868	11	730,703	13	618,287
Washington	6,753,369	2	3,376,685	10	675,337	12	562,781
West Virginia	1,859,815	2	929,908	3	619,938	5	371,963
Wisconsin	5,698,230	2	2,849,115	8	712,279	10	569,823
Wyoming	568,300	2	284,150	1	568,300	3	189,433

SOURCE: The Green Papers, www.thegreenpapers.com/Census10/FedRep.phtml (accessed 2/9/16).

The Question of Slavery: The Three-Fifths Compromise. Many of the conflicts facing the Constitutional Convention were reflections of the fundamental differences between slave and nonslave states, differences that pitted the southern planters and the New England merchants against each other. This was the first premonition of a conflict that would almost destroy the Republic in later years.

Over 90 percent of all slaves resided in five states—Georgia, Maryland, North Carolina, South Carolina, and Virginia—where they accounted for 30 percent of the population. In some places, slaves outnumbered nonslaves by as much as 10 to 1. Were they to be counted as part of a state's population even though they had no rights, thereby giving slave states increased representation in the House? If the Constitution were to embody any principle of national supremacy, some basic decisions would have to address the place of slavery in the general scheme.

Whatever they thought of the institution of slavery, most delegates from the northern states opposed counting slaves in the distribution of congressional seats. Wilson of Pennsylvania, for example, argued that if slaves were citizens, they should be treated and counted like other citizens. If, however, they were property, then why should not other forms of property count toward the apportionment of Congress? But southern delegates asserted that if the northerners refused to give in, they would never agree to the new government. Even southerners such as Edmund Randolph of Virginia, who conceded that slavery was immoral, insisted on including slaves in the allocation of congressional seats. This conflict was so divisive that many delegates came to question the possibility of creating and maintaining a union of the two.

Northerners and southerners eventually reached agreement through the **Three-Fifths Compromise**. The seats in the House of Representatives would be apportioned according to a "population" in which only three-fifths of slaves would be counted. The slaves would not be allowed to vote, but the number of representatives would be apportioned accordingly. This arrangement was supported by the slave states, which included some of the biggest and some of the smallest states at that time. It was also acceptable to many delegates from nonslave states who supported the principle of property representation, whether that property was expressed in slaves or in land, money, or stocks.

The issue of slavery was the most difficult one the framers faced, and it nearly destroyed the Union. Although some delegates considered slavery morally wrong, an evil institution that made a mockery of the ideals and values espoused in the Constitution, morality was not the issue that caused the framers to support or oppose the Three-Fifths Compromise. Northerners even agreed to permit a continuation of the odious slave trade to keep the South in the Union. But in due course, a bloody war broke out when the two sides' disparate interests could no longer be reconciled.

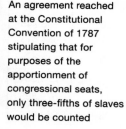

Three-Fifths Compromise

An agreement reached at the Constitutional Convention of 1787 stipulating that for purposes of the apportionment of congressional seats, only three-fifths of slaves would be counted

THE CONSTITUTION

The political significance of the Great Compromise and the Three-Fifths Compromise was to restore the unity of the northern merchants and southern planters, paving the way for the creation of a new government. The Great Compromise reassured those of both groups who feared that their own local or regional influence would be threatened. The Three-Fifths Compromise temporarily defused the rivalry between the merchants and the planters. Their unity secured, members of the alliance supporting the establishment of a new government moved to fashion a constitutional framework consistent with their economic and political interests.

The framers of the Constitution understood that well-designed institutions make it easier to achieve collective goals. They understood also that the institutions they built could affect political outcomes for decades, if not centuries, to come (see the Policy Principle section on p. 48). Accordingly, the framers took great care to construct institutions that over time would help the nation accomplish what they viewed as important political purposes.

First, the framers sought a government strong enough to promote commerce and protect property from radical state legislatures. This goal became the basis for national control over commerce and finance, as well as for the establishment of national judicial supremacy and the effort to construct a strong presidency. Second, the framers sought to prevent the threat posed by the "excessive democracy" of the state and national governments under the Articles of Confederation. Here again the framers' historical experience mattered. This goal led to such constitutional principles as **bicameralism** (division of the Congress into two chambers), checks and balances, staggered terms of office, and indirect election (selection of the president by an electoral college rather than directly by the voters). Third, the framers, lacking power to force the states or the public at large to accept the new form of government, sought to identify principles that would help secure support. This goal became the basis for the constitutional provision for direct popular election of representatives and, subsequently, the basis for the addition of the Bill of Rights to the Constitution. Finally, the framers wanted to ensure that the new government did not use its power to pose even more of a threat to citizens' liberties and property rights than did the radical state legislatures they feared and despised. To prevent the new government from abusing its power, the framers incorporated into the Constitution such principles as the separation of powers and federalism.

 bicameralism

The division of a legislative assembly into two chambers, or houses

The framers provided us with a grand lesson in purposive behavior. They came to Philadelphia united by a common distaste for government under the Articles and animated by the agitation following Shays's Rebellion. They didn't always agree on what they disliked about the Articles or on how to proceed—hence the necessity for the historic compromises. But they did believe that fostering commerce and protecting property could be served better by a set of institutional arrangements other than that provided by the Articles. They agreed that the institutional arrangements of government mattered for their lives and for those of their fellow citizens. They believed that both too much democracy and too much governmental power were threats to the common good, and they felt compelled to find instruments and principles that weighed against them. Let us assess the major provisions of the Constitution's seven articles to see how each relates to these objectives.

The Legislative Branch

The first seven sections of Article I of the Constitution provide for a Congress consisting of two chambers—a House of Representatives and a Senate. Members of the House of Representatives hold two-year terms of office and are to

The Constitution and Policy Outcomes

Large states and small states debated representation at the Constitutional Convention.

The policy principle tells us that political outcomes are the products of individual preferences and institutional procedures. One extension of this principle is the idea that individuals involved in politics try to create institutions that will help them achieve policy outcomes they favor and prevent policy outcomes they oppose. For any political actors, the right institutional arrangements can put them at an advantage, and their opponents at a disadvantage, in conflicts over policy for many years.

This idea is illustrated by the struggles at the constitutional convention. Delegates from the smaller states thought their states had much to gain by creating legislative institutions that gave each state an equal vote regardless of population. The larger states, however, especially Virginia, Massachusetts, New York, and Pennsylvania, were centers of commerce, and their delegates believed that, over time, the new government's commercial policies would be more likely to serve those states' interests if its legislative institutions reflected their advantage in population. Nevertheless, representatives of both groups of states agreed that a new government was likely to produce better policies than those developed under

the Articles of Confederation and so were willing to compromise. They eventually settled, in what is known as the Great Compromise, on an institutional arrangement that gave the large states more weight in the House of Representatives and the small states equality of representation in the Senate.

In a similar vein, the southern delegates knew a system of apportioning House seats that counted slaves as part of their states' population would increase southern states' legislative representation and thereby strengthen their hands in political struggles for years to come. The northern delegates, for their part, were determined not to provide this institutional advantage to the South in future policy making. Again, though, both groups of delegates calculated that the benefits of new national institutions were substantial and thus agreed to the Three-Fifths Compromise, in which, for the purposes of apportionment of House seats, only three-fifths of slaves would be counted.

The Three-Fifths Compromise became moot with the abolition of slavery, but the impact of the Great Compromise continues to be felt today. For example, the Constitution assigns each state a number of electors in the Electoral College equal to its number of senators plus representatives. Because the Great Compromise assigned each state an equal number of senators, small states have more electoral votes *per capita* in presidential elections than large states. One Wyoming voter, for example, has as much influence as three New York voters. Equal representation in the Senate plus a disproportionate share of electoral votes may help explain why some of America's smallest states, such as South Carolina and North Dakota, are leading beneficiaries of federal tax and spending policies, receiving far more in federal spending than their citizens pay in taxes.

be elected directly by the people. Members of the Senate were to be appointed by the state legislatures (this provision was changed in 1913 by the Seventeenth Amendment, which instituted direct election of senators) for six-year terms. These terms, moreover, are staggered so that the appointments of one-third of the senators expire every two years. The Constitution assigns somewhat different tasks to the House and the Senate. Though the approval of each body is required for the enactment of a law, the Senate alone can ratify treaties and approve presidential appointments. The House has the sole power to originate revenue bills.

The character of the legislative branch reflects the framers' major goals. The House of Representatives was designed to be directly responsible to the people, to encourage popular consent for the new Constitution, and to help enhance the power of the new government. At the same time, to guard against "excessive democracy," the power of the House of Representatives was checked by the Senate, whose members are to be appointed rather than elected directly by the people and are to serve long (six-year) terms. The purpose of this provision was to avoid "an unqualified complaisance to every sudden breeze of passion, or to every transient impulse which the people may receive."[15] Staggered terms of service in the Senate, moreover, would make that body even more resistant to popular pressure. Because only one-third of the senators would be selected at any given time, the composition of the institution would be protected from changes in popular preferences transmitted by the state legislatures, thereby preventing what James Madison called "mutability in the public councils arising from a rapid succession of new members."[16] Thus the structure of the legislative branch contributed to governmental power, promoted popular consent for the new government, and at the same time placed limits on the popular political currents that many framers saw as a radical threat to the economic and social order.

The issues of power and consent are important throughout the Constitution. Section 8 of Article I lists the specific powers of Congress, which include the authority to collect taxes, borrow money, regulate commerce, declare war, and maintain an army and navy. By granting it these powers, the framers indicated that the new government would be far more influential than its predecessor. At the same time, by defining the new government's most important powers as belonging to Congress, the framers sought to promote popular acceptance of this critical change by reassuring citizens that their views would be fully represented whenever the government exercised its new powers.

As a further guarantee that the new government would pose no threat to the people, the Constitution implies that any powers not listed are not granted at all. This is the doctrine of **expressed powers**: the Constitution grants only those powers specifically expressed in its text. No new powers can be seized on by the national government without a constitutional amendment. Without such an amendment, any power not enumerated is conceived to be "reserved"

← **expressed powers**

The powers that the Constitution explicitly grants to a branch of the federal government

---

15 Alexander Hamilton, James Madison, and John Jay, *The Federalist Papers*, Clinton Rossiter, ed. (New York: New American Library, 1961), no. 71.

16 *The Federalist*, no. 62.

necessary and proper clause

Article I, Section 8, of the Constitution, which enumerates the powers of Congress and provides Congress with the authority to make all laws "necessary and proper" to carry them out; also referred to as the elastic clause

to the states (or the people). But the framers desired an active and powerful government, so they also included the **necessary and proper clause**, sometimes known as the elastic clause, which signifies that the enumerated powers are meant to be a source of strength to the national government, not a limitation on it—that the government may employ means "necessary and proper" to implement the expressed powers. As we will see, the question of what powers the federal government can or cannot exercise is still debated today. For example, opponents of the 2010 Affordable Care Act (Obamacare) said the federal government lacked the power to require Americans to purchase health insurance. The Supreme Court upheld major provisions of the law, but the debate continued with the High Court upholding the Act again in 2015.[17]

The Executive Branch

The Constitution provides for the establishment of the presidency in Article II. As Alexander Hamilton commented, the presidential article was aimed toward creating "energy in the Executive." It did so in an effort to overcome the natural stalemate that was built into both the bicameral legislature and the separation of powers among the legislative, executive, and judicial branches. The Constitution afforded the president a measure of independence from the people and from the other branches of government, particularly Congress.

Some of the framers had wanted a plural executive or executive council in order to avoid the evils that many associated with a monarch. However, Hamilton argued that "energy" required a single rather than a plural executive. While abuse of power should be guarded against by checks and balances and other devices, energy also required that the executive hold "competent powers" to direct the nation's business.[18] These would include the unconditional power to accept ambassadors from other countries—essentially, the power to "recognize" other countries; the power to negotiate treaties, although their acceptance requires Senate approval; the unconditional right to grant reprieves and pardons, except in cases of impeachment; and the power to appoint major departmental personnel; to convene Congress in a special session; and to veto congressional enactments. (The veto power is not absolute because Congress can override it by a two-thirds vote. The Analyzing the Evidence unit on pp. 52–3 explores the various points at which legislation can be halted in the United States as compared to other countries.)[19]

---

17 *National Federation of Independent Business v. Sebelius,* 135 S.Ct.475 (2014). See also *King v. Burwell,* no. 14-114, 2015.

18 *The Federalist,* no. 70.

19 A modern description of executive-legislature relations is "The president proposes; the Congress disposes." The president may propose to the legislature when the subject is a treaty or a major departmental appointment or a federal judge or justice, which must be approved by the Senate; then the president is a legislative "agenda setter." When, however, it is a proposed law or budget, it is a "suggestion" that the legislature may choose to ignore altogether. Such proposals are then said to be "dead on arrival" because Congress marches to the beat of its own drummer.

The framers hoped to create a presidency that would make the federal government, rather than the states, the agency capable of timely and decisive action to deal with public issues and problems. This goal is the meaning of the "energy" that Hamilton hoped to impart to the executive branch.[20] At the same time, however, the framers sought to help the president withstand (excessively) democratic pressures by making the office subject to indirect rather than direct election (through selection by a separate electoral college). In Chapter 7 we discuss the extent to which the framers' hopes were realized.

The Judicial Branch

In establishing the judicial branch in Article III, the Constitution reflects the framers' preoccupations with enhancing the power of the national government and checking radical democratic impulses while guarding against potential interference with liberty and property from the new national government itself.

The framers created a court that was to be literally a supreme court of the United States and not merely the highest court of the national government. The most important expression of this intention was granting the Supreme Court the power to resolve any conflicts that might emerge between federal and state laws. In particular, the Supreme Court was given the right to determine whether a power was exclusive to the federal government, concurrent with the states, or exclusive to the states. The significance of this was noted by Justice Oliver Wendell Holmes, Jr.: "I do not think the United States would come to an end if we lost our power to declare an act of Congress void. I do think the union would be imperiled if we could not make that declaration as to the laws of the several states."[21]

In addition, the Supreme Court was assigned jurisdiction over controversies between citizens of different states. The long-term significance of this provision was that as the country developed a national economy, it came to rely increasingly on the federal judiciary, rather than the state courts, for the resolution of disputes.

Judges held lifetime appointments to protect them from popular politics and interference by the other branches. To further safeguard judicial independence, the Constitution prohibited Congress from reducing the salary of any sitting judge. This did not mean, however, that the judiciary would remain totally impartial to political considerations or to the other branches, for the president appoints the judges and the Senate approves the appointments. Congress also has the power to create inferior (lower) courts, change the federal courts' jurisdiction, add or subtract federal judges, and even change the size of the Supreme Court.

----

20 *The Federalist*, no. 70.

21 Oliver Wendell Holmes, Jr., *Collected Legal Papers* (New York: Harcourt, Brace, 1920), pp. 295–96.

Constitutional Engineering: How Many Veto Gates?

Contributed by
Steven L. Taylor
Troy University
Matthew S. Shugart
University of California, Davis

Any given constitution contains a number of individual elements that interact to produce a specific policy-making environment. These parameters determine how policy decisions are made as well as which political actors can stop them from proceeding through the process. One area of comparative constitutional structures is how many *veto gates* a system contains. A veto gate is an institution that serves as a point in the legislative process where the progress of a proposal can be halted. This notion conceives of the legislative process as being made up of one or more such gates that have to be opened to allow an idea to "flow" past on its way to becoming law. Each gate, however, is locked and can be opened only by institutional actors who hold the keys.

The simplest possible model of such a system would be an absolute dictator who has to consult only his or her own preferences before acting. Democratic governance, on the other hand, is a system that builds complex (and often multiple) gates and then creates and empowers players to open (or not) those gates.

The exact mix of institutional elements in a given constitution has a profound impact not only on how policy is made but also on what kinds of policies are made. More veto gates and players in a given system will generate more need for negotiation and compromise versus systems with fewer such actors. In counting veto gates, we can ask three questions:

1. **Presidential veto:** Is there an elected president who can veto legislation? In parliamentary systems like the United Kingdom and India, there is no elected presidency at all. Other systems have elected presidents who may be important in some respects but who are not empowered with a veto (for instance, France). The strongest presidents are both elected and have a veto, such as the U.S. president.

2. **Number of legislative chambers:** How many legislative chambers are there? Does the government have one chamber (unicameral) or two (bicameral)? If there is only one legislative chamber, as in Costa Rica and Denmark, then obviously there can be only one veto gate among legislative actors—but we need a final question to differentiate different forms of bicameralism.

3. **Symmetry of chambers:** If there is a second chamber, are they symmetrical in their powers? Many second chambers are less powerful in their systems than the U.S. Senate, which is fully symmetrical. Some other bicameral legislatures are asymmetrical, meaning the second chamber has minimal powers beyond delaying power, as in Austria, or it has substantial powers in some areas but not others, as with the Canadian Senate and the United Kingdom's House of Lords.

We can see from the table of 40 established democracies that there are multiple ways in which national constitutions can configure the lawmaking process in terms of the type and number of veto gates. Moreover, the United States is not typical. It is only 1 of 9 of these 40 democracies to have three veto gates in the lawmaking process. Most other established democracies have fewer veto gates, although several have multiple veto players—such as frequent coalition governments where political parties have to compromise with one another. This combination of veto gates and veto players directly impacts the policies and may help us understand why policies are different across different democracies.

	ELECTED PRESIDENT WITH VETO?	NO. OF LEGISLATIVE CHAMBERS	LEVEL OF CHAMBER SYMMETRY	NUMBER OF VETO GATES
ARGENTINA, BRAZIL, CHILE, COLOMBIA, DOMINICAN REPUBLIC, MEXICO,* PHILIPPINES, UNITED STATES, URUGUAY	Yes	●●	High	✖✖✖
COSTA RICA,** PANAMA, SOUTH KOREA	Yes	●	Unicameral	✖✖
POLAND	Yes	●●	Low 1 strong chamber 1 weak chamber	✖✖
AUSTRALIA, ITALY, **SWITZERLAND**	No	●●	High 2 strong chambers	✖✖
CANADA, GERMANY, INDIA, JAPAN, **NETHERLANDS,** SOUTH AFRICA, **UNITED KINGDOM**	No	●●	Medium 1 strong chamber 1 chamber with limitations	✖✖
AUSTRIA, BELGIUM, CZECH REPUBLIC, FRANCE, SPAIN	No	●●	Low	✖
BULGARIA, DENMAR K, **FINLAND**, GREECE, HUNGARY, IRELAND, ISRAEL, **NEW ZEALAND,** NORWAY, PORTUGAL, SLOVAKIA, **SWEDEN**	No	●	Unicameral	✖

Beyond the legislative process, there are other constitutional factors that can create veto gates for policy implementation: a federal system may empower states to block the implementation of policy passed at the national level; Supreme Courts or constitutional tribunals may have the ability to declare laws unconstitutional, and therefore null and void. All of these factors derive from constitutional design.

SOURCES: Steven L. Taylor, Matthew S. Shugart, Arend Lijphart, and Bernard Grofman, *A Different Democracy: American Government in a Thirty-One-Country Perspective* (New Haven, CT: Yale University Press, 2014); and authors' classifications.

Mexico's second chamber has no power over spending bills.

No veto on budget.

talicized cases are federal.

Bold cases lack judicial review of legislation.

judicial review ➡

The power of the courts to determine whether the actions of the president, the Congress, and the state legislatures are or are not consistent with the Constitution. The Supreme Court asserted the power to review federal statutes in *Marbury v. Madison* (1803)

No direct mention is made of **judicial review**—the power of the courts to render the final decision when a conflict of interpretation of the Constitution or of laws arises between the courts and Congress, the courts and the executive branch, or the federal government and the states. Scholars generally feel that judicial review is implicit in the existence of a written constitution and in the power given to the federal courts over "all Cases . . . arising under this Constitution, the Laws of the United States, and Treaties made, or which shall be made, under their Authority" (Article III, Section 2). The Supreme Court eventually assumed the power of judicial review. Its assumption of this power, as we see in Chapter 9, was based not on the Constitution itself but on the politics of later decades and the membership of the Court.

National Unity and Power

Various provisions in the Constitution address the framers' concern with national unity and power, including Article IV's provisions for comity (reciprocity) among states and among the citizens of all states.

Each state is prohibited from discriminating against the citizens of other states in favor of its own citizens, with the Supreme Court charged with deciding in each case whether a state has discriminated against goods or people from another state. The Constitution restricts the power of the states in favor of ensuring that the national government holds enough power to give the country a free-flowing national economy.

The framers' concern with national supremacy was also expressed in Article VI in the **supremacy clause**, which provides that national laws and treaties "shall be the supreme Law of the Land." This means that all laws made under the "Authority of the United States" are superior to those adopted by any state or any other subdivision, and the states are expected to respect all treaties made under that authority. This provision aimed to keep the states from dealing separately with foreign nations or businesses. The supremacy clause also binds the officials of all state and local, as well as federal, governments to take an oath of office to support the national Constitution if disputes arise between national and state laws.

supremacy clause ➡

A clause of Article VI of the Constitution that states that all laws passed by the national government and all treaties are the supreme laws of the land and superior to all laws adopted by any state or any subdivision

Amending the Constitution

The Constitution establishes procedures for its own revision in Article V. Its provisions are so difficult that Americans have availed themselves of the amending process only 17 times since 1791, when the first 10 amendments were adopted. Many other amendments have been proposed, but fewer than 40 have come even close to fulfilling the Constitution's requirement of a two-thirds vote in Congress, and only a fraction have approached adoption by three-fourths of the states. The Constitution can also be amended by a constitutional convention, but no national convention has been called since the Philadelphia Convention of 1787; Congress has submitted all proposed amendments to the state legislatures for ratification.

Any body of rules, including a national constitution, must balance the need to respond flexibly to changes on the one hand with the caution not to be too flexible on the other. An inflexible body of rules cannot accommodate major change and risks being rebelled against, a circumstance in which the slate is wiped clean and new rules are designed—or ignored altogether. Too much flexibility, however, is disastrous. It invites those who lose in everyday politics to replay battles at the constitutional level. If institutional change is too easy to accomplish, the stability of the political system becomes threatened. This means, as stated in the institution principle, that the institutional arrangements characterized in a constitution should structure politics by providing a framework, not specify explicit political outcomes. To determine whether a constitutional document has the right degree of flexibility, it must pass the test of time. The fact that ours has survived for more than two centuries works as a point in its favor.

Ratifying the Constitution

Rules for ratification of the Constitution of 1787 are set forth in Article VII of the Constitution. This provision actually violated the amendment provisions of the Articles of Confederation. For one thing, it adopts a nine-state rule in place of the unanimity required by the Articles. For another, it provides for ratification to occur in special state conventions rather than in the state legislatures. All the states except Rhode Island eventually did set up state conventions to ratify the Constitution.

Constitutional Limits on the National Government's Power

As we have indicated, although the framers desired a powerful national government, they also wanted to guard against possible misuse of that power. Thus they incorporated two key principles into the Constitution: the **separation of powers** and **federalism** (see Chapter 3). A third set of limitations, in the form of the **Bill of Rights**, was added to the Constitution to help secure its ratification when opponents charged that it paid insufficient attention to citizens' rights.

The Separation of Powers. No principle of politics was more widely shared at the time of the 1787 Founding than the principle that power must be used to balance power. The French political theorist Baron de la Brède et de Montesquieu (1689–1755) believed that this balance was an indispensable defense against tyranny. His writings "were taken as political gospel" at the Philadelphia convention. Although the principle of the separation of powers was not explicitly stated in the Constitution, the entire structure of the national government was built precisely on Article I, the legislature; Article II, the executive; and Article III, the judiciary (Figure 2.1).

 separation of powers

The division of governmental power among several institutions that must cooperate in decision making

 federalism

The system of government in which a constitution divides power between a central government and regional governments

 Bill of Rights

The first 10 amendments to the U.S. Constitution, adopted in 1791; it ensures certain rights and liberties to the people

Figure 2.1
THE SEPARATION OF POWERS

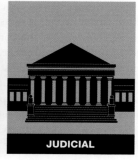

LEGISLATIVE	EXECUTIVE	JUDICIAL
Passes federal laws	Enforces laws	Reviews lower-court decisions
Controls federal appropriations	Serves as commander in chief of armed forces	Decides constitutionality of laws
Approves treaties and presidential appointments	Makes foreign treaties	Decides cases involving disputes between states
Regulates interstate commerce	Nominates Supreme Court justices and federal court judges	
Establishes lower-court system	Pardons those convicted in federal court	

checks and balances

The mechanisms through which each branch of government is able to participate in and influence the activities of the other branches

However, separation of powers is nothing but mere words on parchment without a method table to maintain the separation. The method became known as **checks and balances**. Each branch is given not only its own powers but also some power over the other two branches. Among the most familiar checks and balances are the president's veto as a power over Congress and Congress's power over the president through its control of appointments to high executive posts and to the judiciary. Congress also has power over the president with its control of appropriations and (by the Senate) the right of approval of treaties. The judiciary was assumed to have the power of judicial review over the other two branches.

Another feature of the separation of powers is the principle of giving each branch a distinctly different constituency. Theorists such as Montesquieu called this a "mixed regime," with the president chosen indirectly by electors, the House by popular vote, the Senate (originally) by state legislature, and the judiciary by presidential appointment. By these means, the members of each branch would develop very different outlooks on how to govern, different definitions of the public interest, and different alliances with private interests.

Federalism. Compared with the confederation principle of the Articles of Confederation, federalism was a step toward greater centralization of power. Seeking to place more power at the national level without completely undermining the power of state governments, the delegates devised a system of two sovereigns, or supreme powers—the states and the nation—with the hope that competition between the two would limit the power of both.

The Bill of Rights. Late in the Philadelphia convention, a motion was made to include a bill of rights in the Constitution. After a brief debate, it was almost unanimously turned down. Most delegates felt that because the federal government was already limited to its expressed powers, any further protection of citizens was unnecessary. The delegates argued that the states should adopt bills of rights because their greater powers needed greater limitations. But almost immediately after the Constitution was ratified, there was a movement to adopt a national bill of rights. This is why the Bill of Rights, adopted in 1791, makes up the first 10 amendments to the Constitution and is not incorporated into the body of it. We further explore the Bill of Rights in Chapter 4.

THE FIGHT FOR RATIFICATION: FEDERALISTS VERSUS ANTIFEDERALISTS

The first hurdle faced by the new Constitution was ratification by state conventions of delegates elected by the people of each state. This struggle for ratification encompassed 13 separate campaigns influenced by local as well as national considerations. Two sides faced off throughout the states, however, calling themselves Federalists and Antifederalists (Table 2.2).[22] The Federalists supported the Constitution and preferred a strong national government. The Antifederalists opposed the Constitution and preferred a decentralized federal government; they took their name in reaction to their better-organized opponents. The Federalists were united in their support of the Constitution, whereas the Antifederalists were divided in what they believed the alternative to the Constitution should be.

During the struggle over ratification, Americans argued about great political issues and ideals. How much power should the national government be given? What safeguards were most likely to prevent the abuse of power? What institutional arrangements could best ensure adequate representation for all Americans? Was tyranny to be feared more from the many or from the few?

In political life, of course, ideals—and values—are seldom completely divorced from interests. In 1787, divisions along economic, regional, and political lines influenced Americans' attitudes toward political questions. Many

---

22 An excellent analysis of the ratification campaigns—based on a quantitative assessment of the campaigners' own words as found in campaign documents, pamphlets, tracts, public letters, and the eighteenth-century equivalent of op-ed pieces (such as the individual essays that make up the *Federalist Papers*)—is William H. Riker, *The Strategy of Rhetoric: Campaigning for the American Constitution* (New Haven, CT: Yale University Press, 1996).

Table 2.2

FEDERALISTS VERSUS ANTIFEDERALISTS

	FEDERALISTS	ANTIFEDERALISTS
Who were they?	Property owners, creditors, merchants	Small farmers, frontiersmen, debtors, shopkeepers
What did they believe?	Elites are best fit to govern and "excessive democracy" is dangerous	Government should be close to the people and the concentration of power in the hands of the elites is dangerous
What system of government did they favor?	Strong national government; believed in "filtration" so that only elites would obtain governmental power	Retention of power by state governments and protection of individual rights
Who were their leaders?	Alexander Hamilton, James Madison, George Washington	Patrick Henry, George Mason, Elbridge Gerry, George Clinton

well-to-do merchants and planters favored a stronger central government with the capacity to protect property, promote commerce, and keep the more radical state legislatures in check. At the same time, many powerful state leaders feared that strengthening the national government would reduce their own influence and status. Each of these interests justified its position with an appeal to basic values.

Ideas can be important weapons in political warfare, and seeing how and by whom they are wielded can illuminate their implications. Even if an idea initially serves a given interest, however, once it has been articulated it can take on a life of its own and have implications that transcend the narrow interest it was created to serve. For example, some opponents of the Constitution who criticized the absence of a bill of rights in the initial document did so simply in hopes of blocking the document's ratification. Yet the bill of rights that was ultimately added has proved for over two centuries to be a bulwark of civil liberty in the United States.

As this example shows, truly great political ideas transcend the interests that initially set them forth. The first step in understanding a political value involves understanding who espouses it and why. The second step involves understanding the full implications of the idea itself—implications that may go far beyond the interests that launched it. Whatever clashing interests may have guided them, the Federalists and the Antifederalists presented important alternative visions of America.

During the ratification struggle, thousands of essays, speeches, pamphlets, and letters were presented in support of and in opposition to the proposed Constitution. The best-known pieces supporting ratification were the 85 essays written under the name Publius by Alexander Hamilton, James Madison, and

John Jay in late 1787 and early 1788. The *Federalist Papers*, as they are known today, defended the principles of the Constitution and sought to dispel fears of a national authority. The Antifederalists published essays of their own, arguing that the new Constitution betrayed the Revolution and was a step toward monarchy. Among the best Antifederalist works were the essays, usually attributed to New York Supreme Court justice Robert Yates, that were written under the name Brutus and published in the *New York Journal* at the same time the *Federalist Papers* appeared. The Antifederalist view also appeared in pamphlets and letters written by a former delegate to the Continental Congress, Richard Henry Lee of Virginia, using the pen name the Federal Farmer. These essays highlight the major differences between Federalists and Antifederalists. Federalists appealed to basic principles of government in support of their nationalist vision. Antifederalists cited equally fundamental precepts to support their vision of a looser confederacy of small republics. The two sides engaged in what was almost certainly the first nationwide political campaign in the history of the world.

Representation

One major area of contention was the question of representation. The Antifederalists asserted that representatives must be "a true picture of the people, . . . [possessing] the knowledge of their circumstances and their wants."[23] This could be achieved, argued the Antifederalists, only in small, relatively homogeneous republics such as the existing states. In their view, the size and extent of the entire nation precluded the construction of a truly representative form of government.

The absence of true representation, moreover, would mean that the people would lack attachment to the national government and would refuse to obey its laws. As a result, according to the Antifederalists, the national government described by the Constitution would have to use force to secure popular compliance. The Federal Farmer averred that laws of the remote federal government could be "in many cases disregarded, unless a multitude of officers and military force be continually kept in view, and employed to enforce the execution of the laws, and to make the government feared and respected."[24]

Federalists, for their part, saw no reason that representatives should be precisely like those they represented. In their view, government must be representative *of* the people but must also have some autonomy *from* the people. Their ideal government was to be capable of serving the long-term public interest even if doing so conflicted with the public's current preference. In more contemporary terms, Federalists sought representatives who were *trustees*, whereas Antifederalists sought *delegates*.

---

23 Melancton Smith, quoted in Herbert J. Storing, *What the Anti-Federalists Were For: The Political Thought of the Opponents of the Constitution* (Chicago: University of Chicago Press, 1981), p. 17.

24 "Letters from the Federal Farmer," no. 2, in Herbert Storing, ed., *The Complete Anti-Federalist*, 7 vols. (Chicago: University of Chicago Press, 1981).

Federalists also dismissed the Antifederalist claim that the distance between representatives and constituents in the proposed national government would lead to popular disaffection and compel the government to use force to secure obedience. Federalists replied that the system of representation they proposed was more likely to produce effective government. Competent government, in turn, should inspire popular trust and confidence more effectively than simple social proximity between rulers and ruled.

The Threat of Tyranny

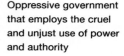

tyranny

Oppressive government that employs the cruel and unjust use of power and authority

A second important issue dividing Federalists and Antifederalists was the threat of **tyranny**—unjust rule by the group in power. Both opponents and defenders of the Constitution frequently affirmed their fear of tyrannical rule. Each side, however, had a different view of the most likely source of tyranny and hence of how best to forestall the threat of it.

From the Antifederalist perspective, the great danger was the tendency of all governments—including republican governments—to become increasingly "aristocratic," with a few individuals in positions of authority gaining more and more power over the general citizenry. In essence, the few would use their power to tyrannize the many. For this reason, Antifederalists were sharply critical of features of the Constitution that divorced governmental institutions from direct responsibility to the people—institutions such as the Senate, the executive, and the federal judiciary.

The Federalists, too, recognized the threat of tyranny. They agreed that individuals could be opportunistic and self-interested. But they believed that the danger associated with republican governments was not aristocracy but, instead, majority tyranny. The Federalists were concerned that a popular majority, "united and actuated by some common impulse of passion, or of interest, adverse to the rights of other citizens," would endeavor to "trample on the rules of justice."[25] From the Federalist perspective, it was precisely those features of the Constitution attacked as potential sources of tyranny by the Antifederalists that offered the best hope of averting the threat of oppression. The size and extent of the nation, for instance, were for the Federalists a bulwark against tyranny. In Madison's famous formulation, reflecting the logic of the collective action principle,

> The smaller the society, the fewer probably will be the distinct parties and interests . . . the more frequently will a majority be found of the same party; and the smaller the number of individuals composing a majority, and the smaller the compass within which they are placed, the more easily will they concert and execute their plans of oppression. Extend the sphere, and you take in a greater variety of parties and interests; you make it less probable that a majority of the whole will have a common motive to invade the rights of other citizens; or if such a common motive exists, it will be more difficult for all who feel it to discover their own strength, and to act in unison with each other.[26]

25 *The Federalist,* no. 10.

26 *The Federalist,* no. 10.

The Federalists understood that in a democracy, temporary majorities could abuse their power. The Federalists' misgivings about majority rule were reflected in the constitutional structure. The indirect election of senators, the indirect election of the president, the judicial branch's insulation from the people, the separation of powers, the president's veto power, the bicameral design of Congress, and the federal system were all means to curb majority tyranny. These features suggest, following the institution principle, the framers' awareness of the problems of majority rule and the need for institutional safeguards. Except for the indirect election of senators (which was changed in 1913), these aspects of the constitutional structure remain in place today.[27] In essence, the Federalists sought to place limits on collective action in order to protect liberty. We shall return to this idea in Chapters 4 and 5.

To some extent, the Federalists and Antifederalists were influenced by different understandings of history. Federalists believed that colonial history, to say nothing of the history of the Greeks, showed that republican governments were often endangered by mob rule. The Antifederalists, by contrast, thought that history revealed the dangers of aristocratic conspiracies against popular liberties. History matters, but it is always subject to interpretation.

Governmental Power

A third major difference between Federalists and Antifederalists was the issue of governmental power. Both groups agreed on the principle of limited government, but they differed on how to place limits on governmental action.

Antifederalists favored limiting and enumerating the powers granted to the national government in relation to both the states and the people at large. To them, the powers given the national government ought to be "confined to certain defined national objects."[28] Otherwise, the national government would "swallow up all the power of the state governments."[29] Antifederalists bitterly attacked the supremacy clause and the necessary and proper clause of the Constitution as unlimited and dangerous grants of power to the national government.[30] They also demanded that a bill of rights be added to the Constitution to place limits on the government's exercise of power over the citizenry.

Federalists favored the construction of a government with broad powers—to defend the nation against foreign foes, guard against domestic strife and insurrection, promote commerce, and expand the nation's economy. Hamilton

---

27 A classic development of this theme is found in James M. Buchanan and Gordon Tullock, *The Calculus of Consent: Logical Foundations of Constitutional Democracy* (Ann Arbor: University of Michigan Press, 1962). For a review of the voting paradox and a case study of how it applies today, see Kenneth A. Shepsle, *Analyzing Politics: Rationality, Behavior and Institutions,* 2nd ed. (New York: Norton, 2010), pp. 53–89.

28 "Essays of Brutus," no. 7.

29 "Essays of Brutus," no. 6.

30 Storing, *What the Anti-Federalists Were For,* p. 28.

pointed out that these goals could not be achieved without allowing the government to exercise the necessary power. Federalists acknowledged, of course, that every power could be abused but argued that the way to prevent misuse of power was not by depriving government of the powers needed to achieve national goals. Instead, they argued, the threat of abuse of power would be mitigated by the Constitution's internal checks and controls. As Madison put it,

> The power surrendered by the people is first divided between two distinct governments, and then the portion allotted to each subdivided among distinct and separate departments. Hence a double security arises to the rights of the people. The different governments will control each other, at the same time that each will be controlled by itself.[31]

The Federalists' concern with avoiding unwarranted limits on governmental power led them to oppose a bill of rights, which they saw as unnecessary restrictions on the federal government. For the Federalists, the issue was one of national versus state power, not substantive rights as such. They feared that a bill of rights would weaken the federal government relative to the states.

The Federalists acknowledged that abuse of power remained a possibility but felt that the risk had to be taken because of the goals to be achieved. "The very idea of power included a possibility of doing harm," said the Federalist John Rutledge during South Carolina's ratification debates. "If the gentleman would show the power that could do no harm," Rutledge continued, "he would at once discover it to be a power that could do no good."[32]

CHANGING THE INSTITUTIONAL FRAMEWORK: CONSTITUTIONAL AMENDMENT

The Constitution has endured for more than two centuries as the framework of government. But it has not endured without change. Without change, the Constitution might have become merely a sacred relic, stored under glass.

Amendments: Many Are Called, Few Are Chosen

The framers of the Constitution recognized the need for change, and provisions for the amendments were incorporated into Article V. Since 1791, when the first 10 amendments—the Bill of Rights—were added, only 17 amendments have

---

31 *The Federalist,* no. 51.

32 Quoted in Storing, *What the Anti-Federalists Were For,* p. 30.

been adopted. And two of them—Prohibition and its repeal—cancel each other out, so that overall only 15 amendments have been added since 1791, despite vast changes in American society and its economy.

Four methods of amendment are provided for in Article V:

1. Passage in House and Senate by two-thirds vote; then ratification by majority vote of the legislatures of three-fourths (now 38) of the states.

2. Passage in House and Senate by two-thirds vote; then ratification by conventions called for that purpose in three-fourths of the states.

3. Passage in a national convention called by Congress in response to petitions by two-thirds (now 34) of the states; ratification by majority vote of the legislatures of three-fourths of the states.

4. Passage in a national convention, as in method 3; then ratification by conventions called for that purpose in three-fourths of the states.

(Figure 2.2 illustrates each of these methods.) Because no amendment has ever been proposed by national convention, however, routes 3 and 4 have never been

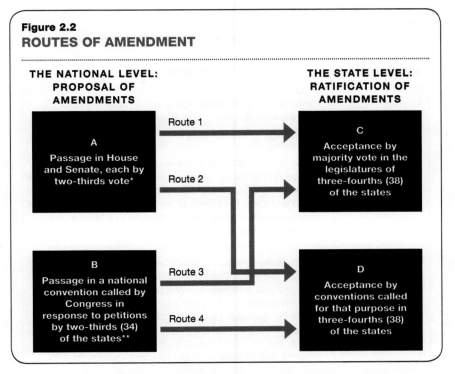

Figure 2.2
ROUTES OF AMENDMENT

THE NATIONAL LEVEL: PROPOSAL OF AMENDMENTS

THE STATE LEVEL: RATIFICATION OF AMENDMENTS

Route 1

A
Passage in House and Senate, each by two-thirds vote*

Route 2

C
Acceptance by majority vote in the legislatures of three-fourths (38) of the states

B
Passage in a national convention called by Congress in response to petitions by two-thirds (34) of the states**

Route 3

Route 4

D
Acceptance by conventions called for that purpose in three-fourths (38) of the states

* In each amendment proposal, Congress has the power to choose the method of ratification, the time limit for consideration by the states, and other conditions of ratification.

** This method of proposal has never been employed. Thus amendment routes 3 and 4 have never been attempted.

employed. And route 2 has been used only once (for the Twenty-First Amendment, which repealed the Eighteenth, or Prohibition, Amendment). Thus route 1 has been used for all the others.

The Twenty-Seven Amendments

The Constitution and its 27 amendments are reproduced at the end of this book. Most share a common characteristic: all but two are concerned with the structure or composition of government. This is consistent with the dictionary definition of *constitution* as the "makeup or composition of a thing." And it is consistent with the concept of a constitution as higher law, because the purpose of a higher law is to establish a framework within which government and the process of making ordinary law can take place. There is great wisdom in this principle. A constitution ought to enable legislation and public policies to take place, but it should not determine what that legislation or those public policies ought to be.

The purpose of the 10 amendments in the Bill of Rights was to give each of the three branches clearer and more restricted boundaries. The First

Table 2.3
THE BILL OF RIGHTS: ANALYSIS OF ITS PROVISIONS

AMENDMENT	PURPOSE
I	Limits on Congress: Congress is not to make any law establishing a religion or abridging the freedom of speech, press, or assembly or the right to petition the government.
II, III, IV	Limits on the executive: The executive branch is not to infringe on the right of people to keep arms (II), is not to force people arbitrarily to let soldiers live in their houses (III), and is not to engage in the search or seizure of evidence or to arrest people without a court warrant swearing to a belief in the probable existence of a crime (IV).
V, VI, VII, VIII	Limits on the courts: The courts are not to hold trials for serious offenses without provision for a grand jury (V), a petit (trial) jury (VII), a speedy trial (VI), presentation of charges, and confrontation of hostile witnesses (VI). Individuals may not be compelled to testify against themselves (V) and are immune from trial more than once for the same offense (V). Neither bail nor punishment can be excessive (VIII), and no property can be taken without just compensation (V).
IX, X	Limits on the national government: All rights not enumerated are reserved to the states or the people.

Amendment clarifies the jurisdiction of Congress. Although its powers under Article I, Section 8, do not justify laws regulating religion, speech, and the like, the First Amendment makes this limitation explicit: "Congress shall make no law . . ." The Second, Third, and Fourth Amendments similarly spell out limits on the executive branch, which were considered a necessity given the abuses of executive power Americans had endured under British rule.

The Fifth, Sixth, Seventh, and Eighth Amendments contain some of the most important safeguards for individual citizens against the arbitrary exercise of governmental power. These amendments define the judicial branch more concretely than had been done in Article III of the Constitution. The Ninth and Tenth Amendments reinforce the idea that the Constitution creates a government of limited powers. The Ninth declares that failure to mention a right does not mean it is not possessed by the people while the Tenth states that powers not granted to the federal government are reserved to the states and the people. Table 2.3 analyzes the 10 amendments included in the Bill of Rights.

Five of the 17 amendments adopted since 1791 are concerned with expansion of the electorate (Table 2.4). These efforts resulted from the Founders being unable to establish a national electorate with uniform voting qualifications. Stalemated on that issue, the delegates decided to evade it by providing in the final draft of Article I, Section 2, that eligibility to vote in a national election would be the same as "the Qualifications requisite for Electors of the

Table 2.4

AMENDING THE CONSTITUTION TO EXPAND THE ELECTORATE

AMENDMENT	PURPOSE	YEAR PROPOSED	YEAR ADOPTED
XIV	Provided, in Section 1, a national definition of citizenship	1866	1868
XV	Extended voting rights to all races	1869	1870
XIX	Extended voting rights to women	1919	1920
XXIII	Extended voting rights to residents of the District of Columbia	1960	1961
XXIV	Extended voting rights to all classes by abolition of poll taxes	1962	1964
XXVI	Extended voting rights to citizens ages 18 and over	1971	1971

Table 2.5

AMENDING THE CONSTITUTION TO CHANGE THE RELATIONSHIP BETWEEN THE ELECTED OFFICES AND THE ELECTORATE

AMENDMENT	PURPOSE	YEAR PROPOSED	YEAR ADOPTED
XII	Provided a separate ballot for the vice president in the electoral college	1803	1804
XIV	Penalized states for depriving freed slaves of the right to vote	1866	1868
XVII	Provided for the direct election of senators	1912	1913
XX	Shortened the time between elections and inauguration of the new president and Congress	1932	1933
XXII	Limited the presidential term	1947	1951
XXV	Provided for presidential succession in case of disability	1965	1967

most numerous Branch of the State Legislature." Article I, Section 4, added that Congress could alter state regulations as to the "Times, Places and Manner of holding Elections for Senators and Representatives." Nevertheless, this meant that any important expansion of the American electorate would almost certainly require a constitutional amendment.

Six more amendments are also electoral in nature, although not concerned directly with voting rights and the expansion of the electorate. These amendments deal with the elective offices themselves (the Twentieth, Twenty-Second, and Twenty-Fifth) or with the relationship between elective offices and the electorate (the Twelfth, Fourteenth, and Seventeenth; Table 2.5).

Another five amendments have sought to expand or limit the powers of the national and state governments (Table 2.6).[33] The Eleventh Amendment

33 The Fourteenth Amendment is included in this table as well as in Table 2.4 because it not only seeks to define citizenship but also *seems* to intend that this definition of citizenship include, along with the right to vote, all the rights of the Bill of Rights, regardless of the state in which the citizen resides. A great deal more will be said about this in Chapter 4.

Table 2.6

AMENDING THE CONSTITUTION TO EXPAND OR LIMIT THE POWER OF GOVERNMENT

AMENDMENT	PURPOSE	YEAR PROPOSED	YEAR ADOPTED
XI	Limited the jurisdiction of federal courts over suits involving the states	1794	1795
XIII	Eliminated slavery and the rights of states to allow property in the form of persons	1865*	1865
XIV	Established due process of law in state courts for all persons; later used to apply the entire Bill of Rights to the states	1866	1868
XVI	Established the national power to tax income	1909	1913
XXVII	Limited Congress's power to raise its own salary	1789	1992

* The Thirteenth Amendment was proposed on January 31, 1865, and adopted less than a year later, on December 6, 1865.

protects the states from suits by private individuals and takes away from the federal courts any power to hear suits by private individuals of one state (or a foreign country) against another state. Three other amendments in Table 2.6 aim to reduce state power (the Thirteenth), reduce state power and expand national power (the Fourteenth), and expand national power (the Sixteenth). The Twenty-Seventh limits Congress's ability to raise its members' salary.

The two missing amendments underscore the meaning of the rest: the Eighteenth, or Prohibition, Amendment and the Twenty-First, its repeal. They represent the only instance in which the country tried to *legislate* by constitutional amendment. In other words, the Eighteenth is the only amendment that was designed to address a substantive social problem. And it was the only amendment ever to have been repealed. Two other amendments—the Thirteenth, which abolished slavery, and the Sixteenth, which established the power to levy an income tax—essentially had the effect of legislation. But the purpose of the Thirteenth Amendment was to restrict the states' power by forever forbidding them to treat any human being as property. As for the Sixteenth Amendment, it is certainly true that income-tax legislation followed immediately; nevertheless, the amendment concerns itself strictly with establishing the power of Congress to enact such legislation. The legislation came later.

For those whose hopes for change center on the Constitution, it must be emphasized that the amendment route to social change is, and always will be, extremely limited. This is "path dependency," as captured in the history principle, with a vengeance. The status quo—the original Constitution—and the arduousness of its amendment process provide durability on the one hand and constrain the prospects for change on the other. Through a constitution it is possible to establish a working structure of government, and through a constitution it is possible to establish basic rights of citizens by placing limitations and obligations on that government's powers. Once these structures have been accomplished, the real problem is how to extend rights to those people who do not already enjoy them.

CONCLUSION: REFLECTIONS ON THE FOUNDING—IDEALS OR INTERESTS?

At the start of this chapter, we stressed the need to look beyond the myths and rhetoric of the Founding era to analyze the Founders' goals, their struggle to resolve their conflicts and reach their collective goals, and the institutions that resulted from their endeavor. The story of the Founding—the initial decision of Britain's New World colonies to chart a separate course (the Declaration of Independence), a successful revolution and the creation of a confederation of states with a weak central government (the Articles of Confederation), and the re-creation of an entirely elaborated new body of institutional arrangements (the Constitution)—is a chronicle of purposeful collective action leading to the creation of a unique political scaffolding for governance.

The revolutionary generation, the politicians of the Articles years, and those who met in Philadelphia to create a new nation were rational actors with specific goals. Northern merchants and manufacturers wanted property protection and security, unfettered opportunities to trade in domestic and international markets, and the financial security of sound currency, low taxes, and limited public debt. Southern planters also wanted property protection (with some of that property human in form), low tariffs to obtain manufactured goods cheaply, and access to international markets for their products and for slaves. Small farmers, tradesmen, and artisans wanted easy credit, relief from onerous taxes, and permissive policies toward debt. Independence, loose federation, and finally a new nation with a central government capable of effective action were the goals, at different times, toward which many of these groups pointed.

To orchestrate a revolution, organize a confederation, or draft a constitution requires a large variety of collective actions. Behaviors must be coordinated, participation must be induced, efforts must be focused on common objectives, and free riding must be discouraged. During the Founding period, political leaders facilitated this process. Jefferson and Adams brought the colonies to the point of separating from the motherland; Washington was pivotal in the revolutionary phase; numerous politicians bargained over the directions to be taken by the Confederation; Madison, Hamilton, Washington, and ultimately Franklin presided over the drafting of the Constitution. In sum, collective action, coordinated by motivated leadership, paved the historical path from colony to new nation.

We've also seen that new institutions were needed to organize the new government successfully. Colonial institutions were satisfactory for 150 years, especially while the mother country was preoccupied with events elsewhere. Independence and self-governance became institutional objectives when the burdens of colonialism began to stifle the colonists' economic circumstances and political freedoms. From roughly 1775 to 1790, the Founders experimented with and ultimately crafted a political order that, in most aspects, has survived more than two centuries. The final product of the Constitutional Convention stands as an extraordinary victory for the groups that most forcefully had sought a new system of government to replace the Articles of Confederation. Antifederalist criticisms forced the Constitution's proponents to accept a bill of rights designed to limit the powers of the national government. In general, however, it was the Federalist vision of America that triumphed. The Constitution adopted in 1789 created the framework for a powerful national government that has defended the nation's interests, promoted its commerce, and maintained national unity in the years since.

Though the Constitution was the product of a particular set of political forces, the form of government it established has significance far beyond its authors' interests. As we have observed, political ideals often take on lives of their own. The great political values incorporated into the Constitution continue to shape our lives in ways that the framers may not have anticipated. For example, when they empowered Congress to regulate commerce among the states, they could hardly have anticipated that this provision would become the basis for many federal regulatory activities in areas as diverse as the environment and civil rights.

Two great constitutional notions, federalism and civil liberties, will be discussed in Chapters 3 and 4, respectively. As we close our discussion of the Founding, though, it is worth reflecting on the Antifederalists. Although they were defeated, they show an important picture of an America that might have been. Would we have been worse off if we had been governed by a confederacy of small republics linked by a national administration with severely limited powers? Were the Antifederalists correct in predicting that a government given great power in the hope that it might do good would, through "insensible progress," inevitably come to serve the interests of the few at the expense of the many? More than two centuries of government under the federal Constitution are not enough to definitively answer these questions. Only time will tell.

For Further Reading

Allison, Robert. *The American Revolution: A Concise History.* New York: Oxford University Press, 2011.

Amar, Akhil Reed. *America's Constitution: A Biography.* New York: Random House, 2005.

Bailyn, Bernard. *The Ideological Origins of the American Revolution.* Cambridge: Harvard University Press, 1967.

Beard, Charles A. *An Economic Interpretation of the Constitution of the United States.* New York: Macmillan, 1913.

Beeman, Richard. *Plain, Honest Men: The Making of the American Constitution.* New York: Random House, 2010.

Chernow, Ron. *Alexander Hamilton.* New York: Penguin, 2004.

Dahl, Robert. *How Democratic Is the American Constitution?* 2nd ed. New Haven, CT: Yale University Press, 2003.

Ellis, Joseph. *Founding Brothers: The Revolutionary Generation.* New York: Knopf, 2000.

Ellis, Joseph. *His Excellency, George Washington.* New York: Knopf, 2004.

Farrand, Max, ed. *The Records of the Federal Convention of 1787.* Rev. ed. 4 vols. New Haven, CT: Yale University Press, 1966.

Ferling, John. *Whirlwind: The American Revolution and the War That Won It.* New York: Bloomsbury Press, 2015.

Glaeser, Edward C. "Revolution of Urban Rebels." *Boston Globe,* July 4, 2008, section A.

Hamilton, Alexander, James Madison, and John Jay. *The Federalist Papers,* no. 10 and no. 51. Clinton Rossiter, ed. New York: New American Library, 1961.

Keller, Morton. *America's Three Regimes: A New Political History.* New York: Oxford University Press, 2007.

Lutz, Donald. *Colonial Origins of the American Constitution.* New York: Liberty Fund, 2010.

Newton, Michael. *Angry Mobs and Founding Fathers: The Fight for Control of the American Revolution.* New York: Eleftheria, 2011.

Riker, William H. *The Strategy of Rhetoric: Campaigning for the American Constitution.* New Haven, CT: Yale University Press, 1996.

Stewart, David O. *Madison's Gift: Five Partnerships That Built America* New York: Simon & Schuster, 2015.

Storing, Herbert J., ed. *The Complete Anti-Federalist.* 7 vols. Chicago: University of Chicago Press, 1981.

3

Federalism and the Separation of Powers

The great achievement of American politics in the eighteenth century was the fashioning of an effective constitutional structure of political institutions. Although it is an imperfect and continuously evolving work in progress, this structure of law and political practice has served well for more than two centuries by managing conflict, providing inducements for bargaining and cooperation, and facilitating collective action. It has had at least one major failure: the cruel practice of slavery, which ended only after a destructive civil war. But the basic configuration of institutions first formulated in Philadelphia in 1787 survived that tragedy and has otherwise stood the test of time.

Two of the United States' most important institutional features are federalism and the separation of powers. Federalism seeks to limit government by dividing it into two levels, national and state, each with sufficient independence to compete with the other, thereby restraining the power of both.[1] The separation of powers seeks to limit the national government's power by dividing government against itself—by giving the legislative, executive, and judicial branches separate functions, thus forcing them to share power.

In Chapter 1 we observed that institutions organize political life. Institutions, however, take many forms and can choreograph collective action in a variety of ways. One important way in which political institutions vary is the manner in which they distribute decision, agenda, and veto powers. Institutions established by authoritarian regimes usually concentrate power in a small group

---

1   The notion that federalism requires separate spheres or jurisdictions in which lower and higher levels of government are uniquely decisive is developed fully in William H. Riker, *Federalism: Origin, Operation, Significance* (Boston: Little, Brown, 1964). This American version of federalism is applied to the emerging federal arrangements in the People's Republic of China during the 1990s in a paper by Barry R. Weingast: "The Economic Role of Political Institutions: Market-Preserving Federalism and Economic Development," *Journal of Law, Economics, and Organization* 11 (1995): 1–32.

of leaders who determine what will be considered, make the final decisions, and seek to block the actions of others. In democratic states, in contrast, political institutions usually allow a variety of groups to participate in decision making and provide at least a measure of agenda and veto power to numerous actors.

In the United States, the framers of the Constitution created institutions that would widely disperse involvement in decision making. Federalism assigns agenda-setting power, decision-making power, and veto powers to the federal government and to each of the 50 states. The separation of powers gives several federal institutions a degree of control over the agenda, the power to affect decisions, and the ability to block the others' actions. The framers feared that concentrating power in a small number of hands would threaten citizens' liberties, and they were correct. Yet, although the dispersion of power among federal institutions and between the federal government and the states may well protect our liberties, it often seems to make it impossible to get anything done collectively. This lack of decisiveness sometimes appears to negate the most important reason for building institutions in the first place.

Since the adoption of the Constitution, politicians have developed various strategies for overcoming the impediments to policy change that inevitably arise in our federal system of separated powers. Most commonly, those seeking to promote a new program may try to find ways of dispersing the program's benefits so other politicians controlling institutional veto powers will find it in their interest to go along. For example, if the executive branch hopes to win congressional support for a new weapons system, it generally ensures that portions of the new system are subcontracted to firms in as many congressional districts as possible. In this way, dispersion of benefits helps overcome the separation of powers between the executive and legislative branches. Similarly, as we see later, federal officials often secure state cooperation with national programs by

CORE OF THE ANALYSIS

 Two of the most important institutional features of America's government are federalism and the separation of powers.

 Federalism assigns agenda-setting, decision-making, and veto powers to the federal government and the 50 states.

 The apportionment of powers between the federal government and the states has shifted over time.

 The separation of powers delineates the authority of the executive branch, Congress, and the courts, giving each a degree of control over the agenda, the power to affect decisions, and the ability to block the actions of the others.

offering the states funding, called grants-in-aid, in exchange for their compliance. These programs help overcome the limitations of federalism. Spending on public works and other pork-barrel projects, a term used to describe federal dollars that members of Congress bring home to their states and districts offers yet another strategy for achieving policies by dispersing their benefits. Thus, consistent with our discussion of the five principles of politics in Chapter 1, America's public policies are shaped by the institutional arrangements through which individual efforts must flow.

However, institutions are not carved in stone. They are subject to modification as competing forces seek new decision rules that will give them an advantage, and as the leaders of institutions seek to strengthen their own power and expand their own jurisdictions at the expense of other institutions. In recent decades, the presidency has increased in power relative to Congress, and the federal government has grown in jurisdiction relative to the states. Nevertheless, these two core institutional features, federalism and the separation of powers, remain at the heart of the American system of government. Let us examine them and assess their consequences for American government.

WHO DOES WHAT? FEDERALISM AND INSTITUTIONAL JURISDICTIONS

federalism

The system of government in which a constitution divides power between a central government and regional governments

sovereignty

Independent political authority. A government holding such authority is a sovereign

Federalism can be defined as the division of powers and functions between the national government and the state governments. Federalism limits national and state power by creating two levels of government—the national government and the state governments, each with significant **sovereignty** and thus the ability to restrain the power of the other. As we saw in Chapter 2, the states existed as individual colonies before independence, and for nearly 13 years they were virtually autonomous units under the Articles of Confederation. In effect, the states had retained too much power relative to the national government, a problem that led directly to the Annapolis Convention in 1786 and to the Constitutional Convention in 1787. Under the Articles, disorder within states was beyond the reach of the national government (see Shays's Rebellion, discussed in Chapter 2), and conflicts of interest between states were not manageable. For example, states were making their own trade agreements with foreign countries and companies, which could then play off one state against another for special advantages. Some states adopted barriers to foreign commerce that were contrary to the interests of other states.[2] Tax and other barriers were also being erected.[3] But even after

2 For a good treatment of these conflicts of interest between states, see Forrest McDonald, *E Pluribus Unum: The Formation of the American Republic, 1776–1790* (Boston: Houghton Mifflin, 1965), chap. 7, esp. pp. 319–38.

3 See David M. O'Brien, *Constitutional Law and Politics,* 3rd ed. (New York: Norton, 1997), I: 602–03.

ratification of the Constitution, the states remained more important than the national government. For nearly a century and a half, virtually all of the fundamental policies governing Americans' lives were made by the state legislatures, not by Congress.

Why Keep the States: The Importance of History. Many of the Constitution's framers, particularly Alexander Hamilton, had hoped to create something close to a unitary national government and to circumscribe severely the power of the individual states. The fact that the framers established a federal system in which the states retained significant powers is an illustration of the importance of history. Each state had well-established governmental institutions staffed by legislators, judges, and executive officials who had no desire to see their power and autonomy submerged in a new national government. At the same time, citizens identified with their own states. The people of North America were not Americans. Instead, they had already had several generations to become Virginians, New Yorkers, Pennsylvanians, and so on. Well-established popular identification with the 13 states was another reason that even the most nationalistic framers had to accept that the states would continue as important entities. In a sense, the framers faced the same historically given realities faced today by advocates of a stronger European Union (EU). The nations of Europe have historically distinct identities, well-entrenched governments, and loyal citizens. Given the force of history, uniting these nations is no easy matter. Like America's Founders, the architects of the EU, bowing to history, have generally sought to erect the new regime on federal foundations. A federal system also allows geographically concentrated groups to wield more power than they could wield in a central system (see the Policy Principle section on p. 76).

Federalism in the Constitution: Who Decides What

American federalism recognized two sovereigns in the original Constitution and reinforced the principle in the Bill of Rights by granting a few expressed powers to the national government and reserving the rest to the states. Thus the Constitution defined the jurisdiction of each level of government.

The Powers of the National Government. As we saw in Chapter 2, the expressed powers granted to the national government are found in Article I, Section 8, of the Constitution. These 17 powers include the powers to collect taxes, coin money, declare war, and regulate commerce (which became a very important power for the national government). Article I, Section 8, also contains an important source of power for the national government: the **implied powers** that enable Congress "to make all Laws which shall be necessary and proper for carrying into Execution the foregoing Powers." Not until several decades after the Founding did the Supreme Court allow Congress to exercise the power granted in this necessary and proper clause, but ultimately the doctrine allowed the national government to expand the scope of its authority. In addition to expressed and implied powers, the Constitution affirms the national government's power in the supremacy clause (Article VI), which makes all national laws and treaties "the supreme Law of the Land."

 implied powers

Powers derived from the necessary and proper clause (Article I, Section 8) of the Constitution; such powers are not specifically expressed but are implied through the expansive interpretation of delegated powers

Federalism and Support for Corn Farmers

An ethanol plant in Missouri.

One of the United States' key institutional arrangements is federalism. Because members of Congress are elected from districts and states rather than chosen on a national basis, and because states also elect governments of their own that possess considerable powers, well-organized local groups often find it possible to work through Congress to develop national government policies that serve their interests.

Take the case of ethanol. Because ethanol (ethyl alcohol) can be made from a renewable resource—agricultural crops such as corn—grown in the United States, ethanol producers have argued that its increased use in motor fuel would help preserve nonrenewable resources such as oil and thus reduce American dependence on energy suppliers in the volatile Middle East.

The U.S. government has been heavily subsidizing the production and use of ethanol since the 1970s by mandating its addition to motor fuel. In 2015, the Environmental Protection Agency proposed increasing the required use of ethanol in motor fuel, but supporters of the product charged that the agency's proposal did not go far enough.

If ethanol could indeed become a renewable, domestically produced substitute for foreign oil, these billions in federal subsidies would have been well spent. However, the claims by pro-ethanol forces may be based more on political considerations than on economic and technological reality. The energy needed to produce a gallon of ethanol from corn is greater than the energy that can be generated by that gallon; thus on balance ethanol production actually consumes rather than creates energy.

If ethanol is not the answer to dependence on foreign oil, why does the government require its use? The answer has to do with the structure of government institutions and how such institutions shape policies. As a federal republic, the United States elects its legislature—Congress—in local contests, rather than national ones (as in some other countries) in which citizens vote for a political party rather than individual candidates, and national party officials select the individuals to fill the number of seats proportional to the party's share of the vote. In addition, in the United States each state has a separate and powerful level of government, whose governor is elected at the state level rather than appointed by the national government. This decentralized system allows geographically concentrated interest groups to wield more power through their local members of Congress and state governments than they could possibly wield in a centralized system where decision making was concentrated at the national level. Ethanol producers are highly organized and concentrated in several Midwestern agricultural states such as Iowa, and the campaign for ethanol subsidies and tax breaks is strongly backed by virtually all the members of Congress and governors representing these states. Thus, federalism magnifies the political influence of the pro-ethanol forces, which would otherwise be minor players, by giving them a chance to wield power within several states.

The Powers of State Governments. One way in which the framers preserved a strong role for the states was through the Tenth Amendment. This amendment presents a decision rule, or general principle governing decisions, stating that the powers the Constitution does not delegate to the national government or deny to the states are "reserved to the States respectively, or to the people." The Antifederalists, who feared that a strong central government would encroach on individual liberty, pressed for such an amendment as a way of limiting national power. Federalists agreed to the amendment because they did not think it would do much harm, given the powers the Constitution already granted to the national government. The Tenth Amendment is also called the **reserved powers** amendment because it aims to reserve powers to the states.

The most fundamental power retained by the states is that of coercion—the power to develop and enforce criminal codes, administer health and safety rules, and regulate the family via marriage and divorce laws. The states have the power to regulate individuals' livelihoods: if you're a doctor or a lawyer or a plumber or a barber, you must be licensed by the state. Even more fundamental, the states have the power to define private property: private property exists because state laws against trespass define who is and who is not entitled to use a piece of property. If you own a car, your ownership isn't worth much unless the state is willing to enforce your right to possession by making it a crime for anyone else to drive your car without your permission. Similarly, your "ownership" of a house or piece of land means that the state will enforce your possession by prohibiting others from occupying the property against your will. At the same time, however, under its power of **eminent domain**, the state may seize your property for anything it deems to be a public purpose. If the state does seize your property, it is required by its own constitution and the federal Constitution to compensate you for your loss. The decision to take the property, though, is well within the states' recognized powers.

A state's authority to regulate these fundamental matters, commonly referred to as the **police power** of the state, encompasses its power to regulate the health, safety, welfare, and morals of its citizens. Policing is what states do—they coerce you in the name of the community in order to maintain public order. And this was exactly the type of power the Founders intended the states to exercise.

In some areas, the states share **concurrent powers** with the national government: they share some power to regulate commerce and affect the currency— for example, by chartering banks, granting or denying corporate charters, and regulating the quality of products or the conditions of labor. This issue of concurrent versus exclusive power has come up at times in our history, but wherever there has been a direct conflict of laws between the federal and the state levels, the issue has generally been resolved in favor of national supremacy.

States' Obligations to One Another. The Constitution also creates obligations among the states. These obligations, spelled out in Article IV, were intended to promote national unity. By requiring the states to recognize actions taken in other states as legal and proper, the framers aimed to make the states less like independent countries and more like parts of a single nation. Article IV, Section 1, calls for "Full Faith and Credit" among states, meaning that each state

 reserved powers

Powers, derived from the Tenth Amendment to the Constitution, that are not specifically delegated to the national government or denied to the states; these powers are reserved to the states

 eminent domain

The right of the government to take private property for public use, with reasonable compensation awarded for the property

 police power

The power reserved to the government to regulate the health, safety, and morals of its citizens

 concurrent powers

The authority possessed by *both* state and national governments, such as the power to levy taxes

is expected to honor the "public Acts, Records, and Proceedings" that take place in any other state. So, for example, if two people are married in Texas—marriage being regulated by state law—Missouri must recognize that marriage even though the couple was not married under Missouri state law.

full faith and credit clause

The provision in Article IV, Section 1, of the Constitution requiring that each state normally honors the public acts and judicial decisions that take place in another state

This **full faith and credit clause** recently became entangled in the controversy over same-sex marriage. In 1996, Congress passed the federal Defense of Marriage Act (DOMA), declaring that states would not have to recognize a same-sex marriage legally contracted in another state. DOMA also barred same-sex couples from receiving federal health, tax, social security, and other benefits available to heterosexual couples. In 2013, however, the Supreme Court in *Windsor v. the United States* struck down the Defense of Marriage Act in part, requiring that same-sex married couples receive equal treatment on issues relating to taxes, inheritance, and other federal laws.[4] After *Windsor,* many state courts struck down the state bans on same-sex marriage. On the second anniversary of the *Windsor* ruling, the Court extended this decision in *Obergefell v. Hodges,* ruling that states were required to issue marriage licenses to same-sex couples and to recognize such marriages performed in other jurisdictions.[5]

comity clause

Article IV, Section 2 of the Constitution, which prohibits states from enacting laws that treat the citizens of other states in a discriminatory manner

Article IV, Section 2, known as the **comity clause**, also promotes national unity. It provides that citizens enjoying the privileges and immunities of one state should be entitled to similar treatment in other states. Essentially, a state cannot discriminate against someone from another state or give special privileges to its own residents. For example, in the 1970s, when Alaska passed a law that gave residents preference over nonresidents in obtaining work on the state's oil and gas pipelines, the Supreme Court ruled the law illegal because it discriminated against citizens of other states.[6] There are many exceptions to the comity clause. For example, states may charge out-of-state students a higher tuition rate at state colleges and universities. The comity clause also regulates criminal justice among the states by requiring states to return fugitives to the states from which they have fled. Thus in 1952, when an inmate escaped from an Alabama prison and sought to avoid being returned on the grounds that he was subject to "cruel and unusual punishment" there, the Supreme Court ruled that he must be returned, according to Article IV, Section 2.[7] This example highlights the difference between the obligations among states and those among different countries. Recently France refused to return an American fugitive because he might be subject to the death penalty, which does not exist in France.[8] The Constitution clearly forbids states from doing something similar.

Limitations on the States. Although most of the truly coercive powers of government are reserved to the states, the Constitution does impose

---

4   *United States v. Windsor,* 135 S.Ct. 2071 (2015).

5   *Obergefell v. Hodges,* 576 U.S. ____ (2015).

6   *Hicklin v. Orbeck,* 437 U.S. 518 (1978).

7   *Sweeney v. Woodall,* 344 U.S. 86 (1953).

8   Marlise Simons, "France Won't Extradite American Convicted of Murder," *New York Times,* December 5, 1997, p. A9.

some significant limitations. As discussed in the previous section, states cannot discriminate against denizens of other states, and states must extradite alleged criminals to the state with jurisdiction. Another potential limit on states is in a clause in Article I, Section 10, that provides that "no State shall, without the Consent of Congress, . . . enter into any Agreement or Compact with another State." Compacts are a way for two or more states to reach a legally binding agreement about how to solve a problem that crosses state lines. In the early years of the Republic, states turned to compacts primarily to settle border disputes. Today with the support of the federal government they are used for a wide range of issues but are especially important in regulating the distribution of river water, addressing environmental concerns, and operating transportation systems that cross state lines.[9] A well-known contemporary example is the Port of New York Authority (now the Port Authority of New York and New Jersey), a compact formed between New York and New Jersey in 1921. Without it, such public works as the bridge connecting Brooklyn and Staten Island, the bridges connecting New Jersey and Staten Island, the Lincoln Tunnel, the George Washington Bridge, and the expansion and integration of the three major airports could not have been financed or completed.[10]

The federal government has occasionally blocked a proposed interstate compact, thus limiting state action in certain spheres. In 1939, for example, President Franklin Delano Roosevelt vetoed a bill that would have granted consent in advance to states to enter into compacts relating to fishing in the Atlantic Ocean. Roosevelt considered the advance authorization to be too vague. In 2001, Congress refused to allow the renewal of a compact among the several New England states that regulated milk prices. The New England compact has been opposed by Midwestern dairy farmers. More often than it prohibits compacts, however, Congress attaches conditions to its approval of proposed interstate compacts. For example, when it approved the compact among Virginia, Maryland, and the District of Columbia establishing the Washington Metropolitan Transit Authority in 1960, Congress set a number of conditions, including requiring the publication of specified data and information by the authority.[11]

Local Government and the Constitution. Local government, including counties, cities, and towns, occupies a peculiar but very important place in the American system. In fact, the status of American local government is probably unique in world experience. First, it must be pointed out that local government has no status in the American Constitution. *State* legislatures created local

---

9 Patricia S. Florestano, "Past and Present Utilization of Interstate Compacts in the United States," *Publius* (fall 1994): 13–26.

10 A good discussion of the status of the New York Port Authority in politics is found in Wallace Sayre and Herbert Kaufman, *Governing New York City: Politics in the Metropolis* (New York: Russell Sage Foundation, 1960), chap. 9.

11 John R. Koza, Barry Fadem, Mark Grueskin, Michael Mandell, Robert Richie, and Joseph Zimmerman, *Every Vote Equal*, 3rd ed. (Los Altos, CA: National Popular Vote Press, 2011), chap. 5.

governments, and *state* constitutions and laws permit local governments to take on some of the responsibilities of the state governments. Most states amended their own constitutions to give their larger cities **home rule**—a guarantee of noninterference in various areas of local affairs. But local governments enjoy no such recognition in the Constitution. Local governments have always been mere conveniences of the states.[12]

home rule

The power delegated by the state to a local unit of government to manage its own affairs

Local governments became administratively important early in the Republic because the states possessed little administrative capability. They relied on cities and counties to implement the state's laws. Local government was an alternative to a statewide bureaucracy. Today, local governments and state bureaucracies both compete and cooperate with one another. Take, for example, the relationship between state and county police forces, which usually involve a mix of collegiality and rivalry.

The Slow Growth of the National Government's Power

dual federalism

The system of government that prevailed in the United States from 1789 to 1937 in which fundamental governmental powers were shared between the federal and state governments, with the states exercising the most important powers

Before the 1930s, America's federal system was essentially one of **dual federalism**, a two-layered system—national and state—in which the states and their local principalities did most of the governing. That is, the jurisdiction of the states was greater than that of the federal government. We call it the traditional system because almost nothing about it changed during two-thirds of America's history (with the exception of the Civil War years, after which we returned to the traditional system).

But there was more to dual federalism than merely the two tiers. They were functionally quite different from each other, and every generation since the Founding has debated how to divide responsibilities between the two. As we have seen, the Constitution delegated specific powers to the national government and reserved all the rest to the states. That left a lot of room for interpretation, however, because of the final, "elastic" clause of Article I, Section 8. The three formal words *necessary and proper* amounted to an invitation to struggle over the distribution of powers between national and state governments. We confront this struggle throughout the book. However, it is noteworthy that federalism remained dual for nearly two-thirds of our history, with the national government remaining steadfastly within a "strict construction" of Article I, Section 8.

The Supreme Court has at times ruled on the debate over the distribution of powers between national and state governments, starting in 1819 with a case favoring national power, *McCulloch v. Maryland*.[13] The issue was whether Congress had the power to charter a bank—in particular the Bank of the United

---

12 A good discussion of the constitutional position of local governments is in York Y. Willbern, *The Withering Away of the City* (Bloomington: Indiana University Press, 1971). For more on the structure and theory of federalism, see Thomas R. Dye, *American Federalism: Competition among Governments* (Lexington, MA: Lexington Books, 1990), chap. 1; and Martha Derthick, "Up-to-Date in Kansas City: Reflections on American Federalism," *PS: Political Science and Politics* 25 (December 1992): 671–75.

13 *McCulloch v. Maryland*, 4 Wheaton 316 (1819).

States (created by Congress in 1791 over Thomas Jefferson's constitutional opposition)—because no express power to create banks exists anywhere in Article I, Section 8. Chief Justice John Marshall stated that such a power could be "implied" from the **commerce clause** plus the final necessary and proper clause. Essentially, Marshall's ruling said that if a goal was allowed in the Constitution and Congress's chosen means to achieve the goal was not prohibited by the Constitution, then Congress could act. Thus the Court created the potential for significantly increased national governmental power.

A second question of national power arose in the same case of whether Maryland's attempt to tax the bank was constitutional. Once again Marshall and the Supreme Court sided with national government, arguing that a bank created by a legislature representing all the people (Congress) could not be taxed out of business by a state legislature (Maryland) representing only a small portion of the American people. Here also the Supreme Court reinforced the supremacy clause: whenever a state law conflicts with a federal law, the state law should be deemed invalid because "the Laws of the United States . . . shall be the supreme Law of the Land." (For more on federal supremacy, see Chapters 2 and 9.)

This nationalistic interpretation of the Constitution was reinforced by *Gibbons v. Ogden* in 1824. At issue was whether the state of New York could grant a monopoly to a steamboat company to operate an exclusive service between New York and New Jersey. Aaron Ogden had secured his license from the company, whereas Thomas Gibbons, a former partner of Ogden's, had secured a competing license from the U.S. government. Chief Justice Marshall argued that Gibbons could not be kept from competing because the state of New York did not have the power to grant this particular monopoly affecting other states' interests. At issue was the commerce clause, which delegates to Congress the power "to regulate Commerce with foreign nations, and *among the several States* and with Indian tribes" [emphasis added]. Marshall insisted that the definition of the commerce clause was "comprehensive" but added that the comprehensiveness was limited "to that commerce which concerns more states than one." This opinion gave rise to the legal concept that later came to be called interstate commerce.[14]

Despite the Court's expansive reading of national power in the Republic's early years, between the 1820s and the 1930s federal power grew slowly. During the Jacksonian period, a states' rights coalition developed in Congress. Among the most important members were state party leaders who often had themselves appointed to the Senate, where they jealously guarded the powers of the states they ruled. Of course, the senators and members of the House from the southern states had a particular reason to support states' rights: so long as the states were powerful and the federal government weak, the South's institution of slavery could not be threatened.

Aside from the interruption of the Civil War, the states' rights coalition dominated Congress, affected presidential nominations—a matter also controlled by the state party leaders—and influenced judicial appointments, which required senatorial acquiescence, as well. Indeed, the Supreme Court turned

 commerce clause

The clause found in Article I, Section 8, of the Constitution that delegates to Congress the power "to regulate Commerce with foreign Nations, and among the several States, and with the Indian Tribes." This clause was interpreted by the Supreme Court to favor national power over the economy

14 *Gibbons v. Ogden,* 9 Wheaton 1 (1824).

away from John Marshall's nationalistic jurisprudence in favor of a states' rights interpretation of the Constitution—especially in cases concerning the commerce clause. For many years, any federal effort to regulate commerce in such areas as fraud, the production of impure goods, the use of child labor, or the existence of dangerous working conditions or long hours was declared unconstitutional by the Supreme Court as a violation of interstate commerce. Regulation in these areas would mean the federal government was entering the factory and the workplace, areas inherently local because the goods produced there had not yet passed into commerce and crossed state lines. Rather, the Court held that regulation of these areas constituted police power, a power reserved to the states. No one questioned the power of the national government to regulate certain kinds of businesses, such as railroads, gas pipelines, and waterway transportation because they intrinsically involved interstate commerce.[15] But well into the twentieth century, most other efforts by Congress to regulate commerce were blocked by the Supreme Court's interpretation of federalism, with the concept of interstate commerce as the primary barrier.

After his election in 1932, President Franklin Delano Roosevelt was eager to expand the power of the national government. His "New Deal" depended on governmental power to regulate the economy and to intervene in every facet of American society. Roosevelt's efforts provoked sharp conflicts between the president and the federal judiciary. After making a host of new judicial appointments and threatening to expand the size of the Supreme Court, Roosevelt managed to bend the judiciary to his will. Beginning in the late 1930s, the Court issued a series of decisions converting the commerce clause from a barrier to a source of national power.

One key case was *National Labor Relations Board v. Jones & Loughlin Steel Company*.[16] At issue was the National Labor Relations Act, which prohibited corporations from interfering with the efforts of employees to organize into unions, to bargain collectively over wages and working conditions, and to go on strike and engage in picketing. The newly formed National Labor Relations Board (NLRB) had ordered Jones & Loughlin to reinstate workers fired because of their union activities. The appeal reached the Supreme Court because the steel company had made a constitutional issue over the fact that its manufacturing activities, being local, were beyond the government's reach. But the Court ruled that a large corporation with subsidiaries and suppliers in many states was inherently involved in interstate commerce and hence subject to congressional regulation. In other decisions, the Court upheld minimum wage laws, the Social Security Act, and federal rules controlling how much of any given commodity local farmers might grow.[17]

....

15 In *Wabash, St. Louis, and Pacific Railway Company v. Illinois*, 118 U.S. 557 (1886), the Supreme Court struck down a state law prohibiting rate discrimination by a railroad; in response, Congress passed the Interstate Commerce Act of 1887, creating the Interstate Commerce Commission (ICC), the first federal regulatory agency.

16 *National Labor Relations Board v. Jones & Loughlin Steel Company*, 301 U.S. 1 (1937).

17 *Wickard v. Filburn*, 317 U.S. 111 (1942).

After 1937, the Court threw out the old distinction between interstate and intrastate commerce. The Court would not even review appeals challenging acts of Congress that protected employees' rights to organize and engage in collective bargaining, regulated the amount of farmland in cultivation, extended low-interest credit to small businesses and farmers, and restricted corporate activities dealing in the stock market as well as many other laws that contributed to the construction of the "regulatory state" and the "welfare state."

Cooperative Federalism and Grants-in-Aid: Institutions Shape Policies

Roosevelt was able to overcome judicial resistance to expansive New Deal programs. Congress, however, forced him to recognize the continuing importance of the states. It accomplished this by crafting particular programs in such a way as to encourage the states to pursue nationally set goals while leaving them some leeway to administer programs according to local needs.

If the traditional system of two sovereigns performing highly different functions can be called dual federalism, then the system that prevailed after the 1930s could be called **cooperative federalism**, which generally refers to supportive relations, sometimes partnerships, between the national government and the state and local governments. It takes the form of federal subsidization of special state and local activities; these subsidies are **grants-in-aid**. Because many of these state and local programs would not exist without the federal grant-in-aid, the grant-in-aid is also an important form of federal influence. (We discuss another form of federal influence, the mandate, in the next section.) Thus the shift from dual federalism to cooperative federalism was a subtle but important institutional change. Whereas dual federalism left decision, agenda, and veto powers in the realm of domestic policy firmly in the hands of the states, cooperative federalism gave the federal government far greater control over the domestic political agenda. Under dual federalism, for example, corporations mainly concerned themselves with state regulation of their business. Most firms hardly even lobbied in Washington. With the emergence of cooperative federalism and a greater federal role in the nation's economy, hardly any firm could afford not to lobby in Washington.

A grant-in-aid is really a kind of bribe, whereby Congress appropriates money for state and local governments with the condition that it be spent for a particular purpose. Congress uses grants-in-aid because it does not have the political or constitutional power to command local governments to do its bidding. Federalism gives the states the power to veto many national government efforts. For example, some states threatened to opt out of the federal No Child Left Behind education law and thus veto it in their own jurisdictions. (No Child Left Behind was replaced in 2015 by the Every Student Succeeds law, which returned much of the control to the states for school performances.) When you can't command, a monetary inducement sometimes works. For instance, the nationwide speed limit of 55 miles per hour became law only after Congress threatened to withdraw

 cooperative federalism

A type of federalism existing since the New Deal era, in which grants-in-aid have been used strategically to encourage states and localities to pursue nationally defined goals; also known as intergovernmental cooperation

 grants-in-aid

A general term for funds given by Congress to state and local governments

federal highway grants-in-aid if the state legislatures did not set that speed limit. In the early 1990s, Congress began to allow the states, under certain conditions, to go back to the 65-mile-per-hour (or higher) limit without losing their highway grants. The grant-in-aid is one more example of the fact that institutions shape policies: being that America's constitutional system gives the states de facto vetoes over many potential national government programs, the central government has learned to craft policies likely to elicit the states' cooperation.

When applying this approach to cities, Congress set national goals in specific policy categories, such as public housing and assistance to the unemployed, and provided grants-in-aid to meet them. World War II temporarily stopped the distribution of these grants. But after the war, Congress resumed making grants for urban development and school lunches. The range of categories has expanded greatly over the decades and the value of such **categorical grants-in-aid** increased from $2.3 billion in 1950 to over $550 billion in 2015 (Figure 3.1). Sometimes the state or local government must match the national contribution, but for some programs, such as the interstate highway system, the congressional grant-in-aid covers much of the cost.

For the most part, the categorical grants created before the 1960s simply helped the states perform their traditional functions, such as educating and

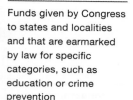

categorical grants-in-aid

Funds given by Congress to states and localities and that are earmarked by law for specific categories, such as education or crime prevention

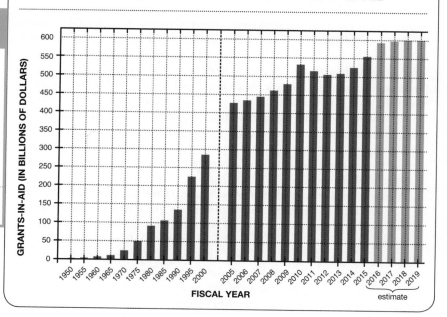

Figure 3.1
THE HISTORICAL TREND OF FEDERAL GRANTS-IN-AID

NOTE: Excludes outlays for national defense, international affairs, and net interest.
SOURCE: Office of Management and Budget, www.whitehouse.gov/omb/budget/historicals (accessed 2/10/16).

Figure 3.2
TWO HISTORIC VIEWS OF FEDERALISM

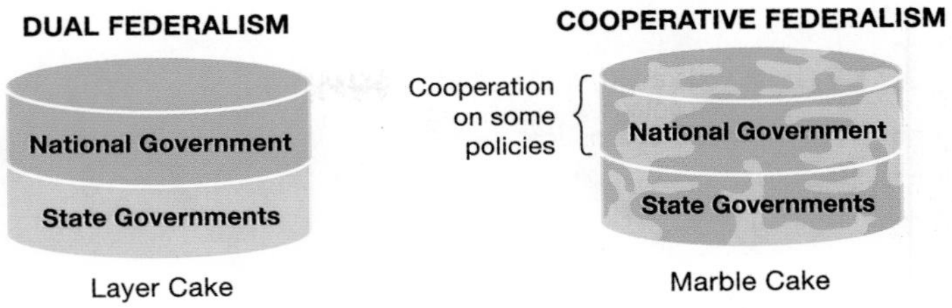

DUAL FEDERALISM

National Government

State Governments

Layer Cake

Cooperation on some policies

COOPERATIVE FEDERALISM

National Government

State Governments

Marble Cake

policing.[18] In the 1960s, however, the national role expanded For example, during the 89th Congress (1965–66) alone, the number of categorical grant-in-aid programs grew from 221 to 379.[19] The grants authorized during the 1960s announced national purposes much more strongly than did earlier grants. Central to that national purpose was the need to provide opportunities to the poor.

Many of the categorical grants enacted during the 1960s were **project grants**, which require state and local governments to submit proposals to federal agencies. In contrast to the older **formula grants**, which used a formula (composed of such elements as need and state and local capacities) to distribute funds, the new project grants made funding available on a competitive basis. Federal agencies would award grants to the proposals they judged to be the best. In this way, the national government acquired substantial control over which state and local governments got money, how much they got, and how they spent it.

The political scientist Morton Grodzins characterized the shift to post–New Deal cooperative federalism as a move from "layer cake federalism" to "marble cake federalism,"[20] in which it is difficult to say where the national government ends and the state and local governments begin. Figure 3.2 demonstrates the basis of the marble cake idea. In the late 1970s, federal aid contributed 25 to 30 percent of the operating budgets of all the nation's state and local governments (Figure 3.3). In 2010, federal aid accounted for more than 35 percent of these budgets (today it accounts for 33 percent). This increase was temporary, resulting from the Obama administration's

 project grants

Grant programs in which state and local governments submit proposals to federal agencies and for which funding is provided on a competitive basis

 formula grants

Grants-in-aid in which a formula is used to determine the amount of federal funds a state or local government will receive

---

18 Kenneth T. Palmer, "The Evolution of Grant Policies," in *The Changing Politics of Federal Grants*, Lawrence D. Brown, James W. Fossett, and Kenneth T. Palmer, eds. (Washington, DC: Brookings Institution, 1984), p. 15.

19 Palmer, "The Evolution of Grant Policies," p. 6.

20 Morton Grodzins, "The Federal System," in *Goals for Americans*, President's Commission on National Goals, ed. (Englewood Cliffs, NJ: Prentice-Hall, 1960), p. 265. In a marble cake, the white cake is distinguishable from the chocolate cake, but the two are streaked rather than arranged in distinct layers.

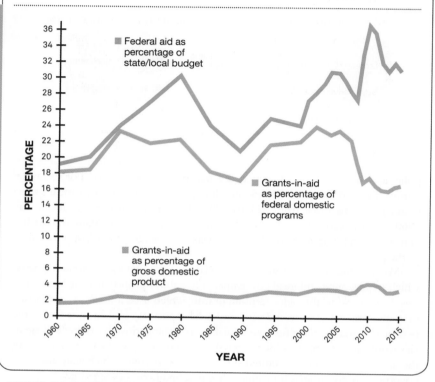

Figure 3.3
THE RISE, DECLINE, AND RECOVERY OF FEDERAL AID

ANALYZING THE EVIDENCE

The extent to which state and local governments rely on federal funding has varied a great deal over time. What difference does it make if the states depend fiscally on the federal government?

■ Federal aid as percentage of state/local budget

■ Grants-in-aid as percentage of federal domestic programs

■ Grants-in-aid as percentage of gross domestic product

PERCENTAGE

YEAR

SOURCE: Robert J. Dilger, Federal Grants to State and Local Governments, CRS, 2015.

$787 billion stimulus package designed to help state and local governments weather the 2008–10 recession. Briefly, however, federal aid became the single largest source of state revenue, exceeding sales and property tax revenues for the first time in U.S. history.

Regulated Federalism and National Standards

Developments from the 1960s to the present have moved well beyond cooperative federalism to what might be called regulated federalism.[21] Regulated federalism is an important new decision rule, enhancing the national

---

21 The concept and the best discussion of this modern phenomenon are found in Donald F. Kettl, *The Regulation of American Federalism* (1983; repr., Baltimore: Johns Hopkins University Press, 1987), esp. pp. 33–41.

government's power. In some areas—especially civil rights, poverty programs, and environmental protection—the national government actually regulates the states by threatening to withhold grant money unless state and local governments conform to national standards. This focus reflects a shift away from federal oversight of economic activities toward "social regulation"—intervention on behalf of individual rights and liberties, environmental protection, workplace safety, and so on. Here the national government provides grant-in-aid financing but sets conditions the states must meet to keep the grants and refers to these policies as "setting national standards." Examples include the Asbestos Hazard Emergency Act of 1986, which requires school districts to inspect for asbestos hazards and remove them from school buildings when necessary, and the Americans with Disabilities Act of 1990, which requires all state and local governments to promote access for the disabled to all government buildings. The net effect of these national standards is that state and local policies are more uniform from coast to coast. National regulations and standards provide coordination across states and localities and solve collective action problems.

However, in other programs the government imposes national standards on the states without providing any funding at all. These are called **unfunded mandates**.[22] These burdens became a major part of the rallying cry that produced the Republican Congress elected in 1994 and its Contract with America. One of that Congress's first measures was the Unfunded Mandates Reform Act (UMRA). Considered a triumph of lobbying efforts by state and local governments, UMRA was "hailed as both symbol and substance of a renewed congressional commitment to federalism."[23] Under this law, any mandate with an uncompensated state and local cost estimated to be above a certain amount can be stopped by a point of order raised on the House or Senate floor. This so-called stop, look, and listen requirement forced Congress to own up to a mandate's potential costs.

UMRA does not prevent members of Congress from passing unfunded mandates; it only makes them think twice before they do. Moreover, the act exempts several areas from coverage. And states must still enforce antidiscrimination laws and meet other requirements in order to receive federal assistance. Nonetheless, UMRA is a serious effort to move the national–state relationship a bit further toward the state side.

 unfunded mandates

National standards or programs imposed on state and local governments by the federal government without accompanying funding or reimbursement

---

22 John J. DiIulio and Donald F. Kettl report that in 1980 there were 36 laws that could be categorized as unfunded mandates. And despite the concerted opposition of the administrations of Ronald Reagan and George H. W. Bush, another 27 laws qualifying as unfunded mandates were adopted between 1982 and 1991. See John DiIulio, Jr., and Donald F. Kettl, *Fine Print: The Contract with America, Devolution, and the Administrative Realities of American Federalism* (Washington, DC: Brookings Institution, 1995), p. 41.

23 Paul Posner, "Unfunded Mandate Reform: How Is It Working?" *Rockefeller Institute Bulletin* (1998): 35.

New Federalism and the National–State Tug-of-War

Federalism in the United States is partly a tug-of-war between those seeking more uniform national standards and those seeking more variability from state to state. Even before UMRA, Presidents Richard Nixon and Ronald Reagan called their efforts to reverse the trend toward national standards and reestablish traditional policy making and implementation the "new federalism." They helped craft national policies that would return more discretion to the states. Examples include Nixon's revenue sharing and Reagan's **block grants**, which consolidated a number of categorical grants into one larger category, leaving the state (or local) government more discretion to decide how to use the money.

President Barack Obama, in contrast, seemed to believe firmly in regulated federalism, with the national government viewing the states more as administrative arms rather than independent laboratories. For example, under the Obama administration's health care reform law, every state was encouraged to establish an insurance exchange where individuals in need of health insurance can shop for the best rate. Citizens purchasing insurance through these exchanges would receive federal tax subsidies. Some states did not establish exchanges, but the Supreme Court ruled that their citizens could receive tax benefits for the policies they purchased through the federal government's exchange.[24] The law also required states to expand their Medicaid programs, adding as many as 15 million Americans to the Medicaid rolls. Several states were concerned that the costs of the new program would fall on their strained budgets, and 12 state attorneys general brought suit, charging that the program's mandates violate the Tenth Amendment. Ultimately, the Supreme Court upheld major provisions of the legislation, although the Court ruled that the federal government cannot require that Medicaid rolls be expanded. As of November 2016, 31 states and Washington, D.C. had decided to expand their rolls. The Analyzing the Evidence unit on pp. 90–1 looks at how health care policy varies across the states.

The Supreme Court as Referee. The courts establish the decision rules that determine the relationship between federal and state power. For much of the nineteenth century, federal power remained limited. The Tenth Amendment was used to bolster arguments about **states' rights**, which in their extreme version claimed that the states did not have to submit to national laws when they believed the national government had exceeded its authority. Arguments in favor of states' rights were voiced less often after the Civil War. But the Court continued to use the Tenth Amendment to strike down laws that it thought exceeded national power, including the Civil Rights Act passed in 1875.

block grants

Federal funds given to state governments to pay for goods, services, or programs, with relatively few restrictions on how the funds may be spent

states' rights

The principle that states should oppose increases in the authority of the national government; this view was most popular before the Civil War

---

24 *King v. Burwell*, 576 U.S.____(2015).

In the early twentieth century, however, the Tenth Amendment appeared to lose its force. Reformers began to press for national regulations to limit the power of large corporations and to preserve the health and welfare of citizens. The Supreme Court approved some of these laws but struck down others, including a law combating child labor. The Court stated that the law violated the Tenth Amendment because only states should have the power to regulate conditions of employment. By the late 1930s, however, the Court had approved such an expansion of federal power that the Tenth Amendment appeared irrelevant.

Recent years have seen a revival of interest in the Tenth Amendment and important Supreme Court decisions limiting federal power. Much of the interest stems from conservatives who believe that a strong federal government encroaches on individual liberties and so power should be returned to the states through the process of devolution. At the same time, the Court has revived the Eleventh Amendment concept of **state sovereign immunity**. This legal doctrine holds that states are immune from lawsuits by private individuals or groups claiming that the state violated a statute enacted by Congress.

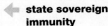

state sovereign immunity

A legal doctrine holding that states cannot be sued for violating an act of Congress

The Supreme Court's ruling in *United States v. Lopez* in 1995 fueled further interest in the Tenth Amendment. Stating that Congress had exceeded its authority under the commerce clause, the Court struck down a federal law that barred handguns near schools. It further limited the federal government's power over the states in a 1996 ruling based on the Eleventh Amendment. That ruling prevented Seminole Indians from suing the state of Florida in federal court. A 1988 law had given tribes the right to sue a state in federal court if the state did not negotiate in good faith issues related to gambling casinos on tribal land. The Court's ruling appeared to signal a much broader limitation on national power by raising new questions about whether individuals can sue a state if it fails to uphold federal law.[25]

Another significant decision was the 1997 case of *Printz v. United States*, in which the Court struck down a key provision of the Brady bill, enacted in 1993 to regulate gun sales. Under the act, state and local law enforcement officers were required to conduct background checks on prospective gun purchasers. The Court held that the federal government cannot require states to administer or enforce federal regulatory programs.[26] Because the states bear administrative responsibility for a variety of other federal programs, this decision could have far-reaching consequences. Overall, rulings such as these signaled a move toward a much more restricted federal government.

This trend continued with the 2006 *Gonzales v. Oregon* case. *Gonzales* involved Oregon's physician-assisted suicide law, which permitted doctors to prescribe lethal doses of medication for terminally ill patients who requested help ending their lives. In 2001, the U.S. attorney general issued an order declaring that

25 *Seminole Tribe v. Florida,* 517 U.S. 44 (1996).

26 *Printz v. United States,* 521 U.S. 898 (1997).

Health Care Policy and the States

Contributed by
Jenna Bednar
University of Michigan

The 2010 Patient Protection and Affordable Care Act (ACA) was an attempt by Congress to standardize access to health care nationally as well as to contain costs. The act raised questions about responsibility for health care policy and poverty relief. The primary federalism question in the ACA was what level of government, state or federal, should set Medicaid eligibility criteria. Medicaid is a program to provide health care coverage to the poor and is jointly financed by the federal and state governments. As enacted, the ACA expanded Medicaid eligibility to adults with incomes at or below 138 percent of the federal poverty level (FPL). In 2015 the FPL was $20,090 for a family of three, making that family eligible for Medicaid if it earned up to $27,724. This provision, however, was effectively made a state option by the Supreme Court's 2012 ruling on the constitutionality of the ACA. States could choose not to accept the Medicaid expansion and instead set their own thresholds for eligibility.

As of November 2015, 31 states and Washington, D.C. had adopted the Medicaid expansion. The first map below shows the 2015 Medicaid eligibility thresholds by state for adults with dependent children. A family of three in Connecticut, a state that extended Medicaid eligibility above the ACA minimum to 155 percent of FPL for parents, could earn up to $31,139 and the family would still qualify for Medicaid benefits. The same family living in Texas, a state that did not adopt the Medicaid expansion, would be ineligible if they earned more than $3,616 (18 percent of FPL). The second map shows the percentage of nonelderly adults who lacked health insurance in each state in 2014.

Medicaid Eligibility Thresholds and Percentage Uninsured*

MEDICAID ELIGIBILITY
Threshold, working adults with dependent children, as percent of FPL

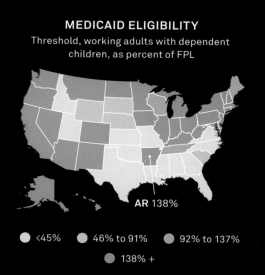

AR 138%

● <45%   ● 46% to 91%   ● 92% to 137%
● 138% +

UNINSURED
Percentage uninsured, 2014

MA 5%

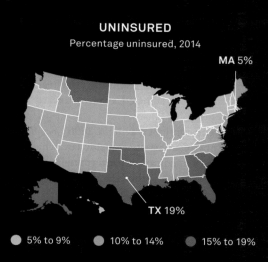

TX 19%

● 5% to 9%   ● 10% to 14%   ● 15% to 19%

When public policy is decentralized in a federal system, not only can states set policy according to their own preferences and capacity, as demonstrated by the variation in Medicaid eligibility, but states may innovate to improve policy. For example, in 2006 Massachusetts enacted a law that required residents to obtain insurance but subsidized or offered free coverage for the poor. In the graph below, we see the proportion of the Massachusetts nonelderly adult population without health insurance compared with the proportion of nonelderly adults without health insurance nationwide. Although Massachusetts already had a far lower rate of uninsured than the national average, the introduction of health policy reform further reduced the percentage of uninsured at a time when the national average was increasing.

The ACA was modeled on the Massachusetts plan. Two aspects were politically controversial: the requirement that all individuals obtain insurance and the standardization of Medicaid eligibility. If states complied with the ACA prescription, access to Medicaid benefits expanded considerably, including extending coverage to all limited-income adults regardless of whether they had dependent children, a population that currently lacks access to Medicaid. However, the ACA did so by centralizing authority, reducing the states' control over health care policy and poverty relief.

Although the federal government would pay the lion's share of the costs of the expanded Medicare coverage through at least 2020, many states were unhappy with the dictum from the central government, and 26 states joined lawsuits to challenge Congress's authority, leading to the 2012 Supreme Court ruling that states need not accept the Medicaid expansion. In 2012 the Supreme Court ruled that states cannot be required to conform their Medicaid eligibility thresholds to the national minimum. As of November 2015, 19 states had indicated that they would not raise their Medicaid eligibility thresholds to meet the ACA minimum. Ultimately, the fate of health care responsibility will rest with the American public, as they grow to accept or reject the arguments made on both sides.

Percentage of Population without Health Insurance**

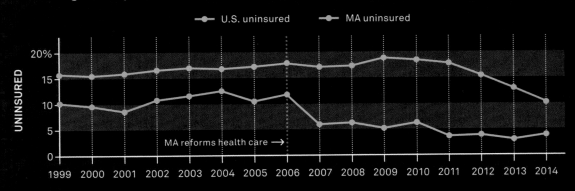

* SOURCE: Kaiser Family Foundation, "Eligibility Limits for Adults as a Percent of the Federal Poverty Level," www.kff.org/health-reform/state-indicator/medicaid-income-eligibility-limits-for-adults-as-a-percent-of-the-federal-poverty-level/#map (accessed 2/11/16); and www.kff.org/other/state-indicator/nonelderly-0-64 (accessed 2/11/16).

** SOURCE: Compiled from U.S. Census Bureau, Current Population Survey, 2012 Annual Social and Economic Supplement, Health Insurance, Table HI05 (2011, 2010), Table HI A-6, Table HI06 (2012); and Kaiser Family Foundation, (2013, 2014) and www.kff.org/other/state-indicator/total-population/#table (accessed 2/11/2016).

any physician involved in such a procedure would be prosecuted for violating the federal Controlled Substances Act. The state of Oregon joined several physicians and patients in a suit against the order. Eventually, the Supreme Court ruled that the federal government could not overrule state laws determining how drugs should be used so long as the drugs were not prohibited by federal law.[27]

In 2012, however, the Court once again seemed to favor the importance of national power in the nation–state tug-of-war. In addition to the Obamacare decision cited earlier, the Court struck down portions of an Arizona immigration law, declaring that immigration was a federal, not a state, matter,[28] and in a 2013 decision it struck down an Arizona law requiring individuals to show documentation of citizenship when registering to vote. The Court ruled that this requirement was preempted by the federal National Voter Registration Act requiring states to use the official federal voter registration form.[29] In two other cases, the Court ruled against state legislatures on questions involving congressional district boundaries.[30]

Of course, shifting interpretations of the Constitution often reflect underlying struggles for political power, and the political forces controlling the national government generally advocate a jurisprudence of nationalism. Those uncertain of their ability to control Capitol Hill and the White House, but more sure of their hold on some states, support respect for state power. In recent decades, Republicans, who control a majority of the states, have expressed respect for states' rights while Democrats, with more power at the national level, have sought to increase the power of the federal government. How different institutional forms will influence decision, agenda, and veto powers is a matter of political principle—and political interest.

THE SEPARATION OF POWERS

As we have noted, the separation of powers enables several different federal institutions to influence the nation's agenda, to affect decisions, and to prevent the other institutions from taking action—dividing agenda, decision, and veto power. The Constitution's framers saw this arrangement, although cumbersome, as an essential means of protecting liberty.

In his discussion of the separation of powers, James Madison quoted the originator of the idea, the French political thinker Baron de Montesquieu:

---

27 *Gonzales v. Oregon,* 546 U.S. 243 (2006).

28 *Arizona v. United States,* 132 S.Ct. 2492 (2012).

29 *Arizona et al. v. Inter Tribal Council of Arizona, Inc.,* 133 S.Ct. 2247 (2013).

30 *Alabama Legislative Black Caucus v. Alabama* 575 U.S. ___ (2015) and *Arizona State Legislature v. Arizona Independent Redistricting Commission* 576 U.S. ___ (2015).

"There can be no liberty where the legislative and executive powers are united in the same person . . . [or] if the power of judging be not separated from the legislative and executive powers."[31] Using the same reasoning, many of Madison's contemporaries argued that there was not *enough* separation among the three branches, and Madison had to backtrack to insist that complete separation was not required:

> Unless these departments [branches] be so far connected and blended as to give to each a constitutional control over the others, the degree of separation which the maxim requires, as essential to a free government, can never in practice be duly maintained.[32]

This is the secret of how Americans have made the separation of powers effective: they have made it self-enforcing by giving each branch of government the means to participate in, and partially or temporarily obstruct, the workings of the other branches.

Checks and Balances: A System of Mutual Vetoes

The means by which each branch of government interacts with the others is known informally as checks and balances. This arrangement gives each branch agenda and veto power, under a decision that requires all the branches to agree on national policies (Figure 3.4). Examples are the presidential power to veto legislation passed by Congress; the power of Congress to override the veto by a two-thirds majority vote; the power of the Senate to approve presidential appointments; the power of the president to appoint Supreme Court justices and other federal judges with Senate approval; and the power of the Court to engage in judicial review (discussed later in this chapter). The framers sought to guarantee that the three branches would use the checks and balances as weapons against each other by giving each branch a different political constituency: direct, popular election of the members of the House and indirect election of senators (until the Seventeenth Amendment, adopted in 1913); indirect election of the president (still in effect, at least formally); and appointment of federal judges for life. The best characterization of the separation-of-powers principle in action is, as we said in Chapter 2, "separated institutions sharing power."[33] This system sometimes gives a measure of agenda power to groups like the corn farmers discussed in the Policy Principle section on page 76. While the corn farmers are a small group, our system of separated powers allows them to exert a

---

31 Alexander Hamilton, James Madison, and John Jay, *The Federalist Papers*, Clinton L. Rossiter, ed. (New York: New American Library, 1961), no. 47, p. 302.

32 *The Federalist*, no. 48, p. 308.

33 Richard E. Neustadt, *Presidential Power and the Modern Presidents: The Politics of Leadership from Roosevelt to Reagan* (1960; rev. ed., New York: Free Press, 1990), p. 33.

Figure 3.4

CHECKS AND BALANCES

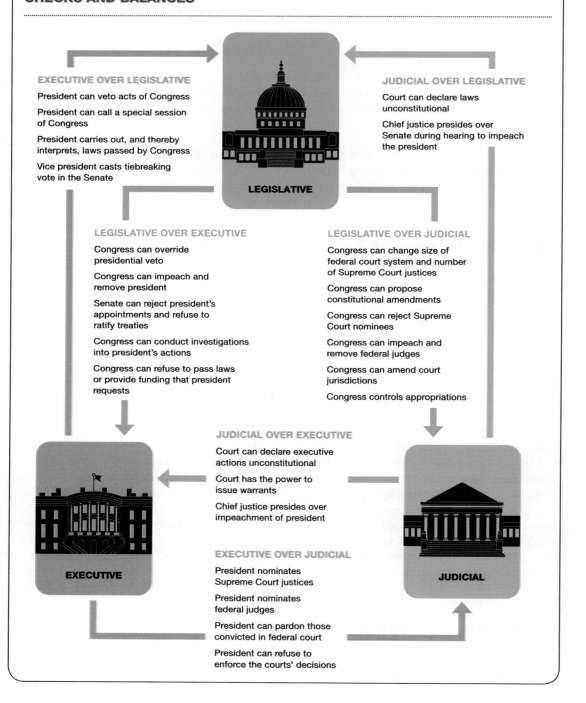

EXECUTIVE OVER LEGISLATIVE

President can veto acts of Congress

President can call a special session of Congress

President carries out, and thereby interprets, laws passed by Congress

Vice president casts tiebreaking vote in the Senate

LEGISLATIVE

JUDICIAL OVER LEGISLATIVE

Court can declare laws unconstitutional

Chief justice presides over Senate during hearing to impeach the president

LEGISLATIVE OVER EXECUTIVE

Congress can override presidential veto

Congress can impeach and remove president

Senate can reject president's appointments and refuse to ratify treaties

Congress can conduct investigations into president's actions

Congress can refuse to pass laws or provide funding that president requests

LEGISLATIVE OVER JUDICIAL

Congress can change size of federal court system and number of Supreme Court justices

Congress can propose constitutional amendments

Congress can reject Supreme Court nominees

Congress can impeach and remove federal judges

Congress can amend court jurisdictions

Congress controls appropriations

JUDICIAL OVER EXECUTIVE

Court can declare executive actions unconstitutional

Court has the power to issue warrants

Chief justice presides over impeachment of president

EXECUTIVE

EXECUTIVE OVER JUDICIAL

President nominates Supreme Court justices

President nominates federal judges

President can pardon those convicted in federal court

President can refuse to enforce the courts' decisions

JUDICIAL

good deal of influence through the members of Congress whose electoral chances they influence.

Legislative Supremacy

Within the system of separated powers, the framers provided for **legislative supremacy** by making Congress the preeminent branch. Legislative supremacy made the provision of checks and balances in the other two branches all the more important.

The framers' intention of legislative supremacy is evident in their decision to place the provisions for national powers in Article I, the legislative article, and to treat the powers of the national government as powers of Congress. In a system based on the rule of law, the power to make the laws is the supreme power. Section 8 provides in part that *"Congress* shall have Power To lay and collect Taxes . . . ; To borrow Money . . . ; To regulate Commerce" [emphasis added]. The Founders also provided for legislative supremacy by giving Congress sole power over appropriations and giving the House of Representatives the power to initiate all revenue bills. Madison recognized legislative supremacy as part and parcel of the separation of powers:

> It is not possible to give to each department an equal power of self-defense. In republican government, the legislative authority necessarily predominates. The remedy for this inconveniency is to divide the legislature into different branches; and to render them, by different modes of election and different principles of action, as little connected with each other as the nature of their common functions and their common dependence on the society will admit.[34]

Essentially, Congress was so likely to dominate the other branches that it would have to be divided against itself, into House and Senate. One almost could say that the Constitution provided for four branches, not three.

Although "presidential government" gradually supplanted legislative supremacy after 1937, the relative power position of the executive and legislative branches since that time has varied with the rise and fall of political parties. It has been especially tense during periods of **divided government**, when one party controls the White House and another controls Congress.

Checks and Balances: The Rationality Principle at Work

The framers' idea that the president and Congress would check and balance each other rests, in part, on an application of the rationality principle. The framers assumed that each branch would seek to maintain or expand its

legislative supremacy

The preeminent position assigned to Congress by the Constitution

divided government

The condition in American government in which the presidency is controlled by one party while the opposing party controls one or both houses of Congress

---

34 *The Federalist,* no. 51, p. 322.

power and would resist "encroachments" by the other branch. This idea seems consistent with the behavior of presidents and congressional leaders, who have battled over institutional prerogatives since at least the Nixon administration. For example, the Watergate struggle began when President Nixon sought a reorganization of the executive branch that would have increased presidential control and reduced congressional oversight powers.[35] After Nixon's resignation, Congress acted to delimit presidential power; but subsequently President Reagan undid Congress's efforts and bolstered the White House. During President George W. Bush's second term, Congress and the president battled constantly over the president's refusals to disclose information on the basis of **executive privilege** and his assertions that only the White House was competent to manage the nation's security. "I am the decider," the president famously averred. Although during Obama's first two years the Democratic leadership in control of both houses cooperated with the new president, this "honeymoon" ended when the GOP took control of the House of Representatives in 2010 and then the Senate in 2014. In the 2016 elections, Americans chose a Republican president and left the GOP in control of both houses of Congress. This development seemed to portend closer cooperation between the executive and legislative branches.

Over time, the president has generally possessed an advantage in this struggle between institutions. The president is a unitary actor, whereas Congress, as a collective decision maker, suffers from collective action problems (see Chapter 13). That is, each member may have individual interests that are inconsistent with the collective interests of Congress as a whole. For example, when Congress initially supported Bush's plan to use force in Iraq in 2003, members were uneasy about his assertion that he did not need congressional approval. The president was using the war to underline claims of institutional power, but few members of Congress thought it politically safe to express that viewpoint when the public was clamoring for action. These considerations help explain why, over time, the powers of the presidency have grown and those of Congress diminished.[36] We will return to this topic in Chapter 7.

The Role of the Supreme Court: Establishing Decision Rules

The role of the judicial branch in the separation of powers has depended on the power of judicial review (see Chapter 9), a power not provided for in the Constitution but asserted by Chief Justice Marshall in 1803:

> If a law be in opposition to the Constitution; if both the law and the Constitution apply to a particular case, so that the Court must either

---

executive privilege ⇨

The claim that confidential communications between the president and the president's close advisers should not be revealed without the consent of the president

---

35 Benjamin Ginsberg and Martin Shefter, *Politics by Other Means,* 3rd ed. (New York: Norton, 2002), chap. 1.

36 Matthew Crenson and Benjamin Ginsberg, *Presidential Power: Unchecked and Unbalanced* (New York: Norton, 2007).

decide that case conformable to the law, disregarding the Constitution, or conformable to the Constitution, disregarding the law; the Court must determine which of these conflicting rules governs the case: This is of the very essence of judicial duty.[37]

Marshall's decision was an extremely important assertion of judicial power: in effect, he declared that whenever there was doubt or disagreement about which rule should apply in a particular case, the Court would decide. In this way, Marshall made the Court the arbiter of all future debates between Congress and the president and between the federal and state governments.

Judicial review of the constitutionality of acts of the president or Congress is relatively rare. For example, there were no Supreme Court reviews of congressional acts in the 50 plus years between *Marbury v. Madison* (1803) and *Dred Scott v. Sandford* (1857). In the century or so between the Civil War and 1970, 84 acts of Congress were held unconstitutional (in whole or in part), but there were long periods of complete Court deference to Congress, punctuated by flurries of judicial review during times of social upheaval. The most significant was 1935–36, when 12 acts of Congress were invalidated, blocking virtually the entire New Deal program.[38] Thereafter no significant acts were voided until 1983, when the Court declared unconstitutional the legislative veto, a practice in which Congress authorized the president to take action but reserved the right to rescind presidential actions with which it disagreed.[39] The Court became much more activist (that is, less deferential to Congress) after the elevation of Justice William H. Rehnquist to the position of chief justice in 1986.[40] Each of the cases in Table 3.1 altered some aspect of federalism by declaring unconstitutional all or an important portion of an act of Congress.

Since the New Deal period, the Court has been far more deferential toward the president, with only five significant confrontations. One was the so-called steel seizure case of 1952, in which the Court refused to permit President Harry Truman to use "emergency powers" to force workers back into the steel mills during the Korean War.[41] In a second case, the Court declared unconstitutional President Nixon's refusal to respond to a subpoena to make available the infamous White House tapes as evidence in a criminal prosecution. The Court argued that although executive privilege protected confidentiality of communications

---

37 *Marbury v. Madison,* 1 Cranch 137 (1803).

38 The Supreme Court struck down 8 out of 10 New Deal statutes. For example, in *Panama Refining Company v. Ryan,* 293 U.S. 388 (1935), the Court ruled that a section of the National Industrial Recovery Act of 1933 was an invalid delegation of legislative power to the executive branch. And in *Schechter Poultry Corporation v. United States,* 295 U.S. 495 (1935), the Court found the National Industrial Recovery Act itself to be invalid for the same reason.

39 *Immigration and Naturalization Service v. Chadha,* 462 U.S. 919 (1983).

40 Cass R. Sunstein, "Taking Over the Courts," *New York Times,* November 9, 2002, p. A19.

41 *Youngstown Sheet and Tube Company v. Sawyer,* 343 U.S. 579 (1952).

Table 3.1

A NEW FEDERAL SYSTEM? THE CASE RECORD, 1995–2016

CASE	DATE	COURT HOLDING
United States v. Lopez, 514 U.S. 549	**1995**	Voids federal law barring handguns near schools: it is beyond Congress's power to regulate commerce
Seminole Tribe v. Florida, 517 U.S. 44	**1996**	Voids federal law giving tribes the right to sue a state in federal court: "sovereign immunity" requires a state's permission to be sued
Printz v. United States, 521 U.S. 898	**1997**	Voids a key provision of the Brady law requiring states to make background checks on gun purchases: as an "unfunded mandate," it violated state sovereignty under the Tenth Amendment
City of Boerne v. Flores, 521 U.S. 507	**1997**	Restricts Congress's power under the Fourteenth Amendment to regulate city zoning and health and welfare policies to "remedy" rights: Congress may not expand those rights
Alden v. Maine, 527 U.S. 706	**1999**	Declares states "immune" from suits by their *own* employees for overtime pay under the Fair Labor Standards Act of 1938 (see also the *Seminole* case)
United States v. Morrison, 529 U.S. 598	**2000**	Extends the *Seminole* case by invalidating the Violence against Women Act: states may not be sued by individuals for failing to enforce federal laws
Gonzales v. Oregon, 546 U.S. 243	**2006**	Upholds state assisted-suicide law over attorney general's objection
National Federation of Independent Business v. Sebelius, 567 U.S. __ (2012)	**2012**	Upholds the Affordable Care Act and expansion of federal control over health care policy
Arizona State Legislature v. Arizona Independent Redistricting Commission 570 U.S. __ (2013)	**2013**	Declares that state voter identification rules are preempted by the National Voter Registration Act

to and from the president, this protection did not extend to data in presidential files or tapes linked to criminal prosecutions.[42] In yet another instance, the Court struck down the Line Item Veto Act of 1996, which allowed the president to veto specific items in spending and tax bills without vetoing the entire bill. The Court held that any such change in the procedures of adopting laws would have to be made by amendment to the Constitution, not by legislation.[43]

Another important confrontation came a few years after the September 11, 2001, terrorist attacks. In 2004 the Court held that the estimated 650 "enemy combatants" detained without formal charges at the U.S. Naval Station at Guantánamo Bay, Cuba, had the right to seek release through a **writ of *habeas corpus*.**[44] However, in Section 7 of the 2006 Military Commissions Act, Congress declared that enemy combatants held at Guantánamo Bay could not avail themselves of the right of *habeas corpus*. Then, in 2008, the Supreme Court responded by striking down Section 7 and affirming that the Guantánamo detainees had the right to challenge their detentions in federal court.[45] The Court noted that *habeas corpus* was among the most fundamental constitutional rights and was included in the Constitution even before the Bill of Rights was added.

 writ of *habeas corpus*

A court order demanding that an individual in custody be brought into court and shown the cause for detention; *habeas corpus* is guaranteed by the Constitution and can be suspended only in cases of rebellion or invasion

CONCLUSION: FEDERALISM AND THE SEPARATION OF POWERS—COLLECTIVE ACTION OR STALEMATE?

As asserted by the institutions principle, institutions are designed to solve collective action problems, but the solutions can take many different forms. The framers believed that agenda, decision, and veto powers should be dispersed among many different institutions. And because history matters and the 13 existing states already possessed significant autonomy when the Constitution was drafted, the framers had little choice but to relinquish considerable agenda, decision, and veto powers to them as well. The result was our federal system of separated powers.

Critics of the American constitutional framework have often pointed to this dispersion of governmental power as a source of weakness and incoherence in America's policy-making processes. Because of federalism, America's national government is often unable to accomplish what might be a matter of course in most other nations. As we saw in *United States v. Lopez,* the Supreme Court invalidated a federal statute prohibiting the possession of firearms near schools, saying that it was an unconstitutional encroachment on the sovereignty of the

---

42 *United States v. Nixon,* 418 U.S. 683 (1974).

43 *Clinton v. City of New York,* 524 U.S. 417 (1998).

44 *Rasul v. Bush,* 542 U.S. 466 (2004).

45 *Boumediene v. Bush,* 553 U.S. 723 (2008).

states. In a country with a unitary system of government, this statute would not face such a hurdle.

Over the course of American history, as we saw, the power of the states has waned relative to that of the national government. Nevertheless, the states still matter and under the terms of what we called the "new federalism," the states can exert a good deal of power over nominally federal programs. Nevertheless, the United States began as a nation of semi-sovereign states and is now closer to being a unitary republic.

As to the separation of powers, the policy principle tells us that political outcomes are the products of individual preferences and institutional procedures. Because of the separation of powers, an institutional procedure, Congress is often stymied by the president—or the president by Congress in their efforts to develop policies. The president can veto congressional action; Congress can, by legislation, limit the powers of the executive. In 2011, for example, the newly elected Republican House of Representatives promised to repeal the president's recently enacted health care program. The Senate, still controlled by Democrats, disagreed, and the president promised to veto any bill that threatened what he viewed as the major achievement of his first term in office. In the meantime, legal challenges to the new law eventually led to a Supreme Court decision upholding the new legislation's main provisions. The dispersion of power among different institutions of government ensures that collective action will be difficult, though not impossible.

At times, however, stalemate between Congress and the president may become so severe that the government is paralyzed. As we saw in 2013, conservative House Republicans refused to allow a vote on any continuing resolution (CR) to extend the government's spending authority that contained funding for the Affordable Care Act (ACA). Senate Democrats and the president said they would not accept a CR that did not provide funding for the ACA. Without a CR, much of the government's spending authority lapsed, such that most federal agencies had to close in a "government shutdown." Republicans also threatened to refuse to raise the nation's debt limit, thereby reducing the government's borrowing power and forcing further cuts in government programs. After a tense 16 days, Republicans and Democrats agreed to a spending bill and a temporary new debt ceiling.

Thus the separation of powers has real political consequences. The framers, though, did not want to make collective action too easy. They thought it was important to provide checks and balances that would protect the nation from the tyrannical actions of a small number of leaders, as well as from precipitous actions on the part of larger groups—"majority tyranny." The framers believed that well-constructed institutions should diminish the likelihood of inappropriate and unwise collective action, even at the cost of occasional stalemate. In recent years, the U.S. government often has been criticized more for what it *has* done, especially in regard to the wars in Iraq and Afghanistan, than what it *has not* done. Many Americans believe that Congress should have done more to thwart presidential war policies and hope the judiciary will do more to delimit presidential war powers in the future. The framers likely would have understood this desire to check the executive branch. Stalemate is not always the worst collective outcome.

For Further Reading

Bednar, Jenna. *The Robust Federation*. New York: Cambridge University Press, 2008.

Crenson, Matthew, and Benjamin Ginsberg. *Presidential Power: Unchecked and Unbalanced*. New York: Norton, 2007.

Ferejohn, John A., and Barry R. Weingast, eds. *The New Federalism: Can the States Be Trusted?* Stanford, CA: Hoover Institution Press, 1997.

Fisher, Louis. *Constitutional Conflicts between Congress and the President*. 7th ed. Lawrence: University Press of Kansas, 2007.

Hamilton, Alexander, James Madison, and John Jay. *The Federalist Papers*, no. 39. Clinton Rossiter, ed. New York: New American Library, 1961.

Karmis, Dimitrios, and Wayne Norman. *Theories of Federalism: A Reader*. New York: Palgrave, Macmillan, 2005.

LaCroix, Alison L. *The Ideological Origins of American Federalism*. Cambridge: Harvard University Press, 2010.

Moellers, Christoph. *The Three Branches: A Comparative Model of Separation of Powers*. New York: Oxford University Press, 2015.

Nolette, Paul. *Federalism on Trial: State Attorneys General and National Policymaking in Contemporary America*. Lawrence: University Press of Kansas, 2015.

Noonan, John T. *Narrowing the Nation's Power: The Supreme Court Sides with the States*. Berkeley: University of California Press, 2002.

Riker, William H. *Federalism: Origin, Operation, Significance*. Boston: Little, Brown, 1964.

Robertson, David. *Federalism and the Making of America*. New York: Routledge, 2011.

Samuels, David, and Matthew Shugart, *Presidents, Parties and Prime Ministers: How the Separation of Powers Affects Party Organization and Behavior*. New York: Cambridge University Press, 2010.

Smith, Rogers M. *Civic Ideals: Conflicting Visions of Citizenship in U.S. History*. New Haven, CT: Yale University Press, 1997.

Van Horn, Carol E. *The State of the States*. 4th ed. Washington, DC: CQ Press, 2004.

Winston, Pamela. *Welfare Policymaking in the States: The Devil in Devolution*. Washington, DC: Georgetown University Press, 2002.

Civil Liberties

Institutions serve to solve collective action problems, and in the United States among the most important constitutional instruments created for this purpose are civil liberties and civil rights. To *solve*, however, does not mean simply to facilitate collective action. Instead, the constitutional principles of civil liberties and civil rights presented in the Bill of Rights also *regulate* collective action. Civil liberties are limitations or restrictions on collective action. In effect, the concept of civil liberties defines certain spheres of activity, such as speech or worship, in which the government's authority to interfere with individual conduct is limited. Civil rights are the rules determining who may participate or be represented in collective decision-making processes as well as regulating the ways in which government can and cannot treat its citizens. Thus, generally speaking, civil liberties limit collective action by restricting the government's jurisdiction. Civil rights, in contrast (as we will see in Chapter 5), regulate collective action by establishing decision rules for government's conduct.

Jurisdiction over civil liberties and civil rights issues is primarily exercised by the courts, which have developed myriad decision rules and procedures to resolve controversies in these realms. The U.S. Supreme Court, in particular, asserts significant agenda and veto power in interpreting constitutional principles. The Court's jurisdiction over constitutional issues is derived from Article III of the Constitution, from statutes, and from prior Court decisions. But consistent with the concept of checks and balances, other actors—particularly Congress—also claim agenda and veto power in these realms. Congress's jurisdiction stems from Article II of the Constitution, which gives Congress the power to make the laws, and from its role in the process of amending the Constitution, as defined in Article V.

In their rulings, the courts are heavily influenced by the history of prior decisions relating to the principles at hand. This use of history is called *precedent*. When issuing decisions, courts constantly refer to the opinions of prior courts to justify their interpretations, logic, and ultimate findings. Seldom will a court depart from established precedent. Even the Supreme Court always justifies its decisions by citing precedents and seldom overturns established legal principles. Because the job of a court is to apply rather than to make the law, history in the form of precedent is an important factor limiting judicial discretion.

As we observed when discussing federalism and the separation of powers, institutional principles are not carved in stone. Over the past century, numerous civil liberties have been strengthened, thereby placing greater limits on collective action. In the realm of civil rights, as Chapter 5 will show, African Americans and others who were once excluded from participation in many collective processes have won the right to be included. In both areas, change resulted from political struggles and from battles within and between Congress and the courts. With these considerations in mind, let us examine the character and evolution of civil liberties in America, to be followed by a discussion of civil rights in the next chapter.

ORIGINS OF THE BILL OF RIGHTS

The history principles tells us that choices made during one point in time can continue to have important consequences decades or even centuries later. The first Congress to meet under the new Constitution in 1789 made a choice— 10 choices to be exact—that help shape our politics today. When the first Congress met, its most important item of business was consideration of a

CORE OF THE ANALYSIS

 Civil liberties are rules that limit the government's authority to interfere in certain spheres of activity. They restrict the government's jurisdiction in areas such as free speech and religion.

 Americans' most important civil liberties are found in the Constitution's Bill of Rights, which might have been called the Bill of Liberties.

 Originally, the limits in the Bill of Rights applied only to the federal government. It took a series of Supreme Court decisions in the twentieth century to apply these limits to the states as well.

 Today's conception of civil liberties has been shaped by their historical development and their interpretation by key political actors, especially the Supreme Court.

proposal to add a bill of rights to the Constitution. Such a proposal had been turned down in the waning days of the Constitutional Convention in 1787 because of arguments by Alexander Hamilton and other Federalists that a bill of rights was irrelevant in a constitution providing the national government with only delegated powers. How could the national government abuse powers not given to it in the first place? Hamilton pointed out that the Constitution's system of checks and balances was designed to prevent tyrannical conduct and pointed to other elements of the Constitution, such as the right of habeas corpus contained in Article 1, Section 9, that already provided guarantees of popular liberties. Hamilton worried that a bill of rights would weaken the new government by limiting its jurisdiction even before it had an opportunity to organize itself. But when the Constitution was submitted to the states for ratification, Antifederalists reiterated Thomas Jefferson's argument that the omission of a bill of rights was a major imperfection of the new Constitution. In response, the Federalists in Massachusetts, South Carolina, New Hampshire, Virginia, and New York made an "unwritten but unequivocal pledge" to add a bill of rights and a promise to confirm the understanding that all powers not delegated to the national government or explicitly prohibited to the states were reserved to the states or to the people.[1]

James Madison, who had been a delegate to the Philadelphia convention and later became a member of Congress, may still have believed privately that a bill of rights was unnecessary. But in 1789, recognizing the urgency of obtaining the Antifederalists' support for the Constitution and the new government, he fought for a bill of rights, arguing that the ideals it embodied would acquire "the character of fundamental maxims of free Government, and as they become incorporated with the national sentiment, counteract the impulses of interest and passion."[2]

"After much discussion and manipulation . . . at the delicate prompting of Washington and under the masterful prodding of Madison," the House adopted 17 amendments; the Senate adopted 12 of these. Ten were ratified by the necessary three-fourths of the states, making them part of the Constitution on December 15, 1791—from the start, these 10 were called the Bill of Rights.[3]

civil liberties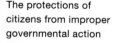

The protections of citizens from improper governmental action

Civil liberties can be defined as protections of citizens from improper governmental action. When adopted in 1791, the Bill of Rights was seen as guaranteeing a private sphere of personal liberty free of governmental restrictions. As Jefferson had put it, a bill of rights "is what people are entitled to against every government on earth." In this sense, we could call the Bill of Rights a bill of

---

1 Clinton L. Rossiter, *1787: The Grand Convention* (New York: Norton, 1987), p. 302.

2 Quoted in Milton Konvitz, "The Bill of Rights: Amendments I–X," in *An American Primer*, 2 vols., Daniel J. Boorstin, ed. (Chicago: University of Chicago Press, 1966), p. I:159.

3 Rossiter, *1787*, p. 303, where he also reports that "in 1941 the States of Connecticut, Massachusetts, and Georgia celebrated the sesquicentennial of the Bill of Rights by giving their hitherto withheld and unneeded assent."

liberties because the amendments focus on what government must *not* do. For example (with emphasis added):

1. "Congress shall make *no* law . . ." (I)

2. "The right . . . to . . . bear Arms, shall *not* be infringed." (II)

3. "*No* Soldier shall . . . be quartered . . ." (III)

4. "*No* Warrants shall issue, but upon probable cause . . ." (IV)

5. "*No* person shall be held to answer . . . unless on a presentment or indictment of a Grand Jury . . ." (V)

6. "Excessive bail shall not be required . . . *nor* cruel and unusual punishments inflicted." (VIII)

Thus the Bill of Rights is a series of "thou shalt nots"—restraints addressed to government, limiting its jurisdiction. Some of these restraints are *substantive*, limiting *what* the government shall and shall not have the power to do, such as establishing a state religion, quartering troops in private homes without consent, or seizing private property without just compensation. Other restraints are *procedural*, addressing how the government is supposed to act. For example, even though the government has the substantive power to declare certain acts to be crimes and to arrest and imprison persons who violate its criminal laws, it may not do so except by fairly meticulous observance of procedures designed to protect the accused. The best-known procedural rule is that a person is presumed innocent until proven guilty. This rule does not question the government's power to punish someone for committing a crime; it questions only the way the government determines who committed the crime.

Substantive and procedural restraints identify the realm of civil liberties. While the distinction between liberties and rights seems clear in theory, in practice several provisions of the Bill of Rights assert both a liberty and right. Proponents of the Bill of Rights wished to ensure that their enumeration of rights and liberties not be deemed exhaustive. The Ninth Amendment addresses this concern, declaring that the enumeration in the Constitution of some rights "shall not be construed" to mean that the people do not retain other rights as well.

NATIONALIZING THE BILL OF RIGHTS

The First Amendment provides that "Congress shall make no law respecting an establishment of religion . . . or abridging the freedom of speech, or of the press; or the right of . . . [assembly and petition]." This is the only amendment that exclusively addresses the national government. For example, the Second Amendment provides that "the right of the people to keep and bear Arms, shall not be infringed." The Fifth Amendment says, among other things, that *no person* "shall . . . be twice put in jeopardy of life or limb" for the same crime, that *no person* "shall be compelled in any criminal case to be a witness against himself," that *no person* shall "be deprived of life, liberty, or property, without due process of law," and that private property cannot be taken "without just compensation."[4] Because the First Amendment is the only part of the Bill of Rights that explicitly limits the national government, a fundamental question arises: Do the remaining amendments of the Bill of Rights put limits on state governments or do they put them only on the national government?

Dual Citizenship

The question of whether the Bill of Rights also limits state governments was settled in 1833 in the case *Barron v. Baltimore.* The facts were simple. In paving its streets, the city of Baltimore had disposed of so much sand and gravel in the water near John Barron's wharf that its value for commercial purposes was virtually destroyed. Barron brought the city into court on the grounds that it had, under the Fifth Amendment, unconstitutionally deprived him of his property.

Here Chief Justice Marshall, in one of the most significant Supreme Court decisions ever handed down, said:

> The Constitution was ordained and established by the people of the United States for themselves, for their own government, and not for the government of individual States. Each State established a constitution for itself, and in that constitution provided such limitations and restrictions on the powers of its particular government as its judgment dictated. . . . If these propositions be correct, *the fifth amendment must be understood as restraining the power of the General Government, not as applicable to the States.*[5] [emphasis added]

In other words, if an agency of the *national* government had deprived Barron of his property, there would have been little doubt about Barron winning his case. But if the constitution of the state of Maryland contained no such provision protecting citizens of Maryland from such action, then Barron had no legal leg to stand on against Baltimore, an agency of the state of Maryland.

Barron v. Baltimore confirmed "dual citizenship"—that each American was a citizen of the national government and separately a citizen of one of the states. This meant that the Bill of Rights did not apply to decisions or procedures of state (or local) governments. Even slavery could continue because the Bill of Rights could not protect anyone from state laws treating people as property.

---

4   It would be useful at this point to review all the provisions of the Bill of Rights to confirm this distinction between the wording of the First Amendment and the wording of the rest (see the Appendix). The emphasis in the examples is not in the original. For an enlightening essay on the extent to which the entire Bill of Rights is about equality, see Martha Minow, "Equality and the Bill of Rights," in *The Constitution of Rights: Human Dignity and American Values,* Michael J. Meyer and William A. Parent, eds. (Ithaca, NY: Cornell University Press, 1992), pp. 118-28.

5   *Barron v. Mayor and City of Baltimore,* 32 U.S. 243 (1833).

In fact, the Bill of Rights did not become a vital instrument for the extension of civil liberties for anyone until after a bloody civil war and the revolutionary Fourteenth Amendment intervened. Even so, nearly another century would pass before the Bill of Rights would truly come into its own. This is a case where America's history has truly mattered. America's states predated the creation of the federal government. The states joined the Union voluntarily, retaining many of their sovereign powers. In contrast, in many other nations, subnational governments were created by and for the administrative convenience of the central government. In the United States, nationalization of governmental powers has proceeded slowly and in fits and starts.

The Fourteenth Amendment

From a constitutional standpoint, the defeat of the South in the Civil War settled one question and raised another. It probably settled forever the question of whether secession was an option for any state. After 1865, there was to be more "united" than "states" to the United States. But this left unanswered just how much the states were obliged to obey the Constitution and, in particular, the Bill of Rights. The words of the Fourteenth Amendment suggest that it was almost perfectly designed to impose the Bill of Rights on the states and thereby reverse *Barron v. Baltimore*. Consider the amendment's first words:

> All persons born or naturalized in the United States, and subject to the jurisdiction thereof, are citizens of the United States and of the State wherein they reside.

This statement provides for a single national citizenship, and at a minimum that means civil liberties should not vary drastically from state to state. That seems to be the spirit of the Fourteenth Amendment: to nationalize the Bill of Rights by nationalizing the definition of citizenship.

This interpretation is reinforced by the next clause:

> No State shall make or enforce any law which shall abridge the privileges or immunities of citizens of the United States; nor shall any State deprive any person of life, liberty, or property, without due process of law.

All of this sounds like an effort to extend the entire Bill of Rights to citizens wherever they might reside. But this was not to be the Supreme Court's interpretation for nearly a century. Within five years of ratification of the Fourteenth Amendment in 1868, the Court was making decisions as though the amendment had never been adopted. The shadow of *Barron* grew longer.

In an important 1873 decision known as the *Slaughter House Cases*, the Supreme Court determined that the federal government was under no obligation to protect the "privileges and immunities" of citizens of a particular state against arbitrary actions by that state's government. The Court argued that the framers of the Fourteenth Amendment could not have intended to incorporate the entire Bill of Rights.[6] Yet when the Civil Rights Act of 1875 attempted to protect blacks from discriminatory treatment by proprietors of hotels, theaters, and other public accommodations, the Court disregarded its own primary argument in the previous case. This time the Court distinguished between state action and private action, declaring that the Fourteenth Amendment applied only to discriminatory actions by state officials, "operating under cover of law," and not to discrimination against blacks by private individuals, even though these private individuals were companies offering services to the public.[7] Thus the Court held that the Civil Rights Act of 1875 was unconstitutional. Such narrow interpretations raised the question of whether the Fourteenth Amendment had incorporated any of the Bill of Rights. The Fourteenth Amendment remained shadowy until the mid-twentieth century. The shadow was *Barron v. Baltimore* and the Court's unwillingness to "nationalize" civil liberties—that is, to interpret the civil liberties expressed in the Bill of Rights as imposing limitations not only on the federal government but also on the states.

It was not until the late nineteenth century that the Supreme Court began to nationalize the Bill of Rights by incorporating its civil liberties provisions into the Fourteenth Amendment. Incorporation can be seen as an expansion of the federal government's power and authority and an erosion of the individual states' autonomy. Thus it is no accident that the major periods of incorporation were the 1930s and the 1960s, when Congress and the president sought to enhance federal power vis-à-vis the states and encouraged the courts to facilitate the effort. During the 1930s, several First Amendment limitations were imposed on states' actions; during the 1960s, the states were compelled to adhere to many of the remaining provisions of the Bill of Rights.

Table 4.1 outlines the major steps in the process of incorporation. The only change in civil liberties during the first 60 years after adoption of the Fourteenth Amendment came in 1897, when the Supreme Court held that the amendment's due process clause did in fact prohibit states from taking property for a public use without just compensation.[8] This effectively overruled *Barron* because it meant that a citizen of Maryland, or any state, was henceforth protected from a "public taking" of property even if the state constitution did not provide such protection. The power of public agencies to seize private property is called eminent domain. According to the Fifth Amendment, private owners must be paid "just compensation" by the government if it decides that it needs their property. In a broader sense, however, *Barron* still cast a shadow because the Supreme Court had "incorporated" into the Fourteenth Amendment only the property protection provision of the Fifth Amendment and no other clause, let alone the other amendments of the Bill of Rights. In other words, although due process applied to the taking

---

6   *The Slaughter House Cases,* 83 U.S. 36 (1873).

7   *The Civil Rights Cases,* 109 U.S. 3 (1883).

8   *Chicago, Burlington, and Quincy Railroad Company v. Chicago,* 166 U.S. 226 (1897).

Table 4.1

INCORPORATION OF THE BILL OF RIGHTS INTO THE FOURTEENTH AMENDMENT

SELECTED PROVISIONS AND AMENDMENTS	DATE "INCORPORATED"	KEY CASES
Eminent domain (V)	1897	Chicago, Burlington, and Quincy Railroad v. Chicago
Freedom of speech (I)	1925	Gitlow v. New York
Freedom of the press (I)	1931	Near v. Minnesota ex rel. Olson
Free exercise of religion (I)	1934	Hamilton v. Regents of the University of California
Freedom of assembly (I)	1937	De Jong v. Oregon
Free Exercise of Religion (I)	1940	Cantwell v. Connecticut
Nonestablishment of state religion (I)	1947	Everson v. Board of Education
Freedom from warrantless search and seizure ("exclusionary rule") (IV)	1961	Mapp v. Ohio
Freedom from cruel and unusual punishment (VIII)	1962	Robinson v. California
Right to counsel in any criminal trial (VI)	1963	Gideon v. Wainwright
Right against self-incrimination and forced confessions (V)	1964	Malloy v. Hogan Escobedo v. Illinois
Right to privacy (III, IV, and V)	1965	Griswold v. Connecticut
Right to remain silent (V)	1966	Miranda v. Arizona
Right against double jeopardy (V)	1969	Benton v. Maryland
Right to bear arms (II)	2010	McDonald v. Chicago

of life and liberty as well as property, only property was incorporated into the Fourteenth Amendment as a limitation on state power.

No further expansion of civil liberties through incorporation occurred until 1925, when the Supreme Court held that freedom of speech is "among the fundamental personal rights and 'liberties' protected by the due process clause of the Fourteenth Amendment from impairment by the states."[9] In 1931, the Court added freedom of the press to that short list of civil rights protected by the Bill of Rights from state action; in 1934, it added freedom of religion; and in 1937, it added freedom of assembly.[10] But that was as far as the Court would go. This one-by-one application of the provisions of the Bill of Rights is known as *selective incorporation*, as distinguished from the notion of *total incorporation* advocated by some scholars. Total incorporation considers that all provisions of the Bill of Rights were applied to the states by the Fourteenth Amendment. As late as 1937, the Court was still loath to nationalize civil liberties beyond the First Amendment. In fact, the Court in that year took an extreme turn backward toward *Barron v. Baltimore*.

The state of Connecticut had indicted a man named Frank Palko for first-degree murder, but a lower court found him guilty of only second-degree murder and sentenced him to life in prison. Unhappy with the verdict, the state of Connecticut appealed the conviction to its highest court and ultimately succeeded in getting Palko convicted of first-degree murder. Palko appealed to the Supreme Court on what seemed an open-and-shut case of **double jeopardy**—being tried twice for the same crime. Yet though a majority of the Court agreed that this could involve double jeopardy, the justices decided that double jeopardy was *not* one of the provisions of the Bill of Rights incorporated into the Fourteenth Amendment as a restriction on states' powers. Justice Benjamin Cardozo rejected the argument made by Palko's lawyer that "whatever is forbidden by the Fifth Amendment is forbidden by the Fourteenth also." Cardozo responded tersely, "There is no such general rule." Palko was eventually executed for the crime—because he lived in Connecticut rather than in a state whose constitution included a guarantee against double jeopardy.

Cases like *Palko* extended the shadow of *Barron* into its second century, despite adoption of the Fourteenth Amendment. The Constitution, as interpreted by the Supreme Court, left standing the framework in which the states had the power to determine their own law on numerous fundamental issues. It left states with the power to pass laws segregating the races—and 13 states chose to exercise that power. The constitutional framework also left states with the power to engage in searches and seizures without a warrant, indict accused persons without benefit of a grand jury, deprive persons of trial by jury, force persons to testify against themselves, deprive accused persons of their right to confront adverse witnesses, and as we have seen, prosecute accused persons

---

9 *Gitlow v. New York,* 268 U.S. 652 (1925).

10 *Near v. Minnesota ex rel. Olson,* 283 U.S. 697 (1931); *De Jonge v. Oregon,* 299 U.S. 353 (1937).

more than once for the same crime, a practice known as double jeopardy.[11] All of these were implicitly identified in *Palko* as "not incorporated" into the Fourteenth Amendment as limitations on the powers of the states.

Before we leave the topic, it is worth mentioning that aside from its implications for the Bill of Rights, one specific part of the Fourteenth Amendment itself is being called into question today: the provision that all persons "born or naturalized" in the United States are citizens. Some politicians and public figures, most notably Donald Trump, have argued that even if born in this country, the children of illegal immigrants should not be considered U.S. citizens and might be subject to deportation. Others say that foreigners come to the United States specifically to have their children born here as citizens and perhaps also thereby provide the parents an advantage in securing their own American citizenship. Though we are a nation of immigrants, the grandchildren of yesterday's immigrants are not always eager to welcome the next group.

The Constitutional Revolution in Civil Liberties

Signs of change in the constitutional framework came after 1954, in *Brown v. Board of Education*, when the Court found state segregation laws for schools unconstitutional.[12] Even though *Brown* was not a civil liberties case, it indicated rather clearly that the Supreme Court was going to be expansive about civil liberties, because with *Brown* the Court had effectively promised that it would actively subject the states and all actions affecting civil rights and civil liberties to strict scrutiny. In retrospect, this constitutional revolution was given a jump-start in 1954 by *Brown v. Board of Education*, even though the results were not apparent until after 1961, when the number of incorporated civil liberties increased (see Table 4.1).

As in the case of the enormous change in the relationship between the federal government and the states as a result of the expansion of the interstate commerce regulation discussed in Chapter 3, the constitutional revolution in civil liberties was a movement toward nationalization. But the two revolutions required opposite motions on the part of the Supreme Court. In the area of commerce (the first revolution), the Court had to assume a passive role by not interfering as Congress expanded the meaning of the commerce clause of Article I, Section 8. This expansion has been so extensive that the national government can now constitutionally reach a single farmer growing 20 acres of wheat or a small restaurant selling barbecue to local "whites only" without the farmer or the restaurant being anywhere near interstate commerce routes. In the second revolution, involving the Bill of Rights and the Fourteenth Amendment, the Court had to assume an active role, which required close review of the laws of state legislatures and the decisions of state courts to apply a single national Fourteenth Amendment standard to the rights and liberties of all citizens.

---

11 *Palko v. Connecticut,* 302 U.S. 319 (1937), was reversed in *Benton v. Maryland,* 395 U.S. 784 (1969), in which the Court said that double jeopardy was in fact incorporated into the Fourteenth Amendment as a restriction on the states.

12 *Brown v. Board of Education,* 374 U.S. 483 (1954).

Table 4.1 shows that until 1961, only the First Amendment had been more or less fully and clearly incorporated into the Fourteenth Amendment.[13] After 1961, several other important provisions of the Bill of Rights were incorporated. Cases that expanded the Fourteenth Amendment's reach include *Gideon v. Wainwright*, which established the right to counsel in a criminal trial, and *Mapp v. Ohio*, which held that evidence obtained in violation of the Fourth Amendment's ban on unreasonable searches and seizures would be excluded from trial.[14] This "exclusionary rule" was particularly irksome to police and prosecutors because it meant that patently guilty defendants sometimes got to go free because the evidence that clearly damned them could not be used. In *Miranda v. Arizona*, the Court's ruling required that arrested persons be informed of the rights to remain silent and have counsel present during interrogation.[15] This is the basis of the **Miranda rule** of reading persons their rights, familiar to most Americans from movies and TV police shows. By 1969, in *Benton v. Maryland*, the Supreme Court had come full circle regarding the rights of the criminally accused, reversing the *Palko* ruling and thereby incorporating double jeopardy.

Beginning in the mid-1950s, the Court expanded another important area of civil liberties: rights to privacy. In 1958, the Court recognized "privacy in one's association" in its decision to prevent the state of Alabama from using the National Association for the Advancement of Colored People (NAACP) membership list in its investigations.[16] As we will see later in this chapter, legal questions about the right to privacy have come to the fore in more recent cases concerning birth control, abortion, homosexuality, and assisted suicide.

Miranda rule

The convention derived from the Supreme Court's 1966 ruling in the case of *Miranda v. Arizona* whereby persons under arrest must be informed of their legal rights, including their right to counsel, before undergoing police interrogation

THE BILL OF RIGHTS TODAY

Because liberty requires restraining the power of government, the general status of civil liberties can never be considered fixed and permanent.[17] Though the Court adheres to law and precedent, every provision in the Bill of Rights

---

13 The one exception was the right to a public trial (the Sixth Amendment), but the 1948 case did not mention the right to a public trial as such; it was cited in a 1968 case as establishing the right to a public trial as part of the Fourteenth Amendment. The 1948 case was *In re Oliver*, 333 U.S. 257, where the issue was put more generally as "due process," and public trial itself was not mentioned. Later opinions, such as *Duncan v. Louisiana*, 391 U.S. 145 (1968), cited the *Oliver* case as the precedent for incorporating public trials as part of the Fourteenth Amendment.

14 *Mapp v. Ohio*, 367 U.S. 643 (1961).

15 *Miranda v. Arizona*, 384 U.S. 436 (1966).

16 *NAACP v. Alabama*, 357 U.S. 449 (1958).

17 This section is taken from Benjamin Ginsberg, Theodore J. Lowi, Margaret Weir, and Caroline J. Tolbert, *We the People: An Introduction to American Politics,* 9th ed. (New York: Norton, 2013).

is subject to interpretation, and interpretations always reflect the interpreter's interest in the outcome. As we have seen, the Court continuously reminds everyone that if it has the power to expand the Bill of Rights, it also has the power to contract it.[18]

One good way to examine the Bill of Rights today is to take the provisions one at a time. Some are settled areas of law; some are not. Any one of them could be reinterpreted by the Court at some point.

The First Amendment and Freedom of Religion

> Congress shall make no law respecting an establishment of religion, or prohibiting the free exercise thereof; or abridging the freedom of speech, or of the press; or the right of the people peaceably to assemble, and to petition the Government for a redress of grievances.

The Bill of Rights begins by guaranteeing freedom of religion, and the First Amendment provides for that freedom in two distinct clauses: "Congress shall make no law [1] respecting an establishment of religion, or [2] prohibiting the free exercise thereof." The first clause is the establishment clause, and the second is the free exercise clause. Let us examine the meaning of each.

Separation between Church and State. The **establishment clause** and the idea of "no law" regarding the establishment of religion could be interpreted in several ways. One interpretation, which probably reflects the views of many of the First Amendment's authors, is that the government is prohibited only from establishing an official church. Official state churches, such as the Church of England, were common in the eighteenth century and seemed to many Americans to be inconsistent with a republican form of government. Indeed, many colonists had fled Europe to escape persecution for having rejected state-sponsored churches. A second possible interpretation, the "non-preferentialist" or "accommodationist" view, holds that the government may not take sides among competing religions but is not prohibited from providing assistance to religious institutions or ideas so long as it shows no favoritism. The United States accommodates religious beliefs in various ways, from the reference to God on U.S. currency to the prayer that begins every session of Congress. These forms of establishment have never been struck down by the courts.

The third view regarding religious establishment, the most commonly held today, is the idea of a "wall of separation" between church and state that the government cannot breach. The concept of a wall of separation was Jefferson's formulation, and it has figured in many Supreme Court cases arising under the establishment clause. For centuries, Jefferson's words have had a powerful

← **establishment clause**

The First Amendment clause that says, "Congress shall make no law respecting an establishment of religion." Today this phrase is generally interpreted as meaning that a wall of separation exists between church and state

---

18 For a lively and readable treatment of the possibilities of restricting provisions of the Bill of Rights without actually reversing earlier decisions, see David G. Savage, *Turning Right: The Making of the Rehnquist Supreme Court* (New York: Wiley, 1992).

impact on our understanding of the proper relationship between church and state in the United States. The Analyzing the Evidence unit on pp. 116–7 explores Americans' attitudes on the separation of church and state.

Despite the absolute sound of the phrase *wall of separation*, there is ample room to disagree on its nature. For example, the Court has been consistently strict in cases of school prayer, striking down such practices as Bible reading,[19] nondenominational prayer,[20] a moment of silence for meditation or voluntary prayer, and pregame prayer at public sporting events.[21] In each case, the Court reasoned that school-sponsored observations, even of an apparently nondenominational character, are highly suggestive of school sponsorship and therefore violate the prohibition against establishment of religion. Yet the Court has been quite permissive (some would say inconsistent) about the public display of religious symbols, such as city-sponsored nativity scenes in commercial or municipal areas.[22] For decades, the Court has faced cases involving government-financed support for religious schools.

In 1971, the Court attempted to specify criteria to guide its decisions and those of lower courts, indicating circumstances under which state financial assistance to religious schools was constitutionally permissible. In *Lemon v. Kurtzman*, the Supreme Court established three criteria to guide future cases. Collectively, these became known as the **Lemon test**. The Court held that government aid to religious schools would be accepted as constitutional if (1) it had a secular purpose, (2) its effect was neither to advance nor to inhibit religion, and (3) it did not entangle government and religious institutions in one another's affairs.[23]

Although these restrictions make it hard to pass the *Lemon* test, imaginative authorities have found ways to do so, and the Supreme Court has demonstrated a willingness to let them, perhaps moving toward a more accommodationist view of the establishment clause. In 1995, for example, the Court narrowly ruled that a University of Virginia student group could not be denied student activities funds merely because it was a religious group espousing a particular viewpoint about a deity. The Court called the denial "viewpoint discrimination" and declared that it violated the group's free speech rights.[24] This led two years later to a more conservative approach to the separation of church and state. In 1997, the Court accepted the practice of sending public-school teachers into parochial schools to provide remedial education to disadvantaged children.[25]

Lemon test ➡

Rule articulated in *Lemon v. Kurtzman* according to which governmental action with respect to religion is permissible if it is secular in purpose, does not lead to "excessive entanglement" with religion, and neither promotes nor inhibits the practice of religion. The *Lemon* test is generally used in relation to government aid to religious schools

---

19 *Abington School District v. Schempp,* 374 U.S. 203 (1963).

20 *Engel v. Vitale,* 370 U.S. 421 (1962).

21 *Wallace v. Jaffree,* 472 U.S. 38 (1985).

22 *Lynch v. Donnelly,* 465 U.S. 668 (1984).

23 *Lemon v. Kurtzman,* 403 U.S. 602 (1971). The *Lemon* test is still good law, but as recently as the 1994 Court term, four justices urged that it be abandoned. Here is a settled area of law that may become unsettled.

24 *Rosenberger v. University of Virginia,* 515 U.S. 819 (1995).

25 *Agostini v. Felton,* 521 U.S. 203 (1997). The case being overruled was *Aguilar v. Felton,* 473 U.S. 402 (1985).

In 2004, the question of whether the phrase *under God* in the Pledge of Allegiance violates the establishment clause came before the Court. Written in 1892, the pledge had been used in schools without any religious references. But in 1954, in the midst of the Cold War, Congress voted to change the pledge, in response to the "godless Communism" of the Soviet Union.

Ever since the change was made, there has been a constant murmuring of discontent from those who object to an officially sanctioned profession of belief in a deity as a violation of the First Amendment's religious freedom clause. In 2003, Michael Newdow, the atheist father of a California kindergartener, brought suit against the local school district, arguing that the reference to God turned the daily recitation of the pledge into a religious exercise. The case was appealed to the Supreme Court, which ruled that Newdow lacked a sufficient personal stake in the case to bring the complaint.[26] This inconclusive decision left "under God" in the pledge while keeping the issue alive for possible resolution in a future case.

In two cases in 2005, the Court ruled, also inconclusively, on government-sponsored displays of religious symbols. Both cases involved displays of the Ten Commandments. In *Van Orden v. Perry*, the Court ruled that a display of the Ten Commandments in the Texas state capitol did not violate the Constitution.[27] However, in *McCreary v. ACLU*, the Court determined that a display of the Ten Commandments inside two Kentucky court houses was unconstitutional.[28] Justice Breyer, the swing vote in both cases, intimated that the difference had been the purpose of the displays. Most legal observers, though, could see little difference between the two and assume that the Court will provide further clarification in future cases.

Free Exercise of Religion. The **free exercise clause** protects the right to believe and practice whatever religion one chooses; it also protects the right to be a nonbeliever. Generally speaking, problems arise under this clause not because the government decides to interfere with religion, but because generally applicable secular laws intrude on the beliefs of one or another group. The precedent-setting case was *West Virginia State Board of Education v. Barnette* (1943), which involved the children of a family of Jehovah's Witnesses who refused to salute and pledge allegiance to the American flag on the grounds that their religious faith did not permit it. Three years earlier, the Court had upheld such a requirement and had permitted schools to expel students for refusing to salute the flag. But the nation's entry into a war to defend democracy, coupled with the ugly treatment to which the Jehovah's Witnesses' children had been subjected, induced the Court to reverse itself and endorse the free exercise of religion even when it may be offensive to the beliefs of the majority.[29]

 free exercise clause

The First Amendment clause that protects a citizen's right to believe and practice whatever religion he or she chooses

---

26 *Elk Grove Unified School District v. Newdow*, 542 U.S. 1 (2004).

27 *Van Orden v. Perry*, 545 U.S. 677 (2005).

28 *McCreary v. ACLU*, 545 U.S. 844 (2005).

29 *West Virginia State Board of Education v. Barnette*, 319 U.S. 624 (1943). The case it reversed was *Minersville School District v. Gobitus*, 310 U.S. 586 (1940).

Americans' Attitudes Toward Church and State

CHAPTER 04

Contributed by
David E. Campbell
University of Notre Dame

Almost all Americans agree that their nation has a separation of church and state, but translating the abstract principle of church–state separation into practice is often contentious. The phrase *separation of church and state* does not actually appear in the Constitution, but religion is mentioned twice in the document.

The first mention of religion is in the First Amendment, which states that "Congress shall make no law respecting an establishment of religion, or prohibiting the free exercise thereof." These two phrases have come to be known as the establishment and free exercise clauses.

A national survey asked Americans about their attitudes toward two applications of the First Amendment: whether the Ten Commandments can be displayed on government property such as courthouses or legislatures (the establishment clause) and whether public schools should be able to ban religious dress such as Muslim head scarves (the free exercise clause). The two graphs below compare the views of Republicans, Independents, and Democrats.

Should the Ten Commandments Be Displayed on Government Property?

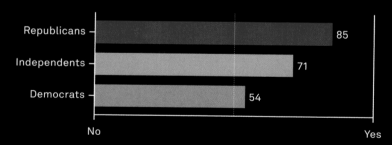

In this study, respondents placed their opinion on a 0–100 scale between "should be allowed" and "should not be allowed." The findings show that most Americans do not have a problem with the display of the Ten Commandments, although Democrats are more likely to object than Republicans. Democrats are also more likely to think that public schools should not be able to prevent students from wearing religious dress at school, but the partisan differences are more muted.

Should Public Schools Be Able to Ban Religious Dress, Such as Muslim Headscarves?

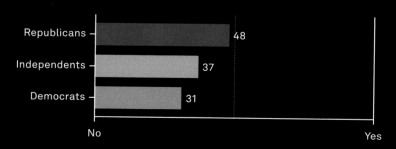

SOURCE: David E. Campbell, Geoffrey C. Layman, and John C. Green, "Secularism in America Study."

The second place that the Constitution mentions religion is Article VI, which says that "no religious test shall ever be required as a qualification to any office or public trust under the United States." Yet while formal religious tests are expressly forbidden, historically some voters have been unwilling to vote for candidates with particular religious backgrounds.

The graph below displays historical trends in the percentage of Americans who say that they would vote for a presidential candidate (from their preferred party) who is Catholic, Jewish, Mormon, Muslim, or Atheist.

Would You Vote for a _____ Candidate?

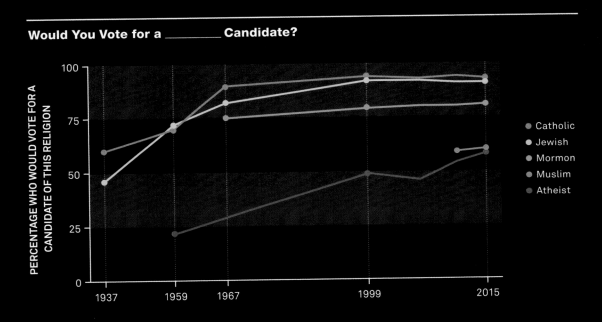

Over the decades, the percentage of Americans who say that they would vote for a Catholic or Jewish presidential candidate has risen steeply (and, of course, in 1960 Americans elected John F. Kennedy, a Catholic). The percentage saying that they would vote for a Mormon has risen only a little since the 1960s. Thus when Mitt Romney, a Mormon, ran for the presidency in 2012, he faced opposition to his religion that was comparable to the anti-Catholicism faced by Kennedy in 1960. While Americans are significantly more willing to vote for an atheist today than in the 1950s, in 2015 only 58 percent of Americans said they would be willing to vote for an atheist. This is comparable to the percentage willing to vote for a Muslim (60 percent). Antagonism toward atheist and Muslim candidates today is about the same as the opposition faced by Catholics and Jews in the 1930s.

SOURCES: Results through 2007: Jeffrey M. Jones, February 20, 2007, www.gallup.com/poll/26611/Some-Americans-Reluctant-Vote-Mormon-72Year%20Old-Presidential-Candidates.aspx (accessed 2/26/2016); 2012 results: Jeffrey M. Jones, June 21, 2012, www.gallup.com/poll/155285/atheists-muslims-bias-presidential-candidates.aspx (accessed 2/26/2016); 2015 results: Frank Newport, September 22, 2015, www.gallup.com/opinion/polling-matters/185813/six-americans-say-yes-muslim-president.aspx (accessed 2/26/2016).
NOTE: Not all religions were included in every year.

Although the Court has been fairly consistent in protecting the free exercise of religious belief, it has distinguished between religious beliefs and *actions* based on those beliefs. The 1940 case of *Cantwell v. Connecticut* established the "time, place and manner" rule. The case arose from the efforts of two Jehovah's Witnesses to engage in door-to-door fund-raising. Americans are free to adhere to any religious beliefs, but the time, place, and manner of their exercise are subject to regulation in the public interest.[30]

In recent years, the principle of free exercise has been bolstered by statutes prohibiting religious discrimination by public and private entities in a variety of realms including hiring, land use, and the treatment of prison inmates. Two recent cases illustrating this point are *Holt v. Hobbs*[31] and *Equal Opportunity Commission v. Abercrombie & Fitch Stores*.[32] The *Holt* case involved a Muslim prisoner in an Arkansas jail. The prisoner, Gregory Holt, asserted that his religious beliefs required him to grow a beard. Thus, according to Holt, an Arkansas prison policy prohibiting beards was a violation of his ability to exercise his religion. The Court held that the prison policy was a violation of the free exercise clause and violated a federal statute designed to protect the ability of prisoners to worship as they pleased. In the second case, the Equal Employment Opportunity Commission (EEOC) brought suit against Abercrombie for refusing to hire a Muslim woman who wore a head scarf in violation of the company's dress code. The Court held that the store's actions amounted to religious discrimination in hiring—something not allowed by federal law.

The First Amendment and Freedom of Speech and the Press

> Congress shall make no law . . . abridging the freedom of speech, or of the press.

Because democracy depends on an open political process and politics is basically talk, freedom of speech and freedom of the press are considered critical. For this reason, they hold a prominence in the Bill of Rights equal to that of freedom of religion. In 1938, freedom of speech (which in all important respects includes freedom of the press) was given extraordinary constitutional status when the Supreme Court established that any legislation attempting to restrict these fundamental freedoms "is to be subjected to a more exacting judicial scrutiny . . . than are most other types of legislation."[33]

---

30 *Cantwell v. Connecticut*, 310 U.S. 296 (1940).

31 *Holt v. Hobbs*, 574 U.S. ____ (2015).

32 *Equal Opportunity Commission v. Abercrombie & Fitch Stores*, 575 U.S. ____ (2015).

33 *United States v. Carolene Products Company*, 304 U.S. 144 (1938), 384. This footnote is one of the Court's most important doctrines. See Alfred H. Kelly, Winfred A. Harbison, and Herman Belz, *The American Constitution: Its Origins and Development*, 7th ed., 2 vols. (New York: Norton, 1991), pp. II:519–23.

The Court was saying that the democratic political process must be protected at almost any cost. This higher standard of judicial review came to be called **strict scrutiny**. It implies that speech—at least some kinds of speech—will be protected almost absolutely. In 2011, for example, the Supreme Court ruled 8–1 that the Westboro Baptist Church, a tiny Kansas institution, had a First Amendment right to picket the funerals of American soldiers killed in action while displaying signs reading "Thank God for Dead Soldiers." Church members believe that these deaths represent divine punishment for America's tolerance of homosexuality and other matters. In his opinion, Chief Justice Roberts wrote, "As a nation we have chosen to protect even hurtful speech on public issues to ensure that we do not stifle public debate."[34] But, even though we do protect many types of speech with which most Americans strongly disagree, only some are fully protected against restrictions. Many forms of speech are less than absolutely protected—even though they are entitled to a preferred position.

Political Speech. Political speech was of greatest concern to the framers, even though they found it the most difficult provision to observe. Within seven years of ratification of the Bill of Rights, Congress adopted the infamous Alien and Sedition Acts (long-since repealed), which, among other things, made it a crime to say or publish anything that might defame or bring into disrepute the U.S. government. The acts' intentions were to criminalize the very conduct given absolute protection by the First Amendment. Fifteen violators, including several newspaper editors, were indicted, and a few were convicted before the relevant portions of the acts were allowed to expire.

The first modern free speech case arose immediately after World War I. It involved persons who had been convicted under the federal Espionage Acts of 1917 for opposing American involvement in the war. The Supreme Court upheld the act and refused to protect the defendants' speech rights on the grounds that their activities—appeals to draftees to resist the draft—constituted a "**clear and present danger**" to security.[35] This is the first and most famous, though since disregarded, test of when government intervention or censorship can be permitted, though courts no longer use it.

It was only after the 1920s that real progress toward a genuinely effective First Amendment occurred. Since then, the courts have protected political speech even when it has been deemed "insulting" or "outrageous." In the 1969 case *Brandenburg v. Ohio*, the Supreme Court rules that as long as speech falls short of actually "inciting or producing imminently lawless action," it cannot be prohibited, even if it is hostile to or subversive of the government and its policies.[36]

This statement was made in the case of a Ku Klux Klan leader, Charles Brandenburg, who had been convicted of advocating "revengent" action against the president, Congress, and the Supreme Court, among others, if they

 strict scrutiny

The most stringent standard of judicial review of a government's actions in which the government must show that the law serves a "compelling state interest"

 clear and present danger

The criterion formerly used to determine whether speech is protected or unprotected, based on its capacity to present a clear and present danger to society

---

34 *Snyder v. Phelps,* 562 U.S. 443 (2011).

35 *Schenck v. United States,* 249 U.S. 47 (1919).

36 *Brandenburg v. Ohio,* 395 U.S. 444 (1969).

continued "to suppress the white, Caucasian race." Although Brandenburg was not carrying a weapon, some members of his audience were. Nevertheless, the Supreme Court reversed the state courts and freed Brandenburg while declaring Ohio's Criminal Syndicalism Act unconstitutional because it punished persons who "advocate, or teach the duty, necessity, or propriety [of violence] as a means of accomplishing industrial or political reform" or who publish materials or "voluntarily assemble . . . to teach or advocate the doctrines of criminal syndicalism." The Court argued that the statute did not distinguish "mere advocacy" from "incitement to imminent lawless action." It would be difficult to go much further in protecting freedom of speech. Typically, federal courts strike down restrictions on speech if they are deemed to be "overbroad," "vague," or lacking "neutrality" in terms of the content of the speech—for example, if a statute prohibited the views of the political left but not the political right, or vice versa, or a statute that seemed to restrict speech broadly without specifying the type of speech or conditions for restrictions.

Additional expansion of political speech, particularly the loosening of limits on spending and donations to political campaigns—occurred in 1976 with the Supreme Court's decision in *Buckley v. Valeo*.[37] Campaign finance reform laws of the early 1970s, addressing the Watergate scandal, sought severe limits on campaign spending, and numerous important provisions were declared unconstitutional on the basis of a new principle that spending money by or on behalf of candidates is a form of speech protected by the First Amendment (as contrasted with contributions to campaigns which Congress has more authority to regulate. The issue arose again in 2003 after passage of a more severe campaign finance law, the Bipartisan Campaign Reform Act (BCRA; 2002). This time, the Court majority seriously reduced the area of speech protected by *Buckley v. Valeo* by holding that Congress was within its power to limit the amounts individuals could spend, the amounts of "soft money" that corporations and their political action committees (PACs) could spend, and the amounts spent on issue advertising before Election Day. The Court argued that "the selling of access . . . has given rise to the appearance of undue influence [that justifies] regulations impinging on First Amendment rights . . . in order to curb corruption or the appearance of corruption."[38] This decision was the anomaly, however. In 2007, the Court struck down a key portion of BCRA, finding that the act's limitations on political advertising violated the First Amendment's guarantee of free speech.[39] In *Citizens United v. Federal Election Commission*, in 2010, the Court ruled that corporate funding of independent election ads could not be limited under the First Amendment.[40] And in 2014, the Court struck down aggregate limits on an individual's contributions to candidates for federal office, political parties, and PACs. The decision stated such limits do not further the government's

---

37 *Buckley v. Valeo,* 424 U.S. 1 (1976).

38 *McConnell v. Federal Election Commission,* 540 U.S. 93 (2003).

39 *Federal Election Commission v. Wisconsin Right to Life,* 551 U.S. 449 (2007).

40 *Citizens United v. Federal Election Commission,* 558 U.S. 310 (2010).

---

interest in preventing corruption and are thus invalid under the First Amendment.[41] In these decisions, the Court maintained that limits on political spending amounted to limits on free speech. As a result of this decision, several wealthy donors contributed more than $10 million to presidential candidates in 2016.

Symbolic Speech, Speech Plus Action, and the Rights of Assembly and Petition. The First Amendment treats the freedoms of assembly and petition as equal to the freedoms of religion and political speech. Freedom of assembly and freedom of petition are closely associated with speech but go beyond it to speech associated with action. Since at least 1931, the Supreme Court has sought to protect actions that are designed to send a political message. (Usually the purpose of a symbolic act is not only to send a message but also to draw spectators and thus strengthen the message.) Generally speaking, state and federal governments may enact reasonable regulations governing the time, place, and manner of speech so long as they do not discriminate against particular messages or messengers. A limitation on political parades after 7 P.M., for example, must apply to *all* parades. Thus the Court held unconstitutional a California statute making it a felony to display a red flag "as a sign, symbol or emblem of opposition to organized government."[42] The ordinance seemed to target one particular political view.

Although today there are limits on how far one can go with actions that symbolically convey a message, the protection of such action is very broad. Thus although the Court upheld a federal statute making it a crime to burn draft cards to protest the Vietnam War on the grounds that the government had a compelling interest in preserving draft cards as part of the conduct of the war itself, it considered the wearing of black armbands to school a protected form of assembly. In such cases, a court will often use the standard articulated in the draft card case, *United States v. O'Brien*, and now known as the *"O'Brien* test."[43] Under this test, a statute restricting expressive or symbolic speech must be justified by a compelling government interest and be narrowly tailored toward achieving that interest.

Another example is the burning of the American flag as a symbol of protest. In 1984, at a rally during the Republican National Convention in Dallas, a political protester burned an American flag in violation of a Texas statute that prohibited desecration of a venerated object. In a 5–4 decision, the Supreme Court declared the Texas law unconstitutional on the grounds that flag burning is expressive conduct protected by the First Amendment.[44] Disagreeing with the Court's decision, Congress passed the Flag Protection Act of 1989. Protesters promptly violated this act, and their prosecution moved into federal district court, which declared the new law unconstitutional. The Supreme Court

---

41 *McCutcheon v. Federal Election Commission,* 572 U.S. _____ (2014).

42 *Stromberg v. California,* 283 U.S. 359 (1931).

43 *United States v. O'Brien,* 391 U.S. 367 (1968).

44 *Texas v. Johnson,* 491 U.S. 397 (1989).

affirmed the lower court's decision.[45] In 2003, the Court struck down a Virginia cross-burning statute, ruling that states could make cross burning a crime as long as the statute required prosecutors to prove that the burning was intended to intimidate rather than simply express an opinion. Justice O'Connor wrote that the First Amendment permits the government to forbid cross burning as a "particularly virulent form of intimidation" but not when the act was "a form of symbolic expression."[46] This decision will likely become a more generalized First Amendment protection of any conduct that can be considered a form of symbolic expression.

Closer to the original intent of the assembly and petition clause is the category of **speech plus**—following speech with physical activity such as picketing, distributing leaflets, and other forms of peaceful demonstration or assembly. Such assemblies are consistently protected by courts under the First Amendment; state and local laws regulating such activities are frequently overturned. But the same assembly on private property is quite another matter and can often be regulated. For example, the directors of a shopping center can lawfully prohibit an assembly protesting a war or supporting a ban on abortion. Assemblies in public areas can also be restricted under some circumstances, especially when the health, safety, or rights of others are jeopardized. This condition was the basis of the Supreme Court's decision to uphold a lower-court order restricting abortion protesters' access to the entrances of abortion clinics.[47]

Freedom of the Press. Freedom of speech includes freedom of the press. With the exception of broadcast media, which are subject to federal regulation, the press is protected under the doctrine prohibiting **prior restraint**. Beginning in 1931,[48] the Supreme Court has held that except under extraordinary circumstances, the First Amendment prohibits government agencies from seeking to prevent newspapers or magazines from publishing whatever they wish. Indeed, in 1971, in *New York Times v. United States*, the so-called Pentagon Papers case, the Court ruled that the government could not even block publication of secret Defense Department documents furnished to the *New York Times* by a Vietnam War opponent who had obtained the documents illegally.[49] In 1990, however, the Court upheld a lower-court order restraining the Cable News Network (CNN) from broadcasting tapes of conversations between former Panamanian dictator Manuel Noriega and his lawyer, supposedly recorded by the American government. The Court held that CNN could be restrained from

speech plus

Speech accompanied by activities such as sit-ins, picketing, and demonstrations. Protection of this form of speech under the First Amendment is conditional, and restrictions imposed by state or local authorities are acceptable if properly balanced by considerations of public order

prior restraint

An effort by a government agency to block the publication of material it deems libelous or harmful in some other way: censorship. In the United States, the courts forbid prior restraint except under the most extraordinary circumstances

---

45 *United States v. Eichman*, 496 U.S. 310 (1990).

46 *Virginia v. Black*, 538 U.S. 343 (2003).

47 For a good general discussion of speech plus, see Louis Fisher, *American Constitutional Law* (New York: McGraw-Hill, 1990), pp. 544–46. The case upholding the buffer zone against the abortion protesters is *Madsen v. Women's Health Center*, 512 U.S. 753 (1994).

48 *Near v. Minnesota ex rel. Olson*, 283 U.S. 697 (1931).

49 *New York Times v. United States*, 403 U.S. 713 (1971).

broadcasting the tapes until the trial court had heard the tapes and decided whether their broadcast would violate Noriega's right to a fair trial.[50]

Libel and Slander. Some speech is not protected at all. If a written statement is made in "reckless disregard of the truth" and is considered damaging to the victim because it is "malicious, scandalous, and defamatory," it can be punished as **libel**. An oral statement of such nature can be punished as **slander**.

Today most libel suits involve freedom of the press. Historically, newspapers were subject to the law of libel, which provided that newspapers printing false and malicious stories could be compelled to pay damages to those they defamed. Recently, however, American courts have narrowed the meaning of libel and made it extremely difficult, particularly for public figures, to win a libel case against a newspaper. In *New York Times v. Sullivan*, the Court held that to be deemed libelous a story about a public official not only had to be untrue but also had to result from "actual malice" or "reckless disregard" for the truth[51]—the newspaper had to *deliberately* print false and malicious material. But this is nearly impossible to prove, and the print media essentially have been able to publish anything they want about a public figure. The courts have been more sympathetic to libel and slander claims made by private individuals.

In at least one case, however, the Court has opened up the possibility of public officials' filing libel suits against the press. In 1985, the Court held that the press was immune from libel only when the printed material was "a matter of public concern." In other words, in future cases a newspaper would have to show that the public official was engaged in activities that were indeed *public*. This new principle has made the press more vulnerable to libel suits, but it still leaves an enormous realm of freedom for the press.

Obscenity and Pornography. If libel and slander cases involve the difficult problem of determining the truth of statements and whether they are malicious and damaging, cases involving pornography and obscenity can be even stickier. It is easy to say that pornography and obscenity fall outside the realm of protected speech, but it is impossible to clearly define where protection ends and unprotected speech begins. The Supreme Court first confronted this problem in 1957 with a definition of obscenity that may have caused more confusion than it cleared up. Justice William Brennan, in writing the Court's opinion, defined obscenity as speech or writing that appeals to "prurient interest"—that is, books, magazines, films, and other material whose purpose is to excite lust as this appears "to the average person, applying contemporary community standards." Even so, Brennan added, the work should be judged obscene only when it is "utterly without redeeming social importance."[52] Brennan's definition, instead of clarifying the Court's view, caused more confusion. In 1964, Justice

 libel

A written statement made in "reckless disregard of the truth" and considered damaging to a victim because it is "malicious, scandalous, and defamatory"

 slander

An oral statement made in "reckless disregard of the truth" and considered damaging to a victim because it is "malicious, scandalous, and defamatory"

50 *Cable News Network v. Noriega,* 498 U.S. 976 (1990).

51 *New York Times v. Sullivan,* 376 U.S. 254 (1964).

52 *Roth v. United States,* 354 U.S. 476 (1957).

Potter Stewart confessed that although he found pornography impossible to define, "I know it when I see it."[53]

All attempts by the courts to define pornography and obscenity have proved impractical because each instance required courts to screen thousands of pages of print material or feet of film alleged to be pornographic. The vague standards meant ultimately that almost nothing could be banned on the grounds that it was pornographic and obscene. An effort to strengthen the restrictions occurred in 1973, when the Supreme Court expressed willingness to define pornography as a work that as a whole is deemed prurient by the "average person" according to "community standards," depicts sexual conduct "in a patently offensive way," and lacks "serious literary, artistic, political, or scientific value." This definition meant that pornography would be determined by local rather than national standards. Thus a local bookseller might be prosecuted for selling a volume that was a best seller nationally but was deemed pornographic locally.[54] This new definition of standards did not help much, and not long after 1973 the Court again began to review all such community antipornography laws, reversing most of them. This area of free speech is far from settled.

Lately the battle against obscene speech has focused on Internet pornography. Opponents argue that it should be strictly regulated because of children's easy access to the Internet. The first significant effort to regulate Internet content occurred in 1996 with major telecommunications legislation. Attached to the Telecommunications Act was an amendment, the Communications Decency Act (CDA), that sought to regulate the online transmission of obscene material. The CDA's constitutionality was immediately challenged by a coalition of interests led by the American Civil Liberties Union (ACLU). In the 1997 case of *Reno v. ACLU*, the Supreme Court struck down the CDA, ruling that it suppressed speech that "adults have a constitutional right to receive."[55] Congress again tried to limit children's access with the 2001 Children's Internet Protection Act, which required public libraries to install antipornography filters on all library computers with Internet access. The law was challenged, and in 2003 the Court upheld it, asserting that its provisions did not violate library patrons' First Amendment rights.[56] Other conflicts have focused on the use of children in pornography rather than their access to it. In 2003, Congress enacted the Prosecutorial Remedies and Other Tools to End the Exploitation of Children Today (PROTECT) Act, which outlawed efforts to sell child pornography via the Internet. The Supreme Court upheld this act in 2008, ruling that criminalizing efforts to pander child pornography did not violate free-speech guarantees.[57]

In 2000, the Court also extended First Amendment protection to cable (not broadcast) television. In *United States v. Playboy Entertainment Group*, the Court

---

53 Concurring opinion in *Jacobellis v. Ohio,* 378 U.S. 184 (1964).

54 *Miller v. California,* 413 U.S. 15 (1973).

55 *Reno v. ACLU,* 521 U.S. 844 (1997).

56 *United States v. American Library Association,* 539 U.S. 194 (2003).

57 *United States v. Williams,* 553 U.S. 385 (2008).

struck down a portion of the Telecommunications Act of 1996 that required cable TV companies to limit the broadcast of sexually explicit programming to late-night hours. In its decision, the Court noted that the law already provided parents with the means to restrict access to sexually explicit cable channels through blocking devices. Moreover, such programming could enter the home only if parents purchased such channels in the first place.[58]

Fighting Words. Speech can also lose its protected position when it moves toward the sphere of action. "Expressive speech," for example, is protected until it moves from the symbolic realm to actual conduct—to direct incitement of damaging conduct with the use of **fighting words**. In 1942, the Supreme Court upheld the arrest and conviction of a man who had violated a state law forbidding the use of offensive language in public. He had called the arresting officer a "goddamned racketeer" and "a damn Fascist." When his case reached the Supreme Court, the arrest was upheld on the grounds that the First Amendment provides no protection for such offensive language because such words "are no essential part of any exposition of ideas."[59] This case was reaffirmed in a case decided at the height of the Cold War, when the Court held that

fighting words

Speech that directly incites damaging conduct

> there is no substantial public interest in permitting certain kinds of utterances: the lewd and obscene, the profane, the libelous, and the insulting or "fighting" words—those which by their very utterance inflict injury or tend to incite an immediate breach of the peace.[60]

Since that time, however, the Court has reversed almost every conviction based on arguments that the speaker had used "fighting words" in a political context. (Abusive language outside a political context is unlikely to be considered protected speech.) But again, this is not an absolutely settled area. The increased activism of minority and women's groups has prompted a movement against words that might be construed as offensive to members of a particular group. This movement is called, derisively, political correctness, or PC. In response, many organizations have imposed codes of etiquette acknowledging these enhanced sensitivities. Such efforts to formalize restraints on the use of certain words in public cause great concern over their possible infringement on freedom of speech. But how should we determine what words are fighting words and therefore fall outside the protections of freedom of speech?

Student Speech. One category of conditionally protected speech is the free speech of high school students in public schools. In 1986, the Supreme Court

---

58 *United States v. Playboy Entertainment Group, Inc.,* 529 U.S. 803 (2000).

59 *Chaplinsky v. State of New Hampshire,* 315 U.S. 568 (1942).

60 *Dennis v. United States,* 341 U.S. 494 (1951), which upheld the infamous Smith Act of 1940, provided criminal penalties for those who "willfully and knowingly conspire to teach and advocate the forceful and violent overthrow and destruction of the government."

backed away from a broad protection of student free speech rights by upholding the punishment of a high school student for making a sexually suggestive speech. The Court held that such speech interfered with the school's goal of teaching students the limits of socially acceptable behavior.[61] Two years later the Court further restricted students' speech and press rights, defining them as part of the educational process and not to be treated with the same standard as adult speech in a regular public forum.[62] A more recent case involving high school students[63] arose from school policies in Juneau, Alaska. In 2002, the Olympic torch relay passed through Juneau on its way to the Winter Olympics. As the torch passed Juneau-Douglas High, a senior, Joseph Frederick, unfurled a banner that read, "Bong Hits 4 Jesus." The school's principal promptly suspended Frederick, who then brought suit, alleging violation of his free speech rights. Like most public schools, Juneau-Douglas High prohibits expressions on school grounds that advocate illegal drug use. Civil libertarians see such policies as restricting students' right to free speech—which the Supreme Court has recognized since a 1969 case in which it said an Iowa public school could not prohibit students from wearing antiwar armbands. However, in Frederick's case, the Court ruled that the First Amendment did not require schools to permit students to advocate illegal drug use.

In addition, scores of universities have attempted to develop speech codes to suppress racial or ethnic slurs. However, the codes may produce more problems than they solve, and speech codes at public universities have been struck down by federal judges as unconstitutional infringements of speech. Similar efforts to formalize "politically correct" speech guidelines have occurred in large corporations, in which many successful complaints and lawsuits have alleged that employers' or supervisors' words create a "hostile or abusive working environment." The Supreme Court has held that "sexual harassment" that creates a "hostile working environment" includes "unwelcome sexual advances, requests for sexual favors, and other *verbal* or physical conduct of a sexual nature"[64] [emphasis added]. A fundamental free speech issue is involved in these regulations of hostile speech.

Hate Speech. Many jurisdictions have drafted ordinances banning forms of expression that assert hatred toward a specific group, be it African Americans, Jews, Muslims, or others. Such ordinances seldom pass constitutional muster. The leading Supreme Court case in this realm is the 1992 decision in *R.A.V. v. City of St. Paul.*[65] Here, a white teenager was arrested for burning a cross on the lawn of a black family in violation of a municipal ordinance that banned cross burning. The Court ruled that such an ordinance must be *content neutral*—that is, not prohibiting actions directed at some groups but not others. The statute

---

61 *Bethel School District No. 403 v. Fraser,* 478 U.S. 675 (1986).

62 *Hazelwood School District v. Kuhlmeier,* 484 U.S. 260 (1988).

63 *Morse v. Frederick,* 551 U.S. 393 (2007).

64 *Meritor Savings Bank v. Vinson,* 477 U.S. 57 (1986).

65 *R.A.V. v. City of St. Paul,* 506 U.S. 377 (1992).

in question prohibited only cross burning, typically an expression of hatred of African Americans. Since a statute banning all forms of hateful expression would be deemed overly broad, the *R.A.V.* standard may suggest that virtually all hate speech is constitutionally protected. In a 1993 case, however, the Court ruled that a state can consider whether a crime was motivated by bias against a minority group. So-called hate crimes can be more severely punished than similar acts committed for other reasons.[66] The Court distinguished this judgment from the *R.A.V.* decision by noting that *R.A.V.* was concerned with expression, whereas the ordinance in question in the 1993 case was aimed at violent action. The question of what constitutes hate speech is often difficult to resolve. To some, a display of the Confederate flag is a symbol of racism and oppression. To others, such a display may constitute respect for regional traditions and heritage.

Commercial Speech. Commercial speech, such as newspaper or television advertising, does not have full First Amendment protection because it cannot be considered political speech. Initially considered entirely outside the protection of the First Amendment, commercial speech made gains during the twentieth century. Some commercial speech is still unprotected and therefore regulated. For example, regulation of false and misleading advertising by the Federal Trade Commission is a well-established power of the federal government. The Supreme Court long ago approved the constitutionality of laws prohibiting the electronic media from carrying cigarette advertising.[67] It also has upheld city ordinances prohibiting the posting of all signs on public property (as long as the ban is total, with no hint of censorship),[68] and Puerto Rico's statute restricting gambling advertising aimed at residents of Puerto Rico.[69]

However, gains far outweigh losses in the effort to expand the protection commercial speech enjoys under the First Amendment. As the scholar Louis Fisher explains, "In part, this reflects the growing appreciation that commercial speech is part of the free flow of information necessary for informed choice and democratic participation."[70] For example, the Court in 1975 struck down a state statute making it a misdemeanor to sell or circulate newspapers encouraging abortions; the Court ruled that the statute infringed on constitutionally protected speech and the reader's right to make informed choices.[71] On a similar basis, the Court reversed its own earlier decisions upholding laws that prohibited lawyers, dentists, and other professionals from advertising their services. For the Court, medical-service advertising was a matter of health that could be

---

66 *Wisconsin v. Mitchell,* 508 U.S. 476 (1993).

67 *Capital Broadcasting Company v. Acting Attorney General,* 405 U.S. 1000 (1972).

68 *City Council v. Taxpayers for Vincent,* 466 U.S. 789 (1984).

69 *Posadas de Puerto Rico Associates v. Tourism Company of Puerto Rico,* 478 U.S. 328 (1986).

70 Fisher, *American Constitutional Law,* p. 546.

71 *Bigelow v. Virginia,* 421 U.S. 809 (1975).

advanced by the free flow of information.[72] In a 1983 case, the Court struck down a congressional statute prohibiting the unsolicited mailing of advertisements for contraceptives. In 1996, it struck down Rhode Island laws and regulations banning the advertisement of liquor prices as a violation of the First Amendment.[73] And in a 2001 case, the Court ruled that a Massachusetts ban on all cigarette advertising violated the tobacco industry's First Amendment right to advertise its products to adult consumers.[74] These instances of commercial speech are significant because they indicate the breadth and depth of the freedom existing today to direct appeals broadly to a large public, whether to sell goods and services or to mobilize people for political purposes.

The Second Amendment and the Right to Bear Arms

A well regulated Militia, being necessary to the security of a free State, the right of the people to keep and bear Arms, shall not be infringed.

The purpose of the Second Amendment is to provide for militias; they were to be the government's backing for the maintenance of local public order. *The framers understood militia* to be a military or police resource for state governments; militias were distinguished from armies and troops, which came within the sole constitutional jurisdiction of Congress. Many individuals, though, have argued that the Second Amendment also establishes an individual right to bear arms.

The judicial record of Second Amendment cases is far sparser than for First Amendment cases, and for almost 60 years, the Court made no Second Amendment decisions. The United States has a higher gun ownership rate than any other developed country (see Figure 4.1 for a comparison with selected countries). Within the United States, there is no single national policy, and different states and localities have very different gun ownership standards. For instance, in Wyoming, there is no ban on owning any type of gun, there is no waiting period to purchase a firearm, and individuals are not required to obtain a permit for carrying a concealed weapon. In California, in contrast, the possession of assault weapons is banned, there is a 10-day waiting period to purchase a firearm, and a permit is required to carry a concealed weapon. In Virginia, individuals may practice "open carry" of handguns without a permit but require a license to carry a concealed weapon.

In a 2008 decision, the Supreme Court ruled that the federal government could not prohibit individuals from owning guns for self-defense in their homes. The case involved a District of Columbia ordinance that made it virtually impossible for residents to possess firearms legally. In the majority opinion, Justice

---

72 *Bates v. State Bar of Arizona,* 433 U.S. 350 (1977).

73 *44 Liquormart, Inc., and Peoples Super Liquor Stores, Inc., Petitioners v. Rhode Island and Rhode Island Liquor Stores Association,* 517 U.S. 484 (1996).

74 *Lorillard Tobacco v. Reilly,* 533 U.S. 525 (2001).

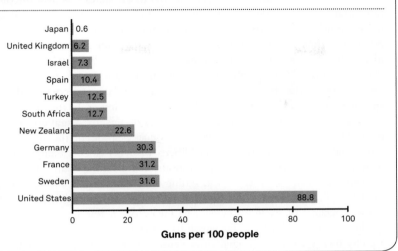

Figure 4.1
GUN OWNERSHIP IN COMPARISON

Country	Guns per 100 people
Japan	0.6
United Kingdom	6.2
Israel	7.3
Spain	10.4
Turkey	12.5
South Africa	12.7
New Zealand	22.6
Germany	30.3
France	31.2
Sweden	31.6
United States	88.8

Guns per 100 people

SOURCE: Sydney Lupkin, "U.S. Has More Guns—And Gun Deaths—Than Any Other Country, Study Finds," ABC News, September 19, 2013, http://abcnews.go.com/blogs/health/2013/09/19/u-s-has-more-guns-and-gun-deaths-than-any-other-country-study-finds/ (accessed 5/23/16).

Antonin Scalia stated that the decision was not intended to cast doubt on all laws limiting firearm possession, such as the prohibition on gun ownership by felons or the mentally ill.[75] In his dissenting opinion, Justice Stephens asserted the Second Amendment protects only the rights of individuals to bear arms as part of a militia force, not in an individual capacity. The District of Columbia is an entity of the federal government, and the Court did not indicate that its ruling applied to state firearms laws. However, in a 2010 case the Court struck down a Chicago firearms ordinance and applied the Second Amendment to the states as well.[76] The case concerned a Chicago ordinance that made it extremely difficult to own a gun within city limits, and the Court's ruling had the effect of overturning the law.[77]

Despite these rulings, the debate over gun control continues to loom large in American politics today. A recent series of tragic shootings (including the killing of 20 elementary school students in Newtown, Connecticut; 9 parishioners at a Charleston, South Carolina, church; and, in the worst mass shooting in U.S. history, 50 people at a nightclub in Orlando, Florida) has kept the issue of gun laws firmly on the national agenda. In 2016, President Obama issued several executive orders designed to expand background checks for gun purchasers and licensure requirements for firearms dealers but these did not end the debate.

75 *District of Columbia v. Heller*, 554 U.S. 570 (2008).

76 *McDonald v. Chicago*, 561 U.S. 3025 (2010).

77 *McDonald v. Chicago*, 561 U.S. 3025 (2010).

Rights of the Criminally Accused

Most of the battle to apply the Bill of Rights to the states was over the protections granted to individuals who are accused of a crime, who are suspects in the commission of a crime, or who are brought before court as witness to a crime. The Bill of Rights entitles every American to **due process** of law, which means that the government must respect all the legal rights to which every individual is entitled. The Fourth, Fifth, Sixth, and Eighth Amendments constitute the essence of due process, even though this fundamental concept does not appear until the very last words of the Fifth Amendment. In the next sections, we consider cases that illuminate the dynamics of this important constitutional issue. The procedural safeguards that we discuss help define the limits of governmental action against the personal liberty of every citizen. Many Americans believe that "legal technicalities" are responsible for setting many criminals free. In many cases, that is true. In fact, setting defendants free is the very purpose of the requirements that constitute due process and a few convictions are actually lost because of excluded evidence. One of our nation's most strongly held juridical values is that "it is far worse to convict an innocent man than to let a guilty man go free."[78] In civil suits, verdicts rest on "the preponderance of the evidence"; in criminal cases, guilt must be proved "beyond a reasonable doubt"—a far higher standard. The provisions for due process in the Bill of Rights were added to improve the probability that the standard of reasonable doubt will be respected.

due process

Proceeding according to law and with adequate protection for individual rights

The Fourth Amendment and Searches and Seizures

> The right of the people to be secure in their persons, houses, papers, and effects, against unreasonable searches and seizures, shall not be violated, and no Warrants shall issue, but upon probable cause, supported by Oath or affirmation, and particularly describing the place to be searched, and the persons or things to be seized.

The purpose of the Fourth Amendment is to guarantee the security of citizens against unreasonable (that is, improper) searches and seizures. In 1990, the Supreme Court summarized its understanding of this Amendment: "A search compromises the individual interest in privacy; a seizure deprives the individual of dominion over his or her person or property."[79] But how do we define what is reasonable and what is unreasonable?

The 1961 case of *Mapp v. Ohio* illustrates the beauty and the agony of one of the most important procedures that have grown out of the Fourth Amendment—the

---

78 *In re Winship,* 397 U.S. 358 (1970). An outstanding treatment of due process in issues involving the Fourth through Seventh Amendments is found in Fisher, *American Constitutional Law,* chap. 13.

79 *Horton v. California,* 496 U.S. 128 (1990).

exclusionary rule, which prohibits evidence obtained during an illegal search from being introduced in a trial. Dollree (Dolly) Mapp was "a Cleveland woman of questionable reputation" (by some accounts), the ex-wife of one prominent boxer, and the fiancée of an even more famous one. Acting on a tip that Mapp was harboring a suspect in a bombing incident, policemen forcibly entered her house, claiming they had a warrant to look for the suspect. They did not find the suspect but did find materials connected to an illegal gambling operation. Although the warrant was never produced, the evidence that had been seized was admitted by a court, and Mapp was convicted of illegal possession of obscene materials.

The question before the Court was whether any evidence produced under the circumstances of the search of her home was admissible. The Court's opinion affirmed the exclusionary rule: under the Fourth Amendment (applied to the states through the Fourteenth Amendment), "all evidence obtained by searches and seizures in violation of the Constitution . . . is inadmissible." Thus even people who are clearly guilty of the crime of which they are accused must not be convicted if the only evidence for their conviction was obtained illegally.

The exclusionary rule is the most severe restraint ever imposed by the Constitution and the courts on police behavior. It is a dramatic restriction because it often rules out the evidence that produces a conviction; it frees those people who are *known* to have committed the crime of which they have been accused. Because it works so dramatically in favor of persons known to have committed a crime, the Court has since softened the rule's application. Recently, federal courts have relied on a discretionary use of the exclusionary rule, whereby they make a judgment as to the "nature and quality of the intrusion." It is thus difficult to know ahead of time whether a defendant will or will not be protected from an illegal search under the Fourth Amendment.[80]

Another issue involving the Fourth Amendment is the controversy over mandatory drug testing. Such testing is most widely used on public employees. In an important case the Supreme Court upheld the U.S. Customs Service's drug-testing program for its employees and[81] approved drug and alcohol tests for railroad workers if they were involved in a serious accident.[82] After Court approvals of those two cases in 1989, more than 40 federal agencies initiated mandatory employee drug tests. The testing was reinforced by a presidential executive order touted as the "campaign for a drug-free federal workplace." These practices gave rise to public appeals against "suspicionless testing" of employees, which seemed to violate the Fourth Amendment. A 1995 case, in which the Court upheld a public school district's policy requiring that all students participating in interscholastic sports submit to random drug tests, surely contributed to the efforts of federal, state, and local agencies to initiate random drug and alcohol testing.[83] A 1997 case suggested, however, that the Court would consider limits on the "war" against

> **exclusionary rule**
>
> The requirement that courts exclude evidence obtained in violation of the Fourth Amendment

---

80 For a good discussion of the issue, see Fisher, *American Constitutional Law,* pp. 884–89.

81 *National Treasury Employees Union v. Von Raab,* 489 U.S. 656 (1989).

82 *Skinner v. Railroad Labor Executives Association,* 489 U.S. 602 (1989).

83 *Vernonia School District v. Acton,* 515 U.S. 646 (1995).

drugs. In an 8–1 decision, the Court applied the Fourth Amendment as a shield against "state action that diminishes personal privacy" when the officials in question are not performing high-risk or safety-sensitive tasks.[84] Using random and suspicionless drug testing as a symbol to fight drug use was, in the Court's opinion, carrying the exceptions to the Fourth Amendment too far.

More recently, the Court found it unconstitutional for police to use trained dogs in roadblocks set up to look for drugs in cars. Unlike drunk-driving roadblocks, where public safety is involved, narcotics roadblocks "cannot escape the Fourth Amendment's requirement that searches be based on suspicion of individual wrongdoing."[85] The Court also ruled that police may not use thermal-imaging devices to detect suspicious patterns of heat emerging from private homes without obtaining a search warrant.[86] In 2012, the Court held that GPS tracking (such as attaching a GPS device to a vehicle to track its movements) also constitutes a search under the Fourth Amendment and therefore requires a warrant.[87] In the 2014 case of *Riley v. California*, the Court held that the police were constitutionally prohibited from seizing and searching the digital contents of a cell phone during an arrest.[88] As new technologies develop, the Court will continue to face the question of what constitutes a reasonable search. In 2016, the FBI sought to compel the Apple Corporation to unlock the contents of the cell phone used by Syed Farook, an alleged terrorist who, along with his wife Tashfeen Malik, killed 14 people in San Bernardino, California, in 2015. Apple refused, arguing that creating new software to enable the FBI to unlock the phone would allow the agency to invade the privacy of millions of iPhone users if it so desired. Civil libertarians applauded the position, but those concerned with the nation's security were aghast at Apple's refusal, believing that the FBI should have access to data that could aid in a terrorist investigation. The case became moot when the FBI was able to unlock the phone without Apple's help.

Fourth Amendment issues have also been raised by aggressive police tactics, particularly the tactic known as "stop and frisk." This is a tactic in which the police confront an individual whom they believe to be acting "suspiciously," question the individual, and conduct a search for weapons. The practice was reviewed by the Supreme Court in the 1968 case of *Terry v. Ohio* and the Court then held that if an officer had "probable cause" to believe the individual was armed, such a search was permitted.[89] In recent years, some police departments, most notably the New York City police, have made stop and frisk a routine practice, searching thousands and thousands of individuals whom they deemed to look suspicious. The police aver that this aggressive tactic has reduced crime rates. In August 2013 a federal judge, Shira Scheindlin, noted that most police stops occurred in minority communities and amounted to a form of racial profiling. The judge's order ending the practice,

84 *Chandler et al. v. Miller, Governor of Georgia et al.,* 520 U.S. 305 (1997).

85 *Indianapolis v. Edmund,* 531 U.S. 32 (2000).

86 *Kyllo v. United States,* 533 U.S. 27 (2001).

87 *United States v. Jones,* 565 U.S. ____ (2012).

88 *Riley v. California,* 573 U.S. ____ (2014).

89 *Terry v. Ohio,* 392 U.S. 1 (1968).

however, was stayed by a federal appeals court that removed Judge Scheindlin from the case and accused her of improper bias. In 2014, the City of New York dropped its appeal and agreed to engage in a process of mediation with community groups to curtail the practice. After his election in 2014, Mayor Bill deBlasio announced an end to aggressive stop and frisk tactics. Critics charged that the mayor's orders were responsible for a subsequent increase in New York crime rates.

The policing tactic of "stop and frisk" is intended to protect communities from violent crime. But opponents view it as invasion of privacy and unreasonable search without sufficient cause. Furthermore, opponents charge that such tactics damage the relationship between the police and the community.

Finally, the Fourth Amendment places limits on government surveillance of individuals, an ongoing and controversial issue in the United States today. For example, a federal judge in Washington, D.C., recently ruled that an NSA program that collected millions of records of telephone calls was impermissible under the Fourth Amendment. The Policy Principle section on p. 134 examines government surveillance in the context of the Fourth Amendment.

The Fifth Amendment and Criminal Proceedings

No person shall be held to answer for a capital, or otherwise infamous crime, unless on a presentment or indictment of a Grand Jury, except in cases arising in the land or naval forces, or in the Militia, when in actual service in time of War or public danger; nor shall any person be subject for the same offense to be twice put in jeopardy of life or limb; nor shall be compelled in any criminal case to be a witness against himself, nor be deprived of life, liberty, or property, without due process of law; nor shall private property be taken for public use, without just compensation.

Grand Juries. The right to have a **grand jury** determine whether a trial is warranted is "the oldest institution known to the Constitution."[90] A grand jury is a body of citizens that must agree the prosecutor has sufficient evidence to bring criminal charges against a suspect. Grand juries play an important role in federal criminal cases. However, the provision for a grand jury is the one important civil liberties provision of the Bill of Rights that the Supreme Court has not incorporated into the Fourteenth Amendment and applied to state criminal prosecutions. Thus some states operate without grand juries; the prosecuting attorney simply files a "bill of information" affirming that there is sufficient evidence available to justify a trial. If the accused person is to be held in custody, the prosecutor must take the available information before a judge to determine whether the evidence shows probable cause.

 grand jury

A jury that determines whether sufficient evidence is available to justify a trial. Grand juries do not rule on the accused's guilt or innocence

Double Jeopardy. "Nor shall any person be subject for the same offense to be twice put in jeopardy of life or limb" is the constitutional protection from

90 E. S. Corwin and Jack Peltason, *Understanding the Constitution* (New York: Wadsworth, 2007), p. 286.

The Fourth Amendment and Government Surveillance

Surveillance at a traffic control center in Colorado.

Policies are usually a product of preferences and institutions, but occasionally immediate preferences clash with institutional constraints. Take the matter of government surveillance. Amid heightened fear of terrorism, government surveillance of communications, travel, and personal conduct has become a fact of American life. Such surveillance can occur through electronic interception of telephone calls, examination of e-mail communications and social media postings, security cameras now tied to crowd-scanning software, traffic monitoring, and airport searches. Modern analytic methods allow the government to process and analyze enormous quantities of data, looking for possible indications of illicit activity.[1]

Many Americans feel that they are the beneficiaries rather than the potential victims of government surveillance.[2] But the framers of the Constitution believed popular government requires citizen privacy and knowledge of government actions: citizens must know what the government is doing to exert influence over it, and they must have considerable protection from the state's scrutiny and the possibility of retaliation and intimidation. For example, the efforts of the party not currently in power can be compromised if the government becomes privy to its plans. In 1972, the Nixon administration thought its surveillance

activities could help undermine Democratic campaign plans. Known political dissidents, moreover, may face some risk of official reprisal. Accordingly, some citizens may refrain from acting on their political beliefs for fear that they will draw attention to themselves and become targets of government efforts to find evidence of misconduct (for example, through tax audits) that can be used against them. Privacy for political activities is, like the secret ballot, an important element of political freedom.

This concept was behind the Constitution's Fourth Amendment prohibiting unreasonable searches. The framers worried that government intrusions into private homes were often aimed at identifying papers, manuscripts, and books that might point to efforts to foment political discontent.[3] While many people today see the Fourth Amendment as related to evidence in criminal cases, its original purpose was to serve as an instrument for protecting liberty of political expression.

Policy makers' preferences for surveillance and secrecy may threaten the institutional constraints established by the Fourth Amendment. Though some of the government's current policies seem inconsistent with these foundational ideas, the United States' institutional arrangements have begun to reshape policies. In recent years, the courts have ruled that the police cannot search cell phones or employ GPS trackers without search warrants, and Congress has sought to rein in the activities of intelligence agencies. Though immediate preferences can clash with institutional constraints, these constraints eventually tend to reassert themselves.

[1] Jennifer Bachner, Katherine Wagner Hill and Benjamin Ginsberg, eds., *Analytics, Policy and Governance* (Baltimore: Johns Hopkins University Press, 2017).

[2] Daniel J. Solove, *Nothing to Hide: The False Tradeoff between Privacy and Security* (New Haven, CT: Yale University Press, 2011).

[3] Thomas P. Crocker, "The Political Fourth Amendment," *Washington University Law Review*, Vol.88, No.2, 2010, 303-79.

double jeopardy, or being tried more than once for the same crime. This protection was at the heart of the *Palko* case in 1937, which, as we saw earlier, also helped establish the principle of selective incorporation of the Bill of Rights. It took another 30 years for the Court to nationalize the constitutional protection against double jeopardy.

◄ **double jeopardy**

The Fifth Amendment right providing that a person cannot be tried twice for the same crime

Self-Incrimination. Perhaps the most significant liberty found in the Fifth Amendment is the guarantee that no citizen "shall be compelled in any criminal case to be a witness against himself." The most famous case concerning self-incrimination is of such importance that Chief Justice Earl Warren assessed its results as going "to the very root of our concepts of American criminal jurisprudence." In 1966, Ernesto Miranda was sentenced to between 20 and 30 years in prison for kidnapping and raping an 18-year-old woman. She had identified him in a police lineup and, after two hours of questioning, Miranda confessed, subsequently signing a statement that his confession had been made voluntarily, without threats or promises of immunity. These confessions were admitted into evidence and served as the basis for Miranda's conviction. After his conviction, Miranda argued that his confession had not been truly voluntary and that he had not been informed of his right to remain silent or his right to consult an attorney. The Supreme Court agreed and overturned the conviction. In one of the most intensely criticized decisions ever handed down by the Court, Miranda's case produced the rules that police must follow before questioning an arrested criminal suspect.

The reading of a person's "Miranda rights" has become a standard scene in every police station and in many dramatizations of police action on television and in the movies. *Miranda* advanced the civil liberties of accused persons not only by expanding the scope of the Fifth Amendment clause covering coerced confessions and self-incrimination but also by confirming the right to counsel. The Supreme Court under Warren Burger and William Rehnquist considerably softened the Miranda restrictions, making the job of the police a little easier, but the Miranda rule still stands as a protection against egregious police abuses of arrested persons.

Eminent Domain. Another fundamental clause of the Fifth Amendment is the "takings clause," which extends to each citizen a protection against the taking of private property "without just compensation." Although this clause is not specifically concerned with protecting persons accused of crimes, it does deal with an important instance where the government and the citizen are adversaries. As discussed earlier, the power of any government to take private property for a public use, such as highway construction is called eminent domain. This power is essential to the very concept of sovereignty. The Fifth Amendment neither invented eminent domain nor took it away; its purpose was to limit that inherent power through procedures that require a demonstration of a public purpose and the provision of fair payment for the seizure of someone's property. This provision is now universally observed in all American principalities, but it has not always been meticulously observed.

The first modern case confronting the issue of public use involved a mom-and-pop grocery store in a rundown neighborhood on the southwest side of the District of Columbia. In carrying out an urban-redevelopment program in the

1950s, the city government of Washington, D.C., took the property as one of many privately owned lots to be cleared for new housing and business construction. The owner of the grocery store and his successors, after his death, took the government to court on the grounds that taking property from one private owner and eventually turning that property back, in altered form, to another private owner was an unconstitutional use of eminent domain. The store owners lost their case, though they received cash compensation for their property. The Supreme Court's argument was that "public interest" can mean virtually anything a legislature says it means. In other words, since the overall slum clearance and redevelopment project was in the public interest, according to the legislature, the eventual transfers of property that were going to take place were justified.[91] In 1984 and again in 2005 the Supreme Court reaffirmed that decision.[92]

The Sixth Amendment and the Right to Counsel

In all criminal prosecutions, the accused shall enjoy the right to a speedy and public trial, by an impartial jury of the State and district wherein the crime shall have been committed, which district shall have been previously ascertained by law, and to be informed of the nature and cause of the accusation; to be confronted with the witnesses against him; to have compulsory process for obtaining witnesses in his favor, and to have the Assistance of Counsel for his defense.

Some provisions of this amendment, such as the right to a speedy trial and the right to confront witnesses before an impartial jury, are not very controversial. The "right to counsel" provision, however, like the exclusionary rule of the Fourth Amendment and the self-incrimination clause of the Fifth Amendment, is notable for freeing defendants who seem to be patently guilty as charged.

Gideon v. Wainwright is the perfect case study because it involved a disreputable person who seemed patently guilty of the crime for which he was convicted. In and out of jails for most of his 51 years, Clarence Earl Gideon received a five-year sentence for breaking into and entering a poolroom in Panama City, Florida. While serving time in jail, Gideon became a fairly well-qualified "jailhouse lawyer," made his own appeal on a handwritten petition, and eventually won the landmark ruling on the right to counsel in all felony cases.[93] *Gideon* was decided in 1963, and in the following year the Supreme Court ruled that suspects had a right to counsel during police interrogations, not just when their cases reached trial.[94]

91 *Berman v. Parker,* 348 U.S. 26 (1954). For a thorough analysis of the case, see Benjamin Ginsberg, "*Berman v. Parker:* Congress, the Court, and the Public Purpose," *Polity* 4 (1971): 48–75.

92 *Hawaii Housing Authority v. Midkiff,* 469 U.S. 2321 (1984), and *Kelo v. City of New London,* 545 U.S. 469 (2005).

93 For a full account of the story of the trial and release of Clarence Earl Gideon, see Anthony Lewis, *Gideon's Trumpet* (New York: Random House, 1964).

94 *Escobedo v. Illinois,* 378 U.S. 478 (1964).

The right to counsel has since been expanded further to encompass the quality of the counsel provided. For example, although at first the right to counsel was met by judges' assigning lawyers from the community as a formal public obligation, most states and cities have now created an office of public defender whose state-employed defense lawyers typically provide poor defendants with legal representation. And although these defendants cannot choose their private defense attorneys, they may have the right to appeal a conviction on the grounds that the counsel provided by the state was deficient. For example, in 2003 the Supreme Court overturned the death sentence of a Maryland death-row inmate, holding that the defense lawyer had failed to fully inform the jury of the defendant's history of "horrendous childhood abuse."[95] Moreover, the right to counsel extends to any trial that holds the possibility of imprisonment.[96]

The Eighth Amendment and Cruel and Unusual Punishment

The Eighth Amendment prohibits "excessive bail," "excessive fines," and "cruel and unusual punishment." Virtually all debate over Eighth Amendment issues focuses on the protection from "cruel and unusual punishment." One of the greatest challenges in interpreting this provision consistently is that what is considered "cruel and unusual" varies from culture to culture and from generation to generation. Unfortunately, it also varies by class and race.

The most important questions concerning cruel and unusual punishment are raised by the use of the death penalty. Some Americans believe that execution is inherently cruel but in its consideration of the death penalty the Supreme Court has generally avoided this question. In 1972, the Supreme Court overturned several state death penalty laws not because they were cruel and unusual but because they were being applied in a capricious manner.[97] Shortly thereafter, a majority of states revised their capital-punishment provisions to provide clear standards.[98] Since 1976, the Court has consistently upheld state laws providing for capital punishment, although it continues to review numerous death penalty appeals each year. In 2015, a Massachusetts jury voted to impose the death penalty on Dzhokhar Tsarnaev, who had been found guilty for his role in the 2013 Boston Marathon bombings. Given the number of appeals likely to be filed, years will elapse before this sentence can be carried out. Between 1976 and October 2016, states executed 1,439 people. Texas led the way with 538 executions. As of 2016,

---

95 *Wiggins v. Smith,* 539 U.S. 510 (2003).

96 For further discussion of these issues, see Corwin and Peltason, *Understanding the Constitution,* pp. 319–23.

97 *Furman v. Georgia,* 408 U.S. 238 (1972).

98 *Gregg v. Georgia,* 428 U.S. 153 (1976).

31 states authorized some form of capital punishment, a penalty approved of by about two-thirds of all Americans.

Although all criminal conduct is regulated by the states, Congress has imposed capital punishment for more than 50 federal crimes. Yet debate about the death penalty remains intense, and cases continue to come before the courts. In 1997, for example, the American Bar Association called for a halt to the death penalty until concerns about its fairness—whether its application violates the principle of equality—and about ensuring due process are addressed. In 2002, the Supreme Court banned all executions of mentally handicapped defendants;[99] in 2008, it declared that death was too harsh a penalty for a child rapist[100] and invalidated a death sentence for a black defendant on the grounds that the prosecutor had improperly excluded African Americans from the jury.[101] In recent years the Court has upheld lethal injection as a mode of execution multiple times, despite arguments that this form of execution was likely to cause considerable pain.

Many death penalty supporters praise its deterrent effects on other would-be criminals, claiming that preventing even one additional murder or other heinous crime is ample justification for such laws. Although studies of capital crimes usually fail to demonstrate a direct deterrent effect, the punishment's "failure" in this regard may be due to the lengthy delays—typically years and even decades—between convictions and executions. Moreover, although constitutional objections to the death penalty often invoke the Eighth Amendment's protection against "cruel and unusual" punishments, supporters claim that the death penalty cannot be considered to violate this protection because it was commonly used in the eighteenth century and most early American leaders supported it.

Death penalty opponents point out that the death penalty has not been proved to deter crime. They also argue that executing criminals debases rather than elevates society by extolling vengeance and that, though most of the Founders supported the death penalty, they also countenanced slavery and lived at a time when society was both less informed about and more indifferent to the human condition. Furthermore, execution is expensive—more expensive than life imprisonment—because the government must make every effort to ensure that it is not executing an innocent person. Curtailing legal appeals would make the possibility of a mistake too great. And although most Americans support the death penalty, people also support life without the possibility of parole as an alternative. Race, too, intrudes in death penalty cases: people of color are disproportionately more likely to be sentenced to death than are whites charged with identical crimes. Finally, according to opponents, a life sentence may be a worse punishment than the death penalty.

---

99 *Atkins v. Virginia,* 534 U.S. 304 (2002).

100 *Kennedy v. Louisiana,* 554 U.S. 407 (2008).

101 *Snyder v. Louisiana,* 552 U.S. 472 (2008).

The Right to Privacy and the Constitution

At times, almost all of us would like to be left alone, to have our own private domain into which no one—friends, family, government, church, or employer—has the right to enter without permission.

Many Jehovah's Witnesses felt that way in the 1930s. As noted earlier in our discussion of the free exercise of religion, they risked serious punishment in 1940 by telling their children not to salute the flag or say the Pledge of Allegiance in school because of their understanding of the first commandment's prohibition of the worship of "graven images." Although these objectors lost their appeal, the children were expelled and the parents punished, the Supreme Court later concluded that the 1940 decision had been "wrongly decided." These cases arose under the First Amendment's freedom of religion provisions, but they were also the first cases to consider the possibility of the right to be left alone. When the Court became more activist in the mid-1950s and 1960s, the idea of a **right to privacy** was revived. In 1958, the Court recognized "privacy in one's association" in its decision to prevent the state of Alabama from using the NAACP membership list in the state's investigations. Although the Constitution does not mention a right to privacy, the Ninth Amendment declares that the rights enumerated by the Constitution are not an exhaustive list.

 right to privacy

The right to be left alone, which has been interpreted by the Supreme Court to entail individual access to birth control and abortions

Birth Control. The sphere of privacy was drawn in earnest in 1965, when the Court ruled that a Connecticut statute forbidding the use of contraceptives violated the right of marital privacy. Estelle Griswold, executive director of the Planned Parenthood League of Connecticut, was arrested by the state of Connecticut for providing information, instruction, and medical advice about contraception to married couples. She and her associates were found guilty as accessories to the crime and fined $100 each. Ultimately, the Supreme Court reversed the lower-court's decisions and declared the Connecticut law unconstitutional because it violated "a right of privacy older than the Bill of Rights—older than our political parties, older than our school system." Justice William O. Douglas, writing the majority decision in *Griswold*, argued that this right of privacy is also grounded in the Constitution because it fits into a "zone of privacy" created by a combination of the Third, Fourth, and Fifth Amendments. A concurring opinion added that "the concept of liberty . . . embraces the right of marital privacy though that right is not mentioned explicitly in the Constitution [and] is supported by numerous decisions of this Court . . . and *by the language and history of the Ninth Amendment*"[102] [emphasis added]. The Ninth Amendment provides that "the enumeration in the Constitution, of certain rights, shall not be construed to deny or disparage others retained by the people." According to Justice Goldberg, this language means, in effect, that just because the Constitution does not specifically mention a particular right to privacy does not mean that the people do not retain that right. The

---

102 *Griswold v. Connecticut,* 381 U.S. 479 (1965), and *Griswold v. Connecticut,* concurring opinion. In 1972, in *Eisenstadt v. Baird,* 405 U.S. 438 (1972), the Court extended the privacy right to unmarried women.

language of the Ninth Amendment, when taken with the evidence provided by the First, Third, Fourth, and Fifth Amendments, was sufficient for the Court to find that the Bill of Rights implies a constitutional right to privacy.

Abortion. The right to privacy was extended in 1973 in one of the most important Supreme Court decisions in American history: *Roe v. Wade*. This decision established a woman's right to seek an abortion and prohibited states from making abortion a criminal act before the point at which the fetus becomes viable which, in 1973, was the 27th week.[103] The Court's decision in *Roe* took a revolutionary step toward establishing the right to privacy and extending it to include women's rights to control their own bodies. The decision was of particular significance in terms of the historical context leading up to it. Most states did not regulate abortions in any fashion until the 1840s, at which time only six states had regulations governing it. In addition, many states had begun to ease their abortion restrictions well before the 1973 *Roe* decision. But none of these prior circumstances had specifically addressed the issue of privacy, although in recent years a number of states have reinstated restrictions on abortion, including lowering the viability standard to 20 weeks (Texas), 12 weeks (Arkansas), and 6 weeks (North Dakota).

By extending the umbrella of privacy, the sweeping ruling in *Roe* dramatically changed abortion practices in America. It also galvanized and nationalized the abortion debate. Groups opposing abortion, such as the National Right to Life Committee, organized to fight the new liberal standard, while abortion rights groups sought to maintain that protection. In recent years, a number of states have reinstated some restrictions on the procedure, and the legal standard has shifted against abortion rights supporters in three key Supreme Court cases.

In 1989, in *Webster v. Reproductive Health Services*, the Court narrowly upheld (by a 5–4 majority) the constitutionality of restrictions on the use of public medical facilities for abortion.[104] And in the 1992 case of *Planned Parenthood v. Casey*, another 5–4 majority upheld *Roe* but narrowed its scope, refusing to invalidate a Pennsylvania law that significantly limits freedom of choice. The Court's decision defined the right to an abortion as a "limited or qualified" right subject to regulation by the states as long as the regulation does not constitute an "undue burden."[105] More recently, the Court had another opportunity to rule on what constitutes an undue burden: in 2000, in *Stenberg v. Carhart*, the Court struck down Nebraska's ban on partial-birth abortions because the law had the "effect of placing a substantial obstacle in the path of a woman seeking an abortion."[106] In 2007, however, the Court upheld a federal ban on partial-birth abortions, essentially overturning the earlier decision.[107]

---

103 *Roe v. Wade,* 410 U.S. 113 (1973).

104 *Webster v. Reproductive Health Services,* 492 U.S. 490 (1989), which upheld a Missouri law that restricted the use of public medical facilities for abortion. The decision opened the way for other states to limit the availability of abortion.

105 *Planned Parenthood v. Casey,* 505 U.S. 833 (1992).

106 *Stenberg v. Carhart,* 530 U.S. 914 (2000).

107 *Gonzales v. Carhart,* 550 U.S. 124 (2007).

Sexual Orientation. In recent decades, the right to be left alone began to include the privacy rights of gay men and lesbians. One morning in Atlanta in the mid-1980s, Michael Hardwick was arrested by a police officer who discovered him in bed with another man. The officer had come to serve a warrant for Hardwick's arrest for failure to appear in court to answer charges of drinking in public. When the officer found Hardwick and another man engaging in "consensual sexual behavior," Hardwick was arrested under Georgia's laws against heterosexual and homosexual sodomy. Hardwick filed a lawsuit against the state, challenging the constitutionality of the Georgia law, and won his case in the federal court of appeals. After the state of Georgia appealed the court's decision to the Supreme Court, the Court's majority decision reversed the lower-court decision, holding against Hardwick on the grounds that "the federal Constitution confers [no] fundamental right upon homosexuals to engage in sodomy" and that there was therefore no basis to invalidate "the laws of the many states that still make such conduct illegal and have done so for a very long time."[108]

Seventeen years later, the Court overturned *Bowers v. Hardwick* with a dramatic pronouncement that homosexuals are "entitled to respect for their private lives" as a matter of constitutional due process. With *Lawrence v. Texas*, state legislatures no longer had the authority to make private sexual behavior a crime.[109] Drawing from the tradition of negative liberty, or freedom from governmental interference. the Court maintained, "In our tradition the State is not omnipresent in the home. And there are other spheres of our lives and existence outside the home, where the State should not be a dominant presence." Explicitly encompassing lesbians and gay men within the umbrella of privacy, the Court concluded that the "petitioners are entitled to respect for their private lives. The State cannot demean their existence or control their destiny by making their private sexual conduct a crime." This decision added substance to the idea that the Ninth Amendment allows for the "right to privacy."

In 2015, the Court took another important step in the protection of gay rights by declaring that state bans on same-sex marriage were unconstitutional.[110] The Court said that the refusal to issue marriage licenses to same-sex couples constituted a violation of the Fourteenth Amendment's equal protection and due process clauses.

The Right to Die. Another area ripe for further litigation and public discourse is the so-called right to die. A number of highly publicized physician-assisted suicides in the 1990s focused attention on whether people have a right to choose their own death and receive assistance in carrying it out. Will this become part of the privacy right, or perhaps be accepted as a new kind of right? In the 2006 case of *Gonzales v. Oregon*, the Supreme Court upheld an Oregon law that allowed doctors to use drugs to facilitate the deaths of terminally ill patients who requested such assistance.[111] This decision is not a definitive ruling on the right-to-die question, but

---

108 *Bowers v. Hardwick,* 478 U.S. 186 (1986).

109 *Lawrence and Garner v. Texas,* 539 U.S. 558 (2003).

110 *Obergefell v. Hodges,* 576 U.S. ____ (2015).

111 *Gonzales v. Oregon,* 546 U.S. 243 (2006).

it does suggest that the Court is not hostile to the idea. In recent years a number of lower-court decisions have reaffirmed this principle. In 2014, for example, a Pennsylvania county judge threw out a case against a nurse who had been accused of homicide for making a bottle of morphine available to her ill 93-year-old father.[112]

CONCLUSION: CIVIL LIBERTIES AND COLLECTIVE ACTION

The Constitution, and especially its Bill of Rights, guarantees Americans a variety of liberties, including freedom of speech and religion and protection against having their homes arbitrarily searched, and a number of procedural rights, including trial by jury, protection against self-incrimination, and the right to counsel in criminal cases. The Bill of Rights initially applied only to the actions of the federal government, but in the twentieth century, under the doctrine of selective incorporation, the Supreme Court gradually applied most of the elements of the Bill of Rights to the states. The most recent such action was incorporation of the Second Amendment's right to bear arms in the 2010 case of *McDonald v. Chicago*.

Constitutional guarantees of civil rights and civil liberties often seem clear in the abstract, but they inevitably produce thousands of complex questions and controversies every year when they are applied to concrete cases. Every government agency, for example, is constitutionally required to respect Americans' civil liberties. The government, though, is also obligated to protect the public's health and safety. This duty, sometimes called the "general police power," is exercised by the governments of the states. The federal government does not have a general police power since the Tenth Amendment limits it to the powers expressly granted by the Constitution. However, the Court has interpreted the Constitution's commerce clause broadly to enable the federal government to protect the public's health and safety by making policies in such realms as health care, education, and crime control.

Suppose that Congress enacts a law allowing national security agencies to sift through millions of phone calls searching for evidence of terrorist plots. Is such a law an unjustified intrusion on civil liberties or a necessary and legitimate effort to prevent bloodshed? In 2008, the Supreme Court declined to hear a case brought by a civil liberties group that wanted to halt a large-scale federal wiretapping program aimed at identifying possible terrorist communications. This action let stand a lower-court ruling that had allowed the program to continue. These concerns surfaced again in 2013, when a National Security Agency (NSA) contract employee released details of an elaborate NSA eavesdropping effort that resulted in the agency accessing the phone and e-mail records of millions of Americans. Civil libertarians charged that NSA had violated the law and the Constitution. President Obama and NSA officials answered that some inadvertent violations of the relevant statutes might have occurred, but that the agency's actions were

---

112 Richard Knox, "Judge Dismisses Assisted Suicide Case against Pennsylvania Nurse," NPR, February 12, 2014, www.npr.org/sections/health-shots/2014/02/12/275913772/judge-dismisses-assisted-suicide-case-against-pennsylvania-nurse?_r50 (accessed 3/3/16).

needed to protect American security. As these examples suggest, the precise character of constitutional limitations on collective action is always open to debate. As part of that debate, we examine our history to identify similar situations in the past and to determine whether the decisions made then still apply to the present. We call this the history principle; the courts call it precedent.

Civil liberties are also important examples of the collective action principle. All politics is collective action but civil liberties are limitations on collective action. They identify spheres of individual autonomy into which the nation as a whole, acting through its government, is not permitted to intrude. The authors of the Bill of Rights agreed that collective action could go only so far. If collective action led to restrictions on speech, religion, assembly, the press and so forth, it would not be allowed. Demonstrating the importance of the history principle, this decision, made more than two centuries ago, has continued to shape our nation. If not for the Bill of Rights, collective action could quickly become tyranny.

For Further Reading

Ackerman, Bruce. *Before the Next Attack: Preserving Civil Liberties in an Age of Terrorism.* New Haven, CT: Yale University Press, 2006.

Dworkin, Ronald. *Justice in Robes.* Cambridge, MA: Belknap Press, 2006.

Koppelman, Andrew M. *Same Sex, Different States: When Same-Sex Marriage Crosses State Lines.* New Haven, CT: Yale University Press, 2006.

Lewis, Anthony. *Freedom for the Thought That We Hate: A Biography of the First Amendment.* New York: Basic Books, 2010.

Lewis, Anthony. *Gideon's Trumpet.* New York: Random House, 1964.

Neuborn, Burt. *Madison's Music: On Reading the First Amendment.* New York: New Press, 2015.

O'Brien, David. *Constitutional Law and Politics: Civil Rights and Civil Liberties.* 9th ed. New York: Norton, 2014.

Smith, Steven D. *The Rise and Decline of American Religious Freedom.* Cambridge: Harvard University Press, 2014.

Waldman, Michael. *The Second Amendment: A Biography.* New York: Simon & Schuster, 2015.

Walker, Samuel. *Presidents and Civil Liberties from Wilson to Obama.* New York: Cambridge University Press, 2012.

5

Civil Rights

civil rights

The legal or moral claims that citizens are entitled to make on the government

As we observed in Chapter 4, civil liberties limit what people may do freely in society. They amount to restrictions on government, and as such they restrain the collective decision making of the people as expressed through the decisions of Congress. **Civil rights** also shape collective action and collective decision making but in a very different way. Civil rights regulate *who* can participate in the political process and civil society and *how* they can participate—for example, who can vote, who can serve in office, who can have a trial or serve on juries, and when and how citizens can petition the government to take action. The scope of civil rights is vast, stretching well beyond voting. Civil rights also define how people are treated in employment, education, and other aspects of American society.

In some nations, citizens have few, if any, civil rights. They have no right to vote, no right to stand for office, and no right to be judged by their peers if accused of a crime. The United States, however, began life as a nation with numerous civil rights guaranteed in both the federal and state constitutions. The federal Constitution provided such rights as representation in Congress (Article I, Section 2), established who can serve in Congress and become president, and guaranteed the privilege of habeas corpus for all people (Article I, Section 9). The Bill of Rights defined civil rights further, especially the right of all persons to due process of the laws, guaranteed in the Fifth Amendment.

The United States' early conception of civil rights was narrower than it is today. Originally, the Constitution did not guarantee a general right to vote; it left voting and many other civil rights to the states. The Founders' initial rules permitted widely disparate treatment of different categories of individuals, including women, minority racial and ethnic groups, owners of property, and others. One way in which states limited civil rights was by linking those rights to property ownership. At the same time, states often put restrictions on who could own property. For instance, women were often not allowed to inherit property or could not own property in their own name if they were married. In addition, women were denied the right to vote and their access to education was limited.

Members of minority racial and ethnic groups also faced many forms of legally sanctioned discrimination, preventing them from voting, owning property, or securing employment. Since the adoption of the Constitution, there has been a tremendous expansion of civil rights to different groups of people and to different spheres of civil life.

The greatest restrictions on civil rights at the time of the Constitution were on black people. Only 5 of the 13 original states were free states in 1789. The other 8 states permitted slavery, and slaves came almost entirely from Africa or the Caribbean. They possessed virtually no civil rights. The Constitution banned the importation of slaves after 1808 but permitted slavery to continue. Immediately before the Civil War, roughly 4 million African Americans were slaves in the southern states where their labor supported the region's agricultural economy. By then slavery was prohibited in most of the northern states, and the issue of whether slavery should be allowed in America's western territories bitterly divided the nation. In the 1857 *Dred Scott v. Sandford* case, the Supreme Court ruled that a slave was not a citizen, could not bring suit in court, and was his master's personal property; moreover, slavery could not be excluded from the territories.[1] This decision inflamed sectional divisions, infuriated antislavery groups in the North, and helped provoke the Civil War.

Following the Civil War, Congress adopted the Thirteenth, Fourteenth, and Fifteenth amendments to the Constitution to protect civil rights that the practice of slavery had violated. The Thirteenth Amendment prohibited slavery and involuntary servitude in the United States. The Fifteenth extended the right to vote to blacks: "The right of citizens of the United States to vote shall not be denied or abridged by the United States or by any State on account of race, color, or previous condition of servitude." The Fourteenth Amendment

CORE OF THE ANALYSIS

 Civil rights are rules that govern collective decision-making processes and outcomes. They curb the power of majorities to exclude or harm individuals on the basis of factors such as race, gender, or ethnic background.

 Today's conception of civil rights has been shaped by the historical development of these ideas and their interpretation by key political actors, especially the Supreme Court.

---

1   *Dred Scott v. Sandford,* 60 U.S. 393 (1857).

asserted the idea of civil rights much more broadly for all citizens. Section 1 of the amendment states:

> All persons born or naturalized in the United States, and subject to the jurisdiction thereof, are citizens of the United States and of the State wherein they reside. No State shall make or enforce any law which shall abridge the privileges or immunities of citizens of the United States; nor shall any State deprive any person of life, liberty, or property, without due process of law; nor deny to any person within its jurisdiction the equal protection of the laws.

equal protection clause

The provision of the Fourteenth Amendment guaranteeing citizens "the equal protection of the laws." This clause has been the basis for the civil rights of African Americans, women, and other groups

The last clause of this section, the **equal protection clause**, has transformed civil rights in the United States because it creates the foundation for asserting equal civil rights for all persons. These words launched a century of political movements and legal efforts to press for racial equality. African Americans' quest for civil rights in turn inspired many other groups—including other racial and ethnic groups, women, people with disabilities, gay men and lesbians, and transgender people—to seek new laws and constitutional guarantees of their civil rights. Their struggles were aided by the simplicity of the equal protection clause, which offers its guarantee to any person. Although the Thirteenth, Fourteenth, and Fifteenth amendments were ratified in the context of the Civil War, the Fourteenth Amendment has been the basis for the expansion of civil rights to many groups in American society.

Under the Constitution today, no American may be excluded from participation or representation in collective decision-making processes or treated adversely by decision makers because of such factors as race, gender, or ethnic background. Legislative actions and legal decrees, however, have rarely been sufficient to guarantee civil rights. Enforcement of this guarantee was hard-won, and debates over the extent of the government's responsibility in ensuring equal protection persist. The reason is that the definition of civil rights depends not only on what laws are passed or how the Constitution's words are interpreted but also on the behavior of people in society. How can we understand historical patterns of discrimination? Do political divisions between whites and racial and ethnic minorities cause a majority of the white population to oppose the preferred candidates of a majority of the black or Hispanic populations? Is there evidence of intentional discrimination in election administration, employment, housing, and other activities?

WHAT ARE CIVIL RIGHTS?

Civil rights are the rules that government must follow in regard to the treatment of individuals when making collective decisions. Some civil rights concern who can be involved in collective decisions and how; others concern how people are treated in civil society, including who has access to public facilities, such as schools and public hospitals. Increasingly, civil rights have extended to private spheres, such as the right to work, the right to marry, and whether clubs and organizations can exclude people on the basis of gender or race. Even when no legal right to something currently exists, such a right may be asserted as a matter of justice or morality. When there is a demand for new civil rights, society must decide whether and how rights should be extended.

Civil rights encompass three features: who, what, and how much. Who has a right and who does not? A right to what? And how much is any individual allowed to exercise that right?

Consider the right to vote. The "what" is the vote. The "who" concerns which persons are allowed to vote. Today all U.S. citizens 18 years of age and older are eligible to vote. The states impose additional criteria for voting, such as requirements in some states that voters show photo IDs or prohibiting voting by ex-felons. The "how much" concerns whether that right can be exercised equally—whether some people's votes count more than others' or whether election laws create greater obstacles for some people and make it easier for others. For instance, until the mid-1960s, the California State Senate had one senator from Los Angeles County, with 6 million people, and one from Inyo County, with 14,000 people. The votes of the 14,000 people translated into the same amount of representation in the state senate as the votes of the 6 million people. The U.S. Supreme Court ruled that such arrangements violated the equal protection clause and hence the civil rights of those in the more populous counties.

Throughout American history, two principles have emerged that answer "who" enjoys civil rights and "how much." First, civil rights ought to be universal— all persons should enjoy them. Second, civil rights ought to be equal—all people who enjoy a civil right ought to be allowed an equal ability or opportunity to practice that right.

Before these principles emerged, however, profound debates and deep divisions in American society concerned *who* has civil rights. At the time of the Founding, most states granted voting rights exclusively to white male property owners. In 1787, many states' constitutions and laws also imposed religious criteria, forbidding Catholics or Jews from voting, running for office, and engaging in other public activities. Subsequent centuries have brought a dramatic expansion of the civil rights of all persons in the nation.

Today, civil rights are guaranteed to all U.S. citizens. One of Congress's first acts was the Naturalization Act of 1790, which provided the rules for granting citizenship to immigrants. Today, any person born in the United States is automatically a citizen (they are called natural-born citizens). In addition, legal immigrants can become citizens through a process of "naturalization." Generally speaking, naturalization requires that the immigrant has been a legal resident of the United States for at least five years; has demonstrated the ability to read, write, and speak English; has passed a basic U.S. civics and history test; and is of good moral standing.[2] Citizens can live in the country and travel to other

2   U.S. Citizenship and Immigration Services, "Citizenship through Naturalization," Department of Homeland Security, last updated, January 22, 2013, www.uscis.gov/naturalization (accessed 3/18/16).

countries with all the privileges and protections of the United States. In addition, citizens who are age 18 or older can vote. Only citizens can serve in Congress. Only a natural-born citizen can be president of the United States. Age is also a criterion for civil rights. Until 1971, the voting age in most states was 21, but in reaction to the draft during the Vietnam War, in which men 18 and older could be conscripted into the military, the Constitution was amended to set the voting age at 18. Also, in terms of seeking office, individuals must be at least age 25 to serve in the U.S. House, age 30 to serve in the Senate, and age 35 to serve as president. Today, the largest groups of people not allowed to participate in American elections are those who are underage and those who are not citizens.

It is interesting that citizenship has not always been a requirement for voting in the United States. At the beginning of the nineteenth century, many states and cities allowed noncitizens to vote. In reaction to the influx of immigrants from Germany and other countries of central Europe, most states imposed citizenship requirements for voting. Even as late as the 1920s, however, there remained some municipalities in which noncitizens could vote in local elections.

The "what" of civil rights covers a wide range of fundamental rights. Perhaps the most basic civil right in any country is the right to be in the country. For much of our nation's first century, there were virtually no restrictions on who could enter the country. In 1875, Congress passed the Page Act, which prohibited some immigrants as "undesirable." The act was introduced by Senator Horace Page to "end the danger of cheap Chinese labor and immoral Chinese women."[3] Subsequent acts have further defined who may enter the country, how, and for how long, including quotas on immigrants from each country that lasted from 1924 to 1966. Today, U.S. immigration law requires that persons wishing to reside in the United States permanently acquire "lawful permanent resident" status (a "green card") through family- or employment-based sponsorship. The law limits the number of green cards that can be approved in a year. Problems arise, however, for people who have illegally entered the country or who have stayed beyond the term allowed for temporary visitors. As discussed later, management of the right to be in the country remains one of the central debates over civil rights.

Political rights are also civil rights. These include the right to vote, the right to run for office, and the right to association. Indeed, much of the historical struggle over civil rights has concerned the expansion of political rights, which today nearly all adult citizens enjoy.

Another class of civil rights is made up of legal rights. The right of *habeas corpus*—the right to be presented before a court if you are accused of a crime— dates back at least to the Magna Carta, the charter of liberties in England adopted in 1215. It is treated as a fundamental civil right granted to any person in the United States or its territories. One of the most powerful rights in the Constitution is the right to due process of law. The Fifth Amendment states that "No person shall . . . be deprived of life, liberty, or property without the Due Process of Law." That is, the federal government must respect the legal

---

3   George Anthony Peffer, "Forbidden Families: Emigration Experiences of Chinese Women under the Page Law, 1875–1882," *Journal of American Ethnic History* 6, no. 1 (fall 1986): 28.

rights that are owed a person; the government cannot harm a person without following the exact course of the law. Later, the Fourteenth Amendment extended due process to state governments as well. The right to due process of law in the Constitution applies to all persons, not just certain types of people. Consequently, due process underlies the assertion of many types of rights and the expansion of rights beyond those favored in a particular state or federal law.

Less obvious are rights to other aspects of civil society. Do you have a right to own property? Do you have a right to education? Do you have a right to a job or to a minimum standard of living or to have access to medical care? Do you have the right to serve in the military or not to serve in the military in the case of a draft? Do you have the right to attend public school and receive various social services if you are an undocumented immigrant. A wide range of economic and civil activities are, in fact, governed by civil rights. We have a right to due compensation if the government takes our property. We have the right to access public schools, and public hospitals cannot turn away people at their emergency rooms. Answers vary as to whether one has a right to employment or to form a union at work to bargain for better wages and benefits. In some states it is exceedingly hard to form a union. In other states and in some industries, one must belong to a union in order to practice a trade.

Medical practice today, for instance, raises complicated questions about the right to work. An immigrant who is a medical doctor, trained and licensed in a foreign country, must still go through the American medical training and licensing procedure in order to practice in the United States. This is a restriction on the right of these people to work.

The question of *how much* individuals can exercise their civil rights is perhaps the subtlest of the three dimensions. Equality is the guiding principle. Americans adhere to a belief in equality, even when it is difficult to impose in practice. The Declaration of Independence begins with the proposition that "all men are created equal." The Constitution establishes the House of Representatives to represent all people (not just citizens, voters, or other subgroups). Perhaps most important, the Fourteenth Amendment establishes the right to equal protection of the laws for all persons. Like due process, equal protection applies regardless of one's race, gender, wealth, residency, or citizenship.

The Fourteenth Amendment's equal protection clause has been instrumental in asserting broad and equal rights for all persons in the United States. The amendment applies to all persons and all laws. One of the first ordinances struck down by the U.S. Supreme Court under the Fourteenth Amendment pertained to discrimination in labor laws, construction permits, and business licenses against Chinese legal residents.[4] In another case, the Court struck down limits on noncitizens' abilities to develop natural resources—in this case the right of an Italian immigrant to have a shotgun for purposes of hunting.[5] And in decisions spanning 1962–68, the Court ruled that the equal protection clause

---

4   *Yick Wo v. Hopkins,* 118 U.S. 356 (1886).

5   *Patsone v. Pennsylvania,* 232 U.S. 138 (1914).

means that all people have equal voting rights: one person's vote cannot have greater say in the country's collective decision making than another person's.

What civil rights we enjoy and who has them is itself a political decision. The Constitution identifies a small number of civil rights. The Bill of Rights asserted a larger number of legal rights. But many of the civil rights we enjoy now were left to Congress and the states to determine. Thus most of our civil rights today are the result of legislation, litigation, and administration that occurred after the country was founded. And getting government action requires collective action by those affected.

THE STRUGGLE FOR CIVIL RIGHTS

Who has what civil rights is a source of contention precisely because those who have civil rights, such as the right to vote, are asked to extend those rights to those who do not. White male property owners had disproportionate political power in 1790 because they alone had voting rights. To expand voting rights to other groups, those in power had to decide to remove property qualifications, extend voting rights to women and blacks, and loosen other restrictions, such as age and religion. Needless to say, the expansion of voting rights has not always gone smoothly. Indeed, democracy can be a barrier to the creation of civil rights.

Consider noncitizens' voting rights. The first constitution of New York State, adopted in 1777, allowed all male inhabitants the right to vote. This meant that noncitizens and blacks could vote, a right they enjoyed for over 40 years. The state then experienced a backlash against growing numbers of European immigrants and black migrants, who were settling in the city of New York. A popular vote authorized a convention to revise the state's constitution, which was rewritten to exclude these groups. The second constitution, adopted in 1821, restricted voting rights to male citizens and removed property qualifications for whites but not for blacks.[6] Most of the people in the state of New York—who were white citizens—feared the growing power of immigrants, blacks, and city dwellers; rather than lose power, they decided to take away the rights of immigrant and black populations. This situation is what James Madison feared during the debate over the Constitution—that a tyranny of the majority would take away the rights of the minority.[7]

American history has many stories akin to the 1821 New York constitution. Since the Founding, legislatures have restricted voting rights via poll taxes, literacy tests, registration, and redistricting. Even today, courts, legislatures,

---

6   For text of the first constitution see http://en.wikisource.org/wiki/New_York_
Constitution_of_1777. For text of the second constitution see http://en.wikisource.org/
wiki/New_York_Constitution_of_1821 (accessed 3/18/16).

7   Alexander Hamilton, James Madison, and John Jay, *The Federalist Papers*, Clinton
Rossiter, ed. (New York: New American Library, 1961), no. 10.

and executive branch departments have determined that some states have imposed new election laws with the effect of disenfranchising poorer people, minorities, seniors, and students.[8] Although we might find such restrictions objectionable, they are acceptable to those in power, who seek to safeguard their own interests by limiting the size of the group that can participate in collective decision making.

More amazing, then, is the fact that Americans have chosen to expand civil rights more than they have chosen to restrict them. Civil rights in legal, political, and civil society have expanded steadily over time, and not always through the ballot or legislation. Often it is the courts that insist on the creation or expansion of civil rights. But, as we will learn in Chapter 9, the courts cannot act alone. They need the concurrence of the people and the support of the legislature and the executive to define and protect civil rights. Often, as with property qualifications and women's suffrage, a public consensus emerges to change our Constitution and our laws and to expand our conception of civil rights. At other times, legal decisions lead to a broader change in the consensus, as the courts insist that democracy respect rights even when the people's instinct runs to the contrary. However, it can take decades, even centuries, to change political cultures and to give political power and other civil rights to those who are powerless.

The Right to Vote

Voting is one of the most basic civic acts in American society; it is the backbone of our representative democracy. But the right to vote (and indeed most civil rights) is not guaranteed in our Constitution, though the Constitution does prohibit restrictions on the right to hold public office based upon religious beliefs. When it comes to the act of voting, however, the Constitution left the power to run elections up to the states, and the states carried over the suffrage rules from their colonial charters. Thus in most states only white men with property had the right to vote; in some, only Protestants had that right. These restrictions have been a source of political conflict ever since the Founding. The right to suffrage and other civil rights cut to the core of what democracy means. Is America a democracy of all people? Can a democracy be legitimate if participation is restricted to less than half of the population? Excluded groups have struggled to gain the right to vote, and those who benefit from restrictions on the franchise have tried to maintain the restrictions. Since the Founding, legislatures and courts have defined and redefined who does and does not have this basic right. This willingness to fight over the right to vote demonstrates how significant a right it is.

---

8   The Department of Justice prevailed in its challenge to voter identification laws in Texas in 2016 because the procedures made getting an appropriate form of identification costly and that, the 5th U.S. Circuit Court of Appeals concluded, would make it more difficult for poor people to vote. That in turn would have a disparate effect on blacks and Hispanics because higher proportions of those groups are very low income.

Property qualifications for voters were the first restrictions to be lifted by the various states. At the time of the Founding, most states required some form of property ownership as a criterion for voting or running for office. The states inherited this practice from Britain, where land created social title, status, and wealth and where democracy was still a practice of the landed elite.[9] Throughout the first half of the nineteenth century, the American states began to shed the requirement that people hold property in order to vote or stand for office, especially as the economy became more industrial and less agricultural, with many people moving to cities for work and thus being less likely to own property. By 1850, property qualifications were eliminated as a requirement for voting and seeking office. Even still, many states (for example, Wisconsin and Texas) had poll taxes well into the twentieth century. Voters had to pay a nominal amount, such as $2, every time they voted. Poll taxes abridged poor people's civil rights and often served to discriminate against blacks. The Twenty-Fourth Amendment eliminated poll taxes in 1964.

Restrictions on the right to vote based on property were removed with relatively little protest. However, the struggle to extend the right to vote to women and to racial and ethnic minorities proved much more contentious, fueling two of the greatest struggles in American political history. Protection of the right to vote as well as other civil rights of blacks and other racial and ethnic minorities remains a struggle today, and the legal guarantee of those rights came relatively recently, with the Civil Rights Act (1964) and the Voting Rights Act (1965). The conflict over race runs so deep in U.S. politics that we will discuss that matter separately. Suffice it to say here that the Voting Rights Act remains an important, yet controversial, tool in fighting discrimination against blacks, Hispanics, and Asians in the administration of elections, and legal cases continue to find evidence of significant discrimination even today.[10]

Women's Suffrage. Early in the 1800s, few municipalities granted women voting rights. It took an entire century of agitation and activism, of protest and political maneuvering, to guarantee women's voting rights. In the decades before the Civil War, attitudes about women's civil rights began to change, in part because of practical problems of maintaining property, inheritance, and settlement in new states and territories. The United States adopted laws of inheritance and property from Britain, which granted men control over all property, and those laws proved problematic in a country of settlers rather than established families and classes. It is no coincidence that many of the newer states, such

---

9 Throughout the nineteenth century and into the twentieth century the United Kingdom changed the voting requirements in England, Scotland, and Wales, most significantly dropping property requirements in the 1832 and 1867 Reform acts. For an excellent history of the politics of electoral reform in nineteenth-century England, see Charles Seymour, *Electoral Reform in England and Wales* (New Haven, CT: Yale University Press, 1915).

10 In *State of Texas v. Holder,* the U.S. District Court of the District of Columbia found that the state had intentionally discriminated against blacks and Hispanics in drawing its district lines. Memorandum Opinion, Civil Action No. 11-1303, August 28, 2012.

as Indiana and Kentucky, were the first to give women economic rights. Around that time, American women began to engage in collective action to advance their political and social rights, including the right to vote. In 1848, women and men attending the Seneca Falls Convention issued the "Declaration of Sentiments and Resolutions," asserting that women were entitled to rights in every way equal to those of men. Present at the meeting were individuals who would lead the movement for women's civil rights—Elizabeth Cady Stanton, Lucretia Mott, Mary Ann McClintock, and the abolitionist leader Frederick Douglass.

In 1869, the National Women's Suffrage Association (NWSA) was formed in New York, and it immediately sought to amend the U.S. Constitution to allow women to vote. By the 1880s, the issue of voting rights for women was the subject of mass meetings, parades, and protests, and as of 1917, NWSA had 2 million members. The change in laws to extend suffrage to women began in the western states and territories. In 1869, Wyoming (still a territory then) was the first to extend women the right to vote, followed by Colorado in 1893 and Utah in 1895. In 1916, Montana became the first state to elect a woman to the U.S. Congress. At last, New York, the home of the women's suffrage movement, granted suffrage to women. By 1918, all of the western states and territories plus Michigan and New York had granted women full suffrage. Soon it was only a matter of time before Congress changed federal law. In 1919, Congress passed the Nineteenth Amendment granting women the right to vote in federal elections.[11] Two months later, the states ratified the amendment, and women nationwide voted in the presidential election of 1920.

The Right to Vote for Black Americans. The struggle to extend full voting rights to racial minorities, especially blacks, reflects even deeper divisions in American society. It took a full century after the Civil War for Congress to guarantee minorities' voting rights with the Voting Rights Act of 1965, and the battle to protect those rights continues today.

The Fifteenth Amendment gives blacks voting rights, and during Reconstruction the federal government enforced those rights. Following withdrawal of federal troops from the South, however, state legislatures and local governments there (and elsewhere) enacted practices that excluded blacks from elections or weakened their political power. In many states, blacks were excluded from primary elections, a practice called the White Primary. Poll taxes, literacy tests, registration list purges, and other tactics served to keep blacks from voting.[12] District and municipal boundaries were drawn to place blacks in jurisdictions in which they had little or no impact on the election of representatives or the approval of public expenditures.[13]

---

11   "Woman Suffrage," *Collier's New Encyclopedia,* X (New York: Collier , 1921), pp. 403–05, http://en.wikisource.org/wiki/Collier%27s_New_Encyclopedia_%281921%29/Woman_suffrage (accessed 3/18/16).

12   V. O. Key, *Southern Politics in State and Nation* (New York: Knopf, 1949).

13   Bernard Taper, *Gomillion v. Lightfoot: The Tuskegee Gerrymander Case* (New York: McGraw-Hill, 1962).

Blacks had little hope of changing state law because state legislators had benefited electorally from them. Congress was also reluctant to pass federal legislation to enforce the Fifteenth Amendment. At last the Supreme Court intervened. It struck down the White Primary in *Smith v. Allwright* in 1944, asserting the federal government's power to intervene in the states' conduct of elections in order to protect blacks' voting rights.[14] The Court acted again in 1960, ruling that state and local governments could not draw election district boundaries so as to discriminate against blacks.[15] At last Congress intervened with the Voting Rights Act, sweeping aside many state laws and practices that served to discriminate against blacks. That act has been amended several times to expand who is covered, including Hispanics (1975) and language groups (1982), and what sorts of activities are prohibited, most notably racially discriminatory districting.

The fight over minority voting rights, however, continues. New administrative procedures, such as laws requiring that voters show a government-issued photo ID, and the redrawing of legislative district maps every 10 years, are subject to intense debate. There are frequent allegations that these practices affect minorities' voting rights adversely and even embody intentional discrimination. Disputes over these laws often end up in federal courts, which must not only examine the circumstances in which the laws were passed but also examine the electoral behavior in the state or area and assess the rules' likely impact on minority voters. Since the 1982 amendments to the Voting Rights Act, this has required consultation with social scientists to develop measures of how blacks, Hispanics, and whites vote, and of the laws' likely effects on minorities' ability to elect their preferred candidates. We discuss how political scientists address these concerns in Chapters 10 and 11. Since the 1960s, the courts—not the legislatures—have become the arena in which minorities, poor people, city dwellers, and many others seek protection of their voting rights.

In 2013 the Supreme Court declared unconstitutional an important section of the Voting Rights Act in *Shelby County v. Holder*. This section—Section 4(b)—obligated jurisdictions in Alabama, Alaska, Arizona, Georgia, Louisiana, Mississippi, South Carolina, and Texas, as well as municipalities and counties in other states, to obtain approval of any change in election administration procedures from the Department of Justice or the Federal District Court in the District of Columbia—a procedure called *preclearance*. Congress had originally used a formula for determining which states needed to obtain preclearance based on the turnout of minorities relative to that of whites. The Supreme Court ruled that the states no longer fit with the facts, as the ratio of minority turnout to white turnout in Alabama was similar to that in Massachusetts. Other parts of the Voting Rights Act still hold, however, and the *Shelby County* decision shifts the legal battles to those other sections.[16] It also puts the question of preclearance back on Congress's agenda.

14   *Smith v. Allwright,* 321 U.S. 649 (1944).

15   *Gomillion v. Lightfoot,* 364 U.S. 339 (1960).

16   *Shelby County v. Holder,* 570 U. S. ____ (2013).

Racial Discrimination in the Nineteenth and Twentieth Centuries

The Supreme Court was initially no more ready to enforce the civil rights aspects of the Fourteenth Amendment than it was to enforce the civil liberties provisions. The Court declared the Civil Rights Act of 1875—a key piece of Reconstruction legislation—to be unconstitutional on the grounds that it sought to protect blacks from discrimination by *private* businesses. The Civil Rights Act of 1875 guaranteed blacks equal treatment in public accommodations, such as public transportation, and prohibited states and local governments from excluding blacks from jury service. According to the Court, the Fourteenth Amendment was intended to protect individuals from discrimination only in the case of actions by *public* officials of state and local governments. This decision gutted much of the legislation needed to make the provisions in the Thirteenth, Fourteenth, and Fifteenth Amendments a reality.

Plessy v. Ferguson: "Separate but Equal."

In 1896, the Court went further, in the infamous *Plessy v. Ferguson* case. It upheld a Louisiana statute that required racial segregation on trolleys and other public carriers (and, by implication, in all public facilities, including schools). Homer Plessy, a man defined as "one-eighth black," had violated a Louisiana law that provided for "equal but separate accommodations" on trains and a $25 fine for any white passenger who sat in a car reserved for blacks or any black passenger who sat in a car reserved for whites. The Supreme Court held that the Fourteenth Amendment's "equal protection of the laws" was not violated by racial distinction as long as the law applied to both races equally. Many people generally pretended that blacks were treated equally as long as some accommodation existed. The Court said that although

> the object of the [Fourteenth] Amendment was undoubtedly to enforce the absolute equality of the two races before the law, . . . it could not have intended to abolish distinctions based on color, or to enforce social, as distinguished from political, equality, or a commingling of the two races upon terms unsatisfactory to either.[17]

In effect, the Court was saying that the use of race as a criterion of exclusion in public matters was not unreasonable. This was the origin of the **"separate but equal" rule**, which was not reversed until 1954.

Challenging "Separate but Equal."

The Supreme Court had begun to change its position on racial discrimination before World War II by defining more strictly the criterion of equal facilities in the "separate but equal" rule.

 "separate but equal" rule

The doctrine that public accommodations could be segregated by race but still be equal

---

17 *Plessy v. Ferguson*, 163 U.S. 537 (1896). The sole dissent to this decision came from Justice John Marshall Harlan, who wrote, "Our constitution is colorblind, and neither knows nor tolerates classes among citizens."

Notably, in 1938, the Court rejected Missouri's policy of paying qualified blacks' tuition to out-of-state law schools rather than admitting them to the University of Missouri Law School.[18]

After the war, modest progress resumed. In 1950, the Court rejected Texas's claim that its new "law school for Negroes" afforded education equal to that of the all-white University of Texas Law School; without confronting the "separate but equal" principle, the Court's decision anticipated *Brown v. Board of Education* by opening the question of whether any segregated facility could be truly equal.[19] The same was true in 1944, when the Court struck down the southern practice of White Primaries, which legally excluded blacks from participation in nominating candidates. Here the Court's decision made parties "an agency of the State," and any discrimination against blacks was therefore "state action within the meaning of the Fifteenth Amendment."[20] The most important pre-1954 decision was probably *Shelley v. Kraemer*, in which the Court ruled against the widespread practice of "restrictive covenants," whereby the seller of a home added a clause to the sales contract requiring buyers to agree not to sell their home to any nonwhite, non-Christian, and so on.[21] The Court ruled that such restrictive covenants could not be judicially enforced because the Fourteenth Amendment prohibits any organ of the state, including the courts, from denying equal protection of its laws.

However, none of these pre-1954 cases confronted "separate but equal" as such and its legal and constitutional support for racial discrimination. Each victory by the NAACP's Legal Defense Fund was just a small victory, not a leading case. The southern states' massive effort to resist direct desegregation and to prevent further legal actions by making a show of equalizing the quality of white and black schools convinced the NAACP that the Supreme Court was not ready for a full confrontation with the constitutional principle sustaining segregation. Congress meanwhile refused to address racial segregation in the South, especially given the power of Southern Democrats inside the U.S. Senate, as we discuss in the next chapter. Thus, even though the NAACP doubted the courts' readiness to tackle segregation, the organization's leadership saw them as its only hope. In 1952, the NAACP brought cases in South Carolina, Virginia, Kansas, Delaware, and the District of Columbia, arguing that the principle of segregation itself was unconstitutional. The strategy was to file suits simultaneously in different federal districts so that inconsistent results between any two states would more quickly lead to Supreme Court acceptance of at least one appeal.[22] The Kansas case became the focal point. It was further along in the adjudicatory process in its district court,

---

18 *Missouri ex rel. Gaines v. Canada,* 305 U.S. 337 (1938).

19 *Sweatt v. Painter,* 339 U.S. 629 (1950).

20 *Smith v. Allwright,* 321 U.S. 649 (1944).

21 *Shelley v. Kraemer,* 334 U.S. 1 (1948).

22 The best reviews of strategies, tactics, and goals is found in John Hope Franklin, *From Slavery to Freedom: A History of Negro Americans,* 4th ed. (New York: Knopf, 1974), chap. 22; and Richard Kluger, *Simple Justice: The History of* Brown v. Board of Education *and Black America's Struggle for Equality* (New York: Vintage, 1977), chaps. 21 and 22.

---

and it had the special advantage of being located in a state outside the South which would lessen local resistance to a decision outlawing segregation.[23]

Brown v. Board of Education. Oliver Brown, the father of three girls, lived "across the tracks" in a low-income, racially mixed Topeka neighborhood. Every school-day morning, Linda Brown took a school bus to the Monroe School for black children, about a mile away. In September 1950, Oliver Brown took Linda to the all-white Sumner School, which was closer to home, to enter her in the third grade, in defiance of state law and local segregation rules. When they were refused, Brown took his case to the NAACP, and soon thereafter *Brown v. Board of Education* was born. In mid-1953, the Court announced that the several cases on their way up would be reargued within the context of questions involving the intent of the Fourteenth Amendment. A year later, the Court responded in one of the most important decisions in its history.

In deciding the case, the Court, to the surprise of many, rejected as inconclusive all the learned arguments about the intent and the history of the Fourteenth Amendment and committed itself to considering only the *consequences* of segregation:

> Does segregation of children in public schools solely on the basis of race, even though the physical facilities and other "tangible" factors may be equal, deprive the children of the minority group of equal educational opportunities? We believe that it does. . . . We conclude that, in the field of public education, the doctrine of "separate but equal" has no place. Separate educational facilities are inherently unequal.[24]

The *Brown* decision altered the constitutional framework protecting civil rights in two fundamental respects. First, after *Brown*, the states would no longer have the power to use race as a criterion of discrimination in law. Second, the national government would from then on have the constitutional basis for extending its power to intervene with strict regulatory policies against discriminatory actions of state or local governments, school boards, employers, and many others in the private sector.

Civil Rights after Brown v. Board of Education. Although *Brown v. Board of Education* withdrew all constitutional authority to use race as a criterion of exclusion, this historic decision was merely a small first step in establishing equal civil rights for blacks. First, most states refused to cooperate until sued, and many ingenious schemes served to delay obedience (such as paying white students' tuition at newly created "private" academies). Second, even as southern

---

23 The District of Columbia case came up too, but because the District of Columbia is not a state, the case did not directly involve the Fourteenth Amendment and its equal protection clause. It confronted the Court on the same grounds, however: that segregation is inherently unequal. Its victory in effect was incorporation in reverse, with equal protection moving from the Fourteenth Amendment to become part of the Bill of Rights. See *Bolling v. Sharpe*, 347 U.S. 497 (1954).

24 *Brown v. Board of Education*, 347 U.S. 483 (1954).

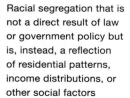

de jure segregation

Racial segregation that is a direct result of law or official policy

de facto segregation

Racial segregation that is not a direct result of law or government policy but is, instead, a reflection of residential patterns, income distributions, or other social factors

school boards began to eliminate their legally enforced **de jure segregation**, extensive actual **de facto segregation** remained in the North and the South as a consequence of racially segregated housing, which the *Brown* principles did not affect. Third, *Brown* did not directly touch discrimination in employment, public accommodations, juries, voting, and other areas of social and economic activity.

A decade of frustration following *Brown* indicated that adjudication alone would not succeed. The goal of equal protection required positive, or affirmative, action by Congress and administrative agencies. And given massive southern resistance and generally negative national public opinion toward racial integration, progress would not be made through courts, Congress, or agencies without well-organized support. The number of peaceful civil rights demonstrations for voting rights and public accommodations increased greatly during the first 14 years after *Brown*.[25]

Organized demonstrations mounted slowly but surely after *Brown v. Board of Education*. In an impressive demonstration of collective political action, hundreds of thousands of Americans, both black and white, exercised their right to peaceably assemble and petition the government for a redress of grievances, demanding that the civil rights guaranteed to white Americans now be recognized and protected for black Americans too. By the 1960s, the many organizations constituting the civil rights movement had accumulated experience and built networks capable of launching massive direct-action campaigns against southern segregationists. The Southern Christian Leadership Conference, the Student Nonviolent Coordinating Committee, and many other organizations had built a movement across the South that used the media to attract nationwide attention and support. In the massive March on Washington in 1963, the Reverend Martin Luther King Jr. staked out the movement's moral claims in his "I Have a Dream" speech. Also in the 1960s, images of protesters being beaten, attacked by police dogs, and set on with fire hoses won broad sympathy for the black civil rights cause and discredited state and local governments in the South. In this way, the movement created intense pressure for a reluctant federal government to take more assertive steps to defend black civil rights.

In recent years, a variety of protests have coalesced under the banner "Black Lives Matter" to focus attention on allegations of police misconduct directed at African Americans. The movement took off in Ferguson, Missouri after the shooting of Michael Brown, an unarmed black teenager, by a white police officer. It spread across the nation as the media carried reports, photos, and videos of police violence against blacks in Chicago, South Carolina, Baltimore, New York, and other cities. African Americans had long asserted that they were often victims of racial profiling and more likely than whites to be harassed, physically harmed, or arrested by the police. Police departments had always replied that blacks were more likely than whites to be engaged in criminal activity. In July 2016, widely publicized deaths of two black men at the hands of police within one day of each other again spurred nationwide protests. While most of the protests were peaceful, a sniper killed five police officers at a protest in Dallas, Texas. The events indicated that nearly two years after the death of Michael Brown, tensions around race relations in the United States remain very high, and protests and civil unrest in response to the issue are unlikely to go away any time soon.

25 Jonathan D. Casper, *The Politics of Civil Liberties* (New York: Harper & Row, 1972), p. 90.

Why Fight for Civil Rights? Collective Action and Selective Benefits. One of the tenets of our five principles of politics from Chapter 1 is that individuals have little incentive to participate in mass-action politics. After all, what difference could one person make by participating in a civil rights protest? Participation is costly in terms of time, and for civil rights marchers even one's health or life was endangered. The risks outweighed the potential benefits, yet hundreds of thousands of people *did* participate. Why?

Even though few scholars have applied this perspective to the civil rights movements,[26] a general answer is available. Most rational analysis sees behavior as *instrumental*—motivated by and directed toward some purpose or objective. But behavior may also be *experiential*. People do things, on this account, because they like doing them—they feel free of guilt, they take pleasure in the activity for its own sake. We maintain that this second view of behavior is compatible with rational accounts. Instrumental behavior may be considered *investment activity*, whereas experiential behavior may be considered *consumption activity*. With the latter, the behavior itself generates utility, rather than the behavior's consequences. As an illustration of collective action, many people certainly attended the 1963 March on Washington because they cared about civil rights. But it is unlikely that many thought their individual participation made a large difference to the fate of the civil rights legislation they supported through the march. Rather, they attended because they wanted to be part of a social movement, hear Martin Luther King Jr. speak, and identify with myriad others who felt the same way. Also—and this should not be minimized— many participated because they anticipated that the march would be a fun adventure.

So experiential behavior is consumption-oriented activity predicated on the belief that the activity in question is fulfilling, apart from its consequences. Individuals are bound to be animated both by the consumption value of a particular behavior and by its instrumental value, the rational (investment) explanation that we have used throughout this book. Insisting on only one of these complementary forms of rationality while excluding the other will provide only a partial explanation.

Opportunity in Education

Education has been the focus of some of the most important battles over civil rights, largely because Americans believe that everyone should have an equal chance to succeed. That commitment to equality is underscored by the centrality of public education in our country. Since the early nineteenth century, American communities and states have provided public education to all persons. That has been essential to help immigrants join our society—to help them learn English, our society's values, and the skills necessary for employment. Universal access to public education has also helped produce one of the world's most productive workforces. Leaving large segments of our population uneducated is potentially bad for the economy, and it is certainly bad for those people. Grossly unequal opportunities for children to receive education will likely mean grossly unequal opportunities for individuals to have a good job, participate in politics, and realize their potential.

....

26 One notable exception is Dennis Chong, *Collective Action and the Civil Rights Movement* (Chicago: University of Chicago Press, 1991).

Cause and Effect in the Civil Rights Movement

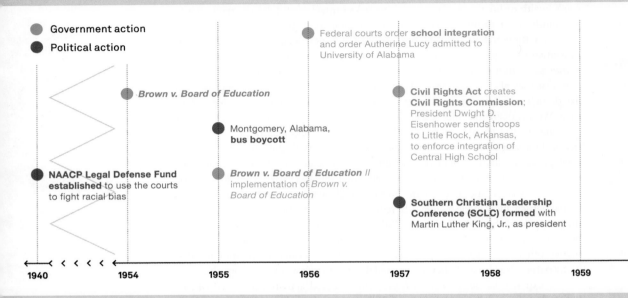

- ● Government action
- ● Political action

Federal courts order **school integration** and order Autherine Lucy admitted to University of Alabama

Brown v. Board of Education

Civil Rights Act creates **Civil Rights Commission**; President Dwight D. Eisenhower sends troops to Little Rock, Arkansas, to enforce integration of Central High School

Montgomery, Alabama, **bus boycott**

NAACP Legal Defense Fund established to use the courts to fight racial bias

Brown v. Board of Education II implementation of *Brown v. Board of Education*

Southern Christian Leadership Conference (SCLC) formed with Martin Luther King, Jr., as president

| 1940 | 1954 | 1955 | 1956 | 1957 | 1958 | 1959 |

Those inequities in educational opportunities were painfully obvious in the 1950s. Poverty rates of blacks far exceeded those of whites. Equal access to quality education, it was thought, would reduce and perhaps eliminate those inequities over the course of a generation.

School Desegregation, Phase One. Although the District of Columbia and some school districts in the border states responded almost immediately to court-ordered desegregation, states in the Deep South responded with a delaying tactic known as *massive resistance*. Southern politicians stood shoulder to shoulder to declare that the Supreme Court's decisions and orders were without effect. These states' legislatures enacted statutes ordering school districts to maintain segregated schools and state superintendents to terminate state funding wherever there was racial mixing in the classroom.

Most of these plans were tested in the federal courts and struck down as unconstitutional.[27] But southern resistance went beyond legislation. Perhaps the most

---

27 The two most important cases were *Cooper v. Aaron*, 358 U.S. 1 (1958), which required Little Rock, Arkansas, to desegregate, and *Griffin v. Prince Edward County School Board*, 377 U.S. 218 (1964), which forced all the schools of that Virginia county to reopen after they had been closed for five years to avoid desegregation.

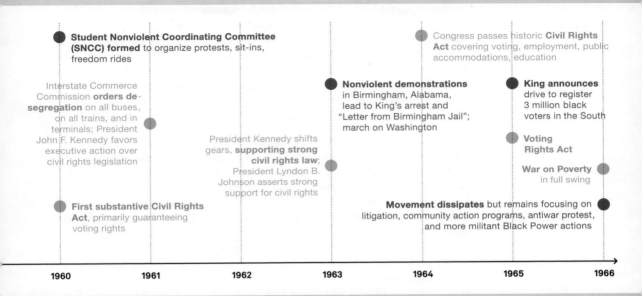

Student Nonviolent Coordinating Committee (SNCC) formed to organize protests, sit-ins, freedom rides

Interstate Commerce Commission **orders de-segregation** on all buses, on all trains, and in terminals; President John F. Kennedy favors executive action over civil rights legislation

President Kennedy shifts gears, **supporting strong civil rights law**; President Lyndon B. Johnson asserts strong support for civil rights

First substantive Civil Rights Act, primarily guaranteeing voting rights

Congress passes historic **Civil Rights Act** covering voting, employment, public accommodations, education

Nonviolent demonstrations in Birmingham, Alabama, lead to King's arrest and "Letter from Birmingham Jail"; march on Washington

King announces drive to register 3 million black voters in the South

Voting Rights Act

War on Poverty in full swing

Movement dissipates but remains focusing on litigation, community action programs, antiwar protest, and more militant Black Power actions

1960   1961   1962   1963   1964   1965   1966

serious incident occurred in 1957, in Arkansas. On the first day of school, a mob assembled at Little Rock Central High School to protest integration and to block black children from attending. Governor Orval Faubus mobilized the Arkansas National Guard to intercede against enforcement of a federal court order to integrate the school. Following a three-week standoff between the Arkansas governor and the federal courts, President Eisenhower was forced to deploy U.S. troops and place the city under martial law. Faubus responded by closing all of the city's public high schools. In December 1959, the Supreme Court ordered them reopened.

The end of massive resistance, however, became the beginning of other strategies, such as "pupil placement" laws.[28] As the southern states continued to avoid desegregation, the federal courts followed with cases and decisions quashing them. That cat-and-mouse game stalled efforts at desegregation. Ten years after *Brown*, fewer than 1 percent of black school-age children in the Deep South were attending schools with whites. The federal courts could not do the job alone. At last,

---

28 *Shuttlesworth v. Birmingham Board of Education,* 358 U.S. 101 (1958), upheld a pupil placement plan purporting to assign pupils on various bases, with no mention of race. This case interpreted *Brown* to mean that school districts must stop explicit racial discrimination but were under no obligation to take positive steps to desegregate. For a while, black parents were doomed to case-by-case approaches.

in 1964, Congress passed the Civil Rights Act of 1964, which outlawed discrimination against racial, ethnic, and religious minorities and against women; it also allowed federal agencies to withhold federal grants, contracts, and loans to states and municipalities found to discriminate or obstruct the law's implementation.

It is important to note the mutual dependence of the courts and the legislatures—not only do the legislatures need constitutional authority to act but the courts also need legislative and political assistance, through the power of the purse, the power to organize administrative agencies to implement court orders, and the ability to focus political support. Consequently, even as Congress finally addressed school desegregation (and other areas of equal protection), the courts continued to exercise their powers, not only by issuing orders against recalcitrant school districts and by extending and reinterpreting aspects of the equal protection clause to support legislative and administrative actions.

School Desegregation: Busing and Beyond. One of the most important judicial extension of civil rights in education after 1954 was the *Swann* decision of 1971, which held that state-imposed desegregation could be brought about by busing children across school districts even when relatively long distances were involved. But the decision also added that under certain circumstances even racial quotas could serve as the "starting point in shaping a remedy to correct past constitutional violations" and that the pairing or grouping of schools and the reorganizing of school attendance zones would also be acceptable (Figure 5.1).[29]

Three years later, however, *Swann* was severely restricted when the Supreme Court determined that only cities found guilty of deliberate and de jure racial segregation (segregation in law) would have to desegregate their schools. This decision was handed down in the 1974 case of *Milliken v. Bradley*, involving the city of Detroit and its suburbs.[30] The *Milliken* ruling had the effect of exempting most northern states and cities from busing because school segregation in northern cities is generally de facto (segregation in fact), resulting from segregated housing and thousands of acts of private discrimination against blacks and other minorities.

Additional progress in school desegregation will likely be extremely slow unless the Supreme Court permits federal action against de facto segregation and the various kinds of private schools and academies that have sprung up for the purpose of avoiding integration. Prospects for further school integration diminished with several Court decisions handed down in the 1990s. In 1995, for example, the Court signaled to the lower courts that they should "disengage from desegregation efforts"[31]—a direct threat to the main basis of the holding in the original 1954 *Brown v. Board of Education* decision. In 2007, the Court went further, declaring unconstitutional programs of the Louisville and Seattle school districts that attempted to achieve racial diversity by using race as a determining factor in admissions. Provocatively, Chief Justice John Roberts quoted the counsel for Oliver Brown in his majority decision, writing, "We have one fundamental

29 *Swann v. Charlotte-Mecklenburg Board of Education,* 402 U.S. 1 (1971).

30 *Milliken v. Bradley,* 418 U.S. 717 (1974).

31 *Missouri v. Jenkins,* 515 U.S. 70 (1995). The quotation is from David M. O'Brien, *Supreme Court Watch 1996* (New York: Norton, 1996), p. 220.

Figure 5.1
PERCENTAGE OF SOUTHERN BLACK CHILDREN ATTENDING SCHOOL WITH WHITES, 1955–73

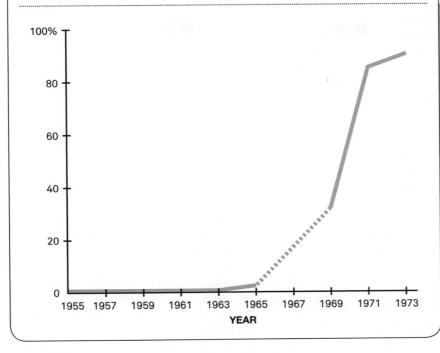

ANALYZING THE EVIDENCE

What happened in 1964 that accounts for the upward trend beginning in 1965?

NOTE: Dashed line indicates missing data.
SOURCE: Gerald N. Rosenberg, *The Hollow Hope: Can Courts Bring About Social Change?* (Chicago: University of Chicago Press, 1991), pp. 50–51.

contention which we will seek to develop in the course of this argument, and that contention is that no state has any authority under the equal protection clause of the Fourteenth Amendment to use race as a factor in affording educational opportunities among its citizens."[32] In recent years, this idea has been important in the realm of college admissions. For example, in the 2013 case of *Fisher v. University of Texas*,[33] the Supreme Court indicated that a school's affirmative action program of admissions that seems to discriminate in favor of black students must be subjected to the same "strict scrutiny" as a program that seems to discriminate against black students and sent the case back to the lower courts for further consideration. In 2016, the Court ruled on the plan and declared that some intrusion on equal protection was warranted by the importance of creating a diverse student body.[34] Strict scrutiny (see Chapter 4) is the most stringent standard of judicial

32 *Parents Involved in Community Schools v. Seattle School District No. 1,* 551 U.S. 701 (2007).

33 *Fisher v. University of Texas* 570 U.S. ____ (2013).

34 *Fisher v. University of Texas* No. 14-981 (2016).

review and requires the government to show that a law furthers a compelling governmental interest and is narrowly tailored to achieve that interest.

Women and Education. Women have also suffered from unequal access to education. Throughout the nineteenth century, relatively few colleges and professional schools admitted women. (Oberlin College was the first to do so.) Even as late as the 1960s, elite universities such as Princeton and Yale did not admit women, and colleges that did admit women offered fewer opportunities to participate in programs, clubs, and athletics. Congress began to remedy these inequities with the Civil Rights Act of 1964, but the most significant federal legislation to guarantee women equal access to education is the 1972 Education Act. Title IX of this act forbids gender discrimination in education. By the mid-1970s most universities had become fully coed. But enforcing equality was more difficult.

Although the act provided weak enforcement provisions, it has proven effective for litigation. A significant step came in 1992, when the Court ruled that violations of the act's Title IX could be remedied with monetary damages.[35] This ruling opened the door for further legal action in the area of education and led to stronger enforcement against sexual harassment, gender inequities in resources (such as lab space, research support for faculty, and athletics), and gender inequities in compensation. In the two years after the ruling, complaints to the Education Department's Office for Civil Rights about unequal treatment of women's athletic programs nearly tripled. Subsequently, some prominent universities have been ordered to create more women's sports programs; many other colleges and universities have added more women's programs to avoid potential litigation.[36]

In 1996, the Supreme Court put an end to all-male schools supported by public funds when it ruled that the Virginia Military Institute's policy of not admitting women was unconstitutional.[37] Along with the Citadel, an all-male military college in South Carolina, Virginia Military Institute (VMI) had never admitted women. It argued that its unique educational experience, including intense physical training and the harsh treatment of freshmen, would be destroyed if women were admitted. The Court, however, ruled that the male-only policy denied "substantial equality" to women. Two days after the Court's ruling, the Citadel announced that it would accept women. VMI considered becoming a private institution in order to remain all male, but ultimately its board voted to admit women.

THE POLITICS OF RIGHTS

The Nineteenth Amendment, *Brown v. Board of Education*, the Civil Rights Acts, and the Voting Rights Act were the signal achievements of the civil rights movements of women and blacks. They helped redefine civil rights in America not just for those

---

35 *Franklin v. Gwinnett County Public Schools,* 503 U.S. 60 (1992).

36 Jennifer Halperin, "Women Step Up to Bat," *Illinois Issues 21* (September 1995): 11–14.

37 *United States v. Virginia,* 518 U.S. 515 (1996).

groups but for all people. They became models for other groups to press civil rights claims, and the NWSA and NAACP strategies have been widely mimicked (see Analyzing the Evidence on pp. 166–7). The principles behind equality in voting and in education have since been applied to other areas, including employment, housing, immigration, access to public facilities, and athletics. With the push for rights in these spheres, there has also been a push back. Just how far do civil rights extend?

Outlawing Discrimination in Employment

The federal courts and the Justice Department entered the arena of discrimination in employment through Title VII of the Civil Rights Act of 1964, which outlaws job discrimination by all private and public employers, including government agencies (such as fire and police departments), that employ more than 15 workers. We have already seen that the Supreme Court gave "interstate commerce" such a broad definition that Congress had the constitutional authority to ban discrimination by virtually any local employers.[38] Title VII makes it unlawful to discriminate in employment on the basis of color, religion, sex, or national origin as well as race.

A potential difficulty with Title VII is that the complaining party must show deliberate discrimination as the cause of the failure to get a job or a training opportunity. Of course, employers rarely admit discrimination on the basis of race, sex, or any other illegal factor. Recognizing this, the courts have allowed aggrieved parties to make their case if they can show that hiring practices had the *effect* of exclusion. A leading case in 1971 involved a class action by several black employees in North Carolina attempting to show with statistical evidence that blacks had been relegated to one department of the Duke Power Company, which involved the least desirable manual-labor jobs, and that they had been kept out of contention for better jobs because the employer had added high school education and passing grades on special aptitude tests as qualifications. The Supreme Court held that although the statistical evidence did not prove intentional discrimination and the requirements were race neutral in appearance, their effects were sufficient to shift the burden of justification to the employer to show that the requirements were a "business necessity" that bore "a demonstrable relationship to successful performance."[39] The ruling was subsequently applied to other hiring, promotion, and training programs.[40] Recently, though, the Court has placed limits on employment discrimination suits. In 2007, for example, it said that a complaint of gender discrimination must be brought within 180 days of the time the discrimination was alleged to have occurred, blocking suits based on events that might have taken place in the past.[41] In 2009,

38 See especially *Katzenbach v. McClung,* 379 U.S. 294 (1964).

39 *Griggs v. Duke Power Company,* 401 U.S. 424 (1971). See also Allan P. Sindler, *Bakke, DeFunis, and Minority Admissions: The Quest for Equal Opportunity* (New York: Longman, 1978), pp. 180–89.

40 For a good treatment of these issues, see Charles O. Gregory and Harold A. Katz, *Labor and the Law,* 3rd ed. (New York: Norton, 1979), chap. 17.

41 *Ledbetter v. Goodyear Tire and Rubber Co.,* 550 U.S. 618 (2007).

Advocacy and Representation for Marginalized Groups

Contributed by
Dara Z. Strolovitch
Princeton University

Historically, women, people of color, and low-income people have faced institutional barriers to participating in collective political processes. When formal avenues of participation, such as voting, are closed, these groups have turned to advocacy organizations as a means to offset this paucity of legislative representation. Indeed, for many years, national advocacy organizations offered some of the only political voice and visibility available to groups such as African Americans in the South and women of all races, who were denied formal voting rights until well into the twentieth century. Long before most women could vote, for example, the National American Woman Suffrage Association mounted protests and lobbied legislators.

The extension of certain formally recognized civil rights to women, people of color, and low-income people has not ended the need for advocacy organizations, however, and the second half of the twentieth century witnessed an explosion in the number of organizations representing these groups. By speaking for marginalized populations on the national political stage, such organizations provide a crucial bridge between the often unheard political voices of underrepresented groups and government institutions, helping reduce racial, gender, and sex-based discrimination and create new resources and opportunities for low-income people.

Number of National Women's, People of Color, and Economic Justice Organizations Founded, by Decade, 1850s–2000s

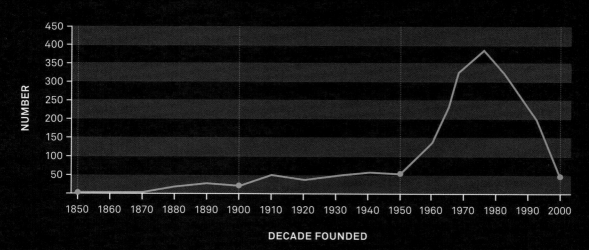

NUMBER / DECADE FOUNDED

SOURCE: Dara Z. Strolovitch, *Affirmative Advocacy: Race, Class, and Gender in Interest Group Politics* (Chicago: Chicago University Press, 2007); and Dara Z. Strolovitch, "Affirmative Advocacy in Hard Times," in *Nonprofic Advocacy*, Steven Smith, Yutaka Tsujinaka, and Robert Pekkanen, eds. (Baltimore, MD: Johns Hopkins Press, in press).

But while the proliferation of advocacy organizations is a striking feature of contemporary American politics, the extent to which these groups have leveled the representational playing field is unclear. First, the growth in the number of social and economic justice organizations has been vastly outpaced by increased numbers of business and professional organizations, and organizations that represent marginalized groups constitute only a modest proportion of the larger interest group universe.

Interests Represented by Organizations in Washington

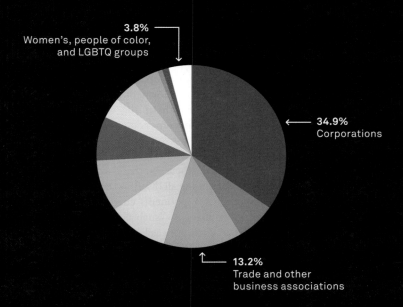

3.8%
Women's, people of color, and LGBTQ groups

← 34.9%
Corporations

↰ 13.2%
Trade and other business associations

Kay Lehman Schlozman and her co-authors collected data about the nearly 12,000 organizations with representatives in Washington, D.C. More than a third of these organizations represent corporations, while labor unions account for 1 percent, social welfare organizations for 0.8 percent, and groups speaking for women, people of color, and LGBTQ people together account for a mere 3.8 percent.

INTERESTS

- Women's, people of color, and LGBTQ groups = **3.8%**
- Unions = **1%**
- Poverty/social welfare = **0.8%**
- Public interest = **4.6%**
- Education = **4.2%**
- Health = **3.5%**
- Foreign = **7.8%**
- Other/unknown = **9.1%**
- State and local governments = **10.4%**
- Trade and other business associations = **13.2%**
- Occupational associations = **6.8%**
- Corporations = **34.9%**

SOURCE: Kay Lehman Schlozman, Sidney Verba, and Henry E. Brady, *The Unheavenly Chorus: Unequal Political Voice and the Broken Promise of American Democracy* (Princeton, NJ: Princeton University Press, 2012), p. 321.

Advocacy organizations that represent women, people of color, and low-income people have also been criticized for focusing on the needs of the more advantaged members of the marginalized constituencies. Research confirms the validity of this criticism: a survey of 286 organizations found that women's and African American groups, for example, were much more active on affirmative action in higher education than they were on the welfare reform legislation that passed in 1996, which had major implications for low-income women and people of color.[1] Although advocacy organizations can fall short, many take deliberate steps to more effectively represent disadvantaged constituents.

1 Dara Z. Strolovitch, *Affirmative Advocacy: Race, Class, and Gender in Interest Group Politics* (Chicago: University of Chicago Press, 2007).

Congress enacted the Ledbetter Fair Pay Act to overturn the Court's decision and give workers more time to file pay discrimination claims. And in two important 2008 decisions, the Court helped individuals who sought to bring employment discrimination complaints by declaring that employers were barred from retaliating against them.[42] Today, several federal statutes enforced by the Equal Employment Opportunity Commission (EEOC) prohibit employer retaliation against workers who file discrimination complaints.

Women and Gender Discrimination

Although women gained voting and property rights long ago, they continue to suffer discrimination in various forms, particularly in employment. Here, women benefited from the civil rights movement and, especially, from Title VII, which in many ways fostered the growth of the women's movement.[43] The National Organization for Women's (NOW) first major campaign involved picketing the EEOC for its refusal to ban sex-segregated employment advertisements.

Building on these victories and the growth of the women's movement, women's rights activists sought an equal rights amendment (ERA) to the Constitution. The proposed amendment's substantive passage stated that "equality of rights under the law shall not be denied or abridged by the United States or by any State on account of sex." Supporters believed that such a sweeping guarantee of equal rights was necessary for ending all discrimination against women and for making gender roles more equal. Opponents charged that it would be socially disruptive and would introduce changes—such as coed restrooms—that most Americans did not want. The amendment easily passed Congress in 1972 and won quick approval in many state legislatures but fell three states short of the 38 needed for ratification by the 1982 deadline.[44]

Despite the ERA's failure, gender discrimination expanded dramatically as an area of civil rights law. In the 1970s, the conservative Burger Court helped establish gender discrimination as a major civil rights issue. Although the Court refused to treat gender discrimination as equivalent to racial discrimination,[45] it made it easier for plaintiffs to file and win suits on the basis of gender discrimination by applying an "intermediate" level of review.[46] This **intermediate scrutiny** is midway between traditional rules of evidence, which put the burden of proof

intermediate scrutiny

The test used by the Supreme Court in gender discrimination cases, which places the burden of proof partially on the government and partially on the challengers to show that the law in question is constitutional

---

42 *CBOC West v. Humphries,* 553 U.S. 442 (2008); and *Gomez-Perez v. Potter,* 553 U.S. 474 (2008).

43 Material in this and subsequent sections is adapted from Benjamin Ginsberg, Theodore J. Lowi, Margaret Weir, and Caroline J. Tolbert, *We the People: An Introduction to American Politics,* 9th ed. (New York: Norton, 2013).

44 See Jane J. Mansbridge, *Why We Lost the ERA* (Chicago: University of Chicago Press, 1986); and Gilbert Steiner, *Constitutional Inequality* (Washington, DC: Brookings Institution, 1985).

45 See *Frontiero v. Richardson,* 411 U.S. 677 (1973).

46 See *Craig v. Boren,* 423 U.S. 1047 (1976).

on the plaintiff, and the doctrine of strict scrutiny, which requires the defendant to show not only that a particular classification is reasonable but also that there is a need or compelling interest for it. Intermediate scrutiny shifts the burden of proof partially onto the defendant, rather than leaving it entirely on the plaintiff.

Elevated awareness of sexual harassment as a form of gender discrimination has also advanced the cause of women's civil rights. In 1986, the Supreme Court recognized two forms of sexual harassment—the quid pro quo type, which involves sexual extortion, and the hostile-environment type, which involves sexual intimidation.[47] In its decision the Court said that sexual harassment may be legally actionable even if the employee did not suffer tangible economic or job-related losses in relation to it. Subsequently the Court said that sexual harassment may be legally actionable even if the employee did not suffer tangible psychological costs as a result of it.[48] In two 1998 cases, the Court further strengthened the law when it said that whether or not sexual harassment results in economic harm to the employee, an employer is liable for the harassment if it was committed by someone with authority over the employee—by a supervisor, for example. But the Court also said that an employer may defend itself by showing that it had a sexual harassment prevention and grievance policy in effect.[49]

The development of gender discrimination as an important part of the civil rights struggle has coincided with the rise of women's politics as a discrete movement in American politics. As with the struggle for racial equality, the relationship between changes in government policies and political action suggests that changes in government policies to a great degree produce political action. Today the existence of a powerful women's movement derives largely from Title VII of the Civil Rights Act of 1964 and from the Burger Court's application of it to the protection of women. Recognition of women's civil rights in many ways transcends the usual distinctions of American political debate. In the heavily partisan debate over the federal crime bill enacted in 1994, for instance, the section enjoying widest support was the Violence against Women Act, which defined gender-biased violent crimes as a matter of civil rights and created a civil rights remedy for women victims of such crimes. But since the Supreme Court ruled key provisions of the act unconstitutional in 2000, the struggle for women's rights will likely remain part of the political debate

Many of the victories won against gender discrimination have, in recent years, been applied to discrimination against transgender individuals. In 2015, President Obama issued an executive order prohibiting federal contractors from discriminating against workers based on their sexual orientation or gender identity. Two months later, the EEOC filed its first-ever lawsuits to protect transgender workers under Title VII of the Civil Rights Act. In late December, Attorney General Eric Holder announced that, going forward, the Justice Department would

---

47 *Meritor Savings Bank v. Vinson*, 477 U.S. 57 (1986).

48 *Harris v. Forklift Systems*, 510 U.S. 17 (1993).

49 *Burlington Industries v. Ellerth*, 524 U.S. 742 (1998); *Faragher v. City of Boca Raton*, 524 U.S. 775 (1998).

consider discrimination against transgender people as covered by the Civil Rights Act's prohibition of sex discrimination.[50] In 2016, gay rights advocates brought a federal suit against the state of North Carolina over the state's new law prohibiting local governments from adopting special protections for lesbian, gay, bisexual, transgender, and queer (LGBTQ) people. The law was enacted in the wake of a Charlotte, N.C., ordinance allowing transgender people to use public restrooms aligned with their gender identity. The state said this would allow sexual predators to enter women's bathrooms. Gay rights groups called this argument false and simply a pretext for discriminatory action by the state. When the Department of Justice warned North Carolina that the law violated the Civil Rights Act, the state sued the federal government in order to defend its new law. As the legal standoff continued, many companies pulled conventions and other events out of the state, costing North Carolina's economy millions of dollars. In the midst of this battle, in June 2016, the U.S. military dropped its ban against openly transgender people serving in the uniformed services. The Policy Principle section on p. 171 looks at changing policy around the transgender movement.

Latinos

The labels *Latino* and *Hispanic* encompass a wide range of groups with diverse national origins, distinctive cultural identities, and particular experiences. For example, the early political experiences of Mexican Americans were shaped by race and region. In 1898, Mexican Americans gained formal political rights, including the right to vote. In many places, however, and especially in Texas, Mexican Americans were segregated and prevented from voting by such means as the White Primary and the poll tax.[51] In addition, before World War II segregated schools were common in Texas and California along with housing and employment restrictions. In 1947, the League of United Latin American Citizens (LULAC) won a key victory in *Mendez v. Westminster*, which overturned an Orange County, California, policy of school segregation aimed at Mexican Americans.[52] *Mendez*, an important precedent for *Brown v. Board of Education*, is a landmark in the civil rights struggle.

Following World War II, LULAC and the American GI Forum worked to stem discrimination against Mexican Americans. By the late 1950s, the first Mexican American had been elected to Congress; four others followed in the 1960s. In the late 1960s, a new kind of Mexican American political movement was inspired by the black civil rights movement. Mexican American students boycotted high school classes in Los Angeles, Denver, and San Antonio; students

---

50 Claire Zillman, "Barnes & Noble Is Latest Retailer to Face Transgender Discrimination Lawsuit," *Fortune*, May 7, 2015, http://fortune.com/2015/05/07/barnes-noble-transgender-lawsuit (accessed 12/23/15).

51 New Mexico had a different history because not many Anglos settled there initially. (*Anglo* is the term for a non-Hispanic white of European background.) Mexican Americans had considerable power in territorial legislatures between 1865 and 1912. See Lawrence H. Fuchs, *The American Kaleidoscope* (Hanover, NH: University Press of New England, 1990), pp. 239–40.

52 *Mendez v. Westminster*, 161 F.2d. 744 (Ninth Cir. 1947).

Transgender Rights and Policy

The campaign for transgender equality, which grew out of the gay and lesbian rights movement, seeks to end discrimination against transgender persons in employment, housing, health care, and public accommodations. Roughly 700,000 Americans openly identify as transgender or gender nonconforming, meaning that they do not necessarily identify with the sex they were assigned at birth. The United States' history of rights advocacy on the part of African Americans, women, and other groups blazed a trail for transgender people to follow, demonstrating tactics and offering potential allies for their cause. Illustrating the history principle, earlier victories by these groups established legal principles, laws, and political institutions that transgender advocates could use to develop and implement policies for their own purposes.

For example, in recent years transgender advocates lobbied effectively to achieve court decisions and executive orders that applied to their own cause laws originally crafted to protect African Americans and women from workplace discrimination. The federal courts, the Justice Department, and the Equal Employment Opportunity Commission have all agreed that Title VII of the 1964 Civil Rights Act, prohibiting sex discrimination in employment, prohibits discrimination against transgender and gender nonconforming individuals as well. Two executive orders, the first by President Bill Clinton in 1998 and the second by President Obama in 2014, prohibit discrimination in federal employment and in hiring by federal contractors, respectively, based on sexual orientation or gender identity. Thus favorable federal policies emerged because transgender individuals could channel their policy preferences through an already-existing set of institutions.

The effort to end gender identity–based discrimination in public accommodations has taken a somewhat different path. Discrimination by hotels, restaurants, theaters, and so forth was not a focus for the women's movement, and thus federal anti-discrimination law for public accommodations covers race, religion, national

An inclusive restroom that people of any gender identity may use.

origin, and disability but not gender. As a result, the transgender movement did not inherit an existing legal framework or set of institutions through which to pursue its policy goals. While continuing to work for federal legislation in this area, advocates have made strides at other levels of government: as of 2016, seventeen states and a number of localities have expressly prohibited discrimination based on gender identity in public accommodations. In this case, preferences channeled through sympathetic state and local institutions rather than federal ones have produced the movement's desired policy outcomes.

These successes have sometimes proved only temporary, however. In 2015, an antidiscrimination ordinance in Houston was repealed in a referendum. And in 2016, a similar measure in Charlotte, North Carolina, was reversed by the state's legislature, which enacted a bill prohibiting transgender individuals from using bathrooms in schools and other government buildings that correspond to their gender identity. The bill also bans any future legislation by local governments to prevent discrimination on the basis of gender identity. After the federal Department of Justice then warned the state that the law violated the Civil Rights Act, the state and the department filed opposing lawsuits over the issue.

in colleges and universities across California joined in as well. Among their demands were bilingual education, an end to discrimination, and greater cultural recognition. In Crystal City, Texas, which Anglo politicians had dominated despite an overwhelmingly Mexican American population, the newly formed La Raza Unida Party took over the city government.[53]

In recent years, Latino political strategy has developed along two tracks. One is a traditional ethnic-group path of voter registration and voting along ethnic lines, because Hispanic voter registration rates typically lag far behind those for whites and blacks. Helping this strategy is the enormous growth of the Latino population resulting in part from immigration. The second is a legal strategy using civil rights laws designed to ensure fair access to the political system. The Mexican American Legal Defense and Education Fund (MALDEF) has played a key role in designing and pursuing the latter strategy.

Asian Americans

The early Asian experience in the United States was shaped by naturalization laws dating back to 1790, the first of which declared that only white aliens were eligible for citizenship. In the 1850s, Chinese immigrants drawn to California by the gold rush faced hostility and virulent antagonism, which led Congress in 1870 to declare them ineligible for citizenship. In 1882, the first Chinese Exclusion Act suspended the entry of Chinese laborers.

At the time of the Exclusion Act, the Chinese community predominantly comprised single male laborers, with few women and children. The few Chinese children in San Francisco were denied entry to the public schools; only after parents of American-born Chinese children pressed legal action were the children allowed to attend. However, they had to attend a separate Chinese school. In 1898 the Supreme Court confirmed that American-born Chinese children could not be denied citizenship, ruling that anyone born in the United States was entitled to full citizenship.[54] Still, new Chinese immigrants were barred from the United States until 1943; China by then had become a wartime ally, and Congress repealed the Chinese Exclusion Act and permitted Chinese immigrants to become citizens.

Immigration climbed rapidly after the 1965 Immigration and Nationality Services Act, which lifted discriminatory quotas. Nevertheless, limited English proficiency barred many Asian Americans and Latinos from full participation in American life. Two developments in the 1970s, however, established rights for language minorities. In 1974, the Supreme Court ruled in a suit filed on behalf of Chinese students in San Francisco that school districts must provide education for students whose English is limited.[55] It did not mandate bilingual education, but it established a duty

---

53 On the La Raza Unida Party, see Carlos Muñoz Jr. and Mario Barrera, "La Raza Unida Party and the Chicano Student Movement in California," in *Latinos and the Political System,* F. Chris Garcia, ed. (Notre Dame, IN: University of Notre Dame Press, 1988), pp. 213–35.

54 *United States v. Wong Kim Ark,* 169 U.S. 649 (1898).

55 *Lau v. Nichols,* 414 U.S. 563 (1974).

to provide instruction that students could understand. The 1970 amendments to the Voting Rights Act of 1965 permanently outlawed literacy tests as a prerequisite to register to vote and mandated bilingual ballots or oral assistance for those who speak Spanish, Chinese, Japanese, Korean, or Native American languages.

Immigration and Rights

The United States has always struggled to define the rights of immigrants and the notion of citizenship. Waves of immigration have led to legislation restricting who can come to the United States legally. These regulations have included quotas, visas, and other controls on how long people can reside here and what privileges they enjoy while here. Approximately one in eight persons in the United States today was born in another country. Such a high level of immigration has led to efforts to stem the influx. It has also raised questions as to whether immigrants should enjoy the same civil rights as citizens, such as the right to vote and equal access to education, or a narrower set of rights. Advocates for immigrants' rights have supported legislation such as the proposed Dream Act, which would open a path to citizenship for undocumented immigrants, and President Obama's controversial executive order in 2014 grating quasi-legal status to millions of individuals who entered the United States illegally as children or who have children who are American citizens. Opponents of increased immigration disputed the executive order, leading to a Supreme Court case in 2016. In the wake of the death of Justice Antonin Scalia, the eight-member Supreme Court split 4–4, which let stand a lower-court decision striking down Obama's order. The lower-court decision, however, did not establish a binding national precedent, and the administration seemed likely to ignore it. Opponents of increased immigration have also proposed banning Syrian refugees from entering the country and reducing the flow of Latinos into the country. During the 2016 presidential election, Donald Trump promised to build a wall along the U.S.–Mexico border and to put in place a temporary ban on Muslim immigration to the United States.

Asian Americans, Latinos, and other groups have been concerned about the impact of immigration laws on their civil rights. Many Asian American and Latino organizations opposed the Immigration Reform and Control Act of 1986 because it imposes sanctions on employers who hire undocumented workers. Such sanctions, they feared, would lead employers to discriminate against Latinos and Asian Americans. Indeed, a 1990 report by the General Accounting Office found that employer sanctions had created a "widespread pattern of discrimination" against Latinos and others who appear foreign.[56] Organizations such as MALDEF and the Asian Law Caucus monitor and challenge such discrimination, also focusing on the rights of legal and illegal immigrants as anti-immigrant sentiment has grown.

The Supreme Court has ruled that undocumented immigrants are eligible for education and medical care but can be denied other social benefits; legal immigrants, however, are to be treated much the same as citizens. But growing numbers of immigrants and mounting economic insecurity have undermined

---

56 Dick Kirschten, "Not Black and White," *National Journal*, March 2, 1991, p. 497.

these practices. Groups of voters nationwide now strongly support drawing a sharper line between immigrants and citizens. The movement to deny benefits to noncitizens began in California, which experienced sharp economic distress in the early 1990s and has the highest levels of immigration of any state. In 1994, Californians voted to deny illegal immigrants all services except emergency medical care. Supporters hoped to discourage illegal immigration and pressure illegal immigrants already in the country to leave. Opponents contended that denying basic services to illegal immigrants risked creating a subclass whose lack of education and poor health would threaten all Americans. In 1994 and 1997, a federal court affirmed previous rulings that illegal immigrants should be granted public education.

The Constitution begins with the phrase "We the People of the United States"; likewise, the Bill of Rights refers to the rights of *people*, not the rights of citizens. Undocumented immigrants are certainly people, though not citizens. Americans continue to be divided on the question of the rights to which these particular people are entitled.

Americans with Disabilities

The concept of rights for people with disabilities emerged in the 1970s as the civil rights model spread to other groups. The seed was planted in a little-noticed provision of the 1973 Rehabilitation Act that outlawed discrimination against individuals on the basis of disabilities. As in many other cases, the law itself helped spark the movement for rights.[57] Mimicking the NAACP's Legal Defense Fund, the disability movement founded the Disability Rights Education & Defense Fund to press its legal claims. The movement's greatest success has been passage of the Americans with Disabilities Act (ADA) of 1990, which guarantees people with disabilities equal employment rights and access to public businesses. Claims of discrimination in violation of this act are considered by the EEOC. The law's impact has been far-reaching as businesses and public facilities have installed ramps, elevators, and other devices to meet its requirements.[58]

Gay Men and Lesbians

The gay rights movement has become one of the largest civil rights movements in contemporary America. Beginning with street protests in the 1960s, it is now a well-financed and sophisticated lobby. The Human Rights Campaign is the primary

---

57 See the discussion in Robert A. Katzmann, *Institutional Disability: The Saga of Transportation Policy for the Disabled* (Washington, DC: Brookings Institution, 1986).

58 For example, after pressure from the Justice Department, one of the nation's largest rental car companies agreed to make special hand controls available to any customer requesting them. See "Avis Agrees to Equip Cars for Disabled," *Los Angeles Times*, September 2, 1994, p. D1.

national political action committee that raises and distributes campaign money to further the gay rights agenda. It provides campaign financing and volunteers to work for candidates endorsed by the group. The movement has also formed legal rights organizations, including the Lambda Legal Defense and Education Fund.

The 1990s witnessed the first national anti-gay laws and the first Supreme Court declaration protecting the civil rights of gay men and women. In 1993, President Bill Clinton confronted the question of whether gays should be allowed to serve in the military. As a candidate, he had favored lifting the ban on gays in the military; but after much controversy and nearly a year of deliberation, his administration enunciated a compromise: its "Don't Ask, Don't Tell" policy, which allowed gay men and lesbians to serve in the military as long as they did not openly proclaim their sexual orientation or engage in homosexual activity. Two years later, in another setback for the movement, Bill Clinton signed the Defense of Marriage Act (DOMA), which recognized a marriage as the union of one man and one woman for the purposes of the application of federal laws, such as taxes and benefits.

As with other civil rights movements, it was the Supreme Court that took a major step in protecting gay men and lesbians from discrimination. This marked an important departure from its earlier jurisprudence. The first gay rights case that the Court decided, *Bowers v. Hardwick* (1986), ruled against a right to privacy that would protect consensual homosexual activity. After the *Bowers* decision, the gay rights movement sought suitable legal cases to test the constitutionality of discrimination against gay men and lesbians, much as the civil rights movement had done in the late 1940s and 1950s.[59] Among the cases tested were those stemming from local ordinances restricting gay rights (including the right to marry), job discrimination, and family law issues such as adoption and parental rights. In 1996, the Court explicitly extended fundamental civil rights protections to gay men and lesbians by declaring unconstitutional a 1992 amendment to the Colorado state constitution that prohibited local governments from passing ordinances to protect gay rights.[60] The decision's forceful language highlighted the connection between gay rights and civil rights as it declared discrimination against gay people unconstitutional.

Finally, in 2003, the Court overturned *Bowers* and struck down a Texas statute criminalizing certain intimate sexual conduct between consenting partners of the same sex.[61] The 2003 decision extended at least one aspect of civil liberties to sexual minorities: the right to privacy. However, it did not undo the exclusions that deprive lesbians and gay men of full civil rights.

Another important victory occurred in 2010, when Congress finally repealed Don't Ask, Don't Tell. Since in 2008 then-candidate Barack Obama had promised to repeal the act should he be elected, gay rights activists

---

59 *Bowers v. Hardwick,* 478 U.S. 186 (1986).

60 *Romer v. Evans,* 517 U.S. 620 (1996).

61 *Lawrence and Garner v. Texas,* 539 U.S. 558 (2003).

criticized him for not doing so early in his administration. After a lengthy study by the Defense Department of the possible consequences of allowing openly gay men and women to serve, Congress voted to repeal Don't Ask, Don't Tell.

Gay Marriage The focal point for the assertion of gay rights soon turned to the right to marry. Unlike women and blacks who fought for equal treatment in education, employment, and voting, gay rights activists targeted marital rights. In part this was symbolic, as same-sex couples sought social and legal recognition of their relationships equal to those of opposite-sex couples. And in part it was economic, as federal and state laws treat married couples differently for such economic policies as taxes, inheritance, and benefits.

The first changes to the right to marry occurred at the state level. In 2004, the Supreme Judicial Court of Massachusetts ruled that under the state's constitution, same-sex couples were entitled to marry. The state senate then requested the court to rule on whether a civil union statute (avoiding the word *marriage*) would, as it did in Vermont, satisfy the court's ruling; in response, the court ruled negatively, asserting that civil unions are too much like the "separate but equal" doctrine that maintained legalized racial segregation from 1896 to 1954. Between 2004 and 2014, same-sex marriage became legal in 35 states. This process occurred through court order, voter initiative, and legislative enactment. However, as with the women's suffrage movement a century earlier, these changes faced pushback. In many states, voters and state legislatures had supported constitutional amendments banning same-sex marriage. By June 2015, same-sex marriage remained illegal in 13 states.

The discrepancy between some state laws, which recognized same-sex marriage, and the federal law under DOMA, which did not, was ultimately the act's undoing. The nation's laws extend to everyone equally; that is the meaning of equal protection under the Fifth and Fourteenth Amendments. In 2013 the Supreme Court ruled DOMA unconstitutional "as a depravation of liberty of the person protected by the Fifth Amendment."[62] In 2015, the Supreme Court ruled definitively on the issue of same-sex marriage. In the case of *Obergefell v. Hodges* the Court ruled that the right to marry is guaranteed to same-sex couples by the due process clause of the Constitution and the equal protection clause of the Fourteenth Amendment.[63] The decision required states to issue marriage licenses to same-sex couples and to recognize same-sex marriages performed in other jurisdictions. Despite scattered local resistance from county clerks, this decision seemed to put an end to the marriage question, though LGBTQ activists continue to fight for equal rights in other arenas.

---

62 *United States v. Windsor*, 570 U.S. ____ (2013). That same day the Court also cleared the way for legalization of gay marriage in California in *Hollingsworth v. Perry*, 570 U.S. ____ (2013).

63 *Obergefell v. Hodges*, 576 U.S. ____ (2015).

AFFIRMATIVE ACTION

Over the past half century or so, the relatively narrow goal of equalizing opportunity by eliminating discriminatory barriers evolved into the broader goal of **affirmative action**—compensatory action to overcome the consequences of past discrimination and encourage greater diversity. In 1965, President Lyndon Johnson issued executive orders promoting minority employment in the federal civil service and in companies doing business with the national government. But affirmative action did not become a prominent goal until the 1970s.

 affirmative action

A policy or program designed to redress historic injustices committed against specific groups by making special efforts to provide members of these groups with access to educational and employment opportunities

The Supreme Court and the Burden of Proof

As this movement spread, it divided civil rights activists and their supporters. The issue of qualification versus minority preference was addressed in the case of Allan Bakke, a white man with no minority affiliation. He brought suit against the University of California Medical School at Davis on the grounds that in denying him admission the school had discriminated against him on the basis of his race. (That year the school had reserved 16 of 100 available slots for minority applicants.) He argued that his grades and test scores ranked him well above many students who were accepted and that he had been rejected because the others were black or Hispanic and he was white. In 1978, Bakke won his case before the Supreme Court and was admitted to the medical school, but he did not succeed in getting affirmative action declared unconstitutional. The Court rejected the procedures at the University of California because its medical school had used both a quota and a separate admissions system for minorities. The Court agreed with Bakke that racial categorizations are suspect categories that place a severe burden of proof on those using them to show a "compelling public purpose." It went on to say that achieving "a diverse student body" was such a public purpose, but the method of a rigid quota of student slots assigned on the basis of race was incompatible with the equal protection clause. Thus the Court permitted universities (and other schools, training programs, and hiring authorities) to continue to consider minority status but limited the use of quotas to situations in which previous discrimination had been shown and the quotas served more as a guideline for social diversity than as a mathematically defined ratio.[64]

For nearly a decade after *Bakke*, the Court was tentative and permissive about efforts by corporations and governments to experiment with affirmative action programs in employment.[65] But in 1989, it returned to the *Bakke* position, ruling that any "rigid numerical quota" is suspect, and further eased the way for

---

64 *Regents of the University of California v. Bakke,* 438 U.S. 265 (1978).

65 *United Steelworkers of America v. Weber,* 443 U.S. 193 (1979); and *Fullilove v. Klutznick,* 448 U.S. 448 (1980).

employers to prefer white men, holding that the burden of proof of unlawful discrimination should be shifted from the defendant (the employer) to the plaintiff (the person claiming to be the victim of discrimination).[66] This decision virtually overruled the Court's prior holding.[67] That same year, the Court ruled that any affirmative action program already approved by federal courts could be challenged by individuals (usually white men) alleging that the program had discriminated against them.[68]

In 1995, another Supreme Court ruling further weakened affirmative action. This decision stated that race-based policies, such as preferences given by the government to minority contractors, must survive strict scrutiny, placing the burden on the government to show that such affirmative action programs serve a compelling government interest and address identifiable past discrimination.[69]

Other developments in the courts and the states also worked to restrict affirmative action. One of the most significant was *Hopwood v. State of Texas*, in which white students charged that the University of Texas Law School's affirmative action program for admissions discriminated against whites. Critics of affirmative action have asserted that the practice amounts to "reverse discrimination," in which the rights of the majority are curtailed through race-conscious policies.

In 2003, affirmative action was challenged in two cases arising from the University of Michigan. The first suit alleged that by automatically awarding 20 points (out of 150) to African American, Latino, and Native American applicants, the university's undergraduate admissions policy discriminated unconstitutionally against white students with otherwise equal or superior academic qualifications. The Supreme Court agreed, arguing that something tantamount to a quota was involved because undergraduate admissions lacked the necessary "individualized consideration," employing instead a "mechanical one," based too much on the favorable minority points.[70]

The second case broke new ground. Barbara Grutter sued the University of Michigan Law School on the grounds that it had discriminated in a race-conscious way against white applicants with grades and law boards equal or superior to those of minority applicants. A 5–4 vote aligned the majority of the Supreme Court with Justice Lewis Powell's opinion in *Bakke* for the first time. Powell had argued that diversity in education is a compelling state interest and that constitutionally, race could be considered a positive factor in admissions decisions. In *Grutter*, the Court reiterated Powell's holding and, applying strict scrutiny to the law school's policy, found that its admissions process was tailored to the school's compelling state interest in diversity because it gave a "highly

---

66 *Wards Cove Packing Company v. Atonio*, 490 U.S. 642 (1989).

67 *Griggs v. Duke Power Company*, 401 U.S. 424 (1971).

68 *Martin v. Wilks*, 490 U.S. 755 (1989).

69 *Adarand Constructors v. Pena*, 515 U.S. 200 (1995).

70 *Gratz v. Bollinger*, 539 U.S. 244 (2003).

individualized, holistic review of each applicant's file," in which race counted but was not used in a "mechanical way."[71]

Today, the subject of affirmative action has not yet been fully settled. In 2009, the Supreme Court ruled that New Haven, Connecticut, officials had discriminated against white firefighters when they threw out a promotions exam because no nonwhite candidate received a high enough score for promotion.[72] The Court said that employers must show "a strong basis in evidence" under Title VII of the Civil Rights Act and may not rely simply on a test's outcome to show racial discrimination. Most recently, in the *Fisher* case discussed earlier, the Court upheld the principles stated in *Grutter* and *Bakke*, ruling that universities, municipalities, and other agencies can engage affirmative action but that those programs are subject to strict scrutiny by the courts.[73]

CONCLUSION: CIVIL LIBERTIES AND CIVIL RIGHTS—REGULATING COLLECTIVE ACTION

Over the past century, America has strengthened its citizens' liberties and expanded their rights. Both civil liberties and civil rights are solutions to collective action problems. Strengthening the former means imposing more restrictions on some forms of collective action. Expanding the later means allowing more individuals to take part in collective decision making and imposing restrictions on the sorts of decisions that can be reached.

Institutions help solve collective action problems, but no solution is carved in stone. Contending political forces continually seek to change institutional rules to serve their particular purposes. In the United States today, for example, some groups seek additional rights for gay men and lesbians, immigrants, and others who have faced political, social, and economic discrimination. Opponents assert that the expansion of civil rights to include such matters as social and educational benefits for illegal immigrants is inappropriate. The Black Lives Matter movement asserts that current police practices violate the rights and endanger the lives of African Americans. Opponents argue that absent aggressive policing, America's streets would be less safe. The outcomes of such struggles over liberties and rights are never certain. Institutions matter, but exactly how they will matter in the years to come is always subject to change.

The case of civil rights also illustrates the history principle in action. The civil rights movement learned tactics from the women's suffrage movement of the nineteenth century. Court victories later won by African Americans helped inspire the contemporary women's movement and provided legal principles that

71 *Grutter v. Bollinger,* 539 U.S. 306 (2003).

72 *Ricci v. DeStefano,* 129 S.Ct. 2658 (2009).

73 *Fisher v. University of Texas,* 570 U.S. ____ (2013).

the federal courts could later apply to gender discrimination, particularly in the realm of employment. Women took advantage of Title VII of the 1964 Civil Rights Act, written to prohibit racial discrimination in employment to demand enforcement against gender discrimination. In a similar vein, other groups facing discrimination relied on the victories of the civil rights and the women's movements to advance their own causes. It was an easy step from the prohibition of gender discrimination to banning transgender discrimination. The history principle tells us that history creates paths, rules, alliances, and points of view. American history certainly created legal paths that successive groups could follow and led to alliances among groups suffering discrimination. The acronym LGBTQ (lesbian, gay, bisexual, transgender, and queer) stands for one such alliance among groups with a variety of sexual and gender identities.

But what about points of view? Has our history made us more tolerant of the rights of individuals with whom we disagree or whom we view as different from ourselves. Has the history of the past century made America more inclusive or more prone to building walls? The history principle cannot provide us with a conclusive answer to this question.

For Further Reading

Baer, Judith, and Leslie Goldstein. *The Constitutional and Legal Rights of Women.* Los Angeles: Roxbury, 2006.

Chavez, Leo. *The Latino Threat: Constructing Immigrants, Citizens, and the Nation.* 2nd ed. Palo Alto, CA: Stanford University Press, 2013.

Davis, Leonard. *Enabling Acts: The Hidden Story of How the Americans with Disabilities Act Gave the Largest US Minority Its Rights.* Boston: Beacon Press, 2015.

Dawson, Michael. *Not in Our Lifetimes: The Future of Black Politics.* Chicago: University of Chicago Press, 2011.

Garrow, David J. *Bearing the Cross: Martin Luther King, Jr., and the Southern Christian Leadership Conference: A Personal Portrait.* New York: Morrow, 1986.

Gerstmann, Evan. *Same-Sex Marriage and the Constitution.* New York: Cambridge University Press, 2004.

Glendon, Mary Ann. *Rights Talk: The Impoverishment of Political Discourse.* New York: Free Press, 1991.

Jackson, Thomas. *From Civil Rights to Human Rights.* Philadelphia: University of Pennsylvania Press, 2006.

Klarman, Michael. *From Jim Crow to Civil Rights: The Supreme Court and the Struggle for Racial Equality.* New York: Oxford University Press, 2004.

Lewis, Anthony. *Gideon's Trumpet.* New York: Random House, 1964.

O'Brien, David. *Constitutional Law and Politics: Civil Rights and Civil Liberties.* 9th ed. New York: Norton, 2014.

Taylor, Jami K., and Donald P. Haider-Markel, eds. *Transgender Rights and Politics.* Ann Arbor: University of Michigan Press, 2015.

Tushnet, Mark, and Michael Olivas. *Colored Men and Hombres Aqui:* Hernandez v. Texas *and the Emergence of Mexican American Lawyering.* Houston: Arte Publico Press, 2006.

Yoshino, Kenji. *Covering: The Hidden Assault on Our Civil Rights.* New York: Random House, 2007.

6

Congress:
The First Branch

The U.S. Congress is the "first branch" of government under Article I of our Constitution and is also among the world's most important representative bodies. Most of the world's representative bodies only represent—that is, their governmental functions consist mainly of affirming and legitimating the national leadership's decisions. The U.S. Congress is one of the few national representative bodies that actually possesses powers of governance. For example, the U.S. Congress never accedes to the president's budget proposals without making major changes, whereas both the British House of Commons and the Japanese Diet always accept the budget exactly as proposed by the government.

This unique status of the American Congress illustrates the institution principle. In the separation-of-powers regime institutionalized by the U.S. Constitution, the American executive cannot govern alone. The legislature, in particular, actively participates. In Richard Neustadt's memorable phrase, the executive and the legislature in the United States are "separated institutions sharing power."[1] In parliamentary regimes, such as Britain and Japan, in contrast, the executive controls its majority in Parliament. These different institutional arrangements give different powers to different players. In the American case, the institutional arrangements were intended to give Congress a great deal of power relative to the president.

Congress controls a formidable battery of powers that it uses to shape policies and, when necessary, defend its prerogatives against the executive branch. Congress has vast authority over the two most important powers given to any government: the power of force (control over the nation's military forces) and the power over money. Specifically, according to Article I, Section 8, Congress

---

1   Richard E. Neustadt, *Presidential Power: The Politics of Leadership* (New York: Wiley, 1960), p. 42.

can "lay and collect Taxes," deal with indebtedness and bankruptcy, impose duties, borrow and coin money, and generally control the nation's purse strings. It also may "provide for the common Defence and general Welfare," regulate interstate commerce, undertake public works, acquire and control federal lands, promote science and "useful Arts" (pertaining mostly to patents and copyrights), and regulate the militia.

In the realm of foreign policy, Congress has the power to declare war, deal with piracy, regulate foreign commerce, and raise and regulate the armed forces and military installations. These powers over war and the military are supreme—even the president, as commander in chief of the military, must obey the laws and orders of Congress *if* Congress chooses to assert its constitutional authority. (In the past century, Congress has usually ceded this authority to the president.) Further, the Senate has the power to approve treaties (by a two-thirds vote) and the appointment of ambassadors. Capping these powers, Congress is charged to make laws "which shall be necessary and proper for carrying into Execution the foregoing Powers, and all other Powers vested by this Constitution in the Government of the United States, or in any Department or Officer thereof."

If it seems to you that many of these powers, especially those having to do with war and spending, actually belong to the president, that is because modern presidents do exercise great authority in these areas. The modern presidency is a more powerful institution than it was two centuries ago, and much of that power has come from Congress, either because Congress has delegated the

CORE OF THE ANALYSIS

 Members of Congress, like all politicians, are ambitious and thus eager to serve the interests of their constituents to improve their chances of reelection.

 Congress is the most important representative institution of American government. In many ways, Congress works because its system of representation harnesses individual legislators' ambitions and puts them to use.

 The internal organization of Congress solves the collective action problems that arise due to the varied goals of individual legislators.

 Rules matter in the legislative process, and the process through which a bill becomes a law affects which proposed bills succeed and in what form.

power to the president by law or because Congress has allowed, or even urged, presidents to be more active in these areas.[2]

Still, the constitutional powers of Congress remain intact in the document and, as we shall see, congressional power cannot be separated from congressional representation. Without its array of powers, Congress could do little to represent effectively the views and interests of its constituents. At the same time, without its capacity to represent important groups and forces in American society effectively, the powers of Congress would be undermined. All five principles of politics from Chapter 1 are important to our understanding of the institutional structure of the contemporary Congress.

We begin our discussion with a brief consideration of representation. Then we examine the institutional structure of the contemporary Congress and the manner in which congressional powers are organized and employed. Throughout, we point out the connections between these two aspects—the ways in which representation affects congressional operations (especially through "the electoral connection") and the ways in which congressional institutions enhance or diminish representation (especially Congress's division-of-labor and specialization-of-labor committee system).

---

constituency

The district making up the area from which an official is elected

---

delegate

A representative who votes according to the preferences of his or her constituency

---

trustee

A representative who votes based on what he or she thinks is best for his or her constituency

REPRESENTATION

Congress is the most important representative institution in American government. Each member's primary responsibility is to the district, to her **constituency**, not to the congressional leadership, a party, or even Congress itself. Yet the task of representation is not simple. Views about what constitutes fair and effective representation differ, and constituents can make very different demands on their representatives. Members of Congress must consider these diverse views and demands as they represent their districts (Figure 6.1).

Legislators vary in the weight they give to personal priorities and to the desires of their campaign contributors and past supporters. Some see themselves as having been elected to do the bidding of those who sent them to the legislature, and they act as **delegates**. Others see themselves as having been selected by their fellow citizens to do what they think is "right," and they act as **trustees**. Most legislators are a mix of these two types. And all need to survive the next election to pursue their chosen role. Rational agents must focus on survival.

---

2   On the issue of congressional delegation to the executive, two valuable sources are D. Roderick Kiewiet and Mathew D. McCubbins, *The Logic of Delegation: Congressional Parties and the Appropriations Process* (Chicago: University of Chicago Press, 1991), and David Epstein and Sharyn O'Halloran, *Delegating Powers: A Transaction Cost Politics Approach to Policy Making under Separate Powers* (New York: Cambridge University Press, 1999).

Figure 6.1

HOW MEMBERS OF CONGRESS REPRESENT THEIR DISTRICTS

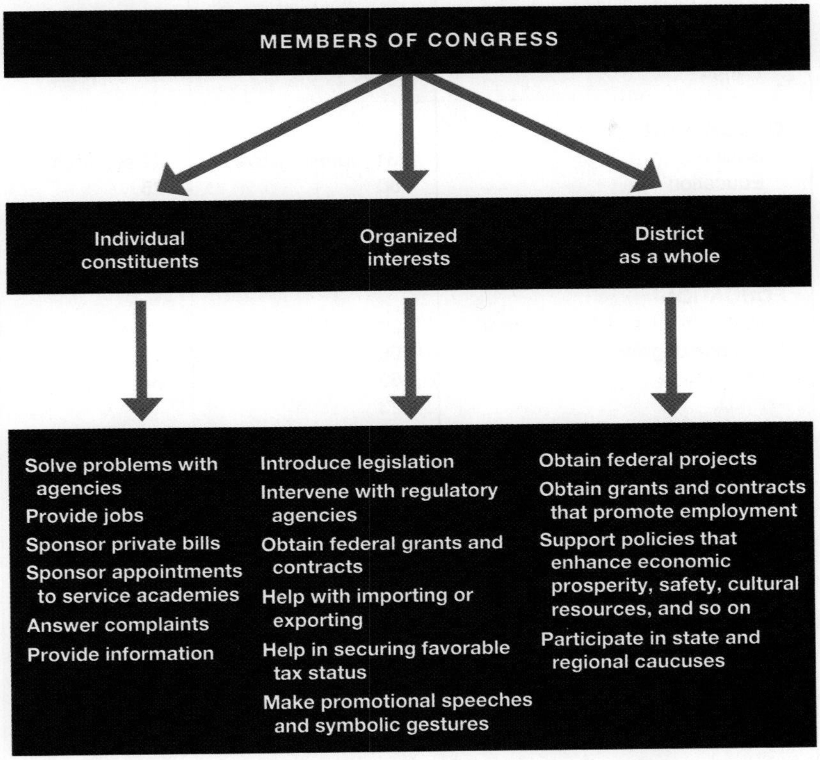

MEMBERS OF CONGRESS

Individual constituents	Organized interests	District as a whole
Solve problems with agencies	Introduce legislation	Obtain federal projects
Provide jobs	Intervene with regulatory agencies	Obtain grants and contracts that promote employment
Sponsor private bills	Obtain federal grants and contracts	Support policies that enhance economic prosperity, safety, cultural resources, and so on
Sponsor appointments to service academies	Help with importing or exporting	
Answer complaints	Help in securing favorable tax status	Participate in state and regional caucuses
Provide information	Make promotional speeches and symbolic gestures	

Legislators not only represent others; they may be representative *of* others as well. The latter point is especially salient in terms of gender and race, where descriptive representation is symbolically significant at the very least. Descriptive characteristics permit women members and representatives drawn from minority groups to serve and draw support from those with whom they share an identity, both inside their formal constituency and in the nation at large. (See Table 6.1 for a summary of demographic characteristics of members of Congress.) Descriptive representation for African American and Hispanic minorities has been facilitated during the process of drawing new district boundaries within states every 10 years after the decennial census, so by creating some districts with these racial or ethnic minorities in the majority—so-called majority-minority districts.

As we discussed in Chapter 1, one person might be trusted to speak for another if the two are formally bound together so that the representative is accountable to those he purports to represent. If representatives can somehow

Table 6.1

DEMOGRAPHICS OF MEMBERS OF THE 114TH CONGRESS

	HOUSE	SENATE
AGE*		
Average	57 years	61 years
Range	30–85 years	37–81 years
OCCUPATION**		
Business	231 representatives	42 senators
Education	80	25
Law	151	51
Public service/politics	271	60
EDUCATION†		
High school is highest degree	20	0
College degree	400	100
Law degree	159	54
Ph.D.	23	1
M.D.	22	3
RELIGION††		
Protestant	251	55
Catholic	138	26
Jewish	19	9
Mormon	9	7
GENDER		
Women	88	20
Men	347	80
RACE/ETHNICITY		
White	340	93
African American	46	2
Hispanic/Latino	34	4
Asian/Pacific Islander	13	1
American Indian	2	0
CONGRESSIONAL SERVICE		
Number serving in first term	61	13
Average length of service	8.8 years (4.4 terms)	9.7 years (1.6 terms)

*Age at time of election (November 4, 2014).

**Most members list more than one occupation.

†Education categories are not exclusive (for example, a representative with a law degree might also be counted as having a college degree).

††Ninety-eight percent of members cite a specific religious affiliation. Other affiliations not listed here include Buddhist, Muslim, Hindu, Greek Orthodox, Unitarian, and Christian Science.

SOURCE: Jennifer E. Manning, "Membership of the 114th Congress: A Profile," Congressional Research Service, March 31, 2015.

be held to account for failing to speak properly for their constituents, then we know they have an incentive to provide good representation even if their own backgrounds, views, and interests differ from those of the people they represent. This is **agency representation**—the sort of representation that occurs when constituents have the power to hire and fire their representatives (who act as their agents). Frequent competitive elections are an important means by which constituents hold their representatives to account and keep them responsive to their own views and preferences. The idea of a representative as agent is similar to the relationship between lawyer and client. True, the relationship between the member of Congress and as many as 700,000 "clients" in the district or that between the senator and possibly millions of clients in the state is very different from that of the lawyer and client. But the criteria of performance are comparable.

We would expect at the very least that each representative will constantly seek to discover the interests of the constituency and will speak for those interests in Congress and other centers of government.[3] We expect this because we believe that members of Congress, like politicians everywhere, are ambitious. For many, this ambition is satisfied by maintaining a hold on their present office and advancing up the rungs of power in that body. Some, however, may be looking ahead to the next level—as when a legislator desires a Senate seat, runs for her state's governorship, or even seeks the presidency.[4] This means that members of Congress may not only be concerned with their present *geographic* constituency. They may want to appeal to a different geographic constituency, for instance, or seek support from a broader gender, ethnic, or racial community. We shall return to this topic shortly in a discussion of elections. But we can say here that in each of these cases the legislator is eager to serve the interests of constituents, either to enhance her prospects of contract renewal at the next election or to improve the chances of moving to another level. In short, the agency conception of representation works in proportion to the ambition of politicians (as "agents") and the capacity of constituents (as "principals") to reward or punish on the basis of the legislator's performance and reputation.[5]

 agency representation

The type of representation according to which representatives are held accountable to their constituents if they fail to represent them properly—that is, constituents have the power to hire and fire their representatives

3   The classic description of interactions between politicians and "the folks back home" is given by Richard F. Fenno Jr., *Home Style: House Members in Their Districts* (Boston: Little, Brown, 1978). Essays elaborating on Fenno are found in Morris P. Fiorina and David W. Rohde, eds., *Home Style and Washington Work* (Ann Arbor: University of Michigan Press, 1989).

4   For more on political careers generally, see John R. Hibbing, "Legislative Careers: Why and How We Should Study Them," *Legislative Studies Quarterly* 24 (1999): 149–71. See also Cherie D. Maestas, Sarah Lutton, L. Sandy Maisel, and Walter J. Stone, "When to Risk It? Institutions, Ambitions, and the Decision to Run for the U.S. House," *American Political Science Review* 100, no. 2 (May 2006): 195–208.

5   Constituents aren't a legislative agent's only principals. He may also be beholden to party leaders and special interests as well as to members and committees in the chamber. See Forrest Maltzman, *Competing Principals* (Ann Arbor: University of Michigan Press, 1997).

House and Senate: Differences in Representation

bicameral legislature

A legislative assembly composed of two chambers, or houses

money bill

A bill concerned solely with taxation or government spending

The framers of the Constitution provided for a **bicameral legislature**—a legislative body consisting of two chambers. As we saw in Chapter 2, the framers intended each chamber to represent a different constituency. Members of the House were to be "close to the people," elected by popular vote every two years. Because they saw the House as the institution closest to the people, the framers gave it a special power. All **money bills**—that is, bills authorizing new taxes or authorizing the government to spend money for any purpose—were required to originate in the House of Representatives. Until the Seventeenth Amendment (1913) provided for direct popular election of senators, members of the Senate were appointed by state legislatures, were to represent the elite members of society, and were to be attuned more to the interests of property than to those of the population. Today members of both the House and the Senate are elected directly by the people. The 435 members of the House are elected from districts apportioned according to population; the 100 members of the Senate are elected by state, with two senators from each. Senators continue to have longer terms in office and usually represent much larger and more diverse constituencies than do their counterparts in the House of Representatives (Table 6.2).

The House and the Senate play different roles in the legislative process. In essence, the Senate is the more deliberative body: it is the forum in which all ideas can receive a thorough public airing. The House is the more centralized and the more organized body: it is better equipped to play a routine role in the governmental process. In part, this difference stems from the different rules governing the two bodies. These rules give House leaders more control over the legislative process and provide for House members to specialize in certain legislative areas. The rules of the much smaller, more freewheeling Senate give its leadership relatively little power and discourage specialization. This is the institution principle at work. The two legislative chambers are organized in very

Table 6.2
DIFFERENCES BETWEEN THE HOUSE AND THE SENATE

	HOUSE	SENATE
Minimum age of member	25 years	30 years
Length of U.S. citizenship	At least 7 years	At least 9 years
Length of term	2 years	6 years (staggered)
Number per state	Depends on population: approx. 1 per 30,000 in 1789; approx. 1 per 700,000 today	2 per state
Constituency	Tends to be local	Is both local and national

different ways, reflecting not only their differences in size but also their differences in electoral rhythm, constituencies, and roles. House members specialize, their specialized activities take place mainly in committees, and deliberations by the full House occur mainly in response to committee proposals. The institution is organized to facilitate expeditious consideration of committee bills. The Senate does many of the same things. But senators are less specialized, partly because of their more heterogeneous constituencies, and therefore address many more areas of policy. Senate proceedings permit wider participation and more open-ended deliberation.

Formal and informal factors also contribute to the differences between the two chambers of Congress. Differences in the length of terms and the requirements for holding office generate differences in how the members of each body develop their constituencies and exercise their powers of office. As a result, members of the House more effectively and more frequently serve as the agents of well-organized local interests with specific legislative agendas—for instance, used-car dealers seeking relief from regulation, labor unions seeking more favorable legislation, or farmers looking for higher subsidies. The small size and relative homogeneity of their constituencies and the frequency with which they must seek reelection make House members more attuned than senators to the legislative needs of local interest groups. This is what the Constitution's framers intended—namely, that the House of Representatives would be "the people's house" and that its members would reflect and represent public opinion in a timely manner.

Senators, in contrast, serve larger and more heterogeneous constituencies. As a result, they are better able than members of the House to serve as the agents of groups and interests organized on a statewide or national basis. Moreover, with longer terms in office, senators have the luxury of considering "new ideas" or seeking to bring together new coalitions of interests, rather than simply serving existing ones. This, too, was the framers' intent—that the Senate should provide a balance to the more responsive House, with its narrower and more homogeneous constituencies. The Senate was said to be the saucer that cools the tea, bringing deliberation, debate, inclusiveness, calm, and caution to policy formulation.

For much of the late twentieth century, the House exhibited more intense partisanship and ideological division than the Senate. Because of their diverse constituencies, senators were inclined to seek compromise positions; but members of the House, with their party's domination in more homogeneous districts, were more willing to stick to their partisan and ideological guns. For instance, the House divided almost exactly along partisan lines on the 1998 vote to impeach President Bill Clinton. In the Senate, by contrast, 10 Republicans joined Democrats to acquit Clinton of obstruction of justice charges, and in a separate vote five Republicans joined Democrats to acquit Clinton of perjury.[6] However, beginning with the presidency of George W. Bush, even the

6   Eric Pianin and Guy Gugliotta, "The Bipartisan Challenge: Senate's Search for Accord Marks Contrast to House," *Washington Post,* January 8, 1999, p. 1.

Senate grew more partisan and polarized—especially on social issues and the war in Iraq.[7] During Barack Obama's presidency, many of the president's initiatives dealing with the economic crisis, health care, gay rights, financial rescues, and most other areas received virtually no Republican support. Initially, Democrats sought compromise but were rebuffed by Republicans who made it their objective to "make Obama a one-term president." Ultimately, neither party was inclined to compromise.

The Electoral System

In light of their role as agents of various constituencies in their states and districts and the importance of elections as a mechanism by which principals (constituents) reward and punish their agents, representatives are significantly influenced by electoral considerations. Three factors related to the American electoral system affect who gets elected and what that person does once in office. The first factor concerns who decides to run for office and which candidates have an edge over others. The second factor is the advantage incumbents have in winning reelection. Finally, the way congressional district lines are drawn can greatly affect the outcome of an election. Let us examine the impact of these considerations on who serves in Congress.

Running for Office. Voters' choices are restricted from the start by who decides to run for office. In the past, local party officials decided who would run for a particular elected office: they might nominate someone who had a record of service to the party, who was owed a favor, or whose turn had come up.[8] Today few party organizations have the power to slate candidates in that way. Instead, the decision to run for Congress is a more personal choice. One

---

7   On the confirmation of Supreme Court nominations, however, even in an atmosphere of elevated partisanship, moderates from both parties in the Senate have prevented partisan extremism from dominating. Chief Justice John Roberts, Justice Samuel Alito, Justice Sonia Sotomayor, and Justice Elena Kagan were all approved with at least some support from both parties. However, lower-court judicial nominees were blocked frequently during the Bush administration and the Obama administration, leaving many vacant seats on the federal bench.

8   In the nineteenth century, it was often considered an *obligation*, not an honor, to serve in Congress. The real political action was back home in the state capital or a big city, not in Washington. So the practice of "rotation" was devised, according to which a promising local politician would do a tour of duty in Washington before being slated for an important local office. This is not to say that electoral incentives—the so-called electoral connection, in which a legislator's behavior was motivated by the desire to retain the seat for himself or his party—was absent in nineteenth-century America. See, for example, Jamie L. Carson and Erik J. Engstrom, "Assessing the Electoral Connection Evidence from the Early United States," *American Journal of Political Science* 49 (2005): 746–57. See also William T. Bianco, David B. Spence, and John D. Wilkerson, "The Electoral Connection in the Early Congress: The Case of the Compensation Act of 1816," *American Journal of Political Science* 40 (1996): 145–71.

of the most important factors is a person's ambition.[9] A potential candidate may also assess whether he can attract enough money to mount a credible campaign through connections to other politicians, interest groups, and the national party organization. Wealthy individuals may finance their own races, although the spiraling cost of campaigns is making this increasingly a relic of the past. One of the biggest spenders in the 2012 election was Elizabeth Warren, who, though not wealthy herself, raised $50 million in her successful campaign for a Senate seat representing Massachusetts.

Features distinctive to each congressional district also affect the field of candidates. Among them is the range of other political opportunities that may lure potential candidates away. In addition, the way the congressional district overlaps state legislative boundaries may affect a candidate's decision to run. A state-level representative or senator who is considering a run for the U.S. Congress is more likely to assess her prospects favorably if the state district largely coincides with the congressional district (because the voters will already know her). For similar reasons, U.S. representatives from small states, whose congressional districts cover a large portion of the state, are far more likely to run for statewide office than are members of Congress from large states. For example, John Thune was elected as the lone representative from South Dakota in 1996. His constituency thus completely overlapped those of Senators Tim Johnson and Tom Daschle. For any candidate, decisions about running must be made early because once money has been committed to declared candidates, it is harder for new candidates to break into a race. Thus the outcome of a November election is partially determined many months earlier, when decisions to run are finalized.[10]

Incumbency. Incumbency plays a key role in the American electoral system and in the kind of representation citizens get in Washington. Once in office, members of Congress are typically eager to remain in office and make politics a career. Over the twentieth century, Congress developed into a professional legislature, one whose members serve full time for multiple terms (Figure 6.2).[11] And incumbent legislators have created an array of tools that stack the deck in favor of their reelection—the rationality principle at work once again. Through effective use of this arsenal of weapons, an incumbent establishes a reputation for competence, imagination, and responsiveness, which are the attributes most principals look for in an agent.

 incumbency

Holding the political office for which one is running

9 See Linda L. Fowler and Robert D. McClure, *Political Ambition: Who Decides to Run for Congress* (New Haven, CT: Yale University Press, 1989); Alan Ehrenhalt, *The United States of Ambition: Politicians, Power, and the Pursuit of Office* (New York: Times Books, 1991); and Jennifer Lawless, *Becoming a Candidate: Political Ambition and the Decision to Run for Office* (New York: Cambridge University Press, 2012).

10 On the thesis of "strategic candidacy," see Gary C. Jacobson, *The Politics of Congressional Elections,* 8th ed. (New York: Pearson Longman, 2012).

11 Nelson W. Polsby, "The Institutionalization of the U.S. House of Representatives," *American Political Science Review* 62, no. 1 (March 1968): 144-68.

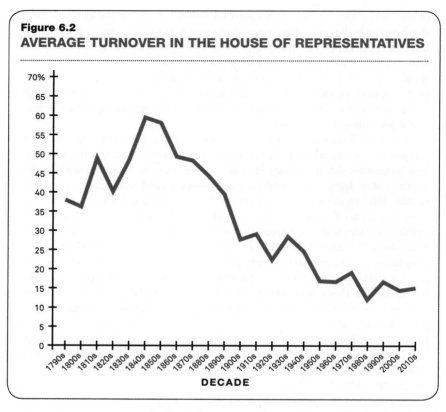

Figure 6.2
AVERAGE TURNOVER IN THE HOUSE OF REPRESENTATIVES

NOTE: Average turnover is the percent of new members in the House averaged over five House elections in a decade. In the period 1790–2012, the mean turnover was 30.7.
SOURCE: Based on John Swain, Stephen A. Borelli, Brian C. Reed, and Sean F. Evans, "A New Look at Turnover in the U.S. House of Representatives, 1789–1998," *American Politics Quarterly* 28 (2000): 435–57, plus author updates.

casework

An effort by members of Congress to gain the trust and support of constituents by providing personal services; one important type of casework consists of helping constituents obtain favorable treatment from the federal bureaucracy

Perhaps the most important advantage of incumbency is the opportunity to serve on legislative committees. Doing so enables legislators to burnish their policy credentials, develop expertise, and help constituents, either by affecting the legislative agenda or by interceding with the bureaucracy. While working on committees, incumbents establish a track record of accomplishments—an especially strategic advantage when a legislator's committees address issues of greatest concern to his constituents. (And, party leaders in Congress are adept at matching their members to the "right" committees—another example of the rationality principle at work.) Finally, continuous service on a committee positions a legislator for committee leadership posts.

The opportunity to help constituents, and thus a boost toward gaining support in the district, goes beyond the particular committees in which a member serves. A considerable amount of his own and of his staff's time is devoted to constituency service (termed **casework**). Not merely a matter of writing and mailing letters, this service includes talking to constituents, providing them with minor services, introducing special bills for them, and attempting to influence decisions by agencies and regulatory commissions on their behalf.

One significant way in which incumbent members of Congress serve as the agents of their constituencies on a larger scale is through **patronage**. Patronage refers to a variety of forms of direct services and benefits that members provide for their districts. One of the most important forms of patronage is **pork-barrel legislation**, through which representatives seek to capture federal projects and federal funds for their home districts (or states in the case of senators) and thus "bring home the bacon."

A common form of pork barreling is the earmark, the practice through which members of Congress insert language into otherwise pork-free bills that provides specific authority or spending for a project that benefits their own constituents.[12] For example, among the more outrageous earmarks in a 2005 transportation bill was a bridge in Alaska that would have cost more than $10 million and would have connected the mainland to an uninhabited island (the so-called bridge to nowhere). This earmark proved so embarrassing to the Republicans once they began receiving adverse publicity that they rescinded the appropriation. Congressional rules now require that any earmark be explicitly associated with the requesting member who must list it on his official website and certify that neither he nor family members benefit financially from it.

Pork-barrel activities by incumbent legislators bring a number of our principles from Chapter 1 into play. Incumbent legislators engage in the practice because it furthers their electoral objectives (the rationality principle). They succeed to the degree that they are able to join with fellow legislators in exchanging support for one another's projects (the collective action principle). These efforts are facilitated by institutional procedures: amendments to appropriations bills, omnibus legislation, and opportunities to insert special provisions into bills (the institution principle). And they influence the mix and location of spending by the federal government (the policy principle). From time to time, as with the "bridge to nowhere," the practice becomes so egregious that Congress establishes procedures to restrict the activity, thereby constraining legislators' future actions (the history principle).

Finally, all of these incumbent benefits are publicized through another incumbency advantage—the franking privilege. Under a law enacted by the 1st Congress in 1789, members of Congress may send mail to their constituents free of charge to keep them informed of governmental business and public affairs. Under current law, members receive an average of about $100,000 in free postage for mailings to their constituents. Although there are restrictions on how members use these funds, especially around election time, the franking

 patronage

The opportunities available to legislators to provide direct services and benefits to their constituents, especially making partisan appointments to offices and conferring grants, licenses, or special favors to supporters

 pork-barrel legislation

Legislative appropriations that legislators use to provide government funds for projects benefitting their home district or state

---

12 For a study of academic earmarking, see James D. Savage, *Funding Science in America: Congress, Universities, and the Politics of the Academic Pork Barrel* (New York: Cambridge University Press, 1999). For a general study of pork-barrel activity, see the excellent book by Diana Evans, *Greasing the Wheels: Using Pork Barrel Projects to Build Majority Coalitions in Congress* (New York: Cambridge University Press, 2004). For a more recent assessment of earmarking, see Scott A. Frisch and Sean Q Kelly, *Cheese Factories on the Moon: Why Earmarks Are Good for American Democracy* (Boulder, CO: Paradigm Publishers, 2010).

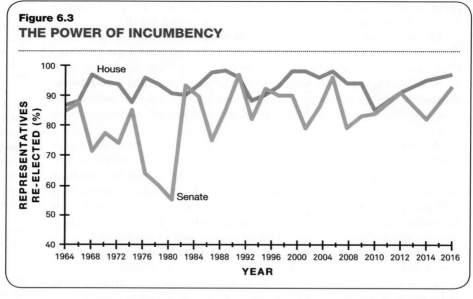

Figure 6.3
THE POWER OF INCUMBENCY

SOURCES: Center for Responsive Politics, www.opensecrets.org/bigpicture/reelect.php?cycle52010 (accessed 3/18/16), and author updates.

privilege helps incumbents publicize their activities and make themselves visible to voters.

The incumbency advantage is evident in the high rates of reelection: over 90 percent for House members and nearly 90 percent for members of the Senate in recent years (Figure 6.3).[13] In 2012, 91 percent of those incumbents running for reelection in each chamber won. In the 2014 House elections, of the 394 incumbents who ran, just 5 lost in a primary and 13 lost in the general election, for a reelection rate of 95 percent. The Senate witnessed more change. Of the 36 contested seats, 12 involved retiring senators (open seats), 19 saw the incumbent reelected, and 5 incumbents were defeated, for a 79% reelection rate.

An additional incumbency advantage is in fund-raising: incumbents are in a position to raise campaign funds throughout their term, often in such quantities as to overwhelm prospective challengers. Members of Congress almost always are able to outspend their challengers (Figure 6.4).[14] Over the past quarter

---

13 The classic study of the incumbency advantage is, Robert S. Erikson, "The Advantage of Incumbency in Congressional Elections," *Polity* 3 (1971): 395–405. A subsequent effort to sort out the causes of the incumbency advantage is Steven D. Levitt and Catherine D. Wolfram, "Decomposing the Sources of Incumbency Advantage in the US House," *Legislative Studies Quarterly* 22 (1997): 45–60.

14 Stephen Ansolabehere and James Snyder, "Campaign War Chests and Congressional Elections," *Business and Politics* 2 (2000): 9–34. Also see Alexander Fouirnaies and Andrew B. Hall, "The Financial Incumbency Advantage: Causes and Consequences," *Journal of Politics* 76 (2014): 711–24.

Figure 6.4
HOUSE AND SENATE CAMPAIGN EXPENDITURES

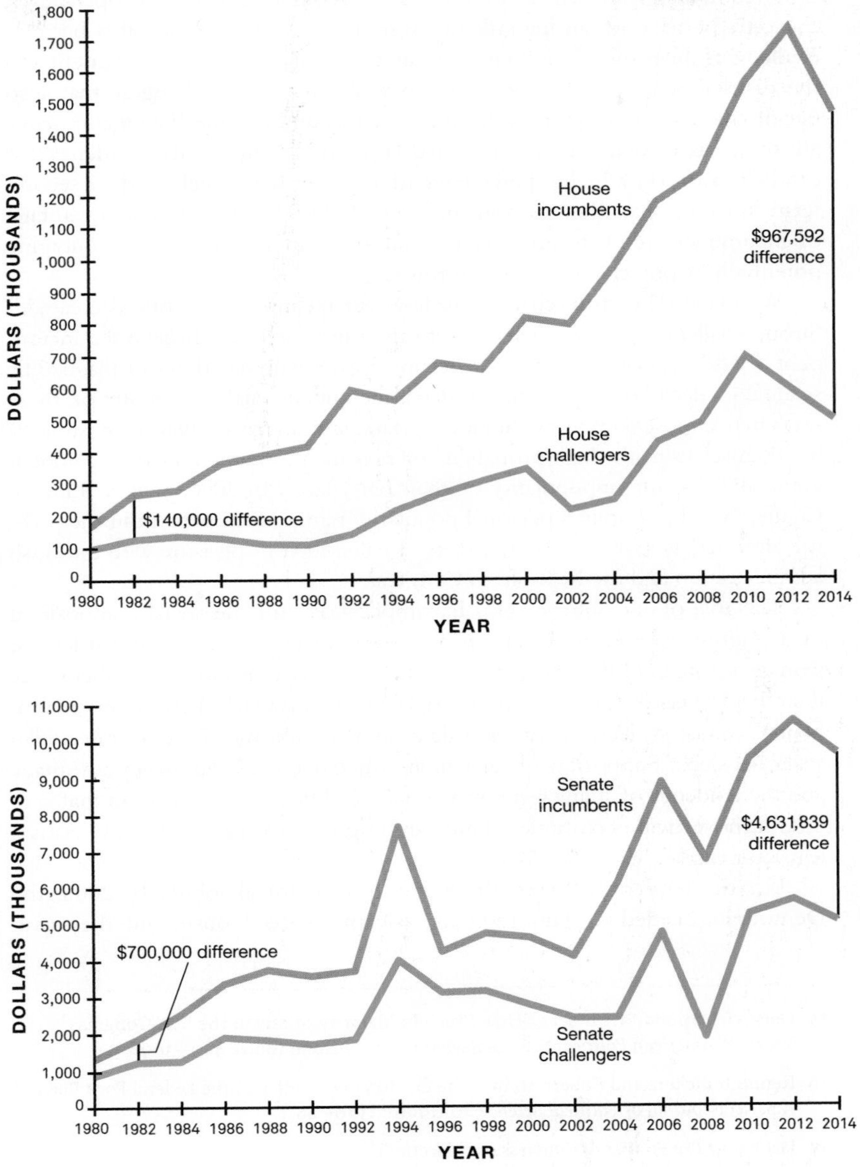

House chart:
Y-axis: DOLLARS (THOUSANDS), from 0 to 1,800
X-axis: YEAR, 1980 to 2014

House incumbents
House challengers
$140,000 difference
$967,592 difference

Senate chart:
Y-axis: DOLLARS (THOUSANDS), from 0 to 11,000
X-axis: YEAR, 1980 to 2014

Senate incumbents
Senate challengers
$700,000 difference
$4,631,839 difference

*Costs in nominal dollars.
SOURCES: Norman J. Ornstein, Thomas E. Mann, and Michael J. Malbin, *Vital Statistics on Congress, 2001–2002* (Washington, DC: American Enterprise Institute, 2002), pp. 87, 93; and Campaign Finance Institute, www.cfinst.org (accessed 6/9/15).

century, and despite campaign finance regulations that aimed to level the playing field, the gap between incumbent and challenger spending has grown. Members of the majority party in the House and Senate are particularly attractive to donors who want access to those in power.[15]

Incumbency can help a candidate by discouraging potential opponents, not only because of an incumbent's war-chest advantages but also because challengers fear the incumbent has simply brought too many benefits to the district or is too well liked or too well known.[16] Challengers may also decide that a district's partisan leanings are too unfavorable. The incumbency advantage is evident in what is called sophomore surge—the tendency for candidates to win a higher percentage of the vote when seeking their second term in office than they won in their initial election victory. The advantage of incumbency tends to preserve the status quo in Congress by discouraging potentially strong challengers from running.

When faced by strong challengers, however, incumbents are often defeated.[17] Strong challengers throw their hat into the ring when they believe the incumbent is weak, out of touch, too preoccupied with national affairs, or plagued by scandal or declining capabilities. Indeed, incumbents afflicted in any of these ways may choose to retire voluntarily (strategic retirement) instead of subjecting themselves to the high probability of defeat. Another source of incumbent vulnerability is the unpopularity of their party label. In 2006, Senator Lincoln Chafee (R-R.I.), despite a personal popularity rating of 62 percent in the polls, was defeated as many Rhode Islanders signaled their displeasure with the Bush administration and the Republican Congress.

The role of incumbency also has implications for the social composition of Congress. For example, the incumbency advantage makes it harder for women to increase their numbers in Congress because most incumbents are men. Female candidates who run for open seats (for which there are no incumbents) are just as likely to win as male candidates, but they have to wait until a seat opens up.[18] Supporters of term limits argue that the incumbency advantage and the tendency of many legislators to view politics as a career mean that very little turnover will occur unless limits are imposed on the number of terms a legislator can serve.

But the tendency toward the status quo is not absolute. In 2006, the Democrats needed to gain 15 seats to capture the House, and they won

---

15 Gary W. Cox and Eric Magar, "How Much Is Majority Status in the U.S. Congress Worth?" *American Political Science Review* 93, no. 2 (June 1999): 299–309.

16 Kenneth Bickers and Robert Stein, "The Electoral Dynamics of the Federal Pork Barrel," *American Journal of Political Science* 40 (1996): 1300–26.

17 Jacobson, *The Politics of Congressional Elections.*

18 See Barbara C. Burrell, *A Woman's Place Is in the House: Campaigning for Congress in the Feminist Era* (Ann Arbor: University of Michigan Press, 1994). An excellent recent study is Sarah F. Anzia and Christopher R. Berry, "The Jackie (and Jill) Robinson Effect: Why Do Congresswomen Outperform Congressmen?" *American Journal of Political Science* 95 (2011): 478–93.

double that number; in the Senate, they captured the six Republican seats they needed to win control of that chamber. The election in 2010 saw a reversal as Republicans easily exceeded the gains required to capture the House and barely fell short of capturing the Senate; in 2014 they finally captured the Senate and in 2016 retained their majority in both chambers. As these elections suggest, the advantages of incumbency, always considerable, are not necessarily decisive.

Congressional Districts. The final factor that affects who wins a seat in Congress is the way congressional districts are drawn. Every 10 years, state legislatures must redraw congressional districts to reflect population changes. In 1929, Congress enacted a law fixing the total number of congressional seats at 435. As a result, when states with fast-growing populations gain districts, they do so at the expense of states with slower population growth. In recent decades, this has meant that the nation's growth areas in the South and West have gained congressional seats at the expense of the Northeast and the Midwest (Figure 6.5).

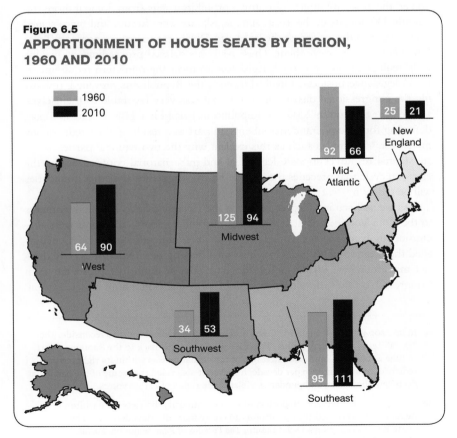

Figure 6.5
APPORTIONMENT OF HOUSE SEATS BY REGION, 1960 AND 2010

1960
2010

West: 64 | 90
Midwest: 125 | 94
Mid-Atlantic: 92 | 66
New England: 25 | 21
Southwest: 34 | 53
Southeast: 95 | 111

SOURCE: U.S. Census Bureau, www.census.gov/prod/cen2010/briefs/c2010br-08.pdf (accessed 2/16/13).

Redrawing congressional districts is a highly political process: in most states, districts are shaped to create an advantage for the majority party in the state legislature, which controls the redistricting process (subject to a possible veto by the governor, who may be of a different party). In this complex process, those charged with drawing districts use sophisticated computer technologies to generate the most favorable district boundaries. Redistricting can create open seats and may pit incumbents of the same party against each other, ensuring that one of them will lose. Redistricting can also give an advantage to one party by clustering voters with some ideological or sociological characteristics in a single district or by separating those voters into two or more districts.

gerrymandering ➡

The apportionment of voters in districts in such a way as to give unfair advantage to one political party

That **gerrymandering** can have a major effect on the outcome of congressional elections. It took an especially dramatic form after the 2000 census. The state of Texas, as elsewhere, drew new congressional districts based on the census, and the 2002 congressional election was the first one under the new redistricting. In 2003, the Texas legislature, controlled by the Republicans, set to work drawing up a *new* set of congressional districts. Ordinarily this exercise is performed once per decade, after the constitutionally required census. But, argued the Texas Republicans, nothing prohibits a state from doing it more frequently. Democrats in the Texas state legislature were furious and twice staged walkouts, even fleeing across the border to Oklahoma to avoid a posse of Texas Rangers sent to retrieve them. These walkouts delayed proceedings by making it difficult to assemble enough legislators to meet the minimum requirements to do legislative business. Finally, however, the Republicans prevailed, redrawing the congressional districts in a way that was very favorable to themselves. In the next election in 2004, the Republicans gained five House seats in Texas, defeating four Democratic incumbents, in part as a result of their redistricting maneuver.[19] Examples such as this explain why the two national parties invest substantial resources in state legislative and gubernatorial contests during the electoral cycle that precedes the year in which congressional district boundaries will be redrawn.

As we will see in Chapter 11, since the passage of the 1982 amendments to the 1965 Voting Rights Act, race has become a major—and controversial—consideration in drawing voting districts. These amendments, which encouraged the creation of districts in which members of racial minorities have decisive majorities, have greatly increased the number of minority representatives in Congress.[20] Yet these developments raise thorny questions about representation.

---

19 In late 2004, the U.S. Supreme Court ordered a lower federal court to reconsider the "extra" Texas redistricting plan. This case worked its way back to the Supreme Court. In June 2006, the Court ruled that the Texas legislature was within its rights to redistrict more than once per decade; however, it also ruled that some of the particular decisions about district boundaries violated the rights of Latino voters.

20 Among the most fervent supporters of the new minority districts were white Republicans, who used the opportunity to create more districts dominated by white Republican voters. David Lublin, *The Paradox of Representation: Racial Gerrymandering and Minority Interests in Congress* (Princeton, NJ: Princeton University Press, 1997).

Some analysts argue that although the system may grant minorities greater descriptive representation (also called sociological representation), it has made it more difficult for them to win substantive policy goals.[21] There is no doubt that descriptive representation has grown. After the 2014 and 2016 elections, the House is more female and minority than ever in its history.[22] But, especially regarding minorities, the creation of a growing number of minority-majority districts has meant that minority voter proportions in other districts have become diluted, opening up the possibility that representatives from these districts will be less responsive to minority policy concerns.

PROBLEMS OF LEGISLATIVE ORGANIZATION

The U.S. Congress is not only a representative assembly. It is also a legislative body. For Americans, representation and legislation go hand in hand. Yet governing is a challenge. It is extraordinarily difficult for a large, representative assembly to formulate, enact, and implement laws. Just the internal complexities of conducting business within Congress—the legislative process—are daunting. In addition, many individuals and institutions have the capacity to influence the legislative process. Because successful legislation requires the confluence of so many factors, it is little wonder that most of the thousands of bills considered by Congress each year are defeated long before they reach the president.

The supporters of legislative proposals often feel that the formal rules of the congressional process are designed to prevent their own deserving proposals from ever seeing the light of day. But these rules allow Congress to play an important role in lawmaking. If it wants to be more than a rubber stamp for the executive branch, which many other representative assemblies around the world are limited to, a national legislature such as Congress must develop a division of labor, set an agenda, maintain order through rules and procedures, and place limits on discussion. If it wants to accomplish these tasks in a representative setting made up of a diversity of political preferences, then it must find the ways and means to facilitate cooperation and to make compromises. We will first take up the general issues that face any legislature or decision-making group possessing diverse preferences: the problems of cooperation, coalitions, and compromises.

---

21 Lani Guinier, *The Tyranny of the Majority: Fundamental Fairness in Representative Democracy* (New York: Free Press, 1995). See also David Epstein and Sharyn O'Halloran, "Measuring the Electoral and Policy Impact of Majority-Minority Voting Districts," *American Journal of Political Science* 42 (1999): 367–95.

22 The Democratic Caucus in 2013 was 53 percent female and minority, whereas the Republican Conference was 90 percent white male. However, as of 2015, the House now has several Republican women of color.

Cooperation in Congress

A number of factors make cooperation difficult in Congress. A popularly elected legislative assembly—the Boston City Council, the Kansas state legislature, the U.S. Congress, the French National Assembly, or the European Parliament—consists of politicians who harbor a variety of political objectives. Because they got where they are by winning an election and many hope to stay where they are or possibly advance their political careers, these politicians are intimately aware of whom they must please to do so:

- Because campaigns are expensive propositions, most politicians are eager to please those who can supply resources for the next campaign: campaign donors, PACs, important endorsers, party officials, volunteer activists.

- The most recent campaign—one that the politicians won—provides information about what categories of voters supported them and may support them again if their performance in office is adequate.

- Many politicians not only aim to please others (campaign contributors and voters) but also have an agenda of their own. Whether for private gain or public good, politicians come to the legislature with policy goals of personal importance. They need to please themselves.

Congress consists of a heterogeneous group of legislators who seek to pursue public policies that are many and varied. They may be considered from two perspectives. First, owing to their different constituencies, legislators will give priority to different realms of public policy. A Cape Cod congressman will be interested in shipping, fishing, coastal preservation, harbor development, tourism, and shipbuilding. An inner-city Philadelphia congresswoman may focus instead on welfare reform, civil rights policy, aid to inner-city school systems, and job-retraining programs. And Montana's sole member of Congress is probably most interested in ranching, agriculture, mining, and public land use. Evidently, Congress encompasses a mélange of legislative priorities.

Second, members' opinions on any given issue are diverse. Although interest in environmental protection, for example, ranges from high among those who count many Sierra Club members among their constituents to low among those who have other fish to fry, once environmental protection is on the agenda there is a broad range of preferences for specific initiatives. Some want pollution discharges to be monitored and regulated by a watchdog agency; others prefer more decentralized and less intrusive means, such as marketable pollution permits—so-called cap-and-trade policies. Still others think the entire issue is overblown and that the country would be best served by leaving well enough alone.

Diversity in priorities and preferences means that the view of no group of legislators predominates. Legislative consensus must be built: support must be assembled, deals consummated, and promises and threats used. In short, legislators intent on achieving their objectives must cooperate, coalesce, and compromise. And these activities are facilitated by rules and procedures. This system leads to the division and specialization of legislative work, the regularization of procedures, and the creation of agenda power. All of these organizational features of Congress arise as part of a governance structure to promote cooperation and coalition building—activities that yield compromise policies.

Underlying Problems and Challenges

Before we can understand why Congress selects particular ways to institutionalize its practices, we need a finer appreciation of other underlying problems with which legislators must grapple. Then we can consider how the U.S. Congress deals with these problems.

Matching Influence and Interest. Legislatures are highly egalitarian institutions. Each legislator has one vote on any issue coming before the body. Whereas a consumer has a cash budget that she may allocate in any way she wishes to categories of consumer goods, a legislator is not given a vote budget in quite the same sense. Instead, his budget of votes is "dedicated"—one vote for each motion before the assembly. He cannot aggregate the votes in his possession and cast all or some large fraction of them for a motion on a subject near and dear to his heart (or the hearts of his constituents). This is a source of frustration because the premise of instrumental behavior dictates that legislators would, if they could, concentrate whatever resources they command on those subjects of highest priority to them. The egalitarian arrangement thus forces legislators to make deals with one another—"I'll support you on this motion if you support me on a future motion."

Information. Legislators do not vote for outcomes directly but, rather, for instruments (or policies) whose effects produce outcomes. Thus legislators must know the connection between the instruments they vote for and the effects they desire. In short, they must have information and knowledge about how the world works.

Few legislators—indeed, few people in general—know how the world works in very many policy domains except in the most superficial of ways. Nearly everyone in the legislature would benefit from the production of valuable information—at the very least, information that would enable them to eliminate ineffectual policy instruments. Producing such information, however, is not a trivial matter. Simply to digest the knowledge that is being produced outside the legislature by academics, scientists, journalists, and interest groups is a taxing task. Clearly, institutional arrangements that provide incentives to some legislators to produce, evaluate, and disseminate this knowledge for others will permit a more effective use of public resources. Because legislatures are in competition with other branches of government—particularly the executive—legislators need to meet certain informational requirements just to keep up with the competition.

Compliance. The legislature is not the only game in town. The promulgation of public policies is a joint undertaking in which judges, executives, bureaucrats, and others participate alongside legislators. If the legislature has no means to monitor what happens after a bill becomes law, then it risks seeing public policies implemented in ways other than those it intended. But it is just not practical for all 435 representatives and all 100 senators to scrutinize the agencies on Pennsylvania Avenue to ensure appropriate implementation by the executive bureaucracy. Like the production and dissemination of reliable information at the policy-formulation stage, the need for oversight of the executive bureaucracy is but an extension of the cooperation that produced legislation in the first place. It, too, must be institutionalized.

We have suggested in this discussion about legislative institutions and practices that the diversity of beliefs and preferences in Congress requires cooperation, coalitions, and compromise to achieve successful policy goals. In addition, there is a mismatch of influence and interest (owing to one person, one vote), information about the effectiveness of alternative policies is in short supply, and the legislature must worry about how the other branches of government treat its product—our public laws. Solving or mitigating these problems requires devising sound institutional arrangements. This is where the rationality principle and the institution principle join forces.

THE ORGANIZATION OF CONGRESS

We now examine the basic building blocks of congressional organization: political parties, the committee system, congressional staff, the caucuses, and the parliamentary rules of the House and Senate. Each of these factors plays a key role in the organization of Congress and in the process through which Congress formulates and enacts laws. We also look at the powers Congress has in addition to lawmaking and explore the future role of Congress in relation to the powers of the executive.

Party Leadership and Organization in the House and the Senate

One significant aspect of legislative life is not even part of the *official* organization: political parties. The legislative parties—primarily Democratic and Republican in modern times, but numerous others over the course of American history—are organizations that foster cooperation, coalitions, and compromise. They are the vehicles of collective action, both for legislators sharing common policy objectives inside the legislature and for the same legislators as candidates in periodic election contests back home.[23] In short, political parties in Congress are the fundamental building blocks from which policy coalitions are fashioned to pass legislation and monitor its implementation, thereby providing a track record on which members build electoral support.

Every two years at the start of a new Congress, the parties in each chamber choose leaders. Consider the House first. There the members gather into partisan groups—called **party caucus** by the Democrats and the **party conference** by the Republicans—to elect leaders and decide other matters of party policy. The elected leader of the majority party is later proposed to the whole House and is automatically elected to the position of **Speaker of the House**, with voting along straight party lines. The House majority caucus (or conference) also elects a **majority leader**. The minority party goes through the same process and selects the **minority leader**. Both parties also elect "whips," who line up party members on important votes and relay voting intentions to the party leaders.

At one time, party leaders strictly controlled committee assignments, using them to enforce party discipline. Today representatives often expect to receive the assignments they want and resent leadership efforts to control assignments. The leadership's best opportunities to use committee assignments as rewards and punishments come when more than one member seeks a seat on a committee.

Generally representatives seek assignments that will allow them to influence decisions of special importance to their districts. Representatives from farm districts, for example, may request seats on the Agriculture Committee.[24] This is one method by which to overcome the egalitarian allocation of power in the legislature: even though each legislator has just one vote on each issue in the full chamber, by serving on the right committees she can acquire extra influence in areas important to her constituents. Seats on powerful committees such as Ways and Means, which is responsible for tax legislation, and Energy and Commerce, responsible for health, energy, and regulatory policy, are especially popular.

In the Senate, the president is pro tempore, a position designated in the Constitution, and exercises mainly ceremonial leadership. Usually the majority party designates the member with the greatest seniority to serve in this capacity.

party caucus, or party conference

A normally closed meeting of a political or legislative group to select candidates or leaders, plan strategy, or make decisions regarding legislative matters

Speaker of the House

The chief presiding officer of the House of Representatives. The Speaker is elected at the beginning of every Congress on a straight party vote. He or she is the most important party and House leader

majority leader

The elected leader of the party holding a majority of the seats in the House of Representatives or the Senate. In the House, the majority leader is subordinate in the party hierarchy to the Speaker

minority leader

The elected leader of the party holding less than a majority of the seats in the House or Senate

---

23 For a historically grounded analysis of the development of political parties as well as a treatment of their general contemporary significance, see John H. Aldrich, *Why Parties? The Origin and Transformation of Political Parties in America* (Chicago: University of Chicago Press, 1995). For an analysis of the parties in the legislative process, see Gary W. Cox and Mathew D. McCubbins, *Legislative Leviathan: Party Government in the House*, 2nd ed. (Berkeley: University of California Press, 2006). See also their *Setting the Agenda: Responsible Party Government in the U.S. House of Representatives* (New York: Cambridge University Press, 2005). A provocative essay questioning the role of parties is Keith Krehbiel, "Where's the Party?" *British Journal of Political Science* 23 (1993): 235–66.

24 For an extensive discussion of the committee-assignment process in the U.S. House, see Kenneth A. Shepsle, *The Giant Jigsaw Puzzle: Democratic Committee Assignments in the Modern House* (Chicago: University of Chicago Press, 1978), and Scott A. Frisch and Sean Q Kelly, *Committee Assignment Politics in the U.S. House of Representatives* (Norman: University of Oklahoma Press, 2006). See also E. Scott Adler, *Why Congressional Reforms Fail: Reelection and the House Committee System* (Chicago: University of Chicago Press, 2002).

Real power is in the hands of the majority and minority leaders, each elected by party caucus. Together they control the Senate's calendar, or agenda, for legislation. In addition, the senators from each party elect a whip.

After winning a majority of Senate seats in the 2006 election, the Democrats named Harry Reid of Nevada majority leader. The Republicans elected Mitch McConnell of Kentucky to the post of minority leader. Both were re-elected to these positions after the 2008, 2010, and 2012 elections. But 2014 witnessed a change in partisan control of the Senate, with the Republicans capturing a majority. Senators Reid and McConnell swapped positions and McConnell remained majority leader after Republicans retained control of the Senate in the 2016 elections.

Party leaders reach outside their respective chambers in an effort to augment their power and enhance prospects for their party programs. One important external strategy involves fund-raising. In recent years, congressional leaders have established their own political action committees. Interest groups are usually eager to contribute to these "leadership PACs" in order to curry favor with powerful members of Congress. The leaders, in turn, use the funds to support the various campaigns of their party's candidates and thereby create a sense of obligation and loyalty among those they help.[25]

In addition to the tasks of organizing Congress, congressional party leaders set the legislative agenda and even regulate deliberation over specific items on the agenda. This aspect of agenda setting is multifaceted. In the House, for example, a bill is initially filed with the Clerk as a legislative proposal. The Speaker then determines which committee has jurisdiction over it. Indeed, since the mid-1970s, the Speaker has been given additional bill-assignment powers, permitting him or her to assign different parts of a bill to different committees or the same parts sequentially or simultaneously to several committees.[26] The steering and agenda setting by party leaders work, however, within an institutional framework consisting of structures and procedures.

Why do members allow themselves to be governed by powerful party leaders? Leaders, after all, are elected by their rank-and-file members, and in their respective party caucuses the rank and file determine how powerful they will permit their leaders to be. Indeed, the power of party leaders has ebbed and flowed over time. The political scientists John Aldrich and David Rohde have sought to understand

---

25 Rank-and-file members, especially those from safe districts who face limited electoral challenges, have also created their own PACs, which enable them to contribute to their party and its candidates. See Eric S. Heberlig, "Congressional Parties, Fundraising, and Committee Ambition," *Political Research Quarterly* 56 (2003): 151–61.

26 For a historical look, see David W. Rohde and Kenneth A. Shepsle, "Leaders and Followers in the House of Representatives: Reflections on Woodrow Wilson's *Congressional Government*," *Congress and the Presidency* 14 (1987): 111–33. An analysis of the House leadership is Eric Schickler and Kathryn Pearson, "The House Leadership in an Era of Partisan Warfare," in *Congress Reconsidered*, Lawrence C. Dodd and Bruce I. Oppenheimer, ed., 8th ed. (Washington, D.C.: CQ Press, 2005), pp. 207–26. A companion piece on the Senate is C. Lawrence Evans and Daniel Lipinski, "Obstruction and Leadership in the U.S. Senate," in *Congress Reconsidered*, 8th ed., pp. 227–48. An update is Kathryn Pearson and Eric Schickler, "The Transition to Democratic Leadership in a Polarized House," in *Congress Reconsidered*, Lawrence C. Dodd and Bruce I. Oppenheimer, eds., 9th ed. (Washington, DC: CQ Press, 2008), pp. 165–89.

---

these ebbs and flows in the power of a party over its members, or what they call "conditional party government." They suggest that the institutional strength of party leaders is conditional: it depends on particular circumstances. The circumstance they emphasize is the degree to which party members share policy goals. If the rank and file are relatively homogeneous in this respect, they will endow their leaders with considerable power to prosecute the shared agenda. If, however, party members are heterogeneous in their goals, they will be less disposed to empower a leader. Thus the Democratic Party of the 1940s and 1950s, with its northern liberal wing and its southern conservative wing, was heterogeneous in the extreme and provided its leaders with few power resources. The effects of the Voting Rights Act of 1965, one of which was that formerly Democratic constituencies in the South started electing Republicans, began to be evident in the 1970s, reducing the diversity in the Democratic ranks and thus rendering the party ideologically more homogeneous. Under this changed circumstance, Democratic Party legislators, who were more focused than before on moderate and liberal goals, were prepared to empower their leaders.[27]

The experience of Democrats in the House just recounted has been experienced by Republicans in that chamber and both parties in the Senate. A half century after the Voting Rights Act, each of the four legislative parties is ideologically more homogeneous than in an earlier era, and it overlaps the other party in its chamber very little. Through this sorting, the parties have become polarized, with Democrats skewed toward the liberal side of the political spectrum and Republicans skewed toward the conservative side. With homogeneity within the ranks of each party, but vast disagreement between them, there is very strong pressure for the majority to push its consensus and very little pressure to compromise with the other party. Polarization has undermined interparty cooperation and compromise.

Polarization was apparent in the attempt to replace Justice Antonin Scalia on the Supreme Court in 2016. After his death in February of that year, Senate majority leader Mitch McConnell made it very clear that the Republicans would refuse to consider any nominee and called on Obama to leave the nomination to the next president. When Obama nominated a moderate Democrat, Merrick Garland of the D.C. Circuit, Republicans refused to hold hearings on the nomination in the hopes that a Republican would be elected to the presidency that year and have the opportunity to appoint another conservative to the Court. Indeed, after the election of Republican Donald Trump to the presidency, the Senate expressed its willingness to act quickly on the new president's nominee.

27 A now-classic treatment of the ebbs and flows of parties and their leaders in the modern era is David W. Rohde, *Parties and Leaders in the Post-Reform House* (Chicago: University of Chicago Press, 1991). For a more historical perspective, see David W. Rohde, John H. Aldrich, and Mark M. Berger, "The Historical Variability in Conditional Party Government, 1877–1986," in *Party, Process, and Political Change in Congress: New Perspectives on the History of Congress,* David W. Brady and Mathew D. McCubbins, eds. (Palo Alto, CA: Stanford University Press, 2002), pp. 17–35. For a development of the analytical argument, see David W. Rohde and John H. Aldrich, "The Logic of Conditional Party Government: Revisiting the Electoral Connection," in *Congress Reconsidered,* 7th ed., Lawrence C. Dodd and Bruce I. Oppenheimer, eds. (Washington, DC: CQ Press, 2001), pp. 265–92. A complementary theoretical perspective is offered by the political scientists Gary Cox and Mathew McCubbins in both *Legislative Leviathan* and *Setting the Agenda.*

The Committee System: The Core of Congress

If the system of leadership in each party and chamber constitutes the first set of organizational arrangements in the U.S. Congress, then the committee system provides a second set of organizational structures. But these are more a division-of-labor and specialization-of-labor system than the hierarchy-of-power system that determines leadership arrangements.

Congress began as a relatively unspecialized assembly, with each legislator participating equally in every step of the legislative process in all realms of policy. By the time of the War of 1812, if not earlier, Congress had begun employing a system of specialists—the committee system—because members with different interests and talents wished to play disproportionate roles in some areas of policy making while ceding influence in areas in which they were less interested.[28] If, Rip van Winkle–like, a congressman had fallen asleep in 1805 and woke up in 1825, he would have found a transformed legislative world. The legislative chambers in the beginning of that period consisted of bodies of generalists; by the end of the period, the legislative agenda was dominated by groups of specialists serving on standing committees. If, in contrast, our legislator had fallen asleep in 1825 and awoke a *century* later, the legislature would not seem so very different. In short, organizational decisions in the first quarter of the nineteenth century affected legislative activity over a long horizon. This is the history principle at work.

The congressional committee system consists of a set of standing committees, each with its own jurisdiction, membership, and authority to act. Each **standing committee** is given a permanent status by the official rules, with a fixed membership, officers, rules, a staff, offices, and above all, a jurisdiction that is recognized by all other committees and, usually, the leadership as well (Table 6.3). The jurisdiction of each standing committee is defined by the subject matter of legislation. Except for the Rules Committee in the House and the Rules and Administration Committee in the Senate, all the important committees receive proposals for legislation and process them into official bills. The House Rules Committee decides the order in which bills come up for a vote and determines the rules that govern the length of debate and opportunity for amendments. The Senate Rules Committee focuses more on administrative matters—managing Senate buildings, the Government Printing Office, the Senate library, and other services—but also on substantive matters, including corrupt practices, presidential succession, and the regulation of federal elections. The jurisdictions of the standing committees usually parallel those of the major departments or agencies in the executive branch. There are important exceptions, but by and large the division of labor is designed to parallel executive-branch organization.

standing committee

A permanent legislative committee that considers legislation within its designated subject area; the basic unit of deliberation in the House and Senate

---

28 The story of the evolution of the standing committee system in the House and the Senate in the early nineteenth century is told in Gerald Gamm and Kenneth A. Shepsle, "Emergence of Legislative Institutions: Standing Committees in the House and Senate, 1810–1825," *Legislative Studies Quarterly* 14 (1989): 39–66.

Table 6.3

STANDING COMMITTEES OF CONGRESS, 2016*

HOUSE COMMITTEES	
Agriculture	Intelligence
Appropriations	Judiciary
Armed Services	Natural Resources
Budget	Oversight and Government Reform
Education and the Workforce	Rules
Energy and Commerce	Science, Space, and Technology
Ethics	Small Business
Financial Services	Transportation and Infrastructure
Foreign Affairs	Veterans' Affairs
Homeland Security	Ways and Means
House Administration	

SENATE COMMITTEES	
Agriculture, Nutrition, and Forestry	Finance
Appropriations	Foreign Relations
Armed Services	Health, Education, Labor, and Pensions
Banking, Housing, and Urban Affairs	Homeland Security and Governmental Affairs
Budget	Judiciary
Commerce, Science, and Transportation	Rules and Administration
Energy and Natural Resources	Small Business and Entrepreneurship
Environment and Public Works	Veterans' Affairs

*These were the committees in the 114th Congress (2015–17). Committee names and jurisdictions change over time, as does the number of committees.

Jurisdiction. The world of policy is partitioned into policy jurisdictions, which become the responsibility of committees. The members of the Armed Services Committee, for example, become specialists in all aspects of military affairs. Legislators tend to have disproportionate influence in their respective committee jurisdictions, not only because they have become the most knowledgeable members in that policy area but also because they exercise various forms of agenda power, a subject we develop further in the next section.

Dividing up institutional activities among jurisdictions, thereby encouraging participants to specialize, has advantages. But it has costs, too. If the Armed Services Committee of the House of Representatives had no restraints, its members would undoubtedly shower their districts with military facilities and contracts. In short, the delegation of authority and resources to specialist sub-units exploits the advantages of the division and specialization of labor but risks jeopardizing the collective objectives of the group as a whole. The monitoring of committee activities thus goes hand in hand with delegation.

Sometimes new issues arise that do not fit neatly into any jurisdiction. Some, such as the issue of energy supplies that emerged during the 1970s, are so multi-faceted that bits and pieces of them are spread across many committee jurisdictions. Other issues, such as the regulation of tobacco products, fall into the gray area claimed by several committees. In this case in the House, the Energy and Commerce Committee, with its traditional claim on health-related issues, fought with the Agriculture Committee, whose traditional domain includes crops such as tobacco, for jurisdiction over this issue. Still others, like Homeland Security, arise at a time of crisis, overlap with the jurisdictions of other committees, and take time to sort out turf responsibilities. Indeed, turf battles between committees of Congress are notorious.[29]

Authority. Committees may be thought of as agents of the parent body to which jurisdiction-specific authority is provisionally delegated. In this section, we describe committee authority in terms of gatekeeping and after-the-fact authority.

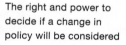

gatekeeping authority

The right and power to decide if a change in policy will be considered

proposal power

The capacity to bring a proposal before the full legislature

Normally any member of the legislature can submit a bill calling for changes in some policy area. Almost automatically this bill is assigned to the committee with jurisdiction, and very nearly always, there it languishes. In a typical session in the House of Representatives, about 8,000 bills are submitted, fewer than 1,000 of which see any action by the appropriate committee with jurisdiction. In effect, then, although any member is entitled to make proposals, committees get to decide whether to allow the bill to be voted on by the full chamber. Related to **gatekeeping authority** is a committee's **proposal power**. After a bill is referred to a committee, the committee may take no further action on it, amend the legislation in any way, or even write its own legislation before bringing the bill to

---

29 An outstanding description and analysis of these battles is found in David C. King, "The Nature of Congressional Committee Jurisdictions," *American Political Science Review* 88, no. 1 (March 1994): 48–63. See also King's *Turf Wars: How Congressional Committees Claim Jurisdiction* (Chicago: University of Chicago Press, 1997).

the floor for a vote. Committees, then, are lords of their jurisdictional domains, setting the table, so to speak, for their parent chamber.[30]

A committee also has responsibilities for bargaining with the other chamber and for conducting oversight, or **after-the-fact authority**. Because the U.S. Congress is bicameral, once one chamber passes a bill, the other chamber must consider it. If the other chamber passes a bill different from the one passed in the first chamber and the first chamber refuses to accept the changes, then the two chambers must resolve the differences; often they meet in a **conference committee**, in which representatives from each chamber hammer out a compromise. In the great majority of cases, conferees are drawn from the committees that had original jurisdiction over the bill.[31] The committee's effective authority to represent its chamber in conference-committee proceedings constitutes the first manifestation of after-the-fact power that complements its before-the-fact gatekeeping and proposal powers.

A second manifestation of after-the-fact committee authority consists of the committee's primacy in legislative **oversight** of policy implementation by the executive bureaucracy. Even after a bill becomes a law, bureaucrats in the career civil service, commissioners in regulatory agencies, and political appointees in the executive branch may not do precisely what the law requires (especially in light of the fact that statutes are often vague and ambiguous). Congressional committees are continuously watchful of the manner in which legislation is implemented and administered. They play this after-the-fact role by allocating staff and resources to track what the executive branch is doing and, from time to time, holding oversight hearings in which particular policies and programs undergo intense scrutiny. Former secretary of state Hillary Clinton, for example, was intensively grilled by a House committee for actions, and the absence of actions, taken by the Obama administration in the wake of the attack on the U.S. consulate in Benghazi, Libya. The power of oversight, in turn, gives congressional committees an additional source of leverage over policy in their jurisdictions. Oversight is discussed further in Chapter 8 on the bureaucracy.

Subcommittees. The standing committees of the U.S. House are divided into about 100 specialized subcommittees. These subcommittees serve their full committees in precisely the same manner as the full committees serve the parent chamber. Thus in their narrow jurisdictions they have gatekeeping, proposal, interchamber bargaining, and oversight powers. For a bill on wheat to be taken up by the full Agriculture Committee, for example, it first has to clear

after-the-fact authority

The authority to follow up on the fate of a proposal once it has been approved by the full chamber

conference committee

A joint committee created to work out a compromise for House and Senate versions of a piece of legislation

oversight

The effort by Congress, through hearings, investigations, and other techniques, to exercise control over the activities of executive agencies

---

30 This setup gives committee members extraordinary power in their respective jurisdictions, allowing them to push policy into line with their own preferences—but only up to a point. If the abuse of their agenda power becomes excessive, the parent body has structural and procedural remedies available to counteract the committee's actions, such as stacking the committee with more compliant members, deposing a particularly obstreperous committee chair, or removing policies from a committee's jurisdiction. These measures rarely have to be employed; their mere presence keeps committees from the more outrageous forms of advantage taking.

31 See Kenneth A. Shepsle and Barry R. Weingast, "The Institutional Foundations of Committee Power," *American Political Science Review* 81, no. 1 (March 1987): 85–104. For a more recent description, see Elizabeth Rybicki, "Conference Committees and Related Procedures: An Introduction," Congressional Research Service Report 7-5700 (2013).

the subcommittee on General Farm Commodities. All of the issues involving assignments, jurisdictions, and authority that we discussed earlier regarding full committees apply at the subcommittee level as well.

Hierarchy. At the committee level, the mantle of leadership falls on the committee chair. She, together with the party leaders, determines the committee's agenda and then coordinates the committee's staff, investigatory resources, and subcommittee structure.[32] This coordination includes scheduling hearings, "marking up" bills—that is, transforming legislative drafts into final versions—and scripting the process by which a bill goes from committee to floor proceedings to final passage. For many years, Congress followed a rigid **seniority** rule for the selection of committee chairs. The benefits of this rule are twofold. First, the chair would be occupied by someone knowledgeable in the committee's jurisdiction, familiar with interest-group and executive-branch players, and politically experienced. Second, the larger institution would be spared divisive leadership contests that reduce the legislative process to efforts in vote grubbing. There are costs, however: senior individuals may be unenergetic, out of touch, even senile. Since the mid-1970s, committee chairs have been elected by the majority-party members of the full legislature, though there remains a presumption (which may be rebutted) that the most senior committee member will normally assume the chair.[33]

Decisiveness on Committees. When a committee goes about its business, its chair exercises agenda power, as noted. But she is not a dictator. Any proposal made by the chair must ultimately secure the support of a committee majority. In this setting, who is *decisive*? That is, whose vote is necessary and sufficient for a motion to pass? The answer is provided by the *median-voter theorem*. This theorem can be stated as follows: (1) if the alternatives under consideration can be represented as points on a line, (2) if individuals have a most-preferred point, and (3) if their preferences decrease steadily for points farther away, then the most-preferred point of the median (middle) voter can defeat any other point in a majority contest.

In Figure 6.6 we have a five-person committee that must choose a point on the line ranging from 0 to 100. Each member has a favorite point, represented by the peak of his curve, and his preferences decline steadily as points farther and farther away are considered. The median-voter theorem asserts that the favorite point of member 3 can beat any other point in a majority contest. A majority comprising members 3, 4, and 5 prefers 3's favorite to any point to its left; a majority comprising members 1, 2, and 3 prefers 3's favorite to any point to its right; therefore 3's favorite can prevail against *any* point. We will discuss the median-voter theorem again in Chapter 11 in the context of elections.

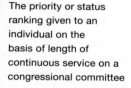

seniority

The priority or status ranking given to an individual on the basis of length of continuous service on a congressional committee

---

32 Because subcommittee chairs do essentially the same things in their narrower jurisdictions, we won't provide a separate discussion of them.

33 Beginning with the Republican takeover of the House in 1995, committee chairs have been term limited. After three terms, a chair must step down. It appears that party leaders exert more authority today in the appointment of new chairs.

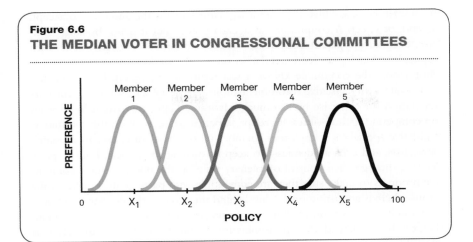

Figure 6.6

THE MEDIAN VOTER IN CONGRESSIONAL COMMITTEES

Monitoring Committees. If unchecked, committees might take advantage of their authority. Indeed, what prevents committees from exploiting their before-the-fact proposal power and their after-the-fact bargaining and oversight authority? As we saw in Chapter 1, in our discussion of the principal-agent problem, principals must be certain that agents are properly motivated to serve the principal's interests, either by actually sharing the principal's interests themselves or by deriving something of value (reputation, compensation, and so on) for acting to advance those interests. Alternatively, the principal will need to have some instruments by which to monitor and validate what her agent is doing, rewarding or punishing the agent accordingly.

Consider again the example of congressional committees. The House or Senate delegates responsibility to its Committee on Agriculture to recommend legislative policy in the field of agriculture. Legislators from farm districts are most eager to get onto this committee, and for the most part their wishes are accommodated. The Committee on Agriculture, consequently, mainly comprises farm legislators. And nonfarm legislators are relieved at not having to spend their time on issues of little interest to them or their constituents. In effecting this delegation, however, the parent legislature is putting itself in the hands of its farm colleagues, benefiting from their expertise on farm-related matters, to be sure, but laying itself open to the danger of planting the fox squarely in the henhouse. The Committee on Agriculture becomes not only a collection of specialists but also a collection of advocates for farm interests. How can the parent body be certain, therefore, that a recommendation from that committee is not more a reflection of its advocacy than a reflection of its expertise? This is the risk inherent in delegation in principal-agent relationships.

And for this very reason the parent legislature maintains a variety of tools and instruments to protect itself from being exploited by its agents. First, it does not allow committees to make final decisions on policy; it allows only recommendations, which the parent legislature retains the authority to accept, amend, or reject. A committee has agenda power, but it is not by itself decisive. Second, the parent body relies on the committee's concern for its own reputation. Making a recommendation on a piece of legislation is not a one-shot action; the committee knows it will return to the parent body time and time again with legislative recommendations, and it will not want to tarnish its reputation for expertise by too much advocacy. Third, the parent body relies on competing agents—interest groups, expert members not on the committee, legislative specialists in the other chamber of the legislature, executive-branch specialists, and even academics—to keep its own agents honest. Fourth, party leaders, through their control of plenary time on the floor, monitor committee products to make sure they are compatible with party goals. Finally, in the House there is an institutional "club behind the door"—the discharge petition. A committee that sits on a bill, not permitting it to be taken up by the full chamber, can be discharged of responsibility for the bill if a petition to that effect is signed by a majority of the chamber.

Nevertheless, a principal will not bother to eliminate *entirely* these prospective deviations from his interests by agents who have interests of their own. A principal will suffer some **agency loss** from having delegated authority to a "hired hand"; therefore, nearly all principal-agent relationships will be imperfect in some respects from the principal's perspective. The Committee on Agriculture, for example, cannot get away with spending huge proportions of the federal budget on agricultural subsidies to farmers. But it can insert small items into agriculture bills from time to time—an experimental grain-to-fuel conversion project in an important legislator's state or district, for example, or special funds to the U.S. trade representative to give priority to agriculture-related trade issues. The parent body will keep an eye on the Agriculture Committee, but it won't be worth its while to take action on every instance of indulgence by the committee. The transaction cost of monitoring and overseeing committee performance gets excessive if perfection is the objective.

Thus we see the institution principle providing some guidance on how a group of legislators organizes itself for business. The legislators take advantage of the division and specialization of labor, dividing themselves into specialized subgroups (committees and subcommittees) and benefiting from these subunits' expertise. But they also guard against the subunits' excessive pursuit of their own narrower interests. The parent legislature in effect uses institutional arrangements to regulate and oversee its subunits' activities.

Committee Reform. Over the years, Congress has reformed its organizational structure and operating procedures. Most changes have served to improve efficiency, but some reforms have also represented a response to political considerations. In the 1970s, a series of reforms substantially altered the organization of power in Congress. Among the most important changes at that time were the election of committee chairs, an increase in the number of subcommittees, greater autonomy for subcommittee chairs, the opening of most

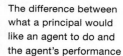

agency loss

The difference between what a principal would like an agent to do and the agent's performance

committee deliberations to the public, and a system of multiple referral of bills that allowed several committees to consider one bill at the same time. One of the driving impulses behind these reforms was an effort to reduce the power of committee chairs.

As a consequence of those reforms, power became more fragmented, making it harder to reach agreement on legislation. In 1995, the Republican leadership of the 104th Congress sought to concentrate more authority in the party leadership (something that had begun in the 1980s when the Democrats were in the majority). One of the ways the House achieved this was by abandoning the principle of seniority in the selection of a number of committee chairs, appointing them instead according to their loyalty to the party. This move tied committee chairs more closely to the leadership. In addition, the Republican leadership eliminated 25 of the House's 115 subcommittees and gave committee chairs more power over their subcommittees. The result was an unusually cohesive congressional majority, which pushed forward a common agenda. House Republicans also imposed a three-term limit on committee and subcommittee heads. As a result, all the chairs were replaced in 2001, with a net result of a redistribution of power in the House of Representatives. Since 2001, however, some of the earlier practices have slowly begun to reassert themselves. Speaker Nancy Pelosi and the Democratic majority in 2007 observed seniority in the appointment of nearly all committee chairs. But it is not automatic, and committee chairs are on notice that significant deviations from a party policy consensus will not be tolerated.

The role of committees in the legislative process was evident during Obama's first term. In the midst of the financial crisis, taxing and spending committees played major roles in shepherding a stimulus package and a rescue of the auto industry through both chambers, as well as follow-up monitoring of the earlier rescue of banks and other financial players. During this period, the banking committees produced major regulatory reforms for their industry. At the same time, the health committees produced what ultimately became Obama's health care policy. Speaker Pelosi and Majority Leader Reid conducted and choreographed all these activities. The legislative record of the 111th Congress was testimony both to an efficient division- and specialization-of-labor committee system *and* to authoritative and strong party leadership. The role of committees and strong party leadership were also evident in Obama's second term. But in this case it was the committees and party leaders of the Republican House majority in the 113th Congress and of the Republican majorities in both the House and Senate in the 114th Congress that thwarted Obama policy efforts.

Finally, we should reiterate that the strengthening of party leaders in each chamber—one of the effects of the homogenization of policy preferences and ideology within parties and the polarization between them—has in turn had effects on the committee system. It may no longer be assumed that senior committee leaders are the movers and shakers in each chamber. Party leaders have accrued powers that once were enjoyed by these senior committee members. The position of committee chair is still consequential, make no mistake about that, but increasingly the committee chairs serve party leaders and their objectives whereas in the past it was just the reverse.[34]

The Staff System: Staffers and Agencies

A congressional institution ranking just below committees and parties in importance is the staff system. Every member of Congress employs a large number of staff members, whose tasks include handling constituency requests and, to a growing extent, dealing with legislative details and the activities of administrative agencies. Increasingly, staffers bear the primary responsibility for drafting proposals, organizing hearings, dealing with administrative agencies, and negotiating with lobbyists. Indeed, legislators typically deal with each other through staff members rather than through direct, personal contact. Representatives and senators together employ nearly 11,000 staffers in their Washington and home offices. In addition, Congress employs roughly 2,000 permanent committee staffers. These individuals, who often stay regardless of turnover in Congress, are responsible for administering the committee's work, doing research, scheduling, organizing hearings, and drafting legislation.

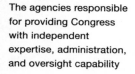

staff agencies

The agencies responsible for providing Congress with independent expertise, administration, and oversight capability

Congress has also established three **staff agencies** that provide resources and expertise independent of the executive branch. These agencies enhance Congress's capacity to oversee administrative agencies and evaluate presidential programs and proposals. They are the Congressional Research Service, which performs research for legislators who wish to know the facts and competing arguments relevant to policy proposals or other legislative business; the Government Accountability Office, through which Congress can investigate the financial and administrative affairs of any government agency or program; and the Congressional Budget Office, which assesses the economic implications and likely costs of proposed federal programs.

Informal Organization: The Caucuses

In addition to the official organization of Congress, an unofficial organizational structure also exists: the caucuses, or legislative service organizations (LSOs). A **congressional caucus** is a group of senators or representatives who share certain opinions, interests, or social characteristics. There are ideological caucuses such as the liberal Democratic Study Group and the conservative Democratic Forum. There are also a large number of caucuses representing particular economic or policy interests, such as the Travel and Tourism Caucus, the Steel Caucus, the Mushroom Caucus, and the Concerned Senators for the Arts. Legislators who share common backgrounds or social

congressional caucus

An association of members of Congress based on party, interest, or social characteristics such as gender or race

---

34 See Andrew B. Hall and Kenneth A. Shepsle, "The Changing Value of Seniority in the U.S. House: Conditional Party Government Revised," *Journal of Politics* 76 (2014): 98–114.

characteristics have organized such caucuses as the Congressional Black Caucus, the Congressional Caucus for Women's Issues, and the Hispanic Caucus. All these caucuses advance the interests of specific groups by promoting legislation, encouraging Congress to hold hearings, and pressing administrative agencies for favorable treatment.

RULES OF LAWMAKING: HOW A BILL BECOMES A LAW

The institutional structure of Congress is one key factor that helps shape the legislative process. An equally important set of factors is made up of the rules of congressional procedure. These rules govern all the procedures from introducing a bill through submitting it to the president for signing. Not only do these regulations influence the fate of every bill, but they also help determine the distribution of power in Congress.[35]

Committee Deliberation

Even if a member of Congress, the White House, or a federal agency has spent months developing a piece of legislation, it does not become a bill until a senator or a representative officially submits it to the clerk of the House or Senate and it is referred to the appropriate committee for deliberation. No floor action on any bill can occur until the committee with jurisdiction over it has taken all the time it needs to deliberate.[36] During its deliberations, the committee typically refers the bill to a subcommittee, which may hold hearings, listen to expert testimony, and amend the proposed legislation before referring it to the full committee for consideration. The full committee may accept the recommendation of the subcommittee or hold its own hearings and prepare its own amendments. Even more frequently, the committee and subcommittee may do little or nothing with a bill and simply allow it to die in committee.

Once a bill's assigned committee or committees in the House of Representatives have acted affirmatively, the whole bill or various parts of it are transmitted to the Rules Committee, which determines the rules under which the legislation will be considered by the full House. Together with the Speaker, it influences

---

35 We should emphasize that a legislature suspends its rules as often as it follows them. There are unorthodox ways to avoid procedural logjams, and the House and, especially, the Senate frequently resort to them. See Barbara Sinclair, *Unorthodox Lawmaking: New Legislative Processes in the U.S. Congress,* 3rd ed. (Washington, DC: CQ Press, 2007).

36 A bill can be pulled from a committee by a discharge petition, but this extreme measure is resorted to only rarely. Other parliamentary tricks may also be attempted, but most of the time it is the committee of jurisdiction that influences the course of a bill.

when debate will be scheduled, for how long, what amendments will be in order, and the order in which they will be considered. The Speaker also rules on all procedural points of order and points of information raised during the debate. A bill's supporters generally prefer a **closed rule**, which puts severe limits on floor debate and prohibits amendments. Opponents of a bill usually prefer an **open rule**, which permits potentially damaging floor debate and makes it easier to add amendments that may cripple the bill or weaken its chances of passing.

Debate

A bill that passes in committee and clears the Rules Committee is then scheduled for debate by the full House. Party control of the agenda is reinforced by the rule giving the Speaker of the House and the majority leader of the Senate the power of recognition during debate on a bill. Usually the chair knows the purpose for which a member intends to speak well in advance of the occasion. Spontaneous efforts to gain recognition are often foiled. For example, the Speaker may ask, "For what purpose does the member rise?" before deciding whether to grant recognition. In general, the party leadership in the House has total control over debate. In the Senate, each member has substantial power to block the close of debate. A simple majority in the House can override opposition, whereas it takes an extraordinary majority (60 votes) to close debate in the Senate. In recent years, with partisanship in both chambers on the rise, prolonging debate, using procedural delays, and generally dragging one's feet have been potent tools for the minority to frustrate the majority.

In the House, the bill's sponsor and his or her leading opponent control virtually all of the time allotted by the Rules Committee for debate on a given bill. These two participants are granted the power to allocate most of the debate time in small amounts to members who seek to speak for or against the measure.

In the Senate, other than the power of recognition, the leadership has much less control over floor debate. Indeed, the Senate is unique among the world's legislative bodies for its commitment to unlimited debate. Once given the floor, a senator may speak for as long as she wishes unless an extraordinary majority votes to end debate, a procedure called **cloture**. Sixty votes are needed for this. On a number of memorable occasions, senators have used the right to continue speaking to prevent action on legislation they opposed. Through this tactic, called the **filibuster**, small minorities or even one individual in the Senate can force the majority to give in to his demands. During the 1950s and 1960s, for example, opponents of civil rights legislation often sought to block its passage by filibustering. The filibuster remains potent today, though Senate rules have reduced its value for blocking the confirmation of executive and judicial appointments (though it still may be used against Supreme Court nominations). The Policy Principle case study on p. 217 gives an example of how Rand Paul used the filibuster and other maneuvers to ensure that the Patriot Act would not be renewed.

Although it is the best known, the filibuster is not the only technique used to block Senate action. Under Senate rules, members have a virtually unlimited ability to propose amendments to a pending bill. Each amendment must be

---

closed rule

The provision by the House Rules Committee that prohibits the introduction of amendments during debate

open rule

The provision by the House Rules Committee that permits floor debate and the addition of amendments to a bill

cloture

A procedure allowing a supermajority of the members of a legislative body to set a time limit on debate over a given bill

filibuster ⮕

A tactic used by members of the Senate to prevent action on legislation they oppose by continuously holding the floor and speaking until the majority backs down; once given the floor, senators have unlimited time to speak, and it requires a cloture vote of three-fifths of the Senate to end a filibuster

From the Patriot Act to the Freedom Act

Shortly after the 9/11 terror attacks in 2001, Congress passed and President George W. Bush signed the USA Patriot Act, which authorized extensive data collection and domestic surveillance by the National Security Agency. This legislation, giving officials tools to forestall acts of terrorism, was reauthorized in 2006 and again in 2011 despite criticisms by both Democrats and Republicans for its disregard of individual liberties and privacy. However, by 2015, when the Patriot Act was again set to expire, significant opposition arose to another reauthorization. This time, opponents worked through the specific institutions of the House and the Senate to produce a different outcome: a new law to replace the Patriot Act.

As we've seen in this chapter, the House and the Senate are organized quite differently, which influences how members' policy preferences are translated into outcomes in each chamber. The House is tightly controlled by its leadership and thus can act expeditiously. There, the Patriot Act was discarded completely, and in its place the USA Freedom Act—an entirely new document intended to place a much higher premium on individual liberties and privacy—passed comfortably with 338 supporters.

The Senate is a much less centralized institution. Senate Majority Leader Mitch McConnell favored a "clean" reauthorization of the Patriot Act, with no amendments. However, his Kentucky colleague, Senator Rand Paul, wanted to allow amendments, which could include protections for privacy and civil liberties. Under Senate rules allowing any senator unlimited time when speaking on the floor, Paul spoke against McConnell's position for 10 hours and 30 minutes, and it appeared his filibuster would cause the Patriot Act to expire before it could be renewed. Paul didn't talk right up to the deadline,

Rand Paul spoke for over 10 hours to prevent the renewal of the Patriot Act in 2015.

but he ensured that those with reservations about the Patriot Act had time to go public about them. Because the rules of the Senate require unanimous consent to bypass committee hearings and bring a bill to the floor, Paul had the power to prevent slight variations of the Patriot Act—McConnell's preferred option—from being considered by forcing the bill to go through committee. Senate rules mattered decisively here, and Paul exploited them smartly.

The Senate then turned to the USA Freedom Act already passed by the House. The act faced stiff opposition from key senators, but eventually agreement was reached to vote on several amendments that satisfied the concerns of opponents. These amendments were ultimately rejected, however, and the Senate passed the unchanged USA Freedom Act by a margin of 67-32 on June 2, 2015, two days after the Patriot Act had expired. Institutional rules and practices, combined with individual preferences and persistence, revised a policy from one that had been permissive of domestic surveillance to one that, at least in the opinion of its proponents, restrained government a bit more.

voted on before the bill can come to a final vote. The introduction of new amendments can be stopped only by unanimous consent. This strategy can permit a determined minority to filibuster by amendment, indefinitely delaying the passage of a bill. Senators can also place "holds," or stalling devices, on bills to delay debate. Senators do this when they fear that openly opposing them will be unpopular. Because holds are kept secret, the senators placing the holds do not have to take public responsibility for their actions.[37]

Once a bill is debated on the floor of the House and the Senate, the leaders schedule it for a vote on the floor of each chamber. Leaders do not bring legislation to the floor unless they are fairly certain it is going to pass. On rare occasions, however, the last moments of the floor vote can be dramatic, as each party's leadership puts its whip organization into action to make sure wavering members vote with the party.

Conference Committee: Reconciling House and Senate Versions of a Bill

Getting a bill out of committee and through both of the houses of Congress is no guarantee that it will be enacted. Frequently bills that began with similar provisions in both chambers emerge at variance to one another. For example, a bill may be passed unchanged by one chamber but undergo substantial revision in the other. If the differences cannot be worked out by passing the revised version back to the other chamber and having it accept any changes, a conference committee composed of the senior members of the committees or subcommittees that initiated the bills may be required to iron out differences. Sometimes members or leaders will let objectionable provisions pass on the floor with the idea that they will be eliminated in conference. Conference agreement requires majority support from each of the two delegations. Legislation that emerges successfully from a conference committee is more often a compromise than a clear victory of one set of forces over another.

When a bill comes out of conference, it faces one more hurdle. Before it can be sent to the president for signing, the House–Senate conference report must be approved on the floor of each chamber. It must be voted up or down; no amendments are in order. Usually such approval comes quickly. Occasionally, however, a bill's opponents use the report as one last opportunity to defeat a piece of legislation.

Presidential Action

Once adopted by the House and the Senate, a bill goes to the president, who may choose to sign the bill into law or **veto** it (Figure 6.7). The veto is the president's constitutional power to reject a piece of legislation. To veto a bill, the president returns it within 10 days to the house of Congress in which it originated, along with objections to it. If Congress adjourns during the 10-day period and the president has taken no action, the bill is considered to have been vetoed by means

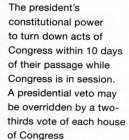

veto

The president's constitutional power to turn down acts of Congress within 10 days of their passage while Congress is in session. A presidential veto may be overridden by a two-thirds vote of each house of Congress

---

37 This and other features of the Senate rules came under intense scrutiny in the 112th Congress (2011–12) and remain on the reform agenda today.

Figure 6.7

HOW A BILL BECOMES A LAW

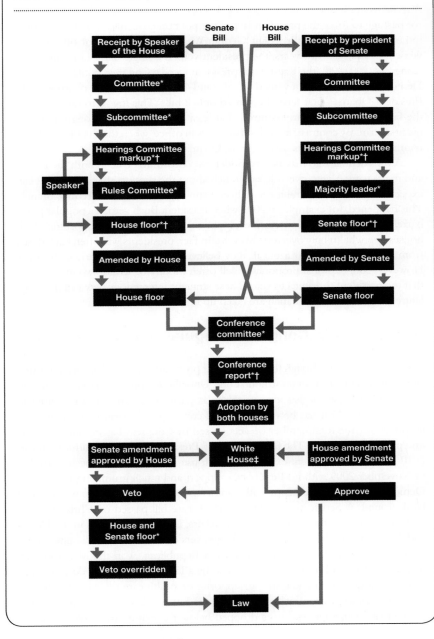

Senate Bill / House Bill

Receipt by Speaker of the House → Committee* → Subcommittee* → Hearings Committee markup*† → Rules Committee* → House floor*† → Amended by House → House floor

Speaker*

Receipt by president of Senate → Committee → Subcommittee → Hearings Committee markup*† → Majority leader* → Senate floor*† → Amended by Senate → Senate floor

Conference committee* → Conference report*† → Adoption by both houses → White House‡

Senate amendment approved by House → Veto → House and Senate floor* → Veto overridden → Law

House amendment approved by Senate → Approve → Law

*Points at which the bill can be amended.
†Points at which the bill can die.
‡If the president neither signs nor vetoes the bill within 10 days, it automatically becomes law.

pocket veto ➡

A veto that is effected when Congress adjourns during the time a president has to approve a bill and the president takes no action on it

of the **pocket veto**. The possibility of a presidential veto affects the willingness of members of Congress to push for different pieces of legislation at different times. If they think a proposal is likely to be vetoed, they might shelve it for a later time. Alternatively, the sponsors of a popular bill opposed by the president might push for passage to force the president to pay the political costs of vetoing it.[38] During the entire first term of President George W. Bush (2001–05), not one bill was vetoed. In the next two years, the president vetoed a single bill. But in the 110th Congress (2007–08), the Republican president faced a Congress controlled by the Democrats. The president vetoed 11 bills, and 4 of his vetoes were overridden. In President Obama's first term, he vetoed only 2 bills. This low veto rate reflected the fact that Obama's party controlled at least one chamber of Congress during his first term. By contrast, in his last two years in office, when the Republican party controlled both chambers of Congress, Obama vetoed 10 bills.

A presidential veto may be overridden by a two-thirds vote in both the House and the Senate. A veto override says much about the support that a president can expect from Congress, and it can deliver a stinging blow to the executive branch. This happened, for example, in 2007 when President Bush vetoed a popular pork-barrel bill, the Water Resources Development Act. Despite his opposition, both houses overwhelmingly overrode his veto. In fact, presidents will often back down from their threat to veto a bill if they believe Congress will override the veto. However, congressional proponents will often modify or withdraw entirely a bill that the president threatens to veto. These strategic interactions between the legislature and the executive branch are taken up in the next chapter.

Procedures in Congress: Regular and Unorthodox

We have noted that although there is a regular procedure in each chamber, it is often abandoned in favor of an unorthodox one. Unorthodox procedures are often seen as necessary to pass legislation, especially as party polarization has increased in recent decades. As it has become more difficult to pass legislation through regular processes, the total number of acts passed by Congress has declined (see the timeplot on pp. 222–3). The final passage of President Obama's health care bill in 2010 provides an excellent example. The House initially passed a health care bill in November 2009 with no Republican support and much grumbling from some Democrats who were unhappy with various aspects. But the Senate was the real battleground. A Senate version of the health care bill passed on Christmas Eve 2009. Upon their return after the holiday recess, Democratic leaders in the House and Senate plotted how to combine the two versions. But a shock disrupted their plans: on January 19, 2010, Scott Brown, a Republican, won the Massachusetts Senate seat that had been temporarily held by a Democrat after the death of Ted Kennedy (a Democrat and a strong supporter of health care reform). The Senate had been filibuster-proof with 60 Democrats but was now no longer since the number of Democratic senators dropped below the cloture threshold. Now the

---

38 John B. Gilmour, *Strategic Disagreement: Stalemate in American Politics* (Pittsburgh, PA: University of Pittsburgh Press, 1995).

Republican minority could block any further vote in the Senate, which would be necessary to approve changes to the bill. What was to be done?

The Democrats took an unusual route. Speaker Pelosi and the Democratic leadership convinced Democrats in the House to support the Senate version of the bill, passing it 219 to 212. The identical bill was thus passed by both chambers, and no further vote was needed in the Senate. House Democrats were not happy with the Senate version, but they were placated by the promise of a second bill in which their concerns would be addressed. The second bill employed the so-called reconciliation procedure, a procedure normally reserved for spending and budgeting subjects and somewhat novel in this context, which requires only a simple majority in each chamber. Thus a filibuster was avoided in the Senate. On March 26, the Senate passed this second bill, 56 to 43; the House passed it, 220 to 207; and the way was clear for Obama to sign health care reform into law.

Before leaving this topic, it is worth noting that normal and abnormal procedures involve either the conventional or the creative application of existing rules. Each chamber, however, is granted by the Constitution the privilege of formulating its own rules of procedure. So from time to time, the House or the Senate will change its rules of procedure. At other times, a dominant coalition in a chamber will threaten to do this unless it is allowed its way under the existing rules. Here we see the confluence of the rationality principle and the institution principle as rational legislators seek to (re)arrange their chamber's institutional procedures in order to accomplish particular purposes or realize particular goals.

This phenomenon was dramatically illustrated in May 2005. Even though Republicans held a majority in the Senate, President Bush's judicial nominations were threatened by a filibuster by Democratic senators. (The Senate must formally approve a president's nominations to the federal judiciary.) In the face of nominations whose approval looked vulnerable to a blocking action by the minority party, the Senate majority leader unveiled the *nuclear option*—a clever parliamentary maneuver in which debate could be brought to a close not by securing the 60 votes normally required (which the Republicans did not control) but by a simple majority. This would be executed by requesting the Senate president to end debate without a cloture vote because the issue was the constitutional one of "advising and consenting" on a presidential judicial nomination. It was expected that any such move by the Republicans would prompt the Democrats to appeal any ruling by the Senate president to end debate. But that ruling required only a majority vote to be sustained. In this manner, the Republicans could end-run the practice of unlimited debate that normally prevails in the Senate. The nuclear option was never implemented, however. The very threat of it induced some moderate senators to support a motion to end debate (thereby producing the 60 needed votes) and bring a presidential nominee forward for a final vote. These senators agreed to accommodate a vote so long as the president and the Republican majority did not abuse this concession by bringing forward "extremist" nominees.[39]

---

39 For a model of the judicial confirmation process, see David W. Rohde and Kenneth A. Shepsle, "Advising and Consenting in the 60-Vote Senate: Strategic Appointments to the Supreme Court," *Journal of Politics* 69 (2007): 664–77.

Acts Passed by Congress, 1789–2014

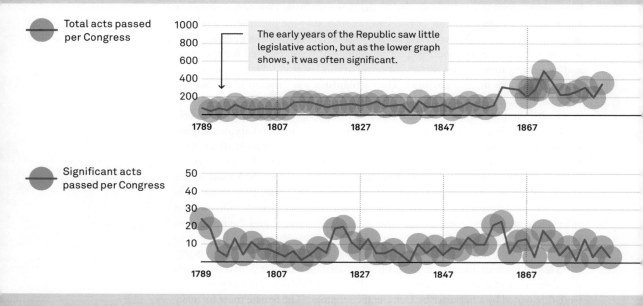

Total acts passed per Congress

The early years of the Republic saw little legislative action, but as the lower graph shows, it was often significant.

Significant acts passed per Congress

This compromise sufficed for a few years, but during the Obama presidency the same issue of nominations blocked by minority obstruction arose. Now a Democratic president was prevented from appointing judges and senior executive branch officials by a determined Republican minority. The Senate Majority Leader, Harry Reid, invoked the nuclear option. As a result, today, most presidential executive appointments and judicial nominations other than for the Supreme Court require only a simple majority to end debate and proceed to a vote on confirmation.

The Distributive Tendency in Congress

To pass a policy, it is necessary to provide statutory authority to a government agency to implement the legislation and then provide appropriations to fund the implementation. The list of politicians whose consent is required in these processes is extraordinarily long. At a minimum, it includes majorities of the relevant committee and subcommittee of each chamber (almost certainly including their chairs), the Appropriations Committee and relevant appropriations subcommittee in each chamber (including their chairs), the House Rules Committee,

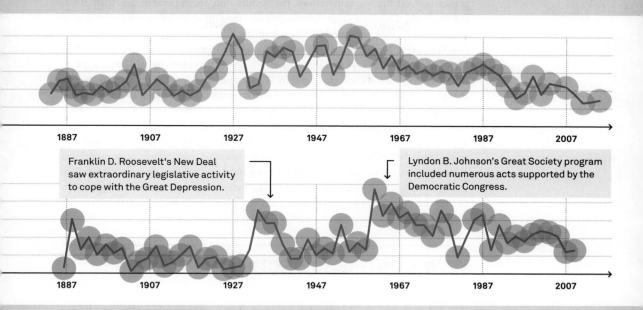

1887   1907   1927   1947   1967   1987   2007

Franklin D. Roosevelt's New Deal saw extraordinary legislative activity to cope with the Great Depression.

Lyndon B. Johnson's Great Society program included numerous acts supported by the Democratic Congress.

1887   1907   1927   1947   1967   1987   2007

chamber majorities (including leaders of the majority party), and the president. Some legislators may go along without requiring much for their states or districts on the assumption that their turn will come on another bill. But most of these politicians negotiate some form of compensation to provide their support.

With so many hurdles to clear before a legislative initiative can become a law, the benefits must be spread broadly. It is as though a bill traveled on a toll road past a number of tollbooths, each one housing a collector with her hand out for payment. On some occasions, the toll takes the form of a personal bribe—a contract to a firm run by a congressman's brother, a job for a senator's daughter, a "military inspection" trip to a Pacific isle for a legislator and his companion. Occasionally there is a wink-and-a-nod understanding, usually given by the majority leader or committee chair, that support from a legislator today will ensure reciprocal support for legislation of interest to her down the road. But most frequently, a bill becomes widely attractive by making its provisions more inclusive, spreading the benefits among a broad set of beneficiaries. This is the **distributive tendency**.

The distributive tendency is part of the American system of representative democracy. In advocating their constituents' interests, legislators are eager to advertise their ability to deliver for their state or district. They maneuver to put

 distributive tendency

The tendency of Congress to spread the benefits of a policy over a wide range of members' districts

themselves in a position to claim credit for good things that happen there and duck blame for bad things. This is the way they earn trust back home, deter strong challengers in upcoming elections, and defeat those who do run against them. It means that legislators must take advantage of every opportunity that presents itself. In some instances, the results may seem bizarre. In April 2003, for example, a senator from Mississippi inserted into the bill funding the war in Iraq language that provided $250 million for "disaster relief" for southern catfish farmers.[40] Most Americans would never have guessed that driving Saddam Hussein from power would have an effect on catfish farming in Mississippi.

This system, which is practiced in Washington and most state capitals, means that political pork gets spread around; it is not controlled by a small clique of politicians. But it also means that public authority and appropriations do not go where they are most needed. The most impoverished cities do not get as much money as appropriate because some of the available money gets diverted to buy political support. The neediest individuals often do not get tax relief, health care, or occupational subsidies for reasons unrelated to philosophy or policy grounds. It is the distributive tendency at work. And it is one of the unintended consequences of the separation of powers and multiple veto points.[41] As the policy principle suggests, rationality combines with institutional practices to leave their marks on the shape of policy.

HOW CONGRESS DECIDES

What determines the kinds of legislation that Congress ultimately produces? The process of creating a legislative agenda, drawing up a list of possible measures, and deciding among them is very complex. In this process, a variety of influences from inside and outside government play important roles. External influences include a legislator's constituency and various interest groups. Influences from inside government include party leadership, congressional colleagues, and the president. Let us examine each of these influences individually and then consider how they interact to produce congressional policy decisions.

Constituency

Because members of Congress want to be reelected, constituents' views influence their decisions. Yet constituency influence is not so straightforward as we might think. In fact, most constituents do not even know what policies their representatives support. The number of citizens who *do* pay attention to such matters—the attentive public—is usually very small. Nonetheless, members of Congress worry about what their constituents think because these representatives realize that their choices may be scrutinized in a future election and used as ammunition

40 Dan Morgan, "War Funding Bill's Extra Riders," *Washington Post,* April 8, 2003, p. A4.

41 See George Tsebelis, *Veto Players: How Political Institutions Work* (Princeton, NJ: Princeton University Press, 2002).

by an opposing candidate. Thus members try to anticipate their constituents' policy views.[42] In this way, constituents may affect congressional policy choices even when there is little direct evidence of their awareness of those choices.[43] For example, because a large number of voters will not support a candidate who opposes cuts to mandatory spending programs such as Medicare, legislators are unwilling to support such cuts even as those programs approach unsustainable levels (see the Analyzing the Evidence unit on pp. 226–7). Similarly, even moderate Republicans in Congress support very conservative positions on issues like gay marriage, abortion, and gun control because they fear that angry voters will support a more conservative Republican in the next primary election.

Interest Groups

Interest groups are another important external influence on the policies that Congress produces. When members are making voting decisions, interest groups that have some connection to constituents in the districts of particular members are most likely to be influential. For this reason, interest groups with the ability to mobilize followers in many congressional districts may be especially influential. The small-business lobby, for example, played an important role in defeating President Clinton's proposal for comprehensive health care reform in 1993–94. The mobilization of networks of small businesses across the country meant that virtually every member of Congress had to take their views into account. In 2009, the Obama administration brought small-business groups and the insurance industry into their planning for health care reform early in the process precisely because of this.

In addition to mobilizing voters, interest groups contribute money. In the 2014 electoral cycle, interest groups and PACs gave many millions of dollars in campaign contributions to incumbent legislators and challengers. What does this money buy? A popular conception is that campaign contributions buy legislative votes. In this view, legislators vote for whichever proposal favors the bulk of their contributors. Although the vote-buying hypothesis makes for good campaign rhetoric, it has little factual support. Empirical studies by political scientists show little evidence that contributions from large PACs influence legislative voting patterns.[44]

....

42 See John W. Kingdon, *Congressmen's Voting Decisions* (New York: Harper & Row, 1973), chap. 3; and R. Douglas Arnold, *The Logic of Congressional Action* (New Haven, CT: Yale University Press, 1990). See also Joshua Clinton, "Representation in Congress: Constituents and Roll Calls in the 106th House," *Journal of Politics* 68 (2006): 397–409.

43 Interest groups from the state or district (which we discuss later) can provide legislators with useful information concerning the significance of particular issues for various constituency groups. See Kenneth W. Kollman, *Outside Lobbying: Public Opinion and Interest Group Strategies* (Princeton, NJ: Princeton University Press, 1998).

44 See Janet M. Grenke, "PACs and the Congressional Supermarket: The Currency Is Complex," *American Journal of Political Science* 33, no. 1 (February 1989): 1–24. More generally, see Jacobson, *The Politics of Congressional Elections.* For a view that interest groups spend too little, not too much, money, see Stephen Ansolabehere, John de Figueiredo, and James Snyder, "Why Is There So Little Money in U.S. Politics?" *Journal of Economic Perspectives* 17 (2003): 105–30.

Why Congress Can't Make Ends Meet

Contributed by
David M. Primo
University of Rochester

For most of the past half century, Congress has chosen to exercise its constitutionally granted "power of the purse" by authorizing spending in excess of revenues. The result of this deficit spending is a federal debt that stood at nearly $19 trillion at the end of 2015.

How did we get here? The answer begins with congressional rules. In the 1970s, Congress constructed a budget process under which entitlement programs, such as Social Security and Medicare, were left to operate on "autopilot," meaning that spending on these programs is mandatory and continues to increase unless Congress intervenes.

Reforming the process is easier said than done. Some scholars point to the success of the U.S. states in balancing their budgets as a model for Congress. Every state except for Vermont requires a balanced budget, and research shows that deficits and spending are lower in states with constitutional, effectively enforced budget rules.[1]

The federal government has no such constitutional rule and is unlikely to implement one anytime soon, meaning that Congress has to rely on internal enforcement of its budget rules. Because it is much easier to break the rules than to reach bipartisan agreement on difficult spending and tax policy questions, Congress has not managed to meet its own budget deadlines in nearly 20 years.

As the population ages and health care costs increase, programs on autopilot are soaking up an increasing share of government spending. In every year since 1990, mandatory spending has exceeded discretionary spending, and the gap is projected to widen significantly in the coming decades.

Federal Government Spending by Category as a Percentage of GDP

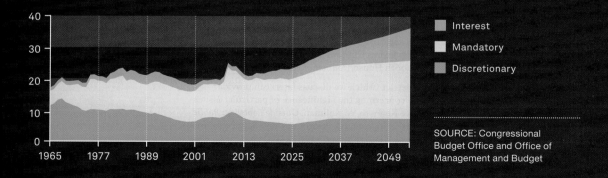

Legend:
- Interest
- Mandatory
- Discretionary

SOURCE: Congressional Budget Office and Office of Management and Budget

1 David M. Primo, *Rules and Restraint: Government Spending and the Design of Institutions* (Chicago: University of Chicago Press, 2007); and Henning Bohn and Robert P. Inman, "Balanced Budget Rules and Public Deficits: Evidence from the U.S. States," *Carnegie Rochester Conference Series on Public Policy* 45 (1996): 13–76.

If Congress is not able to design effective budget rules to overcome institutional inertia, the federal government's debt will continue to grow, with future generations being left with a big bill to pay. Legislators, however, are reluctant to insist on reforms in these areas for fear of upsetting their constituents and losing their seats in Congress. In a 2013 survey, very few voters said they would be more likely to support a candidate who wanted to cut Medicare to reduce the deficit; in fact, a majority of voters in all age groups but one said they would be less likely to support that candidate. The exception? Young people aged 18 to 29, who cast ballots at much lower rates than older voters.

Opposition to Medicare Cuts

This survey asked, "If a candidate for Congress supports making major cuts in Medicare spending to reduce the federal budget deficit, would that make you more likely or less likely to vote for that candidate specifically because of this issue, or would it not make much difference in your vote?"

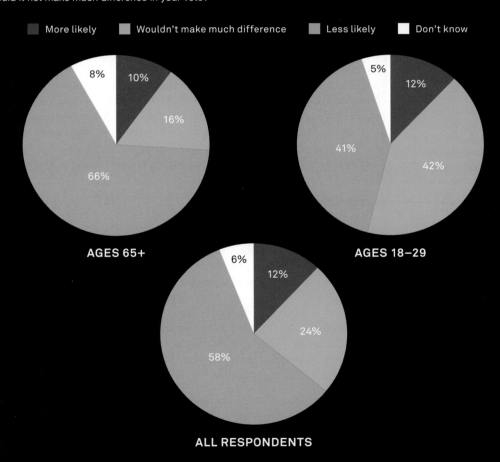

■ More likely   ■ Wouldn't make much difference   ■ Less likely   ■ Don't know

AGES 65+

AGES 18–29

ALL RESPONDENTS

SOURCE: Robert J. Blendon and John M. Benson, "The Public and Conflict over Future Medicare Spending," *New England Journal of Medicine* 369 (2013): 1072.

If contributions don't buy votes, what do they buy? Our claim is that campaign contributions influence legislative behavior in ways that are difficult for the public to observe and political scientists to measure. The institutional structure of Congress provides opportunities for interest groups to influence legislation outside the public eye, which legislators and contributors prefer.

Committee proposal power enables legislators, if they are on the relevant committee, to introduce legislation that favors contributing groups. Gatekeeping power enables committee members to block legislation that harms contributing groups. (The fact that certain provisions are *excluded* from a bill is just as much an indicator of PAC influence as the fact that certain provisions are *included*. The difference is that it is hard to measure what you don't see.) Committee oversight powers enable members to intervene in bureaucratic decision making on behalf of contributing groups.

The point here is that voting on the floor, the alleged object of campaign contributions according to the vote-buying hypothesis, is a highly visible, highly public act, one that could get a legislator in trouble with his broader electoral constituency. The committee system, in contrast, provides numerous opportunities for legislators to deliver to PAC contributors and other donors "services" that are better hidden from public view. Thus we suggest that the most appropriate places to look for traces of campaign-contribution and interest-group influence are in the manner in which committees deliberate, mark up proposals, and block legislation from the floor.[45]

Interest groups mobilize voters and contribute campaign finance, but they also convey information. While it is true that legislators become specialists, acquire expertise, and hire expert staff to assist them, for much specialized knowledge, especially about how aspects of policy will affect local constituencies, they depend on lobbyists. Informational lobbying is a very important inside-the-beltway activity. Interest group expenditures on lobbying dwarf money given in campaign contributions.[46]

Party Discipline

In both the House and the Senate, party leaders have substantial influence over their party members' behavior. This influence, sometimes called party discipline, was once so powerful that it dominated the lawmaking process. Let us define as a **party vote** a vote on which 50 percent or more of the members of one party take one position while at least 50 percent of the members of the other party take the opposing position. At the beginning of the twentieth century, most **roll-call votes** in the House of Representatives were party votes. The frequency of party votes declined through most of the twentieth century as legislative parties grew more ideologically diverse. Democrats included liberals from the

party vote

A roll-call vote in the House or Senate in which at least 50 percent of the members of one party take a particular position and are opposed by at least 50 percent of the members of the other party. Party votes are less common today than they were in the nineteenth century

roll-call votes

Votes in which each legislator's yes or no vote is recorded

---

45 A complementary effect of campaign contributions is not to buy votes that would otherwise be unavailable to a contributor. It is, rather, to increase the likelihood that legislators *already sympathetic* will be reelected. Interest groups thus primarily support their friends with contributions rather than attempting to convert opponents to their cause.

46 See Sven E. Feldmann and Morten Bennedsen, "Informational Lobbying and Political Contributions," *Journal of Public Economics* 90 (2006): 631–56.

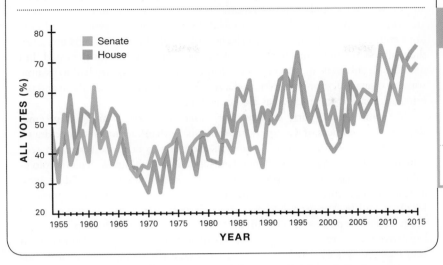

Figure 6.8

PARTY UNITY SCORES BY CHAMBER

ANALYZING THE EVIDENCE

Party voting increased in the 1970s and has remained fairly high since then. What contributes to party voting?

NOTE: The scores represent the percentage of recorded votes on which the majority of one party voted against the majority of the other party.

SOURCE: voteview.com/party_unity.html (accessed 8/15/16) and "2015 Vote Studies: Party Unity Remained Strong," *CQ Weekly*, February 8, 2016.

big cities and conservatives from the South. Republicans included conservatives from the Midwest and West and moderates from the Northeast. The tail end of this decline in party voting is evident in Figure 6.8 between 1955 and 1970.

Beginning in the 1970s, however, legislative parties grew more homogeneous and more polarized. Conservative southern districts began electing Republicans, and liberal northeastern districts began sending Democrats to Congress. This meant that there were fewer conservatives in the ranks of Democratic legislators, and fewer moderates and liberals among Republican legislators. Party members were becoming more alike, but the parties themselves were becoming more different—the very essence of polarization. The data shown in Figure 6.8 reflect this, with party votes ticking upward from the 1970s onward. Some of this change is the result of intense partisan struggles that began during the administrations of Ronald Reagan and George H. W. Bush. Straight party-line voting was also seen briefly in the 103rd Congress (1993–94) after Bill Clinton's election in 1992. The situation soon gave way, however, to the many long-term factors working against party discipline in Congress, as seen in the decline in party voting over the rest of the 1990s.[47] Since the election of George W. Bush, accompanied by Republican congressional control, party voting again ticked upward. And in the first Obama administration, party voting in both chambers was

47 There were fluctuations during George W. Bush's presidency-declines in party voting following September 11 and then surges and declines in subsequent years (see Figure 6.8).

strong—Republican votes supporting Obama initiatives were quite rare. In the last Congress of Obama's first term (the 112th), the Senate minority leader announced that his main objective was to defeat Obama in the 2012 election, and he kept the Republican troops unified in opposition on almost every Senate vote of importance. Hence: gridlock.[48] Obama's second term showed little improvement and, in the midterm election of 2014, the Republicans increased their House majority and won control of the Senate. Gridlock persisted, but with the Republicans now in complete control of Congress, they had to assume some responsibility for governing; a degree of bargaining between them and the minority Democrats emerged as a consequence.

To some extent, party divisions are based on ideology and background. Republican members of Congress are more likely than Democrats to be drawn from rural or suburban areas. Democrats are likely to be more liberal on economic and social questions than their Republican colleagues. This ideological gap has been especially pronounced since 1980 (Figure 6.9).[49] Ideological differences certainly help explain roll-call divisions between the two parties.[50] Ideology and background, however, are only part of the explanation of party unity. The other part has to do with party organization and leadership. Although legislative party organization has weakened throughout most of the twentieth century, there was an uptick in the late 1970s and early 1980s. Today's party leaders have resources at their disposal: (1) committee assignments, (2) access to the floor, (3) the whip system, (4) logrolling, and (5) the presidency. These resources are often effective in securing the support of party members.[51]

Committee Assignments. Leaders can create debts among members by helping them get favorable committee assignments. These assignments are made early in the congressional careers of most members and ordinarily cannot be taken from them if they later balk at party discipline.[52] Nevertheless, if the leadership goes

---

48 One of the hidden consequences of polarization between the parties is what is *not* voted on. In the Senate, especially, the majority leader often pulls from the floor those bills on which unified minority opposition would sink the measure.

49 Figure 6.9 is slightly misleading in showing southern Democrats becoming more liberal. It is true, but for a nonobvious reason: there are fewer and fewer southern Democrats, with the ones remaining most likely to be urban and/or minority legislators.

50 Keith T. Poole and Howard Rosenthal, *Congress: A Political-Economic History of Roll Call Voting* (New York: Oxford University Press, 1997). As a result, it is hard to sort out the effects of party and ideology. On this latter issue, see Krehbiel, "Where's the Party?"

51 Legislative leaders may behave in ways that enhance their reputation for being willing to punish party members who stray from the party line. The problem of developing such a credible reputation is analyzed in Randall Calvert, "Reputation and Legislative Leadership," *Public Choice* 55 (1987): 81–120, and is summarized in Kenneth A. Shepsle, *Analyzing Politics: Rationality, Behavior, Institutions*, 2nd ed. (New York: Norton, 2010), pp. 460–68.

52 There have been occasions in which members have lost their committee posts because of failing to support the leadership. In a bold move at the end of the 112th Congress, for example, as the nation approached an end-of-the-year set of tax and spending deadlines, Speaker Boehner removed several recalcitrant Republicans from the Budget Committee.

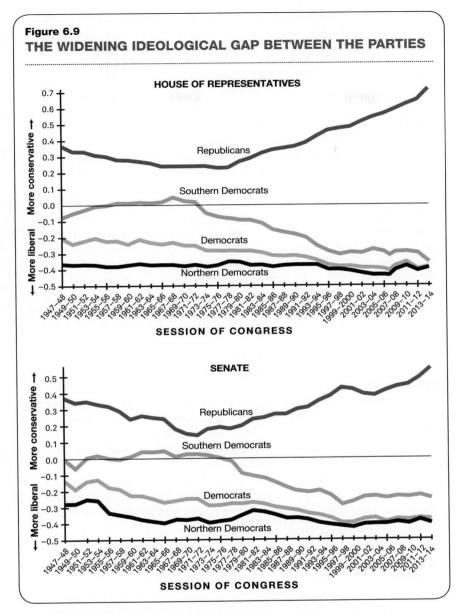

Figure 6.9

THE WIDENING IDEOLOGICAL GAP BETWEEN THE PARTIES

HOUSE OF REPRESENTATIVES

Republicans

Southern Democrats

Democrats

Northern Democrats

More conservative ↑
More liberal ↓

SESSION OF CONGRESS

SENATE

Republicans

Southern Democrats

Democrats

Northern Democrats

More conservative ↑
More liberal ↓

SESSION OF CONGRESS

SOURCE: voteview.com/party_unity.html (accessed 8/15/16).

out of its way to get the right assignment for a member, the effort is likely to create a bond of obligation that can be called on without any other payments or favors.

Access to the Floor. The most important everyday resource available to the parties is control over access to the floor. With thousands of bills awaiting passage and most members clamoring to influence a bill or publicize themselves, floor time is precious. In the Senate, the leadership allows ranking committee members to influence the allocation of floor time—who will speak for how long. In the House, the Speaker, as head of the majority party (in consultation with the minority leader), allocates large blocks of floor time. Thus floor time is allocated in both houses of Congress by the majority and minority leaders. More important, the Speaker of the House and the majority leader in the Senate possess the power of recognition. This formidable authority can be used to stymie a piece of legislation completely or to frustrate a member's attempts to speak on a particular issue. Because the power is significant, members of Congress usually attempt to stay on good terms with the Speaker and the majority leader to ensure that they will continue to be recognized.[53]

The Whip System. Some influence accrues to party leaders through the **whip system**, which is primarily a communications network. Between 12 and 20 assistant and regional whips are selected by geographic zones to operate at the direction of the majority or minority leader and the whip. They take polls of all the members to learn their intentions on specific bills. This information lets the leaders know if they have enough support to allow a vote and whether the vote is so close that they need to put pressure on a few swing votes. Leaders also use the whip system to convey their wishes and plans to the members.

Logrolling. An agreement between two or more members of Congress who have nothing in common except the need for mutual support is called **logrolling**. The agreement states, in effect, "You support me on bill X, and I'll support you on a bill of your choice." Because party leaders are the center of the communications networks in the two chambers, they can help members create large logrolling coalitions. Hundreds of logrolling deals are made each year, and although there are no official records, it would be a poor party leader whose whips did not know who owed what to whom.[54]

In some instances, logrolling produces strange alliances. A seemingly unlikely alliance emerged in Congress in 1994, when 119 mainly conservative senators and representatives from oil-producing states met with President

---

whip system →

A party communications network in each house of Congress by which whips poll the membership to learn their intentions on specific legislative issues and convey to members the wishes and plans of the leaders

---

logrolling →

A legislative practice wherein reciprocal agreements are made between legislators, usually in voting for or against a bill; in contrast to bargaining, logrolling unites parties that have nothing in common but their desire to exchange support

---

53 An analysis of how floor time is allocated is found in Cox and McCubbins, *Setting the Agenda.*

54 For an analysis of the formal problems that logrolling (or vote trading) both solves and creates, see Shepsle, *Analyzing Politics,* pp. 374−76. It is argued there that logrolling cannot be the entire solution to the problem of assembling majority coalitions out of the diverse preferences found in any political party. The reason is that although party leaders can try to keep track of who owes what to whom, the bookkeeping is imperfect and highly complex at best. Nevertheless, if anyone is positioned to orchestrate a system of logrolling, it is the party leaders. And of all those who have tried to facilitate such "cooperation," Robert Byrd (D-W.Va.), who served as both majority whip and majority leader in the Senate, was the acknowledged master. For an insightful analysis of the ways party leaders build majority coalitions through the strategic use of pork-barrel projects, see Evans, *Greasing the Wheels.*

Clinton to suggest that they might be willing to support the president's health care proposals in exchange for his support for certain tax breaks for the oil industry. Another alliance of strange bedfellows was the 1994 "corn for porn" logroll in which liberal urbanites supported farm programs in exchange for rural support for National Endowment for the Arts funding (at a time when many conservatives considered some NEA grantees' art to border on the pornographic). In 2015, to give a third example, the Trans-Pacific Partnership was a trade deal sought by President Obama and supported mainly by *Republicans*. The logroll would open up Asian markets to U.S. exports, something favored by Republicans and their friends in the business community, in exchange for the imposition of environmental restrictions and labor-market liberalization in Asian economies favored by the president and some of his Democratic allies. (Many Democrats and their union supporters, however, opposed the deal because of the fear it would adversely affect manufacturing employment in the United States.) Good logrolling, it would seem, is not hampered by minor ideological concerns. In this case, the rationality principle (exemplified by a willingness to support a policy that one opposes in exchange for reciprocal support for a policy that one cares passionately about) and the institution principle (in which the separation of powers allows the president and legislators to cut deals) work in unusual ways to produce policy outcomes.

The Presidency. Of all the influences that maintain the clarity of party lines in Congress, the influence of the presidency is probably the most important. Indeed, it is a touchstone of party discipline in Congress. Since the late 1940s, under President Harry Truman, presidents each year have identified a number of bills to be considered part of their administration's program. By the mid-1950s, both parties in Congress began to look to the president for these proposals, which became the most significant part of Congress's agenda. Some major presidential initiatives, like Eisenhower's program to build a national highway system in the mid-1950s, persuaded leaders of *both* parties to push their followers to support the program. However, in recent years support for, and opposition to, many presidential initiatives has come to define party loyalty; fellow partisans are expected to support their president's initiatives while opposition party members oppose them. The Patient Protection and Affordable Care Act of 2010 (commonly known as Obamacare) was the classic instance of a presidential initiative that plainly and unmistakably drew party lines and defined party loyalty.

Weighing Diverse Influences

Clearly many factors affect congressional decisions. But at various points in the decision-making process, some are more influential than others. For example, interest groups may be more effective at the committee stage, when their expertise is especially valued and their visibility is less obvious. Because committees play a key role in deciding what legislation reaches the floor of the House or the Senate, interest groups can often put a halt to bills they dislike, or they can ensure that options that do reach the floor are those that the group's members support. Once legislation reaches the floor and members of Congress are deciding among alternatives in visible roll-call votes, to take another example, constituent opinion will become more important.

The influence of the external and internal forces described in the preceding section also varies according to the kind of issue under consideration. On policies of great importance to powerful interest groups—farm subsidies, for example—those groups are likely to have considerable influence. On other issues, members of Congress may be less attentive to narrow interest groups and more willing to consider what they see as the general interest.

Finally, the mix of influences varies according to the historical moment. The Republicans' 1994 electoral victory allowed their party to control both houses of Congress for the first time in 40 years. That fact, combined with an unusually assertive Republican leadership, meant that party leaders became especially important in decision making. Likewise, the historical significance in 2008 of the election of the first African American president gave Democratic party leaders that extra weight and credibility to rally their fellow partisans in support of the new president's agenda.

BEYOND LEGISLATION: ADDITIONAL CONGRESSIONAL POWERS

In addition to the power to make the law, Congress has at its disposal an array of other instruments through which it can influence the process of government. These include advice and consent in several areas, as well as the extreme step of impeachment.

Advice and Consent: Special Senate Powers

The Constitution has given the Senate a special power, one that is not based on lawmaking: the president has the power to make treaties and appoint top executive officers, ambassadors, and federal judges—but only "with the Advice and Consent of the Senate" (Article II, Section 2). For treaties, two-thirds of those senators present must concur; for appointments, a majority is required.

The Senate only occasionally exercises its power to reject treaties and appointments. More common than Senate rejection of presidential appointees is a senatorial "hold" on an appointment. Any member may place an indefinite hold on the confirmation of a mid- or lower-level presidential appointment. The hold may be a signal of a senator's willingness to filibuster a nomination, but it typically aims to wring concessions from the White House on matters unrelated to the appointment in question. Regarding judicial appointments, Senate Democrats actively scrutinized the nominations of President George W. Bush and prevented final confirmation votes on a dozen especially conservative nominees. Of course, Republicans had done the same thing to many judicial nominations in the preceding Clinton administration and continued the practice in the Obama administration.

Senatorial advice and consent is also required on treaties. Thus at the end of the first Congress of the Obama presidency—one featuring frequent obstruction from Republicans—it was surprising that they joined Democrats in consenting to the New START treaty with Russia to reduce nuclear arsenals. Most presidents make every effort to take potential Senate opposition into account in treaty negotiations and frequently resort to **executive agreements** with foreign powers instead of treaties when they find the prospects of Senate advice and consent unlikely. The Supreme Court has held that such agreements are equivalent to treaties, but they do not need Senate approval.[55]

In the past, presidents sometimes concluded secret agreements without informing Congress. In 1972, Congress passed the Case Act, which requires that the president inform Congress of any executive agreement within 60 days of its having been reached. This provides Congress with the opportunity to cancel agreements that it opposes. In addition, Congress can limit the president's ability to conduct foreign policy through executive agreement by refusing to appropriate the funds needed to implement an agreement. In this way, for example, Congress can modify or even cancel executive agreements to provide economic or military assistance to foreign governments.

 executive agreement

An agreement between the president and another country that has the force of a treaty but does not require the Senate's "advice and consent"

Impeachment

The Constitution, in Article II, Section 4, also grants Congress the power of **impeachment** over the president, vice president, and other executive officials. Impeachment means charging a government official (president or otherwise) with "Treason, Bribery, or other high Crimes and Misdemeanors" and bringing him or her before Congress to determine guilt. Impeachment is thus like a criminal indictment in which the House of Representatives acts like a grand jury, voting (by simple majority) on whether the accused ought to be impeached. If a majority of the House votes to impeach, the impeachment trial is held in the Senate, which acts like a trial jury by voting whether to convict and forcibly remove the person from office. (This vote requires a two-thirds majority.)

Controversy over Congress's impeachment power has arisen over the grounds for impeachment, especially the meaning of "high Crimes and Misdemeanors." A strict reading of the Constitution suggests that the only impeachable offense is an actual crime. But a more commonly accepted definition is that "an impeachable offense is whatever the majority of the House of Representatives considers it to be at a given moment in history."[56] In other words, impeachment, especially impeachment of a president, is a political decision.

 impeachment

The charging of a government official (president or otherwise) with "Treason, Bribery, or other high Crimes and Misdemeanors" and bringing him or her before Congress to determine guilt

55 *United States v. Pink,* 315 U.S. 203 (1942). For a good discussion of the problem, see James W. Davis, *The American Presidency: A New Perspective* (New York: Harper & Row, 1987), chap. 8. Also see William G. Howell, *Power without Persuasion: The Politics of Direct Presidential Action* (Princeton, NJ: Princeton University Press, 2003).

56 Carroll J. Doherty, "Impeachment: How It Would Work," *Congressional Quarterly Weekly Report,* January 31, 1998, p. 222.

The United States came closest to impeaching and convicting a president in 1867. Andrew Johnson, a southern Democrat who had battled a congressional Republican majority over Reconstruction, was impeached by the House but saved from conviction by one vote in the Senate. At the height of the Watergate scandal in 1974, the House started impeachment proceedings against President Richard Nixon, but Nixon resigned before the House could proceed. The possibility of impeachment arose again in 1998, when President Clinton was accused of lying under oath and obstructing justice in the investigation into his sexual affair with White House intern Monica Lewinsky. In October 1998, the House voted to impeach the president. At the conclusion of the Senate trial in 1999, Democrats, joined by a handful of Republicans, acquitted Clinton of both charges.

CONCLUSION: POWER AND REPRESENTATION

Because they feared both executive and legislative tyranny, the framers of the Constitution pitted Congress and the president against each other. And as the history principle suggests, this has yielded a legacy of interbranch competition. During the first century of American government, Congress was the dominant institution. American foreign and domestic policy was formulated and implemented by Congress, and generally the most powerful figures in American government were the Speaker of the House and the leaders of the Senate—not the president. During the nineteenth century, the War of 1812 was planned and fought by Congress.[57] The great sectional compromises before the Civil War were formulated in Congress without much intervention from the executive; and even during the Civil War—a period of extraordinary presidential leadership—a joint congressional committee played a role in formulating war plans and campaign tactics and even in promoting officers. After the Civil War, when President Andrew Johnson sought to interfere with congressional plans for Reconstruction, he was summarily impeached, saved from conviction by only one vote.

Congressional preeminence began to diminish in the twentieth century, so that by the 1960s the executive had become the dominant branch of American government. The major domestic policy initiatives of the twentieth century—Franklin Delano Roosevelt's New Deal, Harry Truman's Fair Deal, John F. Kennedy's New Frontier, and Lyndon Johnson's Great Society—were essentially developed, introduced, and implemented by the executive. In foreign policy, although Congress continued to be influential, the focus of decision-making power clearly moved into the executive branch. American entry into World War I, World War II, Korea, Vietnam, Iraq, Afghanistan, and numerous lesser conflicts was initiated essentially by presidential—not congressional—action.

---

57 President Madison's resolve against the war dissolved under relentless pressure from congressional war hawks led by Speaker of the House Henry Clay.

The relationship between the two branches is one of ebb and flow. In the last 40 years, there has been a resurgence of congressional power vis-à-vis the executive. This has occurred in part because Congress has sought to represent many important political forces, specifically the civil rights, women's, environmental, consumer, and peace movements in the 1970s and 1980s, and newer conservative political forces of the social and religious right in the last quarter century. These, in turn, have become constituencies for congressional power. The resurgence of congressional power has also been helped by the creation of congressional agencies to provide informational support independent of the executive branch

As we have seen, the U.S. Congress is a two-chamber legislature with the authority to develop and pass legislation (with the concurrence of the president) on the one hand, and the power to oversee policy implementation by the president and executive bureaucracy on the other hand. It is present at the creation of laws and has a continuing responsibility after laws are crafted. Each chamber keeps an eye on the other chamber and ultimately must come to terms with that other chamber on joint legislative products that are sent to the president for his signature. But each chamber has a life of its own as well. Each is organized by its majority party, itself possessing an organizational structure of leaders and followers. In addition to pursuing substantive policy objectives through legislation by authorizing new programs and reauthorizing existing ones, the two chambers play a special role in the financial realm—raising revenue from taxes and appropriating monies to fund authorized programs. In addition, the Senate's further responsibilities include the approval of treaties and the confirmation of federal judges, Supreme Court justices, and high administrative officers.

In analytical terms, the U.S. Congress is an institutional arrangement. In light of the rationality principle, it arranges itself in accordance with the policy and career ambitions of its members. Politicians are ambitious for themselves, their party, and their constituencies. To accomplish at least some of the personal objectives of 435 individuals in one chamber and 100 in the other, politicians engage in bargaining, coordination, and cooperation that are orchestrated by institutional rules, structures, and procedures. Given the size of majorities required in each chamber to produce results, policy benefits must be distributed widely in what we called the *distributive tendency*. The resulting product isn't always pretty; there are occasional "bridges to nowhere" and other undesirable pork-barrel projects. But this is what it takes to accomplish goals in a diverse, multiperson, elected body. For over more than two centuries, each chamber has created ways of doing business, reformed them, and sometimes engineered entirely new ways of conducting its affairs. The history of what has gone before channels this institutional engineering.

The two chambers of the American legislature do not operate in a vacuum. In front of them are the president, the executive bureaucracy, and the courts, which jointly participate in lawmaking and its implementation. Behind them is public opinion and organized interests, which ultimately render judgment on their efforts by rewarding or punishing individuals and parties through elections. In the next three chapters we take up the presidency, the executive branch, and the court system. In Part 3 we explore public opinion, organized interests, parties, and elections.

For Further Reading

Adler, E. Scott. *Why Congressional Reforms Fail: Reelection and the House Committee System.* Chicago: University of Chicago Press, 2002.

Aldrich, John H., and David W. Rohde. "The Republican Revolution and the House Appropriations Committee." *Journal of Politics* 62 (2000): 1–33.

Binder, Sarah. *Stalemate: Causes and Consequences of Legislative Gridlock.* Washington, DC: Brookings Institution, 2003.

Binder, Sarah, and Paul Quirk, eds. *Institutions of Democracy: The Legislative Branch.* New York: Oxford University Press, 2004.

Brady, David W., and Mathew D. McCubbins, eds. *Party, Process, and Political Change in Congress: New Perspectives on the History of Congress.* Palo Alto, CA: Stanford University Press, 2002 (vol. 1); 2007 (vol. 2).

Brady, David W., and Craig Volden. *Revolving Gridlock: Politics and Policy from Carter to Bush.* 2nd ed. Boulder, CO: Westview Press, 2005.

Cox, Gary W., and Jonathon Katz. *Elbridge Gerry's Salamander: The Electoral Consequences of the Reapportionment Revolution.* Cambridge: Cambridge University Press, 2002.

Cox, Gary W., and Mathew D. McCubbins. *Setting the Agenda: Responsible Party Government in the U.S. House of Representatives.* New York: Cambridge University Press, 2005.

Cox, Gary W., and Mathew D. McCubbins. *Legislative Leviathan: Party Government in the House.* 2nd ed. Berkeley: University of California Press, 2006.

Frisch, Scott A., and Sean Q Kelly. *Committee Assignment Politics in the U.S. House of Representatives.* Norman: University of Oklahoma Press, 2006.

Gamm, Gerald, and Kenneth A. Shepsle. "Emergence of Legislative Institutions: Standing Committees in the House and the Senate, 1810–1825." *Legislative Studies Quarterly* 14 (1989): 39–66.

Harbridge, Laurel, and Neil Malhotra. "Electoral Incentives and Partisan Conflict in Congress: Evidence from Survey Experiments." *American Journal of Political Science* 55 (2011): 494–510.

Jacobson, Gary C. *The Politics of Congressional Elections.* 8th ed. New York: Longman, 2012.

Krehbiel, Keith. *Pivotal Politics: A Theory of U.S. Lawmaking*. Chicago: University of Chicago Press, 1998.

Mayhew, David R. *Congress: The Electoral Connection*. New Haven, CT: Yale University Press, 1974.

Rohde, David W. *Parties and Leaders in the Post-Reform House*. Chicago: University of Chicago Press, 1991.

Smith, Steven S., and Christopher J. Deering. *Committees in Congress*. 3rd ed. Washington, DC: CQ Press, 1997.

Stewart, Charles H. *Analyzing Congress*. 2nd ed. New York: Norton, 2012.

Wawro, Gregory, and Eric Schickler. *Filibuster: Obstruction and Lawmaking in the United States Senate*. Princeton, NJ: Princeton University Press, 2006.

The Presidency as an Institution

America's last eight presidents have left office under political clouds and, in five cases, sooner than they wanted. Lyndon Johnson did not run for reelection in 1968 after the Vietnam War turned much of his own party against him. As the Watergate scandal unfolded and the House prepared to vote impeachment, Richard Nixon chose to resign in 1974 to avoid almost certain conviction. Nixon's appointed successor, Gerald Ford, was defeated for election to a full term in 1976. Jimmy Carter, who ousted Ford, was denied reelection by Ronald Reagan, who himself left office with a reputation damaged by the Iran-Contra scandal. Reagan's successor, George H. W. Bush, was defeated for reelection by Bill Clinton, who served two full terms but faced an impeachment and numerous scandals. Clinton's successor, George W. Bush, will be remembered as the least popular president in the history of opinion polling, leaving office with historically low approval ratings despite having enjoyed very high ones earlier in his presidency. Barack Obama, elected in 2008 as a popular successor to Bush, won reelection in a bruising campaign in 2012, despite presiding over four years of economic sluggishness and indifferent international performance. (He, too, suffered relatively low popularity during the early part of his second term, despite great expectations and high popularity when first elected.)

Yet even as our presidents have limped out of the White House or struggled to remain there, the presidency as an institution has grown in power and prominence. Indeed, over the past century the presidency has become America's most powerful institution in the realms of foreign and military policy and, arguably, domestic policy as well. One reason is that the presidency is America's only political institution characterized by unitary rather than collective decision making. Members of Congress and the judiciary must deliberate, compromise, and vote before reaching decisions. The president may wish to seek advice from many sources but, in the end, exercises the powers of the office either directly on his own authority or it is exercised by those to whom he has delegated this authority. As former president George W. Bush once said, "I am the decider."

Unitary "deciders" are usually better able to accrue power than collective decision makers. To begin with, the unitary decider usually sees a direct relationship between the power of the institution and the ability to achieve his political goals. Presidents Reagan and Bill Clinton, for example, worked diligently to expand the president's power of regulatory review (discussed later in the chapter) so that they could use the bureaucratic rule-making process to achieve their policy goals without the need for congressional approval. In contrast, members of collective decision-making bodies, such as Congress, often confront collective action problems and are motivated to put their immediate political interests ahead of the long-term power of the institution. For example, in 2008 Congress responded to enormous political pressure for quick action on the nation's financial crisis by giving the executive branch unprecedented new economic powers. Several years later, President Obama used this additional authority to promote new rules to refinance federally guaranteed mortgages and to ease repayment schedules for federal student loans in 2008. In his second term he relied on executive orders in the face of a gridlocked Congress.

At the same time, collective decision makers often feel pressure to cede power to unitary deciders when expeditious action seems of paramount importance. During times of crisis, when a quick response is needed and the public is impatient with constitutional limitations on collective action, Congress and the

CORE OF THE ANALYSIS

 The Constitution endows the president with a limited number of expressed powers. Other presidential powers are delegated by Congress or are claimed by presidents without specific statutory authority.

 Over time, the presidency has accumulated more and more power relative to the other institutions of government, partly because the president does not face the same collective action problems as Congress.

 Presidents can broaden their powers through successful execution of the law.

 Presidential power can also be enhanced through strategic interactions with other political actors and through a president's ability to build popular support.

Historic events requiring bold action and leadership by the president, such as the Great Depression, can also contribute to the president's power.

judiciary typically accede to presidential demands for new executive powers to deal with the emergency.

Hence the character of the presidency as an institution—the fact that the president is a unitary decider—helps explain why the position has gained in power at the expense of other institutions, particularly Congress. However, as presidents gain power in more policy spheres, they also have opportunities to make more mistakes and generate more opposition. Thus, ironically, the growing power of the presidency is one reason so many of our recent chief executives have become unpopular after a few years in office. President Obama, for instance, entered office with over 60 percent approval; this dropped to just 38 percent in October 2011. Approval hovered near 50 percent at the start of Obama's second term but fell to the low 40s by 2014. By the end of his presidency his approval had rebounded some, to 55 percent.

Our focus in this chapter is on the development of the institutional character of the presidency, the power of the presidency, and the relationship between the two. First, we review the constitutional origins and powers of the presidency. Second, we review the history of the American presidency to see how the office has evolved from its original status under the Constitution. Third, we assess the means by which presidents can enhance their own ability to govern.

THE CONSTITUTIONAL ORIGINS AND POWERS OF THE PRESIDENCY

The presidency as an institution was established by Article II of the Constitution, which asserts, "The executive Power shall be vested in a President of the United States of America." The article goes on to describe the manner in which the president is to be chosen, qualifications for the office (one must be a natural-born citizen, 35 years of age or older, and a resident of the United States for at least 14 years), and the basic powers of the presidency. By vesting the executive power in a single president, the framers were emphatically rejecting proposals for collective leadership, most of which sought to avoid undue concentration of power in the hands of one individual. While some of the framers favored a multiheaded executive, most hoped the president would be capable of taking quick and decisive action; they thought a unitary executive would be more energetic than some form of collective leadership. They believed that a powerful executive would help protect the nation's interests vis-à-vis other nations and promote the federal government's interests relative to the states. In other words, the framers opted for a decider rather than a deliberative body.

Immediately following the first sentence of Article II, Section 1, of the Constitution, the manner in which the president is to be chosen is defined. This odd sequence says something about the difficulty the delegates to the Constitutional Convention were having over how to provide great power of action to the executive and at the same time balance that power with limitations. This reflected the twin struggles deeply etched in the memories of the founding generation—against the powerful executive authority of King George III and the dismal low energy of the government under the Articles of Confederation. Some delegates wanted the president to be selected by, and thus responsible to, Congress; others preferred that the president be elected directly by the people. Direct popular election would create a more independent and more powerful presidency. But by adopting a scheme of indirect election through an electoral college, in which the electors would be selected by the state legislatures (and close elections would be resolved in the House of Representatives), the framers hoped to achieve a "republican" solution: a strong president responsible to state and national legislators rather than directly responsible to the electorate. This indirect method of electing the president dampened the power of most presidents in the nineteenth century by denying them a political base of support and legitimacy independent of Congress and the state legislatures.

The presidency was strengthened somewhat in the 1830s with the introduction of the national convention system of nominating presidential candidates. Until then, candidates had been nominated by their party's congressional delegates. The convention system was seen as a victory for democracy over the congressional elite, giving the presidency a base of power independent of Congress. This additional independence did not immediately transform the presidency into the office we recognize today, but the national convention did begin to open the presidency to larger social forces and newly organized interests in society.

Article II, Sections 2 and 3, outline the powers and duties of the president. These two sections identify two sources of presidential power. One source is the specific language of the Constitution. For example, the president is specifically authorized to make treaties, grant pardons, and nominate judges and other public officials. These clearly defined powers, called the **expressed powers** of the office, cannot be revoked by Congress or any other agency without an amendment to the Constitution. Other expressed powers include the power to receive ambassadors and to command the nation's military forces.

The second source of presidential power lies in the declaration that the president "shall take Care that the Laws be faithfully executed." Because the laws are enacted by Congress, this language implies that Congress is to delegate to the president the power to implement or execute its will. Powers given to the president by Congress are called **delegated powers**. In principle, Congress delegates to the president only the power to identify or develop the means through which to carry out its decisions. So, for example, if Congress determines that air quality should be improved, it might delegate to a bureaucratic agency in the executive branch the power to identify the best means of bringing about such an improvement, as well as the power to implement the cleanup process. In practice, of course, decisions about how to clean the air are likely to have an enormous effect on businesses, organizations, and individuals throughout the nation. As it delegates power to the executive branch, Congress substantially enhances the importance of the presidency. In most cases, Congress delegates power to bureaucratic agencies in the executive branch rather than directly to the president. As we shall see, however, contemporary presidents have found ways to capture a good deal of this delegated power for themselves.

 expressed powers

The powers that the Constitution explicitly grants to a branch of the federal government

 delegated powers

Constitutional powers assigned to one branch of the government but exercised by another branch with the express permission of the first

inherent powers

Powers claimed by a president that are not expressed in the Constitution but are said to stem from the "rights, duties, and obligations of the presidency," claimed mostly during war and national emergencies.

Presidents have claimed a third source of institutional power beyond expressed and delegated powers. These **inherent powers** are not specified in the Constitution or the law but are said to stem from "the rights, duties and obligations of the presidency."[1] They are most often asserted by presidents in times of war or national emergency. For example, after the fall of Fort Sumter and the outbreak of the Civil War, President Lincoln issued a series of executive orders, although he had no clear legal basis for doing so. Without even calling Congress into session, Lincoln combined the state militias into a 90-day national volunteer force, called for 40,000 new volunteers, enlarged the regular army and navy, diverted $2 million in unspent appropriations to military needs, instituted censorship of the U.S. mail, ordered a blockade of southern ports, suspended the writ of habeas corpus in the border states, and ordered military police to arrest individuals whom he deemed to be guilty of engaging in or even contemplating treasonous actions.[2] Lincoln asserted that these extraordinary measures were justified by the president's inherent power to protect the nation.[3]

Expressed Powers

The president's expressed powers, as defined by Article II, Sections 2 and 3, fall into several categories:

1. *Military.* Article II, Section 2, provides for the power as "Commander in Chief of the Army and Navy of the United States, and of the Militia of the several States, when called into the actual Service of the United States."

2. *Judicial.* Article II, Section 2, provides the "Power to grant Reprieves and Pardons for Offences against the United States, except in Cases of Impeachment."

3. *Diplomatic.* Article II, Section 2, provides the "Power, by and with the Advice and Consent of the Senate, to make Treaties." Article II, Section 3, provides the power to "receive Ambassadors and other public Ministers."

---

1   In the case of *In re Neagle,* 135 U.S. 1 (1890), David Neagle, a deputy U.S. marshal, had been authorized by the president to protect a Supreme Court justice whose life had been threatened by an angry litigant. When the litigant attempted to carry out his threat, Neagle shot and killed him. Neagle was then arrested by local authorities and tried for murder. His defense was that his act was "done in pursuance of a law of the United States." Although the law was not an act of Congress, the Supreme Court declared that it was an executive order of the president and that the protection of a federal judge was a reasonable extension of the president's power to "take Care that the Laws be faithfully executed."

2   James G. Randall, *Constitutional Problems under Lincoln* (New York: Appleton, 1926), chap. 1.

3   E. S. Corwin, *The President: Office and Powers,* 4th ed. (New York: New York University Press, 1957), p. 229.

4. *Executive.* Article II, Section 3, authorizes the president to see to it that all the laws are faithfully executed. Section 2 gives the chief executive power to appoint, remove, and supervise all executive officers and appoint all federal judges.

5. *Legislative.* Article I, Section 7, and Article II, Section 3, give the president the power to participate authoritatively in the legislative process.

Military Power. The president's military powers are among the most important of the powers exercised by the chief executive. The position of **commander in chief** makes the president the highest military authority in the United States, with control of the entire defense establishment. The president is also head of the nation's intelligence network, which includes not only the CIA but also the National Security Council (NSC), the NSA, the Federal Bureau of Investigation (FBI), and a host of less-well-known but very powerful international and domestic security agencies.

Domestic Defense Power. The president's military powers extend into the domestic sphere. Article IV, Section 4, provides that "the United States shall . . . [protect] every State . . . against Invasion . . . and . . . domestic Violence." Congress has made this an explicit presidential power through statutes directing the president as commander in chief to discharge these obligations.[4] The Constitution restrains the president's use of domestic force by providing that a state legislature (or governor when the legislature is not in session) must request federal troops before the president can send them into the state to provide public order. Yet this proviso is not absolute. First, presidents are not obligated to deploy national troops merely because a state legislature or governor makes such a request. And more important, the president may deploy troops in a state or city without a specific request from a state legislature or governor if the president considers it necessary to maintain an essential national service during an emergency, enforce a federal judicial order, or protect federally guaranteed civil rights.

One historic example was the decision by President Dwight Eisenhower in 1957 to send troops into Little Rock, Arkansas, to enforce court orders to integrate Little Rock's Central High School; he did so only after failed negotiations with the state's governor, who had posted the Arkansas National Guard at the entrance of the school to prevent the admission of nine black students. This case makes quite clear that the president does not have to wait for a request by a state legislature or a governor before acting as a domestic commander in chief. More recently, President George W. Bush sent various military units to the Gulf Coast in response to Hurricanes Katrina and Rita in 2005, and in 2010 President Obama sent Coast Guard and teams from other agencies to participate in the rescue and cleanup following the BP *Deepwater Horizon* explosion and oil spill in the Gulf of Mexico. In most instances of domestic disorder—whether a result of human or natural events—presidents tend to exercise unilateral power by declaring a state of emergency, thereby making available federal grants, insurance, and direct assistance.

 commander in chief

The power of the president as commander of the national military and the state national guard units (when called into service)

---

4   These statutes are contained mainly in Title 10 of the United States Code, Sections 331, 332, and 333.

Military emergencies have also led to expansion of the domestic powers of the executive branch. This was true during World Wars I and II and has been the case during the ongoing "war on terrorism" as well. Within a month of the September 11 attacks, the White House had drafted, and Congress had enacted, the USA PATRIOT Act, expanding the power of government agencies to engage in domestic surveillance, including electronic surveillance, and restricting judicial review of such efforts. In the following year Congress created the Department of Homeland Security, combining offices of 22 federal agencies into one huge new cabinet department that would be responsible for protecting the nation from attack. President Obama signed a four-year extension in 2011. In 2015, the USA Freedom Act was passed by Congress and signed by President Obama, renewing expiring sections of the PATRIOT Act but scaling back the domestic surveillance authority of the National Security Agency.

reprieve

Cancellation or postponement of a punishment

pardon

Forgiveness of a crime and cancellation of relevant penalty

amnesty

A pardon extended to a group of persons

executive agreement

An agreement between the president and another country that has the force of a treaty but does not require the Senate's "advice and consent"

Judicial Power. The presidential power to grant **reprieves, pardons,** and **amnesties** involves the power of life and death over all individuals who may be a threat to the nation's security. Presidents may use this power on behalf of a particular individual, as Gerald Ford did when he pardoned Richard Nixon in 1974 "for all offenses against the United States which he . . . has committed or may have committed." Or they may use it on a large scale, as Jimmy Carter did in 1977 when he declared an amnesty for all Vietnam War draft evaders.

Diplomatic Power. The president is America's chief representative in dealings with other nations. As head of state, the president has the power to make treaties for the United States (with the advice and consent of the Senate). When President George Washington received Edmond Genet ("Citizen Genet") as the formal emissary of the revolutionary government of France in 1793 and had his cabinet officers and Congress back his decision, he established a greatly expanded interpretation of the power to "receive Ambassadors and other public Ministers," extending it to the power to "recognize" other countries. That power gives the president the almost unconditional authority to review the claims of any new ruling group to determine whether it indeed controls the territory and population of its country and therefore can, in the president's opinion, legitimately commit it to treaties and other agreements.

In recent years, presidents have expanded the practice of using executive agreements instead of treaties to establish relations with other countries.[5] An **executive agreement** is like a treaty because it is a contract between two countries, but it does not require approval by the Senate. (A treaty requires a two-thirds vote of approval by the Senate.) Ordinarily executive agreements are used to carry out commitments already made in treaties or to arrange for matters well below the level of policy. But when presidents have found it expedient to use an executive agreement in place of a treaty, Congress has typically acquiesced.

....

5   In *United States v. Pink,* 315 U.S. 203 (1942), the Supreme Court confirmed that an executive agreement is the legal equivalent of a treaty despite the absence of Senate approval.

Table 7.1

NOMINATIONS TO FEDERAL DISTRICT AND CIRCUIT COURTS
(First five years of presidency)

PRESIDENT	CIRCUIT NOMINATIONS	SUCCESS RATE	DISTRICT NOMINATIONS	SUCCESS RATE
Bill Clinton (1993–1998)	48	77%	232	85%
George W. Bush (2001–2006)	52	79%	187	97%
Barack Obama (2009–2014)	54	76%	215	80%

SOURCE: Russell Wheeler, "Judicial Nominations and Confirmations: Fact and Fiction," Brookings Institution, December 30, 2013, www.brookings.edu/blogs/fixgov/posts/2013/12/30-staffing-federal-judiciary-2013-no-breakthrough-year (accessed 6/24/16).

Executive Power. The most important basis of the president's power as chief executive is found in Article II, Section 3, which stipulates that the president must see that all the laws are faithfully executed, and Section 2, which provides that the president will appoint and supervise all executive officers and appoint all federal judges (with Senate approval). The power to appoint the principal executive officers and to require each of them to report to the president on subjects relating to the duties of their departments makes the president the true chief executive officer of the nation. In this manner, the Constitution focuses executive power and legal responsibility on the president. The famous sign on President Truman's desk, "The buck stops here," was not merely an assertion of his personal sense of responsibility but was in fact evidence of his recognition of the legal and constitutional responsibility of the president.

The president's executive power is not absolute, however, as many presidential appointments—including ambassadors, cabinet officers and other high-level administrators, and federal judges—are subject to majority approval by the Senate. And in fact, the Senate has often refused to confirm presidential nominees or has held them hostage by failing even to bring them up for an up-or-down vote. This pattern is evident in the confirmation process for federal judges. Table 7.1 shows, for the first five years of the Clinton, Bush, and Obama presidencies, the presidential success rate for federal circuit and district court nominations.

The George W. Bush administration, supported by conservative scholars, argued that Article II of the Constitution vests all executive power in the president, who, by implication, is in full control of the executive branch. This idea is called the theory of the unitary executive. It is controversial in part because it denies Congress a significant role in managing the bureaucracy, concentrating this authority instead in the hands of the executive. This undermines the view of the American separation of powers system that executive and legislature are two branches "sharing powers."[6]

6 For a famous statement of this, see Richard E. Neustadt, *Presidential Power* (1960; rev. ed. New York: Free Press, 1980).

executive privilege

The claim that confidential communications between the president and the president's close advisers should not be revealed without the consent of the president

Another component of the president's power as chief executive is **executive privilege**—the claim that confidential communications between a president and close advisers should not be revealed without the president's consent. Presidents have made this claim ever since George Washington refused a request from the House of Representatives to deliver documents concerning negotiations of an important treaty. Washington refused (successfully) on the grounds that, first, the House was not constitutionally part of the treaty-making process and, second, that diplomatic negotiations required secrecy.

Executive privilege became a part of the checks-and-balances counterpoint between the president and Congress, and presidents have usually had the upper hand when invoking it. Although many presidents have claimed executive privilege, the concept was not tested in the courts until the Watergate affair of the early 1970s, during which President Nixon refused congressional demands that he turn over secret White House tapes that congressional investigators thought would establish Nixon's complicity in illegal activities. In *United States v. Nixon*, the Supreme Court ordered Nixon to turn over the tapes.[7] The president complied with the order and resigned from office to avoid impeachment and conviction. *United States v. Nixon* is often seen as a blow to presidential power, but in actuality the Court's ruling recognized for the first time the validity of a claim of executive privilege, although it held that it did not apply in this instance. Subsequent presidents have cited *United States v. Nixon* in support of their claims of executive privilege. Thus in 2012 the Obama administration appealed to executive privilege in refusing to comply with a subpoena from the House of Representatives for documents related to "Operation Fast and Furious," a Justice Department program to combat drug-trafficking.

Legislative Power. Two constitutional provisions are the primary sources of the president's power in the legislative arena. Article II, Section 3, states that the president "shall from time to time give to the Congress Information of the State of the Union, and recommend to their Consideration such Measures as he shall judge necessary and expedient." The second of the president's legislative powers is the veto power assigned by Article I, Section7.[8]

Delivering a State of the Union address might not appear to be of any great import. It is a mere obligation on the part of the president to make recommendations for Congress's consideration. But as political and social conditions favored an increasingly prominent role for presidents, each president has relied on this provision to become (1) the primary initiator of proposals for legislative action in Congress and (2) the principal source for public

---

7   *United States v. Nixon,* 418 U.S. 683 (1974).

8   There is a third source of presidential power implied in the provision for faithful execution of the laws: the president's power to impound funds—that is, to refuse to spend money Congress has appropriated for certain purposes. One author referred to this as a "retroactive veto power" (Robert E. Goostree, "The Power of the President to Impound Appropriated Funds," *American University Law Review* 11 [1962]: 32–47).

awareness of national issues as well as (3) the most important individual participant in legislative decisions. Few today doubt that the president, together with the executive branch as a whole, is the primary source of many important congressional actions.

The **veto** is the president's constitutional power to turn down acts of Congress (Figure 7.1). It alone makes the president the most important single

 veto

The president's constitutional power to turn down acts of Congress within 10 days of their passage while Congress is in session. A presidential veto may be overridden by a two-thirds vote of each house of Congress

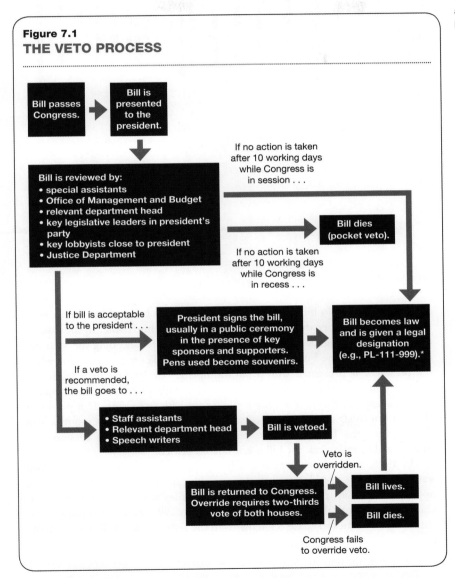

Figure 7.1
THE VETO PROCESS

*PL stands for "public law"; 111 is the Congress (e.g., the 111th Congress was in session in 2009–11); 999 is the number of the law.

Presidential Vetoes, 1789–2016

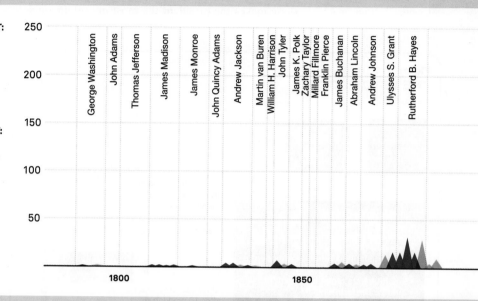

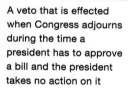
UNIFIED GOVERNMENT: The president's party controlled both chambers during this session of Congress

DIVIDED GOVERNMENT: The president's party controlled one or neither chamber during this session of Congress

---

pocket veto ➡

A veto that is effected when Congress adjourns during the time a president has to approve a bill and the president takes no action on it

---

line-item veto ➡

The power of the executive to veto specific provisions (lines) of a bill passed by the legislature

---

legislative leader.[9] No bill vetoed by the president can become law unless both the House and the Senate override the veto by a two-thirds vote. In the case of a **pocket veto**, Congress does not have the option of overriding the veto but must reintroduce the bill in the next session. A pocket veto can occur when the president is presented with a bill during the last 10 days of a legislative session. Usually if a president does not sign a bill within 10 days, it automatically becomes law. But this is true only while Congress is in session. If a president chooses not to sign a bill presented within the last 10 days that Congress is in session, then the 10-day limit expires while Congress is out of session, and instead of becoming law, the bill is considered vetoed.

In 1996, a new power was added to the president's lineup—the **line-item veto**—giving the president the power to strike specific spending items from appropriations bills passed by Congress unless they were reenacted by a two-thirds vote of both the House and the Senate. In 1997, President Clinton used this power 11 times to strike 82 items from the federal budget. But in 1998 the

....

9 For more on the veto, see Chapter 6. Also see Robert J. Spitzer, *The Presidential Veto: Touchstone of the American Presidency* (Albany: State University of New York Press, 1988); and Charles M. Cameron, *Veto Bargaining: Presidents and the Politics of Negative Power* (New York: Cambridge University Press, 2000).

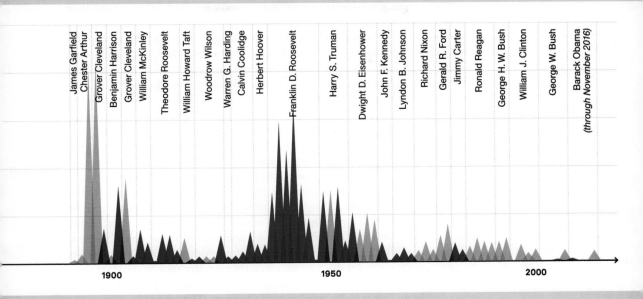

James Garfield
Chester Arthur
Grover Cleveland
Benjamin Harrison
Grover Cleveland
William McKinley
Theodore Roosevelt
William Howard Taft
Woodrow Wilson
Warren G. Harding
Calvin Coolidge
Herbert Hoover
Franklin D. Roosevelt
Harry S. Truman
Dwight D. Eisenhower
John F. Kennedy
Lyndon B. Johnson
Richard Nixon
Gerald R. Ford
Jimmy Carter
Ronald Reagan
George H. W. Bush
William J. Clinton
George W. Bush
Barack Obama
(through November 2016)

1900   1950   2000

Supreme Court ruled that the Constitution does not authorize the line-item veto.[10] Only a constitutional amendment would give this power to the president.

The Games Presidents Play: The Veto. Use of the veto varies according to the political situation that each president confronts. George W. Bush vetoed no bill during his first term and only one bill during the first two years of his second term, both periods during which his party controlled both houses of Congress. In the last two years of his second term, with Congress controlled by the Democrats, he vetoed 11 bills. In President Obama's first term, with Democratic control of both the House and the Senate in the first two years, he vetoed only two bills. In his second term, during which his party did not control the House and controlled the Senate for only one Congress, Republicans pursued the strategy of obstruction, and very little legislation was produced. Obama's vetoes nevertheless increased to the low double digits.[11] In general, presidents have used the veto to equalize or upset

10 *Clinton v. City of New York,* 524 U.S. 417 (1998).

11 For the complete list of presidential vetoes, see www.senate.gov/reference/Legislation/Vetoes/vetoCounts.htm (accessed 10/31/16).

the balance of power with Congress. The politics surrounding the veto is complicated, and it is usually part of an intricate bargaining process between the president and Congress, involving threats of vetoes, the repassage of legislation, and second vetoes.[12] As the timeplot shows, divided government does not necessarily result in more vetoes.

The fact that presidents vetoed only several hundred of the more than 20,000 public bills that Congress sent to them between 1945 and 2015 belies the centrality of the veto to presidential power. Many of these bills were insignificant and not worth the veto effort. Thus it is important to separate "significant" legislation, for which vetoes frequently occur, from insignificant legislation.[13] Vetoes can also be effective because of the rationality principle: individuals will condition their actions on the basis of how they think others will respond.[14] With respect to vetoes, this means that members of Congress will alter the content of a bill to make it more to a president's liking to discourage a veto. Thus the veto power can be influential even when the veto pen remains in its inkwell.[15]

Rhetoric and reputation take on particular importance when vetoes become part of a bargaining process. In fact, bargaining between Congress and the president is strategic and an example of the rationality principle in action. The president tries to influence legislators' beliefs about what they must do to keep him from using the veto power. The key to veto bargaining is uncertainty: legislators are often unsure about the president's policy preferences and therefore don't know which bills he is willing to sign. When the policy preferences of the president and Congress diverge, as they typically do in a divided government, the president tries to convince Congress that his preferences are more extreme than they really are to get Congress to enact legislation that is closer to what he really wants. Thus, through strategic use of veto threats, a president tries to shape Congress's beliefs about his policy preferences in order to gain greater concessions from Congress. Reputation is central to presidential effectiveness in this process.[16] By influencing congressional beliefs, the president is building a policy reputation that will affect future congressional behavior.

During the first year of his presidency, Barack Obama threatened to veto a defense spending bill that contained $369 billion in funding for the production of the F-22 fighter as well as a congressional resolution that would have blocked the release of about $350 billion in economic stimulus funds. After meeting with the president, members of Congress agreed to release the stimulus funds. On the issue of the F-22, however, Congress was reluctant to concede. Nevertheless, on July 21, 2009, with the backing of Defense Secretary Robert Gates

12 Cameron, *Veto Bargaining*. See also David W. Rohde and Dennis Simon, "Presidential Vetoes and Congressional Response: A Study of Institutional Conflict," *American Journal of Political Science* 29 (1985): 397–427.

13 David R. Mayhew, *Divided We Govern: Party Control, Lawmaking, and Investigations, 1946–1990* (New Haven, CT: Yale University Press, 1991).

14 Jack H. Nagel, *The Descriptive Analysis of Power* (New Haven, CT: Yale University Press, 1975).

15 See Rohde and Simon, "Presidential Vetoes and Congressional Response."

16 Neustadt, *Presidential Power*.

and former Republican presidential nominee John McCain, Obama's position was sustained by a vote in the Senate, stripping funds for the F-22 from a defense appropriations measure. The House, which had previously voted to appropriate the funds, followed the Senate's lead on July 30, agreeing to eliminate the funds.

What about the relationship between mass public support for the president and the use of the veto? At least for the modern presidency, a crucial resource for the president in negotiating with Congress has been public approval as measured by opinion polls.[17] In some situations, members of Congress pass a bill not because they want to change policy but because they want to force the president to veto a popular bill that he disagrees with in order to hurt his approval ratings.[18] The key is that the public, uncertain of the president's policy preferences, uses information implied by vetoes to reassess what it knows about his preferences. As a result, vetoes may come at a price to the president. According to the rationality principle, a president must weigh the advantages of using the veto or threatening to do so—to gain concessions from Congress—against the hit he might take in popularity. He may be reluctant to use the veto or the threat of a veto if it will hurt him in the polls; but in some cases, the president will take a hit in his approval ratings by vetoing a bill that is drastically inconsistent with his policies.[19] The Policy Principle case study on the following page looks at Obama's veto of a bill authorizing the Keystone XL pipeline, a project that was supported by a majority of Americans but strongly opposed by Democrats in Congress. In this case, the president risked a dip in public approval in order to promote his own policy preferences and those of the politicians who supported him.

Delegated Powers

Many of the powers exercised by the president and the executive branch are not set forth in the Constitution but are the products of congressional statutes and resolutions. Over the past three-quarters of a century, Congress has voluntarily delegated a great deal of its own legislative authority to the executive branch. To some extent, this has been an almost inescapable consequence of the expansion of governmental activity in the United States since the New Deal. Given the vast range of the federal government's responsibilities, Congress cannot execute and administer all the programs it creates and the laws it enacts. Inevitably Congress must turn to the hundreds of departments and agencies in the executive branch or, when necessary, create new agencies to implement its goals. Thus,

---

17 Theodore J. Lowi, *The Personal President: Power Invested, Promise Unfulfilled* (Ithaca, NY: Cornell University Press, 1985).

18 Timothy Groseclose and Nolan McCarty, "The Politics of Blame: Bargaining before an Audience," *American Journal of Political Science* 45 (2001): 100–19.

19 For a study of the ways presidents mobilize mass public opinion on behalf of policies they pursue, see Brandice Canes-Wrone, *Who Leads Whom? Presidents, Policy, and the Public* (Chicago: University of Chicago Press, 2006). Also see Lawrence R. Jacobs and Robert Y. Shapiro, *Politicians Don't Pander: Political Manipulation and the Loss of Democratic Responsiveness* (Chicago: University of Chicago Press, 2000).

The Veto and the Keystone XL Pipeline

Demonstrators protest the Keystone XL pipeline.

President Obama, despite presiding over congresses with at least one house controlled by Republicans through most of his two terms, did not use his veto pen very often. However, his veto of a 2015 bill concerning the Keystone XL pipeline provides a clear example of how institutions shape policy outcomes.

The Keystone XL pipeline would have taken crude oil from Alberta, Canada, through Montana, South Dakota, and Nebraska and on to refineries in Illinois and along the Gulf Coast. Proponents of the pipeline, including most Republicans and business groups, pointed to its economic benefits, such as construction jobs and ongoing employment at U.S. refineries. Opponents of the pipeline, including environmental groups and many Democrats, argued that the construction jobs would not last and that the project posed serious environmental risks. The proposed pipeline would have traveled through fragile wetlands, threatened large aquifers, and been vulnerable to ruptures.

In 2012, Obama announced his opposition to the pipeline plans because of the environmental dangers. The pipeline corporation adjusted the route in response, and the governor of Nebraska (where the risks were especially alarming) signed off on the new proposal. Obama then announced that any further consideration would be suspended until various lawsuits against the pipeline were resolved. In 2015 the Nebraska Supreme Court allowed the project to go forward. The table was now set for federal action.

In February 2015 a bill approving the Keystone XL pipeline passed the House, was amended by the Senate, and then passed the House again. The institutional rules of Congress mattered: Republican majorities controlled the agenda in both chambers; had the Democrats held a majority in either chamber they could have blocked consideration of the bill. The vote splits on the bill were important too: 62–36 in the Senate and 270–152 in the House. Neither total indicated that the votes were there to override a presidential veto with the two-thirds required under the Constitution.

On February 24, 2015, the bill was sent to President Obama for his signature. Although opinion polls indicated that a majority of the public supported the pipeline, it was not a top public issue. It *was* very important to environmental organizations, however, and thus to their Democratic allies in Congress and in the White House. This was enough to persuade the president to wield his veto pen. On that very same day he communicated to the Senate his decision to veto the bill. A week later the Senate held a vote to override the veto, which failed to reach the necessary two-thirds (62–37).

As the policy principle advises, the institutional features involved shaped how (and whose) preferences were translated into policy. In particular, the very exacting standard for the legislature to override a president's veto means that presidents require only a sufficiently large minority in at least one chamber to block legislative action. Presidents facing a hostile Congress may be handicapped in accomplishing their own policy goals, but these presidents nevertheless may succeed in blocking policies they oppose.

for example, in 2002, when Congress sought to protect America from terrorist attacks, it established the Department of Homeland Security and gave it broad powers in the realms of law enforcement, public health, and immigration.

As they implement congressional legislation, federal agencies interpret Congress's intent; promulgate thousands of rules aimed at implementing that intent; and issue thousands of orders to individuals, firms, and organizations nationwide designed to impel them to conform to the law. When it establishes an agency, Congress sometimes grants it only limited discretionary authority, providing very specific guidelines and standards that the administrators charged with the program's implementation must follow. Consider the Internal Revenue Service (IRS). Most Americans view the IRS as a powerful agency whose dictates can have an immediate and sometimes unpleasant effect on their lives, yet congressional tax legislation is specific and detailed and leaves little to the discretion of IRS administrators.[20] The agency certainly develops rules and procedures to enhance tax collection. It is Congress, however, that establishes the structure of the tax liabilities, exemptions, and deductions that determine each taxpayer's burdens and responsibilities.

In many instances, however, congressional legislation is not very detailed. Often Congress defines a broad goal or objective and delegates enormous discretionary power to administrators to determine how that goal is to be achieved. For example, the 1970 act creating the Occupational Safety and Health Administration (OSHA) states that Congress's purpose is "to assure so far as is possible every working man and woman in the nation safe and healthful working conditions." The act, however, neither defines such conditions nor suggests how they might be achieved.[21] The result is that agency administrators have enormous discretionary power to draft rules and regulations that have the effect of law. Indeed, the courts treat these administrative rules like congressional statutes. Essentially, when Congress creates an agency such as OSHA, giving it a broad mandate to achieve some purpose, it transfers its own legislative power to the executive branch.

In the nineteenth and early twentieth centuries, Congress typically wrote laws that provided fairly clear principles and standards to guide executive implementation. For example, the 1922 Tariff Act empowered the president to increase or decrease duties on certain manufactured goods in order to reduce the difference in cost between products produced domestically and those manufactured abroad. The act authorized the president to make the final determination, but his discretionary authority was quite constrained. At least since the New Deal, however, Congress has tended to give executive agencies broad mandates through legislation that offers few clear standards or guidelines for implementation. The 1972 Consumer Product Safety Act, for example, authorized the Consumer Product Safety Commission to reduce unreasonable risk of injury from household products but offered no suggestions to guide the commission's

---

20 Kenneth F. Warren, *Administrative Law,* 3rd ed. (Upper Saddle River, NJ: Prentice-Hall, 1996), p. 250.

21 Theodore J. Lowi, *The End of Liberalism: The Second Republic of the United States,* 2nd ed. (New York: Norton, 1979), pp. 117–18.

determination of what constitutes reasonable and unreasonable risks or how these are to be reduced.[22]

This shift from issuing relatively well defined congressional guidelines for administrators, to the more contemporary pattern of broadly delegating congressional power to the executive branch, is partially a consequence of the great scope and complexity of the tasks that America's contemporary government has undertaken. During much of the nineteenth century, the federal government had relatively few domestic responsibilities, and Congress could pay close attention to details. Today the operation of an enormous executive establishment and thousands of programs under varied and changing circumstances requires that administrators be allowed considerable discretion to carry out their jobs. Nevertheless, the result is to shift power from Congress to the executive branch.[23]

Inherent Powers

A number of presidential powers are neither expressed explicitly in the Constitution nor delegated by congressional statute or resolution. They are said to be "inherent" powers of a sovereign nation exercised by its chief executive. One inherent power of sovereign nations is self protection. Today, this power is mainly exercised by the White House.

War and Inherent Presidential Power. The Constitution gives Congress the power to declare war. Presidents, however, have gone a long way toward capturing this power for themselves. Congress has not declared war since December 1941, and yet since then American military forces have engaged in numerous campaigns throughout the world under orders of the president. When North Korean forces invaded South Korea in June 1950, Congress was prepared to declare war, but President Harry S. Truman decided not to ask for congressional action. Instead, Truman asserted the principle that the president, and not Congress, could decide when and where to deploy America's military might. Truman dispatched U.S. forces to Korea without a congressional declaration, and in the face of the emergency Congress felt it had to acquiesce. It passed a resolution approving the president's actions, and this sequence of events became the pattern for future congressional-executive relations in the military realm. The wars in Vietnam, Bosnia, Afghanistan, and Iraq, as well as a host of lesser conflicts, were all fought without declarations of war.

In 1973, Congress responded to presidential unilateralism by passing the **War Powers Resolution**—over President Richard Nixon's veto. This resolution reasserted the principle of Congress's power to declare war, required the

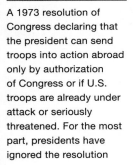

War Powers Resolution

A 1973 resolution of Congress declaring that the president can send troops into action abroad only by authorization of Congress or if U.S. troops are already under attack or seriously threatened. For the most part, presidents have ignored the resolution

---

22 *Lowi, The End of Liberalism,* p. 117.

23 To some extent, though, the shift in power is illusory. What authority Congress delegates, it can recover. The wise president or executive branch administrator is eminently aware of this and conditions her discretionary decisions with one eye cast over a shoulder at a watchful Congress.

president to inform Congress of any planned military campaign, and stipulated that forces must be withdrawn within 60 days in the absence of a specific congressional authorization for their continued deployment. Presidents have generally ignored the War Powers Resolution, however, claiming inherent executive power to defend the nation. Thus, for example, President George W. Bush responded to the 2001 attacks by Islamic terrorists by organizing a major military campaign to overthrow the Taliban regime in Afghanistan, which had sheltered the terrorists. In 2003, Bush ordered a major U.S. campaign against Iraq, which he accused of posing a threat to the United States. Although Congress passed resolutions approving the president's actions, the War Powers Resolution was barely mentioned on Capitol Hill and was ignored by the White House.[24]

However, the fact that presidents since 1974 have ignored the War Powers Resolution, with virtually no objection from Congress, does not mean that tensions stemming from the separation of powers between the president and Congress have ceased. The powers of the purse and of investigation give Congress levers with which to constrain even the most freewheeling executive. For all these reasons, the president restrains himself, often self-censoring to minimize adverse political consequences.[25] Thus in 2013, with public opinion running against him, President Obama sought authorization from Congress for an airstrike on Syria as punishment for its use of chemical weapons, part of an effort to implicate Congress in the action and thereby share accountability. Throughout the last years of the Obama presidency, the president and Congress negotiated over a congressional "authorization for the use of military force" against the Islamic state and debated the legal rationale for a continuing American military effort without such authorization.

Legislative Initiative. Although not explicitly stated, the Constitution provides the president with the power of **legislative initiative**. To initiate means to originate, and in government that can mean power. The framers of the Constitution clearly saw legislative initiative as one of the keys to executive power. Initiative obviously implies the ability to formulate proposals for important policies, and the president, as an individual with a great deal of staff assistance, is able to initiate decisive action more frequently than Congress, with its large assemblies that have to deliberate before taking action. It should be emphasized that Congress is under no constitutional obligation to take up proposals from the president. He can, according to Article II, Section 3, only "recommend to their Consideration such Measures as he shall judge necessary and expedient." Having said that, however, with some important exceptions, Congress banks on the president to set the agenda of public policy. And there is power in being able to set the terms of discourse in the making of public policy.

 legislative initiative

The president's inherent power to bring a legislative agenda before Congress

---

24 These were, in fact, joint resolutions authorizing the use of military force—PL107-40 for Afghanistan and PL 107-243 for Iraq—thus protecting some role for Congress in the deployment of military forces.

25 On this point, see William G. Howell and Jon C. Pevehouse, *While Dangers Gather: Congressional Checks on Presidential Power* (Princeton, NJ: Princeton University Press, 2007).

Table 7.2 A

FINAL PASSAGE VOTE TALLIES, 2009–12: HOUSE OF REPRESENTATIVES

LEGISLATION	TOTAL		DEMOCRATS		REPUBLICANS	
	YEAS	NAYS	YEAS	NAYS	YEAS	NAYS
The Lilly Ledbetter Fair Pay Act	250	177	247	5	3	172
The Children's Health Insurance Program Reauthorization Act of 2009	290	135	250	2	40	133
The American Recovery and Reinvestment Act of 2009	246	183	246	7	0	163
The Fraud Enforcement and Recovery Act of 2009	338	52	224	0	114	52
The Helping Families Save Their Homes Act of 2009	367	54	244	3	123	51
The Credit Card Accountability Responsibility and Disclosure Act of 2009	279	147	105	145	174	2
The Dodd-Frank Wall Street Reform and Consumer Protection Act	237	192	234	19	3	173
The Patient Protection and Affordable Care Act	219	212	219	34	0	178
The Middle Class Tax Relief and Job Creation Act of 2012	293	132	147	41	146	91

SOURCE: Library of Congress, http://thomas.loc.gov/home/rollcallvotes.html (accessed 6/25/13).

For example, during the weeks immediately following September 11, 2001, George W. Bush took many presidential initiatives to Congress, and each won almost unanimous support: from commitments to pursue Al Qaeda and remove the Taliban in Afghanistan all the way to almost unlimited approval to regulate American civil liberties. But in his second term, as Bush faced growing problems (and casualties) in Iraq, administrative scandals, and a financial crisis, his popularity ebbed in the polls and so too did his agenda power.

In 2009, soon after taking office, President Obama presented Congress with a record-breaking $3 trillion budget proposal that included a host of new programs in such areas as health and human services, transportation, housing, and education. Obama told Congress that he would soon be requesting several hundred billion more for the financial bailout to rescue America's banks and revive the nation's credit markets. Not only was Congress responsive to the president's initiatives but lawmakers also expected the president to take the

Table 7.2 B

FINAL PASSAGE VOTE TALLIES, 2009–12: SENATE

LEGISLATION	TOTAL		DEMOCRATS		REPUBLICANS	
	YEAS	NAYS	YEAS	NAYS	YEAS	NAYS
The Lilly Ledbetter Fair Pay Act	61	36	56	0	5	36
The Children's Health Insurance Program Reauthorization Act of 2009	66	32	57	0	9	32
The American Recovery and Reinvestment Act of 2009	60	38	57	0	3	38
The Fraud Enforcement and Recovery Act of 2009	92	5	56	0	36	4
The Helping Families Save Their Homes Act of 2009	91	5	56	0	35	5
The Credit Card Accountability Responsibility and Disclosure Act of 2009	90	5	55	1	35	4
The Dodd-Frank Wall Street Reform and Consumer Protection Act	60	39	57	1	3	38
The Patient Protection and Affordable Care Act	60	39	60	0	0	39
The Middle Class Tax Relief and Job Creation Act of 2012	60	36	46	5	14	31

SOURCE: Library of Congress, http://thomas.loc.gov/home/rollcallvotes.html (accessed 6/25/13).

lead in responding to America's financial emergency and other problems. As a general matter Congress empowered the president, in the Budget Act of 1921, to submit an annual budget, something that has given all subsequent presidents enormous agenda power in the formulation of tax and spending policy. But, as just noted, Congress takes the president's budget recommendations as suggestions, not mandates, and in the world of divided government, many presidential budget proposals are said to be "dead on arrival" on Capitol Hill.

For example, Obama worked with the Democratic 111th Congress to achieve a number of legislative results in his first two years: the Lilly Ledbetter Fair Pay Act, the Children's Health Insurance Program Reauthorization Act of 2009, the American Recovery and Reinvestment Act of 2009, financial reform legislation, and of course, health care reform legislation. Table 7.2 shows how Congress voted on each of these bills. In working strategically to get these bills passed, Obama's team was mindful of the institutional rules and practices that would affect the outcomes. Despite Obama's efforts to assemble bipartisan support, Republicans, with some exceptions, mainly opposed the legislation. After Republicans won control of the House in 2010, the president won fewer major legislative successes. And after the 2012 and 2014 elections, which increased Republican legislative numbers and enabled them to capture the Senate in the latter election, administration legislative successes slowed to a trickle.

There were also legislative disappointments. Obama took on enormous political risks when he staked his presidency on legislative accomplishments. The overarching risk was that he would fail to accomplish what he had set out to do. More specifically, the messy and often ugly process of legislation will frustrate a president's efforts to meet these goals. There is a reason that the German statesman Otto von Bismarck said, "Laws are like sausages. It's better not to see them being made." Compromise is at the heart of politics in a democracy. When the president gives special favors to those whose votes might help his legislation pass or when the majority leader tries to pass amendments that favor a particular senator or representative, the seamy side of politics is rearing its head. During the attempt to pass health care reform, for example, Nebraska was given a Medicare exemption that no other state received solely to secure the vote of the pivotal Nebraska senator—something Obama's opponents took great pains to point out. The Republicans called out the inconsistencies between Democratic pledges for open, honest government and the closed-door negotiations, proposals, and counterproposals that were taking place. Even worse, elements of the coalitions that supported Obama saw their objectives sacrificed or ignored in the quest to get *something* done. In short, the messiness of the political process negatively affected the Democrats and left the Republicans largely unscathed.

Following the 2010 elections, the Democratic Party lost majority control of the House and saw its large Senate majority trimmed to a bare minimum. Thus during the 112th Congress the Republicans shared legislative initiative with the president, pursuing objectives of their own and blocking numerous presidential initiatives. Notably, the president and Congress failed to solve the problem of the debt ceiling or to negotiate a spending-reduction package. The productivity (in terms of legislation produced) of the 113th Congress, with a Republican House and a Democratic Senate still in place, and the 114th Congress, in which Republicans continued their hold on the House and captured the Senate, were well below historic averages. Divided government and gridlock take a toll on legislating.

The president's initiative does not end with policy making involving Congress and the making of laws in the ordinary sense of the term. The president has still another legislative role (in all but name) within the executive branch: the power to issue **executive orders**. The executive order is foremost a normal tool of management, a power virtually any CEO possesses to make company policy—rules-setting procedures, etiquette, chains of command, functional responsibilities, and so on. But evolving from this practice is a presidential power to promulgate rules that have the effect of legislation. Most executive orders of the president provide for the reorganization of structures and procedures or otherwise direct the affairs of the executive branch—either to be applied to all agencies or in some important respect to a single agency or department. The power to issue executive orders illustrates that although reputation

executive orders ⇨

A rule or regulation issued by the president that has the effect of legislation

and persuasion are typically required in presidential policy making, the practice of issuing executive orders, within limits, allows a president to govern without the necessity to persuade.[26] We take a closer look at how modern presidents have used executive orders later in the chapter.

THE RISE OF PRESIDENTIAL GOVERNMENT

Most of the real influence of the modern presidency derives from the powers granted by the Constitution and the laws made by Congress. Presidential power is institutional. Thus any person properly elected and sworn in as president will possess almost all the power held by the strongest presidents in American history. What variables account for a president's success in exercising these powers? Why are some presidents considered great successes, others colossal failures, and most somewhere in between? These questions relate broadly to the very concept of presidential power. Is it a reflection of the attributes of the person, or is it more a characteristic of the political situations that a president encounters? The personal view of presidential power dominated political scientists' thinking for several decades,[27] but recently scholars have argued that presidential power should be analyzed in terms of the strategic interactions that a president has with other political actors.[28] With the occasional exception, it took more than a century before presidents came to be seen as consequential players in these strategic encounters. A bit of historical review will be helpful in understanding how the presidency has risen to its current level of influence.

The Legislative Epoch, 1800–1933

In 1885, a then-obscure political science professor named Woodrow Wilson titled his general textbook *Congressional Government* because American government was just that—congressional government. There is ample evidence that Wilson's description of the national government was consistent not only with nineteenth-century reality but also with the intentions of the framers. Within the system of three separate and competing powers, the clear intent of the Constitution was legislative supremacy. In the early nineteenth century, some

26 This point is developed in both Kenneth R. Mayer, *With the Stroke of a Pen: Executive Orders and Presidential Power* (Princeton, NJ: Princeton University Press, 2001), and William G. Howell, *Power without Persuasion: The Politics of Direct Presidential Action* (Princeton, NJ: Princeton University Press, 2003).

27 Neustadt, *Presidential Power and the Modern Presidents.*

28 Charles M. Cameron, "Bargaining and Presidential Power," in *Presidential Power: Forging the Presidency for the Twenty-First Century,* Robert Y. Shapiro, Martha Joynt Kumar, and Lawrence R. Jacobs, eds. (New York: Columbia University Press, 2000). See also Samuel Kernell, *Going Public: New Strategies of Presidential Leadership,* 4th ed. (Washington, DC: CQ Press, 2006).

observers saw the president as little more than America's chief clerk. Indeed, most historians agree that after Thomas Jefferson and until the beginning of the twentieth century, presidents Andrew Jackson and Abraham Lincoln were the only exceptions to a succession of weak presidents. Both Jackson and Lincoln are considered great presidents because they used their power in momentous ways. But it is important in the history of the presidency that neither of them left his powers as an institutional legacy to his successors. That is to say, once Jackson and Lincoln left office, the presidency reverted to the subordinate role that it played throughout the nineteenth century.

One of the reasons so few great men became president in the nineteenth century is that there was rarely room for greatness.[29] As Chapter 3 indicated, the national government of that period was not a particularly powerful entity. The presidency of the nineteenth century was also weak because during this period the presidency was not closely linked to major national political and social forces. Federalism had fragmented political interests and diverted the energies of interest groups toward the state and local levels of government, where most key decisions were being made.

As discussed earlier in the chapter, the presidency was strengthened in the 1830s when the national convention system of nominating presidential candidates was introduced. However, this additional independence did not change the presidency into the office we see today because once the national election was over the parties disappeared, returning to their states and Congress. In addition, as the national government grew, Congress kept a tight rein on the president's power. For example, when the national government began to exercise authority over an increasingly continentwide, industrial economy (beginning in 1887 with the adoption of the Interstate Commerce Act and in 1890 with the adoption of the Sherman Antitrust Act), Congress sought to keep this power away from the president and the executive branch by placing the new regulatory policies in "independent regulatory commissions" responsible to Congress rather than to the president (see also Chapter 8).

The New Deal and the Presidency

The key moment in the history of American national government came during Franklin Delano Roosevelt's administration. The Hundred Days at the outset of the Roosevelt administration in 1933 had no parallel in U.S. history—but it was only the beginning. The policies proposed by Roosevelt and adopted by Congress during the first 100 days of his administration so changed the size and character of the national government that they constitute a moment in

---

29 For related appraisals, see Jeffrey Tulis, *The Rhetorical Presidency* (Princeton, NJ: Princeton University Press, 1987); Stephen Skowronek, *The Politics Presidents Make: Leadership from John Adams to Bill Clinton* (Cambridge: Harvard University Press, 1997); and Robert J. Spitzer, *President and Congress: Executive Hegemony at the Crossroads of American Government* (Philadelphia: Temple University Press, 1993).

American history equivalent to the Founding or the Civil War. The president's constitutional obligation to see "that the laws be faithfully executed" became, during Roosevelt's presidency, virtually a responsibility to shape the laws before executing them.

Many of the New Deal programs were extensions of the traditional national government approach, which was described in Chapter 3. But the New Deal also adopted types of policies never before tried on a large scale by the national government; it began intervening in economic life in ways that had hitherto been reserved to the states. For example, during the Great Depression the Roosevelt administration created the Works Progress Administration, seeking to put the able-bodied back to work; the federal government became the nation's largest employer at this time. The Social Security Act, to give another example, sought to improve the economic condition of the most impoverished segment of the population—the elderly. In other words, the national government discovered that it could directly regulate individuals as well as provide roads and other services.

The new programs were such dramatic departures from the traditional policies of the national government that their constitutionality was in doubt. The Supreme Court in fact declared several of them unconstitutional, mainly on the grounds that in regulating the conduct of individuals or their employers, the national government was reaching beyond "*inter*state" and involving itself in "*intra*state"—essentially local—matters. Most of the New Deal remained in constitutional limbo until 1937, five years after Roosevelt was first elected and one year after his landslide 1936 reelection.

The turning point came with *National Labor Relations Board v. Jones and Laughlin Steel Corporation*, a Supreme Court case challenging the federal government's authority over the regulation of labor relations. The Court affirmed a federal role in the regulation of the national economy.[30] After the end of the New Deal, the Court has never again seriously questioned the legitimacy of interventions of the national government in the economy or society.[31]

The most important constitutional effect of Congress's actions and the Supreme Court's approval of those actions during the New Deal was the enhancement of presidential power. Most major acts of Congress in this period involved significant exercises of control over the economy, but few programs specified the actual controls to be used. Instead, Congress authorized the president or, in some cases, a new agency to determine what the controls would be. Although some of the new agencies were independent commissions responsible

---

30 *National Labor Relations Board v. Jones and Laughlin Steel Corporation*, 301 U.S. 1 (1937).

31 Some will argue that there are exceptions to this statement. One was *National League of Cities v. Usery*, 426 U.S. 833 (1976), which declared unconstitutional Congress's effort to apply national minimum wage standards to state and local government employees. But the Court reversed itself on this nine years later, in *Garcia v. San Antonio Metropolitan Transit Authority*, 469 U.S. 528 (1985). Cases such as these are few and far between, and they touch on only part of a law, not the constitutionality of an entire program.

to Congress, most of the new agencies and programs were placed in the executive branch directly under presidential authority. The institutional power of the presidency had been greatly increased.

Technically this form of congressional act is the delegation of power. In theory, the delegation of power works as follows: (1) Congress recognizes a problem, (2) Congress acknowledges that it has neither the time nor the expertise to deal with the problem, and (3) Congress therefore sets the basic policies and then delegates to an agency the power to fill in the details. But in practice, Congress was delegating to the executive branch not merely the power to fill in the details but also real policy-making powers—that is, real legislative powers. This level of delegation produced a fundamental shift in the American constitutional framework.[32]

Of course, Congress can rescind these delegations of power, restrict them with subsequent amendments, and oversee the exercise of delegated power through congressional hearings, oversight agencies, budget controls, and other administrative tools. Thus while it is fair to say that presidential government has become an administrative fact of life as government by delegation has expanded greatly over the past century, it is important to remember that Congress still has many "clubs behind the door" with which to influence and contain the executive branch.[33]

PRESIDENTIAL GOVERNMENT

The locus of policy decision making shifted to the executive branch because, as we noted, Congress made delegations of authority to the president. Congress did so for instrumental reasons, much as a principal delegates to an agent. An expanded agenda of political demands, necessitated first by economic crisis—the Great Depression—but also by the effects of nearly a century's worth of industrialization, urbanization, and greater integration into the world economy. Finally World War II confronted the national government, forcing Congress's

---

32 The Supreme Court did in fact *disapprove* broad delegations of legislative power by declaring the National Industrial Recovery Act of 1933 unconstitutional on the grounds that Congress did not accompany the broad delegations with sufficient standards or guidelines for presidential discretion (*Panama Refining Co. v. Ryan,* 293 U.S. 388 [1935], and *Schechter Poultry Corporation v. United States,* 295 U.S. 495 [1935]). The Supreme Court has never reversed those two decisions, but neither has it really followed them. Thus broad delegations of legislative power from Congress to the executive branch can be presumed to be constitutional. See Sotirios A. Barber, *The Constitution and the Delegation of Congressional Power* (Chicago: University of Chicago Press, 1975).

33 David Epstein and Sharyn O'Halloran, *Delegating Powers: A Transaction Cost Politics Approach to Policy Making under Separate Powers* (New York: Cambridge University Press, 1999).

hand. Because the legislature had a limited capacity to undertake these growing responsibilities, delegation proved a natural administrative strategy. These acts of delegation gave a far greater role to the president, empowering this "agent" to initiate in his own right.

Franklin Delano Roosevelt's New Deal launched an era of presidential government. Congress certainly retained many tools with which to threaten, cajole, encourage, and persuade its executive agent to do its bidding. But presidents are not *only* agents of Congress and not *only* dependent on Congress for resources and authority. They are also agents of national constituencies, for whom they are eager to demonstrate leadership in executing constituency policy agendas.[34]

Likewise, congressional delegations of power are not the only resources available to a president. Presidents have at their disposal other formal and informal resources that have important implications for their ability to govern. Indeed, without these other resources, presidents would lack the ability—the tools of management and public mobilization—to make much use of the power and responsibility given to them by Congress. Let us first consider the president's formal, or official, resources and then turn to the more informal resources that affect a president's capacity to govern, in particular, the president's base of popular support.

The Formal Resources of Presidential Power

The Cabinet. In the American system of government, the **Cabinet** is the traditional but informal designation for the heads of all the major departments of the federal government (Figure 7.2). The Cabinet has only a limited constitutional status.[35] In contrast to the United Kingdom and many other parliamentary countries, where the cabinet *is* the government, the American Cabinet is not a collective body. It meets but makes no decisions as a group. Each appointment must be approved by the Senate, but cabinet members are not responsible to the Senate or to Congress at large. Cabinet appointments help build party and popular support, but the Cabinet is not a party organ. It is made up of directors but is not a true board of directors. Because cabinet appointees generally have not shared political careers with the president or with one another and because they may meet each other for the first time after their selection, the formation of an effective governing group out of this disparate collection of appointments is unlikely. Although the Cabinet is not always powerful, it does serve an important role in managing policy for the president and his political associations. For instance, members of the

 Cabinet

The secretaries, or chief administrators, of the major departments of the federal government. Cabinet secretaries are appointed by the president with the consent of the Senate

---

34 See Terry M. Moe, "Presidents, Institutions, and Theory," in *Researching the Presidency: Vital Questions, New Approaches,* George C. Edwards III, John H. Kessel, and Bert A. Rockman, eds. (Pittsburgh, PA: University of Pittsburgh Press, 1993), p. 367.

35 The Twenty-Fifth Amendment gives the Cabinet a formal role in determining presidential disability.

Figure 7.2
THE INSTITUTIONAL PRESIDENCY 2016

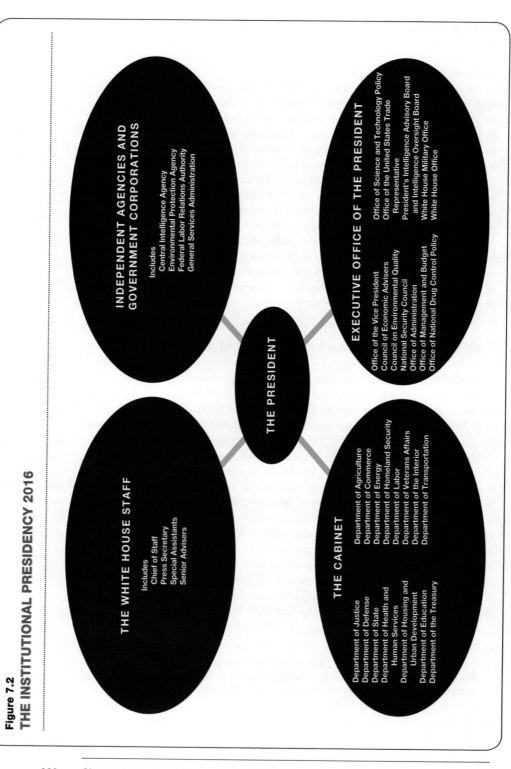

INDEPENDENT AGENCIES AND GOVERNMENT CORPORATIONS

Includes
Central Intelligence Agency
Environmental Protection Agency
Federal Labor Relations Authority
General Services Administration

EXECUTIVE OFFICE OF THE PRESIDENT

Office of the Vice President
Council of Economic Advisers
Council on Environmental Quality
National Security Council
Office of Administration
Office of Management and Budget
Office of National Drug Control Policy
Office of Science and Technology Policy
Office of the United States Trade
Representative
President's Intelligence Advisory Board
and Intelligence Oversight Board
White House Military Office
White House Office

THE PRESIDENT

THE WHITE HOUSE STAFF

Includes
Chief of Staff
Press Secretary
Special Assistants
Senior Advisers

THE CABINET

Department of Justice
Department of Defense
Department of State
Department of Health and
Human Services
Department of Housing and
Urban Development
Department of Education
Department of the Treasury
Department of Agriculture
Department of Commerce
Department of Energy
Department of Homeland Security
Department of Labor
Department of Veterans Affairs
Department of the Interior
Department of Transportation

Cabinet travel on the president's behalf, make policy speeches, and negotiate with other political leaders, both at home and abroad.

Some presidents have relied more heavily on an "inner cabinet," the **National Security Council (NSC)**. The NSC, established by law in 1947, is composed of the president, the vice president, the secretary of state, the secretary of defense, and other officials invited by the president. It has its own staff of foreign policy specialists run by the assistant to the president for national security affairs. For these highest appointments, presidents usually turn to people from outside Washington, often longtime associates. Presidents have been uneven in their reliance on the NSC and other subcabinet bodies because executive management is inherently a personal matter. However, one generalization can be made: presidents have increasingly preferred the White House staff to the Cabinet as their means of managing the gigantic executive branch.

The White House Staff. The **White House staff** is composed mainly of analysts and advisers.[36] Although many of the top White House staff members carry the title "special assistant" for a particular task or sector, the types of judgments they are expected to make and the kinds of advice they are supposed to give are a good deal broader and more generally political than those coming from the Executive Office of the President or the cabinet departments. The members of the White House staff also tend to be more closely associated with the president than other presidentially appointed officials. President Obama, in his early months in office, relied heavily on his chief of staff, Rahm Emanuel; his former chief campaign strategist and then senior adviser, David Axelrod; the deputy chief of staff, Jim Messina; and the press secretary, Robert Gibbs. (However, by Obama's second term, there had been complete turnover in his senior staff.)

The White House staff is a crucial information source and management tool for the president. But it may also insulate the president from other sources of information. Managing this trade-off between in-house expertise and access to independent outside opinion is a major challenge for the president. Sometimes it is botched, as when President George W. Bush depended too heavily on his staff for information about weapons of mass destruction (WMD) in Iraq, leading him to erroneous conclusions.[37] In 2009, President Obama merged the White House Homeland Security staff with the National Security staff to deal with all security problems.

The Executive Office of the President. The development of the White House staff can be appreciated only in its relation to the still-larger **Executive Office of the President (EOP)**. Created in 1939, the EOP is a major part of what is often called the institutional presidency—the permanent agencies that perform

National Security Council (NSC)

A presidential foreign policy advisory council composed of the president; the vice president; the secretaries of state, defense, and treasury; the attorney general; and other officials invited by the president

White House staff

The analysts and advisers to the president, often given the title "special assistant"

Executive Office of the President (EOP)

The permanent agencies that perform defined management tasks for the president; created in 1939, it includes the Office of Management and Budget, the Council of Economic Advisers, the National Security Council, and other agencies

---

36 A substantial portion of this section is taken from Lowi, *The Personal President,* pp. 141–50.

37 See George Krause, "The Secular Decline in Presidential Domestic Policymaking: An Organizational Perspective," *Presidential Studies Quarterly* 34 (2004): 779–92. On the general issue, see James P. Pfiffner, ed., *The Managerial Presidency,* 2nd ed. (College Station: Texas A&M University Press, 1999).

defined management tasks for the president. The most important and the largest EOP agency is the Office of Management and Budget (OMB). Its roles in preparing the national budget, designing the president's program, reporting on agency activities, and overseeing regulatory proposals make OMB personnel part of virtually every presidential responsibility. The status and power of the OMB have grown in importance with each successive president. The process of budgeting at one time was a bottom-up procedure, with expenditure and program requests passing from the lowest bureaus through the departments to "clearance" in OMB and hence to Congress, where each agency could be called in to reveal what its original request had been before it was revised by the OMB. Now the budgeting process is top-down: OMB sets the terms of discourse for agencies as well as for Congress. The director of OMB is now one of the most powerful officials in Washington.

The staff of the Council of Economic Advisers (CEA) constantly analyzes economic trends and attempts to help the president anticipate events, being proactive rather than reactive. The Council on Environmental Quality functions in a similar manner for environmental issues. Members of the NSC meet regularly with the president to give advice on the large national security picture. The staff of the NSC assimilates and analyzes data from all intelligence-gathering agencies (such as the CIA). Other EOP agencies perform more specialized tasks.

Somewhere between 1,500 and 2,000 highly specialized staffers work for EOP agencies.[38] The importance of each agency in the EOP varies according to the personal orientation of the president. For example, the NSC staff was of immense importance under President Nixon, especially because it served essentially as the personal staff of presidential assistant Henry Kissinger before his elevation to the office of secretary of state. But it was of less importance to President George H. W. Bush, who looked outside the EOP for military policy matters, turning much more to the Joint Chiefs of Staff and its chair at the time, General Colin Powell.

The Vice Presidency. The vice presidency is a constitutional anomaly. According to the Constitution, the vice president exists for two purposes only: to succeed the president in case of death, resignation, or incapacitation and to preside over the Senate, casting a tie-breaking vote when necessary.[39]

The main value of the vice presidency as a political resource for the president is electoral. Traditionally a presidential candidate's most important rule for the choice of a running mate is that she should bring the support of at least one state (preferably a large one) not otherwise likely to support the ticket or should provide some regional balance and, wherever possible, some balance among various ideological or ethnic subsections of the party. It is very doubtful that

---

38 The actual number is difficult to estimate because, as with the White House staff, some EOP personnel, especially those in national security work, are detailed to the office from outside agencies.

39 Article I, Section 3, provides that "the Vice President . . . shall be President of the Senate, but shall have no Vote, unless they be equally divided." This is the only vote the vice president is allowed.

John Kennedy would have won in 1960 without his vice-presidential candidate, Lyndon Johnson, and the contribution Johnson made to winning in Texas. In 2016, Donald Trump chose Governor Mike Pence of Indiana as his running mate for several reasons. Pence had been a conservative talk and radio show host and was well known among conservatives. Also, before serving as governor, Pence had served in Congress for twelve years. He worked to reassure skeptical party leaders that Trump was a qualified candidate. Most importantly, as a devout Christian Pence increased Trump's electoral appeal among social conservatives.

As the institutional presidency has grown in size and complexity, most presidents of the past 35 years have sought to use their vice presidents as management resources after the election. George H. W. Bush, as President Reagan's vice president, was kept within the loop of decision making because Reagan delegated so much power. The presidency of George W. Bush resulted in unprecedented power and responsibility for his vice president, Dick Cheney, who was active in cabinet meetings and policy formation as well as in organizing the war on terrorism and launching the Iraq War. Cheney is widely viewed as one of the most—if not the most—influential vice presidents in American history. In the Obama administration, Vice President Joe Biden wielded considerable influence as a liaison to Congress and as a sounding board on matters involving foreign affairs.

The President and Policy. The president's powers and institutional resources, taken together, give the chief executive a substantial voice in the nation's policy-making processes. Strictly speaking, presidents cannot introduce legislation. Only members of Congress can formally propose new programs and policies. However, presidents often do send proposals to Congress, which in turn refers them to the relevant committee of jurisdiction. Sometimes these proposals are said to be dead on arrival, an indication that presidential preferences are at loggerheads with those in the House or Senate. This is especially common during periods of divided government. In such circumstances, presidents and legislators engage in bargaining, although in the end the status quo may prevail—a situation sometimes termed *gridlock*. Presidents are typically in a weak position in these circumstances, especially if they have grand plans to change the status quo.[40] During periods of unified government, the president has fellow partisans in charge of each chamber; in these cases, the president may indeed seize the initiative, seeking to coordinate policy initiatives from the White House. The political scientist Charles Cameron suggests that the distinction between unified and divided government is quite consequential for presidential "style": it makes the chief executive either bargainer in chief or coordinator in chief.[41]

Congress has come to expect the president to propose the government's budget since the Budget Act of 1921, and the nation has come to expect presidential initiatives to deal with major problems. Some of these initiatives have

---

40 D. Roderick Kiewiet and Mathew D. McCubbins, *The Logic of Delegation: Congressional Parties and the Appropriations Process* (Chicago: University of Chicago Press, 1991).

41 Cameron, "Bargaining and Presidential Power."

encompassed multiple programs, such as Franklin Delano Roosevelt's New Deal. Sometimes presidents craft a single program in hopes it will have a significant effect on both the nation and their political fortunes—as George W. Bush did with the war on terrorism. To fight this war, Bush brought about the creation of a new cabinet department, the Department of Homeland Security, and the enactment of legislation such as the USA PATRIOT Act to give the executive branch more power to deal with the terrorist threat. President Obama launched a series of successful legislative initiatives (some listed earlier in Table 7.2), the most important of which was health care. The Patient Protection and Affordable Care Act, known colloquially as Obamacare, was adopted during Obama's first term and remained a contentious issue, both in Congress and in the courts, throughout his second term. In a major decision in 2012, the Court upheld Obamacare by a 5-4 vote.[42] It survived a second major challenge, allowing the government to subsidize the health care premiums of some citizens, by a 6-3 vote in 2015.[43] However, in 2014 the Court affirmed in *Burwell v. Hobby Lobby* a broader interpretation of the "religious exemption" allowed under the ACA; by a 5-4 vote this decision allowed employers to decline to provide no-cost access to contraception services for female employees.[44]

The Contemporary Bases of Presidential Power

In the nineteenth century, when Congress was America's dominant institution of government, its members sometimes treated the president with disdain. Today, however, no one would assert that the presidency is an unimportant institution. This strength is not so much a function of personal charisma or political savvy as it is a reflection of the increasing power of the institution of the presidency. Presidents seek to dominate the policy-making process and claim the inherent power to lead the nation in time of war. The expansion of presidential power over the past century has come about not by accident but as the result of an ongoing effort by successive presidents to enlarge the powers of the office. As the framers of the Constitution predicted, presidential ambition has been a powerful and unrelenting force in American politics.

Generally presidents can expand their power by three means: party, popular mobilization, and administration. In the first instance, presidents may construct or strengthen national partisan institutions with which to influence the legislative process and through which to implement their programs. Alternatively or in addition, presidents may use popular appeals to create a mass base of support that enables them to subordinate their political foes. This tactic has sometimes been called the strategy of going public, or the "rhetorical" presidency.[45] In the third instance, presidents may seek to bolster their control of executive agencies

---

42. *National Federation of Independent Businesses v. Sebelius* 567 U.S. ____ (2012).

43. *King v. Burwell* 576 U.S. ____ (2015).

44. *Burwell v. Hobby Lobby Stores* 573 U.S. ____ (2014).

45 Kernell, *Going Public*; see also Tulis, *The Rhetorical Presidency*.

or create new administrative institutions and procedures that will reduce their dependence on Congress and give them a more independent governing and policy-making capability. The use of executive orders to achieve a president's policy goals in lieu of seeking to persuade Congress to enact legislation is, perhaps, the most obvious example.

Party as a Source of Power. All presidents have relied on the members and leaders of their own party to implement their legislative agendas. But the president does not control his own party; party members have considerable autonomy. President Obama made immigration reform one of his first-term priorities, but he failed to induce the Democratic-controlled Congress to take up the issue. In his second term the Senate did pass a broad immigration reform bill, but the Republican-controlled House did not take up the legislation. Finally, in 2014, Obama announced a series of executive actions on immigration that would expand the number of undocumented immigrants eligible for temporary protection from deportation, among other measures. These actions have received mixed signals from the courts, and Donald Trump vowed to reverse them. An even more significant second-term difficulty for Obama with his own party was on the issue of trade, something on which the president had hoped for a signature accomplishment. The Trans-Pacific Partnership, an effort to cement trade agreements with America's Asian partners by giving the president extraordinary negotiating authority, was initially defeated in the House because too few Democrats would support it. Its ultimate success was the creation of an unusual coalition between Obama and Republican majorities in the two legislative chambers.

When Obama was first elected, he declared his intention to seek bipartisan support for all his programs. Congressional Republicans, however, seeing little to gain from supporting Obama and much to lose if his administration were successful, opposed the president's domestic and foreign policy initiatives. With overwhelming Democratic majorities in both houses of Congress in 2009–11, Obama had no difficulty turning to the Democratic leadership for support. Indeed, Republican opposition helped Democratic leaders unite their fractious followers behind the president's budget proposals in 2009. Many of Obama's successes (see Table 7.2 on pp. 259–260) involved overwhelming Democratic support prevailing over nearly unanimous Republican opposition in his first two years. After the 2010 election, control of the House was captured by the Republicans, who then won the Senate in 2014; neither Democrat-only coalitions nor bipartisan overtures from the president were sufficient to produce major policy victories. The 2015 trade agreement stands out as a notable exception to the policy gridlock that characterized the later Obama years. However, during the 2016 election, Donald Trump promised to withdraw from the agreement.

As Obama's final six years illustrated, in America's system of separated powers, the president's party may be in the minority in Congress and unable to do much for the chief executive's programs (Figure 7.3). This is because the majority party in a legislative chamber may control not only votes on the floor but also *what* is voted on. When it is the minority, the president's party lacks agenda control. Consequently, although their party is valuable to chief executives, it has not been a fully reliable presidential tool. The more unified the president's party

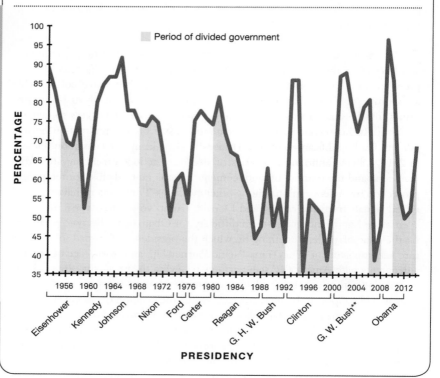

Figure 7.3
THE PRESIDENTIAL BATTING AVERAGE,* 1953–2014

Presidential success ebbs and flows, especially with the partisan character of Congress. Compare success rates when the president and the legislature were of the same party (for example, Clinton's first two years) and when they were not (for example, Clinton's last six years).

Period of divided government

PERCENTAGE

PRESIDENCY

Eisenhower Kennedy Johnson Nixon Ford Carter Reagan G. H. W. Bush Clinton G. W. Bush** Obama

1956 1960 1964 1968 1972 1976 1980 1984 1988 1992 1996 2000 2004 2008 2012

*Percentage of congressional votes in which the president took the position supported by Congress.
**In 2001, the government was divided for only part of the year.
NOTE: Percentages are based on votes on which presidents took a position.
SOURCES: *Congressional Quarterly Weekly Report*, January 3, 2011, pp. 18–24, and authors' update.

is in supporting his legislative requests, the more unified the opposition party is likely to be. The president often poses as being above partisanship to win "bipartisan" support in Congress. But to the extent that he pursues a bipartisan strategy, he cannot throw himself fully into building the party loyalty and the party discipline that would maximize the value of his own party's support in Congress. This is a dilemma for every president, and it is particularly acute with an opposition-controlled Congress.

The role of the filibuster in the Senate should not be underestimated in this context (see Chapter 6). Even a president with a large majority in the House and a good working majority in the Senate may not have the 60 votes needed to shut down debate in the Senate. This is especially apparent in the case of presidential appointments, where individual senators can place a hold on a nomination, putting everyone on notice that the president's pursuit of a particular candidate will trigger a filibuster.[46] Filibuster power was especially prominent in Obama's two terms, when the powerful "senator number 60" was usually a Republican. Frustrated with the frequent use of the filibuster, in particular over President Obama's judicial nominees, in 2013 Senate Democrats changed the rules to eliminate the filibuster for presidential appointments (other than for the Supreme Court).

Going Public. Because a president cannot always rely on his party in Congress, he must consider other methods. One such method is popular mobilization, a technique of presidential power with historical roots in the presidencies of Theodore Roosevelt and Woodrow Wilson. It subsequently became a weapon in the political arsenals of most presidents after the mid-twentieth century. During the nineteenth century, it was considered inappropriate for presidents to engage in personal campaigning on their own behalf or in support of programs and policies. When Andrew Johnson broke this unwritten rule and made a series of speeches vehemently seeking public support for his Reconstruction program, even some of his most ardent supporters were shocked at what was seen as a lack of decorum and dignity.[47]

The president who used public appeals perhaps most effectively was Franklin Delano Roosevelt. The political scientist Sidney Milkis observes that Roosevelt was "firmly persuaded of the need to form a direct link between the executive office and the public."[48] Roosevelt developed a number of tactics aimed at forging such a link. Like his predecessors, he often embarked on speaking trips around the nation to promote his programs. On one such tour, he told a crowd, "I regain strength just by meeting the American people."[49] In addition, Roosevelt made limited but important use of the new electronic medium, radio, to reach millions of Americans. In his famous "fireside chats," the president, or at least his voice, came into living rooms across the country to discuss programs and policies and generally to assure Americans that Roosevelt was aware of their difficulties and working diligently toward solutions.[50]

---

46 A powerful argument that invokes this logic is that of Keith Krehbiel in *Pivotal Politics: A Theory of U.S. Lawmaking* (Chicago: University of Chicago Press, 1998).

47 Tulis, *The Rhetorical Presidency*, p. 91.

48 Quoted in Sidney M. Milkis, *The President and the Parties: The Transformation of the American Party System since the New Deal* (New York: Oxford University Press, 1993), p. 97.

49 Quoted in James MacGregor Burns, *Roosevelt: The Lion and the Fox* (New York: Harcourt, Brace, 1956), p. 317.

50 The distribution of radio ownership in the 1930s was quite uneven, however. Roosevelt reinforced his "going public" radio addresses with a similarly uneven distribution of relief funds during the Depression. Counties with a high concentration of radio ownership received more relief funds, even after controlling for income and unemployment. Popular mobilization and public policy worked hand in hand to burnish the president's reputation. See David Strömberg, "Radio's Impact on Public Spending," *Quarterly Journal of Economics* 119 (2004): 189–221.

Roosevelt was also an innovator in the realm of what now might be called press relations. When he entered the White House, he faced a mainly hostile press typically controlled by conservative members of the business establishment. As the president wrote, "All the fat-cat newspapers—85 percent of the whole—have been utterly opposed to everything the Administration is seeking."[51] Roosevelt hoped to be able to use the press to mold public opinion, but to do so he needed to circumvent the editors and publishers who were generally unsympathetic to his goals. To this end, the president worked to cultivate the reporters who covered the White House: he held twice-weekly press conferences, offering candid answers to reporters' questions and making important policy announcements that would provide the reporters with significant stories to file with their papers.[52] Roosevelt was especially effective in designating a press secretary, who organized the press conferences and made certain that reporters distinguished presidential comments that were off the record from those that could be attributed directly to the president.

Every president since Roosevelt has sought to craft a public relations strategy that emphasized his strengths and maximized his popular appeal. One Clinton innovation was to make the White House Communications Office an important institution within the EOP.[53] In a practice continued by George W. Bush, the Communications Office became responsible not only for responding to reporters' queries but also for developing a coordinated communications strategy: promoting the president's policy goals, developing responses to unflattering news stories, and ensuring that a favorable image of the president would, insofar as possible, dominate the news. Consistent with President Obama's successful use of social networking in his 2008 election campaign, the Obama administration's communications office emphasized social networking techniques to reach newsmakers and the American people directly. The White House posted several tweets a day on topics as varied as immigration reform, climate change, and the Chicago Blackhawks' Stanley Cup win.

In addition to using the media, recent presidents have reached out directly to the American public to gain its approval (Figure 7.4). During his first full month in office, for example, Obama addressed Congress and the American people on the nation's financial crisis, seeking to reassure the public and to mobilize its support for his policies. During his first year in office, Obama made additional major speeches in the United States and abroad designed to generate both domestic and international support for his programs.

---

51 Burns, *Roosevelt,* p. 317.

52 Kernell, *Going Public,* p. 79.

53 The office had first been established in the Nixon administration and was used very effectively by President Reagan.

Figure 7.4

PUBLIC APPEARANCES BY PRESIDENTS

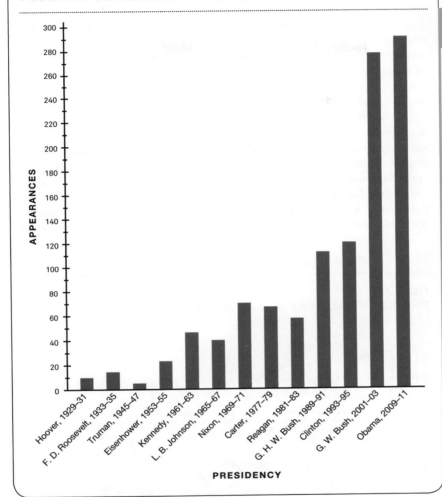

ANALYZING THE EVIDENCE

In the nineteenth century, presidents seldom made public speeches or other public appearances. By the end of the twentieth century, the number of times presidents went public had increased dramatically. What accounts for the growth in public appearances? What do presidents hope to accomplish through speeches and other public events? What risks do presidents take when they seek to develop and use popular support as a political tool?

The Limits of Going Public. Although some presidents have made effective use of popular appeals to overcome congressional opposition, popular support has not been a firm foundation for presidential power. To begin with, it is notoriously fickle. President George W. Bush maintained an approval rating of over 70 percent for more than a year after the September 11 terrorist attacks. By 2003, however, his rating had fallen nearly 20 points as American casualties in Iraq mounted and steadily declined through the remainder of his presidency. Obama began his presidency with a very high approval rating, but after 2010 it hovered in the 40s and 50s. Such declines in popular approval during a president's term in office are nearly inevitable and follow a predictable pattern (Figure 7.5). New presidents generate popular support by promising to undertake important programs that will contribute directly to the well-being of large numbers of Americans, but presidential performance almost always falls short of those promises, leading to a sharp decline in public support and an ensuing collapse of presidential influence. Reagan and Clinton are the exceptions among modern presidents—leaving office at least as popular as when they arrived.

Technological change has affected the tactics of going public. The growing heterogeneity of media outlets—cable stations, streamed radio, the blogosphere, social media such as Twitter—and the declining viewership and readership of mainstream outlets has fragmented the public. This has necessitated newly crafted approaches—"narrowcasting" to reach targeted demographic categories rather than broadcasting to reach "the public." Instead of going "capital P" public, new approaches seek to appeal to myriad "small p" publics (plural). Shrinking and fragmented audiences have raised the costs and cast doubt

Figure 7.5
PRESIDENTIAL PERFORMANCE RATINGS

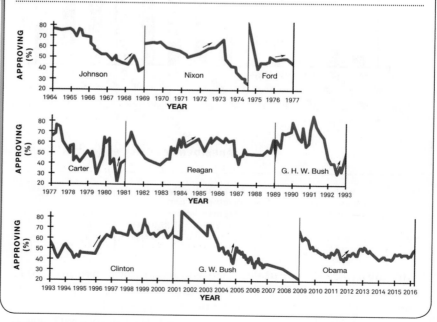

NOTE: Arrows indicate preelection upswings.
SOURCES: Gallup, Presidential Job Approval Center, www.gallup.com/poll/124922/presidential-approval-center.aspx (accessed 5/9/16).

on the effectiveness of presidential efforts to educate and mobilize public opinion. The limitations of going public as a route to presidential power have also led contemporary presidents to make use of a third technique: expanding their administrative capabilities.

The Administrative State

Contemporary presidents have increased the administrative capabilities of their office in two important ways. First, they have sought to increase White House control over the federal bureaucracy. Second, they have expanded the role of executive orders and other instruments of direct presidential governance. Taken together, these components of administrative strategy have given presidents a capacity to achieve their programmatic and policy goals even when they are unable to secure congressional approval. Indeed, some recent presidents have been able to accomplish quite a bit without much congressional, partisan, or even public support.

Appointments and Regulatory Review. Presidents have sought to increase their influence through bureaucratic appointments and **regulatory review**. By appointing loyal supporters to top jobs in the bureaucracy, presidents make it more likely that agencies will follow the president's wishes. As the Analyzing the Evidence unit on the following page shows, recent presidents have increased the number of political appointees in the bureaucracy.

 regulatory review

The OMB function of reviewing all agency regulations and other rule making before they become official policy

Through regulatory review, presidents have tried to control rule making by the agencies of the executive branch (see also Chapter 15). Whenever Congress enacts a statute, its implementation requires the promulgation of hundreds of rules by the agency charged with administering the law. Some congressional statutes are quite detailed and leave agencies with relatively little discretion. Typically, however, Congress enacts a relatively broad statement of legislative intent and delegates to the appropriate agency the power to fill in many important details.[54] In other words, Congress often says to an administrative agency: "Here is the problem. Deal with it."[55]

The discretion Congress delegates to administrative agencies has provided recent presidents with an important avenue for expanding their power. For example, President Clinton believed the president had full authority to order agencies of the executive branch to adopt such rules as the president thought appropriate, and he issued 107 directives ordering administrators to propose specific rules and regulations. Presidential rule-making directives covered a wide variety of topics. For example, after Clinton ordered the FDA to develop rules to restrict the marketing of tobacco products to children, White House and FDA staffers prepared nearly a thousand pages of new regulations affecting tobacco

54 The classic critique of this process is Lowi, *The End of Liberalism*.

55 Kenneth Culp Davis, *Administrative Law Treatise* (St. Paul, MN: West, 1958), p. 9.

Presidential Appointees in the Executive Branch

Contributed by
David Lewis
Vanderbilt University

Article II of the Constitution states that "The executive power shall be vested in a President of the United States of America" and details one of the president's most important constitutional roles: leading the executive branch. Today, this means the president must manage 15 cabinet departments and 55 to 60 independent agencies—and the over 2 million civilian employees who work in the federal government. Given the system of separation of powers, the president often competes with Congress for control of the executive branch. Congress also has a legitimate interest in the actions of executive branch officials since Congress creates programs and agencies and determines their budgets. The stakes of this competition between the branches are increasing. As the scope and complexity of government work have grown, Congress has delegated important policy-making responsibility to government officials working in the executive branch. These officials determine important public policies such as allowable levels of pollutants in the environment, eligibility rules for government benefits like medical care and Social Security, and safety rules in workplaces. Modern presidents have sought to exert more control over these agencies by a number of means, including increasing the number of presidential appointments.

Civil Service Systems

INCREASING PAY AND RESPONSIBILITY

POLITICAL APPOINTMENTS

CIVIL SERVICE

ENTRY LEVEL

Political appointments   Civil service

Government agencies are generally staffed by a mix of two types of employees: civil servants and political appointees. Civil servants staff the lower strata of government agencies and are to be hired, fired, promoted, and demoted on the basis of merit, and they cannot be removed without good cause. Political appointees, however, are generally selected from outside the civil service by the president, and most can be removed at the president's discretion.

SOURCE: David E. Lewis, *The Politics of Presidential Appointments* (Princeton, NJ: Princeton University Press, 2008).

Federal Government Appointees*

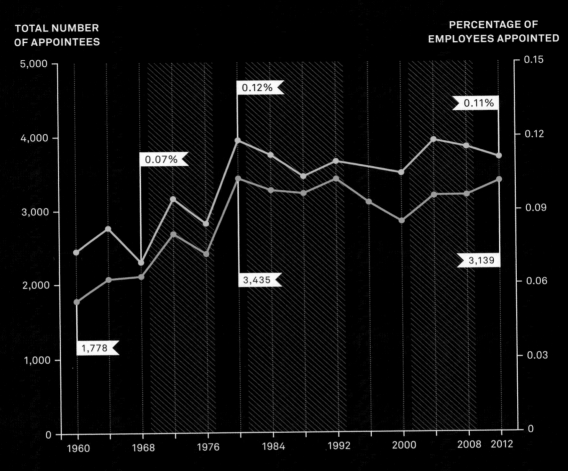

TOTAL NUMBER
OF APPOINTEES

PERCENTAGE OF
EMPLOYEES APPOINTED

0.12%

0.11%

0.07%

3,139

3,435

1,778

* Includes salaried Senate-confirmed appointees and lower-level appointees who do not require
Senate confirmation. Excludes ambassadors, U.S. marshals, U.S. attorneys, and advisory positions.

—●— Percent appointed   —●— Number of appointees   ▨ Republican president

Presidents since the middle of the twentieth century have sought to push down the dividing line between appointees and civil servants in government agencies. The figure above presents the total number of presidential appointees as well as the percentage of appointees in the federal government workforce over the last five decades. First, it should be noted that appointees make up a very small percentage of the federal workforce. However, and interestingly, the proportion of federal employees who are appointees has grown during this time period, as presidents have tried to exert greater influence over the executive branch.

SOURCE: David E. Lewis, www.bepress.com/forum/vol7/iss4/art6 (accessed 10/24/2011).

manufacturers and vendors.[56] Although Republicans denounced Clinton's actions as a usurpation of power,[57] President George W. Bush continued the practice of issuing presidential directives to agencies to spur them to issue new rules and regulations. When he assumed office, President Obama appointed the Harvard law professor Cass Sunstein to head his regulatory review effort; under Sunstein, regulatory review became an even more important arrow in the president's quiver.

Governing by Decree: Executive Orders. Another mechanism through which contemporary presidents have enhanced their power to govern unilaterally is the use of executive orders and other forms of presidential decrees, including executive agreements, national security findings and directives, proclamations, reorganization plans, signing statements, and others.[58] Executive orders have a long history in the United States, serving as the vehicles for a number of important government policies. These include the purchase of Louisiana, the annexation of Texas, the emancipation of the slaves, the internment of the Japanese in World War II, the desegregation of the military, the initiation of affirmative action, and the creation of important federal agencies, among them the Environmental Protection Agency, the Food and Drug Administration, and the Peace Corps.[59]

In the realm of foreign policy, unilateral presidential actions in the form of executive agreements have virtually replaced treaties as the nation's chief foreign-policy instruments.[60] Although wars and national emergencies produce the highest volume of executive orders, such presidential actions also occur frequently in peacetime (Figure 7.6). Of course, presidents may not use executive orders to issue whatever commands they please. If a president issues an executive order, proclamation, directive, or the like, in principle he does so pursuant to the powers granted to him by the Constitution or delegated to him by Congress, usually through a statute. When presidents issue such orders, they generally state the constitutional or statutory basis for their actions. For example, when President Truman ordered the desegregation of the armed services, he did so pursuant to his constitutional powers as commander in chief. In a similar vein, when President Johnson issued Executive Order No. 11246, he asserted that the order was designed to implement the 1964 Civil Rights Act, which prohibited employment discrimination. Where an executive order has no statutory

---

56 Elena Kagan, "Presidential Administration," *Harvard Law Review* 114 (2001): 2265.

57 For example, Douglas W. Kmiec, "Expanding Power," in *The Rule of Law in the Wake of Clinton*, Roger Pilon, ed. (Washington, DC: Cato Institute Press, 2000), pp. 47–68.

58 A complete inventory is provided in Harold C. Relyea, *Presidential Directives: Background and Review*, Congressional Research Service Report for Congress, 98–611 GOV, November 9, 2001.

59 Terry M. Moe and William G. Howell, "The Presidential Power of Unilateral Action," *Journal of Law, Economics, and Organization* 15 (1999): 133–34. Also see William G. Howell, *Power without Persuasion*.

60 Moe and Howell, "The Presidential Power of Unilateral Action," p. 164.

Figure 7.6

SIGNIFICANT EXECUTIVE ORDERS, 1900–95

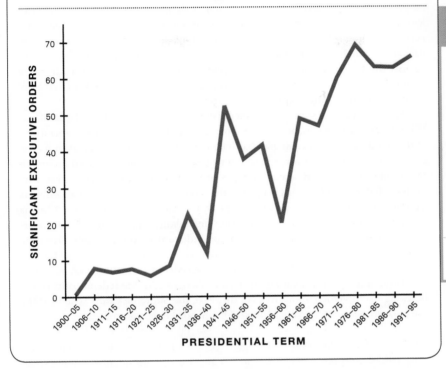

SOURCE: William G. Howell, "The President's Powers of Unilateral Action: The Strategic Advantages of Acting Alone" (Ph.D. diss., Stanford University, 1999).

ANALYZING THE EVIDENCE

During the twentieth century, presidents made increasingly frequent use of executive orders to accomplish their policy goals. What factors explain this development? How have Congress and the courts responded to increased presidential assertiveness?

or constitutional basis, the courts have held it to be void. The most important case illustrating this point is *Youngstown Sheet and Tube Company v. Sawyer*, the so-called steel seizure case of 1952.[61] Here the Supreme Court ruled that President Truman's seizure of the nation's steel mills during the Korean War had no statutory or constitutional basis and was thus invalid.

A number of court decisions, though, have established broad boundaries that leave considerable room for presidential action. By illustration, the courts have held that Congress might approve a presidential action after the fact or through "acquiescence"—for example, by not objecting for long periods or by continuing to fund programs established by executive orders. In addition, the courts have indicated that some areas, most notably the realm of military policy, are presidential in character, and they have allowed presidents wide latitude to make policy by executive decree. Thus, within the very broad limits established by the courts, presidential orders can be important policy tools.

61 *Youngstown Sheet and Tube Company v. Sawyer*, 343 U.S. 579 (1952).

President Clinton issued numerous orders designed to promote a coherent set of policy goals, including protecting the environment and expanding affirmative action programs.[62] Clinton's use of this strategy showed that an activist president could develop and implement a significant policy agenda without legislation—a lesson that was not lost on his successors. Indeed, among other actions, President George W. Bush issued a directive authorizing the creation of military tribunals to try noncitizens accused of involvement in acts of terrorism against the United States, and several years later ordered the National Security Administration to conduct a massive program of domestic surveillance of telephone traffic involving suspected terrorists.[63]

President Obama signed four executive orders on his second full day in office. With the stroke of a pen, he changed government policy on detention operations at the naval base at Guantánamo Bay; clarified his administration's stance on the use of torture and/or controversial interrogation techniques; reversed the previous administration's ban on certain types of stem-cell research; and lifted restrictions on federal funding for groups in other countries that supported abortion as a component of family planning services. By the end of his second term, Obama had issued more than 250 executive orders, including a significant and controversial one that would protect some 4 million undocumented immigrants from the threat of deportation. This order provoked an outcry from congressional Republicans, who declared that the president had exceeded his constitutional authority. The order also spurred a variety of legal challenges and one federal court ruling blocking its implementation. In June of 2016, the Supreme Court sustained the lower-court decision, a major blow to Obama's immigration policy.

Signing Statements. To negate congressional actions to which they objected, recent presidents have made frequent use of presidential signing statements.[64] A **signing statement** is an announcement by the president at the time of signing a congressional enactment into law, sometimes presenting the president's interpretation of the law as well as remarks predicting the benefits the new law would bring to the nation. Occasionally, presidents have used signing statements to point to sections of the law they deemed improper or unconstitutional and to instruct executive branch agencies how to execute the law.[65]

Presidents have made signing statements throughout American history, though many were not recorded and so did not become part of the official legislative record. Ronald Reagan's attorney general, Edwin Meese, is generally

signing statement ⇒

An announcement made by the president when a bill is signed into law

---

62 Todd Gaziano, "The New 'Massive Resistance,'" *Policy Review* (May–June 1998): 283.

63 *Hamdan v. Rumsfeld,* 548 U.S. 557 (2006). In 2006, the Supreme Court determined that the military tribunals established by Bush's executive order to try detainees at the U.S. naval base at Guantánamo Bay, Cuba, violated both the Uniform Code of Military Justice and the Geneva Conventions.

64 Mark Killenbeck, "A Matter of Mere Approval? The Role of the President in the Creation of Legislative History," 48 *University of Arkansas Law Review* 239 (1995).

65 Philip J. Cooper, *By Order of the President: The Use and Abuse of Presidential Direct Action* (Lawrence: University Press of Kansas, 2002), p. 201.

credited with transforming the signing statement into a routine tool of presidential direct action.[66] Meese believed that carefully crafted signing statements would provide a basis for action by executive agencies and, perhaps even more important, would become part of the historical context of a piece of legislation if judicial interpretation ever became necessary. Indeed, to make certain that signing statements became part of the legislative history, Meese reached an agreement with the West Publishing Company to include them in its authoritative texts.[67] Reagan then proceeded to use detailed and artfully designed signing statements—prepared by the Department of Justice—to attempt to reinterpret certain congressional enactments.

Despite subsequent court rulings decrying the notion that the president had the power to declare acts of Congress unconstitutional[68] and stating that the president did not have the authority to "excise or sever provisions of a bill with which he disagrees,"[69] the same tactic of reinterpreting and nullifying congressional enactments was continued by George H. W. Bush[70] and even more so by George W. Bush. The latter challenged more than 800 legislative provisions with his signing statements, including a number of important domestic and security matters, such as a congressional effort to ban the use of torture by American interrogators. During the 2008 presidential campaign, Democrats denounced George W. Bush's use of signing statements. In 2009, however, President Obama made use of the same tactic employed by his predecessors. After signing a $410 billion budget bill into law, Obama declared five provisions of the act to be unconstitutional and nonbinding, including a provision to prevent punishment of whistle-blowers. By the end of his presidency, in November 2016, Obama had issued 36 signing statements in which he offered his own interpretation of portions of the bills he signed into law.

Ed Meese's contrivance has become a full-blown instrument of presidential power. Adding to the importance of this power in recent years, as presidents had hoped, courts have begun giving weight to presidential signing statements when interpreting the meaning of statutes.[71] Still, the legal status of signing statements has not been fully resolved.

The Advantages of the Administrative Strategy. Through the course of American history, party leadership and popular appeals have played important roles in presidential efforts to overcome political opposition, and both continue to be instruments of presidential power. Reagan's tax cuts and Clinton's budget victories were achieved with strong partisan support. George W. Bush,

---

66 Cooper, *By Order of the President,* p. 201.

67 Cooper, *By Order of the President,* p. 203.

68 *Ameron, Inc. v. U.S. Army Corps of Engineers,* 610 F.Supp. 750 (D.N.J. 1985).

69 *Lear, Siegler v. Lehman,* 842 F.2nd 1102 (1988).

70 Cooper, *By Order of the President,* p. 207.

71 Kristy Carroll, "Whose Statute Is It Anyway? Why and How Courts Should Use Presidential Signing Statements When Interpreting Federal Statutes," 16 *Catholic University Law Review* 475 (1997).

lacking the oratorical skills of a Reagan or a Roosevelt, nevertheless made good use of sophisticated communications strategies to promote his agenda. Yet in the modern era parties have waned in institutional strength, and the effects of popular appeals have often proved evanescent. The limitations of the alternatives have increasingly impelled presidents to try to expand the administrative capabilities of the office and their own capacity for unilateral action as means of achieving their policy goals. Recent efforts such as the expansion of the Executive Office, the development of regulatory review, and the use of executive orders, signing statements, and the like have enabled presidents to achieve significant policy results despite congressional opposition.

To be sure, the administrative strategy does not always succeed. In some instances, the federal courts have struck down unilateral actions by the president. And occasionally Congress acts to reverse presidential orders. For example, in 1999, Congress enacted legislation prohibiting the Department of Education from carrying out a presidential directive to administer national tests of reading and mathematics.[72] And before that, in 1996, in response to President Clinton's aggressive regulatory review program, the Republican-controlled Congress moved to strengthen its capacity to block the president's use of administrative directives by enacting the Congressional Review Act (CRA). This legislation requires federal agencies to send all proposed regulations to Congress for review 60 days before they take effect. It also allows the House and Senate to enact a joint resolution of disapproval that would not only void the regulation but also prohibit the agency from subsequently issuing any substantially similar rule.

In principle, perhaps, Congress could respond even more vigorously to unilateral policy making by the president. Certainly a Congress willing to impeach a president should have the mettle to overturn his administrative directives. But the president has significant advantages in such struggles with Congress. In battles over presidential directives and orders, Congress is on the defensive, reacting to presidential initiatives. The framers of the Constitution saw "energy," or the ability to take the initiative, as a key feature of executive power.[73] When the president takes action by issuing an order or an administrative directive, Congress must initiate the cumbersome and time-consuming lawmaking process, overcome internal divisions, and enact legislation that the president may ultimately veto. Moreover, in such battles Congress faces a significant collective action problem insofar as members are likely to be more sensitive to the substance of a president's action and its effects on their constituents than to the more general implications of presidential power for the long-term vitality of their institution.[74]

---

72 Kagan, "Presidential Administration," p. 2351.

73 Alexander Hamilton, James Madison, and John Jay, *The Federalist Papers,* Clinton L. Rossiter, ed. (New York: New American Library, 1961), no. 70, pp. 423–30.

74 Terry M. Moe, "The Presidency and the Bureaucracy: The Presidential Advantage," in *The Presidency and the Political System,* 7th ed., Michael Nelson, ed. (Washington, DC: CQ Press, 2003), pp. 425–57.

The Limits of Presidential Power

Presidents are powerful political actors and have become increasingly so during the past century. This is the take-home point of this chapter. But there are limits to presidential power. Indeed, presidents have had to resort to institutional and behavioral invention—signing statements, executive orders, public appeals—precisely because their official powers are limited. As the framers intended, the separation of powers is a mighty constraint—"the president proposes; the Congress disposes." The president cannot always bend the Congress to his will, though it is an easier task when his party controls the two chambers. And yet, the agendas of powerful congressional players must obtain the president's consent, as the presentment clause of the Constitution requires. Through his veto power the president can defeat—but more important, can influence in advance—congressional aspirations. Presidential power is real, but it is tempered by the necessity of bargaining with the legislature and managing the bureaucracy, along with the constraints imposed by rulings of the federal judiciary. The growth in presidential power over the last hundred years has required the acquiescence if not the outright support of all the other players in the game.

CONCLUSION: PRESIDENTIAL POWER—MYTHS AND REALITIES

We began this chapter by observing that presidents have a distinct institutional advantage vis-à-vis other governmental actors. Presidents are unitary "deciders," whereas other political actors are members of institutions whose decision-making processes are collective, requiring deliberation, debate, compromise, and voting. Unitary actors are advantaged in pursuing their self-interest (rationality principle); actors in collective institutions have to overcome the infirmities of and barriers to collective action (collective action principle). The institutional differences between executives and legislatures determine their relative performance capacities for policy initiative and execution in a complex modern world (institution principle) and have contributed to the steady growth of presidential power. This has occasioned an ongoing debate between the advocates of a strong presidency and those who favor America's traditional separation of powers system. We conclude this chapter with an assessment of this debate in terms of some myths and realities of presidential power.

Myth 1: Executive Superiority in National Emergencies. Advocates of presidential power have typically advanced three arguments for deferring to the White House. The first, which echoes themes articulated by Alexander Hamilton and others among the nation's Founders, is that executive power is needed to deal with emergencies and to ensure the nation's security.[75] Although

---

75 A contemporary statement of this position is Harvey C. Mansfield, Jr., *Taming the Prince: The Ambivalence of Modern Executive Power* (New York: Free Press, 1989), chap. 1.

no one could argue with this position in the abstract, particularly in an age of global terrorism, presidents can sometimes be too anxious to act forcefully in response to what they perceive as security threats. The framers of the Constitution gave Congress, and not the president, the power to make war precisely because they feared that presidents might be too willing to commit the nation to armed conflicts. "The strongest passions and most dangerous weaknesses of the human breast," wrote James Madison, "ambition, avarice, vanity, the honorable or venial love of fame, are all in a conspiracy [within the executive branch] against the desire and duty of peace. Hence it has grown into an axiom that the executive is the department of power most distinguished by its propensity to war."[76]

But if the president is too anxious to go to war, is Congress too reluctant to respond to emergencies? The short answer is no. It would be difficult to identify an instance of the past half century in which the nation's security was compromised because Congress refused to act, though in a number of cases, including perhaps the recent Iraq War, the president was too quick to take vigorous action. When the nation has faced actual emergencies, Congress has seldom refused to grant appropriate powers to the president.

Thus support of presidential power on the grounds of the superior capacity of the executive to respond to emergencies is a false basis on two counts: the legislature is not an obstacle to expeditious responses to emergency, and presidents all too frequently use executive power for myriad purposes other than to respond to emergencies. Executive superiority in national emergencies is Myth 1.

Myth 2: Superior Presidential Responsiveness to the Public Interest. A second argument in favor of expanded presidential power is that the president champions the national interest as opposed to the particularistic interests defended by members of Congress, party politicians, bureaucrats, and most other political actors. This notion that the president is above party politics seems reminiscent of the premodern yearning for a wise and beneficent king who would brush aside the selfish claims of manipulative courtiers and rule in the best interests of all his subjects. Perhaps such kings have existed, but the behavior of the kingly stratum as a whole does not inspire much confidence in the notion that powerful executives are a good antidote to factional selfishness and the entreaties of special interests.

Presidents, to be sure, are unitary actors. As such they may find it more difficult than members of Congress to escape responsibility for their conduct or, through inaction, to become free riders on the efforts of others. And presidents are indeed accountable to a larger, more heterogeneous constituency than most House members or senators. To this extent, the presidentialist argument

---

76 Richard Loss, ed., *The Letters of Pacificus and Helvidius* (Delmar, NY: Scholars Facsimiles and Reprints, 1976), pp. 91–92. It may be noted that the context in which the framers met was one in which English kings had displayed this same propensity to wage war and pursue foreign adventures, a tendency checked by a more activist Parliament only after centuries of disputation with the monarch.

might have some merit. Empirically, however, presidents do not appear much more likely than senators and representatives to set aside personal concerns in favor of some abstract public good. Presidents often enough promote programs designed mainly to reward important political backers and contributors rather than serve the larger public interest. In such instances, personal or political calculations appear to outweigh presidential concern for the public interest. Hence Myth 2, with some qualifications, is superior presidential responsiveness to the public interest.

Myth 3: The Presidency as More Democratic Than Congress.

A third argument in support of enhanced presidential power is the contention that the presidency is a more democratic institution than Congress.[77] This argument has a certain surface plausibility. The president is, of course, the nation's only elected official who can claim to represent all the people. As a decision-making institution, however, the presidency is perhaps America's least democratic entity.

Presidential decision making generally takes place in private and is often shrouded in secrecy. Recent presidents have asserted that the secrecy of the processes leading up to their decisions is shielded by executive privilege. This was the Bush administration's claim when it refused to disclose information regarding the composition or deliberations of the task forces with whom Vice President Cheney met in 2001 to plan the administration's energy policies. The Supreme Court supported the administration's position on the grounds that the "energetic performance" of the executive branch's duties required protection from intrusive requests for information.[78] And the Obama administration resisted requests for transparency in many of its foreign policy pursuits, including the Trans-Pacific Partnership trade deal and negotiations with Iran on ending its nuclear program in 2015. Indeed, sometimes presidential decisions themselves are not revealed to the public or even to Congress. Many so-called national security directives issued by recent presidents have been used to initiate secret missions by intelligence and defense agencies.[79] For many years too presidents have signed secret executive agreements with other governments obligating the United States to various forms of action without congressional knowledge, much less approval.

Arguably, the Congress is inherently a more democratic decision-making institution than the presidency. To exert influence, competing factions in Congress must maintain active relationships with important groups and forces in civil society. Journalists may cluck their tongues at the "senator from Goldman Sachs" or the

77 Grant McConnell, *The Modern Presidency* (New York: St. Martin's, 1976). See also Steven Calabresi, "Some Normative Arguments for the Unitary Executive," 48 *Arkansas Law Review* 23 (1995): 58.

78 *Cheney v. U.S. District Court of the District of Columbia,* 542 U.S. 367 (2004).

79 Christopher Simpson, *National Security Directives of the Reagan and Bush Administrations* (Boulder, CO: Westview Press, 1995).

"congressman from Boeing." But ties to the financial sector, the aerospace industry, or other key constituencies help members of Congress exercise influence on Capitol Hill and strengthen the collective body vis-à-vis the executive branch. Today, indeed, Congress must sometimes mobilize constituency pressure just to compel the president to implement its decisions—for as we have seen, it must depend on the executive to carry out and enforce most of its dictates. As we saw when we discussed presidential signing statements, presidents are increasingly likely to claim they are not required to implement decisions with which they disagree.

Presidents, of course, can also mobilize supporters and interests in order to overwhelm their political opponents at the polls and in the national legislature. When it comes to the routines of governance, however, presidents usually prefer processes that limit political debate and social mobilization. In an open political struggle among many competing forces, presidents may win or they may lose. But where decisions are made discreetly or covertly, in the corridors and offices of the White House with minimal external intervention, then surely the president will prevail. And unlike Congress, the president does not have to rely on an agency outside his sphere of control to implement his decisions. To a far greater extent, presidents control bureaucrats and soldiers and contractors and mercenaries. They view the involvement of other political actors as more likely to hinder their plans than to help them govern. For these reasons, presidents seek to develop institutions and procedures that restrict the number of participants in decision making and limit the scope of political debate. These observations would seem entirely inconsistent with the idea that the presidency is somehow a more democratic institution than the Congress. Institutions matter a great deal, and the claim that the presidency is the more democratic branch is Myth 3.

Our discussion of the presidency, its historical development (history principle), its institutionalization (institution principle), and its capacity for independent and proactive execution relative to institutions like legislatures and multimember courts (collective action principle) suggests something that has evolved into a sleek, efficient, political machine. But it would be a mistake to attribute too much efficiency to the office. The presidency is more than its occupant. While it may have many of the features of a unitary actor, it has become an interconnected complex of separate pieces, often coordinated to be sure by the singular aspirations of the incumbent in office (rationality principle), but is nevertheless an organization rather than an individual. This is no more apparent than when we extend our attention to the full-blown executive branch over which the president presides. This is the topic of the next chapter.

For Further Reading

Cameron, Charles M. *Veto Bargaining: Presidents and the Politics of Negative Power.* New York: Cambridge University Press, 2000.

Canes-Wrone, Brandice. *Who Leads Whom? Presidents, Policy, and the Public.* Chicago: University of Chicago Press, 2006.

Crenson, Matthew, and Benjamin Ginsberg. *Presidential Power: Unchecked and Unbalanced*. New York: Norton, 2007.

Deering, Christopher, and Forrest Maltzman. "The Politics of Executive Orders: Legislative Constraints on Presidential Power," *Political Research Quarterly* 52 (1999): 767–83.

Howell, William G. *Power without Persuasion: The Politics of Direct Presidential Action*. Princeton, NJ: Princeton University Press, 2003.

James, Scott C. *Presidents, Parties, and the State: A Party System Perspective on Democratic Regulatory Choice*. New York: Cambridge University Press, 2000.

Krutz, Glen, and Jeffrey Peake. *Presidential-Congressional Governance and the Rise of Executive Agreements*. Ann Arbor: University of Michigan Press, 2009.

Lowi, Theodore J. *The Personal President: Power Invested, Promise Unfulfilled*. Ithaca, NY: Cornell University Press, 1985.

Milkis, Sidney M. *The President and the Parties: The Transformation of the American Party System since the New Deal*. New York: Oxford University Press, 1993.

Nelson, Michael, ed. *The Presidency and the Political System*. 9th ed. Washington, DC: CQ Press, 2009.

Neustadt, Richard E. *Presidential Power and the Modern Presidents: The Politics of Leadership from Roosevelt to Reagan*. 1960. Rev. ed. New York: Free Press, 1990.

Pfiffner, James P. *The Modern Presidency*. 4th ed. Belmont, CA: Wadsworth, 2005.

Skowronek, Stephen. *The Politics Presidents Make: Leadership from John Adams to Bill Clinton*. Cambridge: Harvard University Press, 1997.

8

The Executive Branch: Bureaucracy in a Democracy

The bureaucracy is the administrative heart and soul of government. It is where the policies formulated and passed into law by elected officials are interpreted, implemented, and ultimately delivered to a nation's citizens. Government touches the lives of ordinary citizens most directly in their interactions with bureaucratic agents—at the Department of Motor Vehicles when obtaining a driver's license; in filing an income tax return with the Internal Revenue Service; at the recruiting center when enlisting in one of the armed services; at the Board of Elections when registering to vote. We examine the federal bureaucracy in this chapter both as an organizational setting within which policies are interpreted and implemented and as a venue in which politicians pursue their own (and sometimes the public's) interests.

As an organizational setting, a bureaucracy is something created by elected politicians. These politicians seek to coordinate governmental effort in order to accomplish public purposes (and private objectives) as well as to solve collective action problems. Sometimes bureaucracies are created in the face of a pressing need or crisis. A good example is the Department of Homeland Security.

In 2003, 22 federal agencies responsible for combating international terrorism in the United States were combined in the DHS (Table 8.1)—the most dramatic reform of the federal bureaucracy since the establishment of the Department of Defense in 1947. Following the catastrophic events of September 11, 2001, both Republicans and Democrats realized that the public was going to demand an ongoing response to the terrorist threat (beyond the immediate military response in Afghanistan).[1] A congressional investigation revealed that serious security lapses and a lack of coordination among agencies

---

1 John W. Kingdon calls events that limit and focus our political options "windows of political opportunity." See his *Agendas, Alternatives, and Public Policies* (Boston: Little, Brown, 1984).

responsible for domestic and foreign intelligence had occurred during the Bill Clinton and George W. Bush administrations. Both political parties might be blamed if the government did not respond aggressively to the terrorist threat. Furthermore, the major alternative solution—creation of a homeland security "czar"—proved inadequate. In the end, Congress created a new cabinet-level department with responsibility for coordinating efforts to protect domestic security in the United States.[2]

Whatever the impetus might be for creating a new bureaucracy, it is shaped by politicians who represent a variety of perspectives and must hammer out an agreement (often involving bargaining and compromise) about the size, scope, and authority of the new entity. The DHS amalgam of 22 major units previously housed in seven cabinet departments and several other independent entities was

CORE OF THE ANALYSIS

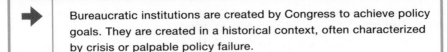 Bureaucratic institutions are created by Congress to achieve policy goals. They are created in a historical context, often characterized by crisis or palpable policy failure.

By implementing the laws and policies passed by elected officials, bureaucrats can be seen as agents of Congress and the presidency. As in any principal-agent relationship, the agent (the bureaucracy) is delegated authority and has a certain amount of leeway for independent action.

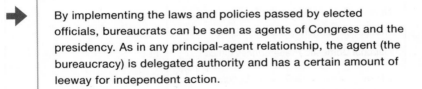 Despite the efforts of elected officials (the principals) to check departments and agencies (the agents), bureaucrats have their own goals and thus exercise their own influence on policy.

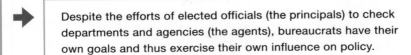 Although controlling the growth of bureaucracy has been a concern in American politics, most Americans benefit in some way from government programs and thus are reluctant to cut back on specific programs.

---

2 It also provided an opportunity for substantive policy change unrelated to national security. The Bush administration included some nonsecurity-based activities within the purview of the DHS—such as coastal environmental enforcement by the U.S. Coast Guard—knowing they would be disadvantaged in the battle for resources within the department and thus reducing their impact (in this case, relaxing the enforcement of environmental regulations). See Dara Kay Cohen, Mariano-Florentino Cuéllar, and Barry R. Weingast, "Crisis Bureaucracy: Homeland Security and the Political Design of Legal Mandates," *Stanford Law Review* 59 (2006): 673–727.

Table 8.1

THE SHAPE OF A DOMESTIC SECURITY DEPARTMENT

DEPARTMENT OF HOMELAND SECURITY	AGENCIES AND DEPARTMENTS NOW PART OF THE MAIN DIVISIONS OF THE DHS	PREVIOUSLY RESPONSIBLE AGENCY OR DEPARTMENT
Border and Transportation Security Directorate	U.S. Customs and Border Protection	Treasury
	U.S. Citizenship and Immigration Services	Justice
	U.S. Immigration and Customs Enforcement	Treasury/Justice
	Federal Protective Service	General Service Administration
	Transportation Security Administration	Transportation
	Federal Law Enforcement Training Center	Treasury
	Animal and Plant Health Inspection Service*	Agriculture
	Office for Domestic Preparedness	Justice
Emergency Preparedness and Response Directorate	Federal Emergency Management Agency**	Health and Human Services
	Strategic National Stockpile and the National Disaster Medical System	Health and Human Services
	Nuclear Incident Response Team	Energy
	Domestic Emergency Support Teams	Justice
	National Domestic Preparedness Office	FBI
Science and Technology Directorate	CBRN (Chemical, Biological, Radiological and Nuclear) Countermeasures Programs	Energy
	Environmental Measurements Laboratory	Energy
	National BW (Biological Warfare) Defense Analysis Center	Defense
	Plum Island Animal Disease Center	Agriculture
Information Analysis and Infrastructure Protection Directorate†	Federal Computer Incident Response Center	General Services Administration
	National Communications System	Defense
	National Infrastructure Protection Center	FBI
	Energy Security and Assurance Program	Energy
Secret Service		Treasury
Coast Guard		Transportation

*Only partially under the aegis of DHS; some functions remain elsewhere.
**Previously independent.
†Established to analyze information provided by the CIA, the FBI, the Defense Intelligence Agency, the NSA, and other agencies.
SOURCE: Department of Homeland Security, www.dhs.gov/who-joined-dhs (accessed 7/3/13).

stitched together through intense negotiations between President Bush's White House and legislators on Capitol Hill. Bureaucracies thus are administrative in purpose but are born through a political process. Their features are designed by politicians who appreciate, as in our institution principle, that the institutional powers with which they endow a bureaucracy have consequences for the kinds of decisions subsequently made.

Bureaucracies are also venues in which bureaucratic actors pursue public and private purposes. Bureaucrats are politicians who make decisions, form coalitions, and engage in bargaining; they bring private preferences to the table as they engage in various administrative processes—just as the rationality principle suggests. The hopes and aspirations they bring to this setting interact with the institutional features with which their bureaucracy has been endowed to produce policies, outcomes, and decisions. And these, as the policy principle tells us, will reflect both the private interests of bureaucrats and the institutional ways in which they conduct their business.

In our focus on the federal bureaucracy—the administrative structure that on a day-by-day basis is the American government—we first describe bureaucracy as a social and political phenomenon. Second, we explore American bureaucracy in action by examining the government's major administrative agencies, their role in the governmental process, and their political behavior.

WHY BUREAUCRACY?

Government bureaucracies touch nearly every aspect of daily life as they implement decisions generated by the political process. Bureaucracies are characterized by routine because routine ensures that services are delivered regularly and that each agency fulfills its mandate. For this reason, students often conclude that bureaucracy is mechanical and cumbersome. But that is a mistake. Bureaucracy is not just about collecting garbage or mailing Social Security checks; it is much more. Mainly, it is a reflection of political deals consummated by elected politicians, turf wars among government agents and private-sector suppliers and contractors, policy-delivery successes and failures in the eyes of the public, and reactions to these by the same officials who cut the deals in the first place. It is politics through and through.

Public bureaucracies are powerful because legislatures and chief executives—and, indeed, the people—delegate to them vast power to make sure a particular job is done, leaving the rest of us freer to pursue our private ends.[3] The public sentiments that emerged after September 11 revealed this underlying appreciation of public bureaucracies. When faced with the challenge of making air

---

3   Private bureaucracies at the heart of modern corporations and nonprofit organizations are also powerful, as students who must deal with college and university bureaucracies well know. In this chapter we focus on *government* bureaucracies.

travel safe again, the public strongly supported giving the federal government responsibility for airport security even though this meant expanding the federal bureaucracy in order to make the security screeners federal workers. A fearful public expressed widespread belief that a public bureaucracy would provide more effective protection than the cost-conscious private companies that had handled airport security in the past.

We can shed light on public attitudes toward government bureaucracy by examining one of the standard questions posed in election years by the American National Election Studies (ANES). In surveying the American public, the ANES asks a range of questions, including "Do you think that people in the government waste a lot of money we pay in taxes, waste some of it, or don't waste very much of it?" Although it doesn't elicit a nuanced assessment of bureaucratic performance, the question allows respondents to register a blunt evaluation. Results from the past several decades appear in Figure 8.1. Public unhappiness with bureaucratic inefficiency grew during the 1960s and 1970s; peaked in 1980, when nearly 80 percent of respondents believed government

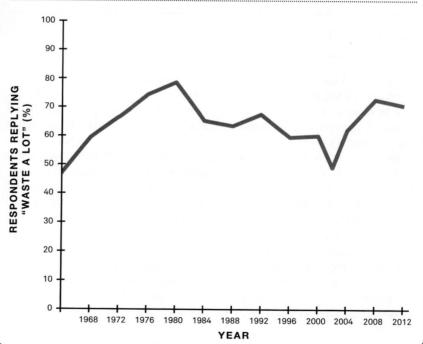

Figure 8.1
PUBLIC OPINION ON WASTE IN GOVERNMENT

SOURCES: American National Election Studies, Cumulative Data File, 1958–2008, www.electionstudies.org/nesguide/toptable/tab5a_3.htm (accessed 12/7/11), and www.electionstudies.org/studypages/anes_timeseries_2012/anes2012TS_codebook.pdf (accessed 6/11/13).

"wastes a lot"; and held steady near the low 60 percent range between 1984 and 2000. There was a significant downward tick in 2002, just after September 11. But whatever honeymoon there might have been after the terrorist attacks, the public is once again increasingly cynical about bureaucratic performance. The poor response of the Federal Emergency Management Agency (FEMA)—part of the DHS—to the Hurricane Katrina crisis in 2005, and domestic terrorist incidents later in the decade that seem to have evaded early detection, contributed to further cynicism.

Bureaucratic Organization Enhances the Efficient Operation of Government

Despite their tendency to criticize bureaucracy, most Americans recognize that maintaining order in a large society is impossible without a large governmental apparatus, staffed by professionals with expertise in public administration. **Bureaucracy** refers to the actual offices, tasks, and principles of organization that large institutions use to coordinate their work. The core of bureaucracy is the division of labor. The key to bureaucratic effectiveness is the coordination of experts performing complex tasks. If each job is specialized to gain efficiencies, then each worker must depend on other workers' output, and that requires careful allocation of jobs and resources. Inevitably bureaucracies become hierarchical, often pyramidal. At the base of the organization are workers with the fewest skills and specializations; one supervisor can oversee a large number of these workers. At the next level of the organization, involving more highly specialized workers, the supervision of work involves fewer workers per supervisor. Toward the top, a handful of high-level executives engages in "management" of the organization, meaning the organization and reorganization of all tasks and functions, plus the allocation of supplies and the distribution of the organization's output to the market (if it is a private-sector organization) or to the public.

 bureaucracy

The complex structure of offices, tasks, rules, and principles of organization that all large-scale institutions use to coordinate the work of their personnel

By dividing up tasks, matching tasks to a labor force that develops appropriately specialized skills, routinizing procedure, and providing the incentive structure and oversight arrangements to get large numbers of people to operate in a coordinated fashion, bureaucracies accomplish tasks and missions in a manner that would otherwise be unimaginable. The provision of an array of "government goods" as broad as the defense of people, property, and national borders or as narrow as a subsidy to a wheat farmer requires organization, routines, standards, and ultimately, the authority for someone to cut a check and put it in the mail. And, of course, delivering the mail is as old as the Republic itself! Bureaucracies are created to do these tasks. Although there are mistakes, a bureaucracy reflects instrumental thinking about how to accomplish particular undertakings; it is the rationality principle at work.

Bureaucracy also consolidates complementary programs and insulates them from opposing political forces. By creating clienteles—in the legislature, the world of interest groups, and public opinion—a bureaucracy establishes a coalition of supporters, some of whom will fight to keep it in place. Clienteles, after all, value consistency, predictability, and durability. It is well known that everyone in the political world cares deeply about certain policies and related agencies and opposes other policies and agencies, but not with nearly the same passion. Opponents, to succeed, must clear many hurdles, while proponents, to maintain the status quo, must marshal their forces only at a few veto points. Opponents typically make the easier decision to give up and concentrate on protecting what they care most deeply about. Politicians appreciate this fact of life. Consequently, both opponents and proponents of a particular set of governmental activities wage the fiercest battles at the time programs are enacted and a bureaucracy is created. Once created, these organizations assume a status of relative permanence, and future developments are shaped, as the history principle suggests, by these "initial conditions."[4]

This raises an interesting dilemma that we will develop in the next section. In principle, bureaucratic agents are "servants" of elected politicians in the White House and on Capitol Hill. They are charged with implementing statutes and policies produced by these "masters." But the bureaucracy's relative permanence is a form of insulation—servants have discretion, and masters have limited ability to control them. Elected officials who might want to steer bureaucracy in a different direction often find substantial obstacles. Only those with intense concern for the jurisdiction of a bureaucracy are likely to persist in efforts to guide it; others have more important objectives in different bureaucratic jurisdictions. Thus bureaucratic agents are most affected by legislators with extraordinary interest in that bureaucracy's mission. Those in opposition succumb to the obstacles and move their attention elsewhere.

So in terms of how bureaucracy makes government possible, efficiency and credibility both play a role. The creation of a bureau is a way to deliver government goods efficiently, and it is a device by which to tie one's hands, thereby providing a credible commitment to the long-term existence of a policy.

Bureaucrats Fulfill Important Roles

Bureaucracy often conveys a picture of hundreds of office workers shuffling millions of pieces of paper. There is truth in that image, but we have to look more closely at what papers are being shuffled and why.

implementation

The efforts of departments and agencies to the development of rules, regulations, and bureaucratic procedures to translate laws into action

Implementing Laws. Bureaucrats, whether in public or in private organizations, communicate with one another to coordinate all the specializations within their organization. This coordination is necessary to carry out the primary task of bureaucracy, which is **implementation**—that is, implementing the organization's objectives as laid down by its board of directors (if a private company) or by law (if a public agency). In government, the bosses are ultimately the legislature and the chief executive. As we saw in Chapter 1, in a principal-agent relationship it is the principal who stipulates what he wants done, relying on incentives

4   For a nuanced discussion of agency creation and persistence, see David Lewis, *Presidents and the Politics of Agency Design* (Redwood City, CA: Stanford University Press, 2003).

and other control mechanisms to secure the agent's compliance. Thus we can argue that legislative principals establish bureaucratic agents—in departments, bureaus, agencies, institutes, and commissions of the federal government— to implement the policies promulgated by Congress and the president.

Making and Enforcing Rules. When the bosses—Congress, in particular, when it is making the law—are clear in their instructions to bureaucrats, implementation is fairly straightforward. Bureaucrats translate the law into specific routines for each employee of an agency. But what happens to routine implementation when there are several bosses who disagree over what the instructions ought to be? The agent of multiple, disagreeing principals often gets caught in a bind. She must chart a delicate course, doing the best she can and trying not to offend any of the bosses too much. This requires yet another job for the bureaucrats: interpretation. Interpretation is a form of implementation in that the bureaucrats have to carry out what they see as the intentions of their superiors. But when bureaucrats have to interpret a law before implementing it, they are in effect engaging in lawmaking.[5] Congress often deliberately delegates to an administrative agency the responsibility of lawmaking: for example, members conclude that some area of industry needs regulating or some area of the environment needs protection, but they are unwilling or unable to specify just how that should be done. In such situations, Congress delegates to the appropriate agency a broad authority within which to make law, through the procedures of **rule making** and administrative adjudication.

 rule making

A quasi-legislative administrative process that produces regulations by government agencies

Rule making is essentially the same as legislation; in fact, it is often called quasi-legislation. The rules issued by government agencies provide more detailed indications of what a policy will actually mean. For example, the Forest Service is charged with making policies that govern the use of national forests. Just before President Bill Clinton left office, the agency issued rules that banned new road building and development in the forests. This was a goal long sought by environmentalists and conservationists. In 2005, the Forest Service relaxed the rules, allowing states to make proposals for building new roads within the national forests. Just as the timber industry opposed the Clinton rule banning road building, environmentalists have challenged the new ruling and have sued the Forest Service in federal court for violating clean-water and endangered-species legislation.

New rules proposed by an agency take effect only after a period of public comment. Reaction from the people or businesses that are subject to the rules may cause an agency to modify them. Public participation involves filing statements and giving testimony in public forums. This occurs after a draft rule or

---

5 When bureaucrats engage in interpretation, the result is what political scientists call *bureaucratic drift*. This occurs because the bosses (in Congress) and the agents (within the bureaucracy) don't always share the same purposes. Bureaucrats also have their own agendas to fulfill. A vast body of political science literature focuses on the relationship between Congress and the bureaucracy. For a review, see Kenneth A. Shepsle, *Analyzing Politics: Rationality, Behavior, and Institutions*, 2nd ed. (New York: Norton, 2010), pp. 420–40.

regulation is announced but before it becomes official, giving the agency time to revise its draft. The rule-making process is thus highly political. Once rules are approved, they are published in the *Federal Register* and have the force of law.[6]

administrative adjudication

The application of rules and precedents to specific cases to settle disputes with regulated parties

Settling Disputes. Administrative adjudication is very similar to what the judiciary ordinarily does: apply rules and precedents to specific cases to settle disputes. In administrative adjudication, the agency charges the person or business suspected of violating the law, and the ruling applies only to the case being considered. Many regulatory agencies use administrative adjudication to make decisions about specific products or practices. For example, the National Labor Relations Board (NLRB) uses administrative adjudication to decide union certification. Groups of workers seek the right to vote on forming a union or the right to affiliate with an existing union as their bargaining agent and are opposed by their employers, who assert that relevant provisions of labor law do not apply. The NLRB takes testimony case by case and makes determinations for one side or the other, acting essentially like a court.

In sum, bureaucrats in government do essentially the same things that bureaucrats in large private organizations do. But because of the coercive nature of government, far more constraints are imposed on public bureaucrats than on private bureaucrats. Public bureaucrats are required to maintain a more thorough paper trail and are subject to more access by the public, such as newspaper reporters. In addition, public access has been vastly facilitated by the Freedom of Information Act (FOIA), adopted in 1966: this act gives ordinary citizens the right of access to agency files and data so that they might determine whether those materials contain derogatory information about them and learn what the agency is doing in general.

Bureaucracies Serve Politicians

We have provided two main answers to the question "Why bureaucracy?": (1) Bureaucracies enhance efficiency, and (2) they are the instruments of policy implementation. But there is a third important answer: legislatures find it valuable to delegate.

In principle, the legislature could make all bureaucratic decisions itself, writing very detailed legislation each year. In some jurisdictions—tax policy, for example—this in fact happens. Tax policy is promulgated in significant detail by the House Ways and Means Committee, the Senate Finance Committee, and the Joint Committee on Taxation. The IRS, the agency charged with implementation, engages in relatively less discretionary activity than many other regulatory and administrative agencies. But it is the exception.

The norm is for statutory authority to be delegated to the bureaucracy, often in vague terms, with the bureaucracy being expected to fill in the gaps. This,

6 The *Federal Register* is the daily journal of the executive branch of the federal government. It is published every day by the Government Printing Office and contains publications and notices of government agencies.

however, is not a blank check for unconstrained discretion. The bureaucracy will be held to account by the legislature's oversight of bureaucratic performance. The latter is monitored by the staffs of relevant legislative committees, which also serve as repositories for complaints from affected parties.[7] Poor performance or the exercise of discretion inconsistent with important legislators' preferences invites sanctions, ranging from the browbeating of senior bureaucrats to the trimming of budgets and the clipping of authority.

HOW IS THE EXECUTIVE BRANCH ORGANIZED?

Cabinet departments, agencies, and bureaus are the operating parts of the bureaucratic whole. They can be separated into four general types: (1) cabinet departments, (2) independent agencies, (3) government corporations, and (4) independent regulatory commissions.

Although Figure 8.2 is an organizational chart of the Department of Agriculture, any other department could serve as an illustration. At the top is the department head, called the secretary of the department. Below him and his deputy are several top administrators, such as the general counsel and the chief economist, whose responsibilities span the various departmental functions and enable the secretary to manage the entire organization. Working alongside these officials are the undersecretaries and assistant secretaries, each with management responsibilities for a group of operating agencies, which are arranged vertically below the undersecretaries.

The next tier, generally called the bureau level, is the highest level of responsibility for specialized programs. These bureau-level agencies are often very well known to the public: the Forest Service and the Food Safety and Inspection Service are examples. Sometimes they are officially called bureaus, as in the FBI, which is a bureau in the Department of Justice. Within the bureaus are divisions, offices, services, and units.

A second type of agency, the independent agency, is established by Congress outside the departmental structure altogether, even though the president appoints and directs these agencies' heads. Independent agencies usually have broad powers to provide public services that are either too expensive or too important to be left to private initiatives. Examples are the National Aeronautics and Space Administration (NASA), the CIA, and the Environmental Protection Agency (EPA). Government corporations are a third type of agency but are more like private businesses performing and charging for a market service, such as transporting railroad passengers (Amtrak).

---

7   See Mathew D. McCubbins and Thomas Schwartz, "Congressional Oversight Overlooked: Police Patrols versus Fire Alarms," *American Journal of Political Science* 28 (1984): 165–79.

Figure 8.2

ORGANIZATIONAL CHART OF THE DEPARTMENT OF AGRICULTURE

Secretary

Deputy Secretary

Director of Communications

Inspector General

General Counsel

Assistant Secretary for Congressional Relations

Assistant Secretary for Administration

Assistant Secretary for Civil Rights

Chief Economist

Director, National Appeals Division

Chief Information Officer

Chief Financial Officer

Executive Operations

Under Secretary for Natural Resources and Environment
- Forest Service
- Natural Resources Conservation Service

Under Secretary for Farm and Foreign Agricultural Services
- Farm Service Agency
- Foreign Agricultural Service
- Risk Management Agency

Under Secretary for Rural Development
- Rural Utilities Service
- Rural Housing Service
- Rural Business Cooperative Service

Under Secretary for Food, Nutrition, and Consumer Services
- Food and Nutrition Service
- Center for Nutrition Policy and Promotion

Under Secretary for Food Safety
- Food Safety and Inspection Service

Under Secretary for Research, Education, and Economics
- Agricultural Research Service
- National Institute of Food and Agriculture
- Economic Research Service
- National Agricultural Library
- National Agricultural Statistics Service

Under Secretary for Marketing and Regulatory Programs
- Agricultural Marketing Service
- Animal and Plant Health Inspection Service
- Grain Inspection Packers and Stockyards Administration

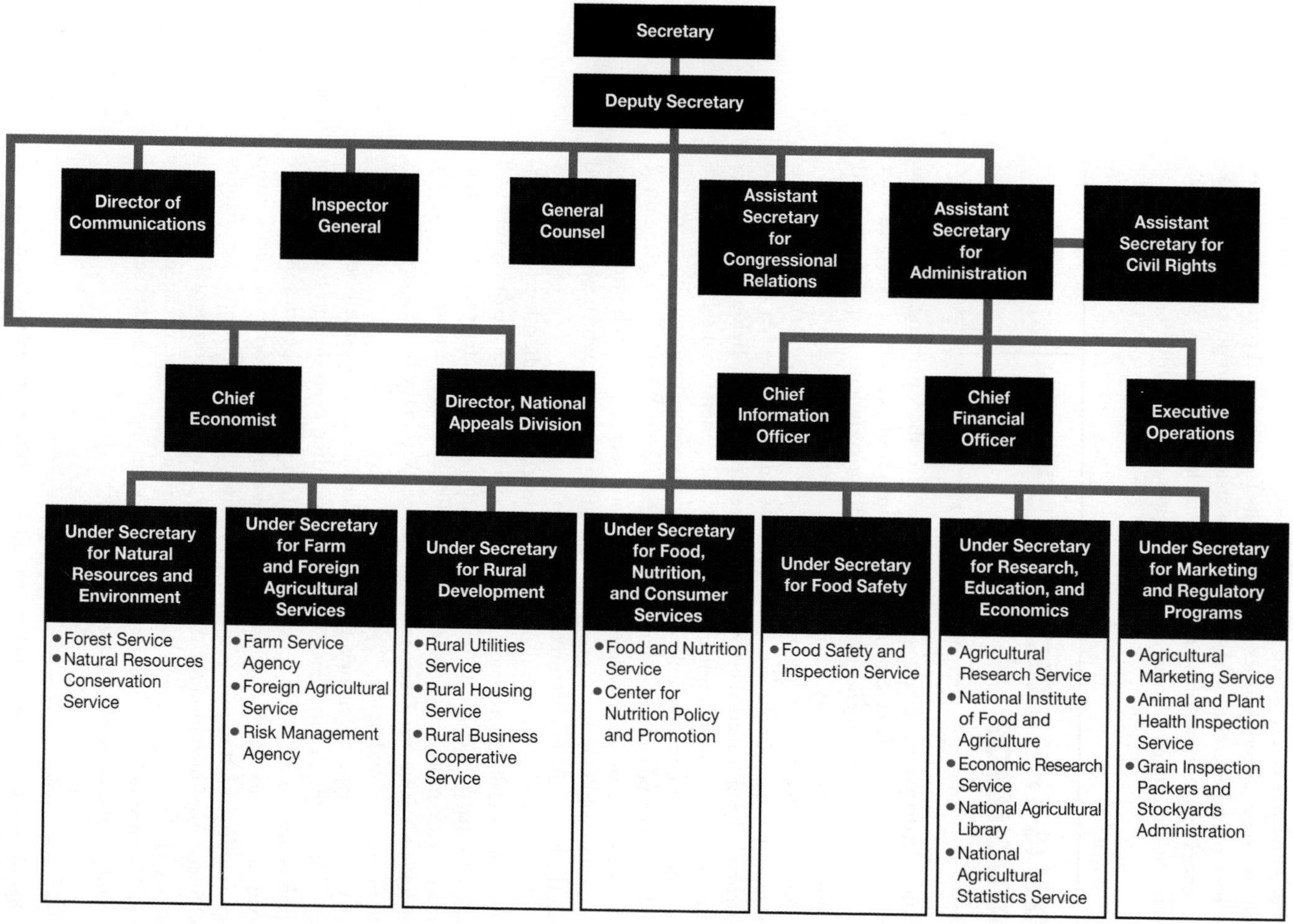

SOURCE: U.S. Department Of Agriculture, www.usda.gov/documents/agencyworkflow.pdf.

Yet a fourth type of agency is the independent regulatory commission, which has broad discretion to make rules. The first regulatory agencies established by Congress, beginning with the Interstate Commerce Commission in 1887, were set up as independent regulatory commissions because Congress recognized that regulatory agencies are mini-legislatures, whose rules and rulings are the same as legislation and legislative interpretation but require the kind of expertise and full-time attention that is beyond the capacity of Congress. Until the 1960s, most of the regulatory agencies set up by Congress, such as the Federal Communications Commission (1934), were independent regulatory commissions. But beginning in the late 1960s and early 1970s, all new regulatory programs, with a few exceptions (such as the Federal Election Commission), were placed within existing departments and made directly responsible to the president. Since then, no new major regulatory programs had been established until the financial crisis of 2008–09. Congress and the president then formulated new arrangements involving the Federal Reserve System, the Federal Deposit Insurance Corporation, the Treasury, and related agencies. The Dodd-Frank Wall Street Reform and Consumer Protection Act of 2010 brought major changes to the regulation of banks and other financial institutions. The act created several new regulatory bodies, including the Financial Stability Oversight Council, the Office of Financial Research, and the Bureau of Consumer Financial Protection.

There are too many agencies in the executive branch to identify them all here, so a simple classification will be helpful. The classification that follows organizes each agency by its mission, as defined by its jurisdiction: clientele agencies, agencies for maintenance of the Union, regulatory agencies, and redistributive agencies.

Clientele Agencies

The entire Department of Agriculture is an example of a **clientele agency**. So are the departments of the Interior, Labor, and Commerce. Although all administrative agencies have clienteles, certain agencies are directed by law to promote the interests of their clientele. For example, the Department of Commerce and Labor was founded in 1903 as a single department "to foster, promote, and develop the foreign and domestic commerce, the mining, the manufacturing, the shipping, and fishing industries, and the transportation facilities of the United States."[8] It remained a single department until 1913, when legislation created the separate departments of Commerce and Labor, with each statute providing for the same obligation: to support and foster each agency's respective clientele.[9] The Department of Agriculture serves the many farming interests that, taken together, are one of the largest economic sectors of the United States.

 clientele agency

A department or bureau of government whose mission is to promote, serve, or represent a particular interest

---

8 *U.S. Statutes at Large* 32 (1903): 825; 15 U.S. Code 1501.

9 For a detailed account of the creation of the Department of Commerce and Labor and its division into separate departments, see Theodore J. Lowi, *The End of Liberalism: The Second Republic of the United States,* 2nd ed. (New York: Norton, 1979), pp. 78–84.

Most clientele agencies locate many of their personnel in field offices dealing directly with their clientele. A familiar example is the Extension Service of the Department of Agriculture, with its local "extension agents" who consult with farmers on farm productivity. The same agencies also provide "functional representation"—that is, they learn what their clients' interests and needs are and then operate almost as a lobby in Washington on their behalf. In addition to the departments of Agriculture, the Interior, Labor, and Commerce, clientele agencies include five of the newest cabinet departments: Housing and Urban Development (HUD, created in 1965), Transportation (DOT, 1966), Energy (DOE, 1977), Education (ED, 1979), and Health and Human Services (HHS, 1979).[10]

Agencies for the Maintenance of the Union

The Constitution entrusts many vital functions of public order, such as the police, to state and local governments. But some agencies vital to maintaining national bonds do exist in the national government, and they can be grouped into three categories: (1) agencies for managing the sources of government revenue, (2) agencies for controlling conduct defined as a threat to internal national security, and (3) agencies for defending American security from external threats. The most powerful departments in these areas are Treasury, Justice, Defense, State, and Homeland Security.

Revenue Agencies. The Treasury Department's IRS is the most important revenue agency and one of the federal government's largest bureaucracies. Over 100,000 employees span 4 regions, 63 districts, 10 service centers, and hundreds of local offices. In 2014, more than 148 million individual tax returns and nearly 2.5 million corporate returns were filed. In the same year, the IRS collected nearly $2.3 trillion in taxes from individuals and corporations.

Agencies for Internal Security. The United States is fortunate to enjoy national unity maintained by civil law rather than imposed by military force. As long as the country is not in a state of insurrection, most of the task of maintaining the Union involves legal work, and the main responsibility for that lies with the Department of Justice. The most important agency in the Justice Department is the Criminal Division, which enforces all federal criminal laws except a few assigned to other divisions. Criminal litigation is actually conducted by the U.S. attorneys. A presidentially appointed U.S. attorney is assigned to each federal judicial district, and he or she supervises the work of assistant U.S. attorneys. The work or jurisdictions of the Antitrust and Civil Rights Divisions are described by their official names. The FBI, another bureau of the Justice Department, serves as the information-gathering agency for all the other divisions.

---

10 Until 1979, the Department of Education and the Department of Health and Human Services were joined in a single department, Health, Education, and Welfare (HEW), which was established by Congress in 1953.

In 2002, Congress created the Department of Homeland Security to coordinate the nation's defense against the threat of terrorism. This department's responsibilities include protecting commercial airlines from would-be hijackers. Most visible to the traveling public are the employees of the Transportation Security Administration (TSA). Consisting of 50,000 security officers and employees protecting airports and rail and bus depots, and staffing security screening operations, TSA is the largest unit of the DHS.

Agencies for External National Security. Two departments occupy center stage here for national security, State and Defense. A few key agencies outside State and Defense also have external national-security functions.

Although diplomacy is generally considered the State Department's primary task, that is only one of its organizational dimensions. The State Department also comprises geographic, or regional, bureaus concerned with all problems within that region of the world; "functional" bureaus, which handle such things as economic and business affairs, intelligence, and research; and relationships with international organizations and bureaus of internal affairs, which handle such areas as security, finance and management, and legal issues.

Despite the State Department's importance in foreign affairs, fewer than 20 percent of all U.S. government employees working abroad are directly under its authority. By far the largest number of career government professionals working abroad are under the authority of the Defense Department.

The creation of the Department of Defense between 1947 and 1949 was an effort to unify the two historic military departments, the War Department and the Navy Department, and integrate them with a new department, the Air Force Department. Real unification did not occur, however. Instead, the Defense Department added more pluralism to national security.

America's primary political problem with its military has been relatively mundane compared to the experience of many other countries, which have struggled to keep their militaries out of the politics of governing. Rather, the American military problem involves pork-barrel politics: defense contracts are often highly lucrative for local districts, so military spending becomes a matter of parochial interests as well as military need. For instance, President Bill Clinton's proposed military-base closings, a major part of his budget-cutting drive for 1993, caused a firestorm of opposition even in his own party and even from some members of Congress who otherwise favored slashing the Pentagon budget. Emphasis on jobs rather than strategy and policy means pork-barrel use of the military for political purposes. This is a classic way for a bureaucracy to defend itself politically in a democracy. It illustrates the distributive tendency, in which the bureaucracy ensures political support among elected officials by distributing things—military bases, contracts, facilities, and jobs—to the states and districts that elected the legislators.

Regulatory Agencies

Federal involvement in the regulation of economic and social affairs did not begin until the late nineteenth century. Until then, regulation was strictly a state

regulatory agency ⇒

A department, bureau, or independent agency whose primary mission is to ensure that individuals and organizations comply with the statutes under its jurisdiction

and local affair. The federal **regulatory agencies** are, as a result, relatively new, most dating from the 1930s. But they have become extensive and important. In this section, we consider them as an administrative phenomenon, with its attendant politics.

The United States has many regulatory agencies. Some are bureaus within departments, such as the Food and Drug Administration in the Department of Health and Human Services, and the Occupational Safety and Health Administration in the Department of Labor. Others are independent regulatory commissions—for example, the Federal Trade Commission (FTC). But whether departmental or independent, an agency or commission is regulatory if Congress delegates to it broad powers over a sector of the economy or a type of commercial activity and authorizes it to make rules governing the conduct of people and businesses within that jurisdiction. Rules made by regulatory agencies have the force of legislation; indeed, such rules are referred to as **administrative legislation**. And when these agencies make decisions or orders settling disputes between parties or between the government and a party, they are acting like courts.

administrative legislation ⇒

Rules made by regulatory agencies and commissions

Because regulatory agencies exercise so much influence and because their rules are a form of legislation, Congress was at first loath to turn them over to the executive branch as ordinary agencies under the president's control. Consequently, most of the important regulatory programs were delegated to independent commissions with direct responsibility to Congress rather than to the White House. This is the basis of the 1930s reference to them as the "headless fourth branch."[11] With the rise of presidential government, most recent presidents have supported more regulatory programs, but have successfully opposed the expansion of regulatory independence. The 1960s and 1970s witnessed the adoption of an unprecedented number of new regulatory programs but only a few new independent commissions.

fiscal policy ⇒

Policies that regulate the economy through taxing and spending powers

Agencies of Redistribution

Welfare, fiscal, and monetary agencies transfer hundreds of billions of dollars annually between the public and the private spheres, and through such transfers these agencies influence how people and corporations spend and invest trillions of dollars annually. We call them agencies of redistribution because they influence the amount of money in the economy and who has it, who has credit, and whether people will invest or save their money rather than spend it.

monetary policy ⇒

Regulation of the economy through manipulation of the supply of money, the price of money (interest rates), and the availability of credit

Fiscal and Monetary Policy Agencies. Governmental activity relating to money makes up fiscal and monetary policy. **Fiscal policy** includes taxing and spending activities. **Monetary policy** focuses on banks, credit, and currency.

---

11 *Final Report of the President's Committee on Administrative Management* (Washington, DC: Government Printing Office, 1937). The term *headless fourth branch* was invented by a member of the committee staff, Cornell University government professor Robert Cushman.

Administration of fiscal policy is primarily a Treasury Department role. It is no contradiction to include the Treasury both here and with the agencies for maintenance of the Union. This duplication indicates that (1) the Treasury performs more than one function of government and (2) traditional controls have been adapted to modern economic conditions and new technologies.

Today, in addition to administering and policing income tax and other tax collections, the Treasury manages the enormous federal debt. The Treasury also prints currency, but that currency is only a tiny portion of the entire money economy. Most of the trillions of dollars exchanged in the nation's private and public sectors exist on printed accounts and computers, not in currency.

Another important fiscal and monetary policy agency is the **Federal Reserve System**, headed by the Federal Reserve Board. The Federal Reserve System (the Fed) has authority over the credit rates and lending activities of the nation's most important banks. Established by Congress in 1913, the Fed is responsible for adjusting the supply of money to both the needs of banks in the different regions and the commerce and industry in each. It also ensures that banks do not overextend themselves by adopting overly liberal lending policies. The basis for this responsibility is the fear of a sudden economic scare that makes dubious loans uncollectible and thus destabilizes the health of the banking system. At its worst, such shocks to the economy could cause another terrible crash like the one in 1929 that ushered in the Great Depression. The Federal Reserve Board sits at the top of a pyramid of 12 district Federal Reserve banks, which are "bankers' banks," serving the hundreds of member banks in the national bank system. The subprime mortgage crisis of 2008 and 2009, caused by banks and other lenders providing risky home mortgages that led to foreclosures, reflected gaps in the regulation of the banking sector. In the midst of the resulting recession, the Fed played a major role by reducing interest rates to lower the price of borrowing and by overseeing support to struggling banks.

Information about and coordination of the nation's finances are provided by the Office of Management and Budget (OMB) in the White House and the Congressional Budget Office (CBO), an arm of the two legislative chambers. OMB organizes the president's budget and plays a coordinating role in clearing spending and regulatory decisions. CBO plays primarily an informational role, providing the legislative chambers and their committees with an assessment of budgetary proposals and conducting long-range forecasts of budget, spending, and tax policies.

Welfare Agencies. No single agency is responsible for all the programs making up the "welfare state." The largest agency in the field is the Social Security Administration (SSA), which manages the social insurance aspects of Social Security and Supplemental Security Income (SSI). These include massive expenditures that finance monthly Social Security checks for retirees as well as payments to the disabled, the unemployed, and some other categories

 Federal Reserve System

A system of 12 Federal Reserve banks that facilitates exchanges of cash, checks, and credit; regulates member banks; and uses monetary policy to fight inflation and deflation

of individuals. These programs are funded by taxes levied on employees and employers. As the baby-boom generation ages, a growing bloc of voters (and their children) worry that without some adjustments in benefit schedules, taxes, or retirement age, the present population will begin drawing down funds in the Social Security Trust Fund in two decades and will exhaust it in 40 years. (See the Analyzing the Evidence unit in Chapter 16 for a discussion of policy options for Social Security.)

Agencies in the Department of Health and Human Services administer Temporary Assistance to Needy Families (TANF) and Medicaid, and the Department of Agriculture is responsible for the Food Stamp Program. With the exception of Social Security, these are *means-tested* programs, requiring applicants to demonstrate that their annual cash earnings fall below an officially defined poverty line. These public-assistance programs carry a large administrative burden. In 1996, Congress abolished virtually all national means-tested public-assistance programs as federal programs, devolving power over them to the state governments (see also Chapter 3).

THE PROBLEM OF BUREAUCRATIC CONTROL

Two centuries, millions of employees, and trillions of dollars after the Founding, we must return to James Madison's observation that "you must first enable the government to control the governed; and in the next place oblige it to control itself."[12] Today the problem is the same, but the form has changed. The problem today is the challenge of keeping the government bureaucracy accountable to elected political authorities.

Motivational Considerations of Bureaucrats

The economist William Niskanen proposed that a bureau or department of government is analogous to a division of a private firm and that a bureaucrat is like the manager who runs that division.[13] In particular, Niskanen stipulated that the behavior of a bureau chief or department head be thought of as following the rationality principle. In this view the bureaucrat is a rational maximizer of her budget (just as the private-sector counterpart is a maximizer of his division's profits).

---

12 Alexander Hamilton, James Madison, and John Jay, *The Federalist Papers*, Clinton L. Rossiter, ed. (New York: New American Library, 1961), no. 51.

13 William A. Niskanen, Jr., *Bureaucracy and Representative Government* (Chicago: Aldine, 1971).

There are many motivational bases on which bureaucratic budget maximizing might be justified. A cynical (though some would say realistic) explanation is that the bureaucrat's own compensation is often tied to the size of her budget. Not only might bureaus with large budgets have higher-salaried executives with more elaborate fringe benefits, but there also may be enhanced opportunities for career advancement, travel, a posh office, possibly even a chauffeured limousine.

A second, related motivation for large budgets is nonmaterial personal gratification. An individual enjoys the prestige that comes from running a major enterprise. Her self-esteem and stature are surely buoyed by the conspicuous fact that her bureau or division has a large budget. Overseeing a large number of subordinates, made possible by a large bureau budget, is another aspect of this ego gratification.

But personal salary, on-the-job consumption, and power tripping are not the only forces motivating a bureaucrat to gain as large a budget as possible. Some bureaucrats, perhaps most, actually *care* about their mission[14] and believe in the importance of helping people in their community. As they rise through the ranks and assume management responsibilities, this mission orientation still drives them. Thus as chief of detectives in a big-city police department, as head of procurement in the air force, as supervisor of the social work division in a county welfare department, or as assistant superintendent of a town school system, individuals try to secure as large a budget as possible to succeed in the mission to which they have devoted their professional lives.

Whether for self-serving motives or for the noblest of public purposes, it is plausible that individual bureaucrats seek to persuade others (typically legislators or taxpayers) to provide them with as many resources as possible. Indeed, it is sometimes difficult to distinguish the saint from the sinner because each sincerely argues that he needs more to do more. This is one nice feature of the rationality principle in general and Niskanen's assumption of budget maximizing in particular: it doesn't matter *why* a bureaucrat is interested in a big budget; what matters is simply that she prefers more resources to fewer.

This does not mean that the legislature has to fork over whatever the bureau requests.[15] In making budget allocations, Congress can evaluate a bureau's performance. Legislative committees hold hearings, request documentation, assign

---

14 John Brehm and Scott Gates, *Working, Shirking, and Sabotage: Bureaucratic Response to a Democratic Public* (Ann Arbor: University of Michigan Press, 1997). For detailed insight about the motivations for government service combining the personal and the patriotic, consider the case of Henry Paulson, a Wall Street financier who became George W. Bush's secretary of the treasury. Paulson's story is described well in Andrew Ross Sorkin, *Too Big to Fail* (New York: Viking, 2009), chap. 2.

15 This and other related points are drawn from Gary J. Miller and Terry M. Moe, "Bureaucrats, Legislators, and the Size of Government," *American Political Science Review* 77, no. 2 (June 1983): 297–323.

investigatory staff to research tasks, and query bureau personnel on the veracity of their data and their use of the lowest-cost technologies. After the fact, the committees engage in oversight, making sure that what the legislature was told at the time when authorization and appropriations were voted actually holds in practice.

Reinforcing the budget-maximization objective of bureaus is the fact that they are intimately associated with interest groups (their clienteles) and legislative committees and subcommittees whose members count those interest groups as major supporters. These close connections among agency, interest group, and legislative committee are known as "cozy little triangles," "policy whirlpools," "unholy trinities," and "policy subgovernments." Interest groups lobby legislators (and provide election support) for large bureau budgets; legislators deliver in providing authority and appropriations for bureaus; and bureaus, in turn, deliver by implementing favorable policies for interest groups. Interest groups express their appreciation by starting the cycle all over again. Sustaining this system of policy making are the weak incentives to oppose it. Indeed, legislators appalled by this arrangement in one policy area are often embedded in a similar arrangement in other areas. The president may try to trim its more outrageous manifestations, but he is not always willing to go to the mat to eliminate the practice entirely.

Before leaving motivational considerations, we should remark that budget maximizing is not the only objective that bureaucrats pursue. We must reemphasize that career civil servants and high-level political appointees are *politicians*. They spend their professional lives pursuing political goals, bargaining, forming alliances and coalitions, solving cooperation and collective action problems, making policy decisions, operating within and interfacing with political institutions—in short, doing what other politicians do. Although they do not have elections to win, elections do affect their conditions of employment by determining the composition of the legislature and the partisan and ideological complexion of the chief executive. Bureaucrats are politicians beholden to other politicians for authority and resources. They are servants of many masters.

Being subject to the oversight and authority of others, bureaucrats must be strategic and forward thinking. Whichever party wins control of the House, Senate, and presidency, whoever chairs the legislative committee with authorization or appropriation responsibility over their agency, bureau chiefs have to adjust to the prevailing political winds. To protect and expand authority and resources, bureaucratic politicians seek, in the form of autonomy and discretion, insurance against political change. They don't always succeed, but they do try to insulate themselves from changes in the broader political world.[16] So their motivations

---

16 For an expanded view of bureaucratic autonomy and insulation with historical application to the U.S. Department of Agriculture and the Post Office, see Daniel P. Carpenter, *The Forging of Bureaucratic Autonomy: Reputations, Networks, and Policy Innovation in Executive Agencies, 1862–1928* (Princeton, NJ: Princeton University Press, 2001).

include budget-maximizing behavior, to be sure, but they also seek the autonomy to weather changes in the political atmosphere and the discretion and flexibility to achieve their goals.

Bureaucracy and the Principal-Agent Problem

As we have mentioned, bureaucrats can be understood as the agents of elected officials (the principals). In any principal-agent relationship, two broad categories of control mechanisms enable a principal to guard against opportunistic or incompetent behavior by an agent. Consider a homeowner (the principal) who seeks out a contractor (the agent) to remodel a kitchen. The first category of control operates before the fact and depends on the agent's reputation. The homeowner guards against selecting an incompetent or corrupt agent (contractor) by relying on various methods for authenticating the agent's promises. These include advice from trustworthy people (neighbors who just had their kitchen remodeled), certification by various official boards (an association of kitchen contractors), credentials (specialized training programs), and interviews. Before-the-fact protection assumes that an agent's reputation is a valuable asset that she does not want to depreciate.

The second category of control mechanisms operates after the fact. Payment may be made contingent on completion of various tasks by specific dates, so that it may be withheld for nonperformance. Alternatively, financial incentives (for example, bonuses) for early or on-time completion may be part of the arrangement. An inspection process, after the work is completed, may lead to financial penalties, bonuses, or legal action. Of course, the principal can always seek legal relief for breach of contract, either through an injunction stipulating that the agent comply or through an order demanding that the agent pay damages.

How does the principal-agent problem apply to the president's and Congress's control of the bureaucracy? Let's suppose that legislation creating the EPA required that after 10 years new legislation be passed renewing the EPA's existence and mandate. The issue facing the House, the Senate, and the president in considering renewal involves how much authority to give this agency and how much money to permit it to spend. Suppose the House is conservative on environmental issues and prefers limited authority and a limited budget. The Senate wants the agency to have wide-ranging authority but is prepared to give it only slightly more resources than the House is (because of its concern with the budget deficit). The president agrees to split the difference between House and Senate on the matter of authority but feels beholden to environmental types and is thus prepared to shower the EPA with resources. Bureaucrats in the EPA want more authority than the Senate is prepared to grant and more resources than the president is willing to grant. Eventually relevant majorities in the House and the Senate (including the support of relevant committees) and the president agree on a policy reflecting a compromise among their various points of view.

The EPA bureaucrats are not pleased with this compromise because it gives them considerably less authority and funding than they had hoped for. If they flout their principals' wishes and implement a policy exactly to their liking, they risk the unified wrath of the House, the Senate, and the president. Undoubtedly the politicians would react with new legislation (and might also replace the current EPA leadership). If, however, the EPA implements some policy located between its own preferences and those of its principals, it might get away with it. That is, at the margin, the bureau tilts policy toward its own preferences, but the tilt is subtle enough so as not to stimulate a legislative response.

Thus we have a principal-agent relationship in which a political principal—a collective principal consisting of the president and coalitions in the House and Senate—formulates policy and creates an implementation agent to execute its details. The agent, however, has policy preferences of its own and, unless subjected to further controls, will inevitably implement a policy that drifts toward its ideal. (The Policy Principle section on the facing page looks at a real case in which the EPA and President Obama worked together against a Republican-controlled Congress to expand the agency's authority. In this case, the shift toward the policy preferences of the bureaucratic agents and the president *did* provoke an outcry from legislators in Congress.)

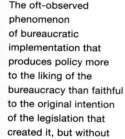

bureaucratic drift

The oft-observed phenomenon of bureaucratic implementation that produces policy more to the liking of the bureaucracy than faithful to the original intention of the legislation that created it, but without triggering a political reaction from elected officials

Various controls might conceivably restrict this **bureaucratic drift**. Indeed, legislative scholars often point to congressional hearings in which bureaucrats may be publicly humiliated; annual appropriations decisions that may serve to punish out-of-control bureaus; and watchdog agents, such as the Government Accountability Office, that may be used to scrutinize the bureau's performance. But these all come after the fact and may be only partially credible threats to the agency.[17]

Before-the-Fact Controls. The most powerful before-the-fact political weapon is the appointment process. The adroit control of a bureau's political stance by the president and Congress, through their joint powers of nomination and confirmation (especially if they can arrange for appointees who share the political consensus on policy), is a mechanism for ensuring reliable agent performance.

A second powerful before-the-fact weapon, following from the institution principle, is procedural controls. The general rules and regulations that direct the manner in which federal agencies operate are specified in the Administrative Procedure Act. This act is almost always the boilerplate of legislation creating and renewing federal agencies. Sometimes, however, an agency's procedures are tailored to suit particular circumstances.

Coalitional Drift as a Collective Action Problem. Not only do politicians want the legislative deals that they strike to be faithfully implemented by the bureaucracy, but they also want those deals to endure. This is especially

---

17 For the classic statement that despite before-the-fact and after-the-fact tools available to the political principals, the bureau-agent will "drift" in policy implementation toward its own preferences, see Mathew D. McCubbins, Roger G. Noll, and Barry R. Weingast, "Structure and Process; Politics and Policy: Administrative Arrangements and the Political Control of Agencies," *Virginia Law Review* 75 (1989): 431–82.

The EPA: Regulating Clean Air

In 1970, Congress passed the Clean Air Act to provide a platform for policy initiatives focused on reducing air pollution across the United States. It was closely aligned with the National Environmental Policy Act, passed earlier that year, which created the Environmental Protection Agency. Congress delegated authority to the EPA to regulate substances deemed harmful to air quality. Originally the list of such substances was limited, including only carbon monoxide, nitrogen oxide, sulfur dioxide, and lead. Over time, as preferences about environmental regulation changed from one presidential administration to another, several institutions shaped (and reshaped) new policies related to air pollution.

On September 20, 2013, more than 40 years after the passage of the Clean Air Act, President Obama announced his intention to extend the EPA's authority to require polluters to cut their emissions of harmful substances, and in particular to begin regulating emissions of carbon dioxide (CO_2). Obama's objective was to reduce CO_2 emissions by 30 percent by 2030. In 2014, the EPA published its proposed plan to achieve this goal and invited commentary from the general public. By December 1, 2014, the end of a 165-day comment period during which the agency received over 2 million responses, the EPA began writing its regulations. In addition, President Obama announced plans for his administration to issue other rules governing CO_2 emissions, such as restricting coal-burning power plants directly or engaging states to devise their own plans for carbon dioxide reduction. This is an example of how the powers delegated to the president and a regulatory agency by the environmental statutes change in response to a change in an administration's goals (reducing carbon emissions).

A coal-burning power plant in Ohio.

Continued pressure to combat greenhouse gases associated with climate change pitted bureaucratic agents in the Obama White House and the EPA against legislators in Congress. Obama sought to leave a legacy of environmental protection, and the EPA wished to interpret its regulatory mandate broadly, but many in Congress were anxious to protect industries in their states and districts that depend on carbon-based fuels. The majority leader in the Senate, Mitch McConnell, from coal-rich Kentucky, was eager to prevent the EPA's expanded interpretation of its authority to regulate CO_2. McConnell's efforts to shape the policies related to carbon dioxide regulation took advantage of the institutional powers available to him. For example, in 2015 he introduced a bill that would block new EPA regulations on carbon emissions from going into effect unless a review by the Labor Department found they would not reduce jobs or the reliability of the electricity supply. Thus, as in many struggles involving the federal bureaucracy, executive, regulatory, and legislative agents all have pressed forward with their respective preferences, producing policy that is never truly settled.

problematic in American political life, with its shifting alignments. Today's coalition transforms itself overnight. Opponents today are partners tomorrow, and vice versa. A victory today, even one implemented in a favorable manner by the bureaucracy, may unravel tomorrow. What is to be done?

To some extent, legislators are disinclined to undo legislation. If a coalition votes for handsome subsidies to grain farmers, say, it is very hard to reverse this policy without the gatekeeping and agenda-setting assistance of members on the House and Senate Agriculture Committees, yet their members undoubtedly participated in the initial deal and are unlikely to turn against it. But even these structural units are unstable; old politicians depart, and new ones are enlisted. For example, by winning control of the House in the 2010 midterm elections, the Republican majority had opportunities to overturn legislation passed in the Democratic-dominated 111th Congress. In particular, Republicans were eager to reverse the 2010 health care reform. While Democratic control of the Senate and presidency through the 112th and 113th Congresses did not allow this to happen, the Republicans took control of both houses in the 114th Congress and vowed to pass legislation hostile to Democrats. However, President Obama had the power to veto any hostile legislation, and in any case the Republicans lacked the 60 votes needed to defeat any Democratic filibuster in the Senate. So, even though politicians come and go—indeed, even though the Republicans now controlled both chambers of the legislature—the new majorities were in no position to reverse the health care reforms of 2010 (popularly known as Obamacare) at that time.[18]

Clearly, legislatively formulated and bureaucratically implemented output is subject to **coalitional drift**.[19] To prevent shifting coalitional patterns from endangering carefully fashioned policies, the legislature might insulate the bureaucracy and its implementation activities from legislative interventions. If an enacting coalition makes it difficult for its *own* members to intervene in implementation, then it also stymies opponents from disrupting the flow of bureaucratic output. This political insulation can be achieved by giving bureaucratic agencies long lives, their heads long terms of office and wide-ranging administrative authority, and other political appointees overlapping terms of office and secure sources of revenue. Such insulation comes at a price, however. The civil servants and political appointees of bureaus insulated from political overseers are thereby

coalitional drift

The prospect that enacted policy will change in the future because the composition of the enacting coalition is temporary and provisional

---

18 In 2015 the Supreme Court validated portions of the health care legislation, making it clear to Republicans that they would get no help in reversing Obamacare through legal challenges.

19 This idea, offered as a supplement to the analysis of bureaucratic drift, is found in Murray J. Horn and Kenneth A. Shepsle, "Administrative Process and Organizational Form as Legislative Responses to Agency Costs," *Virginia Law Review* 75 (1989): 499–509. It is further elaborated in Kenneth A. Shepsle, "Bureaucratic Drift, Coalitional Drift, and Time Consistency," *Journal of Law, Economics, and Organization* 8 (1992): 111–18.

empowered to pursue independent courses of action, meaning an increased potential for bureaucratic drift. This is one of the great trade-offs in intergovernmental relations.

The President as Manager-in-Chief

In 1937, President Franklin Delano Roosevelt's Committee on Administrative Management gave official sanction to an idea that had been growing increasingly urgent: "The president needs help." The national government had grown rapidly during the preceding 25 years, but the structures and procedures necessary to manage the burgeoning executive branch had not yet been established. The response to the call for help for the president initially took the form of three management policies: (1) all communications and decisions related to executive policy decisions must pass through the White House; (2) to cope with such a flow, the White House must have an adequate staff of specialists in research, analysis, legislative and legal writing, and public affairs; and (3) the White House must have additional staff to follow through on presidential decisions—to ensure that those decisions are made, communicated to Congress, and carried out by the appropriate agency.

The story of the modern presidency can be told largely as a series of responses to the plea for managerial help. Indeed, each expansion of the national government into new policies and programs in the twentieth century was accompanied by a parallel expansion of the president's management authority. This pattern began even before Roosevelt's presidency, with the policy innovations of President Woodrow Wilson between 1913 and 1920. Congress responded to Wilson's policies with the 1921 Budget and Accounting Act, which conferred on the White House agenda-setting power over budgeting. The president, in his annual budget message, transmits comprehensive budgetary recommendations to Congress. Because Congress retains ultimate legislative authority, a president's proposals are sometimes said to be dead on arrival on Capitol Hill. Nevertheless, the power to frame deliberations constitutes an important management tool. Each successive president has continued this pattern of setting the congressional agenda, creating what we now know as the managerial presidency.

Along with the managerial presidency came expectations of administrative competence. Presidents are now *expected* to be CEOs and are roundly criticized for ineptitude. For example, President Bill Clinton was often disparaged for the way he managed his administration. (Critics likened his easygoing management style to college bull sessions.) George W. Bush, the first president with a graduate degree in business, followed a standard business-school dictum: select skilled subordinates and delegate responsibility to them. Although Bush followed this model in appointing highly experienced officials to cabinet positions, it was no guarantee of policy success as doubts emerged about the conduct of the Iraq War and the administration's mishandling of relief after Hurricane Katrina. Barack Obama's administrative style fell somewhere in between that of his two predecessors, receiving high marks for the quality of his appointees but heavily dependent on personal staff inexperienced in dealing with Congress and the bureaucracy.

Congressional Oversight and Incentives

Congress is constitutionally essential to responsible bureaucracy because the key to governmental responsibility is legislation. When a law is passed and its intent is clear, then the president knows what to "faithfully execute," and the responsible agency understands what is expected of it. Today, legislatures rarely make laws directly for citizens; most laws are really instructions to bureaucrats and their agencies. But when Congress enacts vague legislation, agencies must rely on their own interpretations. The president and the federal courts step in to tell them what the legislation intended. So do interest groups. But when so many players get involved in interpreting legislative intent, to whom is the agency responsible?

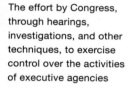

oversight

The effort by Congress, through hearings, investigations, and other techniques, to exercise control over the activities of executive agencies

The answer lies in the process of **oversight**. The more legislative power Congress has delegated to the executive bureaucracy, the more it has sought to get back into the game through committee and subcommittee oversight of the agencies. (See the Analyzing the Evidence unit on pp. 316–7 for a discussion of control of the bureaucracy.) The standing committee system in Congress is well suited for oversight, as most of the congressional committees and subcommittees are organized with jurisdictions roughly parallel to one or more executive departments or agencies. Appropriations committees as well as authorization committees have oversight powers, as do their subcommittees. In addition, there is a committee on government operations in both the House and the Senate, each with oversight powers not limited by departmental jurisdiction.

The best indication of Congress's oversight efforts is the holding of public hearings, at which bureaucrats and other witnesses are required to defend agency budgets and decisions. Committee or subcommittee hearings in 2014, for example, focused on a wide range of topics including the 2012 attack on the U.S. consulate in Benghazi, Libya, the handling of the Ebola crisis, and Internal Revenue Service abuses. In 2015, there were continuing hearings on Benghazi as well as on whether to renew the Export-Import Bank, on job growth performance, and on Hillary Clinton's use of a personal e-mail server for official State Department business. Hearings, in short, apply to the full range of government activities.

However, often the most effective control over bureaucratic accountability is the power of the purse—the ability of congressional committees and subcommittees on appropriations to scrutinize agency performance through the microscope of the annual appropriations process. The process makes bureaucrats attentive to Congress, especially members of the relevant authorizing committee and appropriations subcommittee, because they know that Congress has a chance each year to reduce their authority or funding.[20] This might be another explanation for why there may be some downsizing but almost no terminations of federal agencies.

Oversight can also be carried out by individual members of Congress. Such inquiries addressed to bureaucrats, considered standard congressional "casework," can turn up significant questions of public responsibility even when the motive is only to meet the demand of an individual constituent. Oversight also often occurs through communications between congressional staff and agency staff. Congressional staff has grown tremendously since the Legislative Reorganization Act of 1946, and the legislative staff, especially that of the committees, is just as specialized as the staff of an executive agency. In addition, Congress has created for itself three large agencies that conduct constant research on problems in the executive branch: the Government Accountability Office, the Congressional Research Service, and the Congressional Budget Office. Each gives Congress information independent of what it learns through hearings and other communications directly with the executive branch.[21]

Congressional Oversight: Abdication or Strategic Delegation?

Congress often grants the executive-branch bureaucracies discretion in determining certain features of a policy during the implementation phase. Although the complexities of governing a modern industrialized democracy make the granting of discretion necessary, some argue that Congress delegates too much policy-making authority to the unelected bureaucrats. Congress, in this view, has created a "runaway bureaucracy" in which unelected officials accountable neither to the electorate nor to Congress make important policy decisions.[22] By enacting vague statutes that give bureaucrats broad discretion, so the argument goes, members of Congress abdicate their constitutionally designated roles and remove themselves from the policy-making process. Ultimately this extreme delegation has left the legislative branch ineffectual, with dire consequences for our democracy.

Others claim that Congress fails to use its tools to engage in effective oversight, as we do not see Congress carrying out much oversight

20 See Aaron Wildavsky, *The New Politics of the Budgetary Process*, 2nd ed. (New York: HarperCollins, 1992), pp. 15–16.

21 On the congressional staff more generally, see Robert H. Salisbury and Kenneth A. Shepsle, "Congressman as Enterprise," *Legislative Studies Quarterly* 6 (1981): 559–76. On the role and activities of the Government Accountability Office, see Anne Joseph O'Connell, "Auditing Politics or Political Auditing?" UC Berkeley Public Law Research Paper no. 964656 (2007), http://ssrn.com/abstract=964656 (accessed 12/8/12).

22 Lowi, *The End of Liberalism*; and Lawrence C. Dodd and Richard L. Schott, *Congress and the Administrative State* (New York: Wiley, 1979).

Congressional Design and Control of the Bureaucracy

Contributed by
Sean Gailmard
University of California, Berkeley

Who controls the bureaucracy? Scholars usually argue that political principals try to make bureaucratic agents responsive to their own direction. For example, Congress tries to make agencies choose policies that Congress prefers through oversight and threat of budget reductions. Paradoxically, however, in some cases the best agent for Congress is not one that is controlled by Congress itself but by some other political principal.

When might this be true? On some issues, the president exercises substantially more authority over the direction of public policy than other issues. This is true of foreign policy and defense. The president sets the agenda for U.S. diplomacy, can commit U.S. troops to battle without the prior approval of Congress, and plays an important role in the use of U.S. armed forces as commander in chief.

In order to use this authority effectively, the president needs advice that he trusts. Congress could try to control the bureaucratic agents that advise the president on foreign and defense policy. But if congressional interests conflict with those of the president, such agents might not be effective or trusted advisers to the president. A better alternative for Congress is to let the president control these agents himself. This will build trust and make the agencies' advice more helpful to the president as he exercises his formidable policy authority in foreign affairs and defense. Ultimately, informed use of this policy authority by the president is good for Congress too.[1]

Congress can influence how much control different political principals exert over agencies in its decision about where the agencies are "located" within the executive branch. The location of an agency within the executive branch is determined in the legislation creating that agency.

Organization of the Executive Branch

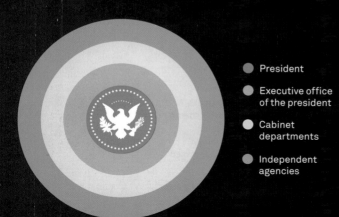

- President
- Executive office of the president
- Cabinet departments
- Independent agencies

The president's closest advisers (e.g., national security adviser, budget director) are in the executive office of the president (EOP). Senior members serve at the pleasure of the president and help him formulate policy. In cabinet departments (e.g., Department of State, Department of Agriculture), senior staff also serve at the pleasure of the president, and major policy decisions are reviewed by the EOP. Independent agencies (e.g., Securities and Exchange Commission, Federal Communications Commission) are the furthest removed from presidential control. Senior officers cannot be dismissed by the president simply for disagreements over policy, and major policy decisions are not reviewed by the EOP.

If Congress wishes the president to have relatively more control over agencies involved in foreign policy and defense than over agencies involved primarily in domestic affairs, then it should locate those agencies closer to the president within the executive branch. This expectation is borne out.[2]

Percentage of Agencies in Each Sphere of the Executive Branch

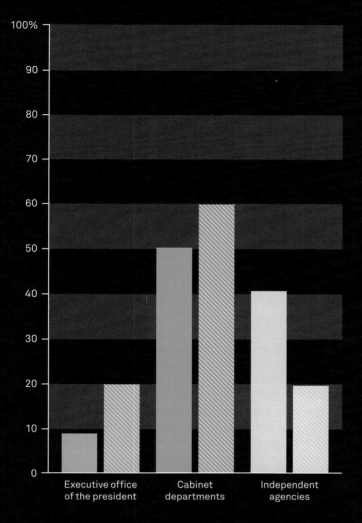

For all agencies created in legislation between 1946 and 2000, Congress was twice as likely to locate foreign and defense policy agencies in the EOP than domestic policy agencies. The reverse is true for independent agencies and commissions. Overall, when Congress designs agencies, it appears to consider the effect of bureaucratic structure on the ease of control by the relevant political principals.

■ Domestic policy agencies

▨ Foreign/defense policy agencies

1 Sean Gailmard and John W. Patty, *Learning While Governing: Institutions and Accountability in the Executive Branch* (Chicago: University of Chicago Press, 2012).

2 Data are from David E. Lewis, *Presidents and the Politics of Agency Design: Political Insulation in the United States Government Bureaucracy, 1946–1997* (Palo Alto, CA: Stanford University Press, 2003).

activity.[23] However, Mathew McCubbins and Thomas Schwartz argue that these critics have missed a type of oversight that benefits members of Congress in their bids for reelection (in accord with the rationality principle).[24] McCubbins and Schwartz distinguish between two types of oversight: police patrol and fire alarm. Under police-patrol oversight, Congress systematically initiates investigation into the activity of agencies. Under fire-alarm oversight, Congress waits for adversely affected citizens or interest groups to bring bureaucratic perversions of legislative intent to the attention of the relevant congressional committee. To ensure that individuals and groups bring these violations to members' attention—to set off the fire alarm, so to speak—Congress helps such parties make claims against the bureaucracy, both granting them legal standing before administrative agencies and federal courts and giving them access to government-held information through the Freedom of Information Act.

McCubbins and Schwartz argue that fire-alarm oversight is more efficient than the police-patrol variety, given costs and the electoral incentives of members of Congress. Why should members spend their scarce resources (mainly time) to initiate investigations without having any evidence that they will reap electoral rewards? Police-patrol oversight can waste taxpayers' dollars too, because many investigations will not turn up evidence of violations of legislative intent. It is much more cost effective for members to conserve their resources and then claim credit for fixing the problem after the fire alarms have been sounded.

In contrast, bureaucratic drift might be contained if Congress spent more time clarifying its legislative intent and less time on oversight activity. If its original intent in the law were clearer, Congress could afford to defer to presidential management to maintain bureaucratic responsibility. Bureaucrats are more responsive to clear legislative guidance than to anything else. But when Congress and the president (or coalitions within Congress) are at odds, bureaucrats can evade responsibility by playing one side off against the other.

Policy Implications. Because the bureaucracy is squarely in the middle of the separation of powers between the legislature and the executive, it often eludes systematic oversight. The institution principle suggests as much. Rational political actors in both branches will pay some attention to the bureaucracy, but their own goals may not be well served by obsessive attention. The result is a bureaucracy that retains some discretion—partly because political actors' specialization warrants it but also because political arrangements permit oversight to fall between the institutional cracks.

---

23 Morris S. Ogul, *Congress Oversees the Bureaucracy: Studies in Legislative Supervision* (Pittsburgh, PA: University of Pittsburgh Press, 1976); and Peter Woll, *American Bureaucracy,* 2nd ed. (New York: Norton, 1977).

24 McCubbins and Schwartz, "Congressional Oversight Overlooked."

Bureaus, in turn, perform their missions in ways that maintain this kind of independence. They produce rulings, interpretations, and implementations of policy that deter after-the-fact oversight, allowing sleeping dogs (potential overseers) to lie.

Rational political adaptations to these institutional arrangements have policy consequences. In particular, bureaucrats will be extraordinarily attentive to the policy needs of those legislators who are in a position to help or harm them. Thus states and districts represented on the House and Senate authorizing committees, as well as on the relevant appropriations subcommittees, can expect government largesse to be steered their way. Legislative lore cites instances in which, for example, a major weapons system is sustained politically by an implicit agreement between Defense Department agents and private-sector contractors to ensure that subcontracts are distributed geographically to politically significant locations.

A repeated pattern of deals among agency officials, powerful legislators, and private-sector special interests over many projects in many policy areas yields a "distributive tendency" in which successful play of the political game by legislators and bureaucrats requires the wide distribution of spending. More efficient targeting of spending takes a backseat to ensuring that the "right" states and districts are taken care of. One classic example is President Lyndon Johnson's attempt in the mid-1960s to focus federal assistance on 10 central cities in direst need of economic stimulus. But 10 was too small a number in a political system with 50 states and 435 legislative districts. By the time Johnson's proposal had worked its way through the legislative process, the relevant bureaucratic entities had won discretion to spread funds to hundreds of distressed cities rather than the 10 most desperate ones and even to tackle rural poverty as well. The policy principle suggests that institutional arrangements (bicameralism and the separation of powers, in this instance) combined with rational political behavior (reelection motivations of legislators and programmatic survival instincts of bureaucrats) produce policy distortions (wide distribution of funds to sustain programs and to avoid the risk of critical oversight).

REFORMING THE BUREAUCRACY

Americans don't like big government because it means big bureaucracy, and bureaucracy means the federal service—about 2.7 million civilian and 1.5 million military employees.[25] Promises to cut the bureaucracy are popular campaign

25 These data are found at Governing, "Military Active-Duty Personnel, Civilians by State," www.governing.com/gov-data/military-civilian-active-duty-employee-workforce-numbers-by-state.html (accessed 7/22/15); and U.S. Census Bureau, "Government Employment & Payroll," www.census.gov/govs/apes (accessed 7/22/15).

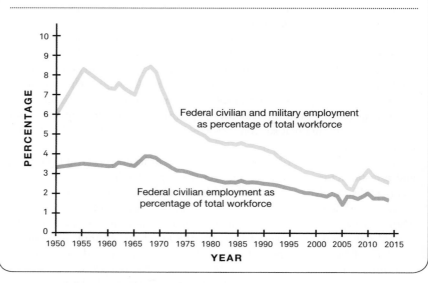

Figure 8.3

EMPLOYEES IN THE FEDERAL SERVICE: TOTAL NUMBER AS A PERCENTAGE OF THE WORKFORCE

Federal civilian and military employment as percentage of total workforce

Federal civilian employment as percentage of total workforce

NOTE: Workforce includes unemployed persons.
SOURCES: Tax Foundation, *Facts and Figures on Government Finance* (Baltimore: Johns Hopkins University Press, 1990), pp. 22, 44; Office of Management and Budget, *Budget of the U.S. Government, Fiscal Year 2009*, table 17.5, https://www.whitehouse.gov/sites/default/files/omb/budget/fy2009/pdf/hist.pdf (accessed 5/9/16); U.S. Bureau of Labor Statistics, http://stats.bls.gov/webapps/legacy/cpsatab1.htm, table A1 (accessed 5/9/16); U.S. Office of Personnel Management, Historical Federal Workforce Tables, www.opm.gov/policy-data-oversight/data-analysis-documentation/federal-employment-reports/historical-tables/total-government-employment-since-1962/ (accessed 5/9/16); and authors' update.

appeals; "cutting out the fat," by reducing the number of federal employees, is touted as a surefire way of cutting the deficit.

Yet the federal service has hardly grown at all during the past 30 years; it reached its peak post–World War II level in 1968 with 2.9 million civilian employees plus an additional 3.6 million military personnel (a figure swollen by the war in Vietnam). The number of civilian federal executive-branch employees has since remained close to that figure. Growth of the federal service is even less imposing when placed in the context of the total workforce and compared to state and local public employment, which was 15 million full-time and 3.7 part-time employees in 2014.[26] Figure 8.3 indicates that since 1950 the ratio of federal service employment to the total workforce has been fairly steady, declining only slightly in the past 25 years.

26 U.S. Bureau of the Census, *Government Employment and Payroll,* https://www.census.gov/govs/apes (accessed 7/22/15).

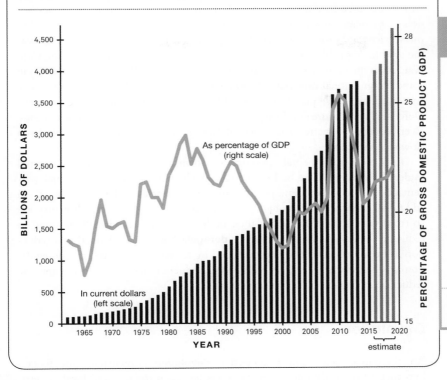

Figure 8.4
ANNUAL FEDERAL OUTLAYS

As percentage of GDP
(right scale)

In current dollars
(left scale)

BILLIONS OF DOLLARS

PERCENTAGE OF GROSS DOMESTIC PRODUCT (GDP)

YEAR

estimate

NOTE: Data for 2016–19 are estimated.
SOURCE: Office of Management and Budget, Historical Tables, Tables 1.1 and 1.2, www.whitehouse.gov/omb/budget/Historicals (accessed 5/9/16).

ANALYZING THE EVIDENCE

Annual federal outlays have increased steadily over time. So has the size of the U.S. economy (not shown in figure). But the ratio of federal expenditures to annual GDP has varied over time. What might explain these fluctuations, and what might be the consequences when the federal government contributes more or less to the economy?

Figure 8.4 offers another useful comparison: although the dollar increase in federal spending shown by the bars looks impressive, the orange line indicates that even here the national government has simply kept pace with the growth of the economy.

In sum, the federal service has not been growing any faster than the economy or the society. The same is roughly true of state and local public personnel. Our bureaucracy keeps pace with our society, despite our seeming dislike for it, because we cannot operate the control towers, the prisons, the Social Security system, and other essential elements of the state without it. And we could not conduct wars in Iraq and Afghanistan without a gigantic military bureaucracy.

Termination

The only *certain* way to reduce the size of the bureaucracy is to eliminate programs. But most agencies have a supportive constituency—people and groups that benefit from the programs—that will fight to reinstate any cuts. Termination is the only way to ensure an agency's reduction, and it is a rare occurrence.

The overall lack of success in terminating bureaucracy is a reflection of Americans' love-hate relationship with the national government. As antagonistic as Americans may be toward bureaucracy in general, they grow attached to the services and protections offered by particular agencies. A good example was the agonizing problem of closing military bases following the end of the Cold War, when the United States no longer needed so many. Because every base is in some congressional member's district, Congress was unable to decide to close any of them. Consequently, between 1988 and 1990, Congress established the Defense Base Closure and Realignment Commission to decide on base closings. Even though the matter is now out of Congress's hands, the process has been slow and agonizing.

In a more incremental approach to downsizing the bureaucracy, elected leaders have reduced the budgets of all agencies across the board by small percentages and have cut some poorly supported agencies by larger amounts. An additional approach targets highly unpopular regulatory agencies, but they are so (relatively) small that cutting their budgets contributes virtually nothing to reducing the deficit. This approach is **deregulation**, simply defined as a reduction in the number of rules promulgated by regulatory agencies. But deregulation is still incremental and, as with budget reduction, has not yielded a genuine reduction in the size of the bureaucracy.

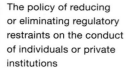

deregulation

The policy of reducing or eliminating regulatory restraints on the conduct of individuals or private institutions

Devolution

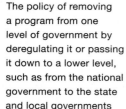

devolution

The policy of removing a program from one level of government by deregulating it or passing it down to a lower level, such as from the national government to the state and local governments

An alternative to genuine reduction is **devolution**—downsizing the federal bureaucracy by delegating program implementation to state and local governments. Indirect evidence for this appears in Figure 8.5, which shows the increase in state and local government employment against a backdrop of flat or declining federal employment. This evidence suggests a growing share of governmental actions taking place on state and local levels.

Devolution often alters the pattern of who benefits most from government programs. In the early 1990s, a major devolution in transportation policy sought to open up decisions to a new set of interests. Since the 1920s, transportation policy had been dominated by road-building interests in the federal and state governments. Many advocates for cities and many environmentalists believed that the emphasis on road building hurt cities and harmed the environment. The 1992 reform, initiated by environmentalists, gave more power to metropolitan planning organizations and lifted many federal restrictions on how the money should be spent. Reformers hoped that through these changes those advocating alternatives to road building, such as mass transit, bike paths, and walkways, would have more influence over how federal transportation dollars were spent. Although change has been slow, devolution has indeed brought new voices to decisions about transportation spending, and alternatives to highways have received increasing attention.

Figure 8.5

GOVERNMENT EMPLOYMENT

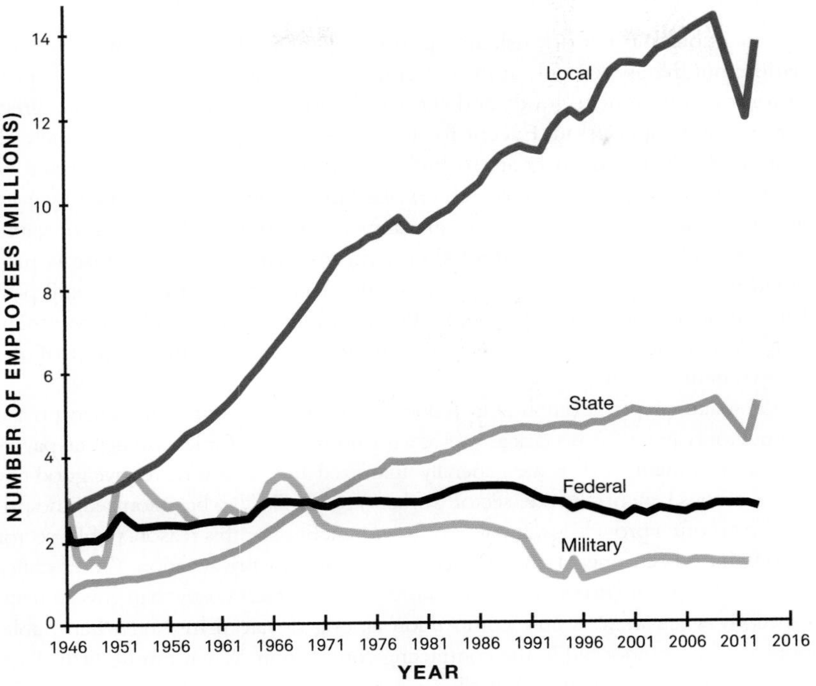

NOTE: Federal government employment figures include civilians only. Military employment figures include only active-duty personnel; 2013 data not available.
SOURCE: U.S. Bureau of the Census, *Statistical Abstract of the United States,* 2011 and 2012 (Washington, DC: Government Printing Office, 2011).

Often devolution seeks to provide more efficient and more flexible government services, yet it entails variation across the states. In some states, government services may improve as a consequence of devolution. In other states, services may deteriorate as devolution leads to spending cuts and reduced services. This has been the pattern in implementation of the welfare reform passed in 1996. Some states, such as Wisconsin, have designed innovative programs that respond to clients' needs; other states, such as Idaho, have virtually dismantled their welfare programs. Because the legislation placed a five-year lifetime limit on receiving welfare, the states will take on an even greater role in the future as existing clients lose their eligibility for federal benefits. Welfare reform has been praised for reducing welfare rolls and responding to the public desire that welfare be a temporary program. At the same time, however, it has placed more low-income women and their children at risk of being left with no assistance at all.

Privatization

Privatization, another downsizing option, may seem like a synonym for termination, but that is true only at the extreme. Most privatization involves the provision of government goods and services by private contractors under direct government supervision. Except for top-secret strategic materials, virtually all military hardware, from boats to bullets, is produced by private contractors. And billions of dollars of research services are bought under contract by government; these private contractors are universities, industrial corporations, and private think tanks. **Privatization** simply means that a public purpose is provided under contract by a private company.[27] But such programs are still paid for and supervised by government. Privatization downsizes the government only in that the workers providing the service are not counted as part of the government bureaucracy.

The aim of privatization is to reduce the cost of government. When private contractors can perform a task as well as a government but for less money, taxpayers win. Government workers are generally unionized and, therefore, receive good pay and generous benefits. Private-sector workers are less likely to be unionized, and private firms often provide lower pay and fewer benefits. For this reason, public-sector unions have been one of the strongest voices against privatization. Other critics observe that private firms may not be more efficient or less costly than government, especially when there is little competition among private firms and when public bureaucracies cannot bid in the contracting competition. When private firms have a monopoly on service provision, they may be more expensive than government.

Moreover, there are important questions about how private contractors can be held accountable. For example, as security has become the nation's paramount concern, some Pentagon officials fear that too many tasks vital to national security have been contracted out and that national security might best be served by limiting privatization.

Indeed, the new demands of domestic security have altered the thrust of bureaucratic reform. Despite strong agreement on the goal of fighting terrorism, the effort to streamline the bureaucracy by focusing on a single purpose is likely to face considerable obstacles. Strong constituencies may attempt to block changes that they believe will harm them, and initiatives for improved coordination among agencies may provoke political disputes if the proposed changes threaten to alter groups' access to the bureaucracy. And groups that oppose bureaucratic changes can appeal to Congress to intervene on their behalf.

privatization

The act of moving all or part of a program from the public sector to the private sector

---

27 A more general term is *outsourcing*. Privatization is outsourcing to the private sector. Devolution is outsourcing to a lower level of government. A third example of outsourcing is the opposite of devolution, as when a small community contracts with a county for, say, police services.

CONCLUSION: PUBLIC BUREAUCRACIES AND POLITICS

Bureaucracy is one of humanity's most significant inventions. It is an institutional arrangement that allows for division and specialization of labor; harnesses expertise; and coordinates collective action for social, political, and economic purposes. It enables governments to exist and perform. In this chapter, we have focused on what public bureaucracies do, how they are organized at the national level in the United States, and how they are controlled (or not) by elected politicians.

At a theoretical level, public bureaucracy is the concrete expression of rational, purposeful, political action (rationality principle). Elected politicians have goals—as broad as defending the realm, maintaining public health and safety, or promoting economic growth; as narrow as securing a post office for Possum Hollow, Pennsylvania, or an exit off the interstate highway for Springfield, Massachusetts. Bureaucracy is the instrument by which political objectives, established by elected legislators and executives, are transformed from ideas and intentions into the actual "bricks and mortar" of implemented policies (policy principle).

At a practical level, this transformation depends on the motivations of bureaucratic agents and the institutional machinery that develops around every bureaucratic entity. Elected politicians engage in institutional design in creating agencies. They have their greatest impact at this point. Once an agency is operating, elected officials only imperfectly control their bureaucratic agents. Institutional arrangements and simple human nature provide some insulation to agencies, enabling bureaucrats to march to their own drummers—at least some of the time. Of course, bureaucrats are not entirely free agents. But control is a constant and recurring problem for elected officials (institution principle).

The policy principle suggests that the combination of bureaucratic arrangements and individual motivations produce evident patterns in policy. Because of its insulation, an agency's policies, once underway, are difficult to reverse. Insulation thwarts only the most intensely expressed interventions in an agency's affairs. This has the benefit of commitment—interested parties are reassured about the continued provision of a bureaucratic product or service. The farmer can rely on his subsidy check, the senior citizen on her monthly Social Security stipend; truckers and other motorists can be confident that the interstate highways will be there for them.

But these commitments have distributive costs. Bureaucrats will be most attentive to the most intensely interested parties. Thus policies will be skewed in particular ways. The efficiency gains arising from the expertise and coordinating services of bureaucracy are thus dissipated by these political pressures. For example, highway funds will find their way disproportionately to the states and districts of legislators who sit on the public works authorizing and appropriating committees.

In describing the federal bureaucracy in this chapter, we have sought to make clear the ways in which rationality, institutional processes, and the resulting policy outputs are a consequence of the way in which agencies straddle the divide produced by the separation of powers. Attuned partly to the executive and partly to the legislature, bureaucratic agents tread a careful line between their several masters, somewhat protected the natural insulation associated with bureaucracy but vulnerable to intense political pressure. Politics is at the very heart of these organizations and the policies they produce.

For Further Reading

Aberbach, Joel, and Bert A. Rockman. *In the Web of Politics: Three Decades of the U.S. Federal Executive.* Washington, DC: Brookings Institution, 2000.

Besley, Timothy. *Principled Agents? Motivations and Incentives in Politics.* Oxford, UK: Oxford University Press, 2006.

Brehm, John, and Scott Gates. *Working, Shirking, and Sabotage: Bureaucratic Response to a Democratic Public.* Ann Arbor: University of Michigan Press, 1997.

Downs, Anthony. *Inside Bureaucracy.* Boston: Little, Brown, 1966.

Fiorina, Morris P. "Legislative Choice of Regulatory Forms: Legal Process or Administrative Process." *Public Choice* 39 (1982): 33–66.

Gailmard, Sean, and John W. Patty. *Learning While Governing: Expertise and Accountability in the Executive Branch.* Chicago: University of Chicago Press, 2013.

Goodsell, Charles. *The Case for Bureaucracy.* 4th ed. Washington, DC: CQ Press, 2003.

Heclo, Hugh. *On Thinking Institutionally.* Boulder, CO: Paradigm, 2007.

Huber, John, and Charles Shipan. *Deliberate Discretion? The Institutional Foundations of Bureaucratic Autonomy.* New York: Cambridge University Press, 2002.

Kerwin, Cornelius M., and Scott R. Furlong. *Rulemaking.* 4th ed. Washington, DC: CQ Press, 2010.

Kettl, Donald F., and James Fesler. *The Politics of the Administrative Process.* 3rd ed. Washington, DC: Brookings Institution, 2005.

Light, Paul C. *The True Size of Government.* Washington, DC: Brookings Institution, 1999.

McCubbins, Mathew, Roger Noll, and Barry Weingast. "Structure and Process; Politics and Policy: Administrative Arrangements and the Political Control of Agencies." *Virginia Law Review* 75 (1989): 431–82.

McCubbins, Mathew, and Thomas Schwartz. "Congressional Oversight Overlooked: Police Patrols Versus Fire Alarms." *American Journal of Political Science* 28 (1984): 165–79.

Meier, Kenneth J., and John Bohte. *Politics and the Bureaucracy.* 5th ed. Belmont, CA: Wadsworth, 2006.

Seidman, Harold. *Politics, Position, and Power: The Dynamics of Federal Organization.* 5th ed. New York: Oxford University Press, 1997.

Wilson, James Q. *Bureaucracy: What Government Agencies Do and Why They Do It.* New York: Basic Books, 1989.

9

The Federal Courts

Courts serve an essential function. When disputes arise, an impartial arbiter is needed to help settle the matter. When laws must be enforced, justice requires an impartial judge to determine guilt and innocence and, if the accused is found guilty, the appropriate punishment. And when questions arise about the meaning of those laws, we rely on the wisdom of judges to interpret what Congress meant and how that meaning applies in a given circumstance. It is not possible, or even wise, to pass a law to cover every contingency. Thus nearly every nation today has established a system of courts to satisfy the need for an arbiter and interpreter.

Perhaps the most distinctive feature of the American judiciary is its independence. The Constitution, as it was written and as it has evolved, established the courts as a separate entity from the legislature, the executive, and the states and insulated it from electoral politics. As we will see, four institutional features of the American judiciary ensure a powerful, independent court system. First, the Constitution establishes the federal courts as a separate branch of government from Congress and the president. Second, authority among the courts is hierarchical, with federal courts able to overturn state courts, and the U.S. Supreme Court as the ultimate authority. Third, the Supreme Court and other federal courts of appeals can strike down actions of Congress, the president, or the states if judges deem those acts to be violations of the Constitution. This authority is the power of *judicial review*. And fourth, federal judges are appointed for life. They are not subject to the pressures of running for reelection and need not be highly responsive to changes in public opinion.[1]

An independent judiciary has been one of our government's most successful institutions. It has settled constitutional crises when Congress and the president are at odds. It has guaranteed that no person is above the law, even members of Congress and the president. It has helped ensure that all people, even noncitizens, enjoy equal protection of the laws. It has enabled small businesses, large

---

1   However, judges in many state and local courts are elected.

corporations, and workers to engage in economic activities and agreements, knowing that their rights will be protected. It has ensured that the branches of government operate in a democratic manner and that every citizen's vote counts equally in selecting the legislature. The independent judiciary has ensured a stable, successful democracy and economy.

Although granting judges lifetime appointments and the power to strike down acts of Congress might seem to permit tyrannical rule by courts, courts lack Congress's power of the purse, the president's ability to move troops or order other branches of the executive to act, or the bureaucracy's power to police. Courts are also passive in that they must wait for people to file lawsuits in order to make decisions or issue decrees. The sources and nature of judicial power in American government are subtle and democratic.

The real power of the courts emanates from their ability to interpret the meaning of the laws in a way that society accepts. Courts are powerful to the extent that the people and groups involved accept judges' decrees in nearly all cases. If people ignored the decrees of judges in local courts or if Congress routinely passed legislation contradicting the Supreme Court, the judicial function in our society would vanish. Herein lies the judiciary's ability not just to interpret but also to make law. Indeed, each court decision or settlement is an

CORE OF THE ANALYSIS

Just like presidents and legislators, judges have preferences about what government should do, and they use their powers to shape public policy.

Judicial decisions are highly constrained by the past, in the form of common law and precedents, but every decision also contributes to the evolution of the law.

The courts maintain their independence from the legislature and executive because federal judges are appointed for life and not elected. Independence allows the courts to act as a check on the democratically chosen branches of government.

Courts can block or overturn political decisions of the legislature or executive if those decisions violate the Constitution or conflict with other laws, a power called judicial review.

However, the courts are also constrained by the checks and balances built into the institutional setting within which they operate.

act of lawmaking, a function as important as the passage of a statute by the legislature. Any decision may serve as a precedent for deciding a future case, and the accumulation of many such decisions, accepted by common practice, eventually becomes the norm.

Common law consists of all past agreements that we accept when reaching any decision. A contract for a real estate sale, for example, comprises many pages of language pertaining to contingencies that might arise, what would happen in each case, and who would bear responsibility. Each clause has been developed through past legal decisions accumulated over centuries, even dating back in some instances to ancient Rome. The Supreme Court is similarly constrained by past decisions. When a majority of justices issues an opinion interpreting the law in a particular way, that opinion has the standing of precedent and constrains future courts. The history principle matters more fundamentally for the judiciary than for the other branches of government. If judges themselves were to ignore precedent, they would undercut the power of the courts and their own authority.

Precedents limit the power of the independent judiciary, but the past does not render the courts impotent. In any decision, a judge is both constrained by the past and contributing to the future meaning of the law. Usually, the courts' influence on American politics is incremental. At times, however, courts have made sweeping changes in the country's law and politics. With industrialization in the late nineteenth century came new ideas about the enforcement of contracts that dominated the courts' thinking. The New Deal eventually won the support of the Supreme Court and with that a new acceptance of government's role in the economy and society. During the 1950s and 1960s, the Supreme Court confronted lingering conflicts over racial and gender equality, religious freedoms, police powers, and legislative redistricting. Today, the courts face new questions, many stemming from rapid changes in information and biological technologies: Who owns your DNA? Do you have a right to privacy when sending an e-mail? As in the past, the courts will settle cases that address such questions, and how the courts do so will shape the meaning of the law and the definition of fundamental rights, such as the rights to property and privacy.

The judiciary's role in our system of government points to a basic lesson about courts worldwide: they are fundamentally political. Just like presidents and legislators, judges have preferences about what government should do, and they use their powers to interpret, apply, and review laws to shape public policy. Judges are also constrained by the institutional setting within which they operate. They know that others in the political process may try to alter or undo a court's rulings.

In this chapter, we examine the judicial process first, including the types of cases that the federal courts consider and the types of laws that they interpret. Second, we assess the structure of the federal court system and explain how judges are appointed. Third, we analyze courts as political institutions and consider their roles in the political system. Fourth, we consider judicial review and how it makes the Supreme Court a lawmaking body. Fifth, we examine the flow of cases through the courts and various influences on Supreme Court decisions. Finally, we analyze the process of judicial decision making and the power of the federal courts in the American political process, looking in particular at the growth of judicial power in our nation.

THE JUDICIAL PROCESS

Many centuries ago a court was the place where a king and his entourage governed. Judging—settling disputes between citizens—was part of governing. Over time the function of settling disputes was slowly separated from the king and his court and became a separate institution of government. Courts have taken over the power to settle controversies by hearing the facts on both sides and deciding which side possesses greater merit. But because judges are not kings, they must have a basis for their authority. That basis in the United States is the Constitution and the law. Courts decide cases by applying the relevant law or principle to the facts. This approach lends authority derived from past law and past social compacts. It also provides a basis for continuing judicial independence, as common law and past precedents evolve on their own, often separate from legislation passed by Congress and the executive. What are these systems of rules that the judiciary has developed? What are the organizations and institutions of the judiciary, and how do they help perform the complex administration and interpretation of the law?

Court cases in the United States proceed under two broad categories of law: criminal and civil. One form of civil law, public law, is so important that we consider it as a separate category (Table 9.1).

In cases of **criminal law** the government charges an individual with violating a statute that has been enacted to protect the public health, safety, morals, or welfare. In criminal cases, the government is always the plaintiff (the party that brings charges) and alleges that a named defendant has committed a criminal violation. Most criminal cases arise in state and municipal courts and involve matters ranging from traffic offenses to robbery and murder. Although much of criminal law is still a state matter, a growing body of federal criminal law addresses such matters as tax evasion, mail fraud, and the sale of narcotics. Defendants found guilty of criminal violations may be fined or sent to prison.

Cases of **civil law** involve disputes between individuals or between individuals and the government where no criminal violation is charged. Unlike criminal cases, the losers in civil cases cannot be fined or sent to prison, although they may be required to pay monetary damages. In a civil case, the one who brings a complaint is the plaintiff and the one against whom the complaint is brought is the defendant. The two most common types of civil cases involve contracts and torts and are often handled by state courts. In a typical contract case, an individual or corporation charges that it has suffered because of another's violation of an agreement between the two. For example, Smith Manufacturing Corporation may charge that Jones Distributors failed to honor an agreement to deliver raw materials at a specified time, causing Smith to lose business. Smith asks the court to order Jones to compensate it for the damage allegedly suffered.

 criminal law

The branch of law that regulates the conduct of individuals, defines crimes, and specifies punishment for proscribed conduct

 civil law

The branch of law that deals with disputes that do not involve criminal penalties

Table 9.1

TYPES OF LAWS AND DISPUTES

TYPE OF LAW	TYPE OF CASE OR DISPUTE	FORM OF CITATION
Criminal law	Cases arising out of actions that violate laws protecting the health, safety, and morals of the community. The government is always the plaintiff.	*U.S. (or state) v. Jones, Jones v. U.S. (or state)* if Jones lost and is appealing
Civil law	Law involving disputes between citizens or between a government and a citizen where no crime is alleged. Two general types are contract law and tort law. Contract cases are disputes that arise over voluntary actions. Tort cases are disputes that arise out of obligations inherent in social life. Negligence and slander are examples of torts.	*Smith v. Jones, New York v. Jones, U.S. v. Jones, Jones v. New York*
Public law	All cases in which the powers of government or the rights of citizens are involved. The government is the defendant. Constitutional law involves judicial review of the basis of a government's action in relation to specific clauses of the Constitution as interpreted in Supreme Court cases. Administrative law involves disputes over the statutory authority, jurisdiction, or procedures of administrative agencies.	*Jones v. U.S. (or state), In re Jones, Smith v. Jones* if a license or statute is at issue in their private dispute

precedents ⇨

Prior cases whose principles are used by judges as the bases for their decisions in present cases

stare decisis ⇨

Literally, "let the decision stand." The doctrine whereby a previous decision by a court applies as a precedent in similar cases until that decision is overruled

public law ⇨

Cases involving the action of public agencies or officials

In a typical tort case, one individual charges that he or she has been injured by another's negligence or malfeasance. Medical malpractice suits are one example of tort cases.

In deciding cases, courts apply statutes (laws) and legal **precedents** (prior decisions). State and federal statutes often govern the conditions under which contracts are and are not legally binding. Jones Distributors might argue that it was not obliged to fulfill its contract with Smith Manufacturing because actions by Smith—the failure to make promised payments—constituted fraud under state law. Attorneys for a physician being sued for malpractice, in contrast, may search for prior instances in which courts ruled that actions similar to their client's did not constitute negligence. Such precedents are applied under the doctrine of **stare decisis**, a Latin phrase meaning "let the decision stand."

A case becomes a matter of **public law** when a plaintiff or defendant in a civil or criminal case seeks to show that his case involves the powers of government or the rights of citizens as defined under the Constitution or by statute. One major form of public law is constitutional law, under which a court will determine whether the government's actions conform to the Constitution as interpreted by the judiciary. Thus what began as an ordinary criminal case may enter the realm of public law if, for example, a defendant claims that the police violated her constitutional rights. Another arena of public law is administrative law, which involves disputes over the jurisdiction, procedures, or authority of administrative agencies. Under this type of law, civil litigation between an individual and the government may become a matter of public law if the individual asserts that the government is violating a statute or abusing its constitutional power. For example, landowners have asserted that federal and state administrative regulations on land use constitute violations of the Fifth Amendment's restrictions on the government's ability to confiscate private property. Recently the Supreme Court has been very sympathetic to such claims, which effectively transform an ordinary civil dispute into a major issue of public law.

Most of the Supreme Court cases we examine in this chapter involve judgments concerning the constitutional or statutory basis of the actions of government agencies. In this arena of public law, Court decisions can have significant consequences for American politics and society.

THE ORGANIZATION OF THE COURT SYSTEM

Types of Courts

In the United States, court systems have been established both by the federal government and by individual state governments. Both systems have several levels (Figure 9.1), though it should be acknowledged that the one federal system and the 50 state systems are all distinctive in a number of ways. Nearly 99 percent of all court cases in the United States are heard in state courts. The majority of criminal cases, for example, involve violations of state laws prohibiting such actions as murder, robbery, fraud, theft, and assault. If such a case is brought to trial, it will be heard in a state **trial court** in front of a judge and sometimes a jury, who will determine whether the defendant violated state law. If the defendant is convicted, he may appeal the conviction to a higher court, such as a state **court of appeals**, and from there to a state's **supreme court**. Similarly, in civil cases, most litigation is brought in the courts established by the state in which the activity in question occurred. For example, a patient bringing suit against a physician for malpractice would file the suit in the appropriate court in the state where the alleged malpractice occurred. The judge hearing the case would apply state law and state precedent to the matter. (However, in both criminal and civil matters, most cases are settled before trial through negotiated agreements between the parties. In criminal cases, these agreements are called plea bargains. Such bargains may affect the severity of the charge and/or the severity of the sentence.)

In addition, the U.S. military operates its own court system under the Uniform Code of Military Justice, which governs the behavior of men and women in the armed services. On rare occasions, the government has constituted special military tribunals to hear cases deemed inappropriate for the civil courts. Such tribunals tried Nazi saboteurs apprehended in the United States during World War II and individuals suspected of acts of terrorism against the

 trial court

The first court to hear a criminal or civil case

 court of appeals (or appellate court)

A court that hears the appeals of trial-court decisions

 supreme court

The highest court in a particular state or in the United States. This court primarily serves an appellate function

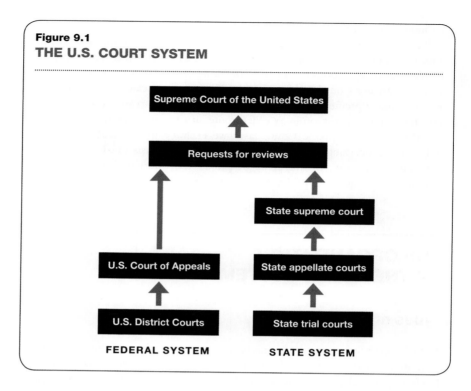

Figure 9.1
THE U.S. COURT SYSTEM

Supreme Court of the United States

Requests for reviews

State supreme court

U.S. Court of Appeals

State appellate courts

U.S. District Courts

State trial courts

FEDERAL SYSTEM

STATE SYSTEM

jurisdiction

The types of cases over which a court has authority

appellate jurisdiction

The class of cases provided in the Constitution and by legislation that may be appealed to a higher court from a lower court

original jurisdiction

The class of cases provided in the Constitution (Article III) that may be taken directly to a federal court

United States after 9/11. More recently, special courts have been created, sometimes in conjunction with the Department of Veterans' Affairs, to hear criminal cases involving military veterans of the recent wars in Iraq and Afghanistan.

Federal Jurisdiction

Cases are heard in the federal courts if they involve federal laws, treaties with other nations, or the U.S. Constitution; these areas constitute the federal courts' official **jurisdiction**. In addition, any case in which the U.S. government is a party is heard in the federal courts. If, for example, an individual is charged with violating a federal criminal statute, such as evading the payment of income taxes, charges would be brought before a federal judge by a federal prosecutor. Civil cases involving the citizens of more than one state and in which more than $75,000 is at stake may be heard in either the federal or the state courts.

But even if a matter belongs in federal court, how do we know which federal court should exercise jurisdiction? The answer is complex. Each federal court's jurisdiction is derived from the Constitution and federal statutes. Article III of the Constitution gives the Supreme Court **appellate jurisdiction** in all federal cases and **original jurisdiction** in cases involving foreign ambassadors and issues in which a state is a party. That is, the Supreme Court may hear cases appealed to it by a party to a case first heard in a lower federal court or a state court (appellate jurisdiction) or the Supreme Court may be the initial destination of cases

Figure 9.2

GEOGRAPHIC BOUNDARIES OF U.S. COURTS OF APPEALS

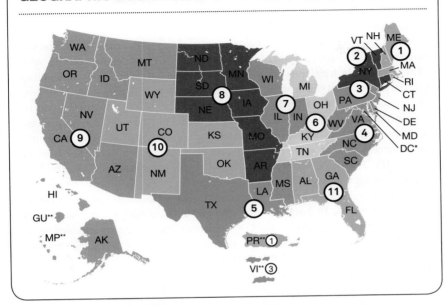

* The District of Columbia has its own circuit, called the D.C. Circuit.

** U.S. Postal Service abbreviations for Guam (GU), Northern Mariana Islands (MP), Puerto Rico (PR), and the U.S. Virgin Islands (VI).

SOURCE: Administrative Office of the U.S. Courts, www.uscourts.gov/uscourts/images/CircuitMap.pdf (accessed 4/2/13).

involving a state or an ambassador (original jurisdiction). Article III assigns original jurisdiction in all other federal cases to the lower courts that Congress was authorized to establish. Over the years, as Congress enacted statutes creating the federal judicial system, it specified the jurisdiction of each type of court it established. Congress generally has assigned jurisdictions on the basis of geography. The nation is currently, by statute, divided into 94 judicial districts, including one court for each of three U.S. territories: Guam, the U.S. Virgin Islands, and the Northern Marianas. Each of the 94 U.S. district courts exercises jurisdiction over federal cases arising within its territorial domain. The judicial districts are, in turn, organized into 11 regional circuits and the District of Columbia circuit (Figure 9.2). Each circuit court exercises appellate jurisdiction over cases heard by the district courts within its region.

Geography is not the only basis for federal court jurisdiction. Congress has also established specialized courts with nationwide original jurisdiction in certain types of cases. These include the U.S. Court of International Trade, which addresses trade and customs issues, and the U.S. Court of Federal Claims, which handles damage suits against the United States. Congress has also established a court with nationwide appellate jurisdiction: the U.S. Court of Appeals for the Federal Circuit, which hears appeals involving patent law and those arising from the decisions of the trade and claims courts. Other federal courts with specialized jurisdictions are the U.S. Court of Appeals for Veterans Claims, which exercises exclusive jurisdiction over cases involving veterans' claims, and the U.S. Court of Appeals for the Armed Forces, which addresses questions of law arising from trials by court martial.

With the exception of the claims court and the Court of Appeals for the Federal Circuit, these specialized courts were created by Congress on the basis of the powers the legislature exercises under Article I. Article III was designed to protect judges from political pressure by granting them life tenure and prohibiting reduction of their salaries while they serve. The judges of Article I courts, by contrast, are appointed by the president for fixed terms of 15 years and are not protected from salary reduction. As a result, these so-called legislative courts are generally viewed as less independent than the courts established under Article III. The three territorial courts were also established under Article I, and their judges are appointed for 10-year terms.

The federal courts' appellate jurisdiction also extends to cases originating in the state courts. In both civil and criminal cases, a decision of the highest state court can be appealed to the U.S. Supreme Court by raising a federal issue. Appellants might assert, for example, that they were denied the right to counsel or otherwise deprived of the **due process** guaranteed by the federal Constitution, or they might assert that important issues of federal law were at stake in the case. The Supreme Court will accept such appeals only if it believes that the matter has considerable national significance. (We return to this topic later in the chapter.) In addition, in criminal cases defendants who have been convicted in a state court may request a **writ of *habeas corpus*** from a federal district court. *Habeas corpus* is a court order to the authorities to show cause for the incarceration of a prisoner. In 1867, Congress's distrust of southern courts led it to authorize federal district judges to issue such writs on behalf of prisoners who they believed had been deprived of their constitutional rights in state court. Generally speaking, state defendants seeking a federal writ of *habeas corpus* must have exhausted all available state remedies and raise issues not previously raised in their state appeals. Federal courts of appeals and, ultimately, the U.S. Supreme Court have appellate jurisdiction over federal district court *habeas* decisions.

Over recent decades, the federal courts' caseload has more than quadrupled, to 450,000 cases annually. This has occurred because Congress has greatly expanded the number of federal crimes, particularly involving drug possession and sale. Behavior that was once a state criminal matter has, to some extent, come within the reach of federal law. In 1999, Chief Justice William Rehnquist criticized Congress for federalizing too many offenses and intruding into areas that the states should handle.[2] About 85 percent of federal cases end in the district courts; the remainder are appealed to the circuit courts. Of these circuit court decisions, thousands annually are appealed to the Supreme Court. Most cases filed with the Supreme Court are dismissed without a ruling on their

due process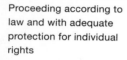

Proceeding according to law and with adequate protection for individual rights

writ of *habeas corpus*

A court order demanding that an individual in custody be brought into court and shown the cause for detention; *habeas corpus* is guaranteed by the Constitution and can be suspended only in cases of rebellion or invasion

2   Roberto Suro, "Rehnquist: Too Many Offenses Are Becoming Federal Crimes," *Washington Post*, January 1, 1999, p. A2.

merits. The Court has broad latitude to decide what cases it will hear and generally listens only to those cases it deems to raise the most important issues. Thus in recent years, fewer than 100 cases annually were given full-dress Supreme Court review (the nine justices actually sitting en banc—in full court—and hearing lawyers argue the case), and 80 or so written opinions were issued.[3]

Although the federal courts hear only a fraction of all civil and criminal cases decided each year, their decisions are extremely important (Table 9.2). It is in the federal courts that the Constitution and federal laws governing all Americans are interpreted and their meaning and significance established. Moreover, it is in the federal courts that the powers and limitations of the increasingly powerful national government are tested. Finally, through their power to review the state courts' decisions, it is ultimately the federal courts that dominate the American judicial system.

Federal Trial Courts

Federal district courts are trial courts of general jurisdiction, and their cases are, in form, indistinguishable from cases in state trial courts.

There are 89 district courts in the 50 states, 1 each in the District of Columbia and Puerto Rico, and 1 in each of three U.S. territories. There are 678 district judgeships. District judges are assigned to district courts through the political process involving both the president and Congress. The number of judgeships on a district court depends in part on workload; the busiest may have as many as 28 judges. Only 1 judge is assigned to each case, except where statutes provide for 3-judge courts to deal with special issues. The procedures of the federal district courts are essentially the same as those of the lower state courts, except federal procedural requirements tend to be stricter. States, for example, do not have to provide a grand jury, a 12-member trial jury, or a unanimous jury verdict. Federal courts must provide all these. As mentioned earlier, in addition to district courts, cases are handled by several specialized courts, including the U.S. Tax Court, the Court of Federal Claims, and the Court of International Trade.

Federal Appellate Courts

Roughly 20 percent of all federal lower-court cases, along with appeals of some federal agency decisions, are subsequently reviewed by a federal appeals court. As noted, the country is divided into 12 judicial circuits, each with a U.S. Court of Appeals. Every state and the District of Columbia are assigned to the circuit in the continental United States that is closest to it. A 13th appellate court, the U.S. Court of Appeals for the Federal Circuit, is defined by subject matter (patent law and decisions of trade and claims courts) rather than geographic jurisdiction.

---

3   www.uscourts.gov/statistics/table/1/judicial-business/2015/09/30 (accessed 8/17/16).

Table 9.2

LANDMARK SUPREME COURT CASES

Not all cases and decisions are equally important. Landmark cases are decisions that revolutionize an area of law and announce new legal standards or have far-reaching political consequences.

Marbury v. Madison (1803). The Court declared part of the Judiciary Act unconstitutional, establishing judicial review.

McCulloch v. Maryland (1819). The Court justified the "implied powers" of the government under the Constitution, enabling Congress and the president to assert their authority beyond those activities explicitly mentioned in the Constitution.

Gibbons v. Ogden (1824). This decision establishes the supremacy of the federal government over the states in the regulation of commerce so as to create uniform business law.

Dred Scott v. Sandford (1857). The Court declared that people of African origin brought to the United States as part of the slave trade were not given the rights of citizenship under the Constitution and could, therefore, claim none of the rights and privileges that the Constitution provides.

Plessy v. Ferguson (1896). The Court interpreted the post–Civil War amendments to the Constitution in such a way as to allow segregation, so long as facilities were "separate but equal."

Lochner v. New York (1905). The Court established a general right to enter freely into contracts as part of business, including the right to purchase and sell labor. The decision made it more difficult for unions to form.

Schenck v. United States (1919). The Court declared that the right to free speech does not extend to words that are "used in such circumstances and are of such a nature as to create a clear and present danger."

Korematsu v. United States (1944). The Court allowed the U.S. government to intern Japanese-Americans in concentration camps during World War II as a safeguard against insurrection or spying.

Brown v. Board of Education (1954). The Court ruled that separate educational facilities could not be equal, overturning *Plessy*, and ordered an end to segregation "with all deliberate speed."

Mapp v. Ohio (1961). The Court ruled that all evidence obtained by searches and seizures in violation of the federal Constitution is inadmissible in a court of law.

Baker v. Carr (1962). The justices established that the Court had the authority to hear cases involving legislative districting, even though that is a "political matter," ultimately guaranteeing equal representation in the state legislatures and the U.S. House of Representatives.

Griswold v. Connecticut (1965). The Court struck down a Connecticut law prohibiting counseling on the use of contraceptives and declared that the Bill of Rights implied a right to privacy.

Brandenburg v. Ohio (1969). The Court ruled that inflammatory speech may not be punished by government unless it is likely to incite imminent lawless action.

Table 9.2

LANDMARK SUPREME COURT CASES—cont'd

Roe v. Wade (1973). The Court held that a mother may abort her baby for any reason up to the point that the fetus becomes "viable" and that any law passed by a state or Congress inconsistent with this holding violated the right to privacy and the right to enter freely into contracts.

Grutter v. Bollinger (2003). The Court held that colleges and universities have a legitimate interest in promoting diversity.

Roper v. Simmons (2005). The Court held that it is cruel and unusual punishment to execute persons for crimes they committed before the age of 18.

Kelo v. City of New London (2005). The Court upheld the power of local government to seize property for economic development.

Boumediene v. Bush (2008). The Court declared that foreign terrorism suspects have the constitutional right to challenge their detention (using the writ of *habeas corpus*) at the Guantánamo Bay naval base in U.S. courts, even though the detainees are not citizens.

Obergefell v. Hodges (2015). The Court held that states must both allow same-sex couples to marry and recognize same-sex marriages from other states.

Except for cases selected for Supreme Court review, decisions made by the appeals courts are final. Because of this finality, certain safeguards have been built into the system. Most important is the provision of more than one judge for every appeals case. Each court of appeals has from 3 to 28 permanent judgeships. Although normally three judges hear appealed cases, in some instances a larger number sit en banc. Another safeguard involves the assignment of a Supreme Court justice as the circuit justice for each of the 12 circuits. The circuit justice addresses requests for special action by the Supreme Court. Circuit justices most frequently review requests for stays of execution when the full Court cannot—mainly during its summer recess.

The Supreme Court

Article III of the Constitution vests "the judicial Power of the United States" in the Supreme Court, which is supreme in fact as well as form. The Supreme Court comprises a chief justice and eight associate justices. The **chief justice** presides over the Court's public sessions and conferences. In the Court's actual deliberations and decisions, however, the chief justice has no more authority than his colleagues. Each justice casts one vote. The chief justice, though, always speaks first when the justices deliberate. In addition, if the chief justice has voted with the majority, he decides which justice will write the formal Court opinion. To some extent, the chief justice's influence is a function of his leadership ability. Some chief justices, such as Earl Warren, have led the Court in

 chief justice

The justice on the Supreme Court who presides over the Court's public sessions

a new direction; in other instances, a forceful associate justice, such as Felix Frankfurter, is the dominant figure.

The Constitution does not specify how many justices should sit on the Supreme Court; Congress has the authority to change the Court's size. In the early nineteenth century, there were six justices; later, seven. Congress set the number at nine in 1869, and the Court has remained that size ever since. In 1937, President Franklin Delano Roosevelt, infuriated by several Court decisions that struck down New Deal programs, asked Congress to enlarge the Court so that he could add sympathetic justices to the bench. Although Congress balked, the Court yielded to Roosevelt's pressure and began to view his policy initiatives more favorably. The president, in turn, dropped his efforts to enlarge the Court. The Court's surrender to Roosevelt came to be known as "the switch in time that saved nine."[4]

How Judges Are Appointed

The president appoints federal judges. Nominees are typically prominent or politically active members of the legal profession—former state court judges or state or local prosecutors, prominent attorneys or elected officials, or highly regarded law professors.[5] Prior experience as a judge is not necessary, either for appointment or, ultimately, success. Many of the greatest Supreme Court justices, including John Marshall, Louis Brandeis, and Earl Warren had no prior experience as judges. They were political and intellectual leaders. Marshall was John Adams's secretary of state. Brandeis was a prominent Boston lawyer and policy advocate. Warren was governor of California.

In general, presidents endeavor to appoint judges who possess legal experience and good character and whose partisan and ideological views are similar to their own. During the presidencies of Richard Nixon, Ronald Reagan, George H. W. Bush, and George W. Bush, most federal judicial appointees were conservative Republicans. Bill Clinton's and Barack Obama's appointees, in contrast tended to be liberal Democrats. George W. Bush made a strong effort to appoint Hispanics. Bill Clinton and Barack Obama also strove to appoint women and African Americans to the federal courts. (See Figure 9.7 for more information on diversity of court appointees.)

The Constitution requires the Senate to "advise and consent" to federal judicial nominations, thus imposing an important check on the president's influence over the judiciary. Before the president formally nominates a candidate for a federal district judgeship, senators from the nominee's state must indicate that they support her. This practice is called **senatorial courtesy**. If

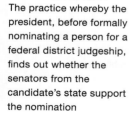

senatorial courtesy

The practice whereby the president, before formally nominating a person for a federal district judgeship, finds out whether the senators from the candidate's state support the nomination

4   The view that the Court "surrendered" to pressure from the elective branches is disputed. For an alternative view, see David R. Mayhew, "Supermajority Rule in the Senate," *PS: Political Science and Politics* 36 (2003): 31–36.

5   Supreme Court justice Thurgood Marshall was the chief counsel for the NAACP and argued *Brown v. Board of Education* before the Court. Felix Frankfurter was a prominent law professor at Harvard University and adviser to Franklin Delano Roosevelt. Hugo Black was an important U.S. Senator.

one or both senators from a prospective nominee's home state belong to the president's political party, the nomination will almost invariably receive their blessing. Because the president's party in the Senate will rarely support a nominee opposed by a home-state senator from their ranks, these senators hold virtual veto power over appointments to the federal bench in their own states. Senators often see this power to grant their support as a way to reward important allies and contributors in their states. If the state has no senator from the president's party, the governor or members of the state's House delegation may make suggestions. Senatorial courtesy is less consequential for appellate court appointments and plays no role in Supreme Court nominations.

Once the president has formally nominated an individual, the appointment must be considered by the Senate Judiciary Committee and confirmed by a majority vote in the full Senate. The politics and rules of the Senate determine the fate of a president's judicial nominees and influence the types of people the president selects for judicial positions. As with any legislation, approval of a nomination must come from the relevant committee, be brought to the Senate floor, and receive a majority of votes. There is always the risk of a filibuster, and cloture of debate requires an affirmative vote of three-fifths of the senators. (See Chapter 6 for discussion of these procedures.) The composition of the Senate Judiciary Committee as well as the Senate as a whole, then, is critical in determining whether a particular nominee will succeed. Moreover, in recent years the most important judicial nominations are given intense scrutiny by the media, thus engaging the broader public in the process.

Before the 1950s, the Senate Judiciary Committee rarely questioned nominees on their judicial views, focusing instead on qualifications. This changed in 1954, however, when President Eisenhower nominated John Marshall Harlan II to succeed Robert Jackson on the Supreme Court. The Senate did not act on his nomination, and Eisenhower had to nominate him a second time. The chairman of the Senate Judiciary Committee, a southerner, and several other southern Democratic senators delayed any hearings, fearing that Harlan would support school integration and further strengthen the Court's efforts to desegregate the South. When the committee finally did hold hearings, the senators grilled Harlan about his views on *Plessy v. Ferguson* and other judicial opinions. All Supreme Court nominees since Harlan have faced questions about their views by the Judiciary Committee.

Since the mid-1950s, judicial appointments have become increasingly partisan and, ultimately, ideological. Today, the Senate Judiciary Committee subjects nominees for the federal judiciary to lengthy questioning about issues ranging from gun rights to abortion to federal power under the commerce clause. Senators' support or opposition turns on the individual's ideological and judicial views as much as on his or her qualifications.

Trends in Presidential Appointments. Presidents nominate individuals who share their own political philosophy. Reagan and George H. W. Bush, for example, sought appointees who believed in reducing government intervention in the economy and supported the moral positions taken by the Republican Party in recent years, particularly opposition to abortion. However, not all Reagan and Bush appointees fulfilled their sponsors' expectations. David Souter, for example, appointed by President George H. W. Bush, was attacked by conservatives as a turncoat for his decisions on school prayer and abortion rights. Nevertheless, through their appointments, Reagan and George H. W. Bush created a strongly conservative Supreme Court. Hoping to counteract the influence of their appointees, President Clinton endeavored to appoint liberal justices, naming Ruth Bader Ginsburg and Stephen Breyer to the Court.

In 2005, President George W. Bush had an opportunity to put his own stamp on the Supreme Court after Justice Sandra Day O'Connor decided to retire and Chief Justice William Rehnquist died. Bush quickly nominated the federal appeals court judge John Roberts, initially to replace O'Connor and then as chief justice after Rehnquist's death. Roberts, a moderate conservative, was confirmed with minimal Democratic opposition. Bush's next nominee, though, sparked an intense battle within the president's own party when he named White House counsel Harriet Miers to replace O'Connor. Opposition among Republicans, many of whom felt she lacked judicial qualifications and was insufficiently conservative, was so intense that she ultimately withdrew from consideration. Bush then turned to a more conventional nominee, the federal appeals court judge Samuel Alito, who pleased conservative Republicans. Barack Obama's nominations of Sonia Sotomayor and Elena Kagan to the Court were easily approved, despite Republican criticisms, thanks to a strong Democratic majority in the Senate (Table 9.3). Because Sotomayor and Kagan replaced liberal justices, they did not affect the balance of power on the Court. In 2016, however, the death

Table 9.3

SUPREME COURT JUSTICES, 2016

NAME	YEAR OF BIRTH	PRIOR EXPERIENCE	APPOINTED BY	YEAR OF APPOINTMENT
John G. Roberts, Jr., *chief justice*	1955	Federal judge	G. W. Bush	2005
Anthony M. Kennedy	1936	Federal judge	Reagan	1988
Clarence Thomas	1948	Federal judge	G. H. W. Bush	1991
Ruth Bader Ginsburg	1933	Federal judge	B. Clinton	1993
Stephen G. Breyer	1938	Federal judge	B. Clinton	1994
Samuel A. Alito, Jr.	1950	Federal judge	G. W. Bush	2006
Sonia Sotomayor	1954	Federal judge	Obama	2009
Elena Kagan	1960	Solicitor general	Obama	2010
(vacant seat)*				

*As of November 2016

of conservative justice Antonin Scalia gave President Obama an opportunity to replace Scalia with a more liberal jurist, and Obama nominated U.S. Appeals Court Judge Merrick Garland. The Senate's Republican leadership, however, refused to take action on the Garland nomination, hoping that the 2016 presidential election would bring a Republican president and a chance to replace Scalia with another Republican conservative. This strategy seemed to pay off when Donald Trump was elected and prepared to nominate a conservative jurist. With only eight justices for most of 2016, several important Supreme Court cases ended in 4–4 ties. A tie lets stand the lower court decision. These struggles over judicial appointments reflect the growing intensity of partisanship today. They also indicate how much importance competing forces attach to Supreme Court appointments.

The increasing role of partisanship or ideology in the nomination process creates a potential danger for the court system. After all, courts derive considerable authority from their position of political independence, as nonpartisan arbiters in our society. The politics of appointments, which increasingly focuses on ideology, risks tainting judges and the judicial process as little more than extensions of the political views of those who nominate them. Fortunately, the individuals appointed to the federal judiciary tend to have a strong independent sense of themselves and their mission. Throughout the history of the federal courts we find instances of judges who have frustrated the presidents who appointed them.

HOW COURTS WORK AS POLITICAL INSTITUTIONS

Judges are central players in important political institutions, and this role makes them politicians. To understand what animates judicial behavior, we need to consider the role of the courts in the political system more generally. In doing so, we emphasize the courts' role as dispute resolvers, coordinators, and interpreters of rules.

Dispute Resolution

Much productive activity occurs in a modern society because its members need not devote substantial resources to protecting themselves and their property or monitoring compliance with agreements. For any potential violation of person or property or defection from an agreement, all parties know that an aggrieved party may take an alleged violator to court. The court, in turn, is a venue in which the facts of a case are established, punishment is meted out to violators, and compensation is awarded to victims. An employee, for example, may sue his employer for allegedly violating the terms of a privately negotiated employment contract. Or a consumer may sue a producer for violating the terms of a product warranty. The court, then, is an institution that engages in fact finding, judgment, and dispute resolution. In criminal cases, the "aggrieved party" is not only the victim of the crime but also the entire society whose laws have been violated.

Coordination

Dispute resolution occurs after the fact—that is, after a dispute has occurred. We may also think of courts and judges as before-the-fact coordination mechanisms inasmuch as the anticipation of legal consequences allows private parties to form rational expectations and thereby coordinate their actions in advance of possible disputes. A prospective embezzler, estimating the odds of getting caught, prosecuted, and punished, may think twice about cheating her partner. Conversely, the legal system can work as an incentive: two acquaintances, for example, may confidently consider going into business together, knowing that the sword of justice hangs over their collaboration.

In this sense, the court system is just as important for what it does indirectly as for its direct effects. The system of courts and law coordinates private behavior by providing incentives and disincentives for specific actions, some of which avoid using the courts altogether. Many cases, for example, are settled out of court, before a judge or court has any role to play. Indeed, the very prospect of litigation discourages disputes and violations of the law, and thus the need for dispute resolution. To the extent that these indirect factors work, there are fewer disputes to resolve (and thus less after-the-fact dispute resolution for courts and judges to engage in) and less frequent violations of law (and thus fewer after-the-fact criminal proceedings).

Rule Interpretation

Dispute resolution and coordination affect private behavior and ordinary citizens' daily lives tremendously. In making these decisions, however, judges are not entirely free agents. In matching the facts of a specific case to judicial principles and statutory guidelines, judges must engage in interpretive activity: they must determine what particular statutes or judicial principles mean, establish which ones fit the facts of a given case, and then ascertain the case's disposition. Does the statute of 1927 regulating the electronic transmission of radio waves apply to television, cellular phones, ship-to-shore radios, fax machines, and e-mail? Does the 1937 law governing the transportation of dangerous substances apply to nuclear fuels, infected animals, and artificially created biological hazards? Often the enacting legislative body has not been clear about the scope of legislation it passed.

Interpreting the rules is probably the most important activity in which higher courts engage. This is because the court system is hierarchical in that higher courts' judgments constrain the discretion of judges in lower courts. If the Supreme Court rules that the 1937 law on transporting dangerous substances covers nuclear fuels, then lower courts must render subsequent judgments in a manner consistent with this ruling.

As the following section explains, courts and judges engage not only in statutory interpretation but in constitutional interpretation as well. In determining, for example, whether the act of Congress regulating the transportation of dangerous substances from one state to another is constitutional, Supreme Court justices might invoke the commerce clause of the Constitution (allowing the federal government to regulate interstate commerce) to justify the act's constitutionality. In contrast, a Court majority might also rule that a shipment of spent fuel rods from a nuclear reactor in Kansas City to a nuclear-waste facility outside St. Louis is not covered by this clause because the shipment occurred within the boundaries of a single state and thus did not constitute interstate commerce.

In short, judges and justices continually elaborate, embellish, and even rewrite the rules by which private and public life are organized. However, judicial interpretation of statutes is subject to review. Statutory interpretation, even if conducted by the nation's highest court, is exposed to legislative review. If Congress disagrees with a specific statutory interpretation, it may amend the legislation to overcome the Court's objection. In 2005, for example, in *United States v. Booker,* the Supreme Court struck down the mandatory sentencing rules enacted in 1984.[6] The rules severely limited judicial discretion in sentencing and had long been resented by the bench. The Court found that mandatory minimum sentences violated the Sixth Amendment, because the latter required that only evidence provided at trial, together with the defendant's previous criminal record, could be used in determining a sentence. In response, members of Congress vowed to reinstate the guidelines through new legislation. Since the *Booker* decision, mandatory sentencing guidelines, at both state and federal levels, remain in flux. However, the thrust of *Booker* remains largely in effect, rendering legislatively constructed guidelines essentially advisory (not mandatory). Of course, if the Court makes a constitutional ruling, Congress cannot abrogate that ruling through new legislation. Congress would need to commence the constitutional amendment process to overturn an interpretation with which it disagrees.

THE POWER OF JUDICIAL REVIEW

The phrase **judicial review** refers to the power of the judiciary to examine and, if necessary, invalidate actions by the legislative and executive branches. The phrase sometimes also describes the scrutiny that appellate courts give to the actions of trial courts, but strictly speaking, that is an improper usage.

The development of judicial review, which is not expressed explicitly in the Constitution, is one of the most powerful expressions of the independent judiciary. In countries without an independent judiciary and without judicial review, the parliament or the executive is the ultimate authority. In English law, for example, the Parliament is sovereign. Judicial review exists only in scrutinizing administration of the laws. An individual cannot challenge an act of Parliament and ask that the courts void that law as a violation of the constitution. But in the U.S. system of government, judicial review is an essential means by which the judiciary checks the legislature and the executive.

 judicial review

The power of the courts to determine whether the actions of the president, the Congress, and the state legislatures are or are not consistent with the Constitution. The Supreme Court asserted the power to review federal statutes in *Marbury v. Madison* (1803)

6   *United States v. Booker,* 543 U.S. 220 (2005).

Judicial Review of Acts of Congress

Because the Constitution does not give the Supreme Court the power of judicial review of congressional enactments, the Court's exercise of it may be considered a usurpation. Among the proposals debated at the Constitutional Convention was one to create a council composed of the president and the judiciary that would share veto power over legislation. Another proposal was to route all legislation through both the Court and the president; overruling a veto by either one would have required a two-thirds vote of the House and the Senate. Those and other proposals were rejected, and no further effort was made to give the Supreme Court review power over the other branches. This does not prove that the framers opposed judicial review, but it does indicate that "if they intended to provide for it in the Constitution, they did so in a most obscure fashion."[7]

Disputes over the framers' intentions were settled in 1803 in *Marbury v. Madison*.[8] In that case, William Marbury sued Secretary of State James Madison for Madison's failure to complete Marbury's appointment to a lower judgeship, which had been initiated by the outgoing administration of President John Adams. Apart from the details of the case, Chief Justice John Marshall used the case to declare a portion of a law unconstitutional. In effect, he stated that although the substance of Marbury's request was not unreasonable, the Court's jurisdiction in the matter was based on a section of the Judiciary Act of 1789, which the Court declared unconstitutional.

Although Congress and the president have often been at odds with the Court, its legal power to review acts of Congress has not been seriously questioned since 1803. One reason is that judicial power has come to be accepted as natural, if not intended. Another reason is that during the early years of the Republic, the Supreme Court used its power sparingly, striking down only two pieces of legislation during the first 75 years of its history. One of these decisions was the 1857 *Dred Scott* ruling, which invalidated the Missouri Compromise and helped precipitate the Civil War. In *Dred Scott v. Sandford*, Chief Justice Roger Taney wrote in the majority opinion that the fact that a slave, Dred Scott, had been transported to a free state (Illinois) and a free territory (Wisconsin) before returning to the slave state of Missouri did not alter the fact that he was property.[9] This ruling had the effect of invalidating a portion of the Missouri Compromise, thus permitting slavery in all the country's territories. More recently, with the power of judicial review accepted, the Court has been more willing to use it. Between 1985 and 2014, the Supreme Court struck down 58 acts of Congress in whole or in part[10] (Figure 9.3).

---

7 C. Herman Pritchett, *The American Constitution* (New York: McGraw-Hill, 1959), p. 138.

8 *Marbury v. Madison*, 1 Cranch 137 (1803).

9 *Dred Scott v. Sandford*, 60 U.S. 393 (1857).

10 For an analysis of the Court's use of judicial review to nullify acts of Congress, see Ryan Emenaker, "Constitutional Interpretation and Congressional Overrides: Changing Trends in Court—Congress Relations," *Journal of Legal Metrics* 2 (2014): 197—223.

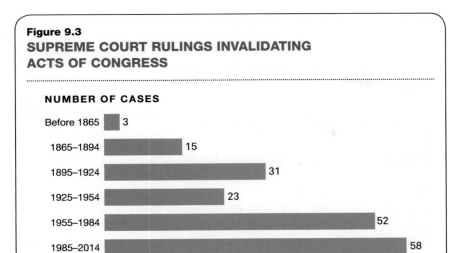

Figure 9.3

SUPREME COURT RULINGS INVALIDATING ACTS OF CONGRESS

NUMBER OF CASES

Before 1865	3
1865–1894	15
1895–1924	31
1925–1954	23
1955–1984	52
1985–2014	58

SOURCE: U.S. Government Printing Office, www.congress.gov/constitution-annotated (accessed 8/17/16).

Judicial Review of State Actions

The power of the Supreme Court to review state legislation or other state action and to determine its constitutionality is neither granted by the Constitution nor inherent in the federal system. But the logic of the **supremacy clause** of Article VI—which declares the Constitution and laws made under its authority to be the supreme law of the land—is very strong. Furthermore, the Judiciary Act of 1789 conferred on the Court the power to reverse state constitutions and laws whenever they are clearly in conflict with the U.S. Constitution, federal laws, or treaties.[11] This power gives the Supreme Court jurisdiction over all of the millions of cases handled by American courts each year.

The history of civil rights protections abounds with examples of state laws that were overturned because the statutes violated the Fourteenth Amendment's guarantees of due process and equal protection. For example, in the 1954 case of *Brown v. Board of Education*, the Court overturned statutes in Kansas, South Carolina, Virginia, and Delaware that either required or permitted segregated public schools, on the basis that such statutes denied black schoolchildren equal protection of the law.[12] In 1967 in *Loving v. Virginia*, the Court invalidated a Virginia statute prohibiting interracial marriages.[13] In 2015 in *Obergefell v. Hodges*, the Court held that "the Fourteenth Amendment

 supremacy clause

A clause of Article VI of the Constitution that states that all laws passed by the national government and all treaties are the supreme laws of the land and superior to all laws adopted by any state or any subdivision

---

11 This review power was affirmed by the Supreme Court in *Martin v. Hunter's Lessee*, 14 U.S. 304 (1816).

12 *Brown v. Board of Education*, 347 U.S. 483 (1954).

13 *Loving v. Virginia*, 388 U.S. 1 (1967).

requires a state to license a marriage between two people of the same sex and to recognize a marriage between two people of the same sex when their marriage was lawfully licensed and performed out-of-state," thus invalidating a Michigan law prohibiting same-sex unions.[14] State statutes in other areas are equally subject to challenge. Thus the Court has overturned state laws that conflict with federal law: in 2012 in *Arizona et al. v. United States,* for instance, the Court struck down parts of an Arizona law regulating immigration on the grounds that it was preempted by federal law.[15]

Judicial Review of Federal Agency Actions

Although Congress makes the law, it can hardly administer the thousands of programs it has enacted and must delegate power to the president and to a huge bureaucracy to achieve its purposes. For example, if Congress wishes to improve air quality, it cannot possibly anticipate all the circumstances that may arise with respect to its general goal. Inevitably Congress must delegate to the executive substantial discretionary power to determine the best ways to achieve improved air quality in the face of changing circumstances. Thus, over time, almost any congressional program will result in thousands and thousands of pages of administrative regulations developed by executive agencies.

The issue of delegation of power has led to a number of court decisions over the past two centuries, generally involving the question of the scope of the delegation. Courts have also been called on to decide whether the rules and regulations adopted by federal agencies are consistent with Congress's express or implied intent.

As presidential power expanded during the New Deal era, one measure of increased congressional subordination to the executive was the enactment of laws that contained few if any principles limiting executive discretion. Congress enacted legislation, often at the president's behest, that gave the executive virtually unfettered authority to address a particular concern. For example, the Emergency Price Control Act of 1942 authorized the executive to set "fair and equitable" prices without indicating what those terms might mean. Although the Court initially challenged such delegations of power to the president during the New Deal, a confrontation with President Franklin Delano Roosevelt caused the Court to retreat from its position. Perhaps as a result, no congressional delegation of power to the president has been struck down as impermissibly broad since then. In the last two decades in particular, the Supreme Court has found that as long as federal agencies developed rules and regulations "based upon a permissible construction" or "reasonable interpretation" of Congress's statute, the judiciary would accept the views of the executive branch. Generally the courts defer to administrative agencies as long as those agencies have undertaken a formal rule-making process and have carried out the conditions prescribed by

---

14 *Obergefell v. Hodges* 576 U.S. ___ (2015). Quotation from SCOTUSblog, "Obergefell v. Hodges," www.scotusblog.com/case-files/cases/obergefell-v-hodge (accessed 9/16/2015).

15 *Arizona et al. v. United States,* 567 U.S. ___ (2012).

statutes governing agency rule making. These statutes include the 1946 Administrative Procedure Act, which requires agencies to notify parties affected by proposed rules and to allow them time to comment before the rules go into effect.

Judicial Review and Presidential Power

The federal courts may also review the actions of the president. As we saw in Chapter 7, presidents have increasingly made use of unilateral executive powers rather than relying on congressional legislation to achieve their objectives. Often, presidential orders and actions have been challenged in the federal courts by members of Congress and by individuals and groups opposing the president's policies. In recent years, the federal bench has generally upheld assertions of presidential power in such realms as foreign policy, war and emergency powers, legislative power, and administrative authority. Indeed, the federal judiciary has sometimes rationalized extraordinary presidential claims made for temporary purposes—that is, the Court has converted them into permanent instruments of presidential government. Consider Richard Nixon's sweeping claims of executive privilege. In *United States v. Nixon*, although the Court rejected the president's refusal to turn over tape recordings to congressional investigators, for the first time the justices recognized the validity of the principle of executive privilege and discussed situations in which such claims might be appropriate.[16] This judicial recognition of executive privilege encouraged presidents Bill Clinton and George W. Bush to base broad claims on that principle during their administrations.[17] Executive privilege has even been invoked to protect the deliberations of the vice president from congressional scrutiny. This pattern of judicial deference to presidential authority was also manifest in the Supreme Court's decisions regarding President Bush's war on terrorism. Perhaps the most important of these cases was *Hamdi v. Rumsfeld*.[18] In 2004, the Court ruled that alleged terrorist and U.S. citizen Yaser Esam Hamdi was entitled to a lawyer and "a fair opportunity to rebut the government's factual assertions." However, the Court affirmed that the president possessed the authority to declare a U.S. citizen an enemy combatant and order that such an individual be held in federal detention. Several justices intimated that once designated an enemy combatant, a U.S. citizen might be tried before a military tribunal, with the normal presumption of innocence suspended. In 2006, in *Hamdan v. Rumsfeld*, the Court ruled that the military commissions established to try enemy combatants and other detainees violated both the Uniform Code of Military Justice and the Geneva Conventions.[19] Thus the Supreme Court did assert that presidential

---

16 *United States v. Nixon*, 418 U.S. 683 (1974).

17 On Clinton, see Jonathan Turley, "Paradise Lost: The Clinton Administration and the Erosion of Executive Privilege," *Maryland Law Review* 60 (2001): 295. On Bush, see Jeffrey P. Carlin, "*Walker v. Cheney*: Politics, Posturing, and Executive Privilege," *Southern California Law Review* 76 (November 2002): 235.

18 *Hamdi v. Rumsfeld*, 542 U.S. 507 (2004).

19 *Hamdan v. Rumsfeld*, 548 U.S. 557 (2006).

actions were subject to judicial scrutiny and placed some constraints on the president's power. But at the same time, it affirmed the president's unilateral power to declare individuals, including U.S. citizens, "enemy combatants" whom federal authorities could detain under adverse legal circumstances.

In June 2016 the Supreme Court sustained an appeals court decision blocking President Obama's ambitious program to prevent millions of undocumented immigrants from being deported. At issue was whether President Obama had abused his office in formulating immigration policy by using an executive order instead of the legislative and administrative processes. The eight-member Court (in the wake of the death of Justice Antonin Scalia) split 4–4, thereby letting stand the lower-court decision.[20] The Court thus thwarted an attempt to create new policy through executive action alone.

Judicial Review and Lawmaking

Much of the courts' work involves applying statutes to particular cases. Over the centuries, however, judges have developed a body of rules and principles of interpretation that are not grounded in specific statutes. This body of judge-made law is called common law.

The appellate courts are in another realm. Their rulings can be considered laws, but governing only the behavior of the judiciary. They influence citizens' conduct only because, in the words of Justice Oliver Wendell Holmes, Jr. (who served on the Supreme Court from 1902 to 1932), lawyers make "prophecies of what the courts will do in fact."[21]

The written opinion of an appellate court is about halfway between common law and statutory law. It is judge made and draws heavily on the precedents of previous cases. In that it tries to articulate the rule of law controlling the case in question and future cases like it, it is like a statute. But a statute addresses the future conduct of citizens, whereas a written opinion mainly addresses the willingness or ability of future courts to take cases and render favorable opinions.

An example may clarify the distinction. In *Gideon v. Wainwright*, the Supreme Court ordered a new trial for Clarence Earl Gideon, an indigent defendant, because he had been denied the right to legal counsel. This ruling said to all trial judges and prosecutors that henceforth they would be wasting their time if they cut corners in the trials of indigent defendants.[22] The Court was thereby predicting what it would and would not do in future cases of this sort. It also invited thousands of prisoners to appeal their convictions.

Many areas of civil law have been constructed in the same way—by judicial messages to other judges, some of which are codified eventually in legislative enactments. It has become "the law," for example, that employers are liable

---

20 *United States v. Texas*, No. 15-674.

21 Oliver Wendell Holmes, Jr., "The Path of the Law," *Harvard Law Review* 10 (1897): 457.

22 *Gideon v. Wainwright*, 372 U.S. 335 (1963).

for injuries in the workplace without regard to negligence. But the law in this instance is simply a series of messages to lawyers that they should advise their corporate clients not to appeal injury decisions.

In the realm of criminal law, almost all the dramatic changes in the treatment of criminals and persons accused of crimes have been made by the appellate courts, especially the Supreme Court. Indeed, the Supreme Court ignited a veritable revolution in the criminal process with three cases over less than five years. The first, *Gideon v. Wainwright*, in 1963, was just discussed. The second, *Escobedo v. Illinois*, in 1964, gave suspects the right to remain silent and the right to have counsel present during questioning.[23] But the decision left confusion that allowed lower courts to make differing decisions. In the third case, *Miranda v. Arizona*, in 1966, the Court cleared up the confusion by setting forth what is known as the Miranda rule: arrested people have the right to remain silent, the right to be informed that anything they say can be held against them, and the right to counsel before and during police interrogation.[24]

One of the most significant changes wrought by the Supreme Court was the revolution in legislative representation unleashed by the 1962 landmark case of *Baker v. Carr*.[25] Here, the Court held that it could no longer avoid reviewing complaints about the apportionment of seats in state legislatures. Following that decision, the federal courts went on to force reapportionment of all state, county, and local legislatures nationwide.

As these cases illustrate, the appellate courts are intimately involved in creating and interpreting laws. Many experts on court history and constitutional law criticize the federal appellate courts for being too willing to introduce radical change. Often these experts are troubled by the courts' willingness (especially the Supreme Court) to jump into such cases prematurely—before the constitutional issues have been fully clarified by decisions of district and appeals courts in many related cases in various parts of the country.[26] But from the perspective of the appellate judiciary, and especially the Supreme Court, the situation is one of choosing between the lesser of two evils: they must take the cases as they come and then weigh the risks of opening new options against the risks of embracing the status quo.

THE SUPREME COURT IN ACTION

The Supreme Court sits at the pinnacle of the U.S. judiciary. It is the only court mentioned in the Constitution, and it is one of the most distinctive political bodies created by the U.S. system. The Court is often the focal point for

---

23 *Escobedo v. Illinois,* 378 U.S. 478 (1964).

24 *Miranda v. Arizona,* 384 U.S. 436 (1966).

25 *Baker v. Carr,* 369 U.S. 186 (1962).

26 See Philip B. Kurland, *Politics, the Constitution, and the Warren Court* (Chicago: University of Chicago Press, 1970).

understanding the judiciary because of its special constitutional status and because it embodies the many principles of the American court system—its independence, its durability, the collective nature of court decision making, and the delicate balance that judges strike between historical precedent and new interpretation. The Court plays a vital role in government as it is part of the structure of checks and balances that prevents the legislative and executive branches from abusing their power. The Court also operates as an institution unto itself, with its own internal rules for decision making. In this way, it has its own version of the policy principle discussed in Chapter 1.

How Cases Reach the Supreme Court

Given the millions of disputes that arise every year, the Supreme Court's job would be impossible if it were not able to control the flow of cases and its own caseload. The Court has original jurisdiction in a limited variety of cases defined by the Constitution, including (1) cases between the United States and one of the states, (2) cases between two or more states, (3) cases involving foreign ambassadors or other ministers, and (4) cases brought by one state against citizens of another state or against a foreign country. The most important of these are disputes between states over land, water, or old debts. Generally the Court deals with these cases by appointing a "special master," usually a retired judge, to hear the case and present a report. The Court then allows the disputing states to present arguments for or against the master's opinion.[27]

Rules of Access. Over the years, the federal courts have developed rules governing which cases within their jurisdiction they will and will not hear. Thus the Court is an institution very much in control of its own agenda, which, according to the institution principle, gives it considerable independence to follow its members' preferences.[28] To have access to the courts, cases must meet certain criteria that are initially applied by the trial court but may be reconsidered by appellate courts. These rules of access fall into three major categories: case or controversy, standing, and mootness.

Both Article III of the Constitution and past Supreme Court decisions define judicial power as extending only to "cases and controversies." That is, a case before a court must involve an actual controversy, not a hypothetical one, with two truly adversarial parties (These criteria are called **ripeness**). The courts have interpreted this language to mean they do not have the power to render advisory opinions to legislatures or agencies about the constitutionality of proposed laws or regulations. Furthermore, even after a law is enacted,

ripeness

A criterion used by courts to avoid hearing cases that depend on hypothetical future events

---

27 Walter F. Murphy, "The Supreme Court of the United States," in *Encyclopedia of the American Judicial System: Studies of the Principal Institutions and Processes of Law*, Robert J. Janosik, ed. (New York: Scribner, 1987).

28 The appellate jurisdiction of the courts is determined by Congress. Currently, this jurisdiction is quite expansive, but Congress may restrict this at any time.

the courts generally refuse to consider its constitutionality until it is actually applied.

Those seeking to bring a case must also have **standing**—they must show a substantial stake in the case's outcome. The traditional requirement for standing has been that one must show injury to oneself; the injury can be personal, economic, or even aesthetic, for example. For a group or class of people to have standing (as in **class-action suits**), each member must show specific injury. This means that a general interest in the environment, for instance, does not provide a group with a sufficient basis for standing.

The third criterion in determining whether the Supreme Court will hear a case is **mootness**. In theory, this requirement disqualifies cases that are brought too late—after the relevant facts have changed or the problem has been resolved by other means. Mootness, however, is subject to the discretion of the courts, which have begun to relax the rules pertaining to this criterion, particularly in cases in which a situation that has been resolved is likely to recur. In the abortion case of *Roe v. Wade*, for example, the Court rejected the lower court's argument that because the pregnancy had already come to term, the case was moot. The Court agreed to hear the case because no pregnancy was likely to outlast the lengthy appeals process.

Putting aside the formal criteria, the Supreme Court is most likely to accept cases that involve conflicting decisions by federal circuit courts, cases that present important questions of civil rights or civil liberties, and cases in which the federal government is the appellant.[29] Ultimately, however, the question of which cases are accepted can come down to the justices' preferences and priorities. If several justices believe that the Court should intervene in a particular area of policy or politics, they are likely to look for a case or cases that will be vehicles for judicial intervention. For several decades, for example, the Court was not interested in considering challenges to affirmative action or other programs designed to provide particular benefits to minorities. Eventually, however, several of the more conservative justices have sought to push back the limits of affirmative action and racial preference and have therefore accepted cases that allow them to do so. In 1995, the Court's decisions in three cases placed new restrictions on federal affirmative action programs, school desegregation efforts, and attempts to increase minority representation in Congress through the creation of "minority districts" (see Chapter 11).[30]

Most cases reach the Supreme Court through a **writ of *certiorari***, a formal request to have the Court review a lower-court decision (Figure 9.4). *Certiorari* is an order to a lower court to deliver the records of a particular case to be reviewed for legal errors. The term is sometimes shortened to *cert*, and cases deemed to merit *certiorari* are referred to as *certworthy*. An individual who loses in

standing

The right of an individual or an organization to initiate a court case

class-action suit

A procedural device that permits a large number of people with common interests to join together under a representative party to bring or defend a lawsuit

mootness

A criterion used by courts to avoid hearing cases that no longer require resolution

writ of *certiorari*

A formal request by an appellant to have the Supreme Court review a decision of a lower court; *certiorari* is from a Latin word meaning "to make more certain"

29 Gregory A. Caldeira and John R. Wright, "Organized Interests and Agenda Setting in the U.S. Supreme Court," *American Political Science Review* 82, no. 4 (December 1988): 1109–27.

30 *Adarand Constructors v. Pena*, 115 U.S. 200 (1995); *Missouri v. Jenkins*, 515 U.S. 70 (1995); *Miller v. Johnson*, 515 U.S. 900 (1995).

Figure 9.4
REACHING THE SUPREME COURT THROUGH *CERTIORARI*

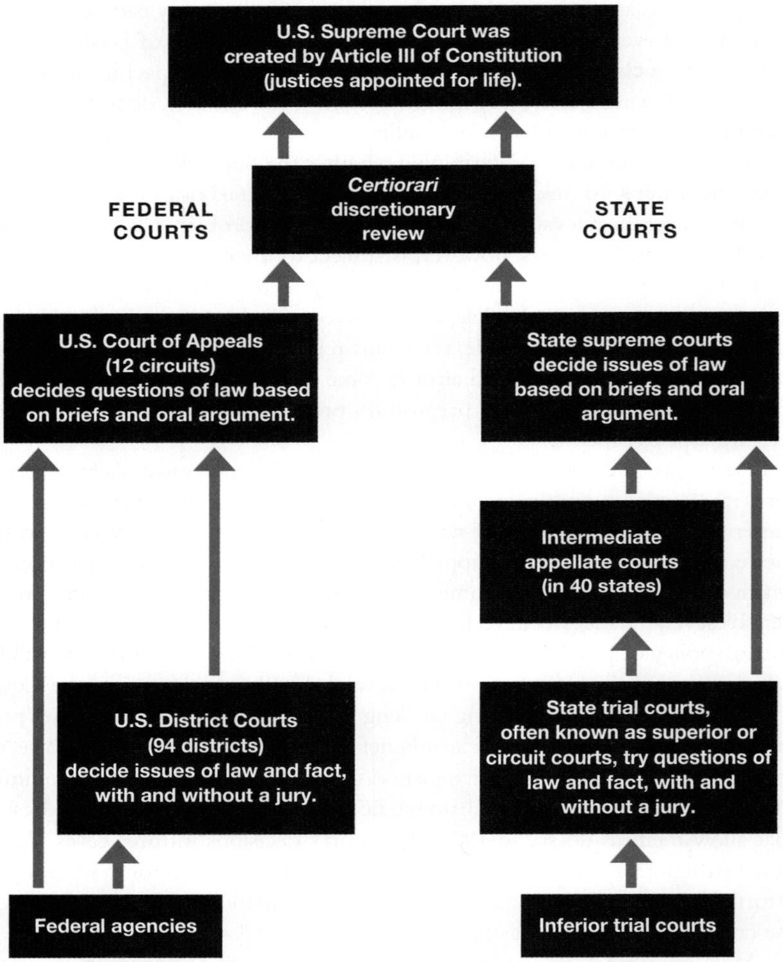

```
                    ┌─────────────────────────────┐
                    │   U.S. Supreme Court was     │
                    │ created by Article III of    │
                    │      Constitution            │
                    │ (justices appointed for life)│
                    └─────────────────────────────┘
                         ▲               ▲
                    ┌─────────────────────────────┐
   FEDERAL          │      *Certiorari*            │      STATE
   COURTS           │   discretionary review       │      COURTS
                    └─────────────────────────────┘
                         ▲               ▲
┌──────────────────────────┐      ┌──────────────────────────┐
│   U.S. Court of Appeals  │      │   State supreme courts   │
│      (12 circuits)       │      │   decide issues of law   │
│ decides questions of law │      │   based on briefs and    │
│ based on briefs and oral │      │      oral argument.      │
│       argument.          │      └──────────────────────────┘
└──────────────────────────┘                ▲
         ▲              ▲           ┌──────────────────────────┐
         │              │           │      Intermediate        │
         │              │           │   appellate courts       │
         │              │           │     (in 40 states)       │
         │              │           └──────────────────────────┘
         │              │                     ▲
         │     ┌──────────────────────┐  ┌──────────────────────────┐
         │     │  U.S. District Courts│  │    State trial courts,   │
         │     │    (94 districts)    │  │ often known as superior or│
         │     │ decide issues of law │  │ circuit courts, try       │
         │     │ and fact, with and   │  │ questions of law and fact,│
         │     │   without a jury.    │  │ with and without a jury.  │
         │     └──────────────────────┘  └──────────────────────────┘
         │              ▲                          ▲
    ┌──────────────────────┐            ┌──────────────────────┐
    │   Federal agencies   │            │  Inferior trial courts│
    └──────────────────────┘            └──────────────────────┘
```

a lower federal court or a state court and wants the Supreme Court to review the decision has 90 days to file a petition for a writ of *certiorari* with the clerk of the Supreme Court. There are two types of petitions: paid petitions and petitions *in forma pauperis* ("in the form of a pauper"). The former requires payment of filing fees, submission of a certain number of copies, and compliance with numerous other rules. For *in forma pauperis* petitions, usually filed by prison inmates, the Court waives the fees and most other requirements.

Since 1972, most of the justices have participated in a "*certiorari* pool" in which their law clerks evaluate the petitions. Each petition is reviewed by one clerk, who writes a memo summarizing the facts and issues and making a recommendation for all the justices participating in the pool. Clerks for the other justices add their comments. After the justices have reviewed the memos, any one of them may place any case on the discuss list, which is circulated by the chief justice. If a case is not placed on the list, it is automatically denied *certiorari*. Cases placed on the list are considered and voted on during the justices' closed-door conference. For *certiorari* to be granted, four justices must be convinced that the case satisfies Rule 10 of the Rules of the U.S. Supreme Court: that *certiorari* is not a matter of right but is to be granted only when there are special and compelling reasons. These include conflicting decisions by two or more circuit courts or by two or more state courts of last resort, conflicts between circuit courts and state courts of last resort, decisions by circuit courts on matters of federal law that the Supreme Court should settle, and a circuit court decision on an important question that conflicts with a Supreme Court decision. The Court usually takes action only when there are conflicts among the lower courts about what the law should be, when an important legal question raised in the lower courts has not been definitively answered, or when a lower court deviates from the principles and precedents established by the high court. The support of four justices is needed for *certiorari*, and few cases satisfy this requirement. In recent sessions, although thousands of petitions have been filed (Figure 9.5), the Court has granted *certiorari* to fewer than 90 petitioners each year—about 1 percent of those seeking a Supreme Court review.

A handful of cases reach the Supreme Court through avenues other than *certiorari*. One is the writ of certification, which can be used when a Court of Appeals asks the Supreme Court for instructions on a point of law that has never been decided. Another avenue is the writ of appeal, which serves to appeal the decision of a three-judge district court.

Controlling the Flow of Cases

In addition to the judges, two other actors are key in shaping the flow of cases through the federal courts: the solicitor general and the federal law clerks.

The Solicitor General. If any person has greater influence than individual justices over the work of the Supreme Court, it is the solicitor general of the United States. This person is third in status in the Justice Department (below the attorney general and the deputy attorney general) but is the top government lawyer in virtually all cases before the appellate courts in which the government is a party. Although others can regulate the flow of cases, the solicitor general has the greatest control, with no review of his or her actions by any higher authority in the executive branch. More than half the Supreme Court's total workload consists of cases under the charge of the solicitor general.

The solicitor general exercises especially strong influence by screening cases involving the federal government long before they approach the Supreme Court; indeed, the justices rely on the solicitor general to do so. Typically, more requests for appeals are rejected than are accepted by the solicitor general. Agency heads

Figure 9.5

CASES FILED IN THE U.S. SUPREME COURT

SOURCES: Years 1938–69: successive volumes of U.S. Bureau of the Census, *Statistical Abstract of the United States* (Washington, DC: Government Printing Office); 1970–79: Office of the Clerk of the Supreme Court; 1980–2010: U.S. Census Bureau, www.census.gov/prod/2011pubs/12statab/law.pdf (accessed 6/11/13); 2010–15: Supreme Court of the United States, Cases on Docket, www.uscourts.gov/statistics-reports/caseload-statistics-data-tables (accessed 7/11/16).

may lobby the president or otherwise try to circumvent the solicitor general, and a few of the independent agencies have a statutory right to make direct appeals, but without the solicitor general's support these are seldom reviewed by the Court.

By writing an ***amicus curiae*** ("friend of the court") brief, the solicitor general can enter a case even when the federal government is not a direct litigant. A friend of the court is not a direct party to a case but has a vital interest in its outcome. Thus when the government has such an interest, the solicitor general can file as *amicus curiae*, or the Court can invite such a brief because it wants an opinion in writing. Other interested parties may file briefs as well.

In addition to influencing the flow of cases, the solicitor general can shape the arguments used before the Court by the way in which he or she characterizes the issues. This individual is the person appearing most frequently before the Court and, theoretically, the most disinterested. The solicitor general's credibility

amicus curiae

"Friend of the court," an individual or group that is not party to a lawsuit but has an interest in influencing the outcome

is not hurt when several times each year he or she withdraws a case with the admission that the government has made an error.[31]

Law Clerks. Every federal judge employs law clerks to research legal issues and assist in preparing opinions. Each justice is assigned four clerks, almost always honors graduates of the nation's most prestigious law schools. A clerkship with a Supreme Court justice generally indicates that the fortunate individual is likely to reach the very top of the legal profession. One of the clerks' most important roles is screening the thousands of petitions for writs of *certiorari* that come before the Court.[32] Some justices likely rely heavily on their clerks for advice in writing opinions and deciding whether an individual case ought to be heard. It is often rumored that certain opinions were actually written by a clerk rather than a justice.[33] Indeed, at the end of long judicial careers, justices such as William O. Douglas and Thurgood Marshall had become so infirm that they had to rely on the judgments of their law clerks.

The Supreme Court's Procedures

The Preparation. The Court's decision to accept a case is the beginning of a lengthy and complex process (Figure 9.6). First, attorneys on both sides must prepare **briefs**—written documents explaining why the Court should rule in favor of their client. The document filed by the individual bringing the case, called the petitioner's brief, summarizes the facts of the case and presents the legal basis on which the Court is being asked to overturn the lower court's decision. The document filed by the side that prevailed in the lower court, called the respondent's brief, explains why the Court should affirm the lower court's verdict. The petitioners then file a brief answering and attempting to refute the points made in the respondent's brief. This document is called the petitioner's reply brief. Briefs contain many references to precedents showing that other courts have frequently ruled in the same way that the Supreme Court is being asked to rule.

As the attorneys prepare their briefs, they often ask sympathetic interest groups for help by means of *amicus curiae* briefs. In a case involving separation of church and state, for example, liberal groups such as the ACLU and People

 brief

A written document in which an attorney explains—using case precedents—why the Court should rule in favor of his or her client

---

31 On the strategic and informational role played by the solicitor general, see Kevin McGuire, "Explaining Executive Success in the U.S. Supreme Court," *Political Research Quarterly* 51 (1998): 505–26. Also see Michael Bailey, Brian Kamoie, and Forrest Maltzman, "Signals from the Tenth Justice: The Political Role of the Solicitor General in Supreme Court Decision Making," *American Journal of Political Science* 49 (2005): 72–85.

32 H. W. Perry, Jr., *Deciding to Decide: Agenda Setting in the United States Supreme Court* (Cambridge: Harvard University Press, 1991).

33 Edward Lazarus, *Closed Chambers: The First Eyewitness Account of the Struggles inside the Supreme Court* (New York: Times Books, 1998).

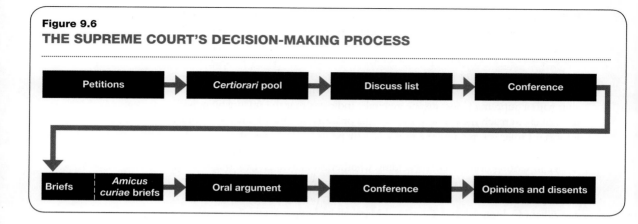

Figure 9.6

THE SUPREME COURT'S DECISION-MAKING PROCESS

Petitions → *Certiorari* pool → Discuss list → Conference

Briefs | *Amicus curiae* briefs → Oral argument → Conference → Opinions and dissents

for the American Way are likely to be asked to file *amicus* briefs in support of strict separation, whereas conservative religious groups—the Family Research Council or Focus on the Family, for example—are likely to file *amicus* briefs advocating increased public support for religious ideas. Often dozens of briefs are filed on each side of a major case.

oral argument

The stage in Supreme Court proceedings in which attorneys for both sides appear before the Court to present their positions and answer questions posed by the justices

Oral Argument. During the next stage, **oral argument**, attorneys for both sides present their positions before the Court and answer the justices' questions. Each attorney has only a half hour to present his case, including interruptions for questions. Oral argument can be very important to the outcome, for it allows justices to better understand the heart of a case and raise questions that the opposing sides' briefs do not address. Sometimes justices go beyond the strictly legal issues and ask opposing counsel to discuss the case's implications for the Court and the nation at large.[34] In oral arguments on the constitutionality of the Defense of Marriage Act in 2013, for example, Justice Kennedy frequently questioned whether the definition of marriage resided with the states rather than with the federal government.

The Conference. After oral argument, the Court discusses the case in its Wednesday or Friday conference. The chief justice presides and speaks first; the others follow in order of seniority. No outsiders are permitted to attend. The justices reach a decision on the basis of a majority vote. As the case is discussed, justices may try to influence one another's opinions. At times, this may result in compromise decisions.

opinion

The written explanation of the Supreme Court's decision in a particular case

Opinion Writing. After a decision has been reached, one of the members of the majority is assigned to write the **opinion**. This assignment is made by the

34 On the consequences of oral argument for decision making, see Timothy R. Johnson, Paul J. Wahlbeck, and James F. Spriggs II, "The Influence of Oral Arguments on the U.S. Supreme Court," *American Political Science Review* 100, no. 1 (February 2006): 99–113.

chief justice or by the most senior justice in the majority if the chief justice is on the losing side. The assignment of the opinion can make a significant difference to the interpretation of a decision, as its wording and emphasis can have important implications for future litigation. Thus in assigning an opinion, the justices must consider the impression the case will make on lawyers and the public, as well as the probability that one justice's opinion will be more widely accepted than another's.[35]

This tactical consideration occurred dramatically in 1944, when Chief Justice Harlan Fiske Stone chose Justice Felix Frankfurter to write the opinion in the "white primary" case *Smith v. Allwright*, which overturned the southern practice of prohibiting black participation in primaries. The day after Stone made the assignment, Justice Robert Jackson wrote a letter to Stone arguing that Frankfurter, a foreign-born Jew from New England, would not win over the South with his opinion, regardless of his brilliance. Stone accepted the advice and substituted Justice Stanley F. Reed, an American-born Protestant from Kentucky and a southern Democrat in good standing.[36]

Once the majority opinion is drafted, it is circulated to the other justices. Some members of the majority may agree with both the outcome and the rationale but wish to highlight a particular point and so draft a concurring opinion, called a regular **concurrence**. Alternatively, one or more justices may agree with the majority but disagree with the rationale. Those justices may draft a special concurrence, explaining their disagreements with the majority. The pattern of opinions that emerge on a case ultimately depends on bargaining among the justices, as suggested by the collective action principle.

Dissent. Justices who disagree with the majority decision may publicize the character of their disagreement in the form of a **dissenting opinion**, which is generally assigned by the senior justice among the dissenters. Dissents can signal to defeated political forces that some members of the Court support their position. Ironically, the most dependable way an individual justice can exercise a direct influence on the Court is to write a dissent. Because there is no need to please a majority, dissenting opinions can be more eloquent and less guarded than majority opinions. The current Supreme Court often produces 5–4 decisions, with dissenters writing long and detailed opinions that, they hope, will convince a swing justice to join their side on the next round of cases addressing a similar topic. Thus, for example, Justice David Souter wrote a 34-page dissent in a 2002 case upholding the use of government-funded school vouchers to pay for parochial school tuition. Souter called the decision "a dramatic departure from basic Establishment Clause principle" and went on to say that he hoped it would be reconsidered by a future court.[37]

 concurrence

An opinion agreeing with the decision of the majority in a Supreme Court case but not with the rationale provided in the majority opinion

dissenting opinion

A decision written by a justice who voted with the minority opinion in a particular case in which the justice fully explains the reasoning behind his or her opinion

---

35 For this and other strategic aspects of the Court's process, see Forrest Maltzman, James F. Spriggs II, and Paul J. Wahlbeck, *Crafting Law on the Supreme Court: The Collegial Game* (New York: Cambridge University Press, 2001).

36 *Smith v. Allwright*, 321 U.S. 649 (1944).

37 Warren Richey, "Dissenting Opinions as a Window on Future Rulings," *Christian Science Monitor*, July 1, 2002, p. 1.

Dissent plays a special role in the work and impact of the Court because it amounts to an appeal to lawyers nationwide to keep bringing cases of the sort at issue. Therefore, an effective dissent influences the flow of cases through the Court as well as the arguments that lawyers will make in later cases.

These rules of collective decision making shape how the Supreme Court addresses cases. But they are just the structure within which judges operate. The rules indicate that judicial authority is restrained and cautious, incremental and rational. But ultimately the rules reveal little about how judges will deal with the great political and social questions of the day. How the courts ultimately decide matters of law depends on the views of those in the judiciary and the nature of the problems they address and on the relationship of the courts to the other branches of government.

JUDICIAL DECISION MAKING

The judiciary is conservative in its procedures, but its effect on society can be radical. That effect depends on numerous factors, two of which stand out above the rest. The first is the individual members of the Supreme Court, their attitudes and goals, and their relationships with one another. The second is the other branches of government, particularly Congress.

The Supreme Court Justices

The Supreme Court explains its decisions in terms of law and precedent. But ultimately the Court itself decides what laws mean and what importance precedents will have. Throughout its history, the Court has shaped and reshaped the law. If any individual judges in the country influence the federal judiciary, the Supreme Court justices are the ones who do.

From the 1950s to the 1980s, the Court was active in such areas as civil rights, civil liberties, abortion, voting rights, and police procedures. It was more responsible than any other governmental institution for breaking down America's system of racial segregation. It virtually prohibited states from interfering with a woman's right to seek an abortion, sharply curtailed state restrictions on voting rights, and placed restrictions on the behavior of local police and prosecutors in criminal cases. But since the early 1980s, resignations, deaths, and new appointments have brought many shifts in the mix of ideologies represented on the Court. In a series of decisions between 1989 and 2001, conservative justices appointed by Ronald Reagan and George H. W. Bush were able to swing the Court to a more conservative position on civil rights, affirmative action, abortion rights, property rights, criminal procedure, voting rights, desegregation, and the power of the national government.

The importance of ideology was very clear during the Court's 2000–01 term. In key decisions, the most conservative justices—Scalia, Thomas, and

Rehnquist, usually joined by Kennedy—generally voted as a bloc.[38] Indeed, Scalia and Thomas voted together in 99 percent of all cases. At the same time, the most liberal justices—Breyer, Ginsburg, Souter, and Stevens—also generally formed a voting bloc.[39] Justice O'Connor, a moderate conservative, was often the swing vote.[40] This ideological division led to a number of important 5–4 decisions. In the case *Bush v. Gore*, which concerned the recounting of ballots in Florida in the 2000 presidential election, O'Connor joined with the conservative bloc to give Bush a 5–4 victory. Indeed, more than 33 percent of all cases heard by the Court in its 2000–01 term were decided by a 5–4 vote. In the Court's 2012–13 term, 7 of the 14 most important cases were decided by a 5–4 margin.

However, precisely because the Court was so evenly split during this period, the conservative bloc did not always prevail. In the 2003 case of *Missouri v. Seibert*, for example, Kennedy joined a 5–4 majority to strengthen Miranda rights.[41] On abortion, women's rights, and affirmative action, Justice O'Connor often joined the liberal bloc. With the departure of O'Connor and her replacement by Alito in 2006, many anticipated a series of new 5–4 decisions favoring the conservatives under new chief justice John Roberts.[42] In 2007, for example, the Court upheld the Partial Birth Abortion Ban Act—a law favored by conservatives—by a 5–4 majority. O'Connor's departure shifted the center of the Court (the pivotal part in formulating opinions) to Justice Kennedy, whose jurisprudence does not significantly differ from O'Connor's. Thus the Court's conservative drift since then has been slight and certainly not as dramatic as the replacement of O'Connor with Alito might have suggested to the untutored eye.[43]

We should note that the liberal-conservative bloc structure on the Court is not always predictive, even in important cases. In *National Federation of Independent Business v. Sebelius*, the 2012 case on the constitutionality of Obama's health care law, it was Chief Justice Roberts, a firm member of the conservative bloc, who joined the four liberals to uphold the law.[44] Roberts again sided with the four liberals on the Court in 2015 to uphold the constitutionality of Obamacare. Writing for the Court majority

---

38 Linda Greenhouse, "In Year of Florida Vote, Supreme Court Also Did Much Other Work," *New York Times*, July 2, 2001, p. A12.

39 Charles Lane, "Laying Down the Law," *Washington Post*, July 1, 2001, p. A6.

40 For an insightful discussion about identifying the swing justice on the Court, see Andrew D. Martin, Kevin M. Quinn, and Lee Epstein, "The Median Justice on the U.S. Supreme Court," *North Carolina Law Review* 83 (2005): 1275–322.

41 *Missouri v. Seibert*, 542 U.S. 600 (2004).

42 Adam Liptak, "Entrances and Exits: The New 5-to-4 Supreme Court," *New York Times*, April 22, 2007.

43 For a development of this argument, see David W. Rohde and Kenneth A. Shepsle, "Advising and Consenting in the 60-Vote Senate: Strategic Appointments to the Supreme Court," *Journal of Politics* 69, no. 3 (August 2007): 664–77.

44 Adam Liptak, "Supreme Court Upholds Health Care Law, 5–4 in Victory for Obama," *New York Times*, June 28, 2012, www.nytimes.com/2012/06/29/us/supreme-court-lets-health-law-largely-stand.html?pagewanted=all&_ro (accessed 7/15/13).

in *King v. Burwell*, Roberts supported a lower-court opinions that millions of Americans were entitled to public subsidies that keep insurance affordable whether the subsidies were established by individual states or the federal government.[45]

Finally, the Court's policy influence comes not from the "horse race" vote results often trumpeted by the media but from the written opinions providing the constitutional or statutory rationale for policy in the future. These opinions establish the guidelines that govern how federal courts must decide similar cases in the future.

Activism and Restraint. One element of judicial philosophy is the issue of activism versus restraint. Over the years, some justices have believed that courts should interpret the Constitution according to the framers' stated intentions and defer to the views of Congress when interpreting federal statutes. Justice Felix Frankfurter, for example, advocated judicial deference to legislative bodies and avoidance of the "political thicket" that arises when deciding questions that are essentially political rather than legal. Advocates of **judicial restraint** are sometimes called strict constructionists because they look strictly to the words of the Constitution in interpreting its meaning.

The alternative to restraint is **judicial activism**, which involves going beyond the words of the Constitution or a statute to consider the broader societal implications of its decisions. Activist judges sometimes strike out in new directions, promulgating new interpretations or inventing new legal and constitutional concepts when they deem them socially desirable. For example, Justice Harry Blackmun's opinion in *Roe v. Wade* was based on a constitutional right to privacy that is not found in the words of the Constitution but was, rather, based on the Court's prior decision in *Griswold v. Connecticut*. Blackmun and the other members of the majority in *Roe* argued that other constitutional provisions imply the right to privacy. In this instance of judicial activism, the Court knew the result it wanted to achieve and was not afraid to make the law conform to the desired outcome.

It is sometimes difficult to discern a difference between restraint and different flavors of activism. The Court's conservative bloc sometimes does try to rein in the more expansive posture of previous activist majorities. In other cases, however, it seeks to move "boldly" and "actively" in areas previously regarded as settled. In *Citizens United* in 2010, for example, the Court held that corporations and unions could not be restricted from financial participation in elections.[46] It did not reverse previous prohibitions on corporate donations directly to candidates, but it did allow independent expenditures—for example, advertising during a campaign—so long as they were not coordinated with any individual campaign. This seems to fit uncomfortably with a philosophy of restraint.

Political Ideology. The second component of judicial philosophy is political ideology. The liberal or conservative attitudes of justices play an important

judicial restraint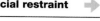

The judicial philosophy whose adherents refuse to go beyond the text of the Constitution in interpreting its meaning

judicial activism

The judicial philosophy that posits that the Court should see beyond the text of the Constitution or a statute to consider broader societal implications for its decisions

---

45 *King v. Burwell*, 576 U.S. ___ (2015).

46 *Citizens United v. Federal Election Commission*, 558 U.S. 310 (2010).

role in their decisions.[47] The philosophy of activism versus restraint is sometimes a smoke screen for political ideology. In the past, liberal judges have been activists, willing to use the law to achieve social and political change, whereas conservatives have been associated with judicial restraint. It is interesting, however, that in recent years some conservative justices have become activists in seeking to undo part of the work of liberal jurists over the past three decades. The Rehnquist Court, dominated by conservatives, was among the most activist Supreme Courts in American history, striking out in new directions in areas such as federalism and election law.

Our discussion of congressional politics in Chapter 6 described legislators as policy oriented. In conceiving of judges as legislators in robes, we are effectively claiming that judges, like other politicians, have policy preferences that they seek to implement. The Analyzing the Evidence unit in this chapter looks at ideology in the Court.

Other Institutions of Government

Congress. At both the national and the state level in the United States, courts and judges are players in the policy game because of the separation of powers. Thus, essentially, the legislative branch formulates policy (defined constitutionally and institutionally by a legislative process), the executive branch implements policy (according to well-defined administrative procedures and subject to initial approval by the president or legislative override of his veto), and the courts, when asked, rule on the faithfulness of the legislated and executed policy, either to the substance of the statute or to the Constitution itself. The courts may strike down an administrative action either because it exceeds the authority granted in the relevant statute (statutory rationale) or because the statute itself exceeds the authority granted the legislature or executive by the Constitution (constitutional rationale).

If the Court declares the administrative agent's act as outside the permissible bounds, the majority opinion can declare whatever policy it wishes. If the legislature is unhappy with this judicial action, it may either recraft the legislation (if the rationale for striking it down was statutory)[48] or initiate a constitutional amendment that would enable the stricken policy to pass constitutional muster (if the rationale for originally striking it down was constitutional).

In reaching their decisions, Supreme Court justices must anticipate Congress's response. As a result, judges do not always vote according to their true preferences because doing so may provoke Congress to enact legislation that moves the policy further from what the judges prefer. By voting for a lesser

---

47 C. Herman Pritchett, *The Roosevelt Court: A Study in Judicial Politics and Values* (New York: Macmillan, 1948); Jeffrey A. Segal and Harold J. Spaeth, *The Supreme Court and the Attitudinal Model* (New York: Cambridge University Press, 1993); Segal and Spaeth, *The Supreme Court and Attitudinal Model Revisited* (New York: Cambridge University Press, 2002).

48 William N. Eskridge, Jr., "Overriding Supreme Court Statutory Interpretation Decisions," *Yale Law Journal* 101 (1991): 331–55.

Ideological Voting on the Supreme Court

Contributed by
Andrew D. Martin
University of Michigan
Kevin M. Quinn
UC Berkeley School of Law

Do the political preferences of Supreme Court justices influence their behavior? The starting point for the analysis of the behavior of Supreme Court justices is to look at their votes.[1] For non-unanimous cases, we can compute agreement scores—the fraction of cases in which a pair of justices vote the same way. We display these agreement scores for the Court's 2014–15 term in the first figure below. If you examine this figure, you will see that two groups of justices emerge. Within each group, the justices agree with one another a lot; almost 90 percent of the time for justices on the left, and between 60 and 70 percent of the time for justices on the right. Voting is more structured than we would expect by chance.

One way to represent that structure is by arranging the justices on a line as in the diagram below to the right.[2] Justices who agree a lot should be close to one another; justices who disagree a lot should be far apart.

Does the fact that there are patterns of agreement mean that the justices are deciding based on political ideology? Not necessarily. These patterns are consistent with ideological decision making, but other things might explain the patterns as well. However, when we read the cases and see who wins or loses, there is a great deal of support for the idea that political ideology influences how justices vote.[3]

Agreement Scores for the 2014–15 Term

	Sotomayor	Ginsburg	Kagan	Breyer	Kennedy	Roberts	Scalia	Alito	Thomas
Sotomayor	1	.85	.85	.89	.72	.49	.31	.36	.13
Ginsburg	.85	1	.9	.89	.62	.49	.31	.31	.23
Kagan	.85	.9	1	.89	.72	.44	.41	.31	.23
Breyer	.89	.89	.89	1	.66	.55	.37	.39	.16
Kennedy	.72	.62	.72	.66	1	.46	.49	.49	.36
Roberts	.49	.49	.44	.55	.46	1	.72	.67	.44
Scalia	.31	.31	.41	.37	.49	.72	1	.64	.62
Alito	.36	.31	.31	.39	.49	.67	.64	1	.67
Thomas	.13	.23	.23	.16	.36	.44	.62	.67	1

- ● < 0.35
- ● 0.35–0.44
- ● 0.45–0.54
- ● 0.55–0.64
- ● 0.65–0.74
- ● 0.75–0.99

POSITION

▶ Sotomayor
▶ Ginsburg
▶ Kagan
▶ Breyer

▶ Kennedy

▶ Roberts

▶ Scalia
▶ Alito

▶ Thomas

The figure to the left contains the agreement scores for the 2014–15 term of the U.S. Supreme Court for all non-unanimous cases. These scores are the proportion of cases when each justice agreed with every other justice. Two justices that always disagreed with each other would get a zero; two justices who always agreed would get a one. Red indicates low agreement scores; green indicates high agreement scores. The policy dimension to the right of the figure is one that best represents the patterns in the agreement scores.

0 = Justices always disagreed
1 = Justices always agreed

This type of analysis can be done for any court, but it becomes more difficult if we are interested in comparing justices across time instead of during just one term. What if we are interested in whether the Supreme Court is becoming more ideologically polarized over time? Or whether individual justices have become more liberal or conservative? Martin-Quinn scores based on a statistical model of voting on the Court help solve this problem.[4]

A number of interesting patterns emerge. Consider the case of Justice Harry Blackmun, who often claimed, "I haven't changed; it's the Court that changed under me."[5] The figure below shows that Justice Blackmun's position did in fact change ideologically over the course of his career. This evidence is consistent with some clear changes in Justice Blackmun's behavior, especially in the area of the death penalty.

We can also look at patterns in the positions of chief justices. While the chief's vote counts just the same as the other justices, he or she plays an important role in organizing the court. Justice Rehnquist was the most conservative justice on the Court when he arrived in 1971, but as the figure below shows, after he was elevated in 1986 he too drifted more toward the middle. This is what we would expect to see of a justice who was working strategically to build coalitions, as any good chief would.

Ideological Trajectories of Selected Justices

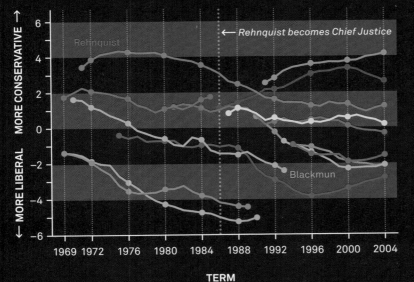

JUSTICES

- Blackmun
- Brennan
- Breyer
- Burger
- Ginsburg
- Kennedy
- Marshall
- O'Connor
- Rehnquist
- Scalia
- Souter
- Stevens
- Thomas

This figure shows the Martin-Quinn score for selected justices serving in the Burger (1969–86) and Rehnquist Courts (1986–2004). Each line represents the trajectory of each justice on the ideological dimension.

1   C. Herman Pritchett, *The Roosevelt Court: A Study in Judicial Politics and Values, 1937–1947* (New York: Macmillan, 1948).
2   Glendon A. Schubert, *The Judicial Mind: The Attitudes and Ideologies of Supreme Court Justices, 1946–1963* (Evanston, IL: Northwestern University Press, 1965).
3   Jeffry A. Segal and Harold J. Spaeth, *The Supreme Court and the Attitudinal Model* (New York: Cambridge University Press, 1993).
4   Andrew D. Martin and Kevin M. Quinn, "Dynamic Ideal Point Estimation via Markov Chain Monte Carlo for the U.S. Supreme Court, 1953–1999," *Political Analysis* 10, no. 2, (2002): 134–53, http://mqscores.wustl.edu (accessed 10/18/11).
5   Linda Greenhouse, *Becoming Justice Blackmun* (New York: Times Books, 2005).

preference, the justices can get something they prefer to the status quo without provoking congressional action to overturn their decision. In short, the interactions between the Court and Congress are part of a complex strategic game.[49]

The President. The president's most direct influence on the Court is the power to nominate justices. Presidents typically nominate those who seem close to their policy preferences and close enough to the preferences of a majority of senators, who must confirm the nomination. In addition to ideological congruence, a president attempts to affect the composition of the district and appellate courts in other respects. As displayed in Figure 9.7, the last six presidents have appointed a number of judges from underrepresented groups.

The president must also confront Congress in shaping the judiciary. By using the filibuster (see Chapter 6), both parties have blocked judicial nominees: when George W. Bush was president, the Democrats repeatedly blocked nominees, and the Republicans did so when Obama was president. Acrimony over judicial nominees has prompted both parties to threaten changing Senate rules to allow their preferred nominees through. In 2013, Senate Democrats carried through with the threat, eliminating the filibuster for most presidential nominees (although filibusters are still allowed for Supreme Court nominees). Of course, opponents of a nomination may block it in other ways. The judiciary committee may refuse to consider the nominee, as in the case of Judge Merrick Garland, President Obama's Supreme Court nominee in 2016.

The Implementation of Supreme Court Decisions

The president and the rest of the executive branch, along with Congress, the states, the lower courts, and a variety of private organizations and individuals, play key roles in the implementation of Supreme Court decisions. Once the high court has made a decision, numerous other government agencies must put it into effect. The lower courts must apply the principles asserted by the Court to new cases. The executive branch must enforce the Court's decision. State legislators and governors must implement the decision in their own jurisdictions. And often individuals and organizations must take action in the courts and in the political arena to demand that the Supreme Court's verdicts be fully implemented. At each of these stages, opposition by relevant actors may delay full national implementation of a decision, sometimes for years.

For example, if lower-court judges strongly disagree with a Supreme Court decision, they may use a variety of tactics to avoid fully implementing it. They may, for example, avoid applying the case by disposing of similar cases on

---

49 A full strategic analysis of the maneuvering among legislative, executive, and judicial branches in the separation-of-powers arrangement choreographed by the U.S. Constitution may be found in William N. Eskridge, Jr., and John A. Ferejohn, "The Article I, Section 7, Game," *Georgetown Law Review* 80 (1992): 523–65. The entire issue of this journal is devoted to the theme of strategic behavior in American institutional politics.

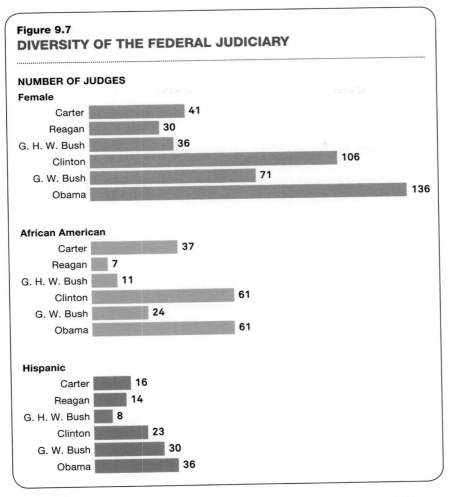

Figure 9.7

DIVERSITY OF THE FEDERAL JUDICIARY

NUMBER OF JUDGES

Female

Carter	41
Reagan	30
G. H. W. Bush	36
Clinton	106
G. W. Bush	71
Obama	136

African American

Carter	37
Reagan	7
G. H. W. Bush	11
Clinton	61
G. W. Bush	24
Obama	61

Hispanic

President	Number
Carter	16
Reagan	14
G. H. W. Bush	8
Clinton	23
G. W. Bush	30
Obama	36

NOTE: Carter appointed 261 federal judges; Reagan appointed 364; G. H. W. Bush appointed 188; Clinton appointed 372; G. W. Bush appointed 321; and Obama appointed 324 (as of March 2016).
SOURCE: The Federal Judicial Center, History of the Federal Judiciary, www.fjc.gov/history/home.nsf/page/judges_diversity.html (accessed 8/17/16).

technical or procedural grounds. Similarly, they may apply the case as narrowly as possible or declare that some portion of the Court's opinion was merely "dicta"—useful as guidance but not binding.

Most Supreme Court decisions must be implemented by federal, state, and local agencies. If these agencies are unsympathetic to a decision, they may obstruct, delay, or even refuse to accept it. In the nineteenth century, President Andrew Jackson famously refused to obey a Supreme Court decision, declaring, "John Marshall has made his decision. Now let him enforce it." In 2015 Kim Davis, clerk of Rowan County, Kentucky, refused to issue marriage licenses to gay and lesbian couples, despite the recent court ruling requiring her to do so in

Obergefell v. Hodges (see the Policy Principle section on p. 369). She spent five days in jail for contempt of court before being released in exchange for agreeing to allow her office to issue licenses (though refusing to issue them herself). Although few officials or agencies have been so defiant, many have quietly ignored or sought to circumvent the Court. For example, many local school boards have searched for years for ways to circumvent the Court's rulings prohibiting religious observance in public schools.

Strategic Behavior in the Supreme Court

In describing the role and effect of the Supreme Court, we have occasionally referred to the strategic opportunities the Court provides. We can divide this strategic behavior into three stages. Stage 1 begins with a period of "normal" politics—in (local or national) legislatures, (local or national) executive and regulatory agencies, political processes like elections, and everyday life involving interactions among public and private entities (citizens, corporations, nonprofits, voluntary associations, governments). Conflict arises, and interested parties must decide what to do: live with the results, pursue normal political channels using legislatures and agencies to resolve the conflict, or move the conflict into the courts. Stage 2 involves a court's response, with judges both reacting to demands from the outside and fashioning their own behavioral strategies within the legal process. Stage 3 involves what happens once a court renders a decision and how the actors in stages 1 and 2 anticipate the decision and adjust their behavior to its expectations. Although our discussion could be developed for all courts, we will primarily address the Supreme Court and its internal strategic environment at stage 2, when it both reacts to developments that preceded its involvement in a conflict (stage 1) and anticipates what will happen if it responds in a particular manner (stage 3).

Stage 1. Assume that a conflict has arisen and appeals have been made through normal channels. Administrative and regulatory agencies, for example, often have well-defined procedures for appealing a ruling within the agency, with the opportunity of a subsequent appeal to a court always being available. Dissatisfied with the outcome, one of the parties moves the dispute to the courts, and at some point in the process the option of appeal to the Supreme Court is available. The aggrieved party has a decision to make. It is a calculated, strategic decision in two respects.

First, an appeal will consume resources that might otherwise serve different purposes. A prospective appellant must weigh an appeal against this "opportunity cost." The Sierra Club, for example, might use resources to appeal a lower-court decision on environmental protection to the Supreme Court or, alternatively, devote some of the same resources to lobbying Congress on other issues.

Second, all options are uncertain propositions whose resolution stretches out over time. Regarding uncertainty, a prospective appellant must recognize that the probability of successfully getting to the Court is slim, and even if it obtains *certiorari*, it may not win on the merits of its case. Regarding the time

Changing Judicial Direction: Gay Marriage

In 1970, Richard Baker and James McConnell applied for a marriage license in Hennepin County, Minnesota. The county clerk, Gerald Nelson, refused to give them a license because they were both men. The couple sued Nelson, claiming that the Minnesota statute barring them from receiving a marriage license was unconstitutional. They appealed the case all the way to the Minnesota Supreme Court, which held in *Baker v. Nelson* (1971) that "The institution of marriage as a union of man and woman, uniquely involving the procreation and rearing of children within a family, is as old as the book of Genesis." In 1972, the U.S. Supreme Court issued a brief affirmation of the Minnesota ruling.

Gay rights advocates celebrate the Court's 2015 decision.

In the years and decades following this setback, the gay rights movement proceeded down other litigation avenues, bringing a series of lawsuits aimed at changing policies that discriminated against gay men and lesbians. Their collective effort to use the institution of the courts to change policy gradually saw results. A quarter of a century after *Baker v. Nelson,* the U.S. Supreme Court struck down a provision of Colorado state law that denied gay and lesbian residents a variety of privileges that the law labeled "special rights." Justice Anthony Kennedy, writing in the 6–3 majority in *Romer v. Evans* (1996) reversing this view, states "We find nothing special in the protections [being withheld]. These protections . . . constitute ordinary civil life in a free society."

The *Romer* opinion, written in the same year Congress passed the Defense of Marriage Act (DOMA) limiting marriage to one man and one woman, shows how the Court can turn away from both its own precedents and congressional policy to actively chart a new direction. As the policy principle suggests, collective action directed toward the courts, combined with new political preferences in the courts, generated a change in policy.

Justice Kennedy went on to author opinions on decriminalizing sodomy in *Lawrence v. Texas* (2003), declaring DOMA unconstitutional in *United States v. Windsor* (2013), and eventually establishing a right for gays to marry across the United States in *Obergefell v. Hodges* (2015). Though by the time of *Obergefell* many states had already legalized gay marriage, the Court was consistently on the front edge of the debate in one of its most consistent shows of judicial activism in recent times. Kennedy's *Obergefell* opinion was aimed at history, not merely at setting a legal precedent. It showed clearly his intention to shape a policy and enshrine a right, rather than argue over semantics or precedent.

Though public opinion on same-sex marriage has been changing rapidly in its favor, the *Obergefell* decision did not silence dissent. In August 2015, post-*Obergefell*, another county clerk (this time in Kentucky) refused to issue a marriage license to a gay couple. Yet, rather than affirming her action, as had happened in Minnesota four decades earlier, a court held her in contempt and jailed her.

dimension, even if the appellant wins, the process may take years, making the delayed victory bittersweet. Ultimately these strategic calculations revolve around what an appellant can expect in pursuing an appeal—that is, what might happen in stages 2 and 3.[50]

Stage 2. Thousands of cases are appealed to the Supreme Court. The nine justices (or, more accurately, their clerks) must sort through these petitions and, according to the **rule of four**, build their docket each session. The Court, in short, has the power to create its own agenda.

In building their docket for the current session, how do justices think about the available options? They support some cases out of a strong belief that an area is ripe for constitutional clarification. They support others out of an interest in the development of legal principles in a particular area—criminal rights, privacy, First Amendment, abortion, affirmative action, federal-state relations, and so on—or in the belief that contradictory decisions in lower courts need to be sorted out. The justices may oppose certain appeals because they believe a particular case will not provide a sufficiently clear-cut basis for clarifying a legal issue. That is, even though a case might attract a justice's interest on substantive grounds or might be perceived by a justice as containing procedural errors that could lead to a reversal, she might not support *certiorari* because of a strategic calculation that it is not a particularly good vehicle or that a better vehicle might come up through the appeals process in a subsequent session.[51]

Once a case is included on the docket and oral arguments have been delivered by the litigants' attorneys and *amicus curiae* briefs filed by other interested parties, the case becomes the subject of two decisions.[52] The first takes place after the justices discuss it in one of their regularly scheduled conferences during the Court's term. When discussion has concluded and all attempts at persuasion have ended, there is a vote on the merits—a vote in favor of the appeal or against it. In principle, this vote affects only the parties to the case, either affirming or reversing the lower-court decision.

The second decision has a wider bearing. Having decided one way or the other, the justices must determine whether there is agreement on the reasons for their decision. This is a highly strategic decision because the Court's impact over and above its effect on the contesting parties depends on the reasons it gives for

rule of four

The rule that *certiorari* will be granted only if four justices vote in favor of the petition

---

50 There are subtleties to the strategies of appellants. They may seek an appeal to the Supreme Court, for example, as a bluff to induce the winner in the lower court to accommodate in advance some of their preferences—in effect, to settle out of court. Why might the lower-court winners be induced to accommodate the losers? There are at least two reasons: first, to avoid the exorbitant costs of fighting an appeal to the Supreme Court and, second, to avoid the prospect that their victory in the lower court may be reversed.

51 An excellent discussion of this facet of Supreme Court decision making is found in Perry, *Deciding to Decide*.

52 On the strategic decisions of *amicus* groups, see Thomas Hansford, "Information Provision, Organizational Constraints, and the Decision to Submit an *Amicus Brief* in a U.S. Supreme Court Case," *Political Research Quarterly* 57 (2004): 219–30.

the decision at hand. A Court majority's reasons set legal precedent for similar cases in the future, thus influencing litigation in lower courts. If the majority cannot agree on why they decided as they did, there is no binding effect on other comparable cases. Drafting an opinion that can attract the signatures of at least five justices is therefore of pivotal significance. A justice on the winning side who stakes out an extreme position relative to the others is unlikely to be able to draft such an opinion, so moderate justices usually do the heavy lifting of opinion drafting for especially controversial cases. Of course, in some cases a majority may agree on the merits of a case but not reach consensus on the reasons. In such cases, there will be no majority opinion, though each justice is free to write his or her own opinion (possibly cosigned by others), either supporting or dissenting from the decision on the merits and giving specific reasons. These opinions have no binding effect on future lower-court cases but may still serve a strategic signaling role, conveying to the lower courts and the legal community where a justice stands on the issues involved.[53]

Stage 3. The Supreme Court is the top rung of one branch in a separation-of-powers system. Its decisions are not automatically implemented; it must depend on executive agencies for implementation and on lower courts for enforcement of its dicta. In fact, it ultimately depends on the willingness of others, especially ordinary citizens, to conform to its rulings. In some instances, the Court may worry about resistance. Throughout the 1940s and 1950s, for example, there were concerns that issues relating to integration would meet with popular disapproval and defiance in the South. Indeed, when writing the majority opinion in the 1954 *Brown* decision desegregating public schools, Chief Justice Earl Warren strategically softened some of its language in order to attract the signatures of all nine justices. The 9–0 decision and opinion were a signal to a potentially defiant South that the Court was united and that it would take a very long time (the time needed to replace at least five justices) before there would be any prospect of reversal.

In addition to compliance, enforcement, and resistance, the Court considers the possibility of reversal. On a decision taken by the Court on a statutory issue—for example, whether an existing law covers a particular situation—majorities in both houses of Congress and the president may pass a new statute reversing the Court's interpretation. If, for example, the Court rules that the Radio Act of 1927 does not cover transmissions by cellular phones and Congress and the president think otherwise, then Congress may pass legislation, and the president may sign it into law, amending the Act so that its provisions do govern the regulation of cell phones.[54] Members of the Court may have no particular stake in being reversed—that is, they may not care whether the "political"

---

53 For an insightful discussion of the strategic elements influencing how the senior justice in the winning coalition assigns opinion writing, see David W. Rohde, "Policy Goals, Strategic Choice, and Majority Opinion Assignments in the U.S. Supreme Court," *Midwest Journal of Political Science* 16 (1972): 652–82.

54 On the strategic interaction among the Court, Congress, and the president, see Eskridge and Ferejohn, "The Article I, Section 7, Game."

branches decide, for example, to allow for cell phones to be covered by the Radio Act of 1927. Indeed, they may feel a certain satisfaction that the act, as originally written, had a narrow scope that only subsequent statutory activity could broaden. Then again, in order to have impact on politics generally, the Court would not want their decisions questioned, reversed, or defied routinely.

For decisions taken on constitutional (as opposed to statutory) grounds, no mere revision of existing law is sufficient to reverse the Court; a constitutional amendment is required. President George W. Bush, for example, gave his blessing to efforts to amend the Constitution to reverse the *Roe v. Wade* decision permitting a woman to choose an abortion in the first two trimesters of her pregnancy.

In the long run, the Supreme Court is the final legal authority on whether governmental and interpersonal practices satisfy statutory or constitutional scrutiny. But the justices are not free agents; the other branches of government must be taken into account as justices vote on cases and write legal opinions. Hence strategic calculation can never be far from their thinking.

CONCLUSION: THE EXPANDING POWER OF THE JUDICIARY

Over the past 50 years, the place of the judiciary in American politics and society has changed dramatically. Demand for legal solutions has increased, and the judiciary's reach has expanded. Some now call for reining in the power of the courts and discretion of judges in areas ranging from criminal law and sentencing to property rights to liability and torts. How our society deals with these issues will shape the judiciary's future independence and effectiveness. Even the most conservative justices now seem reluctant to relinquish their newfound power, authority that has become accepted and thus established.

Let us summarize what we have learned so far. Judges enjoy great latitude because they are not subject to electoral pressures. Judges and justices, more than other politicians in America, can pursue their own goals and preferences, their own ideologies (rationality principle). They are, however, constrained by institutional rules governing access to the courts, by other courts, by Congress and the president, by their lack of enforcement powers, and most important, by the past in the form of precedent and common law (institution principle). For much of its history, the federal judiciary acted very cautiously. The Supreme Court rarely challenged Congress or the president. The justices instead tended to legitimate laws passed by Congress and actions of the president. The scope of the Court's decisions was limited only to those individuals who were granted access to the courts.

Three judicial revolutions have expanded the power and reach of the federal judiciary since World War II. The first revolution brought about the liberalization of a wide range of public policies in the United States. As we saw in Chapters 4 and 5, in certain policy areas—such as school desegregation, legislative apportionment, criminal procedure, obscenity, abortion, and voting rights—the Supreme Court was at the forefront of sweeping changes in the role of the U.S. government and, ultimately, the character of American society (policy principle). The Court put many of these issues before the public long before Congress or the president was prepared to act.

At the same time that the courts forged these policy innovations, they were bringing about a second, less visible revolution. During the 1960s and 1970s, the Supreme Court and other federal courts liberalized the concept of standing to permit almost any group seeking to challenge an administrative agency's actions to bring its case before the federal bench. It thus encouraged groups to come to the judiciary to resolve disputes, rather than to Congress or the executive branch. Complementing this, the federal courts also broadened the scope of relief to permit themselves to act on behalf of broad categories of persons in class-action cases, rather than just on behalf of individuals.[55] The possibility of class-action cases facilitated collective action by allowing legal entrepreneurs to organize an entire group of petitioners who would otherwise face potentially insurmountable coordination and free-rider obstacles (collective action principle).

In a third revolution the federal courts began to employ so-called structural remedies, in effect retaining jurisdiction of cases until a court's mandate had been implemented to its satisfaction.[56]

Through these three judicial mechanisms, the federal courts paved the way for an unprecedented expansion of national judicial power. In essence, liberalization of the rules of standing and expansion of the scope of judicial relief drew the federal courts to link with important social interests and classes. The introduction of structural remedies enhanced the courts' ability to serve these constituencies. Thus during the 1960s and 1970s the power of the federal courts expanded through links with constituencies—such as groups advocating civil rights, consumers' rights, gay rights, women's rights, and environmental issues—that staunchly defended the Supreme Court in its battles with Congress, the executive, or other interest groups.

During the 1980s and 1990s, the Reagan and Bush administrations sought to end the relationship between the Court and liberal political forces. Conservative judges appointed by these Republican presidents modified the Court's position in areas such as abortion, affirmative action, and judicial procedure, though not so completely as some conservative writers and politicians had hoped. Within one week in 2003, for example, the Supreme Court affirmed the validity of affirmative action, reaffirmed abortion rights, strengthened gay rights, offered new protection to individuals facing the death penalty, and issued a ruling in favor of a congressional apportionment plan that dispersed minority voters across several districts—a practice that appeared to favor the Democrats.[57] The Court

---

55 See "Developments in the Law—Class Actions," *Harvard Law Review* 89 (1976): 1318.

56 See Donald L. Horowitz, *The Courts and Social Policy* (Washington, DC: Brookings Institution, 1977).

57 David Van Drehle, "Court That Liberals Savage Proves to Be Less of a Target," *Washington Post*, June 29, 2003, p. A18.

had made these decisions based on the justices' interpretations of precedent and law, not simply personal belief.

Despite its increasingly conservative composition, the current Court has not been conservative in another sense. It has not been eager to surrender the expanded powers carved out by earlier Courts, especially in areas that assert the power of the national government over the states. Indeed, the opponents to the U.S. Constitution (the Antifederalists in Chapter 2) feared the assertion of the national interest over the states through the independent judiciary. Over two centuries of U.S. history, the reach and authority of the federal judiciary has expanded greatly, and the judiciary has emerged as a powerful arm of our national politics (history principle). Whatever their policy beliefs or partisan orientations, judges and justices understand the newfound importance of the courts among the three branches of American government and act not just to interpret and apply the law but also to maintain the power of the courts.

For Further Reading

Abraham, Henry J. *The Judicial Process: An Introductory Analysis of the Courts of the United States, England, and France*. 7th ed. New York: Oxford University Press, 1998.

Baum, Lawrence. *The Puzzle of Judicial Behavior*. Ann Arbor: University of Michigan Press, 1997.

Bickel, Alexander M. *The Least Dangerous Branch: The Supreme Court at the Bar of Politics*. Indianapolis, IN: Bobbs-Merrill, 1962.

Epstein, Lee, and Jack Knight. *The Choices Justices Make*. Washington, DC: CQ Press, 1998.

Kahn, Ronald. *The Supreme Court and Constitutional Theory, 1953–1993*. Lawrence: University Press of Kansas, 1994.

Marbury v. Madison, 5 U.S. (1 Cranch) 137, 1803.

O'Brien, David M. *Storm Center: The Supreme Court in American Politics*. 10th ed. New York: Norton, 2014.

Perry, H. W., Jr. *Deciding to Decide: Agenda Setting in the United States Supreme Court*. Cambridge: Harvard University Press, 1991.

Rosenberg, Gerald. *The Hollow Hope: Can Courts Bring About Social Change?* Chicago: University of Chicago Press, 2008.

Segal, Jeffrey A., and Harold J. Spaeth. *The Supreme Court and the Attitudinal Model Revisited*. New York: Cambridge University Press, 2002.

Silverstein, Mark. *Judicious Choices: The New Politics of Supreme Court Confirmations.* New York: Norton, 1994.

Toobin, Jeffrey. *The Nine: Inside the Secret World of the Supreme Court.* New York: Knopf, 2008.

Whittington, Keith. *Political Foundations of Judicial Supremacy: The President, the Supreme Court, and Constitutional Leadership in U.S. History.* Princeton, NJ: Princeton University Press, 2008.

10

PART 1 2 **X** 4

DEMOCRATIC POLITICS

Public Opinion

• What Is Public Opinion?

• Origins and Nature of Opinion

• Public Opinion and Political Knowledge

• Shaping Opinion: Political Leaders, Private Groups, and the Media

• Measuring Public Opinion

• How Does Public Opinion Influence Government Policy?

• Conclusion: Government and the Will of the People

Public support is the coin of the realm in Washington politics. Popular presidents succeed; unpopular presidents struggle. A president who has the backing of a large majority of the public gains leverage in dealing with Congress and the bureaucracy, but a president who lacks public support often meets resistance from members of Congress, even those in his own party. President George W. Bush described a president's popularity as political capital, an asset that must be spent wisely on a few well-chosen issues.[1]

Members of Congress are perhaps even more attuned than the president to the ups and downs of public opinion. Representatives in the U.S. House must run for reelection every two years, a very short election cycle. They cannot afford to make many unpopular decisions lest their constituents punish them in the next election. Members of Congress and party leaders pay close attention to indicators of public sentiment, including polls; visits to their districts or home states; and letters, phone calls, and e-mails from constituents. A saying among members of Congress goes, "It's okay to be on the losing side of a vote, but you don't want to be on the wrong side."

Even the courts are not immune to the influence of public opinion. Courts lack the power to enforce their decisions; they depend on the compliance of those affected and the cooperation of Congress, the president, and political leaders in the states. That cooperation is not always forthcoming. As we saw in Chapter 5, *Brown v. Board of Education*, perhaps the most important court decision of the twentieth century, met with immediate opposition in the southern states, and desegregation occurred slowly. Only after public opinion turned in support of equal rights for all races did Congress and the president act, accelerating the pace of desegregation.[2]

---

1   Chris Suellentrop, "America's New Political Capital," *Slate*, November 30, 2004, www.slate.com/id/2110256 (accessed 3/18/09). Also see Richard Neustadt, *Presidential Power and the Modern Presidents*, 4th ed. (New York: Free Press, 1990), and Brandice Canes-Wrone, *Who Leads Whom? Presidents, Policy, and the Public* (Chicago: University of Chicago Press, 2006).

2   Gerald Rosenberg, *The Hollow Hope* (Chicago: University of Chicago Press, 1991).

Public opinion is also the standard by which we judge democracy. Ideally, representative democracy approximates what the nation as a whole would choose to do were all 320 million Americans to consider a given matter. Congress and the president are supposed to act as the public's agents, enacting laws that a clear majority of the public wants and rejecting laws that fail to achieve widespread support. If the norms of society shift strongly in one direction for a period of time, so too should the laws of the land. The nature and origins of public opinion are central concerns of modern political science precisely because democratic government is supposed to reflect the will of the people.

Public opinion is, ultimately, the rationale behind democratic government. The public provides democratic government the will to act. The rationality principle applied to the public holds that average people have preferences about what government should and shouldn't do. At stake in many government decisions are individuals' interests and values, and people pursue those goals when voting or engaging in other forms of political action. Democratic politics in its various forms aggregates peoples' preferences and beliefs into an expression of what a majority of people want. How individuals' preferences are transformed into electoral decisions and public policies depends on institutions, problems of collective action, and history. These factors will be emphasized in later chapters on elections, interest groups, political parties, and the media. Public opinion operates through these institutions to determine who serves in government, what problems government must address, and the principles and values that shape public policy. This chapter concerns what people want their government to do and how people understand the political choices that they confront.

CORE OF THE ANALYSIS

 Public opinion is the aggregation of individuals' views. It expresses the range of attitudes and beliefs and on which side of any question a majority of people fall.

 There are a wide range of interests at stake in any question that the government must decide as well as differing preferences, beliefs, and opinions about what ought to be done.

 Politicians follow public opinion as part of the representative process. They take signals from polls and other indicators of public sentiment to gauge whether a particular decision might affect their prospects at the next election.

 Politicians, interest groups, the media, and others try to shape public opinion by influencing what issues are debated, what alternatives are offered, and what information is presented.

While individuals pursue their own interests and values when making decisions about politics, they do not necessarily understand fully the choices they face. People look for information—facts, labels, cues—that can help simplify their decision making. This is quite a different notion of the electorate from what is commonly found in civics books, which generally present an idealized citizenry who closely follow important issues; who are well informed about their representatives' decisions; who understand the consequences of actions; and who participate in public debate, elections, and public decision making. Were we all that attentive, we would have little time for our education, our jobs, our families, and other aspects of daily life. In fact, researchers have long found that most Americans are not highly attentive to the issues before their representatives in their state's capital or in Washington, D.C. Lack of attention to public affairs is a necessary feature of representative democracy, but it also creates a potential problem.

Does public opinion adequately reflect the true preferences of the people? If citizens do not fully know what the choices are, then there is the possibility that elites might manipulate public decisions or that people may simply make the wrong choices. American history contains numerous examples of politicians, newspaper editors, and other elites misleading the public and manipulating public opinion for their own gain.[3] The prospect that elites can readily manipulate the public presents a lingering and difficult problem. The United States continually grapples with this challenge, especially in ongoing struggles to reform electoral rules such as campaign finance. Interestingly enough, the solution to the weaknesses of democracy seems to be more democracy. Most of the legal decisions and electoral laws governing the United States embrace the notion that participation ought to be universal but voluntary and that public discourse ought to be unfettered and wide open. That, so the theory goes, is the best guarantee that government does what society wants.

WHAT IS PUBLIC OPINION?

public opinion

Citizens' attitudes about political issues, leaders, institutions, and events

Public opinion may be understood on two levels—aggregate and individual. The term *public opinion* itself refers to an aggregate—the public. It is, however, the accumulation of millions of individuals' expressions of their opinions, attitudes, and choices.

There are many different procedures for aggregating individual opinion, including voting, town meetings, protests, and other forms of political participation as well as public-opinion polls. The aggregate expression of people's choices or opinions is rarely unanimous; instead, the term *public opinion* is usually shorthand for what most people want or think—in other words, majority rule.

Aggregate opinion may not always appear rational, but there is power in numbers. The basic idea behind democracy holds that the sum of many millions

---

3   William Riker, *The Art of Political Manipulation* (New Haven, CT: Yale University Press, 1986).

of votes produces a better outcome than the decision of a small number of people. This idea is brilliantly expressed in Condorcet's jury theorem. The Marquis de Condorcet, a French political philosopher of the eighteenth century, argued that the majority of a jury would more likely reach the right decision in a trial than would a single individual who heard the same evidence. Every person would like to make the right decision, but there is some chance that an individual will make a mistake. Adding up the judgments of many separate individuals, however, reduces the probability of a mistake. A majority of a jury of 12 people, then, is less likely to reach the wrong decision than a single individual. And millions of voters are even more likely to produce the right verdict.[4] Democracy works, then, because voting efficiently collects the knowledge widely held in society.

This idea was rediscovered at the beginning of the twenty-first century, as new information technology expanded the opportunities and the possibility for millions of people to express their opinions on virtually any matter. Firms such as Amazon aggregate the millions of decisions made by consumers to figure out who is likely to buy particular products. There is wisdom in masses, a lesson borne out in markets and democracy.[5]

Public opinion can also be understood at the level of individuals. For example, votes cast during elections, answers to surveys, and letters and e-mails to members of Congress reflect how individuals think and behave politically. Aggregate public opinion, after all, is the collection of these many expressions. An individual's political opinion depends on three factors: (1) the individual's basic preferences (what he wants), (2) his beliefs about the current circumstances and the consequences of different courses of action, and (3) the choices presented. A person will make a choice among the options presented, say, in an election or on a survey, because she wants a certain outcome (such as higher income or better education) and because she believes that a given option is the best among the alternatives. The choices offered in any situation are usually few—Democrat or Republican, a proposed bill versus the status quo, vote yes or vote no, get involved or stay at home. The significance of the individual's actions depends on why he chooses one of the alternatives.

Preferences and Beliefs

Preferences and beliefs are complex. Preferences reflect what people want, such as material goods and money, and also people's values, such as justice and

---

4 Marquis de Condorcet, "Essai sur l'application de l'analyse à la probabilité des décisions rendues à la pluralité des voix," http://gallica.bnf.fr/ark:/12148/bpt6k417181 (accessed 3/24/09). Condorcet also argued that democracy has a weakness in that it need not always produce a definite majority-rule winner and may be manipulated by a clever agenda setter. This idea was rediscovered in the middle of the twentieth century by the Nobel Prize—winning economist Kenneth Arrow in *Social Choice and Individual Values* (New York: Wiley, 1963).

5 See Cass Sunstein, *Infotopia: How Many Minds Produce Knowledge* (Oxford: Oxford University Press, 2006).

morality. Income is often taken as the basis for political preferences. People want to have higher income: other things being equal, they want lower taxes and more government spending on programs that benefit them directly. But also moral values, which are shaped by religion, family, and social conscience, influence the way Americans behave.[6] These two factors—economic self-interest and social or moral values—are viewed as the basis for people's preferences in the political or public arena.

Preferences also are characterized by intensity—how much individuals want a certain outcome or care about a given issue. It is impossible to compare intensity of preferences directly—to say that one person wants something twice as much as someone else. But some people do have more intense preferences than others. Those who have strong opinions are more likely to express their views and take political action than those who do not. Also, public opinion polls reveal that some people care more about some issues, such as taxes, while others care more about other issues, such as abortion.

Beliefs reflect what people know and how they understand the world and the consequences of their actions. An individual who has developed expertise about a topic usually will have more certainty about the choices involved and the consequences of different actions. However, strong beliefs about politics are not necessarily based only on fact. Often in politics, people have strong convictions about a specific issue that are based on the intensity of their general political views. When the facts don't fit their theories, they may ignore fact and stick with their theory. Thus Democrats and Republicans may observe the same event, such as a political debate, and come to opposite conclusions about who won. And public figures may, in the face of strong scientific evidence, reject the science if it does not favor their own political position. As in other aspects of life, people often find it easier to stick to their political beliefs than to change their minds.

Choices

Whether and how individuals' preferences and beliefs are expressed depends, ultimately, on a third component of opinion: the choice offered. We never really observe an individual's preferences and beliefs. Rather, we observe how she responds to a situation or issue and the alternatives presented. In a public opinion survey, respondents answer the questions put to them, which usually reflect important issues at a given time. In elections, we choose among the candidates or parties. Those candidates have taken stands on many different issues—taxes, spending, national defense, welfare, abortion, and so on. However, we cannot mix and match the different positions. If one candidate is low tax and antiabortion and another is high tax and prochoice, then the only choices are between those two clusters of policies. If a voter wants low taxes and is prochoice, there is no candidate who reflects the cluster of policies (or perhaps ideology) that the voter prefers.

6   Benjamin Wattenberg, *Values Matter Most* (New York: Simon & Schuster, 1995).

Moreover, some issues may not even be on the political agenda. An issue that is potentially of broad concern but has not yet reached the public arena is called *latent*. Because the issue is not on the agenda, there is no opportunity for people to express their preferences on it. Consider the following example. Throughout the 1930s and 1940s, the national Democratic leadership strove to keep race relations out of the Democratic Party platform in order to keep southern Democrats in the party. Yet race in the 1930s and 1940s was an issue on which most people had well-formed opinions. In 1948, when Minneapolis mayor Hubert Humphrey proposed a plank to the Democratic Party's national platform calling for desegregation, certain key southern politicians left the party to form a separate one (the Dixiecrats) espousing states' rights and segregation. These actions moved race from a latent issue to one at the forefront of the national agenda.

In contrast, some issues are so removed from public debate that many people would have difficulty formulating a clear opinion because they have not thought about the matter. The process through which issues are vetted and debated publicly, then, is also key to the formulation and expression of public opinion. Americans had debated the question of race relations for centuries before the 1948 election, and they continue to debate the matter today. Other potentially contentious issues receive little public debate. For example, Spain and the United Kingdom have recently grappled with questions of separatism—whether Catalonia should remain in Spain and whether Scotland should remain in the United Kingdom. One might imagine similar independence movements in the United States, but there has been little serious discussion on the topic. Were separatism to be put on a public opinion poll today, many people likely would decline to give an opinion. But if there were extensive debate on the matter, people would eventually discover where their preferences lie.

The choices offered to people in elections, polls, town meetings, and other venues shape how preferences and beliefs are expressed in democratic politics. Public opinion, then, is never the pure expression of preferences but rather revealed preference—the choices among a given set of issues and alternatives. In this chapter we examine the basis for individuals' preferences and the origins of their beliefs, as well as aggregate public opinion.

Variety of Opinion

The term *public opinion* might suggest that all people are of the same mind. As we've noted, that is rarely the case. The term is really a shorthand description of the variety of opinion in society on a given question. One segment of the population supports the president, a second segment opposes him, and a third is unsure. A percentage of people are for a given bill in Congress, and a percentage are against it.

In some cases, Americans do hold common views on questions vital to governance and society. For example, there is consensus on the legitimacy of the Constitution of the United States, on the principle that no one is above the law, and on the idea that the outcomes of elections determine who governs.

These commonly held opinions and values ensure peaceful transitions of government after each election and respect for laws produced by a legitimately chosen government.

There is also wide agreement on fundamental political values, such as equality of opportunity, liberty, and democracy.[7] Nearly all Americans agree that all people should have equal rights, regardless of race, gender, or social standing. Americans hold a common commitment to freedom. People who live in the United States are free to reside where they want, travel where they want, work where they want, say what they want, and practice whatever religion they wish, including no religion at all. And Americans have an undying belief in democracy—that whenever possible, public officials should be chosen by majority vote.[8]

On most matters that come before the government, however, the public does not hold a single view. Usually, opinions are divided between those who support the government or a proposed action and those who do not. Politicians are still attuned to public opinion when it is divided, but what matters most are the balance and direction of opinion. What do the majority of constituents want? Which way is opinion trending? Is it possible to find a popular middle ground?

People express their views in a variety of ways. Constituents contact their members of Congress through letters, phone calls, e-mails, and even personal visits to the members' offices. Most questions before Congress elicit little reaction from the public, but some questions start a maelstrom of objections. In 2008, when Congress considered a $700 billion bailout of financial institutions, the volume of e-mail related to this bill was so great that at one point the House of Representatives had to limit incoming e-mail to keep its computers from crashing.[9] People also express their opinions more publicly, through blogs, letters to newspapers, and op-ed pieces; in conversations with others; with lawn signs and bumper stickers; by working on campaigns; by giving money to candidates, groups, and party organizations; and most simply, by voting.

Such expressions of opinion are not always easy to interpret. If a constituent votes against a member of Congress, did she do so because of a controversial decision that the legislator made in Congress or because she decided to vote against all politicians from the legislator's party? Or for some other reason?

Political scientists and political consultants try to provide more refined and structured descriptions of public opinion using surveys. Public opinion on a given issue can be thought of as the distribution of opinion across the different options that government might pursue. Likewise, public opinion may represent the division of support for a leader or party. We try to gauge where majority support lies and how intensely citizens across the spectrum hold their views.

---

7   See Louis Hartz, *The Liberal Tradition in America: An Interpretation of American Political Thought since the Revolution* (New York: Harcourt, Brace, 1955).

8   For a discussion of political beliefs of Americans, see Everett Carl Ladd, *The American Ideology* (Storrs, CT: Roper Center, 1994).

9   Jordy Yeager, "House Limits Constituent E-mail to Prevent Crash," *The Hill,* September 30, 2008, http://thehill.com/leading-the-news/house-limits-constituent-e-mails-to-prevent-crash-2008-09-30.html (accessed 3/24/09).

Increasingly, politicians rely on opinion polls to anticipate the effects of their decisions, to identify issues and policies on which they have opportunities to gain political support at the expense of the opposing party, and to develop ways to blunt any objections to controversial decisions. Answering a survey, then, can also be a form of political action, because it may influence political decisions.

Public opinion should be thought of as the variation in opinion across a range of options. A set of exclusive options that capture the range of opinions is called a *variable*. For example, one might want to know whether people support the president. We can do a survey and count how many people support the president. But support alone does not summarize all attitudes toward the president; it is only half of the variable. We can reformulate the question by counting the number of people who *support* the president, the number of people who *do not support* the president, and the number of people who *have no opinion* or *neither support nor oppose* the president. Such a dichotomy is perhaps the simplest variable, but also the most common: support or oppose, favor or not, yes or no.

Often, however, people think about politics in more subtle terms than just yes and no or support and oppose. Consider the debate over the legality of abortion. In the immediate aftermath of the *Roe v. Wade* decision, survey researchers sorted people into two polar positions—prolife and prochoice—and measured the percentage of respondents identifying as prolife or as prochoice or as having no opinion. As social scientists continued to study the politics of abortion, it became clear that people had more nuanced opinions and saw a much wider range of possible government policies on abortion. As a result, survey researchers developed more refined questions to ascertain the conditions under which people would and would not allow abortion. Would a respondent allow abortion for teenagers if parents did not consent? What about cases of rape or incest? What if the pregnancy endangered the mother's life? Such refinements have allowed the public to express its preferences more precisely on this issue.

Opinions take a variety of forms, depending on the issue. It is helpful to keep in mind a few common examples in thinking about this subject.

- **Evaluations of those in government and other institutions.** Survey researchers use a variety of questions to gauge support for or opposition to the government. They ask about approval of the job that the president is doing, the job that Congress is doing and that individual members are doing, and the job the Supreme Court is doing. At elections, voters express their support for and opposition to members of government directly through their votes. In political science as well as other disciplines, similar questions target social and economic institutions and leaders.

- **Assessments of public policies.** Do you support or oppose a given policy? Do you think a problem is important or not? What is the most important problem that government should address? How people answer such questions depends on the choices that are presented and the immediate circumstances. Views on specific issues may follow the same patterns as general political orientations, if they directly affect partisan groups or derive from political debates between parties or ideological groups. For instance, a bill that would alter wages for public employees affects unions directly and thus touches a core constituency of the Democratic Party. So, we might find that Democrats are more likely to view this issue in a certain way.

- **Assessments of current circumstances.** Is the economy performing well or poorly? Is crime high or low? Is the country headed in the right direction? Such questions might seem to have clear-cut, objective answers, but opinions differ depending on each individual's experiences and what she has read or heard through the media.

- **Political orientations.** The two most important indicators of individuals' general political orientations are party identification and ideology. Do you consider yourself a Democrat, a Republican, of another party, or of no party in particular? Do you consider yourself liberal, moderate, or conservative? These concepts capture general political orientations that are usually quite stable. Researchers have shown that party identifications predict voting preferences very well and correlate strongly with evaluations of those in office. Party identification often acts as a filter for information, a tinted lens that colors the way people view the world and interpret information. Immediately after an election, supporters of the winning party express greater optimism about the economy, about global affairs, and even about their own personal finances. Often a Democrat and a Republican will view a presidential debate differently, with the Democrat concluding that the Democratic candidate clearly won and the Republican concluding the opposite.

We can characterize the variation in public opinion by measuring the percentage of people who choose each option of a variable. A bar chart provides one way to display the distribution of public opinion: the height of each bar represents the percentage of people choosing each outcome of a variable, and the sum of these percentages equals 100 percent. Typically, we care about which option receives the most support (a plurality) or the support of a majority. In the 2016 presidential election, Donald Trump won with 46 percent of all votes cast while Hillary Clinton received 48 percent but not enough votes in the electoral college. All other candidates received 6 percent. Political observers view the size of the winner's vote margin as an indication of the support for his or her policies and ideology.

Opinion data, such as the information gathered in surveys, provide an even more subtle and varied measure of public attitudes and political orientations. Consider ideology (which we discuss in more detail later in this chapter). According to a Gallup poll in January 2015, 38 percent of Americans described themselves as conservative, 34 percent as moderate, and 24 percent as liberal. Another 5 percent do not think of themselves in these terms.[10] For an indicator

---

10 Lydia Saad, "U.S. Liberals at Record 24%, but Still Trail Conservatives," Gallup, January 9 2015, www.gallup.com/poll/180452/liberals-record-trail-conservatives.aspx (accessed 6/23/15).

such as ideology, then, no single camp has a clear majority, but we can say that self-described conservatives outnumber self-described liberals.

Polarization. One particularly important debate about public opinion today concerns ideological polarization. Observers have often argued that the public is deeply divided into very conservative and very liberal groups, with relatively few people in the middle, and that this view of "two Americas" holds true for questions about ideology and across a wide range of issues, such as taxation, health care, education, and foreign affairs. The political scientists Morris Fiorina, Jeremy Pope, and Samuel Abrams tackled this alleged polarization in their 2004 book *Culture War? The Myth of a Polarized America.* The co-authors made simple bar charts to describe the distribution of public opinion in the United States. Rather than a deep divide, they found that on most issues Americans are centrists—either moderate or leaning somewhat to the right or left. This finding has important implications about the ability to reach consensus in public debate. It also raises an even more elusive puzzle: although most Americans are centrist, most representatives in Congress vote either on the very liberal or on the very conservative end of the spectrum. The public, then, is not polarized, but Congress is. Why is this the case? Political scientists have suggested that polarization owes to (1) the nature of the debate in Washington and the choices put before Congress; (2) institutional factors, such as the organization of parties in Congress; or (3) the election process, including who votes and who doesn't, primary elections, and campaign contributors. The debate over this question has yet to reach a definitive resolution.[11]

Just as we do not think of public opinion as a consensus, we do not think of the public as monolithic. American society is a hodgepodge of different ethnic and racial groups; Americans differ greatly in educational attainment, income, and religion. The U.S. census, conducted every 10 years, measures variations in housing, family, employment, and other demographic characteristics. The Census Bureau also conducts monthly surveys measuring such activities as communication, employment, and voting. These data provide a rich picture of the diversity and complexity of American society. For example, 18 percent of Americans claim Hispanic ethnicity, 13 percent are black or African American, 6 percent are Asian, 1 percent are Native American, and 62 percent identify themselves as non-Hispanic white. Among people under 18, only 52 percent identify themselves as non-Hispanic white. One person of every eight living

11 For five different views, see Morris Fiorina, Samuel Abrams, and Jeremy Pope, *Culture War?* 2nd ed. (New York: Pearson, Longman, 2005); Nolan McCarty, Keith Poole, and Howard Rosenthal, *Polarization in America: The Dance of Ideology and Unequal Riches* (Princeton, NJ: Princeton University Press, 2007); Gary Jacobson, *A Divider, Not a Uniter: George W. Bush, the American People, the 2006 Election, and Beyond* (White Plains, NY: Longman, 2007); Alan Abramowitz, "Constraint, Ideology, and Polarization in the American Electorate," paper presented at the annual meeting of the American Political Science Association, August 30, 2007; and Stephen Ansolabehere, Jonathan Rodden, and James M. Snyder, Jr., "Purple America," *Journal of Economic Perspectives* 20, no. 2 (spring 2006): 97–118.

in the United States today was not born here. However, among people under 18, only one person in 20 was born elsewhere. Although the large majority of Americans identify with some form of Christianity and most of those are Protestant, the single largest sect is Roman Catholicism. Almost 30 percent of adults in the United States have a college degree; 14 percent did not complete high school. The U.S. is one of the richest nations on earth, but approximately 1 in 7 Americans lives in poverty. The most populous region of the country is the South, home to approximately 35 percent of the population.[12] In describing and understanding the attitudes, opinions, needs, and wants of the American public, we must remember that the public itself is fractured into many sub-groups and interests.[13]

ORIGINS AND NATURE OF OPINION

To understand the meaning and origins of the public's opinions, we must have some sense of the basis for individuals' preferences and beliefs. Opinions are the products of one's personality, social characteristics, and interests. They mirror who a person is, what she wants, and her relationship to family and community as well as to the broader economy and society. But opinions are also shaped by institutional, political, and governmental forces that make it more likely that an individual will hold some beliefs and less likely that he will hold others.

Foundations of Preferences

Self-Interest. Individuals' preferences about politics and public policy are usually rooted in self-interest. Laws and other governmental actions directly affect people's interests—their disposable income, the quality of public services and goods, and personal safety, to give just a few examples. Thus when people express their political opinions, they react to the effects that government actions have on them personally.

---

12 Sandra Colby and Jennifer Ortman, "Projections of the Size and Composition of the US Population: 2014 to 2060," Current Population Reports, P25-1143, March 2015, U.S. Census Bureau, www.census.gov/content/dam/Census/library/publications/2015/demo/p25-1143.pdf (accessed 8/20/16).

13 As an exercise, we recommend consulting the *Statistical Abstract of the United States* and constructing bar charts (distributions) for the following demographic variables: (1) household incomes, (2) residency (urban, suburban, and rural), (3) region, (4) race, and (5) religion. Note the largest category for each variable. For income, calculate the level of income such that half of the people have income below that level and half have income above it (the median).

Economic interests are perhaps the most salient preferences. Government policies, ranging from export and import rules to regulations to spending and taxes, directly affect individual Americans' personal well-being. Taxes, for example, reduce disposable income. The average American family has income of $100,000 (including wages and salaries, income from businesses, investment income, and retirement income) before taxes and $80,000 after taxes.[14] Those taxes, of course, pay for government programs like Social Security and Medicare, national defense, and other public goods. But not all families and individuals are taxed equally, nor do all benefit equally from government programs.

Government regulations also affect people's economic self-interests. Such rules protect people from potentially harmful pollutants, preserve the value of property, protect consumers from potential harm, and create the property rights necessary to maintain a well-functioning market economy. But they also limit how people use their property and may raise the cost of operating a business.

The government is also directly involved in the labor market. Approximately 22 million people, 12 percent of the U.S. civilian labor force, work for federal, state, or local governments; another 1.4 million people are in the armed services.[15] Government spending constitutes a substantial share of the national economy; federal expenditures alone account for about 20 percent of gross domestic product (GDP).[16] Virtually every American has an interest in the government's role in the nation's economy and strong preferences about tax rates and expenditure priorities. Given the enormous influence of the federal government in the economy, assessments of the president and the party in power often correspond to how well the nation's economy performs.

Individuals' attitudes toward government reflect other forms of self-interest as well. Laws affect families, the status of civic and religious organizations, and communities. Zoning laws and urban redevelopment programs shape the nature of neighborhoods, including the mix of commercial and residential housing and the density of low-income housing in an area. Tax laws treat nonprofits, such as universities, religious organizations, and social clubs, differently from for-profit companies, making it easier for nonprofit organizations to exist. Family law affects how easy it is for families to stay together, what happens when they break down, and what rights and responsibilities parents have. Proposed changes in such laws bring immediate reaction from those affected.

---

14 Congressional Budget Office, "The Distribution of Household Income and Federal Taxes, 2013," June 8, 2016, www.cbo.gov/publication/51361 (accessed 8/20/16).

15 Government employment figures are from Robert Jesse Willhide, "Annual Survey of Public Employment & Payroll Summary Report: 2013, U.S. Census Bureau, December 19, 2014, www2.census.gov/govs/apes/2013_summary_report.pdf (accessed 5/23/2016). Figures on number of people in the U.S. armed services are from World Bank, "Armed Forces Personnel, Total," http://data.worldbank.org/indicator/MS.MIL.TOTL.P1 (accessed 5/23/16).

16 The gross domestic product consists of the value of all goods and services produced in the United States. It is one measure of the nation's income.

Values. Much of what individuals want from their government is also rooted in values concerning what is right or wrong—our philosophies about morality, justice, and ethics. Our value systems originate in many places—families, religion, education, groups, and so forth—and often determine our preferences in particular circumstances. For example, values may shape preferences about how government and society distributes or redistributes income—an illustration of economic justice. Americans generally believe in equal opportunity, an idea that has driven our society to try to root out discrimination in employment, housing, and education, and to create a universal public education system. In some states, such as New Hampshire, Ohio, and California, courts have invoked this principle of equality to insist that the states try to equalize public school expenditures per pupil across districts.

Values also shape our notions of what is a crime and what is a suitable punishment. One of the most morally laden debates in American history focuses on capital punishment. Does the government have the right to take an individual's life, even if that individual has taken the life of someone else? An ancient sense of justice seems to call for exactly that: an eye for an eye. Other ideas of morality speak against capital punishment. And our values about government and its appropriate powers say that people must be protected against arbitrary and capricious acts of government. The death penalty is irreversible, and the possibility of a governmental error has led some to claim that the government can never have the power to take the life of an individual.[17]

Our values also reflect established social norms, analogous to common law. What, for example, is marriage? One might consider it an economic convenience, as defined by laws that tie taxes and inheritance to marital status. Most people, however, express more complex ideas of marriage, including whether same-sex marriages ought to be allowed. Such norms change over time. For example, a century ago interracial marriages were deemed unacceptable by most in American society, and most states adopted laws to prevent interracial marriage. It took a Supreme Court decision in 1967, in *Loving v. Virginia*, to eliminate the last of these laws.[18] Gay rights advocates drew similar parallels in their struggle to legalize same-sex marriage, and they too made their arguments in the courts. In the 2015 case of *Obergefell v. Hodges*, the Supreme Court declared same-sex marriage—previously a state-level policy—a fundamental right nationwide.[19]

Values often conflict with one another, as when a law or policy touches on different values and in conflicting ways. A question like capital punishment evokes our notions of how much power government ought to have over individuals, even criminals, and our fundamental ideas of justice and vengeance. A person might support capital punishment as a just response to a heinous crime

---

17 *Furman v. Georgia*, 408 U.S. 238 (1972).

18 *Loving v. Virginia*, 388 U.S. 1 (1967).

19 *Obergefell v. Hodges*, 576 U.S. ___ (2015).

but also think that government should not have the power to kill its citizens. At a societal level, conflicting values are particularly difficult to resolve—especially when the differences strike at fundamental principles of right and wrong.

By the same token, there are many values that unite us. If Americans had few common values or perspectives, it would be very difficult to reach agreement on particular issues. Over the past half century, political philosophers and political scientists have reflected on what those values are and have settled on three important precepts. Americans almost universally agree with (1) the democracy principle (that majority rule is a good decision rule), (2) the importance of equal opportunity, and (3) the idea that that government is best which governs least.

Social Groups. Individuals' preferences about politics and government are rooted in a third source—social groups. We are connected to one another through social characteristics and groupings, including family, neighborhood, language, race, and religion. People often describe themselves using such characteristics. These descriptors tap fundamental psychological attachments that go beyond self-interest and values, though they are often reinforced by our interests and values.

Social groups affect political preferences in two ways. First, people have preferences for political decisions that benefit their group and, indirectly, themselves. Social groups affect our preferences by virtue of simply being members of those groups. A group or organization, such as a union or a church, helps overcome the collective action problem. Each of us usually joins a group for some private benefit, but the group helps us attain a common benefit through collective action that we could not achieve acting alone. Our preferences, then, shift to maintain the group because of the benefits it gains for us.

Second, social groups can change our values and even our view of ourselves. Consider someone who finishes college and takes a job at a corporation as an employee to earn wages. Upon doing so, the person begins to take on the perspective of that organization. On one level, this is a matter of self-interest: as goes the corporation, so goes the person's wages. But on a deeper level, people often internalize the collective value as well: when the corporation does well, we feel proud of our contribution to the corporation and are motivated to work harder still. We identify in this way with our churches, schools, towns and cities, ethnicities, and other groups.

The process through which social interactions and social groups affect our perspectives and preferences is called **socialization**. Most 18-year-olds already have definite political attitudes that they have learned from parents and grandparents, friends, teachers, religious leaders, and others in their social groups and networks. Of course, socialization does not end after leaving home. We continue to learn about politics and what we should think about complex political questions from our family members, co-workers, and others we see and speak with daily.

Socialization works in many ways. First, it is a means of providing information about what is going on in the community and even in national politics. Socialization also takes the form of education or instruction. Parents teach their children how to think about a problem, what is a right or wrong choice or action, and how to participate in politics. This is how we as humans have learned to survive and adapt. But it means that by the time we are adults, we have learned

 socialization

A process through which individuals assimilate community preferences and norms through social interactions

much about what we want government to do, what sorts of people we want in government, and even whether it is worth our while to participate. Sometimes, socialization takes the form of outright pressure to think or behave in a certain way. If an employer asks her employees to vote a certain way or to work for a certain candidate, that employer is using a position of power to influence how others in her social group behave. In these and other ways, social groups shape the way people think and how they behave in politics.

Political Ideology

Political decisions, especially those about public policies, are complex. It can be difficult to see how one's interests and values map into a given vote. Political discourse and debate, however, are often simplified as a conflict between different ideologies. An ideology is a comprehensive way of understanding political or cultural situations; it is a set of assumptions about the way society works that helps us organize our beliefs, information, and reactions to new situations. It ascribes values to different alternatives and helps us balance competing values. Political decisions usually involve trade-offs between values or interests. Belief systems such as conservatism and liberalism help us think through those trade-offs. As such, understanding different political ideologies can help us make decisions in a political, social, or cultural setting. Ideologies are very handy simplifications of an otherwise complex world.

In the United States today, people often describe themselves as liberals or conservatives. Liberalism and conservatism are political ideologies that include beliefs about the role of government, ideas about public policies, and notions about which groups in society should properly exercise power. In earlier times, these terms were defined differently. Before the New Deal in the 1930s, the terms "liberal" and "conservative" were used infrequently in the United States. To the extent that they were used they referred to their European counterparts—where a liberal was someone who favored freedom from government power and laissez faire economic policy, and a conservative was someone who supported the use of governmental power and favored continued influence by the state and aristocracy in national life.

Today, in the United States, the term **liberal** implies support for political and social reform; government intervention in the economy; expansion of federal social services; more vigorous efforts on behalf of the poor, minorities, and women; and greater concern for consumers and the environment. In social and cultural areas, liberals generally support abortion rights and oppose state involvement with religious institutions and religious expression. In international affairs, liberals usually support arms control, oppose the development and testing of nuclear weapons, support aid to poor nations, oppose the use of American troops to influence the domestic affairs of developing nations, and support international organizations such as the United Nations. Of course, liberalism is not monolithic. For example, among individuals who view themselves as liberal, many support American military intervention when it is tied to a humanitarian purpose or in response to a significant threat to the security of the United States, such as the terrorist attacks of September 11, 2001.

liberal

A liberal today generally supports political and social reform; government intervention in the economy; the expansion of federal social services; more vigorous efforts on behalf of the poor, minorities, and women; and greater concern for consumers and the environment

By contrast, the term **conservative** today describes those who generally support the social and economic status quo, favor markets as solutions to social problems, and are suspicious of government involvement in the economy. Conservatives believe that a large and powerful government poses a threat to citizens' freedom. Thus in the domestic arena conservatives generally assert that solutions to social and economic problems can be developed in the private sector. Conservatives claim that government regulation of business is frequently economically inefficient and costly and can ultimately lower the nation's standard of living. As for social and cultural positions, many conservatives oppose abortion and support school prayer. In international affairs, conservatism has come to mean support for the maintenance of American military power. Like liberalism, though, conservatism is far from monolithic. Some conservatives support many government social programs. George W. Bush, a Republican, called himself a compassionate conservative to indicate that he favored programs that assist the poor and the needy. Other conservatives oppose efforts to outlaw abortion, arguing that government intrusion in this area is as misguided as government intervention in the economy. The real political world is far too complex to interpret in terms of a simple struggle between liberals and conservatives.

There are many other ideologies besides liberalism and conservatism. Libertarians, for example, seek to expand liberty above all other principles and wish to minimize government intervention in the economy and society. Other ideologies seek a particular outcome, such as environmental protection, or may emphasize certain issues, such as economic growth, and de-emphasize other issues, such as abortion. Communism and fascism are ideologies that support government control of all aspects of the economy and society; these ideologies dominated politics in many European countries from the 1920s through the 1940s. Political discourse in the United States, however, has revolved around the division between liberals and conservatives for most of the last century.

Liberal and conservative differences manifest themselves in a variety of contexts. For example, the liberal approach to chronically low test scores and high dropout rates at a public high school might be to increase funding for teachers and reduce class sizes. The conservative approach might be to remove administrators or fire teachers from low-performing schools, or even to close such schools. To some extent, contemporary liberalism and conservatism can be seen as blends of the fundamental American political values of liberty and equality. For liberals, equality is often the most important core value; they tolerate government intervention in such areas as college admissions and business decisions to help remedy race, class, or gender inequality. For conservatives, in contrast, liberty is the core value; they oppose most efforts by government, however well intentioned, to intrude into private life or the marketplace. This simple formula for distinguishing liberalism and conservatism is of course not always accurate. Conservatives, for example, sometimes seek more government intervention in social policy realms involving family, marriage, homosexuality, and abortion, whereas liberals tend to resist government regulation of such social relations.

Political scientists often think of liberal and conservative ideologies as anchors on a spectrum of possible belief systems. The Pew Center on People and the Press offers just such a classification in its American Values Survey,

conservative

Today this term refers to those who generally support the social and economic status quo and believe that a large and powerful government poses a threat to citizens' freedoms

conducted annually since 1987.[20] The Pew Survey asks respondents about a wide range of political, social, and cultural preferences, behaviors, and beliefs. Many of these beliefs cluster: for instance, people who believe in the literal truth of the Bible tend to be prolife, favor cuts in taxes, and call themselves conservative. However, the more such questions one asks, the more finely one may sort the respondents. Classifying people this way, the Pew Center finds that a large plurality of Americans have just as many conservative views as liberal views. As discussed earlier, that is essentially what Morris Fiorina and his colleagues concluded about the degree of polarization in the United States—most people are quite moderate. It is interesting that the Pew surveys also document that the number of Americans who choose more liberal policy positions than conservative policy positions is greater than the number of Americans who choose more conservative policy positions than liberal ones. This is true even though the number who choose the conservative label outnumber those who choose the liberal label. Why this is the case is an interesting puzzle.

Identity Politics

Ideology offers one lens through which people can discern where their political interests and values lie. Identity provides an alternative simplification of the political world. Political identities are distinctive characteristics or group associations that individuals carry, reflecting their social connections or common values and interests with others in that group. A harm or benefit to any individual with a given identity is viewed as a harm or benefit to all people with that identity. Common identities in politics include race and ethnicity, religion, and gender.

Identities are both psychological and sociological. At the psychological level these are attachments felt by individuals, and at the sociological level they function at the collective level, such as racial groups, genders, or language groups. Unlike ideological politics, identities are absolutes. A person either is or is not of a certain group. And identity politics are often zero-sum: If one group gains, another group loses. The term *identity politics* is sometimes used today to refer to groups that have been oppressed and that seek to assert their rights. But the concept is much broader. *Political identity* does not simply describe the situation of groups that have suffered some harm; it applies to any collective identity. In fact, political identity often has a very positive side, as the glue that holds society together and as another way to overcome problems of collective action.[21]

Identity politics are quite obvious in the United States today. All citizens and many noncitizens identify themselves as Americans. During international sporting competitions, we root for athletes representing the United States

20 The "American Values Survey" is available at www.people-press.org/values-questions (accessed 5/23/16).

21 Rawi Abdelal, Yoshiko M. Herrera, Alastair Iain Johnston, and Rose McDermott, "Identity as a Variable," *Perspectives on Politics* 4, no. 4 (2006): 695–711.

because we identify with that country; and when those athletes win, as Americans we feel happy and proud. We may feel similarly when an American wins a Nobel Prize or makes a significant scientific discovery. The same is true of people from any country: we feel pride in the accomplishments of others from our country.

One of the most salient political identities in the United States is political party. The authors of *The American Voter* (1960), a classic work of political science research on the social and psychological foundations of electoral behavior in the United States, characterize party identification as a stable psychological attachment usually developed in childhood and carried throughout one's adult life. Party identifications are, of course, shaped by interests and values as well as by current events, but partisanship also has deep roots in family, local culture, and other factors. Moreover, people commonly rely on their partisan identities in filtering information—as in claiming who they think won a presidential debate. Party also has a unique hold on voting behavior. Even after taking into account self-interest, moral values, and other identities, partisanship remains one of the best predictors of how someone will vote.[22] (See the discussion of party voting in Chapters 11 and 12.)

In 2006, Alan Gerber and Gregory Huber of Yale University conducted an ingenious study showing how identity matters to people's preferences. By tracking the consumption behavior of people after elections, the researchers found that individuals who identified strongly with a particular party and whose party won the election spent much more on durable consumer goods, such as washing machines and other appliances, than did individuals whose candidates lost or who did not identify strongly with any party. Behavioral economists and social psychologists have documented other such phenomena, such as the effect of sports teams' victories on feelings of happiness.[23]

This is not to say that party does not reflect ideological choices or self-interest. It does. But it is certainly also the case that party functions as a social identity.

People who hold a specific identity often express strong affinity for others of the same identity—for example, voting for someone of the same ethnicity apart from, or in spite of, the sorts of laws that the particular politician promises to enact. Political scientists call this preference for people of the same identity "descriptive representation," and it is an important subject in the area of race and elections. In fact, the Voting Rights Act tries to protect African Americans, Hispanics, and other racial and ethnic groups against discriminatory electoral practices that prevent those voters from electing their preferred candidates. Since the act was passed in 1965, the percentage of members of Congress who are African American and Hispanic has increased from 1 percent (6 in 1965) to 21 percent (90 in 2015).

---

22 Angus Campbell, Philip Converse, Warren Miller, and Donald Stokes, *The American Voter* (New York: John Wiley, 1960).

23 Alan Gerber and Gregory Huber, "Partisanship and Economic Behavior," *American Political Science Review* 103 (2009): 407–26.

Race, gender, social class, and place all create strong identities that shape voting behavior. So do religion, region of the country, sexual orientation, occupation, and many other distinctive characteristics. In a provocative essay in the *Atlantic Monthly* following the 2000 election, commentator David Brooks wrote that Americans are divided not so much along the lines of ideologies and interests but along cultural lines.[24] His assessment gave rise to the argument that there are red (Republican) and blue (Democratic) areas of the nation, but he also argued that the divisions are based less on ideologies and interests and more on who the voters are, where they live, and how they live. Other differences occur across religious groups, between men and women, and between young and old. Some of these differences may be traced to self-interest, but most cannot. The explanations for differences in opinions and voting behaviors among social groups surely relates to the position of such groups in American society.

Blacks. The practice of slavery in the colonies and early American states created a deep, lasting divide in our society between whites and blacks. That division is reflected in a staggering number of statistics, from wages and education levels to poverty levels to neighborhood integration to political ideals. There are, for example, stark differences between blacks and whites in their beliefs about government's responsibilities for providing shelter, food, and other basic necessities to those in need.[25] Blacks and whites also differ in their views of equality of opportunity in the United States, which can impact their preferences for policies that address perceived disadvantages (Figure 10.1).

More striking, race seems to affect how other factors, like income and education, shape preferences. Among whites, there is a definite correlation between conservatism and income. Higher-income whites tend to support more conservative economic policies and are likely to identify with the Republican Party, while lower-income whites tend to favor more liberal economic policies and align with the Democratic Party. Nearly all African Americans, however, side with the Democrats and support liberal economic policies, regardless of income.

Latinos. Latinos are another major American subgroup with distinctive opinions on some public issues. For instance, in a 2014 poll, 60 percent of Hispanic voters approved of the Affordable Care Act, while 61 percent of non-Hispanic whites disapproved—a significant disparity.[26] In addition, Hispanic voters

24 David Brooks, "One Nation, Slightly Divisible," *Atlantic Monthly,* December 2001, www. theatlantic.com/past/docs/issues/2001/12/brooks.htm (accessed 5/17/13).

25 Pew Research Center for the People and the Press, "The Black and White of Public Opinion," October 31, 2005, http://people-press.org/commentary/?analysisid=121 (accessed 3/24/09).

26 Pew Research Center, September, 2014, "Wide Partisan Differences over the Issues That Matter in 2014," www.people-press.org/files/2014/09/09-12-14-Midterms-Release1.pdf (accessed 12/16/14).

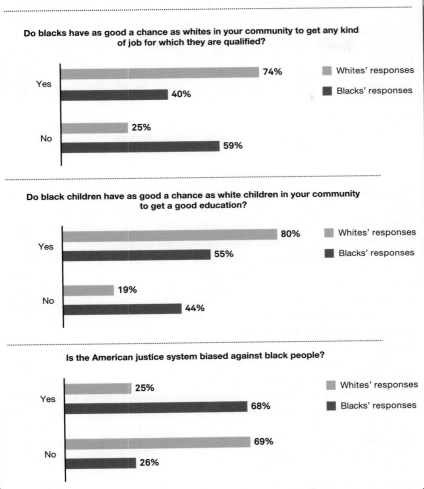

Figure 10.1
DISAGREEMENT AMONG BLACKS AND WHITES

Do blacks have as good a chance as whites in your community to get any kind of job for which they are qualified?

Whites' responses
Blacks' responses

- Yes
  - 74%
  - 40%
- No
  - 25%
  - 59%

Do black children have as good a chance as white children in your community to get a good education?

Whites' responses
Blacks' responses

- Yes
  - 80%
  - 55%
- No
  - 19%
  - 44%

Is the American justice system biased against black people?

Whites' responses
Blacks' responses

- Yes
  - 25%
  - 68%
- No
  - 69%
  - 26%

SOURCE: Gallup Editors, "Gallup Review: Black and White Differences in Views on Race," December 12, 2014, www.gallup.com/poll/180107/gallup-review-black-white-differences-views-race.aspx, (Accessed 6/12/15).

ANALYZING THE EVIDENCE

Although America's system of legally mandated racial segregation ended nearly half a century ago, its effects continue to linger. In contemporary America, blacks and whites have different perspectives on race relations. Do you think that black–white differences have increased or decreased in the past few decades? Are these differences of opinion important?

routinely identify immigration as one of their top concerns, while the issue ranks lower in priority among non-Hispanic white voters.

In one respect, Hispanic and Latino political identities have a different character from those of blacks. Hispanic and Latino group identities are often rooted in particular immigrant communities, such as Mexican American,

Table 10.1

CHANGING PARTY AFFILIATION IN THE LATINO COMMUNITY

ANALYZING THE EVIDENCE

Members of America's Latino community share a linguistic heritage, but they are not politically homogeneous. What factors might account for these differences? Why might so many Cuban Americans have changed their party allegiance between 2004 and 2008?

| BACKGROUND | 2004 | | 2008 | | 2012 | | 2015 | |
	DEM. (%)	REP. (%)	DEM. (%)	REP. (%)	DEM. (%)	REP. (%)	DEM. (%)	REP. (%)
Cuban	17	52	53	20	51	37	38	32
Mexican	47	18	50	18	64	18	48	22
Puerto Rican	50	17	61	11	74	10	56	19

SOURCES: 2004–12: Pew Hispanic Center, www.pewhispanic.org (accessed 11/13/14); 2015: Stephen Ansolabehere and Brian Schaffner, "2015 Cooperative Congressional Election Survey, Common Content," projects.iq.harvard.edu/cces/data (accessed 10/31/16).

Puerto Rican, and Cuban.[27] And, Hispanic and Latino political identities are strongly tied to particular issues of immigration.[28] These differences have led to heterogeneity in opinion on certain issues. Among Latinos, Cuban Americans have long been disproportionately Republican, while those of Mexican, Puerto Rican, and Central American descent identify more often as Democrats (Table 10.1). That difference reflected Cuban Americans' relationship with their homeland and the long-standing policy differences between Republicans and Democrats over U.S. relations with Cuba. It is interesting that the difference had largely vanished by 2008; surveys during the presidential campaign found that Cuban Americans were nearly as Democratic as other Hispanic groups.

As with blacks, Hispanic Latino identity tempers the way other demographic characteristics translate into political identities and values. Although higher-income Hispanics and Latinos identify more as Republican than lower-income Hispanics and Latinos do, the differences are not as stark as among whites, and low-income Hispanics and Latinos are much more likely to identify as Democrats than low-income whites. Hispanics and Latino identity mutes the political effects of other characteristics.

Gender. Men and women express differing political opinions as well. Women tend to be less militaristic than men on issues of war and peace, more likely to favor measures to protect the environment, and more supportive of government social and health care programs (Table 10.2). Perhaps because of these differences, women are more likely than men to vote for Democratic candidates,

27 Gabriel R. Sanchez, "The Role of Group Consciousness in Latino Public Opinion," *Political Research Quarterly* 59, no. 3 (2006): 435–46; and Pamela Johnston Conover, "The Influence of Group Identifications on Political Perception and Evaluation," *Journal of Politics* 46, no. 3 (1984): 760–85.

28 Taeku Lee, "Race, Immigration, and the Identity-to-Politics Link," *Annual Review of Political Science* 11 (2008): 457–78.

Table 10.2

DISAGREEMENTS AMONG MEN AND WOMEN ON ISSUES OF WAR AND PEACE

GOVERNMENT ACTION	APPROVE OF ACTION (%)	
	MEN	WOMEN
Sending U.S. ground troops to fight Islamic militants in Iraq and Syria (2015)	52	41
Support U.S. missile strikes against Syria (2013)	43	30
Use U.S. troops to attack a terrorist camp (2012)	71	55
Support withdrawal of troops from Iraq (2008)	70	52
Use U.S. troops to intervene in a genocide or civil war (2008)	53	42
Go to war against Iraq (2003)	66	50
Broker a cease-fire in Yugoslavia instead of using NATO air strikes (1999)	44	51
Go to war against Iraq (1991)	72	53

SOURCES: Gallup polls, 1991, 1993, and 1999, www.gallup.com/home.aspx; *Washington Post*, 2003, www.washingtonpost.com/politics/polling/; Cooperative Congressional Election Study, 2008 and 2012, projects.iq.harvard.edu/cces/home; Langer Research, 2013, www.langerresearch.com; Pew Center, 2015, www.people-press.org.

whereas men have become increasingly supportive of Republicans.[29] This tendency for men's and women's opinions to differ is called the **gender gap**. The gender gap in voting first became evident in the 1980 election and has persisted, averaging about 8 percentage points. In the 2016 presidential election, Hillary Clinton became the first female major-party candidate. The gender gap was the widest in history: she won 54 percent of the votes of women, but only 41 percent of the votes of men.

Why the gender gap emerged 40 years ago and persists today is a puzzle. Many scholars speculate that reproductive rights and abortion politics lie at the root of this division; yet a Pew Research Center poll from 2006 indicates little or no opinion gap between men and women on the abortion issue.[30] Rather, the gender gap appears to be more attributable to wages, and other differences between the ways that men and women are treated in the economy and society, and to women's shared objective of ensuring equal treatment for all women.[31]

 gender gap

A distinctive pattern of voting behavior reflecting the differences in views between women and men

29 For data, see Center for American Women and Politics, Eagleton Institute of Politics, Rutgers, State University of New Jersey, www.cawp.rutgers.edu/fast_facts/voters/turnout.php (accessed 4/30/09).

30 Pew Research Center for the People and the Press, "Pragmatic Americans Liberal and Conservative on Social Issues: Most Want Middle Ground on Abortion," August 3, 2006, http://people-press.org/report/283/pragmatic-americans-liberal-and-conservative-on-social-issues (accessed 3/24/09).

31 An outstanding research paper along these lines is Ebonya Washington, "Female Socialization: How Daughters Affect Their Legislator Fathers' Voting on Women's Issues," *American Economic Review* 98 (2008): 311–32.

Religion. Religion shapes peoples' values and beliefs and, thus, political ideologies, but it also serves as a strong identity quite apart from what values are at play. One of the clearest examples was the decades-long attachment of Catholics to the Democratic Party. This began in 1924 with the Democratic Party's nomination of Al Smith, a Catholic, for president of the United States. When Democrat John Kennedy became the country's first Catholic president in 1961, that bond was strengthened.[32] The lesson of the Kennedy election is clear: people are much more likely to vote for candidates of the same religion, even after controlling for ideology, party, and other measures of value. This pattern held true for born-again Christians and Jimmy Carter in 1976 and for Mormons and Mitt Romney in 2012.

Geography. Where we live also molds our sense of identity, affecting characteristics such as accent and mode of dress. People from different regions of the country, even from specific states, often strongly identify with others from the same region or state and thus are more likely to trust them and to vote for someone from that background. Also, some people hold negative stereotypes about those from other regions. An unfortunate consequence of the Civil War is a lasting discomfort that many people from the North and South still feel around one another—and that conflict was more than 150 years ago. Yet to this day Americans contest the symbols of that conflict, such as whether a southern state should have a Confederate battle flag as part of its state's symbol.

Other geographic identities are tied to the type of community one lives in. The division between those in urban and rural areas often reflects self-interest—for instance, people from states with predominantly agricultural economies express stronger support for government farm subsidies. But geography also reflects different ways of living, and we tend to identify with people who live like us. Such differences are cultural. Where we shop, which restaurants we frequent, what we do in our spare time, and so forth—all are aspects of local culture that shape our identification with others of similar backgrounds and ways of living.

Residential segregation can also strengthen other aspects of identity politics. People segregate according to income, which might strengthen social class identities, and according to race and ethnicity, which reinforces racial and ethnic identities. Those who live in highly segregated neighborhoods have much stronger identities with their own racial groups, and they also express much stronger prejudices against other groups.[33]

Outgroups. Some groups are defined not by who they are, but by who they are not: they are the outgroups in society. Discrimination is one manifestation of the treatment of an outgroup. In some industries, for example, workers who are not members of a union cannot work in that industry. Such "closed shop" rules benefit union members, but at the cost of nonunion members.

---

32 See Campbell et al., *The American Voter.*

33 Rene R. Rocha and Rodolfo Espino, "Racial Threat, Residential Segregation, and the Policy Attitudes of Anglos," *Political Research Quarterly* 62, no. 2 (2009): 415–26.

Often an outgroup is clearly identifiable and ostracized, leading to systematic discrimination or persecution. When the discrimination is intense, systematic, and long-held, the outgroup can itself develop a particular psychology. Social psychologist James Sidanius expresses this as a social dominance relationship and argues that more numerous groups systematically discriminate against less numerous groups, whose members develop a common identity and see their own situation in the treatment of others of their group.[34] Writing about the particular psychology of African Americans in the United States, Professor Michael Dawson calls this the "linked fate" of African Americans. It has been found in many other societies as well, such as Albanians in Italy.

Discrimination, then, is the collective "bad" against which the identity of all in a given group must act. Even high-income African Americans will, thus, be led by the collective needs and identities of their group to support policies that are likely to help large numbers of low-income or underemployed African Americans. Groups that have experienced severe discrimination over very long periods are most likely to feel a sense of linked fate, which helps account for the persistence of a strong sense of common identity in some groups.[35]

Political, social, and economic discrimination is not limited to race and ethnicity. As we discussed in Chapter 5, the United States has witnessed struggles for equity for many different groups, including women, Catholics, Jews, gay people, divorced fathers, and even urban residents. In all cases, members of these groups had to assert themselves politically to establish or protect their rights to property, to vote, or to equal protection of the laws. Because it is difficult for those with diminished political rights to work inside the legislative process, these people often had to pursue outsider strategies, including protests, propaganda, and litigation. Their rights were abrogated because they were treated as a class or group, and their identity was the target of discrimination. That same identity, however, also served as a source of power, leading these groups to organize and defend their political rights and identities.

PUBLIC OPINION AND POLITICAL KNOWLEDGE

When survey researchers poll the public, they seek to measure what government action the majority of Americans support, or which political party or faction enjoys the support of most people. But what do those responses really mean?

---

34 Being a numerical majority is not necessary. For over a century, blacks in South Africa were oppressed by Afrikkaners, even though the white population accounted for only about 10 percent of all people in the country.

35 Paula D. McClain, Jessica D. Johnson Carew, Eugene Walton, Jr., and Candis S. Watts, "Group Membership, Group Identity, and Group Consciousness: Measures of Racial Identity in American Politics?" *Annual Review of Political Science* 12 (2009): 471–85.

At one level, they might mean that every respondent has weighed all sides of an issue and has made a reasoned judgment about which side is more consistent with his or her interests, values, or identity. Yet, from the advent of public-opinion research, observers have noted that most respondents have a stunning lack of knowledge about specific issues, even about the major political parties. Learned Hand, one of the most distinguished jurists in American history, described the problem of political knowledge as a collective action problem: people have so many other problems to worry about, and most issues are so complex, that simply studying the issues would leave us with little time to do anything else. It is far easier to rely on the wisdom of others.[36] Walter Lippmann, a great American journalist, wrote in the 1920s that this situation creates the opportunity for a learned class of elites to govern—not by winning elections, but by shaping how others think.[37]

One of the most troubling questions about American democracy is this: How is democracy possible when people seem to know so little? Here we present different perspectives on this matter.

Political Knowledge and Preference Stability

People constantly learn of new political events, issues, and personalities as they watch television, surf the web, talk to friends and family, or read the news. In our democracy we expect every citizen to have views about current issues and about who should be entrusted with the nation's leadership, and we expect people to cast informed votes about what government ought to do. Issues, however, come and go, and people are continually learning about new ones.

Some Americans know quite a bit about politics and many hold opinions on several issues. Few Americans, though, devote sufficient time, energy, or attention to politics to really understand or evaluate the myriad issues that face us on a regular basis. Since the advent of polling in the 1930s, studies have repeatedly found that the average American appears to know little about current events or the basic facts of American government.[38]

Low levels of information lead to instability and incoherence in survey responses. Philip Converse, in one of the most widely cited pieces of social science research, noted that most people do not seem to have clear opinions on important issues. Answers they gave to a question one year correlated poorly to answers they gave to the same question two years later; and the answers across issues did not seem to form a consistent pattern or system of belief. The incoherence of respondents' opinions was traceable to their level of education.

36 Learned Hand, "Democracy: Its Presumptions and Realities" in *The Spirit of Liberty: Papers and Addresses of Learned Hand*, Irving Dilliard, ed. (New York: Knopf, 1932).

37 Walter Lippmann, *Public Opinion* (New York: Harcourt, Brace and Company, 1922).

38 Philip E. Converse, "The Nature of Belief Systems in Mass Publics," in *Ideology and Discontent*, David E. Apter, ed. (New York: Free Press, 1964).

Better-educated people gave more coherent answers and more stable answers over time. This research led social scientists to argue that most people are in fact not capable of expressing meaningful opinions on issues because of their low levels of information or cognitive ability.

Converse's views have represented an important pole in the debate over public knowledge and democracy. More recent research, including new analyses of Converse's data, has shown a markedly different picture: it is not that people are incapable of reasoning, but that surveys are imperfect instruments for measuring what people know and how they think. Vague or difficult questions, it turns out, explain much of the apparent incoherence that Converse's respondents expressed. When the data were reanalyzed and further studies were conducted, researchers found much more stability in people's preferences from year to year and much more coherence from issue to issue. Even respondents who had less than a high school education or did not know many common facts about government still expressed fairly coherent and stable preferences.[39] It was the survey, not the people, that failed the test.

Even so, there is something compelling about Converse's account. Why do people seem to know so little, and what might be the consequence of low levels of information about current events and political institutions for the long-run health of democracy?

Attending to the daily goings-on in Washington or the state capital or the city council is costly; it means spending time, and often money as well, to collect, organize, and digest political information.[40] Because individuals anticipate that any informed actions they might take will rarely make much difference and that the costs of informing oneself are rarely trivial, it may be rational to remain ignorant. Thus the rationality principle suggests that people should more profitably devote their personal resources—particularly their time—to more narrowly personal matters. This idea is in turn suggested by the collective action principle, in which the bearing of burdens—such as the cost of becoming informed—is not likely to have much impact in a mass political setting. A more moderate version of "rational" ignorance recognizes that some kinds of information take little time or money to acquire, such as sound bites from television news shows, or tweets from politicians. In such cases, an individual may become partially informed, but usually not in detail.

Precisely because becoming truly knowledgeable about politics requires a substantial investment of time and energy, many Americans seek to acquire political information and to make political decisions by using shortcuts, labels, and stereotypes, rather than by following current events closely. One "inexpensive" way to become informed is to take cues from trusted others—the

39 See Christopher Achen, "Mass Political Attitudes and the Survey Response," *American Political Science Review* 69 (1975): 1281; and Stephen Ansolabehere, Jonathan Rodden, and James M. Snyder, Jr., "The Strength of Issues," *American Political Science Review* 102 (2008): 215–32.

40 Anthony Downs, *An Economic Theory of Democracy* (New York: Harper & Row, 1957).

local minister, the television commentator or newspaper editorialist, an interest-group leader, friends, or relatives.[41] A common shortcut for political evaluation and decision making involves assessing new issues and events through the lenses of one's general beliefs and orientation. Thus if a conservative learns of a plan to expand federal social programs, she might express opposition to the endeavor without bothering to pore over the proposal's details.

These shortcuts are handy, but not perfect. Taking cues from others may lead individuals to accept positions that they would reject if they had more information. And general ideological orientations can be coarse guides to decision making on concrete issues. For example, what position should a liberal take on immigration? Should he favor keeping America's borders open to poor people from all over the world, or should he be concerned that America's open borders create a pool of surplus labor that permits giant corporations to drive down the wages of impoverished American workers? Many other issues defy easy ideological characterization.

Although it is understandable and perhaps inevitable, widespread inattentiveness to politics weakens American democracy in two ways. First, those who lack political information often do not understand where their political interests lie, and thus do not effectively defend them. Second, the large number of politically inattentive or ignorant individuals means that public opinion and the political process can be more easily manipulated by the institutions and forces that seek to do so.

As to the first of these problems, in our democracy millions of ordinary citizens take part in political life, at least to the extent of voting in national elections. But those with little knowledge of the issues, candidates, or voting procedures can find themselves acting against their own preferences and interests. One example is U.S. tax policy. Over the past several decades, the United States has substantially reduced the rate of taxation for its wealthiest citizens.[42] Tax cuts signed into law by President Bush in 2001 and mostly maintained throughout the decade provided a tax break mainly for the top 1 percent of the nation's wage earners, and further tax cuts proposed by the president offered additional benefits to this privileged stratum. Polling data showed that millions of middle-class and lower-middle-class Americans who did not stand to benefit from the president's tax cuts seemed to favor them nonetheless.

These Americans' support for the tax cuts might have been based on principle. As Andrea Campbell argues in her work on the history of public attitudes toward taxes, public opinion toward taxation changed in the 1960s, and since then there has been a consistent, ideological resistance to taxation among

---

41 For a discussion of the role of information in democratic politics, see Arthur Lupia and Mathew D. McCubbins, *The Democratic Dilemma: Can Citizens Learn What They Need to Know?* (New York: Cambridge University Press, 1998).

42 One of the most detailed analyses of the distribution of the tax burden in advanced industrial democracies in the past half century is Thomas Piketty and Emmanuel Saez, "How Progressive Is the U.S. Federal Tax System? Historical and International Perspectives," working paper 12404, National Bureau of Economic Research, 2006, www.nber.org/papers/w12404 (accessed 3/25/09).

political conservatives and most moderates.[43] The support of the 2001 tax cuts among middle- and lower-income people might also have arisen out of ignorance or from following the wrong cue-givers. Larry Bartels, Paul Pierson, and Jacob Hacker, among others, attribute this state of affairs to a lack of political knowledge.[44] Millions of individuals who were unlikely to derive much advantage from President Bush's tax policy thought they would. Bartels has called this phenomenon "misplaced self-interest."[45] Knowledge may not always translate into political power, but lack of knowledge is almost certain to translate into political weakness. And according to the policy principle, the lack of knowledge and concomitant political weakness mean policy disappointment.

Campaigns and other forums for public discourse can change public attitudes on issues by altering the nature of the choices or by informing the public about the effects of policies. Continued debate of the tax issue throughout the 2008 and 2012 presidential campaigns brought about changes in public attitudes toward taxes, especially taxes on the wealthiest segment of the population. During the 2008 presidential election campaign, Barack Obama seized on the tax issue at a time when the economy was worsening and most voters' economic prospects looked bleak. He returned to that theme during the 2012 campaign, promising to raise taxes on the top 2 percent of income earners—those who make at least $250,000 a year. That promise was instrumental in both of Obama's successful election campaigns. In January 2013, staring at potential automatic tax increases on all Americans, he was able to outmaneuver the Republican leadership in Congress and increase taxes on those with incomes over $400,000 per year—an increase that affected only 1 percent of the population, yet nearly failed to make it through Congress.

Stability and the Meaning of Public Opinion

There is a great stability to public opinion in the United States. What people want government to do on specific issues and who people want to have in charge usually changes little from election to election. Benjamin Page and Robert Shapiro's *The Rational Public* (1992) traces public attitudes since the 1950s and finds that on most issues and political attitudes, aggregate public opinion is quite stable. For example, party identification for a large portion of the American public remains stable for life, as do notions of what is right and wrong, racial and ethnic identities, gender identities, and other cultural identities that are formed in childhood. Our occupations and educational achievement also shape our economic interests, which tend to be constant throughout our adult lives. Interests, identities, and values, in turn, influence attitudes about when and how government should act.

---

43 Andrea Campbell, *How Americans Think about Taxes* (Princeton, NJ: Princeton University Press, 2013).

44 Jacob Hacker and Paul Pierson, *Winner Take All Politics* (New York: Simon & Shuster, 2010).

45 Larry M. Bartels, "Homer Gets a Tax Cut: Inequality and Public Policy in the American Mind," *Perspectives on Politics* 3 (2005): 15–31.

One of the most important factors generating stability in public opinion is a fundamental truth about democracy: there is power (and stability) in numbers. Democratic theorists have long understood that aggregation counteracts the effects of political ignorance. When people do not fully know their interests, they will make mistakes. Fortunately, when individuals' opinions and choices are aggregated, in surveys or elections, those errors seem to average out. People may, for example, vote on the basis of how they are doing today, without knowing the macroeconomic indicators such as unemployment and inflation rates. Some people are doing well economically; others are doing poorly. Adding up all those personal experiences, though, will lead to a collective sense of how the society is doing. A wisdom of the masses thus emerges in public opinion polls, election results, and other aggregates of people's preferences. More important, these aggregates are much more stable and more meaningful than individuals' opinions.

But public opinion is not static. At times in American history, the majority of Americans' opinions have changed dramatically and rapidly. Between 1945 and 1965, public opinion toward federal action to promote racial equality swung from majority opposition to majority support for the Civil Rights Act and the Voting Rights Act, as well as for integration of schools and public conveyances. And since the mid-1990s there has been a near about-face in public attitudes toward same-sex marriage. In 1996, Congress passed the Defense of Marriage Act, which defined marriage as a union between one man and one woman for the purpose of federal benefits. A CNN/USA Today/Gallup poll in 1996 showed that 68 percent of Americans opposed same-sex marriage and only 27 percent supported it. By 2015, though, a Pew poll found that 57 percent of Americans supported same-sex marriage and 39 percent opposed it. (See the Analyzing the Evidence unit on pp. 406-7.)

In both cases, public attitudes changed within the span of one or two decades. How and why does public opinion change? In part, the answer lies in the evolving positions of the candidates and parties and elite discourse. As party leaders, celebrities, and other elites debate an issue, the public often follows their cues and shifts sides. The answer also surely lies with public learning. As the public learns about an issue, the implications of government action and inaction become clearer, as does the right thing to do.

In turn, such evolutions in public opinion influence public policy. James Stimson has provided a comprehensive assessment of the link between aggregate public opinion and public policy. His research tracks public opinion on a wide variety of issues from the 1950s to the present. When aggregate public opinion has shifted to the left, as in the 1960s, or to the right, as in the 1980s, public policy has generally followed suit. The high level of responsiveness of policy outcomes to changes in aggregate opinion suggests that the political system follows the general sense of aggregate opinion, or what Stimson calls the policy mood. This result, he argues, strongly suggests that "the magic of aggregation" provides a corrective for the typical citizen's low levels of knowledge.[46]

46 James Stimson, Robert Erikson, and Michael MacKuen, *The Macro Polity* (Cambridge: Cambridge University Press, 1998).

SHAPING OPINION: POLITICAL LEADERS, PRIVATE GROUPS, AND THE MEDIA

The fact that many Americans are inattentive to politics and lack even basic political information means that there is a place for public debate and political discourse. Controversy educates us. Through debate, the average person learns what is important and the information needed to make sensible decisions. The lack of information also creates opportunities to influence how the public thinks. Although direct efforts to manipulate opinion often don't succeed, three forces play especially important roles in shaping opinion. These are the government, private groups, and the news media.

Government and the Shaping of Public Opinion

All governments attempt, to a greater or lesser extent, to influence their citizens' beliefs. But the extent to which public opinion is affected by government public relations efforts is probably limited. The government—despite its size and power—is only one source of information in the United States. Very often government claims are disputed by the media and interest groups, and at times by opposing forces within the government itself. Often too government efforts to manipulate public opinion backfire when the public is made aware of the government's tactics. Thus in 1971 the government's efforts to build popular support for the Vietnam War were hurt when CBS News aired its documentary *The Selling of the Pentagon*, which purported to reveal the extent of government efforts to sway popular sentiment—including planted news stories and faked film footage that had misrepresented the government's activities in Vietnam. These revelations undermined popular trust in government claims.

A hallmark of the administration of President Bill Clinton was the steady use of election-campaign-type techniques to bolster popular enthusiasm for White House initiatives. The president established a political "war room" similar to the one that operated in his campaign headquarters. In the presidential version, representatives from all cabinet departments met daily to discuss and coordinate the president's public-relations efforts. Many of the same consultants and pollsters who directed the successful Clinton campaign were also employed in the selling of the president's programs.[47]

After he assumed office in 2001, George W. Bush asserted that political leaders should base their programs on their own conception of the public interest, not on the polls. This did not mean that Bush ignored public opinion, however. He relied on the pollster Jan van Lohuizen to conduct a low-key operation, sufficiently removed from the limelight to allow the president to

---

47 Gerald F. Seib and Michael K. Frisby, "Selling Sacrifice," *Wall Street Journal*, February 5, 1993, p. 1.

The Contact Hypothesis and Attitudes about Gay Rights

Contributed by
Patrick J. Egan
New York University

Americans' attitudes toward gay rights have evolved significantly over the past 20 years. In 1996, opponents of gay marriage in the United States greatly outnumbered supporters by 65 to 27 percent. By 2015, the year the U.S. Supreme Court established the right to marry for gay couples in *Obergefell v. Hodges,* Americans favored gay marriage by 56 to 39 percent.

Americans' Attitudes toward Same-Sex Marriage, 1996–2015

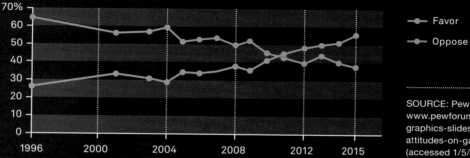

Legend: Favor, Oppose

SOURCE: Pew Research Center, www.pewforum.org/2015/07/29/ graphics-slideshow-changing-- attitudes-on-gay-marriage/ (accessed 1/5/16).

What explains this change in attitudes? A theory from social psychology known as the *contact hypothesis* holds that certain types of contact between in-group and out-group members reduces the stigma directed toward the out-group. In this case, are straight people (the in-group) who know openly gay people (the out-group) more supportive of gay rights? The graphs show that support for gay rights has increased at the same time that more Americans have reported knowing gays and lesbians who have told them personally.

Americans' Contact with Gays and Lesbians, 1985–2013

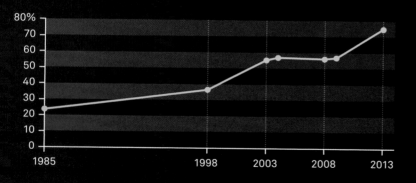

Legend: Americans who report having a gay or lesbian friend, co-worker, or relative who has told them personally

SOURCE: American Enterprise Institute for Public Policy Research, www.scribd.com/doc/ 229377762/Polls-on-Attitudes- on-homosexuality-and-gay-- marriage (accessed 12/29/15).

Furthermore, those who report having gay friends are indeed significantly more supportive of gay rights than those who do not. We can see this by creating a composite score for survey respondents based on their opinions on such issues as gay marriage, adoption, and job discrimination. A score of 100 is fully supportive of all gay rights. Those with gay friends score an estimated 43 on the scale; those who report having no gay friends score only 36 (see graph below).

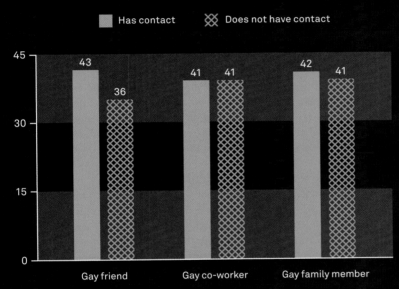

Contact with Gay People and Support for Gay Rights

■ Has contact   ▨ Does not have contact

NOTE: Bars indicate support for gay rights on a 100-point scale after accounting for demographic and political factors that affect the likelihood of contact as well as attitudes on gay rights.

SOURCE: Author's analysis of Newsweek survey data collected by Princeton Survey Research Associates, 2008.

TYPE OF CONTACT

But can we be sure that contact with gay people is actually *causing* increased support for gay rights? One concern is selection bias. Gay people may be selective about disclosing their identity to those friends whom they already know to be supportive, and straight people who hold more tolerant attitudes may be more likely to select gay people as friends.

To further explore this question, we can examine types of contact that are governed less by selection. While we typically do chose our friends, co-workers and family members are essentially chosen for us. These types of contacts thus offer much cleaner tests of the contact hypothesis. As shown in the bar graph above, in these contexts the effect of contact on attitudes is essentially zero (i.e., individuals with gay co-workers or gay family members are no more supportive of gay rights than those without).

This evidence thus runs counter to the contact hypothesis. But it does not entirely settle the question, and some political scientists have presented results in support of the hypothesis. When political scientists find evidence against a hypothesis, they consider different theories. For example, it may be that it is not the *type* but the *quality* of contact that changes attitudes. Definitive answers to these questions await discovery through additional research.

renounce polling while continuing to make use of survey data.[48] At the same time, the Bush White House developed an extensive public-relations program to bolster popular support for the president's policies. Working with a conservative TV personality, the program director coordinated White House efforts to maintain popular support for the administration's war against terrorism. These efforts included presidential speeches, media appearances by administration officials, press conferences, and press releases presenting the administration's views.[49] The White House also sought to sway opinion in foreign countries, even sending officials to present the administration's views on television networks serving the Arab world.

Not all political media strategies work, however. President Obama, striving to maintain the political momentum from his 2008 election campaign, attempted to use social media to keep up the same enthusiasm about his legislative agenda. He brought the expert who developed his campaign's social media strategy into the White House team to organize the effort. The Obama White House maintained a newsy website, a blog, a YouTube channel, a Facebook page, and a Twitter account, but many criticized the low level of actual engagement with the people. Each of these new media was being used like the old media—to talk at people rather than with them, to disseminate information to the press rather than answer reporters' questions. Indeed, many White House reporters felt that the Obama press office was less accessible than its predecessors.[50]

Social media, however, and especially Twitter, has continued to connect the public with politicians in more direct ways. Barack Obama's Twitter account, @BarackObama, had close to 77 million followers as of August 2016; the account for the president of the United States, @POTUS, had 10 million followers. During the 2012 presidential election, Obama had a substantial edge over Republican candidate Mitt Romney in terms of Twitter followers. The Obama campaign boasted 23.6 million followers compared with 1.8 million followers for the Romney campaign. Four years later, in the 2016 presidential primary elections, social media proved to be one of Donald Trump's most distinctive campaign advantages over his Republican opponents. By the end of the primary season, Trump had 10.7 million Twitter followers, while Senators Marco Rubio and Ted Cruz each had 1.5 million follows, and Governor John Kasich had only 400,000.[51]

48 Joshua Green, "The Other War Room," *Washington Monthly*, April 2002.

49 Peter Marks, "Adept in Politics and Advertising, Four Women Shape a Campaign," *New York Times*, November 11, 2001, p. B6.

50 Michael Calderone, "White House News Strategy Causes Concerns about Access," February 15, 2011, http://news.yahoo.com/s/yblog_thecutline/20110215/bs_yblog_thecutline/white-house-media-strategy-causes-concerns-about-access (accessed 8/22/11).

51 Statistica, "Number of Twitter followers of Barack Obama and Mitt Romney as of November 21, 2012," www.statista.com/statistics/243305/number-of-twitter-followers-of-barack-obama-and-mitt-romney/ (accessed 8/26/16).

Private Groups and the Shaping of Public Opinion

The ideas that become prominent in political life are also developed and spread by important economic and political groups seeking to advance their causes. Rational political entrepreneurs pursue strategies that—in an application of the collective action principle—give the groups they lead a decided advantage in the political arena in comparison with latent, unorganized groups. In some instances, in the hope of bringing others over to their side, private groups espouse values they truly believe in—as in the campaign against so-called partial birth abortion, which led to the Partial Birth Abortion Ban Act of 2003. Proponents believed that prohibiting particular sorts of abortions would be a first step toward eliminating all abortions, something they view as a moral imperative.[52] In other cases, groups promote principles designed mainly to further hidden agendas. One famous example is the campaign against cheap imported handguns—dubbed Saturday-night specials—that was covertly financed by the domestic manufacturers of more expensive firearms. The campaign's organizers claimed that cheap handguns pose a grave risk to the public and should be outlawed. The real goal, though, was to protect the economic well-being of the domestic gun industry. A more recent example is the campaign against the alleged sweatshop practices of some American companies manufacturing their products in third world countries. This campaign is mainly financed by U.S. labor unions seeking to protect their members' jobs by discouraging American firms from manufacturing their products abroad.[53]

Typically, ideas are marketed most effectively by groups that have access to financial resources and sufficient skill to promote agendas that will win support. Thus the development and promotion of conservative ideas in recent years have been greatly facilitated by the millions of dollars that conservative corporations and business organizations (such as the U.S. Chamber of Commerce and the Public Affairs Council) spend each year on public information and "issues management." In addition, conservative business leaders have contributed millions of dollars to such conservative institutions as the Heritage Foundation, the Hoover Institution, and the American Enterprise Institute.[54] Many of the ideas that helped the right influence political debate were first articulated by scholars associated with institutions such as these.

Although they usually lack access to financial assets that match those available to their conservative opponents, liberal intellectuals and professionals have ample organizational skills, access to the media, and practice in communicating and using ideas. During the past three decades, the chief vehicle through which liberal intellectuals and professionals have advanced their ideas has been the "public interest group," an institution that relies heavily on voluntary contributions of time and effort from its members. Such groups include Common

---

52 Cynthia Gorney, "Gambling with Abortion," *Harper's Magazine*, November 2004, pp. 33–46.

53 David P. Baron and Daniel Diermeier, "Strategic Activism and Nonmarket Strategy," *Journal of Economics and Management Strategy* (2006).

54 See David Vogel, "The Power of Business in America: A Reappraisal," *British Journal of Political Science* 13 (1983): 19–44.

Cause, the National Organization for Women, the Sierra Club, Friends of the Earth, and Physicians for Social Responsibility.[55] In addition, research conducted at universities and liberal think tanks such as the Brookings Institution often provides the ideas on which liberal politicians rely.

The Media and Public Opinion

The communications media are among the most powerful forces operating in the marketplace of ideas. Most Americans say that their primary source of information about public affairs is news media—newspapers, broadcast and cable news, radio, and Internet news providers. Alternative sources are direct contact with politics, information provided by groups, and information conveyed by family members or co-workers. Certainly, few people actually go to Washington to find out what's going on in American politics, and the population's broad access to media outlets dwarfs the number of households that receive direct mail from organizations and elected officials. Personal conversation is also an important source for information, but people generally avoid controversial political topics in casual conversation.

The mass media, as the term suggests, can be thought of as mediators. They are the conduits through which much information flows. Through newspapers, radio, television, magazines, and the Internet we can learn about what's going on in the world and in our government. Providing this opportunity to learn about the world and politics is the most important way the media contribute to public opinion.

Media outlets also are ubiquitous. More households in the United States have television than have indoor plumbing. Nearly every community has a newspaper. The number of news programs has also expanded tremendously in recent decades. In the 1960s there were only three television news outlets—CBS, NBC, and ABC. They aired evening and nightly news programs and allowed a half-hour slot for news from local affiliates. The rise of cable television in the 1980s brought a 24-hour news station, CNN; expanded news programming through the Public Broadcasting System (PBS); and a network devoted exclusively to broadcasting proceedings of Congress and government agencies, C-SPAN. Important competitors to the big three networks emerged, including Fox and the Spanish-language networks Univision and Telemundo. Today there is no shortage of televised news programming available at all hours.[56]

Technological innovations continue to push change in political communication in the United States. Today, almost 75 percent of Americans have Internet access.[57] Conventional media—from the United States and around the

---

55 See David Vogel, "The Public Interest Movement and the American Reform Tradition," *Political Science Quarterly* 96 (Winter 1980): 607–27.

56 See Stephen Ansolabehere, Roy Behr, and Shanto Iynger, *The Media Game* (New York: Macmillan, 1993).

57 These figures are tracked regularly by the Pew Internet and American Life Project, www.pewinternet.org/Static-Pages/Trend-Data/Whos-Online.aspx (accessed 7/14/11). See also Pew Research Center, "Three Technology Revolutions," www.pewinternet.org/three-technology-revolutions (accessed 6/21/15).

world—have moved much of their content online, often provided for free. The Internet has also spawned new forms of communications, most notably blogs and Twitter, which provide platforms for anyone to have their say. Several websites, such as Google News and RealClearPolitics, are clearinghouses for traditional media, newswire stories, and blogs. This new, highly competitive media environment has radically changed the flow and nature of communication in the United States and the availability of information to the public. In Chapter 14, we discuss the media as a democratic institution at greater length. Our concern here is the media's role in how people learn about politics and public affairs.

Learning through mass media occurs both actively and passively. Active learning occurs when people search for a particular type of program or particular information: you turn on the nightly news to find out what has happened in national and international affairs, or you search the web for information about your member of Congress. Passive learning may be just as important. Many entertainment programs discuss current affairs and issues, such as social issues or an election: you watch the program for entertainment but gain information about politics at the same time. One study found that people learned as much from Oprah as from the evening news.[58] Political advertising is perhaps the most common form of passive information. During the last month of national political campaigns, three or four political advertisements often air during one commercial break in a primetime television program.

Mass media are our primary source for information about current affairs. They influence how Americans understand politics not just through the volume of information available but also through what is presented and how. Editors, reporters, and others involved in preparing the content of the news must ultimately decide what topics to cover, what facts to include, and whom to interview. Journalists usually try to present issues fairly, but it is difficult, perhaps impossible, to be perfectly objective. In fact, psychologists have identified two potential pathways through which media coverage shapes what people think. First, the news sets the public's agenda. Through this **agenda-setting effect**, the media cues people to think about some issues rather than others; it makes some considerations more salient than others. Suppose, for example, that the local news covers crime to the exclusion of all else. When someone who watches the local news regularly thinks about the mayoral election, crime is more likely to be his or her primary consideration, compared with someone who does not watch the local news. Psychologists call this **priming**.

Second, news coverage of an issue frames the way the issue is defined. Coverage of crime, to continue the example, may include a report on every murder that happens in a large city. Such coverage would likely make it seem that murder occurs much more often than it actually does. This in turn might heighten viewers' sense of insecurity or threat, leading to an exaggerated sense of risk of violent crime and increased support for tough police practices.[59] **Framing** refers to the media's power to influence how events and issues are interpreted.

agenda-setting effect

The power to bring attention to particular issues and problems

priming

A process of preparing the public to take a particular view of an event or a political actor

framing

The power of the media to influence how events and issues are interpreted

---

58 See Matthew Baum, *Soft News Goes to War* (Princeton, NJ: Princeton University Press, 2006).

59 The seminal work on priming and framing in public policy and politics is Shanto Iyengar and Donald Kinder, *News That Matters* (Chicago: University of Chicago Press, 1987).

Priming and framing are often viewed as twin evils. One can distract us from other important problems, and the other can make us think about an issue or a politician in a biased way. The cumulative effects on public opinion depend ultimately on the variety of issues covered and the diversity of perspectives represented. That, after all, is the idea behind the guarantee of a free press in the First Amendment to the Constitution. Free and open communication media allow the greatest likelihood that people will learn about important issues, that they will gain the information they need to distinguish good ideas from bad ones, and that they will learn which political leaders and parties can best represent their interests.

In this regard, the most significant framing effects take the form of the balance in the information available to people. Those in politics—elected officials, candidates, leaders of organized groups—work hard to influence what the news covers. A competitive political environment usually translates into a robust flow of information. However, in some political environments only one view gets expressed and is reflected in the media. Congressional elections are a case in point. Incumbent politicians today raise about three times more money than their challengers. As a result, House elections often have a gross imbalance in the amount of advertising and news coverage between the two campaigns, that of the incumbent and that of the challenger. This will likely affect public opinion, because voters hear the incumbent's views and message more often than the challenger's.

A further example of an imbalance in news coverage arises with the president and Congress. Presidential press conferences and events receive much more coverage than the press events of the leaders of the House or Senate. This gives the president the upper hand in setting the public agenda through the media, because the public is more likely to hear the president's arguments for a particular policy. Of course, a president who pursues an ill-advised policy can easily squander this advantage. If the policy fails, the president's media advantage can be short-lived. In 2002, for example, President George W. Bush convinced the nation that Iraq was developing weapons of mass destruction and the United States needed to topple Saddam Hussein's regime immediately. The invasion occurred and Hussein's regime quickly fell, but large caches of chemical and nuclear weapons were never found, and the United States remained in Iraq for a decade. The backlash against these policies cost the Republicans support among the public, contributing to their loss of control of Congress in the 2006 election, and ultimately the presidency in 2008. The power of the president is the power to persuade, but control of information for political aims must be used with caution.

It is often difficult to measure bias in the media. Ultimately, judgment about media bias rests with the consumers—do they get the coverage they demand? Do they get too much coverage of some issues or candidates, and too little of others? During the 2016 primary elections, the Pew Research Center conducted a public opinion survey to ascertain whether some candidates received too much attention from the media and others too little. Seventy-five percent of respondents said that news organizations gave Donald Trump "too much coverage" and only 19 percent said news coverage of Trump was "just about right." Most respondents felt that Ted Cruz and John Kasich, Trump's main Republican rivals, received about the right amount of coverage or too little coverage. Respondents felt that coverage of the Democratic primary was more balanced.

Forty-eight percent said that news organizations gave Hillary Clinton about the right amount of coverage, while 53 percent said the same about her Democratic rival, Bernie Sanders.[60]

Today, it is easy to learn about public affairs and to hear different opinions—even when we don't want to. Furthermore, new forms of media likely have facilitated learning and have muted some of the biases that may emerge through priming and framing. No one voice or perspective dominates our multifaceted media environment and competitive political system. And biases in the media often reflect not the lack of outlets or restrictive editorial control but, rather, failures of political competition.

MEASURING PUBLIC OPINION

A century ago, American political leaders gauged public opinion by people's applause and the size of crowds at meetings. This did not necessarily produce accurate knowledge of public opinion. It did, however, give political leaders confidence in their public support—and therefore confidence in their ability to govern by consent.

Abraham Lincoln and Stephen Douglas debated each other seven times in the summer and autumn of 1858, two years before they became presidential nominees. Their debates took place before audiences in parched cornfields and courthouse squares. A century later most presidential debates, although seen by millions, take place before a few hundred people, usually in auditoriums at university campuses, but they are really staged for national television audiences. The public's response cannot be experienced firsthand. This distance between leaders and followers is one of the agonizing problems of modern democracy. The media provide information to millions of people, but they are not so efficient at providing leaders with feedback from the public. Is government by consent possible when the scale of communication is so large and impersonal? To compensate for the decline in their ability to experience public opinion for themselves, leaders have turned to science—in particular, the science of opinion polling.

It is no secret that politicians and public officials make extensive use of **public-opinion polls** to help them decide whether to run for office, what policies to support, how to vote on important legislation, and what types of appeals to make in their campaigns. President Lyndon Johnson was famous for carrying the latest Gallup and Roper poll results in his pocket, and it is widely believed that he began to withdraw from politics because the polls reported losses in public support. All recent presidents and other major political figures work closely with pollsters and consultants who themselves are steeped in the polls.

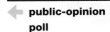

public-opinion poll

A scientific instrument for measuring public opinion

60 Pew Research Center, "Views of the primaries, press coverage of candidates, attitudes about government and the country," www.people-press.org/2016/03/31/1-views-of-the-primaries-press-coverage-of-candidates-attitudes-about-government-and-the-country/ (accessed 8/26/16).

Constructing Public Opinion from Surveys

The population that we are interested in studying is usually quite large, such as all adults or all voters in the United States. To conduct their polls, survey researchers first identify the relevant population and choose a **sample** of the total population. The selection of this sample is important. Above all, it must be representative: the views of those in the sample must accurately and proportionately reflect the views of the whole. To a large extent, the validity of the poll's results depends on the sampling procedure used.

Sampling Techniques and Selection Bias. The most common techniques for choosing such a sample are probability sampling and random digit dialing. In the case of **probability sampling**, the pollster begins with a list of the population to be surveyed. This list is called the sampling frame. After each member of the population has been assigned a number, a table of random numbers or a computerized random selection process is used to pick those members of the population to be surveyed.

It is important to emphasize, first, that a sample selected in this manner produces a subset of the population that is representative of the population. It is also important that whatever is learned about this representative sample can also be attributed to the larger population with a high level of assurance. Random sampling helps ensure that the way in which people are chosen for the study is not related to the individuals' characteristics, such as their level of education.

This technique for constructing a sample is appropriate when the entire population can be identified. For example, all students registered at Texas colleges and universities can be identified from college records, and a sample of them can easily be drawn. For a national sample of Americans, however, this technique is not feasible, because no complete list of Americans exists.[61]

Exit polls conducted during national elections use areas to construct their sample. The polling organization randomly selects a set of precincts (voting stations) within each state throughout the nation—usually, between 50 and 150 such locations. The polling organization trains individuals to conduct the exit poll on Election Day at the voting stations. The pollster approaches people as they leave the voting area and persuades them to fill out the exit poll questionnaire. To guard against biases, the pollster is instructed on how many people to choose and which people to approach, such as every seventh person. As the day progresses, the pollsters tally the results of the exit poll and report them to the organization, which tallies those figures and distributes them to the media outlets that use them on election night.

For the typical public-opinion poll today, national samples are usually drawn using **random digit dialing**, in which a computerized random-number generator produces a list of as many 10-digit numbers as the pollster deems necessary. The pollster is trained how to interview people and record responses. Because there are biases in who answers the phone in a given home, pollsters randomly choose an adult in the house, such as the "oldest female adult," "oldest male

Margin glossary

sample

A small group selected by researchers to represent the most important characteristics of an entire population

probability sampling

A method used by pollsters to select a representative sample in which every individual in the population has an equal probability of being selected as a respondent

random digit dialing

A poll in which respondents are selected at random from a list of 10-digit telephone numbers, with every effort made to avoid bias in the construction of the sample

---

61 Herbert Asher, *Polling and the Public* (Washington, DC: CQ Press, 2001), p. 64.

adult," or "youngest adult male." Given that more than 95 percent of American households have telephones, this technique provides very good coverage. Randomization—of which household is chosen and of which person is interviewed in each household—helps guard against potential biases.

Recently, however, with the growth in cell phone use and the enactment of "do-not-call" legislation to discourage telemarketers, random digit dialing has become less reliable. Computerized methods of random digit dialing have difficulty reaching households that are registered on the do-not-call list or that have only cell phones. In addition, some people are simply more willing than others to talk to pollsters. If pollsters could be certain that those who respond to their surveys simply reflect the views of those who refuse to respond, there would be no problem. Some studies suggest, however, that the views of respondents and nonrespondents can differ, especially along social-class lines. Middle- and upper-middle-class individuals are more likely to respond to surveys than their working-class counterparts.[62] The experience with cell phones and random digit dialing phone polls points to a general feature of public-opinion research, driven by the ways that people communicate in today's society.

Innovations in technology and the spread of new modes of communication may create problems for establishing research methods, but they can also create opportunities. These new methods often offer much cheaper ways to contact people and conduct research, but their newness usually means that not everyone uses them equally. The challenge for capturing the potential of new technologies is to figure out how to reach an acceptably broad segment of the population using these methods and how to ensure the representativeness of the resulting samples.

Over the past 10 years a new set of firms have begun conducting survey research over the Internet. They use a variety of techniques to enlist people into their surveys, such as pop-up ads on websites. However, not everyone uses the Internet, and people respond to pop-ups differently. To correct for such issues, Internet survey firms try different ways of reaching different audiences over the Internet and different sorts of appeals to potential respondents. After collecting survey responses, Internet survey firms (indeed, all polling firms) further adjust their data to correct for segments of the population that they over- or underrepresent.

Although these technical aspects of how surveys are constructed may seem obscure, the importance of sampling was brought home early in the history of political polling. A 1936 *Literary Digest* poll predicted that the Republican presidential candidate, Alf Landon, would defeat the Democrat, Franklin Delano Roosevelt, in that year's election. But the election ended in a Roosevelt landslide. The main problem with the survey was **selection bias** in drawing the sample: pollsters had relied on telephone directories and automobile registration rosters to produce a sampling frame. During the Great Depression, however, only wealthy Americans owned telephones and automobiles. Thus the millions of working-class Americans who constituted Roosevelt's principal base of support were excluded from the sample.

A more recent instance of polling error caused by selection bias occurred during the 1998 Minnesota gubernatorial election. A poll conducted by the *Minneapolis Star*

◀ **selection bias**

A polling error in which the sample is not representative of the population being studied, so that some opinions are over- or underrepresented

---

62 John Goyder, Keith Warriner, and Susan Miller, "Evaluating Socio-Economic Status Bias in Survey Nonresponse," *Journal of Official Statistics* 18, no. 1 (2002): 1–11.

Tribune just six weeks before the election showed the former professional wrestler Jesse Ventura running a distant third to the Democratic candidate, Hubert Humphrey III (who seemed to have the support of 49 percent of the electorate), and the Republican, Norm Coleman (whose support stood at 29 percent). Only 10 percent of those polled said they were planning to vote for Ventura. But on Election Day, Ventura outpolled both Humphrey and Coleman. Why had the preelection poll been so wrong? It was conducted only among individuals who had voted in the previous election in an effort to take account of the likelihood that respondents would actually vote. Ventura, however, brought to the polls not only individuals who had not voted in the last election but also many people who had never voted before in their lives.[63] Selection bias may also have contributed to inaccurate predictions that Hillary Clinton would win the 2016 presidential election, as many groups turned out to vote for Donald Trump at higher-than-usual rates (see Figure 10.2).

Polling organizations are ever mindful of these fateful stories. Their business depends on producing accurate representations of the American public's opinions and behavior. The challenges are to keep pace with the ever-changing ways that people communicate and to anticipate the sometimes surprising nature of the American electorate.

Sample Size. The degree of reliability in polling is also a function of sample size. In U.S. polls, a typical sample ranges from 450 to 1,500 respondents. This number reflects a trade-off between cost and degree of precision desired. A larger and hence more costly sample size is associated with greater precision in making generalizations to the full population than is a smaller sample size.

The chance that the sample does not accurately represent the population from which it is drawn is the **sampling error**, or *margin of error*. The margin of error acknowledges that any given sample may not perfectly represent the full population. A typical survey of 1,500 respondents, for example, will have a sampling error of approximately 3 percent. Thus, for example, when a preelection poll indicates that 51 percent of voters surveyed favor the Republican candidate and 49 percent support the Democratic candidate, the margin of error tells us that in fact between 48 and 54 percent of voters in the population favor the Republican, and between 46 and 52 percent support the Democrat. The precision of the poll in this case does not permit a clear prediction of a winner.

Attempts to predict the final outcome of an election allow us to examine whether some survey methods are more accurate than others and which surveys should be viewed as most credible.[64] Figure 10.2 shows the results from

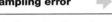

sampling error

A polling error that arises on account of the small size of the sample

---

63 Carl Cannon, "A Pox on Both Our Parties," in *The Enduring Debate: Classic and Contemporary Readings in American Politics*, 2nd ed., David T. Canon, Anne Khademian, and Kenneth R. Mayer, eds. (New York: Norton, 2000), p. 389.

64 For a discussion of the difficulties with polls, especially in trying to assess the preferences of specific subgroups in the population, see David Leal, Matt Barreto, Jongho Lee, and Rodolfo O. de la Garza, "The Latino Vote in the 2004 Election," *PS: Political Science and Politics* 38 (January 2005): 41–9.

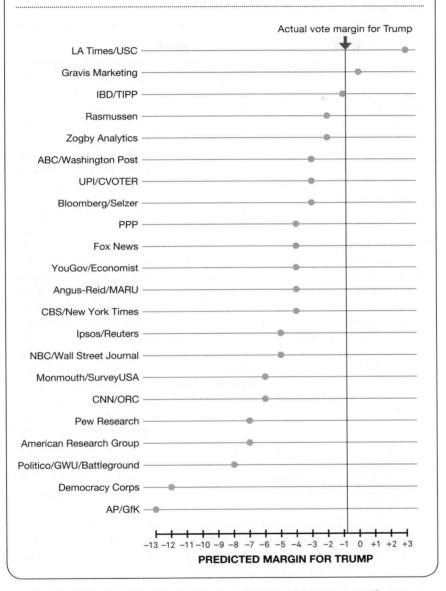

Figure 10.2

ACCURACY OF FINAL PREELECTION POLLS, 2016

Actual vote margin for Trump

LA Times/USC	
Gravis Marketing	
IBD/TIPP	
Rasmussen	
Zogby Analytics	
ABC/Washington Post	
UPI/CVOTER	
Bloomberg/Selzer	
PPP	
Fox News	
YouGov/Economist	
Angus-Reid/MARU	
CBS/New York Times	
Ipsos/Reuters	
NBC/Wall Street Journal	
Monmouth/SurveyUSA	
CNN/ORC	
Pew Research	
American Research Group	
Politico/GWU/Battleground	
Democracy Corps	
AP/GfK	

−13 −12 −11 −10 −9 −8 −7 −6 −5 −4 −3 −2 −1 0 +1 +2 +3

PREDICTED MARGIN FOR TRUMP

SOURCES: All poll data, except LATimes/USC, from HuffPost Pollster: www.elections.huffingtonpost.com/pollster (accessed 11/10/2016). Poll results are from the most recent polls prior to election day in the database. USC/LATimes data from: www.cesrusc.org/election/ (accessed 11/11/2016). Popular vote margin data from 'CNN 2016 Election Results:' www.cnn.com/election/results (accessed 11/11/2016).

22 different organizations' final preelection polls before the 2016 presidential election. The vertical line is the actual election outcome, and each dot is a survey organization's estimate of Trump's margin of victory. Most polls were correct in predicting the direction of the popular vote in Clinton's favor (even though she did not win in the electoral college). But polls were much less accurate in predicting the size of the vote margin.

Survey Design. Much of the science of public-opinion research concerns the appropriate way to ask questions. If a question is vague or confusing or doesn't match an individual survey respondent's opinion, the respondent will likely skip the question or answer in a confused way. Thus researchers frame questions in a balanced way and offer as full a set of options as possible. Moreover, leading questions prompt respondents to give answers that fit with the questions' bias or that match what they think the surveyor would like them to say. The challenge is to discover ways of asking questions that allow people to express their own views.

Sometimes, seemingly minor differences in the wording of a question can convey vastly different meanings to respondents and thus produce quite different response patterns (Figure 10.3). For example, for many years the University of Chicago's National Opinion Research Center has asked respondents whether they think the federal government is spending too much, too little, or about the right amount of money on "assistance for the poor." Answering this question, about two-thirds of all respondents say that the government is spending too little. However, the same survey also asks whether the government spends too much, too little, or about the right amount for "welfare." When the word *welfare* is substituted for *assistance for the poor*, about half of all respondents indicate that too much money is being spent.[65]

Vague or poorly worded questions create **measurement error**, which can skew data analyses away from the true results. Suppose that on a given piece of legislation 75 percent of people support the bill and 25 percent oppose it. In a poorly designed survey question about the legislation, the wording is so confusing that one in five respondents misinterprets the meaning. In this case, then, one-fifth of the 75 percent (or 15 percent of all respondents) who support the bill will say they oppose it, and one-fifth of the 25 percent who oppose the bill (or 5 percent) will say they support it. As a result, only 65 percent of those surveyed will say that they support the bill and 35 percent will say that they do not.[66] In this way, measurement error can bias survey results.

You, as a savvy consumer of political data, should be mindful of what surveys ask of respondents and of possible confusion or slant in any question. As our discussion has shown, the challenge is to ask questions that allow people to express their preferences and that capture what people really think about important issues. It is a good exercise to try writing a survey. The typical public-opinion survey over the

measurement error

→

The failure to identify the true distribution of opinion within a population because of errors such as ambiguous or poorly worded questions

---

65 Michael R. Kagay and Janet Elder, "Numbers Are No Problem for Pollsters, Words Are," *New York Times*, August 9, 1992, p. E6.

66 The calculation is that the percentage who say they support it are four-fifths of the 75 percent who really support it (60 percent of all people in the survey) plus one-fifth of the 25 percent (5 percent of all people in the survey) who do not support it but mistakenly say that they do. The total percentage who say they support the bill is 60 percent plus 5 percent.

Figure 10.3
IT DEPENDS ON HOW YOU ASK

Variation 1:
The AP reported classified information about U.S. anti-terrorism efforts and prosecutors have obtained AP's phone records through a court order. Do you think this action by federal prosecutors is or is not justified?

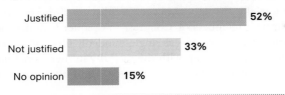

Justified	52%
Not justified	33%
No opinion	15%

Variation 2:
As you may have heard, the U.S. Justice Department secretly seized extensive telephone records of calls on both work and personal phones for reports and editors working for the Associated Press in the spring of 2012. At the time, the news organization, using government leaks, had broken a story about an international terrorist plot. The government obtained the phone records without giving the news organization prior notice, as is customary. Do you think the government was probably justified in taking these actions or does this sound more like the government went too far?

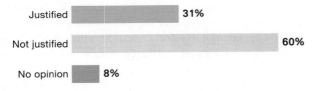

Justified	31%
Not justified	60%
No opinion	8%

SOURCE: Pew Research Center, www.pewresearch.org/fact-tank/2013/05/22/polling-when-public-attention-is-limited-different-questions-different-results (accessed 5/1/16).

ANALYZING THE EVIDENCE

In 2012, the federal government subpoenaed the phone records of Associated Press journalists as part of an investigation after AP reported classified information regarding U.S. anti-terrorism efforts. Pollsters asking whether the government's actions were justified got different results, depending on the specifics of the question. What differences in the two versions of the question do you think account for the different answers?

phone lasts 5 to 10 minutes, and each question takes about 15 seconds to ask and answer. The typical survey consists of 20 to 40 questions that not only cover a broad set of current issues but also take into account respondents' demographic characteristics. Each question, then, must summarize the issue at stake in few words and capture the full range of possible or likely answers in a reasonably small set of options.

HOW DOES PUBLIC OPINION INFLUENCE GOVERNMENT POLICY?

In democratic nations, leaders should pay heed to public opinion, and most evidence suggests that they do. Although public policy and public opinion do not always coincide, in general the government's actions are consistent with citizens' preferences. There are three important ways in which public opinion influences government policy.

Electoral Accountability.

Electoral Accountability. The Constitution of the United States gives the public the power to change government by voting their representatives out of office. Originally this means of popular control extended only to the public for the House of Representatives, but it has since been extended to the U.S. Senate, and there are increasing calls to eliminate the last vestige of indirect representation, the Electoral College. We discussed the power that constituents have on their members of Congress in Chapter 6. Today, political scientists see members of Congress as single-mindedly focused on reelection. Legislators who are out of step with the majority in their constituency quickly find themselves out of office. We will discuss how elections work in the next chapter.

Building Coalitions. Legislative politics, however, goes beyond a member's own constituency. In order for legislation to pass, it is important that any bill have public support (or at least, no intense public opposition) in a majority of House districts and a majority of states (the Senate's constituencies) and for a majority of people in the nation (the president's constituency). It is not enough, then, for a legislator to be attentive to her own constituency; she must be attuned to public opinion nationwide. Likewise, no president can push his agenda in Congress without having the support of the public, at least in a majority of states and districts (see the Policy Principle case study on President George W. Bush's attempt to reform Social Security on p. 421). Some presidents have managed to pass major legislation even in the face of public opposition, but the consequences have usually been disastrous for his party. In January 2010, for example, in the face of stiff public opposition, President Obama pushed through the Affordable Care Act. Ten months later, the Democratic Party suffered a stunning defeat in the House and nearly lost its nine-seat majority in the Senate. As Republicans continued to campaign against the act, in 2014 the Democrats lost their majority in the Senate as well as additional seats in the House.

Input in Rule-Making and Legal Decisions. Some laws explicitly rely on public opinion or social science evidence concerning political behavior. The federal and state governments have various open meeting and sunshine laws that allow for public commentary on new rules and new laws. Federal advisory committees consist of experts and stakeholders—such as scientists, industry representatives, public interest group advocates, and people who are very interested in a subject—who advise federal agencies on the likely impact of particular rules or laws. These committees cover an enormous range of subjects and agencies, from approval of drugs by the Food and Drug Administration (FDA) to space exploration by NASA to licensing of telecommunications under the Federal Communications Commission (FCC). Such committees operate in an open manner, posting public notices

Public Opinion and Reforming Social Security

Presidents consider many institutional and political factors when putting together a major policy initiative, including likely support for the proposed law in Congress, reactions of organized interests, the coherence of the policy, and whether the public supports or opposes the law. Presidents need to muster public support behind a law in order to move forward, and failing to do so can lead to the end of important presidential initiatives.

Reform of Social Security has been particularly difficult because of widespread support for the benefit program. The looming surge in retirements of baby boomers (those born between 1946 and 1964) has threatened to bankrupt Social Security, as payments to retirees exceed contributions made by younger workers into the fund. President George W. Bush decided to take on the Social Security problem.

The president made Social Security reform the centerpiece of his domestic policy agenda at the start of his second term. His plan was to "privatize" Social Security. Younger workers would have the option to invest some of their Social Security tax in private accounts. Those workers would earn the interest on that investment, but would get a smaller check from the government when they retired. Bush's State of the Union address in January 2005 emphasized the need for reform and the promise of private retirement accounts, and over the succeeding months his administration undertook a massive campaign, orchestrated by Karl Rove and Kevin Mehlman, to promote the privatization plan.

However, the campaign failed to win over the American public. A Pew Research survey conducted in 2005 noted that "Despite Bush's intensive campaign to promote the idea, the percentage of Americans who say they favor private accounts has tumbled to 46% in Pew's latest nationwide survey, down from 54% in December and 58% in September. Support has declined as the public has become increasingly aware of the president's plan. More than four-in-ten (43%) say they have heard a

Demonstrators protest Social Security reform proposed in 2005.

lot about the proposal, nearly double the number who said that in December (23%)."[1]

Eventually the negative public reaction to the plan started to drag down the president's approval ratings. Conservative commentator Bill Kristol, editor of the *Weekly Standard*, put the matter bluntly, "The negative effect of the Social Security [campaign] is underestimated. Once you make that kind of mistake, people tend to be less deferential to your decisions."[2]

The public had spoken. By summer of 2005, it was evident that the plan, however sound it was as a policy, had failed to muster the public support needed to win approval in Congress. Fearing further damage to President Bush's reputation and to his efforts on other policies, the administration decided to drop what had been, just six months earlier, the central focus of his domestic policy agenda. Even a popular president with the institutional advantage of a unified government usually cannot get his policy agenda enacted into law without public support for those specific policies.

[1] Pew Research Center, "Bush Failing in Social Security Push," March 2, 2005, www.people-press.org/2005/03/02/bush-failing-in-social-security-push (accessed 4/8/16).
[2] Jim VandeHei and Peter Baker, "President Struggles to Regain His Pre-Hurricane Swagger," September 24 2005, *Washington Post*, www.washingtonpost.com/wp-dyn/content/article/2005/09/23/AR2005092302182.html (accessed 5/23/16).

of meetings, hearings, or proposed rules; and they collect public commentary on proposed rules.

As a somewhat different example, under the Voting Rights Act (discussed in Chapters 5 and 11) federal courts rely heavily on information about the political preferences of ethnic and racial groups, including electoral and survey data, and on historical patterns of discrimination. Historians and political scientists have been vitally important in conveying what is known about how different racial groups vote in a given state or county, and how they are viewed and treated in politics and other settings. This information is crucial in deciding whether states have discriminated against racial minorities in the administration of election laws.[67]

Public opinion and public policy, however, are not always in alignment. The institutions of American government were designed to have significant public influence and accountability, but they were also designed to work slowly and deliberately, to protect individual rights and property. The complex institutions of the American government, then, often create disparities between what the public wants and what the government does (or does not do).

Inconsistencies between opinion and policy might be reduced if the federal government of the United States used ballot initiatives nationwide, as many states do. This procedure allows propositions to be voted into law by the electorate, bypassing most of the normal machinery of representative government. Ballot measures in the states have been used to restrict property tax increases; ban the use of racial or gender preferences in government employment, contracting, and university admissions; enact environmental regulations; legalize marijuana; limit campaign spending; regulate auto insurance; change the rules governing redistricting; and opt out of the Affordable Care Act.[68] Some states even use initiatives to pass budget agreements when the legislature does not want to be held responsible for casting unpopular votes.[69]

However, government by initiative offers little opportunity for reflection and compromise. Voters are presented with a proposition, usually sponsored by a special interest group, and must take it or leave it. Perhaps the true will of the people lies somewhere between the positions held by various interest groups. In a representative assembly, as opposed to a referendum campaign, a compromise position might be more satisfactory to all voters. This capacity for compromise is one reason the Founders strongly favored representative government rather than direct democracy.

---

67 David Epstein, Richard Pildes, Rudolfo de la Garza, and Sharyn O'Haloran, eds., *The Future of the Voting Rights Act* (New York: Russell Sage Foundation, 2006).

68 David Broder, *Democracy Derailed: Initiative Campaigns and the Power of Money* (New York: Harcourt, 2000).

69 Robert Tomsho, "Liberals Take a Cue from Conservatives: This Election, the Left Tries to Make Policy with Ballot Initiatives," *Wall Street Journal*, November 6, 2000, p. A12.

CONCLUSION: GOVERNMENT AND THE WILL OF THE PEOPLE

Representative democracy was a novel form of government when the framers created the Constitution. Behind this radical system lies one central idea—that the government reflects the will of the people. People have the opportunity to express their preferences through elections, public meetings and organizations, and free expression and debate. Public deliberations and public choices, it is conjectured, aggregate individuals' preferences and opinions to form the collective "will of the people" that would guide those in office. This chapter has explored the meaning of this idea today.

We no longer speak of the people of the United States as an organic whole with a coherent will. Rather, we characterize the "people" as the aggregation of individuals' preferences about the choices presented to them—in a phrase, public opinion. The individual is the foundation of public opinion. Politicians assume that individuals will pursue their own preferences; will protect and expand their own property and wealth; will express their own ideologies about what is right; will pursue their own happiness above the interests of the state or the community. The aggregation of all those actions expresses the public's opinion.

Politicians take risks when attempting to convince the public to follow them, for they cannot anticipate which way the public will break on any given issue; they must hope they have chosen issues that people care about and have framed policies in ways that seem consistent with the interests and values of a majority of voters. Politicians do this through speeches and op-eds, political advertising, and working with the media to present issues in a certain way. Of course, their opponents also try to influence how people think. The public benefits from competition among politicians, as it brings out the best arguments for and against a given policy or government action. This is the real testament to the power of public opinion.

Public opinion and public policy are not always in agreement, and several factors contribute to this lack of consistency. First, the nominal majority on a particular issue may not be as committed as the intensely committed minority, which may be more willing to commit time, energy, and resources to the affirmation of its opinions. In the case of gun control, although proponents are in the majority by a wide margin, most do not regard the issue as critically important to themselves and are unwilling to commit much effort to advancing their cause. Opponents, by contrast, are intensely committed, well organized, and well financed; as a result, they usually carry the day. In accordance with the institution principle, the collective action principle, and the policy principle, intense commitment, organization, and financial resources are potent assets in the legislature, the executive bureaucracy, and the courts.

Second, the framers of the Constitution, as we saw in Chapter 2, sought to create a system of government that was based on popular consent but did not invariably and automatically translate shifting popular sentiments into public policies. As a result, the American governmental process includes arrangements such as an appointed judiciary that can produce policy decisions that may run contrary to prevailing popular sentiment—at least for a time.

The succeeding chapters will consider how public opinion manifests itself through different institutions of democracy—elections, parties, organized interests, and communications media. As we discuss these institutions, it will be useful to keep in mind how we have described public opinion in this chapter. Most people in the United States hold fairly centrist or moderate views on most questions. Neither right nor left nor center commands an outright majority of public support on any issue of importance. Anyone adhering to one of these views must reach out beyond her particular ideological slant in order to find a coalition large enough to capture the support of a majority.

Democracy is complicated further by the heterogeneity of American society. The nation's political institutions tolerate all manner of religious and political beliefs and all manner of social and economic relations, and the United States has long been a refuge for immigrants seeking asylum or a better way of life. As a result, ours is one of the most diverse societies in the world, with freedom to practice every major religion, with a wide spectrum of political and social organizations, and with great concentrations of wealth and poverty. This would seem to be a recipe not for consensus but for disagreement and conflict, even civil conflict.

The open society in the United States, however, has worked for over two centuries because its members have a strong commitment to democracy itself. Americans, in essence, agree to disagree. We agree that it is best to tolerate many different opinions. We value liberty and restrain the government from imposing itself on how people think or express themselves politically. We further agree to allow the institutions of democracy to help us reach collective decisions about who should govern and how they should govern. The next four chapters examine in detail those institutions—the institutions of elections, of political parties, of interest groups, and of the media and communications technologies.

For Further Reading

Althaus, Scott. *Collective Preferences and Democratic Politics*. New York: Cambridge University Press, 2003.

Ansolabehere, Stephen, Jonathan Rodden, and James M. Snyder, Jr. "Purple America." *Journal of Economic Perspectives* 20, no. 2 (spring 2006): 97–118.

Bartels, Larry. *Unequal Democracy: The Political Economy of the New Gilded Age.* Princeton, NJ: Princeton University Press, 2008.

Berinsky, Adam. *In Time of War: Understanding Public Opinion from World War II to Iraq.* Chicago: University of Chicago Press, 2009.

Erikson, Robert S., and Kent L. Tedin. *American Public Opinion: Its Origins, Content, and Impact.* 8th ed. New York: Pearson, 2010.

Fiorina, Morris, Samuel Abrams, and Jeremy Pope. *Culture War?* 3rd ed. New York: Pearson, 2010.

Ginsberg, Benjamin. *The Captive Public: How Mass Opinion Promotes State Power.* New York: Basic Books, 1986.

Jacobson, Gary. *A Divider, Not a Uniter: George W. Bush, the American People, the 2006 Election, and Beyond.* White Plains, NY: Longman, 2007.

Kinder, Donald, and Cindy Kam. *Us against Them: Ethnocentric Foundations of American Opinion.* Chicago: University of Chicago Press, 2010.

Lee, Taeku. *Mobilizing Public Opinion.* Chicago: University of Chicago Press, 2002.

Lupia, Arthur, and Mathew D. McCubbins. *The Democratic Dilemma: Can Citizens Learn What They Need to Know?* New York: Cambridge University Press, 1998.

McCarty, Nolan, Keith Poole, and Howard Rosenthal. *Polarized America: The Dance of Ideology and Unequal Riches.* Princeton, NJ: Princeton University Press, 2007.

Page, Benjamin I., and Robert Y. Shapiro. *The Rational Public: Fifty Years of Trends in Americans' Policy Preferences.* Chicago: University of Chicago Press, 1992.

Stimson, James A. *Public Opinion in America: Moods, Cycles, and Swings.* 2nd ed. Boulder, CO: Westview Press, 1999.

Zaller, John R. *The Nature and Origins of Mass Opinion.* New York: Cambridge University Press, 1992.

11

PART 1 2 ✖ 4

DEMOCRATIC POLITICS

Elections

Chapter Outline

- Institutions of Elections
- How Voters Decide
- Campaigns: Money, Media, and Grass Roots
- The 2012 and 2014 Elections
- Conclusion: Elections and Accountability

The most profound expression of an individual's political preferences is the vote. It is a blunt but effective instrument for controlling the government. Citizens usually cannot decide directly what laws are enacted, what the tax or interest rates will be, or whether to declare war. Citizens can affirm a commitment to stay the course or to change their government when they think a new direction is needed. It is our way of reining in government and ensuring that elected officials remain attentive to public preferences. Elections have proved remarkably successful at ensuring continual renewal of government through peaceful means.

Frequent, regular elections are the hallmark of democracy. The United States embraces this idea more intensely than any other democracy. America has elections very frequently, with great regularity, and for all manner of governments. Voters elect the president, governors, and other executive officers every four years,[1] federal and state legislators every two years, and thousands of local mayors, councilors, and commissioners with similar frequency. All told there are over 90,000 governments at the federal, state, and local levels in the United States, nearly all of them run by elected bodies.[2] A typical election involves choosing among candidates as well as deciding bond issues and other local questions, and in any given year a typical voter has the opportunity to vote three or four times.

How is it that elections create a government that reflects and responds to the preferences of the public? The simple idea behind democracy is that there is power, and perhaps even wisdom, in numbers. Voting allows each of us to express our preferences, and election procedures aggregate those

---

1   Vermont and New Hampshire elect their governors every two years.

2   One federal government, 50 state governments, over 3,000 county governments, about 36,000 municipal and town governments, about 13,500 school districts, and over 35,000 special districts (for example, water or utility). www.census.gov/govs/www/cog2007.html (accessed 3/26/09; site discontinued).

426   **Chapter 11:** Elections

votes into a legitimate collective choice. Election laws determine how votes are counted and translate into a government—who wins seats in the legislature, who is elected to the executive, and, in many states, who will serve as judges.

Elections in the United States work by choosing who will govern, not what they should do or what the laws should be. We do not have direct democracy in federal elections, although many states and municipalities allow voting on bonds and a small number of laws. For the most part, elections are occasions when multiple principals—the citizens—choose political agents to act on their behalf.

Two problems immediately arise for the principals (the citizens). First, are we selecting the best people for the job? This problem of **adverse selection** stems from hidden information. We want to choose people who have the competence to write smart legislation or who have our interests at heart, but we may not have the information to judge which candidate possesses those characteristics.

 adverse selection

The problem of incomplete information— of choosing alternatives without fully knowing the details of available options

CORE OF THE ANALYSIS

 The United States holds frequent elections as a means of keeping politicians close to the preferences of a majority of the people.

 The United States uses a system of plurality rule in which the candidate with the most votes wins the electoral district. Plurality rule creates a strong pressure toward two-party politics and makes it difficult for third parties to succeed.

 Plurality rule also shapes the incentives facing candidates and parties. It creates strong pressure on the parties or candidates to take centrist policies so as to appeal to the median voter among the electorate as a whole.

 Most voters develop strong attachments to political parties, based on agreement on policy, social pressure, and/or upbringing. Those who identify with a party, vote with that party nearly all of the time.

 Campaigns try to mobilize their candidate's supporters and persuade undecided voters. In the process, they provide information that helps solve some of the informational problems inherent in representative democracy.

moral hazard

The problem of not knowing all aspects of the actions taken by an agent (nominally on behalf of the principal but potentially at the principal's expense)

Second, once elected, do the politicians do the job as we wish them to? This problem of **moral hazard** stems from hidden actions. Once selected, representatives cannot easily be monitored. When political leaders engage in acts that do not attract public attention, such as making deals with colleagues to build a winning coalition for a particular bill, we need to ensure that the politicians' decisions are the ones we want them to make. However, voters cannot know everything about the candidates for office or about politicians' actions once they are elected. In fact, the incentives to be highly knowledgeable are minimal. In a nation of 155 million registered voters or even a district of 700,000 voters, surely one's own ballot is unlikely to make a difference in the outcome and the cost of making a mistake is nil. Why, then, bother to find out the details of the candidates' backgrounds and personalities or to learn about the goings-on in Congress?

Voters use simple rules to solve these problems. They usually vote out of office any politicians caught in scandals or seen to be responsible for economic downturns through mismanagement of economic policy, as occurred in 2008, 2010, and 2014. They also reward a party for economic good times and express their desire to continue with current economic policies, as occurred in 2004. In other years, when economic signals are mixed, such as 2016, elections are quite close. But given the simplicity of these rules, how do we hold politicians accountable for the details of legislation?

Ultimately, elections work through competition. The public relies on competition among politicians, the parties, interest groups, and the media to inform them. This chapter focuses on the politicians; later chapters address parties, interest groups, and the media.

In the United States politicians are central. Rival politicians or teams of politicians (parties) seek to hold elective office—we consider that their primary motivation. They formulate positions on important policies that appeal to the greatest number of voters; they develop personal appeals; they advertise their ability to do the job at hand, their strength of character, and their fidelity to the public. Likewise, politicians draw attention to their rivals' failings. Candidates and parties use advertisements, press conferences, speeches, and other modes of reaching the public to highlight their opponents' policy decisions as being out of step with most voters' wishes, and they expose scandalous behavior and play up political gaffes. Politicians themselves bear much of the cost of informing the public about their performance and ideas and those of their opponents. Competition, then, creates strong incentives for those vying for office to reveal information to the electorate.

Competition alone does not cure all. Proponents of electoral reform criticize many features of U.S. election laws, including the campaign finance system, redistricting procedures, the lack of third parties, and the relatively low levels of voter turnout. In this chapter, we consider how the institutional features of American elections shape the way that citizens' goals and preferences are reflected in their government and how voters decide among the candidates and questions put before them on the ballot. Democracy is a work in progress. Americans constantly tinker with the rules to make it a better system.

INSTITUTIONS OF ELECTIONS

Elections are formal institutions for making collective decisions. As in Congress, the executive branch, and the courts, rules (institutions) determine who is allowed to vote, how votes are cast and counted, and how we determine who wins office. Election rules consist of a mix of state and federal laws, legal decisions, and local administrative practices. Federal laws regulate the time of congressional and presidential elections, the qualifications for office, the allocation of seats, the structure of electoral districts, and the qualifications and rights of voters. State laws determine a wider range of factors, including how votes are cast and counted, the procedures for registering voters, candidate qualifications for most elected officials, the procedures for nominating candidates and getting on the ballot, the operations of the parties, and the conduct of all state and local elections. The responsibility for making all of this go smoothly on Election Day falls on the roughly 5,000 local election offices in counties and municipalities. These workers manage the registration lists, prepare the ballots and voting machinery, set up polling places, recruit and train poll workers, and tally and certify the votes. And at the nation's polling places on Election Day, roughly 1 million volunteer poll workers administer the election. The Policy Principle case study on p. 430 shows how the decisions by local officials can affect the outcomes.

The laws and procedures governing elections have important consequences. They can skew the electorate toward one interest or another; they can impede certain political organizations; and they can create a legislature that either reflects the population's diversity or allows one segment of society to dominate.

Election laws, as the rules under which a given election is conducted, manifest the institution principle. Viewed over the long arc of history, however, election laws are also a product of the political system and exemplify the policy and rationality principles. Like any law, an election law reflects the politics inside the legislature as a product of the bargaining and negotiation among elected officials. The rationality principle is at work in that it is interests and values that motivate elected officials and voters. Finally, election laws also exhibit a great deal of stickiness: they typically change slowly, and laws passed decades, even centuries, ago continue to shape the way American democracy operates.

Four features of U.S. election laws deserve particular emphasis:

- First, *who*. The United States provides for universal adult suffrage—all citizens over the age of eighteen have the right to vote.[3]

- Second, *how*. Americans vote in secret and choose among candidates for particular office using a form of the ballot called the "Australian ballot."

---

3 In addition, there is the restriction that those currently serving sentences for felonies cannot vote; some states prohibit ex-felons from voting.

Local Control of Elections and Voter ID Laws

Voters show IDs before casting a ballot.

Through elections, Americans choose their leaders and, in doing so, which policies are likely to be enacted. We saw in Chapter 1 that political behavior is purposive and that institutions "choreograph" political activity, making some outcomes more likely and others less likely. This concept applies to even the most basic aspects of the electoral process. In this chapter we discussed the major institutions of elections, including who votes, how we vote, where we vote, and what it takes to win; but the nuts and bolts of *running* elections also affect the results. Someone must register voters, certify the eligibility of the candidates, print the ballots, manage the polling places, count the votes, and, ultimately, ascertain who won and lost. Each of these functions requires many tasks, such as selecting voting technologies, programming voting machines to read voters' ballots, finding voting locations, setting up polling places, and recruiting poll workers.

The U.S. Constitution gives the authority to organize national elections to the states, as it gives the states the power to determine the "time, place, and manner" of federal elections. States, in turn, generally shift the task of running elections to the county

and municipal governments. There are 8,000 local election offices in the United States, each of which is responsible for choosing voting equipment, software, polling place locations, and staff for running elections. Though some offices have large staffs and budgets, most are led by minor officials who manage elections as only one of many other responsibilities.

The decisions that state and local officials make in organizing their electoral machinery affect voter turnout, the composition of the electorate, and thus the outcomes of elections. Officials are very much aware of these implications. For example, the location of polling places may increase turnout of voters for whom the location is convenient and decrease turnout of those who have more difficulty reaching the polls. Similarly, understaffing a polling place will produce long lines that may discourage people from voting. In every state, these seemingly routine decisions frequently become hot button issues as their potential to affect election results is assessed by competing political forces.

Currently, one of the most controversial topics in election administration is the matter of voter ID laws. Some states have adopted laws requiring voters to show some form of photo identification at the polling place. Proponents of these laws say that identification is necessary to prevent voting fraud. Opponents of voter ID laws, on the other hand, assert that such laws are designed to reduce voting on the part of poor (often minority) voters who may not have drivers' licenses or other required forms of identification.

This ongoing debate demonstrates that institutions matter. Even the most ordinary aspects of electoral machinery that we hardly notice when we go to cast our votes can be used to influence who wins, and thus the policies that will be prioritized by the government.

- Third, *where*. The United States selects almost all elected offices through single-member districts that have equal populations—one person, one vote.

- Fourth, *what* it takes to win. For most offices in the United States, the candidate who wins the most votes among all of those competing for a given seat wins the election.

We will see that these rules create a two-party system that broadly encompasses the entire adult population but that exaggerates the political power of the majority. Other features of election laws and procedures, including rules governing campaign expenditures and fund-raising, party nominations, and ballot access, further shape political competition in the United States.

Also notable are rules that the United States does not have. Federal and state laws do not limit the amount of television and other forms of advertising, total campaign spending, the activities of groups and parties on behalf of candidates, or how the media cover the campaigns. Most other countries limit the use of television or forbid it altogether, restrict how candidates can campaign and how much they can spend, and tightly regulate the activities of organized interest groups. Compared with other countries, then, the United States has a relatively unregulated electoral system that allows candidates to run on their own, separate from the parties, and to spend quite freely on media and other aspects of their campaigns. We turn to these activities in the next section, especially as they bear on the important question of voter learning through campaigns. The features of election law considered here regulate the nature of the electorate and the choices that voters face.

The rules governing elections are not static, having evolved over time through legislation, court decisions, administrative rulings of agencies, and public agitation for electoral reform. The nation has gradually converged on our present system of universal suffrage with secret voting and the use of single-member districts with plurality rule. The future will likely bring further innovations. With waves of immigration, new communication technologies, and other changes reshaping society, the institutions of democracy must change as well. Perhaps the most dramatic changes under way involve the rise of "convenience voting"—voting by mail or voting early at a polling center or town hall. In 1972, approximately 5 percent of all votes nationwide were cast in absentia; in 2012, almost 40 percent of all votes were absentee or early ballots. Oregon and Washington State vote entirely by mail. Colorado is entirely vote by mail as well but allows people to vote at voting sites early and on election day. Twenty-three states and the District of Columbia accept absentee ballots sent by e-mail or fax, which is particularly convenient for military personnel. These new modes of voting give rise to questions about secrecy and the form of the ballot; they also provide new opportunities for reform and modes of voting (such as instant runoff voting). Such changes rarely come about through federal legislation. Rather, new election institutions emerge out of the experiences and experiments of local election officials and state laws.

The Growth of the American Electorate, 1790–2016

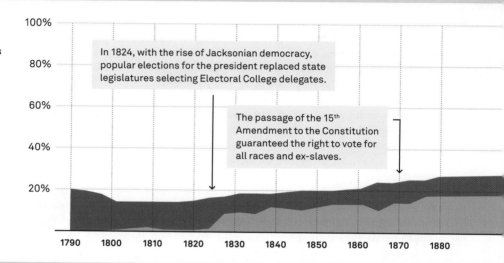

- ■ % of population eligible to vote in national elections

- ■ % of population that did vote in national election

In 1824, with the rise of Jacksonian democracy, popular elections for the president replaced state legislatures selecting Electoral College delegates.

The passage of the 15th Amendment to the Constitution guaranteed the right to vote for all races and ex-slaves.

Who Can Vote: Defining the Electorate

Over the course of American history the electorate has expanded greatly. At the beginning of the Republic, voting rights in most states were restricted to white men over 21 years of age, and many states further required that those people own property. Today, all citizens over 18 years of age are allowed to vote, and the courts and Department of Justice and activist organizations actively ferret out discrimination in elections.[4] The timeplot above compares the percentage of the American population eligible to vote with the percentage of the population that did vote in national elections.

While the right to vote is universal, the exercise of this right is not. In a typical U.S. presidential election, approximately 60 percent of those eligible to vote in fact do so; in midterm elections for Congress, around 45 percent of the eligible electorate votes. And in local elections the percentage of people who vote can be quite low: in some locales, city elections attract only 10 to

---

4   There are further restrictions in some states that prohibit ex-felons from voting and impose residency requirements.

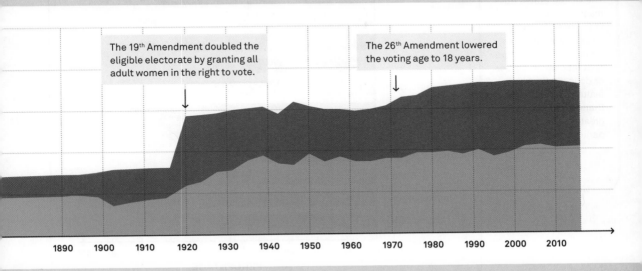

The 19th Amendment doubled the eligible electorate by granting all adult women in the right to vote.

The 26th Amendment lowered the voting age to 18 years.

1890   1900   1910   1920   1930   1940   1950   1960   1970   1980   1990   2000   2010

20 percent of the eligible electorate. Some of the most basic questions about the functioning and health of our democracy concern the exercise of the franchise. Who votes and why? How does nonparticipation affect election outcomes, and would election outcomes be different if everyone voted? Does low voter turnout threaten the legitimacy of government?

It is also important to point out that voting in the United States is a right, not a requirement. If we do not feel strongly about government, we do not have to participate. If we want to express dissatisfaction, one way to do so is not to vote. Of course, if no one voted, it would be a disaster for American democracy, signaling the end of Americans' commitment to their form of government.

Participation Rates. Not all nations take the same view of democracy. While most democracies view voting as a right and a voluntary act, some also treat it as a responsibility of citizenship. In Mexico and Australia, for example, adult citizens are required to vote in national elections; those who fail to vote must either receive a medical exemption or pay a fine. That guarantees turnout rates in the range of 90 percent and it makes election results a reflection of the preferences of all citizens. Universal voting in the United States, however, is not viewed favorably: nonvoters don't want to face a potential fine, and those who do vote may not want the

Figure 11.1
VOTER TURNOUT AROUND THE WORLD

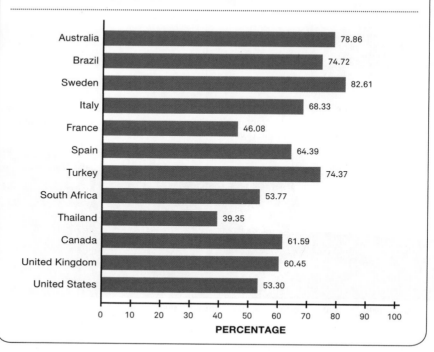

Country	Percentage
Australia	78.86
Brazil	74.72
Sweden	82.61
Italy	68.33
France	46.08
Spain	64.39
Turkey	74.37
South Africa	53.77
Thailand	39.35
Canada	61.59
United Kingdom	60.45
United States	53.30

PERCENTAGE

NOTE: Turnout as a percentage of voting-age population in the most recent national presidential or parliamentary election as of 2016.
SOURCE: International Institute of Democracy and Electoral Assistance, www.idea.int/vt/ (accessed 11/1/16).

nonvoters diluting their power. Moreover, most Americans simply do not like the notion that the government can compel us to do something. Even without compelling participation, the United States is one of the world's most participatory democracies. For example, citizens can participate in electoral politics by blogging and posting on social media, speaking with others, joining organizations, giving money, and of course voting. For nearly all of these activities, Americans participate in politics at much higher rates than people in nearly every other country.[5]

That said, levels of U.S. voter participation in the latter half of the twentieth century were quite low as compared with voter participation in other democracies (Figure 11.1)[6] and as compared with earlier eras of

5   Sidney Verba, Kay Schlozman, and Henry Brady, *Voice and Equality: Civic Volunteerism in America* (Cambridge: Harvard University Press, 1995).

6   See Walter Dean Burnham, "The Changing Shape of the American Political Universe," *American Political Science Review* 59, no. 1 (March 1965): 7–28. It should be noted that other democracies, such as India and Switzerland, have even lower turnout rates, as do some of the new democracies in eastern Europe.

Figure 11.2
VOTER TURNOUT IN U.S. PRESIDENTIAL ELECTIONS

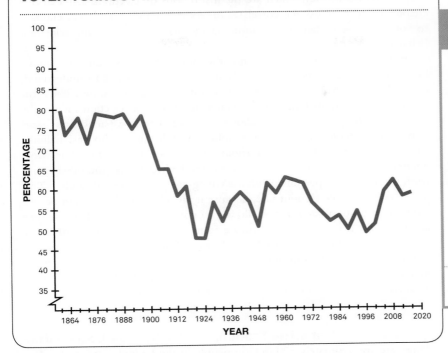

NOTE: Data reflect the population of eligible voters; the percentage of the voting-age population that voted would be smaller.
SOURCES: For 1860–1928, U.S. Bureau of the Census, www.census.gov/prod/www/abs/statab.html (accessed 3/26/09); pt. 2, p. 1071; for 1932–92, U.S. Bureau of the Census, *Statistical Abstract of the United States,* 1993 (Washington, DC: Government Printing Office, 1993), p. 284; for 1996–2016, U.S. Census Bureau data.

ANALYZING THE EVIDENCE

Voter turnout for American presidential elections was significantly higher in the nineteenth century than in the twentieth. What institutional change caused the sharp decline in turnout between 1890 and 1910? Why did this change have such a dramatic effect? Did it have any positive outcomes?

American history, especially the late nineteenth century (Figure 11.2).[7] The five decades after World War II saw a steady erosion of voter turnout in the United States, with voter participation in presidential elections falling below 50 percent in 1996. That decline stirred Congress to reform voter registration rules in the mid-1990s. Turnout rates have grown since then, in response both to legal changes and to the observation by political parties and candidates that there was an opportunity to influence elections by bringing people back to the polls. In 2016, 59 percent of adult citizens in the United States voted.

---

7 See statistics of the U.S. Bureau of the Census and the Federal Election Commission. For voting statistics for 1960 to 2004, see "National Voter Turnout in Federal Elections: 1960–2004," at www.infoplease.com/ipa/A0781453.html (accessed 3/26/09).

Who Votes and Why? The answers to the questions of who votes and why lie partly in the motivations and behavior of individuals and party with the laws of democracy, which are the institutions of elections. Later in this chapter we will discuss the correlates of voting to understand who chooses to vote. We discuss here the institutions and how they define and constrain behavior.

First we must explain one term—the *turnout rate*. It is simple to define, but some of the subtleties of the definition are important to understand, especially when making comparisons over time or across countries. The turnout rate is the number of people who vote in a given election divided by the number of people who are allowed to vote. The first part of this ratio is relatively uncontroversial—the number of individuals who cast ballots.[8] The appropriate baseline in the turnout ratio is more difficult to define. Most commonly, the turnout rate presented for the United States (and other countries) is turnout as a percentage of the voting-age population (all adults). This understates the true turnout rate, because it includes noncitizens and people who are institutionalized or not allowed to vote in some states because they are ex-felons. It is possible to estimate from census reports the numbers of noncitizens and institutionalized populations, though getting reliable figures for these populations is difficult. Following the usual conventions, we focus here on the voting-age population. However, the eligible electorate is somewhat smaller owing to other restrictions on the franchise.[9]

The Electorate and the Franchise. How big is the U.S. electorate? There are approximately 320 million people in the United States today. But not all of them are allowed to vote. These include children under age eighteen, noncitizens, and people in prison. In addition, ex-felons are not allowed to vote in most states. The biggest restriction on the size of the electorate is age. There are approximately 74 million people under age eighteen in the United States. Noncitizenship reduces the eligible electorate by another 13 million adults.[10] Finally, the total ineligible prison and felon population is

---

8 Not all states report such figures in their certified tally of the vote. In fact, 11 states do not report the number of ballots cast, and researchers must substitute the total votes for all candidates for the presidency or another office on the top of the ballot. So, for example, if an individual voter in one of these states does not cast a vote for president but does turn out to vote on other questions on the ballot, this voter might not be counted in the total. However, since nearly all voters who turn out do vote on the races at the top of the ticket, counting those totals is a reasonably accurate substitute for official turnout records.

9 Michael McDonald and Samuel Popkin, "The Myth of the Vanishing Voter," *American Political Science Review* 95 (December 2001): 963–74.

10 These figures exclude undocumented, illegal immigrants, of which there are estimated to be another 12 million persons.

approximately 3.3 million persons. Hence the eligible electorate is approximately 237 million persons, or about two-thirds of the people living in the United States. Of course, throughout the nineteenth and much of the twentieth century there were even more restrictions on the franchise, including gender, race, and property. Perhaps the most significant changes in election institutions over the nation's 200-year history have been to break down historical barriers to voting.

To put the changes in election laws in perspective, suppose that the nineteenth century's restrictive rules applied today—that only white male citizens over 21 were allowed to vote. If that had been the case in 2016, the eligible electorate would have totaled only about 76 million—about one in four people. Those restrictions would have made for a very different electorate in terms of interests, values, and preferences; they would have altered the political parties' strategies; and they would have yielded very different election outcomes.

Other restrictions on the franchise relate to how local officials run elections. As Figure 11.2 indicates, voter turnout declined markedly in the United States between 1890 and 1910. These years coincided with two changes in the institutions of elections. Many states (1) imposed rules such as literacy tests to keep immigrants, blacks, and other groups out of the electorate and (2) began to create registration systems and lists, so that people had to be on a formal list of eligible voters in order to establish that they were allowed to vote on Election Day. Personal registration was one of several "progressive" reforms initiated early in the twentieth century, ostensibly to discourage fraud and "corruption"—a category in which reformers included machine politics in large cities, where political parties had organized immigrant and ethnic populations. Election reforms not only tried to reign in corruption but also sought to weaken the urban factions' power and keep immigrants and blacks from voting.

Voter Registration. Over the years, voter registration restrictions have been modified somewhat to facilitate the process. In 1993, for example, Congress approved and President Bill Clinton signed the National Voter Registration Act, commonly known as the "motor voter" law, which allows individuals to register when applying for driver's licenses, as well as in public assistance and military recruitment offices.[11] In many jurisdictions, casting a vote automatically registers the voter for the next election. In Europe, in contrast, the government automatically handles voter registration. This is one reason voter turnout rates there are higher than those in the United States.

The mere requirement that people register in order to vote affects turnout rates. Today, we can get reliable counts of the number of persons who are actually registered as well as the percentage of registered persons who vote.

---

11 Helen Dewar, "'Motor Voter' Agreement Is Reached," *Washington Post*, April 28, 1993, p. A6.

Studies of contemporary voter registration lists find that almost 90 percent of registered voters in fact vote, but only about 80 percent of the eligible electorate is currently registered to vote. In other words, the eligible electorate is really only about 189 million people—those who are actually registered to vote. There are approximately 47 million eligible voters who have not yet registered—disproportionately those ages 18 to 29 (Figure 11.3). Getting those people into the registration system, and keeping them on the rolls, is an important way to increase the turnout rate. If you are not registered to vote, you cannot vote.[12]

Why, then, have a registration system? Such systems contain a fairly reliable list of all people who are interested in voting. Local election offices and campaigns use the lists to communicate with voters about when, where, and how to vote. Campaigns use them to prepare grassroots organizing efforts and direct-mail campaigns.

Today, registration lists are the basis for administering elections. Local election offices rely on their registration databases to format ballots, set up precincts, determine which voters should vote in which place, and communicate with people. Any given area contains many overlapping election jurisdictions, creating many different combinations of unique sets of offices. For example, one voter might reside in Congressional District 1, State Senate District 7, State Representative District 3, City Council District 1, and so forth. Variations in district boundaries may mean that a few blocks away, another voter lives in entirely different districts. Although they live in the same city, these voters must vote on different ballots. The first voter is not supposed to vote in Congressional District 2, for instance. Registration lists have become vitally important in sorting out where people should vote. Using the definitions of the boundaries, local election offices determine how many distinct ballots they must prepare. Each distinct ballot is assigned to a precinct: only one ballot constellation per precinct. The local election office then uses the registration list to assign individuals to precincts and to communicate to each voter exactly where he or she is supposed to vote. Without this means of assigning voters to precincts and communicating with voters, there would be considerable confusion on Election Day. Efforts to eliminate or reform registration requirements must confront this very practical problem.

Some states, such as Minnesota and Wisconsin, allow registration at the polls on Election Day (called same-day registration or Election Day registration). These states have noticeably higher turnout but also must recruit additional poll workers to handle the new registrants in the precincts. Recently, five states, California, Connecticut, Oregon, Vermont, and West Virginia, have gone even further by adopting laws to automatically register eligible residents to vote. These states will mail a ballot to any citizen with a driver's license who is not currently registered. Other states, such as Colorado, are trying to eliminate traditional precincts in favor of vote centers. Electronic voting equipment now makes it possible to program many different ballots on a single machine, so that each voter keys in his or her

12 Stephen Ansolabehere and Eitan Hersh, "Validation: What Big Data Tell Us about the Actual Electorate," *Political Analysis* 20 (2012): 437–459.

Figure 11.3

VOTER REGISTRATION RATES BY DEMOGRAPHIC, 2012

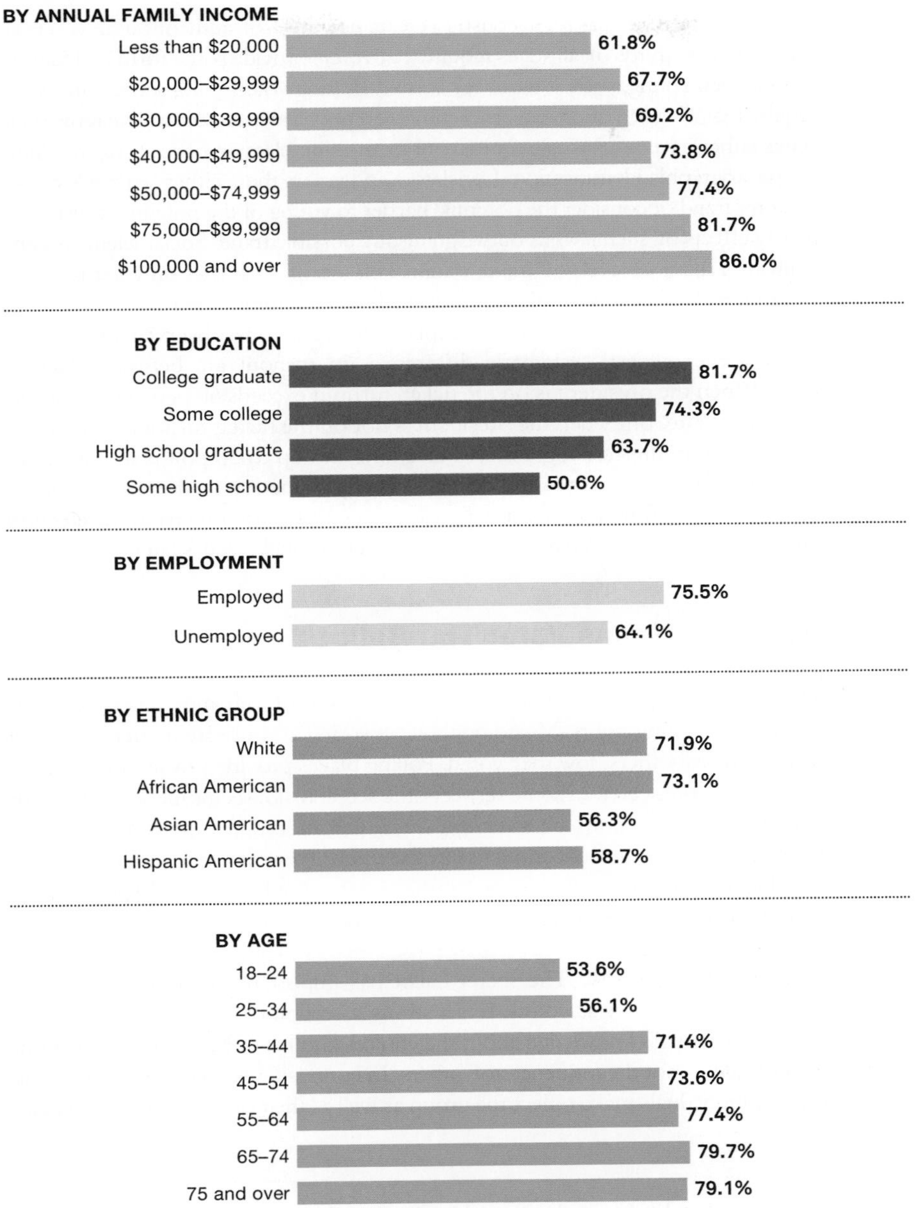

BY ANNUAL FAMILY INCOME

Less than $20,000	61.8%
$20,000–$29,999	67.7%
$30,000–$39,999	69.2%
$40,000–$49,999	73.8%
$50,000–$74,999	77.4%
$75,000–$99,999	81.7%
$100,000 and over	86.0%

BY EDUCATION

College graduate	81.7%
Some college	74.3%
High school graduate	63.7%
Some high school	50.6%

BY EMPLOYMENT

Employed	75.5%
Unemployed	64.1%

BY ETHNIC GROUP

White	71.9%
African American	73.1%
Asian American	56.3%
Hispanic American	58.7%

BY AGE

18–24	53.6%
25–34	56.1%
35–44	71.4%
45–54	73.6%
55–64	77.4%
65–74	79.7%
75 and over	79.1%

SOURCE: U.S. Bureau of the Census, " www.census.gov/hhes/www/socdem/voting/publications/ p20/2012/tables.html (accessed 7/15/13).

address to get the appropriate ballot and vote. Such machines enable people to vote anywhere and lessen the need for lists to assign voters to precincts. These innovations may lead ultimately to an election system that does not require or rely heavily on registration before Election Day, but even these mechanisms still require the voter to register.

The past decade has seen a push to create new ways of authenticating voters at the polls. Two-thirds of all states require that voters provide some form of identification when voting, such as a driver's license. Fearing voter fraud, some states now require that all voters show government-issued photo identification. The remaining states either have no formal requirement or prohibit election officials from asking for photographic identification. Legislators and voters there either sense a low risk of voter fraud or consider the potential barrier to voting or the potentially discriminatory effects of such laws as outweighing any possible fraud. Social scientists generally find minimal levels of fraud, minimal effects of such laws on voter turnout, and minimal effects on people's confidence in the electoral system.[13]

Laws alone, however, cannot explain the variations observed in turnout. Perhaps the biggest, systematic differences in turnout are between election years. When the president is on the ticket, turnout exceeds 60 percent of the eligible electorate. But when the president is not on the ticket, turnout drops 15 to 20 points in midterm congressional elections and up to 50 points in local elections. This pattern of surge and decline is partly a function of the election calendar and partly a function of campaign activities and voter interest in the election outcomes. These are behavioral matters, which we will discuss later.

How Americans Vote: The Ballot

The way Americans cast their votes reflects some of our most cherished precepts about voting rights. Most people view voting as a private matter, choosing whether to tell others how they voted. Polling places provide privacy and keep an individual's vote secret. In some respects, the secret ballot seems incongruous with voting, because elections are a very public matter. Indeed, for the first century of the Republic, voting was conducted in the open. However, public voting led to vote buying and voter intimidation, so the secret ballot became widespread at the end of the nineteenth century in response to such corrupt practices.

The Secret Ballot. The secret ballot has important implications for how people see themselves as voters. It is a strong assertion of the individual, reflecting the individual's knowledge about the choices and his or her preferences about government—not the influences of others. In contrast, when voting is public, the choices individuals make reflect the group as well as their own thinking. American

---

13 Stephen Ansolabehere and Nathaniel Persily, "Vote Fraud in the Eye of the Beholder," *Harvard Law Review* 121 (2008): 1737; and Stephen Ansolabehere, "Effects of Identification Requirements on Voting: Evidence from the Experiences of Voters on Election Day," *PS* (January 2009): 127–30.

elections still have vestiges of public voting, in town meetings in New England states and at party-nominating caucuses, such as in Iowa, Nevada, and Minnesota.

Attend a caucus or town hall meeting, and you will appreciate the difference between these events and voting in the seclusion of a voting booth. Town meetings and caucuses often exhibit the tendency of groups to follow particular individuals or to reflect a public conversation rather than each person's private information. Public voting also demands more of the individual—more time, more attention to the decision-making process—and thus draws in a much smaller and more committed electorate. These two methods can lead to very different results. A good example comes from the Democratic nominating process in Texas during the 2008 election. The Texas Democratic Party allocates one-half of its delegates through a primary election involving secret ballots and the other half through caucuses. Primary voting runs throughout the day; the caucuses begin in the evening immediately after polls close. In 2008, Hillary Rodham Clinton won a decisive victory over Barack Obama in the primary voting in Texas, but Obama won the caucuses by an equally large margin. The caucuses are reminiscent of an older style of democracy in which people took a stand publicly for what they believed. Today, secrecy in voting is the norm.

The Australian Ballot. With the secret ballot came another innovation, the **Australian ballot:** it lists the names of all candidates running for a given office and allows the voter to select any candidate for any office. This procedure was introduced in Australia in 1851, and in the United States today it is universal. Before the 1880s some Americans voted in public meetings; others voted on paper ballots printed by the political parties or by slates of candidates. Voters chose which ballot they wished to submit—a Republican ballot, a Democratic ballot, a Populist ballot, a Greenback ballot, and so forth. The ballots were often printed on different-colored paper so that voters could easily distinguish them—and so that local party workers could observe who cast which ballots. With these party ballots, voters could not choose candidates from different parties for different offices; they had to vote the party line.

In the 10-year period 1885–1895, nearly every state adopted the Australian ballot and, with it, the secret ballot. This new form of voting occurred in an era of administrative reform in government throughout the United States. County governments took on the job of formatting and printing ballots, and conducting elections became an administrative task of government rather than a political activity of the parties. The change also reflected state governments' efforts to break the hold of local political organizations. All ballots are identical under the Australian form, making it difficult to observe who votes for which party. More important, voters could choose any candidate for any office, breaking the hold of parties over the vote. The introduction of the Australian ballot gave rise to the phenomenon of split-ticket voting, in which some voters select candidates from different parties for different offices.[14]

 Australian ballot

An electoral format that presents the names of all the candidates for any given office on the same ballot; introduced at the end of the eighteenth century, it replaced the partisan ballot and facilitated split-ticket voting

---

14 Jerold G. Rusk, "The Effect of the Australian Ballot Reform on Split Ticket Voting, 1876–1908," *American Political Science Review* 64, no. 4 (December 1970): 1220–38.

The secret and Australian ballot enabled voters to choose candidates as well as parties and facilitated the rise of the personal vote and the incumbency advantage in American electoral politics. (See the discussion of the incumbency advantage in Congress in Chapter 6.) In contrast, under the party ballot voters could not choose particular candidates without voting for all candidates nominated by a party or slate. Voters could not choose, say, one party's nominee for president and another party's nominee for the House of Representatives. In the absence of a real possibility of split-ticket voting, a desire for change could manifest only as a vote against all candidates of the party in power. When the electorate voted to oust those in power at the national level, the opposing party or slate at state and local levels would sweep into office as well. As a result, elections in the United States before 1896 were highly partisan, often producing wholesale changes in control of government at all levels. Today, the Australian ballot allows voters to judge the performance both of individual officeholders and of the political parties as a whole. And the possibility of split-ticket voting has led to increasingly divided control of government as well as the rise of personal voting.

Where Americans Vote: Electoral Districts

Elected officials in the United States represent places as well as people. Today, the president, representatives, senators, governors, and many other state and local officials are elected through geographic areas called electoral districts. Generally speaking, the United States employs **single-member districts** with equal populations. This means that the U.S. House of Representatives, almost all state legislatures, and almost all local governments have their own districts that each elect one representative, and all of the districts for a given legislative body must have equal populations.[15]

Representation in the Electoral College. Elections for the U.S. Senate and the presidency are the odd cases. In the Senate, the states are the districts. Senate districts, then, have multiple members and unequal populations. In presidential elections, every state is allocated votes in the **Electoral College** equal to its number of U.S. senators (two) plus its number of House members. The District of Columbia is assigned three electors. The states are the districts, and

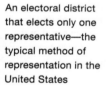

single-member district

An electoral district that elects only one representative—the typical method of representation in the United States

Electoral College

The presidential electors from each state who meet in their respective state capitals after the popular election to cast ballots for the president and vice president

---

15 The exceptions in the state legislatures are Arizona, Idaho, Maryland, New Hampshire, New Jersey, North Dakota, South Dakota, Vermont, Washington, and West Virginia. These states use multimember districts in either their state house of representatives or their state senate. In some cases legislators are elected en bloc: if there are two seats in a district, the top vote getters win the seats, as in both chambers in Vermont and the lower chambers in Arizona, Maryland, New Hampshire, New Jersey, North Dakota, and West Virginia. In some cases, there are multiple posts for each district, candidates must declare which post they are running for, and the top vote getter for a given post wins that seat, as in the lower chambers in Idaho, Maryland (also uses bloc), South Dakota (also uses bloc), and Washington.

each state chooses all of its electors in a statewide vote. The electors commit to casting their votes for a certain candidate in the Electoral College.[16] Within the political parties, the nomination process in most states allocates delegates to the parties' national conventions on the basis of House districts, and thus population. However, some states choose delegates on a statewide basis, with all districts selecting multiple delegates to the party conventions.

The system of single-member districts with equal populations was not part of the Founders' original design. Rather, it evolved over nearly two centuries, from 1790 to 1970. Article II of the Constitution designed the House to represent the people, with the number of seats elected by each state allocated on the basis of population following each decennial census, and the Senate to represent the states. The Constitution originally specified that the state legislatures would choose the U.S. senators, with each state choosing two senators to staggered six-year terms. That system was jettisoned in 1913 with the adoption of the Seventeenth Amendment, providing for direct election of senators.

The Constitution said nothing about the election of individual House members or electors to the Electoral College. That task fell to the states, and in early times the states used many different electoral systems for choosing their House delegations. Most of the early state laws adopted single-member districts: the states divided their territory into as many districts as they had House seats, and each district elected one member. Some states created multimember districts, in which a district would elect more than one legislator. This was common in urban counties and cities, where the population exceeded the number required for two or more districts, but the legislature did not want to draw district boundaries. And some states elected all their House members in a single, statewide election (an at-large election). An even greater hodgepodge of election procedures applied to the state legislatures and local councils.[17]

Congress tried to bring order to the election of House members with the 1842 Apportionment Act. Through an amendment from Representative John Campbell of South Carolina, the act included an additional requirement on districts:

> [I]n every case where a State is entitled to more than one Representative, the number to which each State shall be entitled under this apportionment shall be elected by districts, composed of contiguous territory, equal in number to the number of Representatives to which said State may be entitled; no one district electing more than one Representative.[18]

---

16 The exceptions are Maine and Nebraska, which choose the House electors in individual House districts and the Senate electors in a statewide vote.

17 For a history of districting politics, see Stephen Ansolabehere and James Snyder, Jr., *The End of Inequality: One Person, One Vote and the Transformation of American Politics* (New York: Norton, 2008).

18 Congressional Globe, 27th Cong., 2d sess., 1842, 11, Part 1:471, 348.

Most states complied with this provision, even though it made them responsible for creating appropriate districts, especially around urban areas. Some states, however, insisted on using at-large and multimember districts up to the 1960s. Finally, in the 1967 Apportionment Act, Congress forbade the use of anything but single-member districts.

A second important change in the nature of U.S. political districts occurred at that time as well. In a series of decisions beginning with *Baker v. Carr* in 1962, the Supreme Court ruled that all federal and state legislative districts must have equal populations: one person, one vote. That simple aphorism today rings as the very definition of democracy, but before 1962 state legislative districts often had highly unequal populations, which meant that some votes in effect counted more than others. In the California state senate, Los Angeles County elected as many seats as Alpine County, even though Los Angeles had almost 500 times as many people. As a result, voters in Alpine County had greater representation (500 times greater) relative to their population than did voters in Los Angeles County. Similar inequities reigned in every state legislature, producing a pattern of overrepresentation of rural areas and underrepresentation of most urban areas and, especially, suburban counties.

In most states these inequalities arose from neglect. Most state constitutions require redistricting to keep district populations equal, but as urban populations grew, especially in the first half of the twentieth century, those in power realized that redistricting might jeopardize their own reelection. As a result, the legislatures chose to do nothing. With each successive decade, representation in the United States became more unequal, and there seemed to be no way to force the state legislatures to act. Finally, the U.S. Supreme Court ruled, in a series of important cases, that unequal representation violated the Fourteenth Amendment's guarantee of equal protection under the law. By 1971, nearly every legislative district in the United States elected one representative, and the populations of the districts for each legislative chamber were equal. By now, single-member districts with equal populations have become the rule in the United States, from city councils and school districts to the House of Representatives.[19]

The U.S. Senate and the Electoral College remain the two great exceptions to the requirements of single-member districts with equal populations. The apportionment of Senate seats to states makes that chamber inherently unequal. California's 39 million people have the same number of senators as Wyoming's 586,000 people. The allocation of Electoral College votes creates a population inequity in presidential elections, with larger states selecting fewer electors per capita than smaller states. In the 1960s, the Supreme Court let stand the unequal district populations in the Senate and the Electoral College, because the representation of states in the Senate is specified in the Constitution. The reason lies in the politics of the Constitutional Convention (see Chapter 2), which consisted of delegations of states, each of which held equal numbers of votes under the Articles of Confederation. In order to create a House of Representatives to

---

19 The story of this transformation is told in Ansolabehere and Snyder, *The End of Inequality*.

reflect the population's preferences, the large states had to strike a deal with the smaller states, which stood to lose representation with the initial plan of a single chamber that reflected population. That deal, the Connecticut Compromise, created the U.S. Senate to balance representation of people with representation of places and led to a clause in Article V of the Constitution that guarantees equal representation of the states in the Senate.

Nonetheless, the Senate and the Electoral College share the salient feature of elections for the House and for state and local offices: the use of districts to select representatives. All elections in the United States and all elected officials are tied to geographically based constituencies rather than to the national electorate as a whole. This is certainly true for the House and Senate. It applies also to presidential elections, in which candidates focus on winning key states in the Electoral College rather than on winning a majority of the popular vote.

Electoral Districts and Majority Rule. Electoral districts have a particularly important political consequence: the use of districts tends to magnify the power of the majority. In a system like ours with two parties and single-member districts, the party that wins a majority of the vote nationwide tends to win a disproportionate share of the seats. In 2016, Republicans won 51.7 percent of the two-party vote nationwide for the U.S. House, but 55.4 percent of the seats. As an empirical matter, when the election is a tie, the parties win equal shares of the vote, and for every 1 percent of the vote above 50 percent a party gains an additional 2 percent of the seats. This pattern has been observed in data on U.S. House elections over the last 60 years. In 2012, however, Democrats and Republicans finished in a virtual tie for popular votes cast in House races, but the GOP won 54 percent of the seats. This anomaly was partly the result of the Republican advantage at the time in redrawing district boundaries, and partly the result of candidate recruitment, retirements, and reapportionment. The Electoral College tends to magnify the votes even more dramatically, and can even turn the popular vote on its head. In 2016, Donald Trump won 46 percent of the popular vote, but captured 57 percent of the electoral votes. Electoral districts, then, create a very strong tendency toward majority rule.

This magnifying effect has caused problems for smaller parties and minority groups. Just as districts magnify the number of seats won by the majority party, they shrink the representation of small parties. If a party wins 5 percent of the vote nationwide, it has difficulty winning any seats or Electoral College delegates unless the support for that party is concentrated in a particular geographic area. The most successful third party in recent U.S. history was the Reform Party, started by Ross Perot in 1992. Perot won 19 percent of the presidential vote nationwide that year, but no Electoral College delegates.

The majoritarian tendency of districts also makes it very difficult for racial minorities to gain representation. Blacks and Hispanics constitute roughly a quarter of the population. Districts crafted without regard to race would spread the minority vote across many districts, making it unlikely for a sufficiently large segment in any one district to elect proportionate numbers of blacks or Hispanics to the legislature. This problem, compounded by the historic discrimination against blacks and Hispanics, led Congress to amend the Voting

Rights Act in 1982 to provide for the creation of legislative districts with sufficient numbers of black and Hispanic voters to elect House members representative of those groups. This law has been interpreted and implemented to mean that the state legislatures must create majority-minority districts, containing majorities of black or Hispanic people, whenever possible. As we discuss later, that provision has proved highly controversial in each subsequent round of districting, but the Voting Rights Act has been renewed repeatedly and has withstood legal challenges.[20] Even with this rule, blacks and Hispanics make up only 9 percent of members of the Congress, even though they accounted for 17.6 percent of the population in 2016.

Periodic Redistricting. House districts and state legislative districts are not static. To ensure equal population representation, they must be remade every decade. Responsibility for drawing new district boundaries rests, in most states, with the state legislatures and the governors, with the supervision of the courts and sometimes with the consultation of commissions (Figure 11.4). Every 10 years, the U.S. census updates the states' official population figures, as well as population counts, to a fine level of geographical detail. The politicians and others with a stake in the outcome use the census data to craft a new district map; ultimately, the legislatures must pass and the governors must sign a law defining new U.S. House and state legislative districts. This job is forced on the legislatures by their constitutions and by the courts. However, periodic redistricting, although it corrects one problem, invites another. Those in charge may manipulate the new map to increase the likelihood of a particular outcome, such as the election of a majority of seats for one party or interest group. This problem arose with some of the earliest congressional district maps. A particularly egregious map of the 1812 Massachusetts House districts drawn with the imprimatur of Governor Elbridge Gerry prompted a *Boston Gazette* editorial writer to dub a very strangely shaped district the "Gerry-Mander." The term stuck, and **gerrymandering** refers broadly to any attempt at creating electoral districts for political advantage.

gerrymandering

The apportionment of voters in districts in such a way as to give unfair advantage to one political party

It is easy to intentionally draw an unfair electoral map, especially with the sophisticated software and data on local voting patterns and demographics that are available today. To facilitate districting, the Census Bureau divides the nation into very small geographic areas, called census blocks, which typically contain a few dozen people. U.S. House districts contain over 700,000 people. Political mapmakers combine various local areas, down to census blocks, to construct legislative districts. Those seeking political advantage try to make as many districts as possible that contain a majority of their own voters, maximizing the number of seats won for a given division of the vote. There are constraints on

20 In 2013, the Supreme Court struck down Section 4 of the Voting Rights Act, which determined which states were automatically subject to preclearance. The remaining sections, including this one and the prohibition against intentional discrimination (Section 2), were not affected. See *Shelby County, Alabama v. Holder,* 570 U.S. ____ (2013).

Figure 11.4
CONGRESSIONAL REDISTRICTING

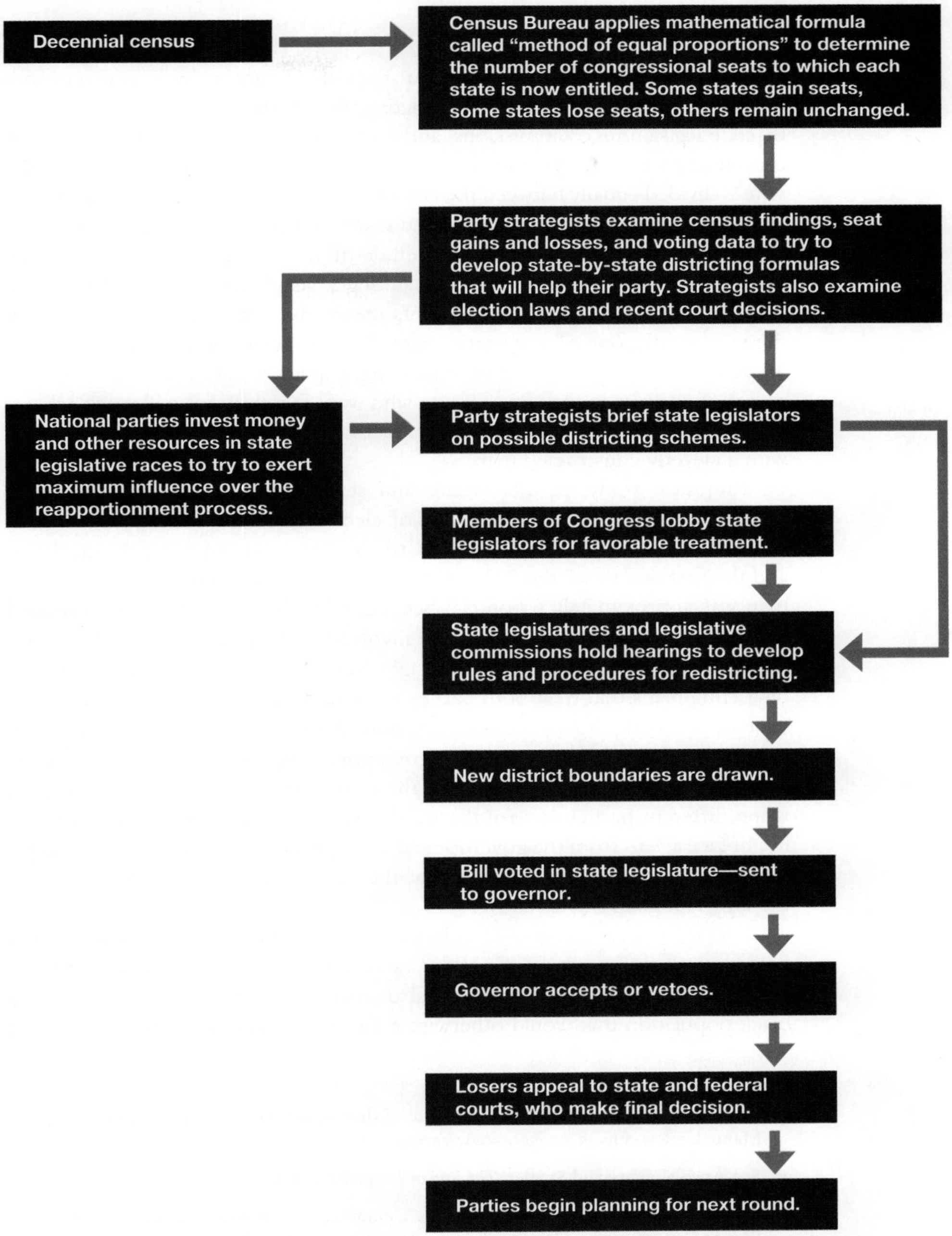

Decennial census →

Census Bureau applies mathematical formula called "method of equal proportions" to determine the number of congressional seats to which each state is now entitled. Some states gain seats, some states lose seats, others remain unchanged.

↓

Party strategists examine census findings, seat gains and losses, and voting data to try to develop state-by-state districting formulas that will help their party. Strategists also examine election laws and recent court decisions.

National parties invest money and other resources in state legislative races to try to exert maximum influence over the reapportionment process. →

Party strategists brief state legislators on possible districting schemes.

Members of Congress lobby state legislators for favorable treatment.

↓

State legislatures and legislative commissions hold hearings to develop rules and procedures for redistricting.

↓

New district boundaries are drawn.

↓

Bill voted in state legislature—sent to governor.

↓

Governor accepts or vetoes.

↓

Losers appeal to state and federal courts, who make final decision.

↓

Parties begin planning for next round.

political cartography: the district populations must be equal, and all parts of the district must touch (be contiguous). Even with those constraints, the number of possible maps that could be drawn for any one state's legislative districts is extremely large.[21] Gerrymandering exemplifies the policy principal at work in the area of elections.

Fairness and Bias. Political scientists examine fairness by assessing quantitatively the features of any given districting plan. Such measures are widely used by state legislatures, commissions, and courts in assessing districting plans. Of central importance is the notion of bias. In a hypothetical election where the vote is divided equally between the two major parties, what share of seats do we expect each party to win? An unbiased districting plan would give both parties half of the seats. To gauge the magnitude of the bias, political scientists then simulate such hypothetical elections among a state's electorate under a given districting plan. A bias of, say, 5 points means that when the two parties split the vote evenly, one of the parties wins 55 percent of the seats and the other 45 percent. With each round of districting, experts weigh in with their assessments of the bias in the plans. Those who want fair elections will try to achieve no bias. Those who want to gain the upper hand try to inject bias into elections with a cleverly constructed map.

Empirical study of U.S. House and state legislative elections has documented important patterns in the bias of electoral districts. First, there is significant evidence of partisan bias in redistricting maps passed today. In the 1990s and the first decade of the 2000s, the bias in the average state legislative district map was approximately 5 points.[22] Second, while bias remains, it has dropped substantially since the courts became involved in the process. Since the 1960s, frequent redistricting and court oversight has forced state legislatures to create districting plans that treat both parties more fairly. Third, the bias is the largest in states where the legislature conducts redistricting and one party controls both chambers of the legislature and the governor's office: the legislature can create a map biased toward that party, and the governor will likely sign it. However, when different parties control the legislature and the executive, the legislature might face a veto from the governor and must create districts that will be acceptable to the other party.[23] This is one of the benefits of divided party control of the legislature and the executive.

Politicians can use gerrymandering to dilute the strength not only of a party but also of a group. Consider racial minorities. One common strategy has involved redrawing congressional district boundaries so as to disperse a black population that would otherwise constitute a majority within the original

---

21 For definitions of these units, see Bureau of the Census, Geographic Area Reference Manual, www.census.gov/geo/www/garm.html (accessed 3/27/09).

22 See Ansolabehere and Snyder, *The End of Inequality*, chap. 11.

23 See Gary King and Robert X. Browning, "Democratic Representation and Partisan Bias in Congressional Elections," *American Political Science Review* 81, no. 4 (December 1987): 1252–73.

---

district. This form of gerrymandering was used in Mississippi during the 1960s and 1970s to prevent the election of black candidates to Congress. Historically, the state's black population was clustered along the Mississippi River Delta. From 1882 until 1966, the Delta constituted one congressional district with blacks a clear majority; but discrimination in voter registration and at the polls guaranteed the continual election of white congressmen. With passage of the Voting Rights Act in 1965, this district would almost surely have gone to a black candidate or one favored by the black majority. To prevent that, the Mississippi legislature drew new House districts that split the black population across three districts so that it constituted a majority in none. This gerrymandering scheme helped prevent the election of any black representative until 1987, when Mike Espy became the first African American since Reconstruction to represent Mississippi in Congress.

Continuing controversies about the legislatures' involvement in drawing their own districts have raised deep concerns about the fairness of the process. Even with some states creating commissions or appointing "special masters" to draw the maps or even using independent commissions, it has proved difficult to find a satisfactory reform for redistricting. Perhaps the most creative attempt to engage the issue was that proposed by former Ohio secretary of state Jennifer Brunner. Working with the League of Women Voters of Ohio, Common Cause, and state representatives Joan Lawrence and Dan Stewart, Brunner created a public contest in 2009 to develop the best districting plan—the Ohio Redistricting Competition. The purpose was not to produce a new districting law but to show how "a robust public conversation about the process can occur, leading to the development of the best possible redistricting recommendations for consideration by the Ohio General Assembly."[24] This was a way to inform the legislature and courts about what the public wanted in the districting plans and to produce a blueprint to guide those who would draw the official maps.

The Ohio experiment was just the beginning in an important transformation in districting. In 2011, the Public Mapping Project, led by Michael McDonald and Harvard researcher Micah Altman, conducted similar contests in a dozen states. And independent software developer David Bradlee developed Dave's Redistricting App, a powerful tool that is easy to use and free.[25] The State of Texas and the State of Florida posted on their districting website all of the districting tools and data that were available to the legislative committees that drafted the maps. The technology has created a new era of open redistricting.

During the redistricting process in 2010 and 2011, these new tools and public mapping projects generated many different plans that the legislatures and commissions examined as part of their deliberations. Interest groups and the minority party within legislatures now wield the information and technology to propose alternative configurations of districts during the legislative process (not

---

24 The contest was available at www.ohioredistricting.org, sponsored by the Ohio secretary of state (accessed 8/31/11; site discontinued).

25 Dave's Redistricting, http://gardow.com/davebradlee/redistricting (accessed 8/31/11); Public Mapping Project, www.publicmapping.org (accessed 8/31/11).

just after the fact). Before the 2011 redistricting, the districting committee in the legislature and the majority party in most states controlled the technology and shaped the political debate in the legislature. As controversies over district plans moved into the courts, the public mapping projects and open-source districting tools empowered plaintiffs, who could point to alternative and (arguably) fairer maps, and the courts, who could see the range of possible maps that could have been constructed and contrast those with what the legislatures produced. Such evidence is especially powerful when allegations of racial discrimination are at stake.

For two centuries, the districting process has been closed to the public, to interest groups, even to members of the minority party within the legislature. Now, new developments in geographic information systems (GIS) software and provision of census data enable anyone to draw credible district maps. Opening up the process, it is hoped, will lessen the extent and effect of gerrymandering.

What It Takes to Win: Plurality Rule

plurality rule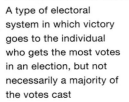

A type of electoral system in which victory goes to the individual who gets the most votes in an election, but not necessarily a majority of the votes cast

The fourth prominent feature of U.S. electoral law is the criterion for winning. Although Americans often embrace majority rule as a defining characteristic of democracy, the real standard is **plurality rule**. The candidate who receives the most votes in the relevant district or constituency wins the election, even if that candidate doesn't receive a majority of votes. Suppose three parties nominate candidates for a seat and divide the vote such that one wins 34 percent and the other two each receive 33 percent of the vote. Under plurality rule, the candidate with 34 percent wins the seat, even though he did not win a majority of votes (more than 50 percent). There are different types of plurality systems. The system most widely used in the United States combines plurality rule with single-member districts and is called *first past the post*. In choosing delegates for the Electoral College, most states use a plurality system in which the candidate who receives the most votes wins all of the delegates. This is called *winner take all*.[26] In state-wide elections, two states, Louisiana and Georgia, require a candidate to receive at least 50 percent of all votes in order to win. This is **majority rule**. If no candidate receives a majority, a runoff election is held about one month later between the two candidates who received the most votes in the first round. Other systems also use plurality- and majority-rule criteria. For instance, some city councils still have multimember districts. The top vote getters win the seats. If there are, say, seven seats to fill, the seven candidates who win the most votes each win a seat.

majority rule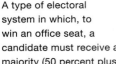

A type of electoral system in which, to win an office seat, a candidate must receive a majority (50 percent plus one) of all the votes cast in the relevant district

Plurality rule is often criticized for yielding electoral results that do not reflect the public's preferences. Votes for the losing candidates seem wasted, because they do not translate into representation. Indeed, as the example of the three-candidate race above suggests, it is possible that a majority of voters wanted someone other than the winner. In the aggregate, plurality rule with

---

26 Over the centuries, many systems for voting and determining electoral outcomes have been devised. For an excellent analysis of voting systems and a complete classification, see Gary Cox, *Making Votes Count* (New York: Cambridge University Press, 1997).

single-member districts tends to inflate the share of seats won by the largest party and deflate the others' shares. A striking example comes from Great Britain. In 2015, the British Conservative Party won 37 percent of the vote and 51 percent of seats, while the Labour party placed second with 30 percent of the vote and 36 percent of seats. The remainder of the votes and seats were distributed very unevenly among three other parties. For example, the UK Independence Party came in third with 13 percent of the vote, but only won one seat. Nevertheless, plurality rule offers certain advantages. It enables voters to choose individuals to represent them personally, not just political parties, and it picks a definite winner without the need for runoff elections.

Proportional Representation.

Among the world's democracies, the main alternative to plurality rule is **proportional representation**, or PR. Under proportional representation, competing parties win legislative seats in proportion to their share of the popular vote. For example, if three parties running for seats in the legislature divide the vote such that one wins 34 percent and the other two receive 33 percent of the vote, the first party receives 34 percent of the seats and the other two receive 33 percent of the seats.

proportional representation (PR)

A multiple-member district system that awards seats to political parties in proportion to the percentage of the vote each party won

PR is used rarely in the United States. The most substantial elections in which it is employed are the Democratic presidential primary elections. During the 1988 primary season, Jesse Jackson routinely won 20 percent of the vote in the primaries but garnered only about 5 percent of the delegates. To make the Democratic National Convention and the party more representative of its disparate voting groups, Jackson negotiated with other party leaders to change the delegate allocation rules so that delegates within congressional districts would be assigned on a proportional basis. If a district elects five delegates, a candidate wins a delegate if the candidate receives at least 20 percent of the vote in the district, two delegates if the candidate wins at least 40 percent of the vote, and so forth. Before this rule change the Democratic Party awarded all delegates from a given congressional district to the candidate who won a plurality of the vote. Like any districted system with plurality rule, this created a strong majoritarian tendency.

Plurality rule in single-member districts has a very important consequence. It is the reason for two-party politics in the United States. Worldwide, countries with plurality rule in single-member districts have far fewer political parties than other nations. Typically, elections under plurality rule boil down to just two major parties that routinely compete for power, with one of them winning a majority of legislative seats outright. Proportional representation systems, in contrast, tend to have many more than two parties. Rarely does a single party win a majority of seats. Governments form as coalitions of many different parties. The political scientist Maurice Duverger described that pattern in a path-breaking book, *Party Politics* (1951). Duverger formalized his law of politics quite simply: plurality rule creates two-party politics; proportional representation encourages more than two parties.

Duverger's Law

Law of politics, formalized by Maurice Duverger, stating that plurality-rule electoral systems will tend to have two political parties

The rationale behind **Duverger's Law** has two components: the strategic behavior of politicians and the behavior of voters. Consider, first, how politicians would think about the prospects of forming a new party. Suppose that there already are two parties, a center-right party and a center-left party. For a politician from the far right, for example, the parties do not represent the ideals she espouses. She wants a far-right policy most, a center-right policy less, and least of all a center-left policy. One solution is for her to leave the center-right party and form a far-right party. But doing that helps the center-left party by splitting the vote of those on the right without affecting the vote for the center-left party. Under plurality rule, the center-left party would almost certainly win, an outcome that the far-right politician likes even less. Thus politicians on the extremes cannot gain by forming a new party. A politician with a centrist orientation also cannot win the election if the center-right and center-left parties are not too extreme. The center-right party would win all votes of voters on the right and on the center right. The same is true for the center-left party. That would leave only a small segment of true centrists for a potential centrist party. Hence, if the current parties are not too extreme, there is no incentive for a third party to enter a two-party system when plurality rule is the criterion for winning.

Voters follow a similar logic. They do not want to waste their votes. If voters understand that the extremist party or candidate cannot win, they will vote for the more moderate alternative. Although second best for extremist voters, the moderate has a better chance of winning. This logic leads the extremist voters to choose the moderate party or candidate in order to have a better chance of selecting a candidate more to their liking. Extremist parties and candidates, then, have little incentive to enter a race, and when they do they usually attract few votes.

Such sophisticated voting occurs often in U.S. primary elections. Mitt Romney was significantly more moderate than Rick Santorum, Newt Gingrich, or Ron Paul in the 2012 Republican presidential primaries, and he was more moderate than the typical Republican primary election voter. Nevertheless, he won the nomination easily because many Republicans understood that Romney represented their best chance in the general election.

Proportional representation, in contrast, creates an incentive for more parties and candidates to enter because they will win seats in proportion to their support among the national electorate. PR systems often have a multitude of parties, none of which represents a decisive majority. Elections in such systems often lead to coalition governments, because no one party wins enough seats to govern. In the Democratic Party, proportional representation has the further effect of stretching out the nominating season. If a candidate wins a plurality of 40 percent of the vote in a state's Democratic primary, he wins roughly 40 percent of the delegates. As a result, it usually takes many more victories in the Democratic primaries to accumulate sufficient delegates to lock the nomination. In 2016 Hillary Clinton and Bernie Sanders split the vote and delegates relatively evenly. The election contest was not decided until the final day of the primaries. By contrast, plurality rule and winner take all in the Republican primaries means that even when there are many candidates, the primary elections are usually decided more quickly. By the end of the primary season, Donald Trump had won less than 47 percent of popularly cast votes, but 62 percent of delegates. At the beginning of May, with more than a month to go in the primaries, CNN declared Trump the GOP's presumptive nominee.

How votes are cast and counted and what it takes to win a seat, then, have substantial consequences for American politics. Plurality rule with single-member districts creates strong pressures toward two-party politics and majority rule in the legislature.

Direct Democracy: The Referendum and the Recall

Twenty-four states also provide for referendum voting. The **referendum** process allows citizens to vote directly on proposed laws or other governmental actions. Referendums may come about in two ways. First, some state constitutions and laws require that certain types of legislation (such as bonds or property tax increases) be approved by popular vote. Second, people may get a measure put on the ballot by obtaining enough signatures of registered voters to a petition. Recently, voters in several states have voted to set limits on tax rates, block state and local spending proposals, define marriage, and prohibit social services for illegal immigrants. Although it involves voting, a referendum is not an election. The election is an institution of representative government through which voters choose officials to act for them. The referendum process, by contrast, is an institution of direct democracy; it allows voters to govern directly without intervention by government officials. The validity of referendum results, however, are subject to judicial action. If a court finds that a referendum outcome violates the state or national constitution, it can overturn the result. For example, in 2008 California voters passed Proposition 8, which stated, "Only marriage between a man and a woman is valid or recognized in California." A federal district court ruled Proposition 8 unconstitutional in 2010. The Supreme Court let stand the district court's ruling in and in 2015, the Supreme Court ruled in *Obergefell v. Hodges* that marriage is a fundamental right guaranteed to all people.[27]

There are other means to place issues on the ballot besides the referendum. Twenty-four states also permit various forms of the initiative. Whereas the referendum process enables citizens to affirm or reject a policy already produced by legislative action, the **initiative** provides citizens with a way forward when no legislative action has been taken. They can place a policy proposal (legislation or a state constitutional amendment) on the ballot to be approved or rejected by the electorate. To gain a place on the ballot, a petition must be accompanied by a minimum number of voters' signatures—a requirement that varies from state to state—that have been certified by the state's secretary of state.

The initiative process has both potential advantages and disadvantages. Ballot propositions involve policies that the state legislature cannot (or does not want to) resolve. Like referendum issues, these are often highly emotional and, consequently, not well suited to resolution via popular voting. However, one of the "virtues" of the initiative is that it may force action: legislative leaders may induce recalcitrant colleagues to move on controversial issues by raising the possibility that a worse outcome will result from inaction.[28]

 referendum

A measure that is decided by the vote of the electorate for approval or rejection

 initiative

A process by which citizens may petition to place a policy proposal on the ballot for public vote

---

27 *Hollingsworth et al. v. Perry et al.,* 570 U.S. 12 (2013); *Obergefell v. Hodges,* U.S. ____ (2015).

28 This point is developed in Morton Bennedsen and Sven Feldmann, "Lobbying Legislatures," *Journal of Political Economy* 110 (2002): 919–46.

recall ⇒

The removal of a public official by popular vote

Legal provisions for **recall** elections exist in 18 states. The recall is an electoral device that allows voters to remove governors and other state officials from office before the expiration of their term. Federal officials such as the president and members of Congress are not subject to recall. Generally speaking, a recall effort begins with a petition campaign. For example, in California—the site of a tumultuous recall battle in 2003—if 12 percent of those who voted in the last general election sign petitions demanding a special recall election, the state board of elections must schedule one. Such petition campaigns are relatively common, but most fail to garner enough signatures to bring the matter to a statewide vote. In California in 2003, however a conservative Republican member of Congress led a successful effort to recall Governor Gray Davis, a Democrat. Voters were unhappy about the state's economy and dissatisfied with Davis's performance, blaming him for the state's $38 billion budget deficit. After enough signatures were gathered to force a vote in October 2003, Davis became the second governor in American history to be recalled (the first was North Dakota governor Lynn Frazier, recalled in 1921). Under California law, voters in a special recall election also choose a replacement for the official whom they dismiss. Californians elected the movie star Arnold Schwarzenegger to be their governor. The recall campaign greatly increased voter interest and involvement in the political process: more than 400,000 new voters registered in California in 2003. More recently, labor unions campaigned to recall Wisconsin governor Scott Walker following cuts in state employee benefits and collective bargaining rights of unions. In the June 2012 special election, Governor Walker managed to fend off the challenge from Milwaukee mayor Tom Barrett. Scott Walker's political successes catapulted him to the national stage and a bid for the Republican nomination for president in 2016.

Direct democracy can change legislative, executive, and even judicial decision making. The referendum, initiative, and recall all entail shifts in agenda-setting power. The referendum gives an impassioned electoral majority the opportunity to reverse legislation that displeases it, thus affecting the initial strategic calculations of institutional agenda setters (who want to get as much of what they want without its being subsequently reversed). The initiative has a similar effect, but here it motivates institutional agenda setters toward action rather than inaction. Combining the two, an institutional agenda setter faces a dilemma: Do I act, risking a reversal via referendum, or do I maintain the status quo, risking an overturn via initiative? The recall complements both of these choices, keeping institutional agenda setters on their toes to avoid being ousted. As the institution principle implies, these arrangements do not just provide citizens with governance tools. They also affect the strategic calculations of institutional politicians—legislators and governors.

While initiatives and referendums are often touted as a means of ensuring that the legislature represents the public's preferences, they are also criticized for being expensive, for slowing down government action, and for making bad laws. The issues brought before the public are often emotional matters, which require deliberation and reflection, and many more complicated questions, such as public spending, might be better addressed in a legislative setting where trade-offs can serve to maintain balance in the overall policy area (such as the budget). Many critics of direct democracy point to the fiscal problems that confront California, where a long history of ballot measures restrict how California can raise revenue and how it must distribute expenditures. This leaves the legislature and governor little flexibility when facing an economic downturn.

HOW VOTERS DECIDE

An election expresses the preferences of millions of individuals about whom they want as their representatives and leaders. Electoral rules and laws—the institutional side of elections—impose order on that process, but ultimately elections are a reflection of the people's preferences about politics. The rationality principal comes into play in elections in understanding what voters want and how they think. The policy principle reflects how they behave in the presence of electoral institutions. Do they choose to change government or keep the present government in place, to change the direction of public policy making broadly speaking or stay the course?

The voter's decision can be understood as two linked decisions: whether to vote and for whom to vote. Social scientists have examined both factors by studying election returns, survey data, and laboratory experiments as well as field experiments conducted during elections. Generations of research into these questions yields a broad picture of how voters decide. First, the decision to vote or not correlates strongly with individuals' social characteristics, especially age and education, but it also depends on the electoral choices and context. An individual who knows nothing about the candidates or dislikes all of the choices is unlikely to vote. Second, which candidates or party the voters choose depends primarily on partisan loyalties, issues, and candidate characteristics. Partisan loyalties appear to be the strongest predictor of the vote, though party attachments also reflect issues and individuals' experience with candidates. Party, issues, and candidates act together to shape vote choice.

Voters and Nonvoters

According to the Census Bureau's Current Population Survey, 65 percent of adults were registered voters in 2012, and 57 percent of adults voted that year. Excluding noncitizens, who are ineligible to vote in federal elections, 80 percent of the adult citizen population is registered, and 62 percent of citizens of voting age turned out in 2012. Thus almost 40 percent of those who could have voted did not. Why do so many people not vote?

A general explanation is elusive, but social scientists find that a few demographic characteristics are strong predictors of who votes. Most important are age, education, and residential mobility. Other factors, such as gender, income, and race, also matter, but to a much smaller degree. According to the 2012 Current Population Survey, only 41 percent of those under age 25 voted that year; by comparison, 71 percent of those over age 65 years voted. The difference between these groups was 30 percentage points, and the effect of age on voting surely translated into an electoral difference. The interests of retirees are much more likely to receive attention by the government than are the interests of those in college or just entering the labor force.

Education shows similarly large differences.. More than 75 percent of people with a college education voted, and the rate was 81 percent among those with a professional degree. In contrast, slightly fewer than 40 percent of those without a high school diploma voted, and 52 percent of those with only a high school degree voted. Finally, consider residency and mobility. Only 51 percent of people who had lived in their current residence less than a year report voting, compared with 76 percent of people who lived in their residence at least five years. Those who own their home or apartment vote at a 67 percent rate, but only 49 percent of those who rent vote.[29] Turnout patterns were similar in the 2016 election. Politicians listen to those who vote, and they are disproportionately older, better educated, and more rooted in their communities.

As discussed earlier, election laws have historically had a large effect on the size and character of the electorate. The decision to vote itself consists of two steps: registration and turnout. Minimizing registration requirements may increase participation, as the option of Election Day registration has shown. As of 2016, 14 states plus the District of Columbia allow people to register on Election Day at the polls or at a government office.[30] The three states with the longest experience with same-day registration—Minnesota, Wisconsin, and Maine—do have higher turnout than most other states, and most studies suggest that in a typical state adopting such a law would increase turnout by about 3 to 5 percent.[31]

Demographics and laws are only part of what accounts for voting and nonvoting. The choices presented to voters are also important. The problem is that many people do not feel engaged by current elections or dislike politics altogether. People who are disinterested, "too busy to vote," or do not like the candidates tend not to vote. The Census Bureau survey asks registered nonvoters why they did not vote. The top four reasons are "too busy," "sick or disabled," "not interested," and "did not like the choices."

Not voting may also stem partly from a sense that the election does not hinge on how any individual votes. As advanced by Anthony Downs in *An*

---

29 The most reliable source of information about the demographics of voting is the Current Population Survey, conducted by the Census Bureau. For these and other statistics see U.S. Census Bureau, "Voting and Registration in the Election of November 2012," www.census.gov/hhes/www/socdemo/voting/publications/p20/2012/tables.html (accessed 7/17/13).

30 Hawaii has passed an election day registration law, but it will not be implemented until 2018.

31 The classic study in this area is Raymond Wolfinger and Steven Rosenstone, Who Votes? (New Haven, CT: Yale University Press, 1978). See also Steven Rosenstone and John Mark Hansen, *Participation, Mobilization and American Democracy* (New York: Macmillan, 1993).

Economic Theory of Democracy,[32] rational citizens may decide whether to participate in voting based on the calculation of potential benefits and costs of voting plus their personal sense of civic duty or psychological compunction to vote. There are, however, strong differences in voting rates across demographic groups, and these might have political consequences. What if everyone voted? In some domains, universal voting would certainly alter government policy. Increasing the voting rate of younger cohorts would probably affect government policy on Social Security, for instance. But 100 percent turnout would not likely lead to electing a different person for president or putting a different party in control of Congress. Voters and nonvoters, for all of their demographic and political differences, hold fairly similar partisan views, ideological orientations, and preferences about the candidates.[33] Voters are somewhat more conservative and more Republican than nonvoters, as a result of the higher income levels and higher home ownership incidence of voters, but the median voter would be only slightly more liberal if everyone voted.

Partisan Loyalty

The strongest predictor of how a person will vote is that individual's attachment to a political party. The American National Election Study (ANES), exit polls, and media polls have found that even in times of great political change, the overwhelming majority of Americans identifies with one of the two major political parties and votes almost entirely in accordance with that identity. Survey researchers ascertain **party identification** with simple questions along the following lines: "Generally speaking, do you consider yourself to be a Democrat, a Republican, an Independent, or what?"[34] Survey researchers further classify respondents by asking of those who choose a party whether they identify strongly or weakly with that party, and by asking independents whether they lean toward one party or another.

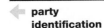

party identification

An individual's attachment to a particular political party, which might be based on issues, ideology, past experience, or upbringing

Over the past three decades, party identifications have broken evenly between Democrats and Republicans. Figure 12.2 in Chapter 12 shows the historical fluctuations in party identifications. From the 1930s to the 1970s, Democratic identifiers outnumbered Republican identifiers; but from the 1980s through 2000, the balance was stable. From 2002 through mid-2009, Democrats gained in overall party identification and Republicans lost ground, because of generational changes and the backlash against the Iraq War.[35] In Obama's first term, however, partisan battles over health care and other legislative initiatives, continuing wars in Iraq and

---

32 Anthony Downs, *An Economic Theory of Democracy* (New York: Harper & Row, 1957).

33 See, for instance, Sidney Verba, Kay Schlozman, and Henry Brady, *Voice and Equality* (Cambridge: Harvard University Press, 1995).

34 This is the wording used by the Gallup Poll. Others ask "In politics today . . ." or offer "or another party" instead of "or what."

35 Jeffrey M. Jones, "More Independents Lean GOP; Smallest Gap since '05," September 30, 2009, www.gallup.com/poll/123362/independents-lean-gop-party-gap-smallest-since-05.aspx (accessed 8/30/11).

Afghanistan, and high unemployment eroded public support for the Democrats. Today, public support for the parties is fairly evenly split, with a slight edge for the Democrats. Since 2005, the percentage of independents has crept steadily upward—and is now the largest group in the electorate, though many Independents lean toward one of the two parties.[36] As of June 2016, the Gallup Poll reported that 41 percent of Americans are Republicans or lean Republican and 48 percent of Americans are Democrats or lean Democratic.[37]

Party identifications capture the voters' predisposition toward their party's candidates. Many of these predispositions are rooted in public policies, such as those on taxes or abortion or civil rights. Those long-standing policy positions lead to divisions in party identifications and voting patterns among different demographic groups. Large majorities of African Americans and Hispanics, for example, identify and vote with the Democratic Party. Since 1980 there has also been a gender gap in voting. Women identify more and vote more with the Democrats than men do. That gap has persisted, averaging 7 percentage points over the past three decades. The 2016 election saw the widest gender gap in history, with the first female candidate running for a major party—Democrat Hillary Clinton: Clinton received 54 percent of the vote of women, but only 41 percent of the vote among men, a difference of 13 points. That difference is also significant because women now make up a majority (53 percent) of voters.

It is a subject of considerable debate as to why the gender gap arose in the late 1970s and early 1980s and why it has persisted. The timing of its emergence is consistent with the two parties' alignment on a range of civil rights issues that affect women. On issues such as pay equity, divorce law, abortion, and women's health, the Democratic administrations and Congress have pursued policies much more favorable to the interests of women. In 2016, Hillary Clinton asserted an absolute right of a woman to choose to have an abortion, and stressed her support for Planned Parenthood as a provider of many different women's health services. Donald Trump promised to end funding of Planned Parenthood and said abortion is only acceptable when the pregnancy threatens the life of the mother or was due to rape or incest. These views alienated many women voters and likely contributed to the increase in the gender gap in the fall election. It is, however, hard to pin down the exact causes of the shifts as so many of these issues emerged at the same time (the 1970s) and shifts in party attachments tend to be subtle and complex.[38] Issues played some part in the rise of the gender gap, but cultural, racial, and regional differences might also explain some of this phenomenon.

---

36 Marc Hetherington, "Resurgent Mass Partisanship: The Role of Elite Polarization," *American Political Science Review* 95, no. 3 (September 2001): 619–31. Pew Research Center, "Party Identification," www .pewresearch.org/data-trend/political-attitudes/party-identification (accessed 11/11/14).

37 Gallup Poll, "Party Affiliation," www.gallup.com/poll/15370/party-affiliation.aspx (accessed 6/29/16).

38 Christina Wohlbrecht, *The Politics of Women's Rights* (Princeton, NJ: Princeton University Press, 2000).

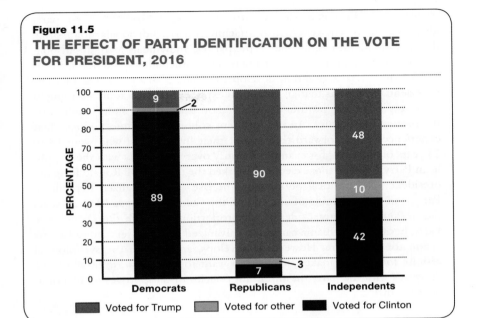

Figure 11.5

THE EFFECT OF PARTY IDENTIFICATION ON THE VOTE FOR PRESIDENT, 2016

Democrats: 89, 9, 2
Republicans: 90, 7, 3
Independents: 48, 10, 42

■ Voted for Trump   ■ Voted for other   ■ Voted for Clinton

Although specific features of the choices and context matter as well, party identifications express how the voter would likely vote in a "neutral" election. Party identifications are extremely good predictors of voting behavior in less prominent elections, such as for state legislatures or lower-level statewide offices, about which voters may know relatively little. Even in presidential elections, with their extensive advertising and thorough news coverage, party predispositions predict individual voting behavior. Figure 11.5 displays the percentages of Democratic identifiers, Republican identifiers, and self-described independents who voted for Clinton, Trump, or someone else in 2016. The 2016 election was typical in that partisan loyalty is usually in the range of 90 percent. Approximately 90 percent of party identifiers voted for their own party's standard bearer. Independents broke 48 to 42 for Trump. Sometimes, the independent vote decides the election. However, in this case, Hillary Clinton's popular vote victory was due to Democrats making up the single largest group in the electorate. She won 90 percent of Democrats and enough independents to give her a majority of all votes (even though Donald Trump still won the Electoral College).

Since the discovery of its importance in the 1950s, party identification has raised deeper questions about its origins and meaning. There are three distinct views about what party identification is, and they point to very different understandings of the nature of party identification and its effect on elections.[39] Debate over the meaning of party identification cuts to the heart of the meaning of elections.

39 For an excellent treatment of the meanings of party identification and analysis of the implications of different theories, see Donald Green, Bradley Palmquist, and Eric Schickler, *Partisan Hearts and Minds* (New Haven, CT: Yale University Press, 2003).

Party Identification as Psychological Attachment. First, party identification is a psychological attachment that individuals hold, often throughout adulthood, to one of the parties. Individuals learn about politics as children and adolescents from parents, other adults, and peers, and as part of that socialization they develop attachments to a party. The first few presidential elections that an individual experiences as an adult are thought to have particularly profound influence on that voter's understanding of the parties and politics. And as different cohorts come into politics, their experiences carry forward throughout their lives. Those who were 18 to 24 years old in 1984, for example, identify overwhelmingly with the Republican Party, because those elections marked the triumph of Ronald Reagan's presidency and political philosophy, the rise of a revitalized Republican Party, and the beginning of the end of the Cold War. Those 18 to 24 years old in 2008, in contrast, identify disproportionately with the Democratic Party, because the Obama campaign galvanized young voters around a new vision for the future. However it develops, an individual's psychological affinity for a party makes that person want to support it, even when she disagrees with the party on important policies or disapproves of its nominees for office.

Party Identification as Ideological Affinity. Of course, the Democratic and Republican parties are quite different entities today than they were 40 years ago or 80 years ago. On matters of race relations, for example, the Democratic Party has moved over the past century from supporting segregation to spearheading civil rights. The Republican Party, once a bastion of economic protectionism, has championed free trade for the past several decades. During the 2016 campaign, however, Donald Trump questioned the basic principles of free trade and sought to lead the GOP back to its protectionist roots. However strong generational transmission of party identifications may be, the dissonance between identities and issues must surely weaken the pull of party, which suggests a second theory: that party identification reflects underlying ideologies of voters and policy positions of parties.

Parties in government are meaningful organizations for producing public policies. The relatively high degree of party loyalty in Congress and other branches of government means that voters can reasonably anticipate how politicians will act in office. Citizens identify with parties that pursue public policies more to their liking. For example, a union worker will feel a stronger attachment to the Democratic Party because the Democrats have historically protected union interests. A high-income earner may feel a strong pull toward the Republican Party because that party pushes lower taxes overall, whereas the Democrats promote higher tax rates for higher-income households. The party labels act as brand names and help voters choose the candidates that will best match their preferences. As such, party labels provide an informational shortcut. In part, party identifiers feel that one party represents their interests better than others; hence an identifier is highly likely to vote for that party without even knowing a candidate's voting record or campaign promises.[40]

Not all people fit neatly into one ideological camp or another. Some people do not think about politics in ideological or policy terms. Others are indifferent to the parties ideologically. A significant portion of Americans consider themselves centrists and feel that the Democrats are somewhat too liberal and the Republicans somewhat too conservative. They do not have a strong affinity for either party. Other people feel pulled in different directions by different issues and concerns. A union member who strongly opposes abortion, for example, is drawn to the Democrats' labor policies and the Republicans' abortion policies. Campaigns target such cross-pressured voters, who are often pivotal in elections.[41]

Party Identification as Tally of Experiences. A third explanation is that party identification reflects experiences with political leaders and representatives, especially presidents. Americans hold their presidents, and to a lesser extent Congress, accountable for the country's economic performance and success in foreign affairs. A bad economy or a disastrous military intervention will lead voters to disapprove of the president and to lower their assessment of the president's party's ability to govern. Parties are, by this account, teams seeking to run the government: they consist of policy experts, managers, and leaders who will conduct foreign policy, economic policy, and domestic policies (such as environmental protection and health care). When things go well, voters infer that the incumbent party has a good approach to running national affairs; but when things go badly, they learn that the party lacks the people needed to run the government competently or the approach needed to produce economic prosperity, international peace, and other desirable outcomes. With each successive presidency and their experience of it, individuals update their beliefs about which party is better able to govern.

Psychological attachments, ideological affinities, and past experiences combine to form an individual's current party identification. But party is not the only factor in voting. We consider next how issues and candidates shape voting behavior.

Issues

Voting on issues and policies cuts to the core of our understanding of democratic accountability and electoral control over government. A simple, idealized account of **issue voting** goes as follows. Governments make policies and laws

issue voting

An individual's propensity to select candidates or parties based on the extent to which the individual agrees with one candidate more than others on specific issues

---

40 For a detailed assessment of the political use of information-economizing devices such as party labels, see Arthur Lupia and Mathew D. McCubbins, *The Democratic Dilemma: Can Citizens Learn What They Need to Know?* (New York: Cambridge University Press, 1998).

41 For a more in-depth discussion of independent voters, policy indifference, and cross pressure, see Sunshine Hillygus and Todd Shields, *The Persuadable Voter: Wedge Issues in Presidential Campaigns* (Princeton, NJ: Princeton University Press, 2008).

on a variety of issues that affect the public. Voters who disagree with those policies and laws on principle or who think those policies have failed will vote against those who made the decisions. Voters who support the policies or like the outcomes will support the incumbent legislators or party. It is important to note that politicians' choices of what laws to enact and what administrative actions are made with the express aim of attracting electoral support. Voters choose the candidates and parties that stand for the policies and laws most in line with voters' preferences. Even long-term factors like party identification are related to voters' preferences.

Voters' choice of issues usually involves a mix of their judgments about the past behavior of competing parties and candidates and their hopes and fears about candidates' future behavior. Political scientists call choices that focus on future behavior **prospective voting** and those based on past performance **retrospective voting**. To some extent, whether prospective or retrospective evaluation is more important in a particular election depends on the strategies of the competing candidates. Candidates always endeavor to define election issues in terms that will serve their interests. Incumbents running during a period of prosperity will seek to take credit for the strong economy and define the election as revolving around their record of success. This strategy encourages voters to make retrospective judgments. By contrast, an insurgent running during a period of economic uncertainty will tell voters it is time for a change and ask them to make prospective judgments. Thus Barack Obama focused on the need for change in 2008, but the White House repeatedly stressed the need to stay the course in 2010 and 2012. In 2016, Hillary Clinton campaigned on staying the course with Obama's policies, a stance buoyed by President Obama's rising popularity in the final two years of his second term.

Not all issues, however, are alike. Politics involves different sorts of issues, such as economic concerns, moral questions, and foreign affairs. Voters may hold different views on each. Some voters might favor low taxes and no government restrictions on abortion (a libertarian perspective), while others want low taxes and a prohibition on abortion; still others may prefer high taxes and no restrictions on abortion; and so on. Moreover, some voters weigh economics more heavily; others give the greatest weight to social issues; still others are national security voters. In 2016, Edison Research, which conducts the national exit polls for the primary media outlets, presented voters with four issues: foreign policy, immigration, the economy, and terrorism. The exit poll found that 60 percent of those who selected foreign policy and 52 percent of those who identified the economy as the most important issue voted for Clinton, while 64 percent of those who selected immigration and 57 percent of those who identified terrorism as the most important issue voted for Trump.[42]

prospective voting

Voting based on the imagined future performance of a candidate

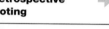

retrospective voting

Voting based on the past performance of a candidate

42 Exit polls, CNN Politics, www.cnn.com/election/results/exit-polls (accessed 11/12/16).

Issues differ in another important respect: the extent to which the policy principle is invoked. Broadly speaking, issues may be distinguished as spatial issues and valence issues. **Spatial issues** are those on which voters have preferences over what policy is pursued; they have beliefs about which policies will lead to the best outcomes, or they have moral convictions that lead them to value the means, not just the ends. Valence issues are those on which voters do not care about the means (the policy), only the ends (the outcome). Voters care about having peaceful and prosperous lives, quite apart from how they are achieved.

Spatial Issues. When issues elicit conflicting preferences over policies and outcomes, we call these spatial preferences because the choices can be mapped along a continuum or line, such as tax rates or size of government. Abortion rights provide an excellent example. At one extreme are those who defend the legality of abortion under all circumstances; at the other extreme are those who want to ban the procedure under all circumstances. Between those two poles lie a range of policy alternatives, from putting some restrictions on access, to regulating the time during pregnancy and procedures used, to allowing the practice only when the mother's life is threatened. Research has demonstrated that public preferences are distributed across such policy options, with many people favoring a moderate approach of placing some restrictions on the practice. Abortion laws exemplify the features of spatial issues—a range of policy options and a lack of consensus on the right policy.

Politicians compete for votes by pursuing policies that they think will attract the most voters. In the 2016 presidential election, Donald Trump promised to cut taxes, reduce government spending on social programs, and repeal NAFTA and other trade agreements in order to stimulate the economy. Hillary Clinton proposed eliminating tax breaks used by very wealthy people and increasing marginal tax rates on those making more than $1 million a year. On health care, Trump promised to repeal the Affordable Care Act, while Clinton promised to revise the act to make it more like Medicare and Medicaid. Voters made judgments on a head-to-head comparison of these and many other issues as well as the candidates' overall ideologies and views about government.

Spatial voting is one way that voters solve the adverse selection problem. Adverse selection arises if, due to a lack of information about the candidates, we choose people for office who do not fit with our interests. Party identities might lead us to this situation, for the "one price fits all" label of the parties may not correctly reflect how an individual candidate will vote on legislation. If, instead, voters choose on the basis of what policies the candidates represent or promise to support, then voters can choose the right people to represent their interests and values. Spatial voting also helps correct for moral hazard, which arises if there is no accountability for legislative decisions. However, politicians must run for reelection. People who are attentive to what laws the politicians supported and opposed can vote against politicians with whom they disagree. Recent research on congressional roll-call voting suggests that this is a strong

 spatial issue

An issue for which a range of possible options or policies can be ordered, say, from liberal to conservative or from most expensive to least expensive

factor in U.S. House elections and accounts for a significant portion of party identification.[43]

When voters engage in issue voting, competition between two candidates pushes the candidates' issue positions toward the middle of the distribution of voters' preferences. This is known as the **median-voter theorem**, made famous by economists Duncan Black and Anthony Downs.[44] (Chapter 6 discussed the median-voter theorem in the context of congressional committees.) To see the logic of this claim in the context of elections, imagine a series of possible stances on a policy issue as points along a line, stretching from 0 to 100 (Figure 11.6). A voter is represented by an "ideal" policy and preferences, which decline as policy moves away from this ideal. Thus voters in group 1 prefer policy X_1 most, and their preference declines as the policy moves to the left or right of X_1. Voters whose ideal policy lies between, say, 0 and 25 are said to be liberal on this policy (groups 1 and 2), those whose ideal lies between 75 and 100 are conservative (groups 4 and 5), and those whose favorite policy is between 25 and 75 are moderate (group 3). An issue voter cares about only issue positions, not partisan loyalty or candidates' characteristics, and would, therefore, vote for the candidate whose announced policy is closest to his or her own most preferred policy.

Consider now an electorate of 125 voters evenly distributed among the five groups shown in Figure 11.6.[45] The middle group contains the median voter because half or more of this electorate has an ideal policy at or to the left of X_3 (groups 1, 2, and 3), and half or more has an ideal policy at or to the right of X_3 (groups 3, 4, and 5). Group 3 is in the driver's seat, as the following reasoning suggests. If a candidate announces X_3 as her policy—the median voter's most preferred alternative—and if her opponent picks any point to the right, then the median voter and all those with ideal policies to the left of the median voter's (groups 1–3) will support the first candidate. They constitute a majority, by definition of the median, so this candidate will win. Suppose instead that the opponent chose as his policy some point to the left of the median ideal policy. Then the median voter and all those with ideal policies to the right of the median voter's (groups 3–5) will support the first candidate—and she wins, again. In short, the median-voter theorem says that the candidate whose policy position is closest to the ideal policy of the median voter will defeat the other candidate in a majority contest. We can conclude from this brief analysis that issue voting encourages candidate convergence (in which both candidates cozy up to the position of the median voter). Even when voters are not exclusively

43 See Stephen Ansolabehere and Philip Jones, "Constituents' Responses to Congressional Roll-Call Voting," *American Journal of Political Science* 54 (July 2010): 583–97.

44 See Duncan Black, *The Theory of Committees and Elections*, 2nd ed. (Boston: Kluwer, 1998); and Anthony Downs, *An Economic Theory of Democracy* (New York: Harper & Row, 1957). A general, accessible treatment of this subject is found in Kenneth A. Shepsle, *Analyzing Politics: Rationality, Behavior, and Institutions*, 2nd ed. (New York: W.W. Norton and Company), chap. 5.

45 For the sake of this illustration, 25 voters have been included in each group. This argument holds true with any distribution of voters among the groups.

---

median-voter theorem

A proposition predicting that when policy options can be arrayed along a single dimension, majority rule will pick the policy most preferred by the voter whose ideal policy is to the left of half of the voters and to the right of exactly half of the voters. (See Chapter 6 for further discussion.)

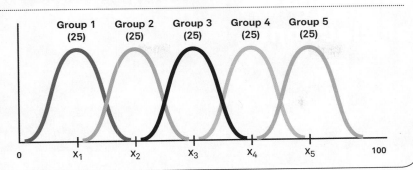

Figure 11.6

THE MEDIAN-VOTER THEOREM

Group 1 (25) Group 2 (25) Group 3 (25) Group 4 (25) Group 5 (25)

0 X_1 X_2 X_3 X_4 X_5 100

issue voters, two-candidate competition still encourages a tendency toward convergence, although it may not fully run its course.[46]

Valence Issues. Some issues lack conflict: all people want the same outcome. All people want less crime, more prosperity and less poverty, less inflation, better health, peace, and security. They may have different beliefs about how to attain those objectives, but they don't really care about the means; they care about the outcome.

In the context of elections, economic conditions are the most important **valence issue**. If voters are satisfied with their economic prospects, they tend to support the party in power, while voters' unease about the economy tends to favor the opposition. Richard Nixon, Ronald Reagan, Bill Clinton, and George W. Bush won reelection easily in the midst of favorable economies. Jimmy Carter in 1980 and George H. W. Bush in 1992 ran for reelection in the midst of economic downturns, and both lost. The Analyzing the Evidence unit on pp. 466–7 explores voters' perceptions of the economy in relation to their support for the incumbent party.

How bad must the economy be in order for the incumbent to get turned out of office? Social scientists have developed several rules of thumb based on historical correlations between economic performance and the vote. A common sort of empirical analysis uses economic growth (annual percentage changes in gross domestic product) to predict the vote. The idea is that large numbers of individuals vote against the incumbent party in bad times and with the incumbent party in good times. Adding up the 100 million or so votes will aggregate every individual's experiences and reflect roughly what is going on in the economy and how that affects his voting. The correlation between economic growth and votes for the incumbent

◄ **valence issue**

An issue or aspect of a choice for which all voters prefer a higher value, in contrast to a spatial issue—for example, voters prefer their politicians to be honest, and honesty is a valence issue

---

46 This convergence will also be a moderating force as candidates move toward what they believe will appeal to voters in the middle. But if the middle of the voter distribution of preferences tilts toward the right or the left, it may not be very moderate. If X_3, for example, were barely to the left of X_4, then the median voter would be fairly right wing rather than in the middle of the issue dimension.

Economic Influence on Presidential Elections

Contributed by
Robert S. Erikson
Columbia University

The state of the economy is a key factor in presidential elections. When the United States prospers, the presidential party performs much better than when economic conditions are poor. The economic influence on presidential elections can be seen by predicting the vote based on objective indicators such as GDP growth leading up to the election. The simplest measure, however, is a subjective one—voters' responses when asked in polls whether the economy has been performing well or badly. When survey respondents are asked early in the election year how they plan to vote, candidate and party preferences show little relationship to economic perceptions at that time. By election day, however, the national vote falls surprisingly in line with the voters' perceptions of economic performance. In short, the election campaign increases the importance of the economy to voters.

The precise indicator of economic perceptions used here is the average response to the following question, asked regularly by the Survey of Consumers at the University of Michigan in April and November of the election year: "Would you say that at the current time business conditions are better or worse than they were a year ago?"

April Poll Results

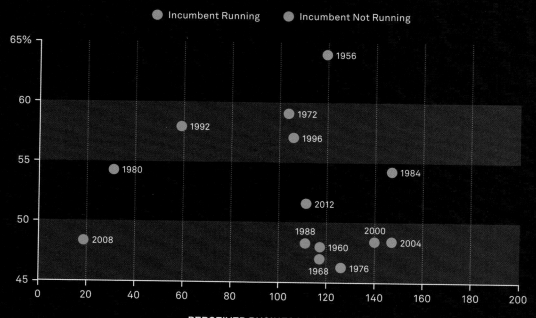

● Incumbent Running   ● Incumbent Not Running

PERCENT INCUMBENT PARTY

- 65%
- 60
- 55
- 50
- 45

1956
1972
1992
1996
1980
1984
2012
2008
1988
2000
1960
2004
1968
1976

PERCEIVED BUSINESS CONDITIONS
(0 = worst, 200 = best)

0 20 40 60 80 100 120 140 160 180 200

The lack of any consistent pattern in the first graph (at left) shows that what voters think about the economy in April of an election year has little bearing on their vote intentions at that time—as if voters had not yet thought about the November election sufficiently to factor in the economy. Especially noteworthy examples are 1980 and 1992 when incumbents Jimmy Carter and George H. W. Bush, respectively, were favored in the early polls, despite being seen as presiding over poor economies. Both lost the general election. John McCain (representing the incumbent Republican Party) was only slightly behind Barack Obama in early 2008, despite an economy that already was almost universally seen as worsening.

The clear pattern in the second graph (below) shows that by November, the vote fell into rough alignment with economic perceptions: The better the average perception of business conditions, the greater the support for the incumbent party. The three weakest economies in terms of perceptions (1980, 1992, 2008) all saw the incumbent party lose.

November Poll Results

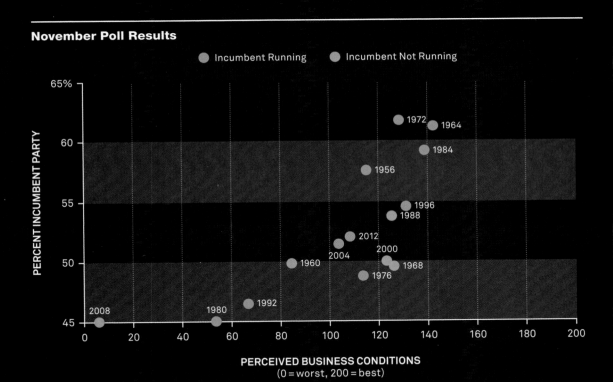

SOURCE: Surveys of Consumers, www.sca.isr.umich.edu/tables.html (accessed 12/16/2015); and author's compilation.

party is sufficient to allow statistically minded political scientists to make forecasts. Roughly speaking, every additional 1 percent growth in GDP corresponds to a 1 percentage point increase in the incumbent president's party's vote.[47]

Another approach relies on the Consumer Confidence Index, which is calculated by the Conference Board, a business research group. The Consumer Confidence Index is based on a public opinion survey that measures people's sense of the economy in their area and their expectations over the coming months. A score above 100 means that most respondents are optimistic about the economy and that growth is strong. A score below 100 means that most respondents are pessimistic about the economy and job growth is weak. It has proven a fairly accurate predictor of presidential outcomes. A generally rosy view, indicated by a score greater than 100, augurs well for the party in power. An index score of less than 100, suggesting that voters are pessimistic about the economy, suggests that incumbents should worry about their job prospects. In October 2016, the Consumer Confidence Index stood at 87.2, and the Democrats lost control of the White House and failed to retake the Senate and the House of Representatives.

Economic voting is one way that voters solve the moral hazard problems inherent in representative democracy. They cannot monitor every policy that the government initiates. They do, however, have a rudimentary way to hold the government accountable—staying the course when times are good, and voting for change when the economy sours.

Candidate Characteristics

Candidates' personal attributes always influence voters' decisions. The more important characteristics are race, ethnicity, religion, gender, geography, and social background. In general, voters presume that candidates who are close to themselves in terms of these attributes will likely have views close to their own. Moreover, they may be proud to see someone of their ethnic, religious, or geographic background in a position of leadership. This is why, for many years, politicians sought to "balance the ticket," making certain that their party's ticket included members of as many important groups as possible.

Just as a candidate's personal characteristics may attract some voters, so they may repel others. Many voters are prejudiced against candidates of certain ethnic, racial, or religious groups. For most of American history, an African American or woman president seemed unthinkable, but those barriers fell in 2008 and 2016 respectively.

Voters also consider candidates' personality characteristics, such as their competence, honesty, and vigor because they figure that politicians with these attributes are likely to produce good outcomes—such as laws that work, fair and honest administration of government, and ability to address crises. Candidates emphasize certain qualities that they think all voters will value. An excellent

---

47 Perhaps the most comprehensive study of the responsiveness of elections to fluctuations in the U.S. economy is Robert Erikson, Michael MacKuen, and James Stimson, *The Macro-Polity* (New York: Cambridge University Press, 2002).

example arose in the 2008 primary election between Hillary Clinton and Barack Obama. Clinton ran an ad that intended to show her experience and ability to solve crises. "It's 3 a.m. and your children are safely asleep. But there's a phone in the White House and it's ringing. Something's happening in the world. Your vote will decide who answers that call. . . . Whether it's someone tested and ready to lead in a dangerous world. . . ." This ad sought to tap voters' belief in the need for a certain set of competencies in the White House.

Other personal characteristics are important as well. In 2016, Hillary Clinton became the first woman nominated by a major party to be president. Throughout the general election, public opinion polls showed a significant shift among women, especially white women, toward her candidacy, and of white men toward Trump. The gap between the vote choice of white men and of white women grew from a 6-point difference in 2012 to an 11-point difference in 2016.

One of the most distinctive features of American politics is the incumbency advantage, as we saw in Chapter 6. Why this advantage has emerged and grown remains a puzzle. Redistricting is almost certainly not the explanation: incumbency effects are as large in gubernatorial elections, where there are no districts, as in House elections. It is thought that about half of the incumbency advantage reflects the activities of the legislator in office; it is the result of voters rewarding incumbents for their performance. The other half of the incumbency advantage evidently reflects the incumbents' opponents.[48] The typical challenger may not have the personal appeal of the typical incumbent, who, after all, has already won office once. Moreover, challengers usually lack the experience and resources that the incumbent has for running a campaign. This is critical. The ability to communicate with the voters can give a politician the edge in close elections.

Although party, issues, and candidate characteristics are perhaps the three most important factors shaping voting decisions, political scientists debate the relative importance of each. Problems of measurement and the limitations of research methods complicate the assessment. Recent scholarship suggests that the three factors have roughly equal weight in explaining the division of the vote in national elections.[49] Part of the difficulty in understanding their importance is that the extent to which these factors matter depends on the electorate's information levels. In the absence of much information, most voters rely almost exclusively on party cues. A highly informed electorate relies more heavily on issues and candidate characteristics.[50]

---

48 The partitioning of the incumbency effect into officeholder advantages and challenger qualities begins with the important work of Gary C. Jacobson. See, for example, his text *The Politics of Congressional Elections*, 7th ed. (White Plains, NY: Longman, 2008). Estimating exactly what fraction of the incumbency effect is due to officeholder benefits is tricky. See Stephen Ansolabehere, James M. Snyder, Jr., and Charles H. Stewart III, "Old Voters, New Voters, and the Personal Vote: Using Redistricting to Measure the Incumbency Advantage," *American Journal of Political Science* 44, no. 1 (January 2000): 17–34.

49 See Stephen Ansolabehere, Jonathan Rodden, and James M. Snyder, Jr., "Issue Voting," *American Political Science Review* 102, no. 2 (May 2008): 215–32.

50 The classic study showing this is Philip Converse, "The Nature of Belief Systems in Mass Publics," in *Ideology and Discontent*, David Apter, ed. (New York: Free Press, 1964).

CAMPAIGNS: MONEY, MEDIA, AND GRASS ROOTS

American political campaigns are freewheeling events with few restrictions on what candidates may say or do. Candidates in hotly contested House and Senate races spend millions of dollars to advertise on television, radio, and the Internet, as well as direct mail and door-to-door canvassing. Those seeking office are in a race to become as well known and as well liked as possible and to get more of their supporters to vote. Federal laws limit how much an individual or organization may give to a candidate but, with the exception of presidential campaigns, place no restrictions on how much a candidate or party committee may spend.

Adding to the freewheeling nature of campaigns is their organizational structure. Most political campaigns are temporary organizations, formed for the sole purpose of winning the coming elections and disbanding shortly afterward. To be sure, political parties in the United States have permanent, professional campaign organizations that raise money, strategize, recruit candidates, and distribute resources. These are, on the Republican side, the Republican National Committee, the National Republican Senatorial Committee, and the National Republican Congressional Committee. On the Democratic side are the Democratic National Committee, the Democratic Senatorial Campaign Committee, and the Democratic Congressional Campaign Committee. They account for roughly one-third of the money in politics and have considerable expertise. But most campaigns are formed by and around individual candidates, who often put up the initial cash to get the campaign rolling and rely heavily on family and friends as volunteers. During an election thousands of such organizations are at work, with relatively little coordination among them. The two presidential campaigns operate 50 different state-level operations, with other campaigns competing for 33 or 34 Senate seats, 435 House seats, dozens of gubernatorial and other statewide offices, and thousands of state legislative seats. All simultaneously seek to persuade as many people as possible to vote for their candidate on Election Day.

What It Takes to Win

All campaigns face similar challenges—how to mobilize volunteers, how to raise money, how to coordinate activities, what messages to run, how to communicate with the public. There is no single best way to run a campaign. There are many tried-and-true approaches, especially building up a campaign from local connections, from the grass roots. Candidates have to meet as many people as possible and get their friends and their friends' friends to support them. In-person campaigning becomes increasingly difficult in larger constituencies. Candidates continually experiment with new ways of reaching large segments of the electorate: in the 1920s, radio advertising eclipsed handbills and door-to-door canvassing; in the 1960s, television began to eclipse radio; in the

1980s and 1990s, cable television, phone polling, and focus groups allowed targeting of specific demographic groups. The great innovation of the Obama campaign was to meld Internet networking tools with old-style organizing methods to develop a massive communications and fund-raising network, what came to be called a "netroots" campaign. The Clinton campaign in 2016 capitalized on the infrastructure built by Obama and sought the advice of many of the same consultants. The Trump campaign, by contrast, relied heavily on Twitter and media coverage, and ignored the typical organization and mobilization activities considered essential for modern campaigns.

Campaigns play an essential role in American democracy. They enable politicians to present themselves to the public to explain who they are, what they have accomplished, and what they will do in office. Television advertisements, get-out-the-vote activities, and direct mail provide voters with factual information about the candidates' personal characteristics and ideologies, about the meaning of the party labels, and about what issues distinguish the politicians.

Campaigns are also a time when the foibles and failures of those in office may be revealed. Challengers claim that a new direction is needed, arguing that the incumbent is the wrong person to represent the constituency (a case of adverse selection) or has failed to do the job as constituents wanted (a case of moral hazard). Incumbents, for their part, appeal to voters on the basis of their ideological fit with their constituents and their performance in office. It has become an assumption of American elections and election law that candidates and parties will mount competitive campaigns to win office. They will spend millions, even billions, of dollars to persuade people to vote and how to vote. And because of those efforts voters will understand better the choices they face. In short, campaigns inform voters through competition.

In addition to being costly, American political campaigns are long. Presidential campaigns officially launch a year and a half to two years in advance of Election Day. Serious campaigns for the U.S. House of Representatives begin at least a year ahead of the general election date and often span the better part of two years. To use the term of the Federal Election Commission, an election is a two-year *cycle*, not a single day or even the period between Labor Day and Election Day loosely referred to as "the general election."

Long campaigns are due largely to the effort required to mount them. There are roughly 320 million people in the United States, and the voting-age population exceeds 245 million people. Communicating with all of those individuals is expensive and time-consuming. In the 2016 election cycle, the Clinton campaign and allied committees spent $1.3 billion; the Trump campaign and allied committees spent $800 million—a combined total of just over $2 billion. Approximately half of that sum purchased airtime for television advertising. The money was raised through personal and political networks that the campaigns and candidates built up over months, even years, of effort.

The campaign season is further extended by the election calendar. American national, state, and local elections proceed in two steps: the party primary elections and the general election. General elections for federal offices are set by the U.S. Constitution to take place on the first Tuesday after the first Monday in November. The first presidential caucuses and primaries come early in January and last through the beginning of June. State and congressional primaries do not follow the same calendar; most occur in the spring and early summer, with some states waiting to hold their nominating elections until September of the election year. The result of this calendar of elections is to stretch the campaigns over the entire election year.

American electoral campaigns contrast starkly with those in other democracies, such as Germany, France, Japan, and the United Kingdom. Parliamentary systems have short campaigns: once the government calls for an election, the campaign proceeds for a few months, and an election is held. The years-long gestation of an American election is considered unseemly in most other democracies, which also limit candidates' campaign expenditures and fund-raising activities. Money and other resources in other democracies flow through party organizations, often with little government oversight. Most democracies also regulate how candidates and parties campaign; while posters, billboards, and public campaign forums are common in other democracies, very few permit television advertising, phone banks, or door-to-door canvassing. The restrictions make the campaigns themselves less important and make media coverage of the parties, the candidates, and the government more prominent.

Campaign Finance

The expense, duration, and chaos of American campaigns have prompted many efforts at reform, including attempts to limit campaign spending, shorten the campaign season, and restrict what candidates and organizations can say in advertisements. The most sweeping campaign reforms came in 1971, when Congress passed the Federal Elections Campaign Act (FECA). It limited the amounts that a single individual could contribute to a candidate or party to $1,000 per election for individuals and $5,000 for organizations (these limits have since been increased, as Table 11.1 indicates). It further regulated how business firms, unions, and other organizations could give money, prohibiting donations directly from the organization's treasury and requiring the establishment of a separate, segregated fund—a **political action committee (PAC)**. It established public funding for presidential campaigns and tied those funds to expenditure limits. And it set up the Federal Election Commission (FEC) to oversee public disclosure of information and to enforce the laws.[51]

Congress has amended FECA several times, most importantly in the Bipartisan Campaign Reform Act of 2002 (also called the McCain-Feingold Act, after senators John McCain and Russell Feingold, its primary sponsors). The McCain-Feingold Act prohibited unlimited party spending (called soft money) and banned certain sorts of political attack advertisements from interest groups in the last weeks of a campaign. Table 11.1 presents a summary of some of the rules governing campaign finance in federal elections.

political action committee (PAC)

A private group that raises and distributes funds for use in election campaigns

---

51   The FEC's website is an excellent resource for those interested in U.S. campaign finance (www.fec.gov).

Table 11.1

FEDERAL CAMPAIGN FINANCE CONTRIBUTION LIMITS

	To each candidate or candidate committee per election	To national party committee per calendar year	To state, district, and local party committee per calendar year	To each pac* (ssf and nonconnected) per calendar year
Individual may give	$2,700**	$33,400**	$10,000 (combined limit)	$5,000
National party committee may give	$5,000	No limit	No limit	$5,000
State, district, and local party committee may give	$5,000	No limit	No limit	$5,000
PAC (multicandidate)* may give**	$5,000	$15,00	$5,000 (Combined limit)	$5,000
PAC (not multicandidate) may give	$2,700	$33,400**	$10,000 (combined limit)	$5,000
Candidate committee may give	$2,000	No limit	No limit	$5,000

* PAC refers to a committee that makes contributions to other federal political committees. Super PACs may accept unlimited contributions.
**Indexed for inflation in odd-numbered years
***A multicandidate committee is a political committee with more than 50 contributors that has been registered for at least six months and, with the exception of state party committees, has made contributions to five or more candidates for federal office.
SOURCE: Federal Election Commission, www.fec.gov/pages/brochures/contrib.shtml#Chart (accessed 7/2/15).

FECA also established public funding for presidential campaigns. If a candidate agrees to abide by spending limits, her campaign is eligible for matching funds in primary elections and full public funding in the general election. The general election amount was set at $20 million in 1974 and allowed to increase with inflation. Until 2000, nearly all candidates bought into the system. But George W. Bush chose to fund his 2000 primary election campaign outside this system and spent $500 million to win the Republican nomination. Barack Obama and Hillary Clinton ignored the public financing system in their 2008 primary contest, and Obama opted out of the public system in the general election as well, allowing him to spend several hundred million more dollars than the Republican nominee, John McCain. In 2016, only Martin O'Malley (Democrat) and Jill Stein (Green Party) received public funding for their presidential campaigns.

The FECA originally went much further than the law that survives today. Congress originally passed mandatory caps on spending by House and Senate candidates and prohibited organizations from running independent campaigns on behalf of or in opposition to a candidate (and not coordinated with any candidate). James Buckley, a candidate for U.S. Senate in New York, challenged the law, arguing that the restrictions on spending and contributions limited his rights to free speech and that FEC had excessive administrative power. In the 1976 landmark case *Buckley v. Valeo*, the U.S. Supreme Court agreed in part.[52] The Court ruled that "money is speech," but the government also has a compelling interest in protecting elections from corrupt practices, such as bribery through large campaign donations. The justices declared the limits on candidate spending unconstitutional because they violated free speech rights of candidates and groups. However, the need to protect the integrity of the electoral process led the justices to leave contribution limits in place. The presidential public-funding system was also validated because it is voluntary. Candidates are not required to opt into the system; hence there is no violation of free speech. What survived *Buckley* is a system in which candidates, groups, and parties may spend as much as they like to win office, but donations must come in small amounts. This is a more democratic process of campaign finance, but it increases the effort and time needed to construct a campaign.

The Supreme Court's decision in *Buckley* rests on an essential truth of American democracy and elections. The First Amendment right to free speech amounts to a "profound national commitment to the principle that debate on public issues should be uninhibited, robust, and wide-open."[53] Furthermore, in 2010 the Court reinforced its reasoning in *Buckley* in the case *Citizens United v. Federal Election Commission*.[54] Here the justices ruled that the BCRA of 2002 had erred in imposing restrictions on independent spending by corporations. It overturned key components of the BCRA and reversed its ruling in the case that had upheld BCRA.[55] The majority opinion struck down limits on independent expenditures from corporate treasuries but kept in place limits on direct contributions from corporations and other organizations to candidates; it also solidified corporations' right to free political speech, on par with the right to free speech of individuals. Following this decision, two sorts of organizations formed—501c(4) organizations, which derive their title from the section of the tax code that allows such entities, and Super PACs. Each can raise and spend unlimited amounts on campaigns, though Super PACs are subject to more disclosure laws. Super PACs spent approximately $1.2 billion in 2016, mostly on

---

52 *Buckley v. Valeo*, 424 U.S. 1 (1976).

53 The majority opinion in *Buckley* quotes an earlier landmark case, *New York Times Co. v. Sullivan*, 376 U.S. 254 (1964).

54 *Citizens United v. Federal Election Commission*, 558 U.S. 310 (2010).

55 *McConnell v. Federal Election Commission*, 540 U.S. 93 (2003).

the presidential election. In 2014, Super PACs spent $339.4 million, substantially more than all independent spending in 2010, the prior midterm election.

Congressional Campaigns

Congressional campaigns share a number of important features with presidential campaigns, but they are also distinctive—especially in terms of the incumbency advantage. Incumbency advantage is more important for congressional representatives, who have no term limits. Beginning around 1970, political scientists noted that congressional incumbents were winning reelection at higher rates than in previous generations and by wider margins, and that this phenomenon appeared due to incumbency itself. As a simple experiment, Robert Erikson compared the same politician running for election not as an incumbent and as an incumbent. In the first sort of election, the politician ran for a seat left vacant by an incumbent's retirement or against an incumbent and won. In the second sort of election, the politician had just won the previous election and had to defend the seat in the next election as a "sophomore." Erikson called the increase in the politician's vote share from the first election to the second the "sophomore surge"—attributable solely to the fact that the politician ran as an incumbent rather than as a nonincumbent. Erikson found an incumbency effect of approximately 5 percentage points around 1970. If the party division of the vote in a congressional district without an incumbent is, say, 50–50, then in a race where one candidate is the incumbent, the same district would vote for the incumbent with 55 percent to 45 percent.

The incumbency advantage has increased in both magnitude and importance in U.S. elections. Incumbency advantages in House elections grew from 1 or 2 percentage points in the mid-1950s to 5 or 6 points by the late 1960s. Today, almost every elective office at the state and federal level exhibits an incumbency advantage. Those advantages have ranged from about 5 percent in state legislative elections to 10 percent for U.S. House, U.S. Senate, and governor. A 10 percent incumbency advantage is a massive electoral edge. It turns a competitive race into a blowout for the incumbent.[56]

Congressional incumbents' advantages arise in campaign spending as well as votes. Like presidential campaigns, congressional campaigns have witnessed increased spending over time. The average U.S. House incumbent in 2014 spent $1.5 million, compared to the $650,000 spent by the typical challenger.[57]

---

56 See Stephen Ansolabehere and James M. Snyder, Jr., "The Incumbency Advantage in U.S. Elections: An Analysis of State and Federal Offices, 1942–2000," *Election Law Journal* 1 (2002): 315–38.

57 Center for Responsive Politics, "Overall Spending Inches Up in 2014: Megadonors Equip Outside Groups to Capture a Bigger Share of the Pie," October 29, 2014, www.opensecrets.org/news/2014/10/overall-spending-inches-up-in-2014-megadonors-equip-outside-groups-to-capture-a-bigger-share-of-the-pie (accessed 6/10/16).

A successful campaign builds on early successes, often starting small by holding meetings with various groups and then bringing in more supporters and volunteers and culminating with intensive advertising campaigns in the final months or weeks before Election Day. The personal style of political campaigning that Americans have come to appreciate reflects an enormous investment of time and resources that takes the better part of a year to grow. Incumbent members of Congress have particular advantages in campaign fund-raising: they have already been tested, they have campaign organizations in place, and they have connections in their constituencies as well as in Washington, D.C.

Effectiveness of Campaigns

Campaigns address the information problems discussed at the beginning of this chapter. Candidates and parties bear much of the responsibility for disseminating electoral information and for creating an informed electorate. Indeed, voters would otherwise have little incentive or opportunity to find information about the many candidates and ballot measures at issue. Through advertising and other campaign efforts, politicians try to shape the electorate and the election outcome. Parties and candidates spend money in order to present voters with the information they need to make a decision come Election Day—what the candidates and parties have done and what they promise to do, who they are, and which person is right for the job and the challenges the country faces.

Political scientists have long wondered how much that money matters, given the high rates of party loyalty among most people. Research on the effectiveness of campaign spending and advertising began in earnest in the 1970s with the path-breaking studies of Gary Jacobson. He found that challengers did better in races in which they spent more money, holding constant the underlying partisan division of the district, but that incumbents who spent higher amounts did no better. Part of the explanation, Jacobson reasoned, was that vulnerable incumbents would have to raise and spend more money, so the observation of high spending reflected the eventual outcome as much as it influenced it. It was impossible to tell how much money influenced votes and how much votes influenced money.[58] A decades-long debate over how to measure the effectiveness of campaign spending has ensued, most of it focusing on the same sort of aggregate data that Jacobson used.

In the 1990s, political scientists turned to experiments. Rather than look at the correlation between votes received and money spent, we could manipulate who sees TV commercials or receives mailers and then measure respondents' attitudes toward the candidates, whether they vote, and how they vote. The first such study was conducted by Stephen Ansolabehere and Shanto Iyengar, who found that seeing a single TV commercial from a candidate in the context of a news program increased support for that candidate by, on average, 7 percentage

---

58 Gary C. Jacobson, *Money in Congressional Elections* (New Haven, CT: Yale University Press, 1980).

points. That holds constant how much the other candidate spends and other important features of the electoral context. It is interesting that the effect of advertising was found to vary across people. Those who were ideologically hostile to a candidate could not be persuaded to change their opinions and cross party lines. Rather, the ads affected independent voters and people of the same party or ideological orientation as the candidate who aired the ad. This finding echoes a much older argument owing to the social psychologist Paul Lazarsfeld, who found in the 1940s that political messages and conversations tended not to *convert* people but to *reinforce* their beliefs. Such is the case today. TV ads strengthen support for a candidate among that candidate's partisans and among independents.[59]

Following on this project, Alan Gerber and Donald Green undertook a measure of the effectiveness of canvassing, direct mail, and other means of voter mobilization. Working with political campaigns, they conducted dozens of field experiments in which some households and precincts received get-out-the-vote messages and some did not. They then measured the participation rates and vote shares of those households and precincts. Although the effects on rates of participation and candidates' vote shares were somewhat smaller than the TV advertising studies, they were still significant.[60] These research projects provide strong evidence of the effectiveness of campaigns, a conclusion masked by studies of aggregate election patterns.

Elections, of course, fail to serve the important function of informing the electorate when competition is weak or lacking all together. Perhaps the most infamous example took the form of Democratic dominance in the South from the 1890s through 1960s—a political arrangement termed the Solid South. During this period, election laws excluded blacks and many poor whites from primary elections, and Republicans made up a relatively small part of the electorate. As a result, Democrats won nearly every House seat, Senate seat, and gubernatorial race in the South from the end of Reconstruction through the passage of the Voting Rights Act in 1965. Shifting political alignments in the South during the 1960s and 1970s brought a rapid rise in Republican fortunes in the South and with that the benefits of electoral competition.

Today, some observers fear that the incumbency advantage stifles electoral competition. As noted earlier, incumbents enjoy a sizable electoral advantage—some of which reflects the voters' reward of the incumbents' performance in office and some of which reflects an imbalance in campaign politics. That imbalance is most obvious in campaign funds. The average House challenger in 2016 raised and spent a little over $200,000; the typical incumbent raised and spent more than six times as much, approximately $1.5 million. Incumbents' funding advantages allow them to communicate more extensively with constituents than their opponents.

59 Stephen Ansolabehere and Shanto Iyengar, *Going Negative* (New York: Free Press, 1996).

60 Alan Gerber and Donald Green, *Get Out the Vote,* 2nd ed. (Washington, DC: Brookings Institution, 2008).

THE 2016 ELECTIONS

In the fall of 2016, 136 million Americans went to the polls to elect a new president. After long primary campaigns in both parties and a bruising general election campaign, Donald Trump defied the expectations of most pundits and other observers to defeat Hillary Clinton. The outcome reflected a unique feature of American presidential elections: because of the Electoral College system, the winner is not necessarily the candidate who receives the most votes. In 2016, one candidate, Hillary Clinton, won the popular vote and another candidate, Donald Trump, won the Electoral College vote (see Figure 11.7).

The result of the 2016 presidential election highlighted the distortions that can occur with electoral systems in which the winner is determined by who wins a majority of many districts or states, rather than by who wins a majority of votes, as discussed earlier in this chapter. But, as we will see in this section, the election outcomes more broadly were not solely a result of the Electoral College.

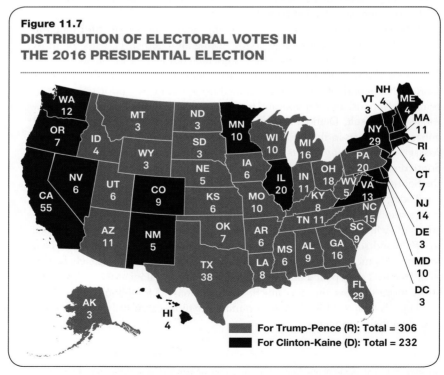

Figure 11.7
DISTRIBUTION OF ELECTORAL VOTES IN THE 2016 PRESIDENTIAL ELECTION

For Trump-Pence (R): Total = 306
For Clinton-Kaine (D): Total = 232

NOTE: Maine and Nebraska allocate Electoral College votes by congressional district. Donald Trump won one of Maine's four electoral votes.
SOURCE: "Presidential Election Results: Donald J. Trump Wins," *New York Times*, www.nytimes.com/elections/results/president (accessed 11/18/16).

Political Parties in 2016

The American political landscape experienced a national realignment of political forces in the 1960s and 1970s, as we discuss in Chapter 12. Over time, the Democratic Party has become increasingly liberal, and the Republican Party increasingly conservative. This ideological realignment of the two parties is one reason partisan struggles in government have become especially intense in recent years.

The growing ideological split between the two parties has not meant that each party is ideologically uniform, however. Disputes among the various liberal groups within the Democratic Party and among the disparate conservative groups in the Republican Party have also been quite heated. In 2016, the factional splits in both parties deepened. For the first time in recent history, both parties had primary election fights that were not settled until the last primary election votes were cast in June.

Initially, it appeared that Hillary Clinton would coast to the Democratic nomination. Clinton was one of the most prominent Democratic leaders, having served as first lady, then as a U.S. senator from New York, and later as secretary of state under President Obama. On the issues, Clinton seemed politically well positioned to take on most Republican opponents. She represented a more moderate approach to public policy, as a Democrat who embraces free trade rather than protectionism, and is known for being hawkish on national defense. Clinton, however, was challenged from the far left wing of the party when Bernie Sanders, a senator from Vermont and self-described Democratic Socialist, emerged as her biggest rival. Sanders proved to be a formidable opponent. He seized on economic issues that energized key segments of the Democratic electorate. In particular, he championed free college tuition, a message that won 80 percent of the votes of people under 30 in the Democratic primaries.[61] Clinton, meanwhile, emphasized health care, racial and gender equality, and her experience. She won strong support among minority voters and older voters.

The Democratic nomination season started with a shockingly close Iowa caucus contest in which Clinton beat Sanders by less than 1 percentage point. Throughout the spring, the race for the Democratic nomination remained close. By the time the last votes were cast in California's primary in June 2016, Sanders had won 23 caucuses or primaries compared to Clinton's 34, and 1,865 delegates compared to her 2,842. It was a highly unusual primary contest for the Democrats. Sanders, a relatively unknown "outsider" candidate, tapped into many Democratic voters' sense of unrest and unease with their party. Sanders's loss left some of his supporters feeling frustrated with the primary system and the results.

---

61 Aaron Blake, "More Young People Voted for Bernie Sanders Than Trump and Clinton Combined—by a Lot," *Washington Post,* June 20, 2016, www.washingtonpost.com/news/the-fix/wp/2016/06/20/more-young-people-voted-for-bernie-sanders-than-trump-and-clinton-combined-by-a-lot (accessed 11/28/16).

The Republican nomination contest was more unusual still. The Republican field attracted 17 candidates for president. Florida Governor Jeb Bush, son of President George H. W. Bush and brother of President George W. Bush, was the early pick of many experts. Bush was a popular governor of a key state, and his Super PAC had over $118 million to spend at the start of the primary season in January 2016.[62] His campaign, however, failed to gain much traction. Through the last six months of 2015 and into 2016 the consistent leader in the polls was not Bush, nor any of the establishment candidates, but real estate mogul and TV personality Donald Trump.

Trump launched his campaign in June 2015 at Trump Tower in Manhattan. He promised to make America great again, a phrase later adopted as his campaign's slogan. The Trump campaign was widely dismissed by the media and most party leaders as a gimmick. The heart of his appeal, however, was not to the media elite or the party establishment, but to working-class conservative white voters in the United States.

Working-class white voters had long been aligned with the Democrats, especially when unionization rates were higher. Although many of them came over to Ronald Reagan's Republican coalition in 1980, they were always treated as outsiders—so-called Reagan Democrats—by the Republican establishment. Not since Reagan had they found another standard bearer in the Republican Party, until Donald Trump. Trump campaigned strenuously against free trade, promising to bring jobs back to America. He also promised to cut taxes on individuals and corporations. He took a staunch stand against immigration, proposing to build a wall at the U.S.–Mexican border and to place a temporary ban on Muslim immigration and create a database of Muslim Americans. These kinds of provocative statements soon came to characterize Trump's campaign. While many called Trump's style offensive and labeled him as xenophobic and racist, to many Americans he seemed an authentic candidate unafraid to assert his views and defy a politically correct culture. Trump seemed to represent a large subset of Americans who have felt disenfranchised and left behind as the status quo is changing.

As Trump's many controversial and inflammatory comments continued to dominate headlines, the field of 17 Republican candidates was winnowed to 4: Donald Trump, Senator Ted Cruz (Texas), Senator Marco Rubio (Florida), and Governor John Kasich (Ohio). Trump won only 45 percent of all votes cast in the primaries, but that was sufficient to earn him 1,441 delegates, 204 more than were needed to secure the nomination.

The primary campaign was a divisive one. Trump's strategy was to challenge the Republican establishment directly. His attacks on a number of prominent party leaders left many in the GOP reluctant to embrace their party's nominee. Heading into the general elections, both parties' nominees needed to heal rifts among their rank-and-file voters.

---

62 Mateo Gold, "Nearly $100 Million in Super PAC Money Couldn't Save Jeb Bush," *Washington Post,* February 20, 2016, www.washingtonpost.com/news/post-politics/wp/2016/02/20/nearly-100-million-in-super-pac-money-couldnt-save-jeb-bush (accessed 11/28/16).

The General Election

The general election season began at the parties' nominating conventions. In 2016, each night of the national conventions drew 30 million viewers.[63] Both parties put on a show aimed to inspire their supporters and to demonize their opponents. The main message of the Trump campaign was to "make America great again" by reversing eight years of Obama's policies, and to bridge the divisions within the party by focusing on their common enemy. The benediction by preacher Mark Burns launched the Republican convention: "Our enemy is not other Republicans, but is Hillary Clinton and the Democrats."[64] And with that prayer, one of the most negative campaign seasons in modern political history began.

The Democrats followed suit with a convention filled with attacks on Trump. One notable example was when Khizr Khan, father of a Muslim American soldier who was killed in Iraq, rebuked Trump for his xenophobic statements and implored Trump to read the Constitution. When not attacking Trump, the Democratic convention focused on appealing to nonwhite voters as well as to women, emphasizing the potential to elect the first woman president and to make sweeping changes in public policies, from health care to education.

As the summer rolled into August, the campaigns shifted from a broad national message to a direct appeal to voters in swing states. Most states leaned either strongly Democratic or strongly Republican. Both campaigns calculated that the cost of flipping these states (for example, turning Texas blue or Illinois red) was too high compared with the cost and potential reward of focusing on a smaller number of swing states that were more evenly divided between Democrats and Republicans. Fourteen swing states—Arizona, Colorado, Florida, Iowa, Maine, Michigan, Minnesota, Nevada, New Hampshire, North Carolina, Ohio, Pennsylvania, Virginia, and Wisconsin—loomed large in the campaigns' strategies, but the two campaigns went about appealing to swing state voters in very different ways.

Trump's general election campaign focused on motivating his core supporters. During the primaries, Trump had proved masterful in the use of social media, especially Twitter, in stirring controversy and attracting news coverage. He used Twitter to call out his opponents and was skillful at the pithy turn of phrase. For example, Trump turned Clinton's main motto I'm with Her around to "I'm with you," cleverly changing her message of progress and inclusion to one of exclusion. As effective as his mastery of the "short media" was, Trump was perhaps even more at home giving hour-long stump speeches. Trump held energetic rallies, each typically lasting several hours, throughout the swing states. He also took to the airwaves and spent a significant amount on advertising,

---

63 Michael O'Connell "TV Ratings: Hillary Clinton's DNC Speech Falls Just Shy of Trump's with 33 Million Viewers," *Hollywood Reporter*, July 29, 2016, www.hollywoodreporter.com/live-feed/tv-ratings-hillary-clintons-dnc-915706 (accessed 11/22/16).

64 Steve Benen, "At This Convention, Even the Benediction Sparks Controversy," MSNBC, July 19, 2016, www.msnbc.com/rachel-maddow-show/convention-even-the-benediction-sparks-controversy (accessed 11/22/16).

though far less than the Clinton campaign. Ultimately, it was Trump's use of social media and campaign rallies to motivate his core supporters that proved to be the staple of his campaign.

The Clinton campaign focused on a strategy of mobilization, following more closely the strategy of the Obama campaigns. Drawing on many of Obama's 2012 campaign consultants and the resources developed under his campaigns, the Clinton team invested heavily in targeted get-out-the-vote activities in key swing states as well as on extensive broadcast advertising. Get-out-the-vote, or mobilization, campaigns target specific people to make sure they are registered to vote and to remind them to vote. This strategy was a stark contrast to the motivational approach that Trump employed, which was designed to inspire enthusiasm among potential supporters more broadly. The Clinton campaign's efforts to create enthusiasm relied heavily on television advertising. Their strategy, however, may have misfired. One analysis of the campaign's advertising expenditures revealed that the Clinton camp took Wisconsin's and Michigan's electoral votes for granted. Clinton spent more on ads in Omaha, Nebraska, seeking a single electoral vote in that state, than she spent in the swing states of Michigan, Wisconsin, and Virginia.[65]

Clinton and Trump squared off in three presidential debates. By most pundits' accounts, Clinton won the debates handily.[66] In addition, scandals that emerged in the fall, including the release of a 2005 video in which Trump was heard boasting that his celebrity status allowed him to touch women inappropriately and his acknowledgment that he had avoided paying federal income tax for decades, raised questions about his electability. Clinton, however, was embroiled in controversy of her own, having been under investigation by the FBI for her use of a private email server during her tenure as secretary of state, a fact that Republicans seized on as evidence that Clinton was not trustworthy. The November exit polls revealed that although Clinton held a strong lead among voters coming into the general election season, the debates, rallies, Tweets, ads, and other activities of the general election campaigns in fact helped push undecided voters toward Trump.[67]

Republican Victory

Based on preliminary tallies, Clinton received 65.2 million votes, or around 48 percent of the popular vote, while Trump won 62.7 million votes, or around 46 percent of the popular vote. However, Trump carried states totaling 306 votes in the Electoral College and thus won the presidency.

---

65 Jim Tankersley "The Advertising Decisions That Helped Doom Hillary Clinton," *Washington Post,* November 12, 2016, www.washingtonpost.com/news/wonk/wp/2016/11/12/the-advertising-decisions-that-helped-doom-hillary-clinton (accessed 11/22/16).

66 Alan Rappeport, "Who Won the Debate? Hillary Clinton, the 'Nasty Woman,'" *New York Times,* October 20, 2016, www.nytimes.com/2016/10/21/us/politics/who-won-the-third-debate.html (accessed 12/7/16).

67 Exit Polls, CNN Politics, www.cnn.com/election/results/exit-polls (accessed 11/21/16).

Five times in U.S. history (1824, 1876, 1888, 2000, and 2016), the Electoral College outcome has flipped the result of the popular vote. The reason for the reversal in 2016 was that Clinton won big in states where Democrats safely win, and Trump racked up electoral votes in key swing states by narrow margins. Clinton had large leads in California, New York, and Illinois, states rich in electoral votes, while Trump had a significant lead in one large state, Texas, and many midsize and small states, especially in the South, the Plains states, and the Mountain West. Among the states deemed relatively safe for one party or the other, Clinton did well. In these 36 safely Democratic or safely Republican states, a total of 86 million votes were cast. Clinton won 49 percent of the popular vote in these states combined and 190 electoral votes. Trump, on the other hand, won 45 percent of the popular vote in these states and 178 electoral votes. The 14 swing states, however, held the key to the election. A total of 50 million votes were cast in swing states. Trump won 48 percent of the popular vote in these states and 125 electoral votes, while Clinton won 47 percent of the popular vote in these states for just 42 electoral votes.[68] In the end, the election was determined by four states where Trump won by 1 percentage point or less: Florida, Michigan, Wisconsin, and Pennsylvania.

In the 2016 election, Americans also elected all members of the House of Representatives, a third of the Senate, new state legislatures in 43 states, and new governors in 12 states. Before the election, Democrats had high hopes of taking back the U.S. Senate and making significant inroads into the state governments. But the election cemented the gains that the Republican Party had made in congressional and state elections in 2010 and 2014. Republicans fended off the Democratic Party's electoral efforts and held onto their position of power in American government. Republicans suffered only minor losses in the congressional elections, retaining their majority in both the House of Representatives and the Senate. Before the 2016 election, the Republicans held 54 seats in the Senate and 247 seats in the House; after the election they held 52 seats in the Senate and 241 in the House (see Tables 11.2A and 11.2B). The GOP gained ground in the state governments in 2016. Before the election Republicans controlled both chambers of the state legislatures in 30 states, and after the election, they controlled both chambers in 32 states. Finally, the Republicans picked up three governorships in 2016, increasing the total number of governorships they control from 31 to 34. The results of the congressional and state elections, in addition to the loss of the presidency, were hugely disappointing for Democrats.

The 2016 election signaled a shift to the right in U.S. politics and public policy making, but a shift with strong populist overtones. The 2016 elections in the United States had an eerie similarity to recent elections in Europe. In the United Kingdom, France, and Germany, right-wing and populist parties, whose messages were centrally against immigration and were nationalist and isolationist, scored stunning victories in 2016 elections. One of the most

---

68 David Wasserman, "2016 National Popular Vote Tracker," Cook Political Report, November 16, 2016, http://cookpolitical.com/story/10174 (accessed 11/16/16).

Table 11.2A

HOUSE ELECTION RESULTS, 2000–2016

YEAR	TURNOUT (%)	PARTY RATIO	SEAT SHIFT	DEMOCRATS REELECTED (%)	REPUBLICANS REELECTED (%)
2000	54.2	212 D, 222 R	+1 D	98.0	97.5
2002	39.5	205 D, 229 R	+8 R	97.4	97.5
2004	60.3	201 D, 232 R	+3 R	97.4	99.0
2006	40.2	233 D, 202 R	+30 D	100.0	89.6
2008	61.0	257 D, 178 R	+24 D	97.9	92.1
2010	37.8	193 D, 242 R	+64 R	78.8	98.7
2012	54.0	201 D, 234 R	+8 D	89.0	90.0
2014	36.4	188 D, 247 R	+13 R	94.0	98.9
2016	58.0	194 D, 241 R	+6 D	97.0	95.1

SOURCE: United States Election Project, www.electproject.org/home/voter-turnout/voter-turnout-data; and information for reelection rates from Wikipedia, https://en.wikipedia.org/wiki/United_States_House_of_Representatives_elections,_2014 (accessed 6/15/15) and authors' updates.

surprising was the referendum vote in June 2016 in the United Kingdom to leave the European Union.[69] The pollsters got the "Brexit" vote wrong, widely predicting that Britons would not vote to leave the E.U. and isolate themselves from Europe.[70] Forecasters and pollsters were similarly wrong in their predictions for the presidential election in the United States. In the week leading up to the election, for example, the Upshot put Hillary Clinton's chances of winning at 85 percent, FiveThirtyEight gave her a 71 percent chance of winning, and the Princeton Election Consortium put her chances at greater than 99 percent. As for the polls, survey-based estimates of the national vote for Clinton and Trump were within the margin of error. The typical poll put her lead at 3 to 4 points. She won by 2 percentage points in the popular vote nationwide.

69 Daniel Korski, "Why We Lost the Brexit Vote," *Politico,* October 20, 2016, www.politico.eu/article/why-we-lost-the-brexit-vote-former-uk-prime-minister-david-cameron (accessed 11/22/16).

70 Chris Hanretty, "Here's Why Pollsters and Pundits Got Brexit Wrong," *Washington Post,* June 24, 2016, www.washingtonpost.com/news/monkey-cage/wp/2016/06/24/heres-why-pollsters-and-pundits-got-brexit-wrong (accessed 11/22/16).

Table 11.2B

SENATE ELECTION RESULTS, 2000–2016

YEAR	TURNOUT (%)	PARTY RATIO	SEAT SHIFT	DEMOCRATS REELECTED (%)	REPUBLICANS REELECTED (%)
2000	54.2	50 D, 50 R	+5 D	93.3	64.3
2002	39.5	48 D, 51 R	+1 R	83.3	93.3
2004	60.3	44 D, 55 R	+4 R	92.9	100.0
2006	40.2	50 D, 49 R	+6 D	100.0	57.1
2008	61.0	59 D, 41 R	+8 D	100.0	66.7
2010	37.8	53 D, 47 R	+6 R	76.9	100.0
2012	54.0	55 D*, 45 R	+2 D	100.0	71.0
2014	36.4	44 D*, 54 R	+9 R	64.7	100.0
2016	58.0	48 D*, 52 R	+2 D	100.0	90.9

*Includes two Independents who caucus with the Democrats.
SOURCE: United States Election Project, www.electproject.org/home/voterturnout/voter-turnout-data; and information for re-lection rates from Politico, www.politico.com/2014-election/results/map/senate/#.VYmi-_lVhBd (accessed 6/15/16) and authors' updates.

Where the polls erred was in the states, especially the upper Midwest. The most likely problem with the state polls is that they used the 2012 presidential election as their baseline estimates of the composition of the electorate. In states where there had been a significant and unexpected shift in the composition of the electorate and the voting behavior of white working-class voters, the survey estimates were biased. That differential shift in turnout made it difficult for pollsters to measure who was likely to vote (perhaps the trickiest aspect of election polling). It may also have made it difficult for polls to elicit how people who were in the process of changing their minds were actually going to vote. The states where many such changes occurred, it turns out, were in the upper Midwest, and the shift reflected the jump in enthusiasm among white working-class voters for Trump compared with the 2012 Republican nominee, Mitt Romney (see Figure 11.8).

The broader economic and political context in the United States may also shed light on Trump's victory. From 2008 to 2016, the U.S. economy never grew faster than 2.5 percent a year and averaged 7 percent unemployment. Growth in GDP from January to October of 2016 was less than 1.5 percent. Against this background of tepid economic growth and relatively high unemployment, many

Figure 11.8
VOTE SHIFTS BETWEEN 2012 AND 2016

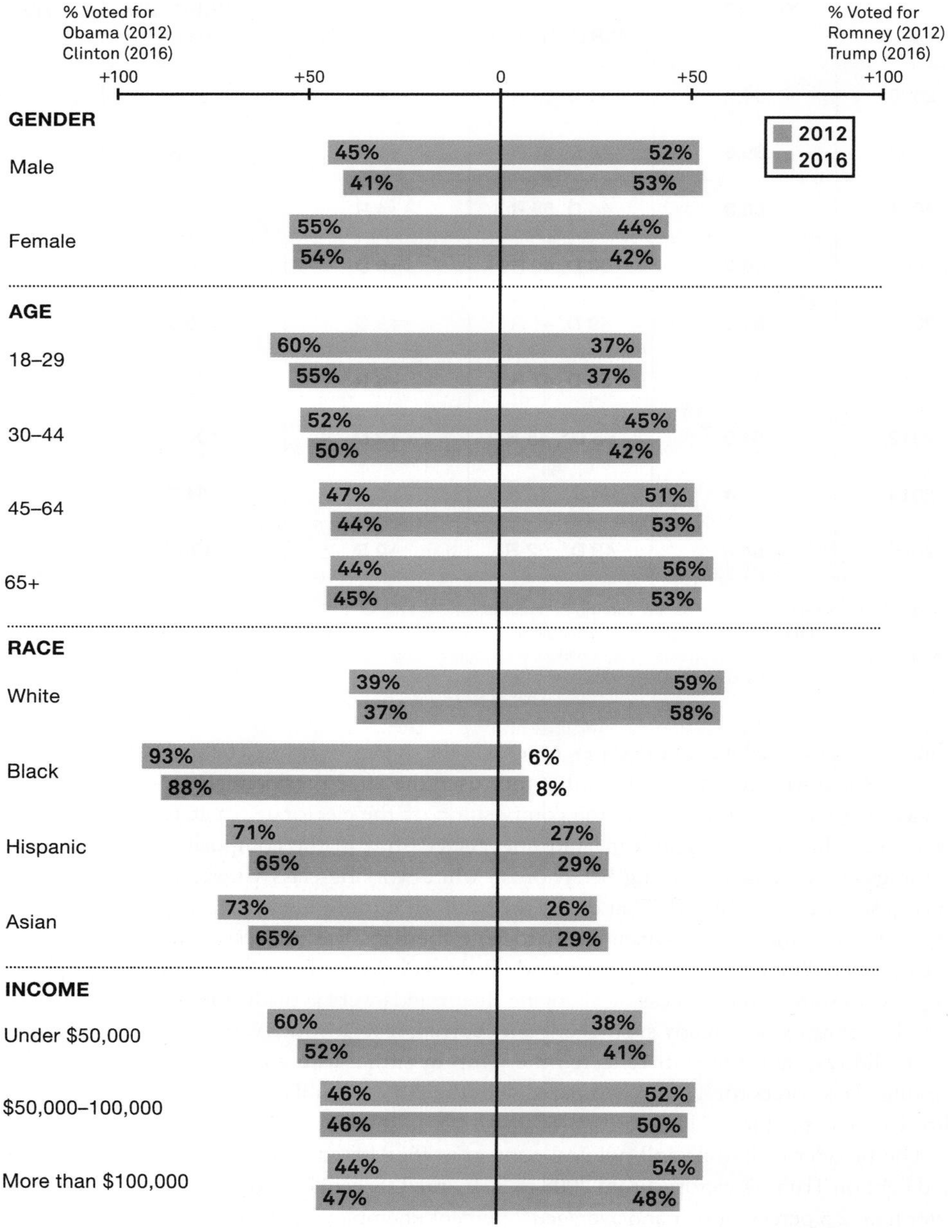

% Voted for
Obama (2012)
Clinton (2016)

% Voted for
Romney (2012)
Trump (2016)

+100   +50   0   +50   +100

GENDER

2012
2016

Male
45% 52%
41% 53%

Female
55% 44%
54% 42%

AGE

18–29
60% 37%
55% 37%

30–44
52% 45%
50% 42%

45–64
47% 51%
44% 53%

65+
44% 56%
45% 53%

RACE

White
39% 59%
37% 58%

Black
93% 6%
88% 8%

Hispanic
71% 27%
65% 29%

Asian
73% 26%
65% 29%

INCOME

Under $50,000
60% 38%
52% 41%

$50,000–100,000
46% 52%
46% 50%

More than $100,000
44% 54%
47% 48%

SOURCE: *Washington Post*, www.washingtonpost.com/wp-srv/special/politics/2012-exit-polls/table.html (accessed 11/28/12) and www.washingtonpost.com/graphics/politics/2016-election/exit-polls/ (accessed 11/28/16).

Americans wanted change. In fact, economic models of the election forecasted a very close race. Economic models of elections typically explain the election results as a function of peace and prosperity: whether we are at war and how strongly the economy is growing. A growth rate of 2.5 percent or better usually bodes well for the incumbent party's candidate.[71] The weak 1.5 percent growth rate in 2016 created a strong headwind into which the Democratic nominee would have to sail.

Looking toward the Future

The months following the election saw deep soul searching among Democrats. How did the party lose an election that seemed in its grasp? What could the party do moving forward? The Republican Party had conducted a similar inquiry after the 2012 election and used their loss to develop a road map for the future.

The Democratic Party leadership not only looked to the future but also saw immediate opportunities to work with President Trump on shared issues. For example, one of Trump's main policy promises during the campaign was a massive increase in spending on infrastructure, such as highways and airports, legislation the Democrats in Congress have long championed.[72]

Looking further ahead, Trump's victory may put the Democratic Party in a strong position for the 2018 midterm elections. The president's party almost always loses seats in the midterm elections. Since 1934, the incumbent president's party has lost, on average, 27 seats in the midterm elections. Those losses extend down the ballot to governorships and state legislative seats. The 2018 midterm will elect most states' governors and most states' legislatures. A strong showing in 2018 will be essential for rebuilding the Democratic Party, not just for the 2020 presidential campaign but beyond.

The 2018 elections will also shape which party controls the states leading into the 2021 redistricting process. Following the 2020 census, the United States will reapportion its congressional seats among the states and every congressional district and state legislative district in the country will be redrawn. In nearly every state, the state legislature passes a redistricting law, and the governor may sign the law or veto it. Whoever controls the state legislatures and governorships in 2021, then, will determine the contours of representation in the states and U.S. Congress for the next decade.

---

71 Michael Lewis-Beck and Charles Tien, "The Political Economy Model: 2016 US Election Forecasts," *PS: Political Science & Politics* 49 (October 2016): 661–63, www.cambridge. org/core/journals/ps-political-science-and-politics/article/the-political-economy-model-2016-us-election-forecasts/B4907EFC1CC6D8CC781E575B824F15CE/core-reader (accessed 11/22/16).

72 Jennifer Steinhauer, "Senate Democrats' Surprising Strategy: Trying to Align with Trump," *New York Times*, November 16, 2016, www.nytimes.com/2016/11/17/us/politics/democrats-house-senate.html (accessed 11/28/16).

CONCLUSION: ELECTIONS AND ACCOUNTABILITY

Elections should stir wonder in even the most jaded person. In an election, no one person matters much, and each person acts in apparent isolation, indeed secrecy. The individual voter's decisions reflect diverse experiences, opinions, and preferences about government and public policy. Yet the millions of votes cumulate into an expression of whom the majority wants to have as its representatives in state government, in Congress, and in the presidency. Through the institutions of elections, hundreds of millions of Americans collectively choose their government. That choice shapes all manner of subsequent public policy making. It indicates whether people want to stay the present course or whether they want government to go in a new direction.

The founders designed the institutions of American elections to facilitate majority rule. Single-member districts and plurality rule create strong pressures toward a two-party system and majoritarianism. Even in elections in which one party wins a plurality but not a majority, that party typically wins an outright majority of legislative seats. The election itself, then, determines the government. Other systems often produce multiparty outcomes, resulting in a period of negotiation and coalition formation among the parties in order to determine who will govern.

The significance of elections derives not so much from the laws as from the voters' expression of their preferences. Voting behavior depends in no small part on the tendency to vote for a given party as a matter of ingrained personal identity. If that were all there is to voting behavior, then elections might not provide a meaningful way of governing. However, voters' preferences are as strongly rooted in the issues at hand as in the choices themselves, the candidates. Voting decisions reflect individuals' assessments about whether it makes sense to keep public policies on the same track or to change direction; whether those in office have done a good job and deserve to be reelected, or whether they have failed and it is time for new representation. The aggregation of all voters' preferences responds collectively to fluctuations in the economy, to differences in the ideological and policy orientations of the parties, and to the personal attributes of the candidates.

For Further Reading

Ansolabehere, Stephen, and James M. Snyder, Jr. *The End of Inequality: One Person, One Vote and the Transformation of American Politics*. New York: Norton, 2008.

Brady, David W. *Critical Elections and Congressional Policy Making*. Palo Alto, CA: Stanford University Press, 1988.

Carmines, Edward G., and James A. Stimson. *Issue Evolution: Race and the Transformation of American Politics*. Princeton, NJ: Princeton University Press, 1989.

Fowler, Linda L. *Candidates, Congress, and the American Democracy*. Ann Arbor: University of Michigan Press, 1994.

Gelman, Andrew. *Red State, Blue State, Rich State, Poor State: Why Americans Vote the Way They Do*. Princeton, NJ: Princeton University Press, 2008.

Ginsberg, Benjamin, and Martin Shefter. *Politics by Other Means: Politicians, Prosecutors, and the Press from Watergate to Whitewater*. 3rd ed. New York: Norton, 2002.

Green, Donald, and Alan Gerber. *Get Out the Vote: How to Increase Voter Turnout*. Washington, DC: Brookings Institution, 2008.

Jacobson, Gary, C. *The Politics of Congressional Elections*. 8th ed. Boston: Pearson, 2013.

McCarty, Nolan, Keith Poole, and Howard Rosenthal. *Polarized America: The Dance of Ideology and Unequal Riches*. Cambridge: MIT Press, 2006.

Reichley, A. James, ed. *Elections American Style*. Washington, DC: Brookings Institution, 1987.

Rosenstone, Steven, and John Mark Hansen. *Mobilization, Participation, and Democracy in America*. New York: Macmillan, 1993.

Witt, Linda, Karen M. Paget, and Glenna Matthews. *Running as a Woman: Gender and Power in American Politics*. New York: Free Press, 1994.

12

Political Parties

Political parties are teams of politicians, activists, and voters whose goal is to win control of government. They do so by recruiting and nominating candidates to run for office; by accumulating the resources needed to run political campaigns, especially manpower and money; and by pursuing a policy agenda that can appeal to large numbers of voters and secure electoral majorities. Once in office, parties attempt to put their stamp on the laws passed by Congress and the president. Their potential political power is immense.

The prospect of "party rule" has long made Americans suspicious of these organizations. Indeed, the separation of powers into different branches was meant to blunt any attempts by a "faction" or party to gain control of government, as might more readily occur in a parliament.[1] Divided government, in which one party controls the presidency and the other has a majority in at least one chamber of the legislature, has been the norm in American national and state politics. In some elections, one party wins a landslide victory for the presidency but still fails to capture control of Congress. And in some midterm elections, voters give control of Congress to the party opposing the president in order to rein in the executive. Our political system intentionally makes it difficult for any party or organized interest to gain complete control of American government, and when one does, unified government is often short lived. Separation of powers and divided government have not, however, put the parties out of business.

The Democratic and Republican parties remain essential to the day-to-day operation of the legislature and the conduct of elections. It is difficult to imagine how candidates would emerge and how individuals would vote without political parties to organize the electoral system. Our inability to conceive of democracy without parties reflects a law of democratic politics. Parties form to solve

---

1 James Madison famously made this argument in *Federalist* 51 during the campaign to ratify the Constitution of the United States. Alexander Hamilton, James Madison, and John Jay, *The Federalist Papers*, Clinton Rossiter, ed. (New York: New American Library, 1961), no. 51.

key problems of rationality and collective action in a democracy. They offer clear choices to voters, lowering the costs of collecting information about the candidates and making it easier for voters to hold government accountable. Parties also ease the transition from elections to government. They bear the costs of bringing together representatives of disparate constituencies into coherent coalitions that can act collectively in government. Thus parties link elections to governing. Throughout this chapter we highlight some of the general functions of parties in any democracy, but we are especially attentive to party politics in the United States.

The simplest observation about American parties is also perhaps the most important: the United States has just two major parties, the Democrats and the Republicans. The American two-party system is impressive in its durability and flexibility. Sustained third parties have not been able to compete with the Democrats and Republicans since the 1850s. The Democratic and Republican parties have, for the past 150 years, elected every president and nearly every member of Congress, governor, and state legislator in the country. Occasionally,

CORE OF THE ANALYSIS

 Political parties are teams of politicians, activists, and interest groups organized to win control of government.

 The United States has a two-party system in which Democrats and Republicans compete for most offices. This two-party system is a consequence of the form of government (presidential-congressional as opposed to parliamentary) and election laws, especially the use of single-member legislative districts.

 Parties offer distinctive views about how government ought to operate and what laws ought to be enacted. They often serve distinct interests and communities.

 Parties help solve an important informational problem for voters. By offering distinctive "brands," the parties simplify the choices that voters must make and reduce the costs of gathering information about how to vote.

 The legislative and executive branches of the U.S. government are organized by the parties, with the party that won a majority of seats controlling most of the key positions and levers of power, especially congressional committees, the congressional agenda, and the appointment of agency heads.

a governor or legislator runs as a third-party candidate, but those independent candidacies usually fail unless the person eventually attaches him- or herself to one of the parties. In the 2016 presidential election, two anti-establishment "outsider" candidates, reality-TV star and businessman Donald Trump and self-described socialist Bernie Sanders, attached themselves to the Republican and Democratic Parties respectively and gained widespread support. Sanders posed a serious challenge to Hillary Clinton in the Democratic primaries. Trump won the Republican nomination, defeating a field of established Republican politicians. He went on to defeat Clinton in the general election, running as the voice of change, and became the first president who had not previously held elected office or been a general. Trump's and Sanders' success exposed many Americans' frustrations with and lack of trust in the establishment. Neither candidate, however, would likely have been as successful without affiliating with one of the two major parties.

When a faction does break from one of the parties, it generally returns to the fold eventually or moves into the other party. The parties have not remained static, however. For instance, the Democrats have shifted from a southern base of support to a northern one, and the Republicans' base has moved increasingly from the Northeast and Midwest to the South. And the two parties have adapted to radical changes in the ideologies and social structure of American society.

The institutions of a two-party system, combined with majority rule, mean that the choice between the parties translates into the choice of government. Whichever party wins a majority of seats in House or Senate elections wins control of that chamber. Whichever party wins a majority of electoral votes wins the presidency. At election time, we choose between those who are in power and those who would like to be. Choosing to change the government means voting against the party that currently holds the presidency and Congress.

In contrast, most parliamentary systems, especially those that allocate seats to parties based on the proportion of votes won nationwide, have more than two parties. In such systems, no party regularly wins a majority, and governments consist of coalitions of several parties. It is difficult to anticipate which coalitions might form, and it is hard to assign blame to any one party in a coalition government. In contrast, there is great simplicity in having a two-party system.

The Democratic and Republican parties have proved adept at accommodating diverse sets of interests while still presenting distinctive visions for governing. They each capture a range of ideological views while keeping successful third parties at bay. This situation largely reflects the electoral and governmental institutions of the United States and the strategic skills of party leaders. The opportunity for a third party to enter races and win many congressional seats or the presidency is very limited.

The French political scientist Maurice Duverger laid out the reason for this state of affairs in his classic book *Political Parties*. Duverger relied on both the institution principle and the rationality principle. As we discussed in Chapter 11, any third-party movement that attempts to enter the American party system would likely fail to win, or worse, would improve the electoral fortunes of the party it most opposes. Also, no voter would want to waste a vote on a losing cause. Hence the number of successful parties is two.

U.S. government institutions and electoral rules create strong pressures to maintain just two parties, distinctive in their plans for governing but expansive in the interests that they encompass. This simplifies politics inside governing institutions, because one party will have a majority and control that institution (the presidency or one or both chambers of Congress). It also simplifies vote choice, because voters can identify with one of the two major parties or use the party labels to figure out the most effective way to vote.

Parties, however, are not benevolent. They don't solve the rationality and collective action problems simply to make democracy work. In fact, these problems represent opportunities for party members to secure elected office, to influence public policy, even to make a profit. For politicians, the parties provide a clear path to office through the nominating system and to power through the party organization. For activists, the party is a potential way to pull government policies in a direction more favorable to the party's views. For interest groups, the parties offer the potential benefits of being closer to power and influencing what government does. At times, the influence of activists, party leaders, organized interests, and local bosses becomes too great. Regulations on campaign contributions and government contracting, sunshine laws and federal advisory rules, and even civil-service reforms have all come about through efforts to prevent party bosses and interest groups from taking advantage of their power. Party organizations have been weakened by these reforms, but they have invariably found new resources to draw on. As a result of these actions and reactions, American history has witnessed eras of very strong party organization and periods of relative party weakness.

Today, American politics is characterized by relatively strong party organizations and disciplined legislative parties. They offer the American voter meaningful electoral choices and a simple strategy for changing the direction of government.

WHY DO POLITICAL PARTIES FORM?

Political parties, like interest groups, are organizations seeking influence over government. Ordinarily, they can be distinguished from interest groups on the basis of their orientation. A party seeks to control the entire government by electing some of its members to office, thereby controlling the government's personnel. Interest groups, through campaign contributions and other assistance, are also concerned with electing politicians—in particular, those who are inclined in their policy direction. But interest groups ordinarily do not sponsor candidates directly, and between elections they usually accept government and its personnel and try to influence government policies through them.

Political parties form to solve three problems. The first is the problem of collective action: a candidate for office must attract campaign funds, assemble a group of activists and workers, mobilize prospective voters, and persuade them to vote

 political party

An organized group that attempts to influence government by electing its members to office

for her. The second problem is the collective choice of policy.[2] The give-and-take within a legislature and between the legislature and the executive can make or break policy success and subsequent electoral success. The third problem is power sharing and competition among politicians. Like members of any organization, politicians seek success simultaneously for the organization and for themselves. In furthering their own ambitions, politicians can act in ways that serve their own interests but that can undermine the collective aspirations of fellow partisans unless astutely managed. We briefly examine each of these problems in the following sections.

Ultimately, each is a problem faced by politicians, especially those already in office. This fact reveals an important reason that parties form—to serve politicians' interests. Ultimately, the political parties in the United States were formed by politicians to serve their aims. Parties make easier the basic tasks of political life—running for office, organizing one's supporters, and forming a government.

To Facilitate Collective Action in the Electoral Process

Political parties as we know them today developed along with the expansion of suffrage and can be understood only in the context of elections. Parties and elections are so intertwined that American parties actually take their structure from the electoral process. Party organization in the United States has followed a simple rule: for every district where an election is held, there should be some kind of party unit. These units provide the brand name, the resources (human and financial), the buzz, and the link to the larger national organization, which all help arouse interest in the party's candidates and stimulate commitment by voters. These activities facilitate collective action as they enable voters to understand the choice of candidates and ultimately overcome the free riding that diminishes turnout in general elections.

Party organization also enables electoral competition by groups. The Republican Party has long been the party of business interests (among other groups), especially small business and peak associations (organizations of organizations) such as the Chamber of Commerce and the National Association of Manufacturers. Since the 1930s, the Democratic Party has been aligned with labor unions and reformers who want to regulate the economy. Often, large groups that lack substantial economic and institutional resources find their voice in the party system. For example, women's organizations worked closely with the Progressive faction inside the Republican Party in the 1900s and 1910s in the struggle to gain suffrage for women. By the 1970s, changing social issues and party strategies led many newer women's groups, such as the National Organization for Women, to align with the Democratic Party. Throughout American history, immigrant groups

---

2   A slight variation on this theme is emphasized by Gary W. Cox and Mathew D. McCubbins in *Legislative Leviathan: Party Government in the House* (Berkeley: University of California Press, 1993). They suggest that parties in the legislature are electoral machines that serve to preserve and enhance party reputation, thereby giving meaning to the party labels when elections are contested. By keeping order within their ranks, parties ensure that individual actions by members do not discredit the party label. This is an especially challenging task for party leaders when there is diversity within each party, as has often been the case in American political history.

have also aligned with the parties. Irish immigrants attached themselves to the Democrats, whose urban political organizations helped them find jobs and negotiate the immigration system, Italian immigrants tended toward Republicans, most Hispanic groups have gravitated to the Democrats because of the party's immigration policies, and Cubans aligned with the Republicans because that party took a harder line against the Castro regime. In the 1970s, disaffection with liberal policies concerning school prayer, funding of religious schools, abortion, and other social issues led fundamentalist Christians to align with the Republican Party.

The relationship between collective action by groups and party electoral strategy is clearly a two-way street. Groups that align with a party provide essential electoral resources, including a reliable voting bloc, money, personnel, and even candidates. When their party wins, these interests gain influence over public policy. Of course, there are risks as well: an organized interest may suffer if the party it supports loses the election.

To Resolve Problems of Collective Choice in Government

Political parties are also essential in the process of making policy. Within government, parties are coalitions of individuals with shared or overlapping interests who generally support one another's programs and initiatives. Even though there may be disagreement within each party, a common party label gives members a reason to cooperate. Because they are permanent coalitions, parties greatly facilitate the policy-making process. If alliances had to be formed from scratch for each legislative proposal, the business of government would slow to a crawl or halt altogether. Parties create a basis for coalition and thus sharply reduce the time and effort needed to advance a legislative proposal. Every president works closely with his party's leadership in the House and Senate, even if the party is in the minority, to ensure that the executive's agenda will be introduced into Congress and supported. Without party support, the president would have to undertake the probably impossible task of forming a completely new coalition for every policy proposal.

Party cohesion, however, sometimes breaks down over the need for action on a crucial issue. For instance, in 2008, facing a collapse of the financial industry, President George W. Bush proposed a $700 billion intervention to unlock frozen credit markets. Democratic leaders in the House twisted enough arms to produce a majority of Democratic votes in favor of the Republican president's plan. But Republican leadership in the House failed to produce enough Republican votes to pass the measure. Those voting against the bill argued that the plan would increase the size of government, reward irresponsible investors, and violate the free-market principles underlying the Republican policy agenda. The failure of the president and his party to come to agreement on this plan in advance doomed the president's proposal.[3] Even when party coalitions appear to agree on an issue, the road to enacting actual policy can be complex (see the Policy Principle section on p. 496).

---

3   Carl Hulse and David M. Herszenhorn, "Defiant House Rejects Huge Bailout; Next Step Is Uncertain," *New York Times*, September 29, 2008, www.nytimes.com/2008/09/30/business/30cong.html (accessed 4/3/09).

Party Coalitions and Abortion Policy

An antiabortion protest in Washington, D.C., in 2016.

Political action is collective. It involves merging people's individual preferences in order to pursue some collective purpose. For interest groups, collective action is relatively straightforward: people who share a common policy goal work together to achieve that goal. For political parties, however, collective action is more complicated. Parties hope not only to achieve policy goals but also to capture public offices. In some instances, party leaders find that they must subordinate policy goals in order to enhance the party's overall electoral chances.

To complicate matters, the two major American political parties, the Republican Party and the Democratic Party, are coalitions of disparate forces and individuals who agree on some things but not on others. The Republican Party, for example, includes economic conservatives who favor lower taxes, social and religious conservatives who oppose abortion and same-sex marriage, libertarians who seek a smaller government, populists who oppose free trade policies, and a number of other factions.

Every four years, the parties write platforms summarizing their core principles and policy positions. Platforms are declarations of collective policy preferences, but the road from collective policy statement to policy action can be complex. Take the case of abortion. In 1973, the Supreme Court affirmed, in the case of *Roe v. Wade*, that women have the right to seek an abortion under the Fourteenth Amendment. Until that time, neither party had mentioned abortion in its platform, but in 1976, the first presidential election following the Court decision, both parties issued broad statements on the issue. Republicans opposed abortion but called it "a moral and personal issue," on which people might disagree.

Over time, the Republican position hardened. By 1980, the Republican platform stated that the party supported a constitutional amendment protecting "the right to life for unborn children." The 2012 and 2016 Republican Party platforms called for a constitutional amendment to overturn *Roe v. Wade*, opposed the use of public funds for abortion, demanded the prohibition of "partial birth abortion," called on the president to appoint judges who opposed abortion, and demanded an end to federal funding of embryonic stem cell research.

The Republicans' increasingly staunch opposition to abortion reflected the growing importance of social conservatives in the electorate and the recognition that the party needed their support in many districts. On the other hand, despite electing three presidents since 1980 and frequently controlling the House, the Senate, or both, Republicans in government have enacted few policies to actually bring an end to abortion.

The explanation for this apparent contradiction between principles and practices is rooted in the complexities of collective action. Antiabortion rhetoric energizes one faction of the party, but antiabortion action runs counter to the views of many other Republicans and might offend moderate and independent voters whom the party also needs at the polls. This example illustrates how engaging in successful collective action in the electoral arena may preclude collective action in the policy arena.

To Deal with the Problem of Ambition

Parties enable individual politicians to achieve their ambitions. The very "brand names" that parties provide are often a significant electoral asset. Moreover, once their candidates are elected, parties provide these politicians, who share principles, causes, and constituencies, with a basis for coordination, common cause, cooperation, and joint enterprise. But individual ambition constantly threatens to undermine any bases for cooperation. Political parties, by regulating career advancement, providing for the orderly resolution of ambitious competition, and attending to the post-career care of party officials, do much to rescue coordination and cooperation and permit fellow partisans to pursue common causes where feasible. Simple devices such as primaries, for example, provide a context in which to resolve clashing electoral ambitions. Representative partisan bodies, like the Democratic Committee on Committees in the House (with comparable bodies for the Republicans and for both parties in the Senate), resolve competing claims for power positions. And centralized fund-raising by organizations, such as the Democratic and Republican National Committees, provide incentives for politicians to conduct their campaigns and vote in the legislature in line with their party. In short, politics consists not of foot soldiers walking in lockstep but, rather, of ambitious and autonomous individuals seeking power. The unchecked burnishing of individual careers is a formula for destructive competition in which the dividends of cooperation are rarely reaped. Political parties constitute organizations of relatively kindred spirits who try to capture some of those dividends by providing a structure in which ambition is not suppressed altogether but is not so destructive either.

WHAT FUNCTIONS DO PARTIES PERFORM?

Parties are mainly involved in nominations and elections, recruiting the candidates for office, getting out the vote, and making it easier for citizens to choose their leaders. That is, they help solve the problems of collective action and ambition. They also influence the institutions of government, providing leadership as well as organization of the various congressional committees and activities on the floor in each chamber. That is, they help solve problems of collective choice concerning institutional arrangements and policy formulation.

Recruiting Candidates

One of the most important party activities is the recruitment of candidates for office. Each election year, candidates must be found for thousands of state and local offices as well as for congressional seats. When an incumbent is not seeking reelection or when an incumbent in the opposing party appears vulnerable, party leaders identify strong candidates and interest them in entering the campaign. The recruiting season begins early because the dates by which candidates must file for office come as early as January in some states. Candidate recruitment in the spring shapes the parties' message and fortunes in the November general election. In 2014, a weak economy and low popularity ratings for President Obama made it difficult for Democrats to recruit candidates for congressional races. Immediately following the 2014 election, the Democratic Congressional Campaign Committee began an aggressive effort to recruit new candidates. The parties also use their recruitment efforts to target segments of the electorate where they would like to strengthen their appeal. The Republican Party, for example, established project GROW—Growing Republican Opportunities for Women—in 2013 in order to improve recruitment of women candidates for state legislatures and Congress.[4]

An ideal candidate will be charismatic, organized, knowledgeable, and an excellent debater; have an unblemished record; and possess the ability to raise enough money to mount a serious campaign. Party leaders usually will not provide financial backing for candidates who cannot raise substantial funds on their own. For a House seat, this can mean between $500,000 and $1 million; for a Senate seat, several million dollars; and upward of $1 billion for the presidency.[5] Often party leaders have difficulty finding attractive candidates and persuading them to run. In recent years, many potential congressional candidates declined to run, saying they were reluctant to leave their homes and families for the hectic life of a member of Congress. Candidate recruitment has become particularly difficult in an era when political campaigns often involve mudslinging and the candidates' personal lives are scrutinized in the press.[6]

Nominating Candidates

Article I, Section 4, of the Constitution makes only a few provisions for elections. It delegates to the states the power to set the "Times, Places and Manner of holding Elections," even for U.S. senators and representatives. It does, however, reserve to Congress the power to make such laws if it chooses to do so. The Constitution has been amended at times to expand the right to participate in elections, and Congress has occasionally passed laws regulating elections, congressional districting, and campaign practices. But the Constitution and the laws are almost completely silent on nominations, setting only citizenship and age requirements for candidates. The president must be at least 35 years of age, a natural-born citizen, and a resident of the United States for 14 years. A senator

4 Nicole Puglise, "GOP Women's Recruitment Effort Adapts for 2016," *Roll Call,* July 6, 2015, www.rollcall.com/news/home/gop-womens-recruitment-effort-adapts-2016 (accessed 8/26/16).

5 Kenneth P. Vogel, Dave Levinthal and Tarini Parti, "Barack Obama, Mitt Romney Both Topped $1 billion in 2012," *Politico,* December 12, 2012, www.politico.com/story/2012/12/barack-obama-mitt-romney-both-topped-1-billion-in-2012-84737.html (accessed 6/10/16).

6 For an excellent analysis of the parties' role in recruitment, see Paul S. Herrnson, *Congressional Elections: Campaigning at Home and in Washington* (Washington, DC: CQ Press, 1995).

Figure 12.1
TYPES OF NOMINATION PROCESSES

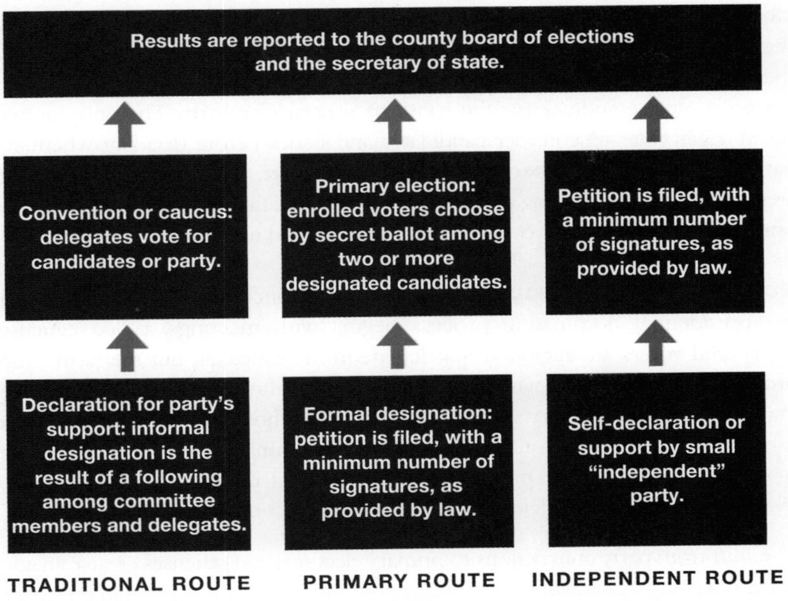

Results are reported to the county board of elections and the secretary of state.		

TRADITIONAL ROUTE

Convention or caucus: delegates vote for candidates or party.

Declaration for party's support: informal designation is the result of a following among committee members and delegates.

PRIMARY ROUTE

Primary election: enrolled voters choose by secret ballot among two or more designated candidates.

Formal designation: petition is filed, with a minimum number of signatures, as provided by law.

INDEPENDENT ROUTE

Petition is filed, with a minimum number of signatures, as provided by law.

Self-declaration or support by small "independent" party.

must be at least age 30, a U.S. citizen for at least 9 years, and a resident of the state he or she represents. A member of the House must be at least age 25, a U.S. citizen for 7 years, and a resident of the state he or she represents.

Nomination is the process by which a party selects a single candidate to run for each elective office. Nomination is the parties' most serious and difficult business. The nominating process can precede the election by many months (Figure 12.1), as it does when many presidential candidates are eliminated through a grueling series of debates and state primaries, caucuses, and conventions until there is only one survivor in each party—that party's nominee.

Nomination by Convention. A nominating convention is a formal meeting of members of a political party that is bound by rules that govern participation and nominating procedures. Conventions are meetings of delegates elected by party members from the relevant county (a county convention) or state (a state convention). Delegates to each party's national convention (which nominates the party's presidential candidate) are chosen by party members on a state-by-state basis; there is no single national delegate selection process.

Nomination by Primary Election. In primary elections, party members select the party's nominees directly rather than selecting convention delegates, who then select the nominees. Primaries are imperfect replacements for

 nomination

The process by which political parties select their candidates for election to public office

conventions because rarely do more than 25 percent of enrolled voters participate.[7] Nevertheless, primaries have replaced conventions as the dominant method of nomination.[8]

Primary elections fall mainly into two categories—closed and open. In a **closed primary**, participation is limited to individuals who have previously declared their affiliation by registering with the party. In an **open primary**, individuals declare their affiliation on the day of the primary election. To do so, they simply go to the polling place and ask for the ballot of a particular party. The open primary allows each voter to consider candidates and issues before deciding whether to participate and in which party's contest to participate. Open primaries, therefore, are less conducive to strong political parties. But in either case, primaries are more open than conventions or caucuses to new issues and new types of candidates.

Nomination by Caucus.
In several states, including Iowa and Nevada, the presidential nominating process begins with meetings, called caucuses. Registered voters are eligible to participate in the caucuses, but the nomination process consists of extensive discussions among those present, and the meetings can last several hours. At the local caucuses, those present select delegates to county-level conventions, and, in turn, the county conventions select delegates to go to the state party convention. It is at the state party convention where these states elect delegates to the party's national convention.

The shift from party conventions to primary elections and caucuses creates an additional screening of candidates: they must now win both the primary and the general election in order to hold office. As a result the introduction of primary elections may have contributed to the rise of candidate-centered politics by creating advantages for politicians who are particularly strong campaigners but who may be less effective at governing.[9] Thus a "selection" effect results from the particular institutional arrangement a state employs. Institutions matter in this case because they encourage or discourage particular types of candidates, as the institution principle suggests.

Getting Out the Vote

The election period begins immediately after the nominations. Historically, this has been a time of glory for the political parties, whose popular base of support is fully displayed. All the paraphernalia of party committees and all the committee members are activated in the form of local party workforces.

---

closed primary

A primary election in which only those voters who registered with the party a specified period before the primary election day can participate

---

open primary

A primary election in which voters can choose on the primary election day itself which party's primary to vote in

---

7 Anthony King, *Running Scared: Why America's Politicians Campaign Too Much and Govern Too Little* (New York: Martin Kessler Books, 1997).

8 At the present time, only a small number of states, including Connecticut, Delaware, and Utah, provide for state conventions to nominate candidates for statewide offices, and even those states also use primaries whenever a substantial minority of delegates has voted for one of the defeated aspirants.

9 Matthew Crenson and Benjamin Ginsberg, *Presidential Power: Unchecked and Unbalanced* (New York: Norton, 2007).

The first step in the electoral process involves voter registration, which takes place all year round. At one time party workers were responsible for this activity, but they have been supplemented (and in many states displaced) by civic groups such as the League of Women Voters, unions, and chambers of commerce.

Those who have registered must decide on Election Day whether to go to the polling place, stand in line, and vote for the various candidates and referendums on the ballot. Political parties, candidates, and campaigning can make a big difference in persuading eligible voters to vote. Because it is costly for voters to participate in elections (because they have to take time off work or spend the time to learn about the issues and candidates in a campaign) and because many of the benefits that winning parties bestow are public goods (that is, parties cannot exclude any individual from enjoying them), people often free ride by enjoying the benefits without incurring the costs of electing the party that provides the benefits. Parties help overcome this free-rider problem (see Chapter 1) by mobilizing the voters to support the candidates.

In recent years, the parties themselves and not-for-profit groups have mobilized large numbers of people to vote and raised millions of dollars for election organizing and advertising. Legions of workers, often volunteers, have used new technologies to build and communicate with networks of supporters. They are the "netroots" organizations of politics. To comply with federal election and tax law, groups must maintain independence from the political parties,[10] although they have the same objectives as the parties and strive to elect politicians from a particular party. Such organizations act as shadow appendages of the two parties, mobilizing supporters for one or the other. The netroots have become integral to campaign organizations, and these new forms of direct campaigning have produced a noticeable uptick in voter turnout.

Facilitating Electoral Choice

Parties make the electoral choice much easier for voters. It is often argued that we should vote for the best person regardless of party affiliation. But on any general-election ballot, only a handful of candidates are likely well known to the voters—namely, certain candidates for president, U.S. Senate, U.S. House, and governor. As one moves down the ballot, voters' familiarity with the candidates declines. Without party labels, voters would constantly confront a bewildering array of new choices and might have difficulty making informed decisions. Without a doubt, candidates' party affiliations help voters make reasonable choices.

Parties lower the information costs of participating in elections by providing a recognizable "brand name." Without knowing much about a given candidate, voters can infer from party labels how the candidate will likely behave once elected. In the United States, the Democratic Party is associated with greater government regulation of the economy and a larger public sector; the

---

10 If a group coordinates its activities with a political party, it is subject to additional reporting requirements and contribution limits, and political action can violate the conditions for tax-exempt status of nonprofits.

Republican Party favors a limited government role in the economy and reduced government spending paired with tax reductions. The Democrats favor aggressive protection of civil rights for women and for sexual and racial minorities and a secular approach to religion in public life. The Republicans generally support banning abortion and favor government participation in expanding the role of religious organizations in civil society. The parties' positions on the economy were cemented in the 1930s, and their division on social issues emerged during the 1960s and 1970s. The Democratic positions are loosely labeled liberal and those of the Republicans conservative.

Most Americans identify with one of the two parties and are likely to vote with that party, but even those who do not can derive value from the party labels. Nonpartisan voters are more conflicted about which party or candidate best represents their interests, but if a voter tried to learn about every politician running for every office, she would spend an enormous amount of time tracking down the information. Party labels, then, help simplify the voter's choice to an evaluation of two competing policy positions or the performance of those in office. The independent voter may ask "Which of the two parties will better represent my ideals and interests?" and then choose the party that offers the best option today. Or the voter may ask "Am I better off now than four years ago?" If not, she will vote against the president's party up and down the ballot. If yes, she will vote to keep the president and his party in power. Whichever strategy the independent voter uses, parties are essential for simplifying an otherwise bewildering choice.

For all voters, partisans and independents alike, the parties make it easier to hold government accountable. People can vote against the party in power in bad times and for the party in power in good times. They can vote against the party in power if it enacts unpopular legislation. Thus political parties solve one of the most important collective action problems facing American democracy, the problem of collective responsibility. If every politician ran on her own, without regard to other candidates, districts, or the nation at large, each race for legislator or executive would become an isolated event. In such a setting it would be exceedingly difficult for voters to send a message that they want government to go in a different direction. Parties, then, lend coherence to government and meaning to elections.[11]

Party labels also benefit the politicians. By having recognizable labels, candidates in most districts and states are spared the great expense of educating voters about what they stand for. The labels Democrat and Republican are usually sufficient. The labels' content is sustained because like-minded people identify with the respective organizations. People who broadly share the principles espoused by a party and who wish to participate on a high level will attend party meetings, run for leadership positions in local and state party organizations, attend state and national conventions, and even run for elected office.[12] Each

11 Morris Fiorina, "The Decline of Collective Responsibility in American Politics," *Daedalus* 109, no. 3 (summer 1980): 25–45.

12 Comprehensive studies of delegates were conducted by Walter J. Stone and Ronald B. Rapoport from 1980 through 1996. See Ronald B. Rapoport and Walter J. Stone, *Three's a Crowd: The Dynamic of Third Parties, Ross Perot, and Republican Resurgence* (Ann Arbor: University of Michigan Press, 1999). Surveys of candidates find similar sorting.

party, then, draws on a distinct pool for activists and candidates. Each successive election reinforces the division between the parties.

Influencing National Government

The two major parties are often called "big tents," attracting as many groups and ideas as possible. Positioning themselves as broad coalitions prevents effective national third parties from emerging and guarantees that the Democrats and Republicans vie for control of Congress.

The coalitions that come together in the Democratic and Republican parties shape the parties' platforms on public policy. The political coalitions that party leaders assemble determine what interests and social groups align with the parties and what sorts of issues emerge. The Democratic Party today embraces a philosophy of active government intervention in the economy, based on the premise that regulation is necessary to ensure orderly economic growth, to prevent the emergence of monopolies, and to address certain costs of economic activity, such as pollution, poverty, and unemployment. In addition, the Democratic Party seeks expansion and protection of civil rights, especially for women and racial minorities. The Republican Party espouses a philosophy of laissez-faire economics and a minimal government role in the economy. The coalition that Ronald Reagan built in the late 1970s paired this vision of limited intervention in the economy with an expanded role for religion in society and opposition to immigration, affirmative action, and abortion, views that continue to represent the party today.

Many European observers regard the American parties as odd amalgams of contradictory ideas. Liberalism, as it developed as a political philosophy in Europe, naturally pairs laissez-faire economics with liberal views on civil rights. Conservatism, which maintains a respect for social and political order, prefers a stronger role for social organizations, especially religions; a greater respect for social hierarchies, most notably social classes and higher-educated elites; and government power in the economy. The American parties, partly because of their histories, have scrambled these traditional views. In the Republican Party today, laissez-faire economics goes hand in hand with conservative views on civil rights and religion in society. In the Democratic Party today, liberal views on civil rights are tied to an expansive view of government in the economy. The American parties have mixed and matched different ideas in response to evolving issues and party leadership. For example, the coalition that President Franklin Delano Roosevelt assembled in the 1930s consisted of Progressive Republicans, who favored greater economic regulation; old-line Democrats, especially in the South; and urban political machines in northern and midwestern cities. This peculiar coalition gave rise to the political philosophy and public policies pursued under the New Deal. It also constrained what Roosevelt could do on some issues. Most important, he could not push for expanding civil rights for blacks without losing the support of southerners. The meaning of Democratic liberalism in the United States, then, was very much a function of the history of the parties.

Even though American liberalism and conservatism do not coincide neatly with their European counterparts, they still represent distinct views about how government ought to act, and they appeal to distinctly different constituencies. The Democratic Party at the national level seeks to unite organized labor, the poor, racial minorities, and liberal upper-middle-class professionals. The Republicans, by contrast, appeal to business, upper-middle-class and upper-class groups in the private sector, and social conservatives. Often party leaders seek to develop issues that they hope will add new groups to their constituent base. During the 1980s, for example, under President Reagan, the Republicans devised a series of "social issues," including support for school prayer, opposition to abortion, and opposition to affirmative action, designed to cultivate the support of white southerners. This effort was extremely successful in increasing Republican strength in the once solidly Democratic South. In the 1990s, under President Clinton, the Democratic Party sought to develop social programs designed to solidify the party's base among working-class and poor voters and somewhat conservative economic programs aimed at attracting middle-class and upper-middle-class voters.

As these examples suggest, party leaders can act as policy entrepreneurs, seeking ideas and programs that will expand their party's base of support while eroding that of the opposition. Both parties, for example, have aggressively sought the support of Hispanic and Latino voters, one of the fastest growing segments of the electorate. Both President George W. Bush and President Obama supported policies to ease immigration restrictions, which are popular with Hispanic and Latino voters. It can, however, be difficult to balance appeals to a party's primary electorate and the general electorate. Throughout the 2016 presidential primary season, Donald Trump proposed restrictive immigration rules, such as building a wall along the U.S.-Mexico border. He also blamed undocumented illegal immigrants for problems related to drugs, rape, and other crimes in the United States. His rhetoric alienated many Hispanic voters but was supported by many Republican primary voters. At the beginning of the general election, Democratic candidate Hillary Clinton led Donald Trump by 45 percentage points among Hispanic voters.[13] To broaden his campaign's appeal among Hispanics, Trump and the Republican National Committee established the National Hispanic Advisory Council to guide their message.[14] Nonetheless, November exit polls revealed that Clinton won 65 percent of the Hispanic vote compared to Trump's 29 percent.

Both parties translate their general goals into concrete policies through the members they elect to office. Republicans, for example, implemented tax cuts, increased defense spending, cut social spending, and enacted restrictions on abortion during the 1980s and 1990s. Democrats defended consumer and environmental programs against Republican attacks and sought to expand domestic social programs

---

13 Andrew O'Reilly, "Fox News Latino Poll: Clinton Holds 46-point lead over Trump among Hispanics," August 11, 2016, www.latino.foxnews.com/latino/politics/2016/08/11/fox-news-latino-poll-clinton-holds-46-point-lead-over-trump-among-hispanics/ (accessed 8/26/16).

14. Eli Watkins, "Trump campaign, RNC convene Hispanic outreach effort," CNN, August 21, 2016, www.cnn.com/2016/08/20/politics/rnc-donald-trump-national-hispanic-advisory-council/ (accessed 8/26/16).

in the late 1990s. In 2009, President Obama and a Democratic-controlled Congress created a national health insurance system that guarantees all people access to health care, a key item on the Democratic Party's platform since the 1940s. In 2016, Democratic candidates pledged to expand national health care if elected.

PARTIES IN GOVERNMENT

Parties operate in three spheres: elections, political institutions, and government. The ultimate test of a political party is its influence on the institutions of government and the policy-making process. We begin there.

Most parties originate inside the government. Political parties form as those who support the government's actions and those who do not; in the United Kingdom, these groups are called Government and Opposition.[15] In the American context, parties vie to control both Congress and the presidency.

The Parties and Congress. The two major American political parties have a profound influence on the organization and day-to-day operation of Congress. The Speaker of the House, perhaps the most powerful person in Congress, is essentially a party officer. All House members participate in electing the Speaker, but the actual selection is made by the **majority party**. When the majority party caucus presents a nominee to the entire House, its choice is invariably ratified in a straight party-line vote.

The parties also organize the committee system of both houses of Congress. Although the whole membership adopts the rules organizing committees and defining the jurisdiction of each committee, all other features of the committees are shaped by the party leadership and caucuses. For example, each party is assigned a quota of members for each committee, depending on the percentage of total seats held by the party. On the rare occasions when an independent or third-party candidate is elected, the leaders of the two parties must agree against whose quota this member's committee assignments will count. Presumably, the member will not be able to serve on any committee until the quota question is settled.[16] As we saw in Chapter 6, the assignment of individual members to congressional committees is a party decision, as is the choice of who advances to committee chair. Since the late nineteenth century, most advancements have been automatic, based on the length of continuous service on the committee. This seniority system has survived only because of the support of the two parties, and each party can depart from it by a simple vote. During the 1970s, both parties reinstituted the practice of reviewing each chairmanship, voting anew every two years on whether to

 majority party

The party that holds the majority of legislative seats in either the House or the Senate

---

15 Maurice Duverger, *Political Parties* (New York: John Wiley, 1951).

16 Scott A. Frisch and Sean Q. Kelly, *Committee Assignment Politics in the U.S. House of Representatives* (Norman: University of Oklahoma Press, 2006).

continue each chair. In 2001, Republicans limited House committee chairs to three terms. Existing chairs are forced to step down but are generally replaced by the next most senior Republican member of each committee.[17]

President and Party. The president carries the mantle of leader of his or her party, and the electoral fortunes of the parties rise and fall with the success of the president. During midterm congressional elections, when the president is not on the ballot, voters hold the president's party accountable for current problems. When the economy does poorly, Americans punish the president's party, even when the opposing party controls Congress.

The president of the United States also relies heavily on fellow party members in organizing the executive and passing legislation. Unlike parliamentary governments, such as in the United Kingdom, the heads of executive departments are not sitting members of the legislature. With few exceptions, heads of executive departments and other key presidential appointments are people loyal to the president and his political party; most have served as governors of states or members of Congress or are close advisers who worked with the president in previous offices or campaigns.

The president and White House staff also work closely with congressional party leaders to shepherd legislation through Congress. The president cannot introduce legislation and must rely on members of Congress to do so. (There are a few exceptions such as nominations and treaties.) Nearly all of the president's legislative initiatives begin as bills introduced by fellow party members in the House and Senate. The party leadership of the president's party also negotiates with individual members of Congress to construct majority support for a White House–sponsored bill. Sometimes even the president will try to persuade individual legislators to support a particular bill.

The president's ability to prevail in Congress depends on which party controls the House and Senate. When the president's party enjoys majorities in both chambers, his legislative agenda succeeds most of the time. A typical president will win in excess of 80 percent of the time on bills if his party controls the House and Senate. President Obama, during his first year in office, had the highest degree of support for a president since World War II, with a majority of Congress supporting his position 96 percent of the time.[18] When another party controls at least one chamber, however, the president has a much more difficult time. In the 113th Congress (2013–2015), Democrats controlled the Senate and Republicans controlled the House. Bills supported by President Obama were passed in the Senate 93 percent of the time and in the House only 15 percent of the time.[19]

---

17 Daniel Newhauser, "Brain Drain: Self-Imposed Term Limits Shuffle Committees, House GOP Leadership," *Roll Call*, April 22, 2014, www.rollcall.com/news/home/republican-committee-term-limits-shuffle-house-gop-leadership (accessed 8/26/16).

18 Don Gonyea, "CQ: Obama's Winning Streak on Hill Unprecedented," NPR, January 11, 2010, www.npr.org/templates/story/story.php?storyId=122436116 (accessed 5/28/13).

19 Shawn Zeller, "Running on Empty," CQ Weekly, March 15, 2015, pages 26–36, library.cqpress.com/cqweekly/file.php?path=/files/wr20150316-2014_Presidential.pdf (accessed 8/26/16).

PARTIES IN THE ELECTORATE

Political parties are more than just political leaders; they comprise millions of people and organizations, such as labor unions, corporations, and other interest groups. Individuals align with the parties when they volunteer for campaigns, give money, register as a partisan, or vote in a party's primary. Many groups have close connections to political parties, often providing money and organizing people for campaigns.

Party Identification

As we saw in Chapter 11, individual voters tend to develop **party identification** with one of the political parties. Party identification partly reflects a psychological attachment developed in childhood or adolescence and carried throughout life. Party identification also has a rational component, rooted in evaluations of the performance of the parties in government, the policies they pursue, and an individual's interests and ideology.[20] Voters generally form attachments to parties that reflect their views and interests. Once those attachments are formed, they are likely to persist and even be handed down to children, unless certain very strong factors convince individuals to disavow their party. In some sense, party identification is similar to brand loyalty in the marketplace: consumers choose a brand of automobile for its appearance or mechanical characteristics and stick with it out of loyalty, habit, and unwillingness to reexamine their choices, but they may eventually switch if the old brand no longer serves their interests.

Although the strength of partisan ties in the United States seemed to decline in the 1960s and 1970s, most Americans continue to identify with either the Republican Party or the Democratic Party (Figure 12.2). Party identification gives citizens a stake in election outcomes that goes beyond the race at hand. This is why people who identify strongly with one party are more likely than other Americans to go to the polls and, of course, to support their party. **Party activists** are those who not only vote but also volunteer their time and energy to party affairs. Activists ring doorbells, stuff envelopes, attend meetings, and contribute money to the party cause—essential work that keeps the organization going. It is worth noting that attachment to a party does not guarantee voting for that party's candidates, though it does reflect a tendency. During the 2016 presidential election, many Republican leaders and politicians, including the party's 2012 nominee Mitt Romney, refused to endorse Donald Trump

party identification

An individual's attachment to a particular political party, which might be based on issues, ideology, past experience, or upbringing

party activist

A partisan who contributes time and energy beyond voting to support a party and its candidates

20 For what is perhaps still the best discussion of the bases of party identification, see Arthur S. Goldberg, "Social Determinism and Rationality as Bases of Party Identification," *American Political Science Review* 63, no. 1 (March 1969): 5–25. For a more recent article weighing in on economic versus social determinants of party attachments, see Larry M. Bartels, "What's the Matter with *What's the Matter with Kansas?*" *Quarterly Journal of Political Science* 1 (2006): 201–26.

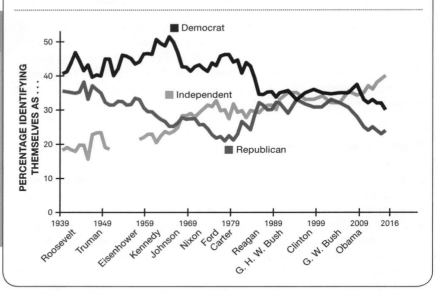

Figure 12.2
AMERICANS' PARTY IDENTIFICATION

NOTE: Independent data not available for 1951–56.
SOURCES: Pew Research Center, www.people-press.org/interactives/party-id-trend/ and
www.pewresearch.org/data-trend/political-attitudes/party-identification/ (accessed 10/11/16).

ANALYZING THE EVIDENCE

In 1952, Democrats outnumbered Republicans significantly. Since the late 1980s, the two parties appear to have similar numbers of loyalists. What factors might account for this partisan transformation?

as the GOP's nominee; some even crossed party lines to endorse Democrat Hillary Clinton.[21] In general, however, strong identifiers vote for their party's candidate almost always, and weak identifiers do so most of the time. For example, according to the 2016 exit polls, 90 percent of those who called themselves Republicans voted for Donald Trump, the Republican Party's nominee, and 89 percent of people who called themselves Democrats voted for Hillary Clinton, the Democratic Party's nominee.[22]

Group Basis of Parties

The Democratic and Republican parties are America's only national parties, drawing support from most regions of the country and from Americans of every racial, economic, religious, and ethnic group. The two parties do not draw equal support from members of every social stratum, however. When we refer

21 David Graham, "Which Republicans oppose Donald Trump? A Cheat Sheet,"
    The Atlantic, August 18, 2016, www.theatlantic.com/politics/archive/2016/08/
    where-republicans-stand-on-donald-trump-a-cheat-sheet/481449/ (accessed 8/26/16).

22 "Election 2016: Exit Polls," *The New York Times*, www.nytimes.com/interactive
    /2016/11/08/us/politics/election-exit-polls.html (accessed 11/12/16).

to the Democratic or Republican coalition, we mean the groups that generally support one or the other party.

One view of political parties, a Pluralist view, is that they consist of coalitions of many organized groups. The leaders of organizations such as the American Federation of Labor and the Christian Coalition may choose to side with a party in an effort to affect what government does by influencing the party's policy orientation. A group can offer resources such as campaign workers, contributions, and votes; the party, in exchange, can pursue policies in line with what the groups want. Once aligned with a party, a group's leaders can then signal to members for whom they should vote. The more disciplined the group and the more resources it can offer, the more power it will have in the party. Party leaders try to build coalitions consisting of many different groups, each seeking a distinct policy or political benefit. The Reagan Coalition consisted of corporate political leaders who wanted to minimize taxes, the Christian Coalition and other fundamental Christian groups that wanted changes in various social policies, and activists in western states who wanted open access to land. The challenge for political parties is to build coalitions that can win majorities in elections but not create too many conflicting demands.[23]

Broader social groups are equally important. Parties can appeal to different types of voters through distinct policy promises. A person with a particularly strong social group attachment might find one of the parties appealing because it aligns well on the social group's pet issue. For instance, the Republican Party's hard line toward Cuba and Communism meant that most Cuban Americans identified as Republican, even while other Hispanic and Latino groups lined up with Democrats over issues such as immigration and education. In the United States today, a variety of group characteristics are associated with party identification. These include race and ethnicity, gender, religion, class, region, and age.

Race and Ethnicity. Since the 1960s and Democratic support for the Civil Rights Movement, African Americans have been overwhelmingly Democratic in party identification. More than 90 percent of African Americans describe themselves as Democrats and support Democratic candidates in national, state, and local elections. Approximately 25 percent of the Democratic Party's support in presidential races comes from African American voters.

Republicans, on the other hand, depend heavily on the support of white voters. Roughly 55 percent of the white electorate has supported the GOP in recent years. In 2016, Donald Trump appealed heavily to white working class voters on issues of trade and immigration, hoping to increase the Republican percentage of the white vote.

Latino and Hispanic voters comprise people whose ancestors came from many different countries, with disparate political orientations. Mexican Americans, the largest group, have historically aligned with the Democratic Party, as

---

23 A recent formulation of the Pluralist model of parties is Kathleen Bawn, Martin Cohen, David Karol, Seth Masket, Hans Noel, and John Zaller, "A Theory of Political Parties: Groups, Policy Demands, and Nominations in American Politics," *Perspectives on Politics* 10 (2012): 571–97.

have Puerto Ricans and Central Americans. Historically, Cuban Americans have voted heavily and identified as Republican. Recently, however, Cubans have shifted toward the Democratic Party. This trend appears to reflect generational differences, as younger Cuban Americans look to be as Democratic as other Hispanic and Latino groups. Asian Americans tend to be divided as well, though more support the Democrats than the Republicans. Japanese, Chinese, Filipino, and Korean communities have been long established in the United States and have influential business communities. Higher-income Asians tend to be as Republican as higher-income whites. It is unclear whether newer Asian immigrant groups, such as the Hmong, the Vietnamese, Thais, and Indians, will follow the same trajectory as the Japanese and Chinese communities.

Gender. Women are somewhat more likely to support Democrats, and men to support Republicans. This difference, known as the **gender gap**, is fairly new in American politics. Early studies of the women's vote in the 1920s, shortly after the extension of the franchise, found little difference in voting behavior between men and women. If anything, women tended to be slightly more Republican, and they more strongly favored the prohibition of alcohol than men did. The modern gender gap emerged in the 1980 presidential election and has ranged from a difference of 4 percentage points in 1992 to a high of 11 percentage points in 1996.[24] The 2016 election saw the first female presidential candidate for a major party—Democrat Hillary Clinton—which contributed to the especially large gender gap that year. Exit polls showed that Clinton won 54 percent of the women's vote and 41 percent of the men's vote, a 13-point gap.

Religion. Jews are among the Democratic Party's most loyal constituent groups. Nearly 90 percent of all Jewish Americans describe themselves as Democrats, although the percentage is declining among younger Jews. Catholics were once strongly pro-Democratic as well but more conservative white Catholics have been shifting toward the Republican Party since the 1970s, when the Republicans began to focus on abortion and other social issues deemed important to Catholics. More religiously conservative Protestant denominations tend to identify with the Republicans, while Protestants who are religiously liberal, such as Unitarians and Episcopalians, tend to identify as Democrats. Evangelical Protestants, in particular, have been drawn to the Republicans' conservative stands on social issues, such as gay marriage and abortion. (See the Analyzing the Evidence unit for a discussion of candidate religion and partisan voting.)

Class. Upper-income Americans are likely to affiliate with the Republicans, whereas very low income Americans are likely to identify with the Democrats. Middle-class voters split evenly between Democrats and Republicans. This divide reflects the parties' differences on economic issues. In general, Republicans support cutting taxes and social spending—positions that reflect the

---

gender gap

A distinctive pattern of voting behavior reflecting the differences in views between women and men

---

24 Susan Carroll, *Women and American Politics: New Questions, New Directions* (Oxford: Oxford University Press, 2003).

interests of the wealthy. Democrats, however, favor increased social spending, even if this requires increasing taxes—a position consistent with the interests of less-affluent Americans. One important exception is that relatively affluent individuals who work in the public sector or for foundations and universities also tend to affiliate with the Democrats. Such individuals are likely to appreciate the Democratic Party's support for an expanded role of government and high levels of public spending. White voters with less than a college education (a measure of class) have become less strongly affiliated with the Democrats over time. Indeed, in the 2016 presidential election, white voters without a college degree strongly supported Republican Donald Trump over Democrat Hillary Clinton. Sixty-seven percent of whites without a college degree voted for Trump, compared to just 28 percent for Clinton.[25]

Region. Between the time of the Civil War and the 1960s, the "Solid South" was a Democratic bastion. Today much of the South has become solidly Republican in national elections, although it is more divided in state elections. The areas of greatest Democratic Party strength are the Northeast and the Far West (especially California, Washington, Oregon, and Hawaii). The Midwest is a battleground, more or less evenly divided between the two parties.

The explanations for these regional variations are complex. The parties' legislative agendas certainly play differently in the regions, with the Republican agenda of social conservatism, low taxes, and high military spending appealing more to voters in the South and Mountain West and the Democratic agenda of social liberalism and high domestic spending (especially on Medicare and Social Security) appealing more in urban areas and in the Northeast and Far West. Republican strength in the South and Mountain West is related to the weakness of organized labor in these regions, as well as to the regions' dependence on military programs supported by the Republicans. Democratic strength in the Northeast reflects the continuing influence of organized labor in the region's large cities, as well as its large population of minority and elderly voters, who benefit from Democratic social programs.

Age. Age is also associated with partisanship, mainly because individuals from the same age cohort likely experienced a similar set of events during the period when their party loyalties were forming. Thus Americans in their sixties and seventies came of political age (that is, became aware of political issues and ideas) during the Cold War, the Vietnam War, and the civil rights movement. Voters whose initial perceptions of politics formed during these periods generally responded favorably to the role played by the Democrats than to the actions of the Republicans. This is thought to reflect the strong effects of a person's first experiences voting, a person's first impression of politics. It is fitting that among young Americans in their twenties and thirties, who came of age during an era of political scandals that tainted both parties, most describe themselves as independents.

----

25 "Election 2016: Exit Polls," *The New York Times,* www.nytimes.com/interactive/2016/11/08/us/politics/election-exit-polls.html (accessed 11/13/16).

Candidate Religion and Partisan Voting

Contributed by

Geoffrey C. Layman
University of Notre Dame

John C. Green
University of Akron

David E. Campbell
University of Notre Dame

Jeremiah J. Castle
University of Notre Dame

Individuals identify with a political party for many reasons, including their own social group memberships and feelings toward other social groups.[1] To what extent do the social group characteristics of political candidates affect the connection between citizens' party identifications and their support for those candidates? One important social group for many people is religion. In recent decades, the American public has come to view the Republican Party as the party of religious people and the Democratic Party as the party of nonreligious people.[2]

Public Perception of Religious Groups' Party Ties

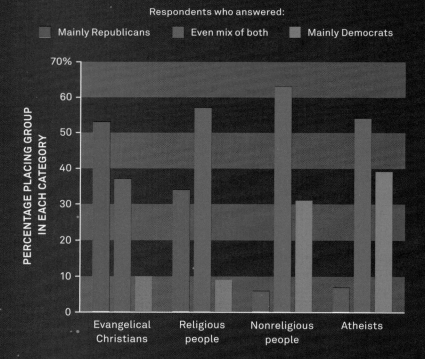

Respondents who answered:

■ Mainly Republicans   ■ Even mix of both   ■ Mainly Democrats

We asked survey respondents whether they considered Evangelical Christians, religious people, nonreligious people, and atheists to be "mainly Republicans, mainly Democrats, or a pretty even mix of both." Americans overwhelmingly view Evangelicals as Republican, tend to view religious people as Republican, and more often perceive nonreligious people as Democrats.

SOURCE: 2010 Secular America Study (conducted online by GfK/Knowledge Networks).

1 Angus Campbell, Philip E. Converse, Warren E. Miller, and Donald E. Stokes, *The American Voter* (Chicago: University of Chicago Press); Donald Green, Bradley Palmquist, and Eric Schickler, *Partisan Hearts and Minds* (New Haven, CT: Yale University Press, 2002).

2 Geoffrey Layman, *The Great Divide: Religious and Cultural Conflict in American Party Politics* (New York: Columbia University Press, 2001); John C. Green, *The Faith Factor: How Religion Influences American Elections* (Westport, CT: Praeger, 2007).

How does the public's perception of political parties' social group profiles affect the connection between individuals' party ties and their voting decisions? To find out, we presented survey respondents with descriptions of candidates that were identical except for what they said about the candidate's religion.[3] We found that the support of Republican and Democratic identifiers for the candidate changed markedly with the candidate's religious profile. Our findings suggest that because voters make assumptions about candidates' political orientations based on their social characteristics, these characteristics are quite important for electoral behavior.

The Electoral Impact of Candidate Religiosity

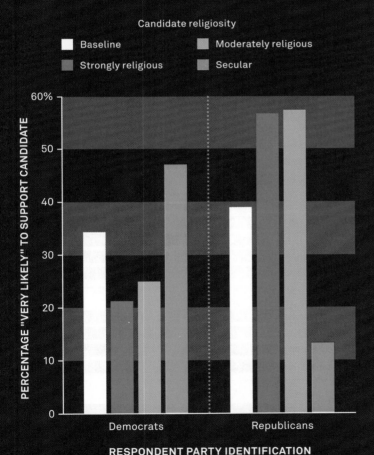

Candidate religiosity

- Baseline
- Strongly religious
- Moderately religious
- Secular

We randomly varied what we told survey respondents about the religiosity of a hypothetical state legislative candidate with a nonpartisan issue profile (focusing on goals such as good jobs, a strong economy, and efficient government) and no identified party affiliation. In the baseline (or control) condition, no mention was made of the candidate's religious orientation. When we told respondents that the candidate was moderately religious ("a man of faith") or strongly religious (a "deeply religious" person with a "personal relationship with God"), support decreased among Democrats and increased among Republicans. When we described the candidate as a secular critic of religion in public life (a "man of science" belonging to Americans United for the Separation of Church and State), support strongly increased among Democrats and strongly decreased among Republicans.

SOURCE: 2009 Cooperative Congressional Election Study (conducted online by YouGov/Polimetrix).

3 David E. Campbell, John C. Green, and Geoffrey C. Layman, "The Party Faithful: Partisan Images, Candidate Religion, and the Electoral Impact of Party Identification," *American Journal of Political Science* 55, no. 1 (2011): 42–58; and Jeremiah J. Castle, Geoffrey C. Layman, David E. Campbell, and John C. Green, "Survey Experiments on Candidate Religiosity, Political Attitudes, and Vote Choice," *Journal for the Scientific Study of Religion*, forthcoming.

Figure 12.3 indicates the relationship between party identification and various social criteria. Race, religion, income, and ideology seem to have the greatest influence on Americans' party affiliations. None of these characteristics is inevitably linked to partisan identification, however. There, for example, are union Republicans and business Democrats. The general party identifications just discussed are broad tendencies that both reflect and reinforce the issue and policy positions the two parties take in national and local political arenas. They reflect the general tendency of groups—organized and unorganized—to sort into partisan camps.

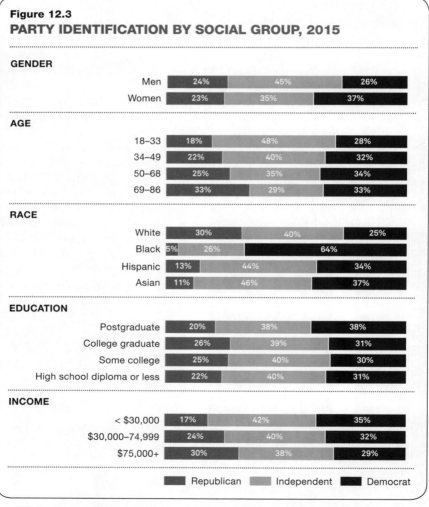

Figure 12.3
PARTY IDENTIFICATION BY SOCIAL GROUP, 2015

GENDER

	Republican	Independent	Democrat
Men	24%	45%	26%
Women	23%	35%	37%

AGE

	Republican	Independent	Democrat
18–33	18%	48%	28%
34–49	22%	40%	32%
50–68	25%	35%	34%
69–86	33%	29%	33%

RACE

	Republican	Independent	Democrat
White	30%	40%	25%
Black	5%	26%	64%
Hispanic	13%	44%	34%
Asian	11%	46%	37%

EDUCATION

	Republican	Independent	Democrat
Postgraduate	20%	38%	38%
College graduate	26%	39%	31%
Some college	25%	40%	30%
High school diploma or less	22%	40%	31%

INCOME

	Republican	Independent	Democrat
< $30,000	17%	42%	35%
$30,000–74,999	24%	40%	32%
$75,000+	30%	38%	29%

■ Republican ■ Independent ■ Democrat

NOTE: Percentages do not add to 100 because the category "Other/don't know" is omitted.
SOURCE: Pew Research Center, www.people-press.org/2015/04/07/a-deep-dive-into-party-affiliation (accessed 2/27/16).

PARTIES AS INSTITUTIONS

Political parties in the United States today are not tightly disciplined, hierarchical organizations. Indeed, they never have been. Rather, they comprise extensive networks of politicians, interest groups, activists and donors, consultants, and, ultimately, voters. Some elements of the parties, such as the party caucuses in Congress, seem to have more influence than others over the policies and strategies pursued by the parties, but each political player shapes the party's ability to influence what government does. Party campaign finance committees may, for example, work with the congressional caucus to maximize the party's appeal to donors. National party leaders must work with state and local party officials and activists to coordinate the many campaign activities in presidential and congressional elections. If parties are such wide-flung networks, how do they make their most momentous decisions, nominating candidates for offices and choosing a policy platform? Such decisions happen at every level of government in party committees, conventions, and primary elections, and it is through these institutions that the parties truly come together to make collective decisions.

Contemporary Party Organizations

The United States has party organizations at virtually every level of government (Figure 12.4). These are usually committees made up of a number of active party members. State law and party rules prescribe how such committees are constituted. Usually, committee members are elected at a local party meeting—a **political caucus**—or as part of the regular primary election. The best-known examples are the Democratic National Committee and the Republican National Committee.

 political caucus

A normally closed meeting of a political or legislative group to select candidates, plan strategy, or make decisions regarding legislative matters

The National Convention. At the national level, the party's most important institution is the national convention. Delegates from each of the states attend; as a group, they nominate the party's presidential and vice-presidential candidates, draft the party's campaign platform for the presidential race, and approve changes in the rules and regulations governing party procedures. Before World War II, presidential nominations occupied most of the convention's time, requiring days of negotiation and compromise among state party leaders and many ballots before a nominee was selected. In recent years, however, presidential candidates have essentially nominated themselves by garnering enough delegate support in primary elections to win the official nomination on the first ballot. The convention itself has played little or no role in selecting the candidates.

The convention's other two tasks, establishing the party's rules and establishing its platform, remain important. Party rules can determine the relative influence of competing factions within the party as well as the party's chances for

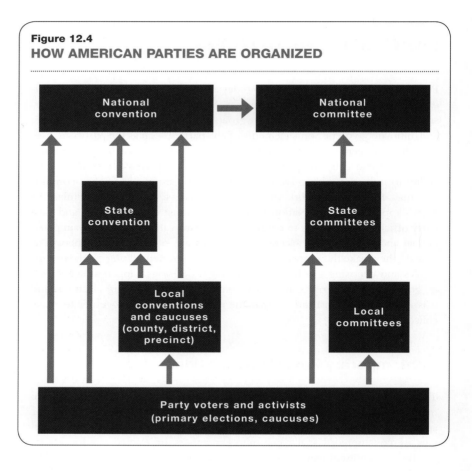

Figure 12.4
HOW AMERICAN PARTIES ARE ORGANIZED

electoral success. In the 1970s, for example, the Democratic National Convention adopted new rules favored by the party's liberal wing, according to which state delegations to the Democratic convention are required to include women and minority group members in rough proportion to those groups' representation among the party's membership in their state. The convention also approves the party platform. Platforms are often dismissed as platitude-laden documents that voters seldom bother to read. Furthermore, the parties' presidential candidates make little use of the platforms in their campaigns; usually they promote their own themes. Nonetheless, the platform should be understood as a "treaty" in which the various party factions state their terms for supporting the ticket.

The National Committee. Between conventions, each national party is technically headed by its national committee: the Democratic National Committee (DNC) and the Republican National Committee (RNC). These committees raise campaign funds, head off factional disputes within the party, and endeavor to enhance the party's media image. Since 1972, the size of staff and the amount of money raised have increased substantially for both national committees. The actual work of each committee is overseen by its chairperson. Other committee members are generally major party contributors or fund-raisers.

For the party that controls the White House, the national committee chair is appointed by the president. Under a first-term president, the committee focuses on the reelection campaign. The national committee chair of the party that does not control the White House is selected by the committee itself; this person usually raises money and performs other activities on behalf of the party's members in Congress and the state legislatures. In 2006, the DNC was headed by former presidential contender Howard Dean, who crafted a midterm election strategy to recruit quality candidates in all 50 states. Barack Obama's 2008 and 2012 presidential campaigns capitalized on Dean's 50-state strategy. Obama developed extensive grassroots organizations in every state, which registered many new Democratic voters in traditionally Republican areas. Following the 2012 presidential election, the Republican National Committee, under the leadership of Reince Priebus, conducted an extensive election "autopsy," called the Growth and Opportunity Project. Out of that comprehensive post-election review came a roadmap for retaining the House and regaining the Senate and the presidency. The Growth and Opportunity Project called for major investments in campaign and fundraising technology, including the launch of Para Bellum Labs, a lab for testing and development digital campaign tools and building "a permanent ground campaign."[26] In the wake of Hillary Clinton's surprising defeat and the Democrats' disappointing showing in the Senate elections in 2016, the Democratic Party immediately launched an effort to evaluate what went wrong and how they could improve their chances in the 2018 midterm elections and the 2020 presidential race.

Congressional Campaign Committees. Each party forms House and Senate campaign committees to raise funds for the House and Senate election campaigns. The Republicans call their House and Senate committees the National Republican Campaign Committee (NRCC) and the National Republican Senatorial Committee (NRSC). The Democrats call their House and Senate committees the Democratic Congressional Campaign Committee (DCCC) and the Democratic Senatorial Campaign Committee (DSCC). These organizations also have professional staff devoted to raising and distributing funds, developing strategies, recruiting candidates, and conducting on-the-ground campaigns. These organizations, however, are accountable to the caucuses inside the House and Senate. The chairs of these committees come from within their respective chambers and rank high in the party leadership hierarchy. The national committees and the congressional committees are sometimes rivals. Both groups seek donations from the same pool of people but for different candidates: the national committee seeks funds primarily for the presidential race, whereas the congressional campaign committees focus on House and Senate seats.

---

26 Jason Linkins, "RNC Touts Past Year's Progress from Grim 'Autopsy' in 2012," *Huffington Post,* March 18, 2014, www.huffingtonpost.com/2014/03/18/rnc-autopsy-video_n_4986508.html (accessed 8/26/16).

State and Local Party Organizations. Each major party has a central committee in each state. The parties traditionally also have county committees and, in some instances, state senate district committees, judicial district committees, and in larger cities, citywide party committees and local assembly district "ward" committees. Congressional districts may also have party committees. Some cities also have precinct committees.[27]

These organizations are very active in recruiting candidates, conducting voter registration drives, and providing financial assistance to candidates. Federal election law permits them to spend unlimited amounts of money on "party-building" activities such as voter registration and get-out-the-vote drives—with the result that the national party organizations, which are limited in the amount they can spend on candidates, transfer millions of dollars each year to the state and local organizations. The state and local parties, in turn, spend these funds, sometimes called soft money, to promote national, state, and local candidates. As local organizations have become linked financially to the national parties, American political parties have grown more integrated and nationalized than ever before. At the same time, the state and local party organizations have come to control large financial resources and play important roles in elections despite the collapse of the old patronage machines.

The Contemporary Party as Service Provider to Candidates

Party leaders have adapted to the modern age. Parties as organizations are more professional, better financed, and better organized than ever before.[28] Political parties have evolved into "service organizations," without which it would be extremely difficult for candidates to win and hold office. For example, the national organizations of the political parties collect information, ranging from lists of likely supporters and donors in local areas to public opinion polls in states and legislative districts, and they provide this information directly to their candidates for state and federal offices. They also have teams of experienced campaign organizers and managers who provide assistance to local candidates who are understaffed.

Parties provide assistance to candidates in tight races. The national parties' campaign committees today target the closest 50 or so House races and the closest 5 to 10 Senate races, spending large sums on advertising and other campaign activities as well as providing tactical support. Consultants from the DCCC, NRCC, NRSC, and DSCC are often deployed to specific campaigns to assist with get-out-the-vote efforts, direct mail, and the like. The party organizations also maintain

---

27 Well-organized political parties—especially the famous old machines of New York, Chicago, and Boston—provided for "precinct captains" and a fairly tight group of party members around them. Precinct captains were usually members of long standing in neighborhood party clubhouses.

28 John Aldrich, *Why Parties? The Origin and Transformation of Party Politics in America,* Cambridge University Press: New York, NY, 1995.

voter contact lists for the entire nation and can provide candidates with access to such information. Occasionally the party organizations put in place an entire campaign operation if there is the prospect of pulling off an upset.

The rise of party campaign organizations is fairly new. In the 1970s, the organizations (at least nationally) were extremely weak and underfunded, and incapable of providing candidates with large-scale support. Congressional campaigns in the 1970s and 1980s were built entirely from the ground up by each candidate. Those who were unusually good at raising money, organizing volunteers, and attracting media attention prevailed. In the late 1980s, however, party leaders in Congress and in their national organizations saw that they could do better in national elections if they could somehow redistribute campaign resources to close races and away from safe seats.

The rise of party campaign organizations over the past two decades has altered the politics of swing districts. In the 1970s and 1980s, incumbents in the swing districts built up personal electoral advantages based on prior elections and their prowess as fund-raisers. This allowed these incumbents to vote in Congress less with their party and more with their districts.[29] The independence of legislators in swing districts frustrated party leaders in Congress, as conservative Democrats and liberal Republicans might very well cross party lines on important votes. Since the early 1990s, the parties have poured resources into the most competitive seats in order to improve their chances of winning control of the legislature. The winners became more beholden to their party, as their electoral fortunes depend more heavily on support from the national party organizations and congressional leadership.

PARTY SYSTEMS

Our understanding of political parties would be incomplete if we considered only their composition and roles. America's political parties compete with each other for offices, policies, and power. The struggle for control of government shapes the policies the parties put forth, the coalitions of interests they represent, and the ability of the parties, indeed the government, to respond to the demands of the time. In short, the fate of each party is inextricably linked to that of its major rival.

Political scientists often call the constellation of parties that are important at any given moment a nation's party system. The most obvious feature of a party system is the number of major parties competing for power. Usually the United States has had a two-party system, meaning that only two parties have a serious chance to win national elections.

---

29 This argument is developed in great detail in David W. Rohde, *Parties and Leaders in the Post-Reform House* (Chicago: University of Chicago Press, 1991), and in the two books by Gary W. Cox and Mathew D. McCubbins, *Setting the Agenda: Responsible Party Government in the U.S. House of Representatives* (New York: Cambridge University Press, 2005) and *Legislative Leviathan*.

There are both institutional and psychological reasons why the United States has just two parties. The American electoral system is winner take all. Whoever gets the most votes wins the congressional seat. Whoever gets the most electoral votes wins the presidency. The Democratic and Republican parties have positioned themselves as center-left and center-right, respectively, neither extremely liberal nor extremely conservative. Their ideological positions maintain their policy distinctiveness and still divide the electorate about equally. If, for example, a far-left party (such as the Green Party) decided to pursue the presidency, it would split votes with the Democratic Party. It would not decrease Republican Party votes but would divide the left-leaning voters between the Democrats and the Greens, effectively guaranteeing a Republican victory. A third party that entered in the middle, however, would be squeezed between the two parties with no hope of gaining sufficient support to win. Understanding this situation, most third parties stay out. Getting on the ballot, recruiting candidates, building an organization—all carry tremendous costs. The best that the party could do would be to come in a distant third. Even worse, it could cause the major party it likes less to win. Voters also appear to understand this situation. Those who would normally want to vote for the third party see that by doing so, they end up boosting the electoral prospects of the major party that they favor less.

The same forces are less likely to influence elections in parliamentary systems, those that allocate legislative seats to parties in proportion to their share of the national vote. In parliaments, if no party wins a majority, the smaller parties can join with larger parties in a coalition. Systems that divvy up power based on the percentage of the vote won, rather than winner take all, occasionally have to form coalitions in order to form a government. That creates an incentive for small parties to fracture off from larger parties or to form on their own.

The term *party system* refers to more than just the number of parties competing for power. It also connotes the parties' organization, the balance of power between and within party coalitions, the parties' social and institutional bases, and the issues and policies around which party competition is organized. The idea of a party system implies a sense of stability, of equilibrium. Voters can reliably expect that the Democrats and Republicans will be the main parties in the next election, that Democrats will generally be ideologically liberal and Republicans ideologically conservative, that Democrats will align with unions and urban interests while Republicans will align more with corporations and rural areas.

That equilibrium is itself an outcome of the political system, reflecting the policies and coalitions of interest that those in office choose to champion. The stability of the U.S. party system, however, does not mean that the system is static. Within each party there exists a tension between moderate and extreme factions. Conflicts among the factions are worked out in state and national conventions, in the caucuses inside Congress and the state legislatures, and in primary elections. Those involved in the political struggle inside the parties, however, always have an ultimate goal to control government, to gain the upper hand. The party system reflects the balance of the political struggles within parties and the political struggles between them. Within this balance, from year to year, the alignment between parties changes, but only a little. Those who have the greatest influence over party policy making are already in office—the president and members of Congress—and they hesitate to embrace new principles or fundamentally alter the party coalitions, lest such radical changes harm their own position.

The character of a nation's party system changes as the parties realign their electoral coalitions and alter their public philosophies. Such realignment sometimes comes subtly and sometimes suddenly. Today's American party system is very different from the party system of 1950, even though the Democrats and the Republicans continue to be the major competing forces (Figure 12.5). Half a century ago, the Democrats' political strength lay in the South and the Republicans' in the North. Democrats favored racial desegregation in the South, and Republicans wanted protectionist trade policies and dismantling of Social Security. Over the past 60 years, gradual social and economic changes forced a shift in the parties' policy orientations and political coalitions. Political scientists have referred to this gradual change as a creeping realignment. One key issue driving the most recent realignment was race. Democratic leaders of the 1940s, such as Harry Truman and Hubert Humphrey, pulled their party to embrace a new platform to end racial desegregation. That change in policy redefined the Democratic Party and took the better part of a generation.[30]

Change has also come suddenly to the party system, as in response to the American Civil War and the economic depressions of the 1890s and 1930s. Those events brought lasting changes to the balance of power between the parties and to the policies they represent. The parties in power and their response to those events redefined their image among the electorate.

Over the course of American history, changes in political forces and alignments have produced six party systems, each with distinctive political institutions, issues, and patterns of political power and participation. Of course, some political phenomena persist across party systems—such as conflicts over the distribution of wealth, an enduring feature of American political life. But even such phenomena manifest themselves in different ways during different political eras.

The First Party System: Federalists and Democratic-Republicans

Although George Washington and, in fact, many other leaders of the time deplored partisan politics, the two-party system emerged early in the history of the new Republic. Competition in Congress between northeastern mercantile and southern agrarian factions led Alexander Hamilton and the northeasterners to form a voting bloc within Congress. The southerners, led by Thomas Jefferson and James Madison, responded by cultivating a popular following to change the balance of power within Congress. When the northeasterners replied to this southern strategy, the result was the birth of America's first national parties—the Democratic-Republicans, whose primary base was in the South,

---

30 Edward Carmines and James Stimson, *Issue Evolution* (Princeton, NJ: Princeton University Press, 1989).

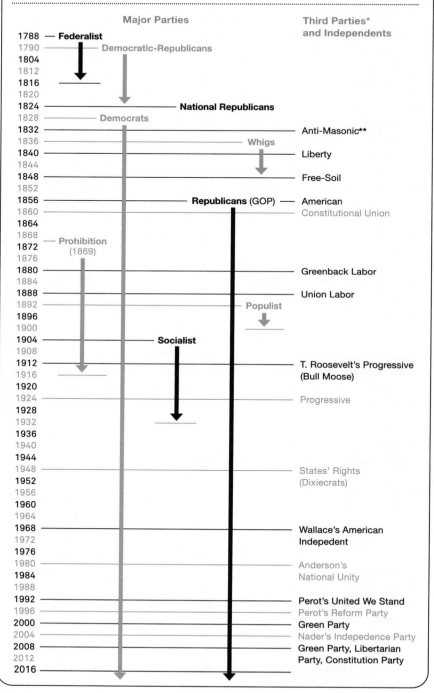

Figure 12.5
HOW THE PARTY SYSTEM EVOLVED

Major Parties

Third Parties*
and Independents

1788 — **Federalist**
1790 — Democratic-Republicans
1804
1812
1816
1820
1824 — **National Republicans**
1828 — Democrats
1832 — Anti-Masonic**
1836 — Whigs
1840 — Liberty
1844
1848 — Free-Soil
1852
1856 — **Republicans** (GOP) — American
1860 — Constitutional Union
1864
1868
1872 — Prohibition (1869)
1876
1880 — Greenback Labor
1884
1888 — Union Labor
1892 — Populist
1896
1900
1904 — **Socialist**
1908
1912 — T. Roosevelt's Progressive (Bull Moose)
1916
1920
1924 — Progressive
1928
1932
1936
1940
1944
1948 — States' Rights (Dixiecrats)
1952
1956
1960
1964
1968 — Wallace's American Independent
1972
1976
1980 — Anderson's National Unity
1984
1988
1992 — Perot's United We Stand
1996 — Perot's Reform Party
2000 — Green Party
2004 — Nader's Indepedence Party
2008 — Green Party, Libertarian Party, Constitution Party
2012
2016

*In some cases, there was even a fourth party. Most of the parties listed here existed for only one term.
**The Anti-Masonics not only had the distinction of being the first third party but also were the first party to hold a national nominating convention and the first to announce a party platform.

and the Federalists, whose strength was greatest in New England. The Federalists spoke mainly for New England mercantile groups and supported protective tariffs to encourage manufacturers, the assumption of the states' Revolutionary War debts, the creation of a national bank, and resumption of commercial ties with England. The Democratic-Republicans opposed these policies, favoring instead free trade, the promotion of agrarian over commercial interests, and friendship with France.

The rationale behind the formation of both parties was primarily that they would create stable voting blocs within Congress around cohesive policy agendas. Although the Federalists and the Democratic-Republicans competed in elections, their ties to the electorate were loose. In 1800, the American electorate was small, and voters generally followed the lead of local political and religious leaders and community notables. Local party leaders would gather the party elites and agree on the person, usually one of them, who would be the candidate. Meetings where candidates were nominated were called caucuses. In this era, before the secret ballot, many voters were reluctant publicly to defy influential members of their community by voting against them. In this context, the Democratic-Republicans and the Federalists organized political clubs and developed newspapers and newsletters to mobilize elite opinion and draw in more followers. In the election of 1800, Jefferson defeated the incumbent Federalist president, John Adams, and led the Democratic-Republicans to power. Over the ensuing years, the Federalists weakened. The party disappeared after the pro-British sympathies of some Federalist leaders during the War of 1812 led to charges that the party was guilty of treason.

The Second Party System: Democrats and Whigs

From the collapse of the Federalists until the 1830s, America had only one political party, the Democratic-Republicans. This period of one-party politics is sometimes known as the Era of Good Feeling, to indicate the absence of party competition. Throughout this period, however, there was intense factional conflict within the Democratic-Republican Party, particularly between supporters and opponents of General Andrew Jackson, America's great military hero of the War of 1812. Jackson, one of five significant candidates for president in 1824, won the most popular and electoral votes but a majority of neither, throwing the election into the House of Representatives. Jackson's opponents united to deny him the presidency, but he won election in 1828 and again in 1832.

Jackson was greatly admired by millions of ordinary Americans living on the nation's farms and in its villages, and the Jacksonians made the most of the general's appeal to the common people via a program of suffrage expansion that would give Jackson's impecunious but numerous supporters the right to vote. To bring more voters to the polls, the Jacksonians built political clubs and held mass rallies and parades, laying the groundwork for a more popular politics. Jackson's vice president and eventual successor, Martin Van Buren, was the organizational genius behind the Jacksonian movement, establishing a central party committee, state party organizations, and party newspapers. In response to complaints about cliques of party leaders dominating the nominations at party caucuses, the Jacksonians also established state and national party conventions as the forums for nominating presidential candidates. The conventions gave control of the presidential nominating process to the new state party organizations that the Jacksonians had created and expected to control. Unlike any political leader before him, Van Buren appreciated the possibilities for mass mobilization and the necessity of a well-oiled national organization to overcome free riding and other collective action problems.[31] He produced institutional solutions to these problems, leaving as a historical legacy the blueprint for the modern mass-based political party.

The Jacksonians, whose party became known as the Democratic Party, were not without opponents, especially in the New England states. During the 1830s, groups opposing Jackson for reasons of personality and politics united to form the Whig Party—thus giving rise to the second American party system. During the 1830s and 1840s, the Democrats and the Whigs built party organizations throughout the nation and sought increased support by expanding suffrage through the elimination of property restrictions and other barriers to voting—although voting was still restricted to white men. Support for the Whigs was strongest in the Northeast and among mercantile groups. Hence to some extent the Whigs were the successors of the Federalists. Many Whigs favored a national bank, a protective tariff, and federally sponsored internal improvements. The Jacksonians opposed all three policies.

Yet conflict between the parties revolved around personalities as much as policies. The Whigs were a diverse group, united more by opposition to the Democrats than by agreement on programs. In 1840, the Whigs won their first presidential election under the leadership of General William Henry Harrison, a military hero. The election marked the first time in American history that two parties competed for the presidency in every state in the Union. The Whig campaign avoided issues—because different party factions disagreed on most matters—and emphasized the candidate's personal qualities and heroism. The Whigs also invested heavily in campaign rallies and entertainment to win voters. The 1840 campaign came to be called the hard-cider campaign to denote the practice of using food and, especially, drink to elicit electoral favor.

In the late 1840s and early 1850s, conflicts over slavery produced sharp divisions within both parties, despite party leaders' efforts to develop sectional compromises that would bridge the widening gulf between North and South. By 1856, the Whig Party had all but disintegrated under the strain. The 1854 Kansas-Nebraska Act overturned the Missouri Compromise of 1820 and the Compromise of 1850, which together had hindered the expansion of slavery in the American territories. The Kansas-Nebraska Act gave each territory the right to decide whether to permit slavery. Opposition to this policy led to the formation of a number of antislavery parties, with the Republicans emerging as the strongest.[32] They drew their membership from existing political groups—former Whigs, Know-Nothings of the American Party, free soilers, and antislavery

---

31 See Aldrich, *Why Parties?*, chap. 4.

32 See William E. Gienapp, *The Origins of the Republican Party, 1852–1856* (New York: Oxford University Press, 1994).

Democrats. In 1856, the party's first presidential candidate won one-third of the popular vote and carried 11 states.

The early Republican platforms appealed to commercial as well as anti-slavery interests. The Republicans favored homesteading, internal improvements, construction of a transcontinental railroad, and protective tariffs as well as the containment of slavery. In 1858, the Republican Party won control of the House of Representatives; in 1860, the Republican presidential candidate, Abraham Lincoln, was victorious. Lincoln's victory strengthened southern calls for secession from the Union and led, soon thereafter, to all-out civil war.

The Third Party System: Republicans and Democrats, 1860–96

During the Civil War, President Lincoln depended heavily on Republican governors and state legislatures to raise troops, provide funding, and maintain popular support for a long and bloody military conflict. Although the South's secession had stripped the Democratic Party of many of its leaders and supporters, it nevertheless remained politically competitive and nearly won the 1864 presidential election due to war weariness on the part of the northern public. With the defeat of the Confederacy in 1865, some congressional Republicans sought to convert the South into a Republican bastion through Reconstruction, a program that enfranchised newly freed slaves while disenfranchising many white voters and disqualifying many white politicians from seeking office. The enfranchisement of black voters, it was believed, would create a sizable pro-Republican voting bloc in the South, and federal reconstruction funds, it was hoped, would bring many white Southerners to the Grand Old Party. Reconstruction collapsed in the 1870s as a result of divisions within the Republican Party in Congress and violent resistance by southern whites.

With the end of Reconstruction, the former Confederate states regained full membership in the Union and full control of their internal affairs. Throughout the South, African Americans were deprived of political rights, including the right to vote, despite post–Civil War constitutional guarantees to the contrary. The post–Civil War South was solidly Democratic, enabling the national Democratic Party to confront the Republicans on a more or less equal basis. From the end of the Civil War to the 1890s, the Republican Party remained the party of the North, with strong business and middle-class support, while the Democratic Party was the party of the South, with support from working-class and immigrant groups in the North.

Party Machines as a Strategic Innovation. It was during the third party system that party organizations became well-oiled machines. In the nineteenth and early twentieth centuries, many cities and counties, and even a few states, had such well-organized parties that they were called **party machines** and their leaders were called bosses. Party machines depended on the patronage of the spoils system, the party's power to control government jobs. Patronage worked as a selective benefit for anyone the party wished to attract to its side. With thousands of jobs to dispense to the party faithful, party bosses were able to recruit armies of political workers, who in turn mobilized millions of voters.

 party machine

In the late nineteenth and early twentieth centuries, the local party organization that controlled local politics through patronage and the nomination process

During the height of the party machines, party and government were virtually interchangeable. Just as the creation of mass parties by Van Buren and other political entrepreneurs of the second party system solved a collective action problem, the well-oiled machines applied the selective incentives of patronage and nomination to maintain their organizations and diminish free riding. Many organizational aspects of party politics, in short, involve the ingenuity of rational politicians and leaders grappling with problems of coordination and collective action, as the rationality principle and the collective action principle suggest.

Many critics condemned party machines as antidemocratic and corrupt. They argued that machines served the interests of powerful businesses and did not help the working people who voted for them. But one of the most notorious machine leaders in American political history, George Washington Plunkitt of New York City's Tammany Hall, considered machine politics and the spoils system to be "patriotic." Plunkitt grasped a central fact about purposeful behavior and overcoming the collective action problem. To create and retain political influence and power, "you must study human nature and act accordin'." He argued that the country was built by political parties, that the parties needed such patronage to operate and thrive, and that if patronage was withdrawn, the parties would "go to pieces." As we see shortly, this observation was prescient.

Institutional Reforms of the Progressives. As the nineteenth century gave way to the twentieth, the excessive powers and abuses of party machines and their bosses led to one of the great reform movements in American history, the so-called Progressive Era. Many Progressive reformers undoubtedly desired to rid politics of corruption and improve the quality and efficiency of government. But simultaneously, from the perspective of middle- and upper-class Progressives and the financial, commercial, and industrial elites with whom they were often associated, the weakening or elimination of party organization would also mean that power could more readily be acquired and retained by the "best men"—that is, those with wealth, position, and education.

The list of antiparty reforms of the Progressive Era is a familiar one. As we saw in Chapter 11, the introduction of voter registration laws required eligible voters to register in person well before an election. The Australian-ballot reform took away the parties' privilege of printing and distributing ballots and thus introduced the possibility of split-ticket voting (see also Chapter 11). The introduction of nonpartisan local elections eroded grassroots party organization. The extension of "merit systems" for administrative appointments stripped party organizations of their access to patronage, thus reducing party leaders' capacity to control the nomination of candidates. These reforms substantially weakened party organizations in the United States. Early in the twentieth century, the strength of American political parties gradually diminished, and voter turnout declined precipitously. Between the two world wars, organization remained the major tool available to contending electoral forces, but in most regions the "reformed" state and local parties gradually lost their organizational vitality and became less effective campaign tools. Although most areas of the nation continued to boast Democratic and Republican Party groupings, reform did mean the elimination of the permanent mass organizations that had been the parties' principal campaign weapons.

The Fourth Party System, 1896–1932

During the 1890s, profound social and economic changes led to the emergence of a variety of protest parties, including the Populist Party, which won the support of hundreds of thousands of voters in the South and the West. The Populists appealed mainly to small farmers but also attracted western miners and urban workers. In the 1892 presidential election, the Populist Party carried four states and elected governors in eight states. In 1896, the Democrats in effect adopted the Populist Party platform and nominated William Jennings Bryan, a Democratic senator with Populist sympathies, for the presidency. The Republicans nominated the conservative senator William McKinley. In the ensuing campaign, northern and midwestern business interests made an all-out effort to defeat what they saw as a radical threat from the Populist-Democratic alliance. When the dust settled, the Republicans had won a resounding victory. In the nation's metropolitan regions, especially in the Northeast and upper Midwest, workers became convinced that the Populist-Democratic alliance threatened the industries that provided their jobs, while immigrants feared the nativist rhetoric of some Populist orators and writers. The Republicans carried the northeastern and midwestern states and confined the Democrats to their bastions in the South and the Far West. For the next 36 years, the Republicans were the nation's majority party—very much the party of American business, advocating low taxes, high tariffs, and minimal government regulation. The Democrats were too weak to offer much opposition. Southern Democrats, moreover, were more concerned with maintaining the region's autonomy on issues of race than with challenging the Republicans on other fronts.

The Fifth Party System: The New Deal Coalition, 1932–68

Soon after the Republican candidate Herbert Hoover won the 1928 presidential election, the nation's economy collapsed. The Great Depression, which produced unprecedented economic hardship, had a variety of causes, but millions of Americans blamed the Republican Party for not having done enough to promote economic recovery. In 1932, Americans elected Franklin Delano Roosevelt and a solidly Democratic Congress. Roosevelt's program for economic recovery, the New Deal, led to substantial increases in the size and reach of the national government. The federal government took responsibility for economic management and social welfare to an extent that was unprecedented in American history. Designing many of his programs specifically to expand the Democratic Party's political base, Roosevelt rebuilt the party around a nucleus of unionized workers, upper-middle-class intellectuals and professionals, southern farmers, Jews, Catholics, and northern African Americans (few blacks in the South could vote) that made the Democrats the nation's majority party for 36 years. Republicans groped for a response to the New Deal but often wound up supporting its popular programs such as Social Security in what was sometimes derided as "me-too" Republicanism.

The New Deal coalition was severely strained during the 1960s by conflicts over President Lyndon Johnson's Great Society initiative, the African American civil rights movement, and the Vietnam War. A number of Johnson's Great Society programs, targeting poverty and racial discrimination, involved the empowerment of local groups that were often at odds with city and county governments. These programs sparked battles between local Democratic political machines and the national administration that split the Democratic coalition. For its part, the struggle over civil rights initially divided northern Democrats, who supported the civil rights cause, and white southern Democrats, who defended racial segregation. Subsequently, as the movement launched a northern campaign seeking access to jobs and education and an end to discrimination in such realms as housing, northern Democrats also split, with blue-collar workers tending to vote Republican. The struggle over the Vietnam War further divided the Democrats, with upper-income liberal Democrats opposing the Johnson administration's decision to involve U.S. forces in Southeast Asia. These schisms within the Democratic Party provided an opportunity for the Republican Party to return to power, which it did in 1968 under Richard Nixon.

The Sixth Party System, 1968–Present

In the 1960s, conservative Republicans argued that me-tooism was a recipe for continual failure and sought to reposition the party as a genuine alternative to the Democrats. In 1964, for example, the Republican presidential candidate, Barry Goldwater, author of a book titled *The Conscience of a Conservative*, argued in favor of substantially reduced levels of taxation and spending, less government regulation of the economy, and the elimination of many federal social programs. Although Goldwater was defeated by Lyndon Johnson, the ideas he espoused continue to be major themes of the Republican Party.

Goldwater's message, however, was not enough to lead Republicans to victory. It took Richard Nixon's "southern strategy" to end Democratic dominance of the political process. Beginning with his successful 1968 presidential campaign, Nixon appealed to disaffected white southerners, promising to reduce federal support for school integration and voting rights. With the help of the independent candidate and former Alabama governor George Wallace, sparked the voter shift that eventually gave the once-hated "party of Lincoln" a strong position in all the states of the former Confederacy. In the 1980s, under Ronald Reagan, Republicans added another important group to their coalition: religious conservatives who were offended by Democratic support of abortion rights as well as alleged Democratic disdain for traditional cultural and religious values.

While Republicans built a political base with economic and social conservatives and white southerners, the Democratic Party maintained support among unionized workers and upper-middle-class intellectuals and professionals. Democrats also appealed strongly to racial minorities. The 1965 Voting Rights Act had greatly increased the participation of black voters in the South and helped the Democratic Party retain some congressional and Senate seats there. And while the GOP appealed to social conservatives, the Democrats appealed to voters concerned about abortion rights, gay rights, feminism, environmental-ism, and other progressive causes. The results have been something of a draw. Democrats have won the presidency 5 out of the 13 elections since passage of the Voting Rights Act and held at least one chamber of Congress for most of that time. Interestingly, that apparent stalemate masked dramatic changes in the parties' regional bases. Republicans surged in the South but lost ground in the Northeast. New England, once the bedrock of the party, had only one Republi-can U.S. House member (of 22 seats) after the 2016 election.

The electoral realignment that began in 1968 laid the foundations for the polit-ical polarization that has come to characterize contemporary politics. As southern Democrats and northeastern Republicans faded, the two parties lost their mod-erate wings. Southern white Democrats tended to come from rural areas; they were socially conservative but strongly aligned with the New Deal. As the rural population in the South declined, and the suburbs rose in the 1970s, the southern Democrats were replaced by suburban Republicans, and these areas are much more economically conservative than their predecessors. The opposite dynamic was at work in the North. Republicans in places like New York and New England tended to be socially moderate and fiscally conservative. Social and political shifts in the northeastern states marginalized the Republican Party and led to the emer-gence of a strong liberal faction within the Democratic Party.[33] As a result, the moderate wings of both parties were substantially reduced, leaving Congress with a void among its moderate ranks and with a more polarized political alignment.

Ideology and Parties. The shift of much of the South from the Demo-cratic to the Republican camp, along with the other developments mentioned earlier, meant that each political party became ideologically more homogeneous after the 1980s. Today there are few liberal Republicans or conservative Demo-crats. Consequently party loyalty in Congress has become a more potent force, leading to a dramatic resurgence of party-line voting. A simple measure of party developed by Professor Stuart Rice in the 1920s and tracked by *Congressional Quarterly* since the 1950s is the party unity score. This is the percentage of bills on which a majority of one party votes against a majority of the other party. Between the 1950s and the 1970s, unity hovered around 70 percent. Since the 1980s, it has regularly exceeded 90 percent.[34]

To some extent, ideology has replaced organization as the glue holding together each party's coalition. But in the long run, ideology is often an unreliable basis for party unity. Although party activists are united by some beliefs, ideological divisions also plague both camps. Within the Republican coalition, social conservatives are often at odds with economic conservatives, whereas among Democrats, propo-nents of regulatory reform and economic internationalism are frequently at odds

----

33 Matthew Levendusky, *The Partisan Sort* (Chicago, IL: University of Chicago Press, 2009).

34 The classic statement of the connection between cohesive legislative parties and ideological homogeneity within party ranks is found in Rohde, *Parties and Leaders in the Post-Reform House*. An elaboration of this argument is presented in Cox and McCubbins, *Setting the Agenda*. See also Nolan McCarty, Keith Poole, and Howard Rosenthal, *Polarized America: The Dance of Inequality and Unequal Riches* (Cambridge: MIT Press, 2006).

Parties' Share of Electoral Votes, 1789–2016

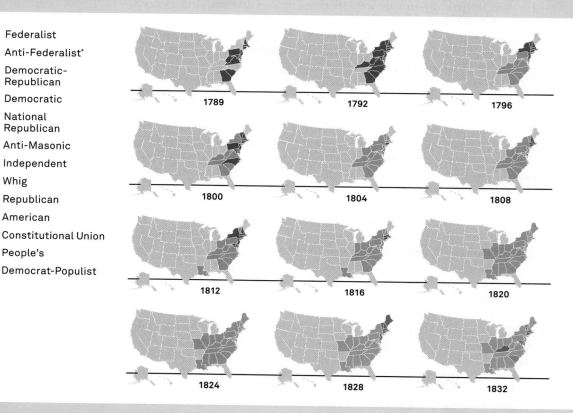

Legend:
- Federalist
- Anti-Federalist*
- Democratic-Republican
- Democratic
- National Republican
- Anti-Masonic
- Independent
- Whig
- Republican
- American
- Constitutional Union
- People's
- Democrat-Populist

Maps: 1789, 1792, 1796, 1800, 1804, 1808, 1812, 1816, 1820, 1824, 1828, 1832

with traditional liberals, who favor big government and protecting American workers from foreign competition. While the party workers of yesteryear supported the leadership almost no matter what, today's more ideologically motivated party activists withhold support if they disagree with the leadership's goals and plans. Because of internal divisions in the Republican Party, for example, Republican congressional leaders have adopted a strategy of avoiding votes on the many issues that might split the party.[35] The price of unity based on ideology can be the inability to act.

The ideological gap between the two parties has been exacerbated by two other factors: each party's dependence on ideologically motivated activists and

35 Isaiah J. Poole, "Votes Echo Electoral Themes," *Congressional Quarterly Weekly Report*, December 11, 2004, pp. 2906–08.

(continued on next page)

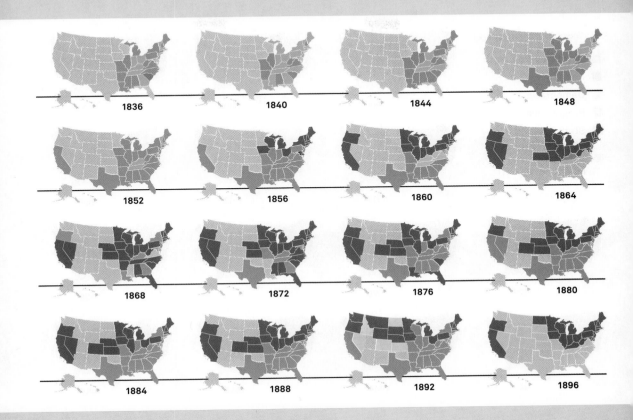

1836   1840   1844   1848

1852   1856   1860   1864

1868   1872   1876   1880

1884   1888   1892   1896

the changes in the presidential nominating system that were introduced during the 1970s. Regarding the first factor, Democratic political candidates depend heavily on the support of liberal activists—such as feminists, environmentalists, and civil libertarians—to organize and finance their campaigns, while Republican candidates depend equally on the support of conservative activists, including religious fundamentalists. In the nineteenth century, political activists were motivated more by party loyalty and political patronage than by programmatic concerns. Today's issue-oriented activists, by contrast, demand that politicians demonstrate strong commitments to moral principles and political causes in exchange for their support. Such demands have pushed Democrats further to the political left and Republicans further to the political right. Often politicians' efforts to reach compromises on key issues are attacked by party activists as "sellouts," leading to stalemates on such matters as the budget and judicial appointments.

Parties' Share of Electoral Votes, 1789–2016

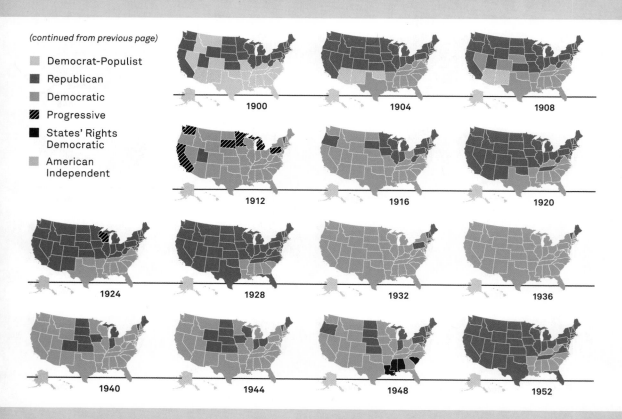

(continued from previous page)

- Democrat-Populist
- Republican
- Democratic
- Progressive
- States' Rights Democratic
- American Independent

1900   1904   1908

1912   1916   1920

1924   1928   1932   1936

1940   1944   1948   1952

The second factor exacerbating the parties' ideological split, the changes in the presidential nominating system, took place in response to the Democratic Party's defeat in 1968. Liberal forces succeeded in changing the rules governing Democratic presidential nominations to reduce the power of party officials and party professionals while increasing the role of issue-oriented activists. Among other changes, the new rules required national convention delegates to be chosen in primaries and caucuses rather than by each state party's central committee. Subsequently, Republican activists wrought similar changes in the Republicans' rules, so that today both parties' presidential nominating processes are strongly influenced by precisely the sorts of grassroots activists who oppose centrist or pragmatic politicians in favor of those who appear to show ideological purity. As a result, elections have generally pitted liberal Democrats against conservative Republicans. The two parties today differ sharply on social, economic, and

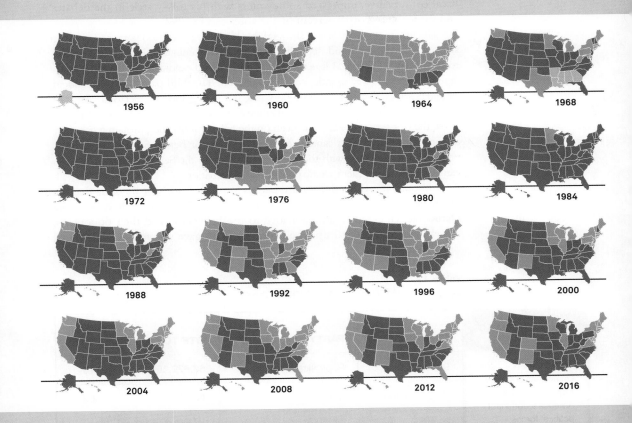

1956 1960 1964 1968

1972 1976 1980 1984

1988 1992 1996 2000

2004 2008 2012 2016

foreign policy issues and are deeply divided over questions concerning taxation and government spending.

American Third Parties

 third party

A party that organizes to compete against the two major American political parties

Although the United States is said to possess a two-party system, we have always had more than two parties. Typically, **third parties** in this country have represented social and economic protests that were not given voice by the two major parties.[36] Third parties have definitely influenced ideas and elections. The

36 For a discussion of third parties in the United States, see Daniel A. Mazmanian, *Third Parties in Presidential Elections* (Washington, DC: Brookings Institution, 1974).

Populists, centered in rural areas of the West and the Midwest during the late nineteenth century, and the Progressives, spokesmen for urban middle classes in the late nineteenth and early twentieth centuries, are important examples. More recently, Ross Perot, who ran for president in 1992 and 1996 as an independent fiscal conservative, impressed some voters with his folksy style in the debates and garnered almost 19 percent of the votes cast in 1992.

The timeplot on pp. 530–3 shows that while in the past third parties won entire states, the Democratic and Republican parties have dominated the electoral map in recent decades. Table 12.1 lists the parties that offered candidates in the 2016 presidential election as well as independent candidates. The third-party and independent candidates together polled 6,957,000 votes, but they gained no electoral votes for president. Third-party candidacies also arise at the state and local levels. In New York, the Conservative Party has been on the ballot for decades, though it generally endorses the Republican candidates. Vermont senator Bernie Sanders is an Independent who caucuses with the Democratic Party in the Senate. In 2016, Sanders campaigned for the Democratic presidential nomination.

Although it is difficult for third parties to survive, it is worth noting that the two major parties today themselves started as third parties. As we have seen, the Democrats emerged as an alternative to the Federalists and their opponents, loosely, the Anti-Federalists. The Federalist Party gave way to the Whig Party,

Table 12.1

PARTIES AND CANDIDATES, 2016*

ANALYZING THE EVIDENCE	CANDIDATE	PARTY	VOTE TOTAL	PERCENT OF VOTE
Though the Democrats and the Republicans are America's dominant political forces, many minor parties nominate candidates for the presidency. Why are there so many minor parties? Why don't these parties represent much of a threat to the major parties?	Donald Trump	Republican	62,679,259	46.16
	Hillary Clinton	Democrat	65,224,847	48.03
	Gary Johnson	Libertarian	4,460,030	3.28
	Jill Stein	Green	1,432,077	1.05
	Evan McMullin	Independent	620,384	0.46
	Darrell Castle	Constitution	197,431	0.15
	Gloria LaRiva	Socialism and Liberation	72,385	0.05
	Rocky de la Fuente	American Delta	33,103	0.02
	Others		135,142	0.10

*As of December 2, 2016.
SOURCE: "2016 Presidential General Election Results," U.S. Election Atlas, "http://www.uselectionatlas.org/RESULTS/national.php?year=2016&minper=0&f=0&off=0&elect=0" (accessed 12/2/16).

which was replaced by the Republicans. In some sense, then, the two major parties today started as alternative parties, and they have reinvented themselves ideologically to change with the times and to co-opt supporters of emerging parties. The Democratic Party, for example, became more liberal when it adopted most of the Progressive program early in the twentieth century. Many socialists felt that the New Deal had adopted most of their party's program, including old-age pensions, unemployment compensation, an agricultural marketing program, and laws guaranteeing workers the right to organize into unions.

The major parties' ability to evolve is one explanation for the short lives of third parties. Their causes are usually eliminated as the major parties absorb their programs and draw their supporters into the mainstream. There are, of course, additional reasons for the short duration of most third parties. One is the typical limitation of their electoral support to one or two regions—Populist support, for example, was primarily midwestern; the 1948 Progressive Party drew nearly half its votes from the state of New York; the American Independent Party, although in 1968 garnering the most electoral votes ever for a third-party candidate (George Wallace), primarily represented the Deep South. Moreover, voters usually assume that only the candidates nominated by one of the two major parties have any chance of winning. Thus a vote for a third-party or an independent candidate is often considered wasted. For instance, there is evidence in the 2000 race between Al Gore, the Democrat, and George W. Bush, the Republican, that the third-party candidate Ralph Nader did better in those states where either Bush or Gore was nearly certain of winning, whereas Nader's support dwindled in more closely contested states. Third-party candidates must struggle—usually without success—to overcome the perception that they cannot win.

As many scholars have asserted, third-party prospects are also hampered by America's single-member-district plurality election system. In many other nations, several individuals are elected to represent each legislative district. With this system of multiple-member districts, weaker parties' candidates have a better chance of winning at least some seats. For their part, voters are less concerned about wasting ballots and usually more willing to support minor-party candidates.

Reinforcing the effects of the single-member district (as noted in Chapter 11), plurality voting rules generally have the effect of setting a high threshold for victory. To win a plurality race, candidates usually must secure many more votes than they would need under most European systems of proportional representation. For example, to win an American plurality election in a single-member district with only two candidates, a politician must win more than 50 percent of the votes cast. To win a seat in a European multimember district under proportional-representation rules, a candidate may need only 15 or 20 percent of the votes cast. This high threshold in American elections discourages minor parties and encourages the various political factions that might otherwise form minor parties to minimize their differences and remain within the major-party coalitions.[37]

---

37 See Maurice Duverger, *Political Parties: Their Organization and Activity in the Modern State*, Barbara North and Robert North, trans. (New York: Wiley, 1954).

It would nevertheless be incorrect to assert (as some scholars have maintained) that America's single-member plurality election system guarantees that only two parties will compete for power in all regions of the country. All one can say is that American election law depresses the number of parties likely to survive over long periods of time. There is nothing magical about two.

CONCLUSION: PARTIES AND DEMOCRACY

Political parties help make democracy work. Americans value a broadly participatory democracy and an effective government, but these are often at odds with each other. Effective government implies decisive action and the creation of well-thought out policies and programs. Democracy, however, implies an opportunity for all citizens to participate fully in the governmental process. And, full participation by everyone is usually inconsistent with getting things done in an efficient and timely manner. Strong political parties help the United States balance the ideals of democracy and efficiency in government. Parties can both encourage popular involvement and convert participation into effective government. However, as we have seen, the parties' struggle for political advantage can also lead to the type of intense partisanship that cripples the government's ability to operate efficiently and in the nation's best interest.

As we've seen, parties simplify the electoral process. In essence, political parties function as an informal political institution in elections and in government. They set the electoral agenda via party platforms, recruit candidates, accumulate and distribute campaign resources, and register and mobilize people to vote. Party control of the nominating process and the pressures toward two-party politics in the United States mean that most voters must decide between just two choices in any election—two competing candidates, two ideas about what public policy should be. They both structure electoral choices and, as we saw in Chapter 5, manage the legislative agenda. In that way, parties serve as a bridge between elections and government.

Political parties also facilitate voters' decision making. Voters can reasonably expect what sorts of policies a candidate carrying a party's endorsement will represent if elected. Even before a candidate has received the nomination, most voters have already determined themselves to be Democratic or Republican and know for whom they will vote. This may seem like a gross simplification of politics. It reduces our society's many complex interests to just two competing teams, whose platforms must accommodate the many subtle differences or ideological nuances among groups inside the party. It further reduces politics into warring factions that have little hope of finding common ground. However, the two-party system does give meaning to the vote. It empowers the voter to say, "I want to stay the course with the party in power" or "I want to go in a new direction."

But there is a downside. Simplification of the choices leaves some voters without an effective voice and without a party that approximates what they would like government to do. Parties also try to monopolize politics, seeming to act as teams seeking to control government for their own purposes and not necessarily the interests of the whole. And the competition for control between just two parties in a system with separation of powers can lead to gridlock and stalemate. George Washington, James Madison, John Adams, and Thomas Jefferson all viewed parties with disdain. Washington's farewell address warned "against the baneful effects of the spirit of party." Jefferson wrote, "If I could not go to Heaven but with a party, I would not go there at all." Nonetheless, all of the Founding Fathers ended up in one way or another involved with the founding of the political parties: Washington, Adams, and Hamilton, the Federalists; Jefferson and Madison, the Democrat-Republicans. They could not help but fall into parties because of the nature of politics and the need for an organization to solve the problems of selecting candidates, organizing elections, and simplifying electoral choice.

For Further Reading

Aldrich, John H. *Why Parties? A Second Look*. Chicago: University of Chicago Press, 2011.

Campbell, Angus, Philip E. Converse, Warren E. Miller, and Donald E. Stokes. *The American Voter*. Chicago: University of Chicago Press, 1980.

Chambers, William N., and Walter Dean Burnham, eds. *The American Party Systems: Stages of Political Development*. 2nd ed. New York: Oxford University Press, 1975.

Coleman, John J. *Party Decline in America: Policy, Politics, and the Fiscal State*. Princeton, NJ: Princeton University Press, 1996.

Cox, Gary W., and Mathew D. McCubbins. *Legislative Leviathan: Party Government in the House*. Berkeley: University of California Press, 1993.

Cox, Gary W., and Mathew D. McCubbins. *Setting the Agenda: Responsible Party Government in the U.S. House of Representatives*. New York: Cambridge University Press, 2005.

Hershey, Marjorie Randon. *Party Politics in America*. 15th ed. New York: Pearson, 2013.

Hofstadter, Richard. *The Idea of a Party System: The Rise of Legitimate Opposition in the United States, 1780–1840*. Berkeley: University of California Press, 1969.

Levendusky, Matthew. *The Partisan Sort*. Chicago: University of Chicago Press, 2009.

Mayhew, David. *Electoral Realignments: A Critique of an American Genre*. New Haven, CT: Yale University Press, 2007.

Rohde, David W. *Parties and Leaders in the Post-Reform House*. Chicago: University of Chicago Press, 1991.

13

Groups and Interests

Democratic politics in the United States does not end with elections. Federal, state, and local governments provide many additional avenues through which individuals and organizations can express their preferences. People may, for example, contact elected officials, their staff, and bureaucrats directly about a particular decision or problem. They may participate in public meetings about legislation or administrative rulings; some private citizens are even selected to serve on special government commissions because of their expertise or particular concerns. People may file lawsuits to request that a government agency take a particular action or to prevent it from doing so. They may express their opinions in newspapers, on television, and the Internet, or through other venues, and hold public protests, all without fear of persecution. Individuals, organizations, and even governments make frequent use of these many points of access. Many such encounters are episodic, as when an individual contacts an agency to solve a particular problem. But much political activity in the United States occurs through enduring, organized efforts that bring together many individuals into collective action to seek a common goal.

Both a pull and a push drive organized political activity in the United States. The pull comes from the government's need to collect information about the impact of decisions on various constituencies. A responsive government needs refined information about how a decision will affect society or about the best way to implement a law. Legislators, judges, and bureaucrats typically do not have the time or resources to study all potential problems. Instead they rely on information from individuals and organizations to gauge the importance of a given problem and to learn about the consequences of particular decisions. The solution in American government is to allow many points of access for competing views.

The push comes from people's willingness to contact government. Individuals and organizations express their concerns with some purpose in mind, to gain some benefit. Those benefits often involve a better understanding of government regulations and actions. When a commission or department issues a new regulation, firms that are potentially affected must determine whether the regulation applies to them, how to comply, and the exact interpretation of the regulations. Firms frequently hire representation in Washington or the state capital just to stay on top of such matters. But many of those involved in direct political action want more than information; they want to change laws and policies to favor their particular interests. They want targeted appropriations or favorable regulatory rulings, potentially worth millions, even billions, of dollars.

Interest group politics in the United States involves thousands of organizations and individuals competing for the attention of elected representatives and government officials and then, having gained that attention, competing with other groups and individuals to influence particular government decisions. There are roughly 12,000 registered lobbyists in Washington, D.C., and many more in state capitals and city governments. In the din of day-to-day politics, it can be hard to get a particular concern before Congress or the bureaucracy, and one group's "special interest" may not seem so special in comparison with others. The institutions of American government further shape the political outcomes that interest groups can achieve. Groups strategically seek out institutional venues most hospitable to their interests, but our system of government often means that one must win in many different domains in order to change public policy. A group may succeed in a House committee, for example, only to be blocked in the analogous Senate committee.

CORE OF THE ANALYSIS

 Individuals, firms, and other organizations engage in a wide variety of political activities, including contacting elected officials, attending government meetings, participating in campaign activities, and contributing money to shape how office holders make and implement laws.

 These activities help government solve an important problem—how to learn about what problems are important to society and how government actions might affect society.

 There is a clear orientation of interest groups toward segments of society with better education or more economic resources, and those most directly affected by government actions, especially corporations.

 Collective organization of interests is difficult, as there are strong incentives for any single individual to free ride. As a result, interests in society, especially very broad interests such as "all consumers" or "the middle class," often lack effective organizations that can express their preferences.

This is pluralism at work. It is messy and often unpopular, but it is an essential feature of American government. The U.S. Constitution embraces this idea fully. The more competition there is among many interests, the less likely it is that any one will triumph and the more likely it is that representatives and government officials will learn what they need to know.[1] There is always a risk, however, that organized interests will have excessive influence over the government. Regulation of lobbying and campaign contributions, as well as ethics rules in government, aim to prevent government from serving particular interests to the detriment of the common good.

One of the most difficult questions about the U.S. system of government is whether the separation of powers and free and open political competition provide sufficient safeguards against excessive influence by certain groups. How much should American governments limit what individuals and organizations say and do in order to prevent certain interests from having too much influence? In short, how should we manage the trade-off between free speech and the potential corrupting influence of groups? Other countries severely limit lobbying and campaign spending. Should we do so as well? Or does open political competition limit the power of special interests? These questions are continually debated in American government, from city councils to the Supreme Court.

In this chapter we analyze the social basis of organizations, the problems inherent in collective action, and some solutions to these problems. We discuss the character and balance of the interests promoted through our nation's pluralistic political system. We further examine the tremendous growth of interest groups in number, resources, and activity in recent decades. Finally, we examine the strategies that groups use to influence politics and whether their influence has become excessive.

WHAT ARE THE CHARACTERISTICS OF INTEREST GROUPS?

interest group

An organized group of individuals or organizations that makes policy-related appeals to government

An **interest group** is an organized group of individuals or organizations that makes policy-related appeals to government. Individuals form groups and engage in collective action to increase the chances that their views will be heard and their interests treated favorably by government. Interest groups are organized to influence governmental decisions; they are sometimes called lobbies.

Interest groups are sometimes confused with political action committees (PACs; see Chapter 11). The difference is that PACs focus on helping certain candidates win elections, and interest groups focus on influencing elected officials. Interest groups also differ from political parties: interest groups concern

---

1   This sentiment is expressed most eloquently in Alexander Hamilton, James Madison, and John Jay, *The Federalist Papers*, Clinton L. Rossiter, ed. (New York: New American Library, 1961), no. 10.

themselves primarily with the policies of government; parties tend to concern themselves primarily with the personnel of government.

Interest Groups Not Only Enhance Democracy . . .

There are an enormous number of interest groups in the United States, and millions of Americans are members of one or more, paying dues or attending an occasional meeting. By representing the interests of such large numbers of people and encouraging political participation, organized groups enhance American democracy. They educate their members about relevant issues, lobby members of Congress and the executive branch, engage in litigation, and generally represent their members' interests in the political arena. Groups mobilize their members for elections and grassroots lobbying efforts, thus encouraging participation. Interest groups also monitor government programs to ensure that they do not adversely affect their members. In all these ways, organized interests promote democratic politics.

. . . But Also Represent the Evils of Faction

The framers of the U.S. Constitution feared the power that organized interests could wield. James Madison wrote:

> The public good is disregarded in the conflict of rival [factions], . . .citizens . . . who are united and actuated by some common impulse of passion, or of interest, adverse to the rights of other citizens, or to the permanent and aggregate interests of the community.[2]

Yet the Founders believed that interest groups thrived because of the freedom, enjoyed by all Americans, to organize and express their views. To the framers, this problem presented a dilemma. If government had the power to regulate or forbid efforts by organized interests to interfere in the political process, it would in effect have the power to suppress freedom. Madison presented the solution to this dilemma:

> Take in a greater variety of parties and interest [and] you make it less probable that a majority of the whole will have a common motive to invade the rights of other citizens. . . .[Hence the advantage] enjoyed by a large over a small republic.[3]

According to Madison's theory, a good constitution encourages multitudes of interests so that no single interest can ever tyrannize the others. The assumption is that competition will produce balance and compromise, with all the interests

2   *The Federalist,* no. 10, p. 78.

3   *The Federalist,* no. 10, p. 83.

pluralism

A condition or system in which many groups, interests, or ideas co-exist in a nation and share political power

regulating one another.[4] Today this principle of regulation is called **pluralism.** According to pluralist theory, all interests are and should be free to compete for influence in the government. Moreover, the outcome of this competition is compromise and moderation, because no group is likely to achieve any of its goals without accommodating some of the views of its many competitors.[5]

There are tens of thousands of organized groups in the United States today, competing to be heard and to influence government, but not all interests are fully and equally represented in the political process. The political deck is heavily stacked in favor of those that wield substantial economic, social, and institutional resources on behalf of their cause. Thus, within the universe of interest group politics, it is political power—not some abstract conception of the public good—that is likely to prevail. Moreover, this means that interest group politics, as a whole, works more to the advantage of some types of interests than to others. In general, a politics in which interest groups predominate is a politics with a distinctly upper-class bias.

Organized Interests Are Predominantly Economic

Most people think of interest groups as having a direct and private economic interest in governmental actions; and indeed, economic interest is one reason individuals and groups engage in political action. Interest groups are generally supported by groups of producers or manufacturers in a particular economic sector. Examples include the National Petrochemical Refiners Association, the American Farm Bureau Federation, and the National Federation of Independent Business, which represents small-business owners. At the same time that broadly representative groups such as these are active in Washington, specific companies—such as Disney, Shell, Microsoft, and General Motors—may be active on other issues.

Labor organizations, although fewer in number and more limited in financial resources, are extremely active lobbyists. The AFL-CIO, the United Mine Workers, and the International Brotherhood of Teamsters are examples of groups that lobby on behalf of organized labor. Recently, lobbies have arisen to further the interests of public employees, the most significant being the American Federation of State, County, and Municipal Employees.

Professional lobbies such as the American Bar Association and the American Medical Association have been particularly successful in furthering their interests in state and federal legislatures. The "gun lobby," made up of representatives of firearms manufacturers and dealers as well as gun owners, is represented by the National Rifle Association (NRA). This group mobilized furiously in 2012 and 2013 to thwart gun control efforts introduced in Congress in the wake of the December 2012 shooting of 20 first graders in a Connecticut elementary school. Financial institutions, represented by organizations such as the American Bankers Association and America's Community Bankers, also are important in shaping legislative policy.

4   *The Federalist,* no. 10.

5   The best statement of the pluralist view is in David B. Truman, *The Governmental Process: Political Interests and Public Opinion* (New York: Knopf, 1951), chap. 2.

Recent decades have witnessed the growth of a powerful "public interest" lobby purporting to represent interests not addressed by traditional lobbies. These groups have been most visible in the consumer protection and environmental policy areas, although public interest groups cover a broad range of issues, from nuclear disarmament to civil rights to abortion. The Natural Resources Defense Council, the Union of Concerned Scientists, the National Association for the Advancement of Colored People, the Christian Coalition of America, and Common Cause are all examples.

The perceived need for representation on Capitol Hill has generated a public-sector lobby, including the National League of Cities, and a "research" lobby. The latter group comprises universities and think tanks—such as Harvard University, the Brookings Institution, and the American Enterprise Institute—that desire government funds for research and support. Indeed, universities have expanded their lobbying efforts even as they have reduced faculty positions and course offerings and increased tuition.[6] Even with the greater number of interests, most organizations involved in politics in Washington, D.C., and in the state capitals represent economic interests. The Policy Principle section on p. 544 gives an example of how the National Association of Realtors and other groups have successfully opposed any changes to the mortgage interest tax deduction, a policy that is in their own economic interests even though it is not in the interest of most homeowners.

Most Groups Require Members, Money, and Leadership

Although there are many kinds of interest groups, most share certain key organizational components. First, most groups must attract and keep members. Usually, groups appeal to members not only by promoting certain political goals but also by providing direct economic or social benefits. Thus, for example, AARP (formerly the American Association for Retired Persons), which promotes senior citizens' interests, also offers insurance benefits and commercial discounts. Similarly, many groups with primarily economic or political goals also seek to attract members through social interaction and good fellowship. Thus the local chapters of many national groups provide a congenial social environment while collecting dues that finance the national office's efforts.

Second, every group must build a financial structure capable of sustaining an organization and funding its activities. Most interest groups rely on yearly dues and voluntary contributions. Many also sell ancillary services, such as insurance and vacation tours. Third, every group must have a leadership and decision-making structure. For some, this structure is very simple. For others, it can involve hundreds of local chapters that are melded into a national apparatus.

---

6   Betsy Wagner and David Bowermaster, "B.S. Economics," *Washington Monthly* (November 1992): 19–21. Benjamin Ginsberg, "The Administrators Ate My Tuition," *Washington Monthly* (September–October 2011), www.washingtonmonthly.com/magazine/septemberoctober_2011/features/administrators_ate_my_tuition031641. php?page=all (accessed 6/24/16).

The Mortgage Interest Tax Deduction

A home for sale in Durham, North Carolina.

When individuals and groups form coalitions to engage in collective action, players may not have equal access to information. Interest groups, for example, are generally better informed than individuals and are thus better able to benefit from collective action in the political arena. Individuals who are poorly informed may find themselves acting in a manner inconsistent with their interests. Take the case of the mortgage tax credit.

Under current U.S. tax law, individuals who file itemized personal income tax returns may deduct the interest on as much as $1 million in mortgage indebtedness plus the interest on another $100,000 in home equity loans. Though the average deduction is only about $1,680 for homeowners who itemize, this law can result in thousands of dollars in savings for an upper-bracket taxpayer with a large mortgage. A family with $1 million mortgage, for example, currently realizes an average annual tax savings of about $21,000 per year.[1]

Proponents of the mortgage interest tax deduction argue that its chief purpose is to encourage home ownership, which they believe gives people a stake in the community and the nation, making them better neighbors and citizens. However, nearly 80 percent of the benefits provided by the mortgage-interest deduction and other housing tax credits accrue to the wealthiest 20 percent of Americans. Less than 5 percent of these tax benefits are received by the bottom 60 percent of Americans. About half of all families with residential mortgages receive no tax benefit at all.

The mortgage interest deduction is politically almost untouchable. Organized groups representing the housing and lending industries vehemently oppose changing this policy. They have access to information and analyses that show that the deduction drives up home sales and prices. The availability of a tax deduction encourages wealthier Americans to purchase second homes, to purchase more expensive homes, and to borrow against the value of their homes. From the perspective of the housing and lending industries, cuts in the mortgage-interest deduction would shrink these lucrative markets.

The housing industry, though, is not alone in its opposition to eliminating the deduction. Most Americans, even those who are not currently eligible for the mortgage-interest deduction, seem to think that they can benefit from its provisions—if not now, then at some future time.

Though many Americans think the mortgage-interest deduction results in a savings for them, the deduction also hurts them. It drives up home prices by allowing purchasers to assume larger mortgages. If the subsidy had not existed, most Americans would probably have been able to purchase the same house they currently own at a lower price. Americans overwhelmingly support a program they think benefits them, when in fact their taxes pay for a program to reward a wealthy industry. Thus well-organized industry groups with greater access to information than individuals can better engage in collective action to translate their preferences into policy outcomes.

[1]Christian A. L. Hilber and Tracy M. Turner, "The Mortgage Interest Deduction and Its Impact on Homeownership Decisions," *The Review of Economics and Statistics* 96 (October 2014): 618–37, www.mitpressjournals.org/doi/abs/10.1162/REST_a_00427#.V9bT0vkrLIV (accessed 9/12/16).

Finally, most groups include an agency that actually carries out the group's tasks. This may be a research organization, a public relations office, or a lobbying office in Washington or a state capital.

Group Membership Has an Upper-Class Bias

Membership in interest groups is not randomly distributed in the population. People with higher incomes, higher levels of education, and managerial or professional occupations are much more likely to join interest groups than are those on the lower rungs of the socioeconomic ladder.[7] Well-educated upper-income professionals are more likely to have the time, money, and skills needed to play a role in a group or association. Moreover, for business and professional people, group membership may provide personal contacts and access to information that can help advance their careers. At the same time, corporate entities—businesses and trade associations—usually have ample resources to form or participate in groups that seek to advance their causes.

The result is that interest group politics in the United States has a pronounced upper-class bias. Although many groups and political associations have a working-class or lower-class membership—labor organizations or welfare-rights organizations, for example—the great majority of interest group members are middle and upper-middle class. In general, interest groups serve the interests of society's "haves." Even when groups take opposing positions on issues, the conflicting positions they espouse usually reflect divisions among upper-income strata rather than conflicts between upper and lower classes.

Even groups associated with a progressive political agenda and support for the rights of the poor tend, in their own membership, to reflect middle- and upper-middle-class interests. Consider the National Association for the Advancement of Colored People (NAACP) and the National Organization for Women (NOW). Both groups advocate for the rights of the poor, but both have a middle-class membership and focus on issues relevant to that membership. The NAACP is concerned with minority access to universities and the professions, a topic primarily of concern to its middle-class supporters. NOW seeks gender equality in education and access to positions in business and the professions—again, matters mainly of interest to its largely middle- and upper-middle-class membership. (See the Analyzing the Evidence unit in Chapter 5 for research on interest group advocacy of marginalized groups.)

In general, to obtain adequate political representation, forces low on the socioeconomic ladder must be organized on the massive scale associated with political parties. Indeed, parties can mobilize the collective energies of large numbers of people who, as individuals, may have very limited resources. Interest

---

7   Sidney Verba, Kay Schlozman, and Henry Brady, *The Unheavenly Chorus* (Princeton, NJ: Princeton University Press, 2013). Martin Gilens, *Affluence and Influence: Economic Inequality and Political Power in America* (New York & Princeton, NJ: Russell Sage Foundation and Princeton University Press, 2012).

groups, in contrast, generally organize smaller numbers of the better-to-do. Thus the relative importance of political parties and interest groups has far-ranging implications for the distribution of political power.. To use the language of the 2012 campaign, active interest groups generally empower the "1 percent." Strong political parties give the "99 percent" a chance as well.

Groups Reflect Changes in the Political Environment

As long as there is government, as long as government makes policies that add value or impose costs, and as long as there is liberty to organize, interest groups will abound. And if government expands, so will interest groups. For example, a spurt of growth in the national government occurred during the 1880s and 1890s, arising largely from government efforts to fight large monopolies and regulate some aspects of interstate commerce. In the latter decade, a parallel spurt occurred in national interest groups, including the imposing National Association of Manufacturers and other trade associations. Many groups organized around agricultural commodities as well. This period also marked the beginning of the expansion of trade unions as interest groups. Later, in the 1930s, interest groups with headquarters and representation in Washington began to grow significantly, concurrent with that decade's expansion of the national government.

The past 50 years has seen an enormous increase both in the number of interest groups seeking a role in the political process and in the extent of their opportunity to influence that process. The total number of interest groups in the United States today is not known. There are certainly tens of thousands of groups at the national, state, and local levels. One indication of the proliferation of their activity is the growing number of political action committees (PACs), the vehicle by which most interest group money is spent to influence elections. Nearly three times as many PACs operated in 2014 as in the 1970s, increasing from fewer than 500 to more than 7,000.[8] A *New York Times* report, for example, noted that during the 1970s, expanded federal regulation of the automobile, oil, gas, education, and health care industries impelled each of these interests to increase its efforts to influence the government's behavior. These efforts, in turn, spurred the organization of other groups to augment or counter the activities of the first.[9] The rise of PACs exhibits one of the most common features of business political activity: businesses are reactive. They are usually drawn into politics in response to regulations, rather than to create a new program.

Similarly, federal social programs have occasionally sparked (1) political organization and action on the part of clientele groups seeking to influence the distribution of benefits and, in turn, (2) the organization of groups opposed

---

8   "Number of Federal PACs Increases," Federal Election Commission, www.fec.gov/press/press2009/20090309PACcount.shtml (accessed 9/6/16).

9   John Herbers, "Special Interests Gaining Power as Voter Disillusionment Grows," *New York Times*, November 14, 1978.

to the programs or their cost. AARP, perhaps the nation's largest membership organization, owes its emergence to the creation and expansion of Social Security and Medicare. Once older Americans had guaranteed retirement income and health insurance, they had a clear stake in protecting and expanding these benefits. AARP developed in response to attempts to pare back the program.[10]

Another factor promoting the recent explosion of interest group activity was the emergence of new social and political movements. The civil rights and antiwar movements of the 1960s, and the reactions against them, created a generation of upper-middle-class professionals and intellectuals who have seen themselves as a political force opposing the public policies and politicians associated with the nation's postwar regime. Following these movements came the decade-long debate over the Equal Rights Amendment, the Sagebrush Rebellion (concerning land use in the West), the nuclear disarmament movement, and the antiabortion movement. More recent social movements include the antitax Tea Party movement and Black Lives Matter, protesting racial discrimination and the social condition of African Americans. Such groups sought to make changes in social behavior and public policy, usually through civil disobedience.

Members of these movements—collectively known as the new politics movement—constructed or strengthened public interest groups such as Common Cause, the Sierra Club, the Environmental Defense Fund, Physicians for Social Responsibility, NOW, and the various organizations formed by consumer activist Ralph Nader. These groups influenced the media, Congress, and even the judiciary and enjoyed remarkable success during the late 1960s and early 1970s in securing enactment of policies they favored. Activist groups also played a major role in promoting the enactment of environmental, consumer, and occupational health and safety legislation.

Among the factors contributing to the rise and success of public interest groups is technology. Computerized direct-mail campaigns in the 1980s were perhaps the first innovation that allowed organizations to reach out to potential members. Today, e-mail, Facebook, Twitter, and other electronic media enable public interest groups to reach hundreds of thousands of potential sympathizers and contributors. Relatively small groups can now efficiently identify and mobilize adherents nationwide. Individuals with perspectives in a small, anonymous minority can connect and mobilize for national political action through social networking tools that were unheard of even 30 years ago.

Latent Groups

Of course, many individuals who share a common interest do not form interest groups. For example, although college students share an interest in the cost and quality of education, they have not organized to demand lower tuition, better facilities, or more effective faculty. Students could be called a "latent group," of

---

10 Andrea Campbell, *How Policies Make Citizens: Senior Citizen Activism and the American Welfare State* (Princeton, NJ: Princeton University Press, 2003).

which there are many in American society. Often, the failure of a latent group to organize reflects individuals' ability to achieve their goals without joining an organized effort. Individual students, for example, are free to choose among colleges that, in turn, compete for patronage. Where the market or other mechanisms allow individuals to achieve their goals without joining groups, they are less likely to do so.

HOW AND WHY DO INTEREST GROUPS FORM?

Pluralist theory argues that because individuals in the United States are free to join or form groups that reflect their common interests, interest groups should readily form whenever a change in the political environment warrants it. If this argument is correct, groups should form roughly in proportion to people's interests. We should find a greater number of organizations around interests shared by a greater number of people. Evidence for this hypothesis is weak, however. In the 1980s, political scientists Kay Schlozman and John Tierney examined interest groups representing people's occupations and economic roles.[11] Using census data and lists of interest groups, they compared the number of people in particular economic roles with the number of organizations representing those roles in Washington. For example, they found that in the mid-1980s 4 percent of the population was looking for work, but only a handful of organizations represented the unemployed in Washington, making up 0.1 percent of total organizations.[12] There was a considerable disparity in Washington representation across categories of individuals in the population. Schlozman and Tierney noted, for example, at least a dozen groups representing senior citizens but none for the middle-aged. Their original study was repeated using data from the 2012 Statistical Abstract of the U.S. Census Bureau and the 2011 Washington Representatives Study (see Table 13.1).

The observation that groups form only around some interests creates a problem for the pluralist notion of democracy. If there is a bias in the sorts of groups that form, such as only wealthy groups, then political decisions may reflect the bias in who is organized and who is not. Mancur Olson's work, discussed later in this chapter, is the best-known challenge to pluralist theory. It is in Olson's insights that we find the basis for interest group formation.

---

11 Schlozman and Tierney, *Organized Interests and American Democracy* (New York: Harper & Row, 1986).

12 Of course, the number of organizations is at best only a rough measure of the extent to which various categories of citizens are represented in the interest group world of Washington.

Table 13.1

WHO IS REPRESENTED BY ORGANIZED INTERESTS?

WORKFORCE STATUS OF THE INDIVIDUAL	U.S. ADULTS (%)	ORGS. (%)	TYPE OF ORG. IN WASHINGTON	RATIO: % OF ORGS. TO % OF ADULTS
Executives	8.5	70.3	Business association	8.27
Professionals	13.0	23.7	Professional association	1.82
White collar workers	14.0	1.1	White collar union	0.08
Blue collar workers	22.2	.4	Blue collar union	0.02
Farm workers	.9	1.6	Agricultural workers' organization	1.78
Unemployed	6.2	1.7	Unemployment organization	0.27
Not in workforce	35.3	1.2	Senior citizens organization, organization for the handicapped, educational organization	0.03

SOURCE: Kay Lehman Schlozman, Sidney Verba, and Henry E. Brady. *The Unheavenly Chorus: Unequal Voice and the Broken Promise of American Democracy* (Princeton, NJ: Princeton University Press, 2012), p. 329. Updated data supplied by Schlozman, Verba, and Brady.

ANALYZING THE EVIDENCE

What types of interests are most likely to be represented by interest groups? If interest group politics is biased in favor of the wealthy and the powerful, should we curb group politics? What was James Madison's answer? Do you agree with Madison?

Interest Groups Facilitate Cooperation

Groups that pursue a common interest or shared objective—maintenance of a hunting and fishing habitat, creation of a network for sharing computer software, lobbying for favorable legislation, and so on—consist of individuals who bear some cost on behalf of the joint goal. Each member of the Possum Hollow Rod and Gun Club may, for example, pay annual dues and devote one weekend a year to cleaning up the rivers and forests of the club-owned game preserve.

We can think of this as an instance of two-person cooperation writ large. Accordingly, each one of a large number of individuals has, in the simplest situation, two options: "contribute" or "don't contribute" to achieving the shared objective. If the number of contributors to the group enterprise is sufficiently large, a group goal is achieved. However, there is a twist. If the group goal is achieved, then every member enjoys the benefits, whether or not she contributed to its achievement.

The Prisoner's Dilemma and Free Riding. Researchers often rely on the metaphor of the prisoner's dilemma when theorizing about social situations of collective action. The prisoner's dilemma, a famous hypothetical problem from game theory, is used to discuss why people rationally take actions that may not be optimal or in the best interests of all. This is similar to the fence-mending example in Chapter 1's discussion of bargaining failure.

In the prisoner's dilemma, two prisoners are accused of jointly committing a crime. They are kept in separate interview rooms. The police have only minimal evidence, however, so they want (at least) one prisoner to snitch on the other so that the prosecutor's case becomes a slam dunk. Each prisoner is offered the same plea bargain: "Testify against the other prisoner in exchange for your freedom, provided that your accomplice does not also testify against you. Remain silent, and you will possibly get the maximum sentence if your accomplice testifies against you." Figure 13.1 displays Prisoner A's options along the rows and Prisoner B's along the columns; in each cell are the sentences (incentives) that each prisoner receives for each combination of actions. If neither snitches, each gets one year; if both snitch, each gets three years; and so on. The outcome of the plea bargain depends on what the other person does. Before reading on, study the table and think about what you would do if you were Prisoner A.

The prisoners face an unpleasant choice. They are self-interested, rational actors who will choose the alternative that offers the best deal. They prefer less jail time to more, and the police, understanding their motivations, have structured the choice so that each prisoner will rat on the other. Notice that in Figure 13.1, Prisoner A is better off choosing to snitch no matter what Prisoner B does. If B chooses to snitch, then A's choice to snitch gets A a three-year jail term, but a don't-snitch choice by A results in six years for A—clearly worse. In contrast, if B chooses not to snitch, then A gets no jail time if he snitches instead of one year if he also chooses not to snitch. In short, A is always better off snitching. But this situation is symmetrical, so it follows that B is better off snitching, too. If both prisoners snitch, the prosecutor can convict both of them, and each serves three years. If they had both kept silent, they would have gotten only one year each. In terms of game theory, each player has a dominant strategy—snitching is best no matter what the other player does—and this leads paradoxically to an outcome in which each player is worse off.

The prisoner's dilemma provides the insight that rational individual behavior does not always lead to the best collective results. The logic is compelling: if A appreciates the dilemma and realizes that B also appreciates the dilemma, then A will still be drawn to the choice of snitching. The reasons for this are the temptation to get off scot free (if he testifies and his accomplice doesn't) and the fear

Figure 13.1
THE PRISONER'S DILEMMA

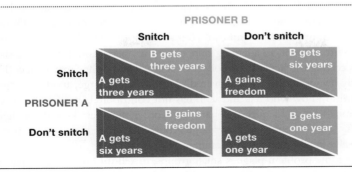

ANALYZING THE EVIDENCE

Given these incentives, what should Prisoner A do? Can you think of other scenarios with a similar pattern of incentives?

of being suckered (if his accomplice testifies and he doesn't). The prisoner's dilemma carries a brilliant yet troubling insight about collective decision making: people often have difficulty achieving objectives that are in the collective good because the incentive to shirk, to defect, to free ride is just too strong.

Consider the swamp-clearing example described in Chapter 1, in which each person benefits from a drained swamp even if she does not provide the required effort. As long as enough other people do so, any individual can ride free on the others' efforts. This is a multiperson prisoner's dilemma because not providing effort, like snitching, is a dominant strategy; yet if everyone chooses not to contribute, an unwanted outcome results: a mosquito-infested swamp. The prospect of free riding, as we see next, is the bane of collective action.

The Logic of Collective Action. The economist Mancur Olson, writing in 1965, essentially took on the political science establishment by noting that the pluralist assumption—that individuals' common interests automatically transform into group organization and collective action—was problematic. Individuals wishing to engage in collective action face the prisoner's dilemma. They are tempted to free ride on the efforts of others, making it exceedingly difficult to achieve outcomes that are best for all.

Olson was most persuasive when talking about large groups and mass collective action, such as the antiwar and civil rights movements of the 1960s. Although these groups mobilized large rallies, most individuals who sympathized with the causes failed to participate; they followed a rational strategy of not contributing. The logic of collective action makes it difficult to induce participation in and contribution to collective goals.

Olson claimed that this difficulty is most severe in large groups for three reasons. First, such groups tend to be anonymous. For example, each household in a city is a taxpaying unit and may share the desire for lower property taxes, but it is difficult to forge a group identity or a group effort toward lowering taxes on such a basis. Second, in the anonymity of the large-group context, it is especially plausible to claim that no single individual's contribution makes much difference. Should an individual citizen kill the better part of a morning writing a letter to his city council member in support of lower property taxes? If hardly anyone else writes, the council member is unlikely to pay much heed to this one letter; then again, if the council member is inundated with letters, would one more have a significant additional effect? Third, there is the problem of enforcement. In a large group, other members cannot prevent a slacker from receiving the benefits of collective action, should they materialize. (Every property owner's taxes will be lowered.) Moreover, in a large, anonymous group it is hard to know who has and who has not contributed, and because there is such limited group identity, it is hard to identify, much less take action against, slackers. As a consequence, many large groups that share common interests fail to mobilize at all—they remain latent.

The same problem plagues small groups, too. But Olson argued that small groups manage to overcome the problem of collective action more frequently and to a greater extent than their larger counterparts. Because small groups are more personal their members are more vulnerable to interpersonal persuasion. Individual contributions may make a more noticeable difference, so individuals feel that their contributions are more essential. Contributors in small groups, moreover, often know who the slackers are. Thus punishment, ranging from subtle judgmental pressure to social ostracism, is easier to effect.

Contrasting large groups that often remain latent to smaller ones, Olson called the small groups privileged, because of their advantage in overcoming the free-riding, coordination, and conflict-of-interest problems of collective action. It is for these perhaps counterintuitive reasons that small groups often prevail over, or enjoy greater privileges relative to, larger groups. These reasons help explain why we so often see producers win out over consumers, owners of capital win out over labor, and a party's elite win out over its mass members.

Selective Benefits: A Solution to the Collective Action Problem

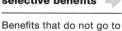

selective benefits

Benefits that do not go to everyone but, rather, are distributed selectively— to only those who contribute to the group enterprise

Despite the free-rider problem, interest groups offer numerous incentives to join. Most important, as Olson noted, they make various **selective benefits** available only to their members. This removes the free-riding option for certain benefits, which makes participation more attractive for the individual. The benefits can be informational, material, solidary, or purposive. Table 13.2 gives examples in each category.

Informational benefits are the most important category of selective benefits offered to group members. Information is provided through conferences, training programs, and printed materials sent automatically to those who have paid dues. Material benefits include anything that can be measured monetarily, such as discount purchasing, shared advertising, and—perhaps most valuable—health and retirement insurance. For example, the AARP, one of the largest groups in the United States, offers insurance packages to its members.

Table 13.2

SELECTIVE BENEFITS OF INTEREST GROUP MEMBERSHIP

CATEGORY	BENEFITS
Informational benefits	Conferences and publications Professional contacts Training programs Coordination among organizations Research Legal help Professional codes Collective bargaining
Material benefits	Travel packages Insurance Discounts on consumer goods
Solidary benefits	Friendship Networking opportunities
Purposive benefits	Advocacy Representation before government Participation in public affairs

ANALYZING THE EVIDENCE

Given these incentives, what should Prisoner A do? Can you think of other scenarios with a similar pattern of incentives?

SOURCE: Adapted from Jack L. Walker, Jr., *Mobilizing Interest Groups in America: Patrons, Professions, and Social Movements* (Ann Arbor: University of Michigan Press, 1991), p. 86.

Among solidary benefits, most notable are the friendship and networking opportunities that membership provides. Another benefit in this category that has been important to nonprofit and citizens' groups is consciousness-raising. For example, many women's organizations claim that active participation conveys to each member an enhanced sense of her own value and a stronger ability to advance individual as well as collective civil rights.

Purposive benefits involve the appeal of the interest group's purpose. Religious interest groups provide good examples of such benefits. The Christian right is a powerful movement made up of numerous interest groups that offer virtually no material benefits to their members. Instead, the growth and success of these groups depend on their members' religious identification and affirmation. Many such religiously based interest groups have arisen, especially at state and local levels, throughout American history. For example, both the abolition and the prohibition movements were driven by religious interest groups whose main attractions were their nonmaterial benefits. The sharing of a common ideology is another important nonmaterial benefit. In fact, many of the most successful citizens' or public interest groups of the past 20 years have coalesced around shared ideological goals, including government reform, election and campaign reform, civil rights, economic equality, "family values," even opposition to government itself.

Of course, some groups use coercion in addition to selective benefits to address the collective action problem. Labor unions, for example, call workers who refuse to join a strike "scabs." At one time, unions employed violence and intimidation against scabs.

Political Entrepreneurs Organize and Maintain Groups

In a 1966 review of Olson's book, the economist Richard Wagner observed that Olson's arguments about groups and politics in general, and his theory of selective incentives in particular, said little about the internal workings of groups.[13] In Wagner's experience, groups often formed and then were maintained not only because of selective incentives but also because of the extraordinary efforts of specific individuals—leaders, or "political entrepreneurs," in Wagner's more colorful terminology.

Wagner raised the issue of leaders because, in his view, Olson's theory was too pessimistic. Mass organizations in the real world—labor unions, consumer associations, senior citizens' groups, environmental organizations—all exist, some persisting over long periods. Contrary to Olson's suggestions, they seem somehow to get jump-started in the real world; therefore, Wagner suggested, a special kind of theory of selective incentives is called for. He argued that certain selective benefits may accrue to those who organize and maintain otherwise latent groups.

Senator Robert Wagner (no relation) in the 1930s and Congressman Claude Pepper in the 1970s each had private reasons—electoral incentives—to organize laborers and the elderly, respectively. Wagner, a Democrat from New York, had a large constituency of working men and women who would reelect him if he bore the cost of organizing workers (or at least of facilitating their organization). And this he did. The law that bears his name, the Wagner Act of 1935, made it much easier for unions to organize in the industrial North.[14] Likewise, Claude Pepper, a Democratic congressman with many elderly constituents in his South Miami district, knew it would serve his own electoral interests to provide the initial effort to organize the elderly as a political force.

---

13 Richard Wagner, "Pressure Groups and Political Entrepreneurs," *Papers on Non-Market Decision Making* 1 (1966): 161–70.

14 The Wagner Act made it possible for unions to organize by legalizing the so-called closed shop. If a worker took a job in a closed shop or plant, she was required to join the union there. "Do not contribute" was no longer an option, so that workers in closed shops could not free ride on the efforts made by others to improve wages and working conditions.

In general, a political entrepreneur is someone who sees a prospective dividend from facilitating cooperation. In other words, he recognizes that if a latent group were to become manifest, it would enjoy the fruits of collective action. For a price, whether in votes (as with Wagner and Pepper), a percentage of the dividend, nonmaterial glory, or other perks, the entrepreneur bears the costs of organizing, expends effort to monitor for slacker behavior, and sometimes even imposes punishment on slackers (such as expelling them from the group and denying them its selective benefits).

Thus political entrepreneurs may be thought of as complements to Olsonian selective incentives in that both motivate groups to accomplish collective objectives. Indeed, if selective incentives resolve the paradox of collective action, then political entrepreneurs dissolve the paradox. Both are helpful—and sometimes necessary—to initiate and maintain collective action. Groups that manage, perhaps on their own, to organize with a low level of activity often take the next step of creating leaders and leadership institutions to increase the activity level and the resulting cooperation dividends. Richard Wagner, in other words, took Olson's theory of selective incentives and suggested an alternative explanation, one that made room for institutional solutions to the problem of collective action.

HOW DO INTEREST GROUPS INFLUENCE POLICY?

By being organized, interest groups improve the probability that all levels of government will hear their policy concerns and treat them favorably. The quest for political influence of power takes many forms. We can roughly divide these actions into "insider strategies" and "outsider strategies."

Insider strategies include gaining access to key decision makers and using the courts. Of course, influencing policy through traditional political institutions requires understanding how those institutions work. A lobbyist who wishes to address a problem with legislation will seek a sympathetic member of Congress, preferably on a committee with jurisdiction over the problem area, and will work directly with the member's staff. Likewise, an organization that decides to bring suit in the courts will sue in a jurisdiction where it has a good chance of getting a sympathetic judge or where the appellate courts are likely to support it. Gaining access is not easy. Legislators and bureaucrats have many requests to juggle; courts have full dockets. Interest groups themselves have limited budgets and staff. They must choose their battles well and map out the insider strategy most likely to succeed.

Outsider strategies include going public and using electoral tactics. Just as politicians can gain an electoral edge by informing voters, so can groups. A well-planned public information campaign, or targeted campaign activities and contributions, can have as much influence as working the corridors of Congress.

Many groups employ a mix of insider and outsider strategies. For example, environmental groups such as the Sierra Club lobby members of Congress and key congressional staff, participate in bureaucratic rule making by offering suggestions to agencies on new environmental rules, and bring lawsuits under various environmental acts, such as the Endangered Species Act. At the same time, the Sierra Club attempts to influence public opinion through media campaigns and to influence electoral politics by supporting candidates who share their environmental views and by opposing those who do not. The Analyzing the Evidence unit on pp. 558–9 considers the relative influence of different groups.

Direct Lobbying

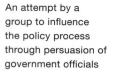

lobbying

An attempt by a group to influence the policy process through persuasion of government officials

Lobbying is an attempt by a group to influence the policy process through persuasion of government officials. Most Americans believe that interest groups exert their influence through direct contact with members of Congress, but lobbying encompasses a broad range of activities with all sorts of government officials and the public as a whole.

Organized advocacy of political interests, known as lobbying, is a multibillion-dollar-a-year industry in Washington, D.C., alone, involving 10,000 individuals, firms, and other organizations.[15] Who is a lobbyist? The 1946 Federal Regulation of Lobbying Act defined a lobbyist as "any person who shall engage himself for pay or any consideration for the purpose of attempting to influence the passage or defeat of any legislation of the Congress of the United States." According to the 1995 Federal Lobbying Disclosure Act, any person who makes at least one lobbying contact with either the legislative or the executive branch in a year, any individual who spends 20 percent of his time in support of such activities, or any firm that devotes 10 percent of its budget to such activities must register as a lobbyist. They must report what topics they discussed with the government, though not which individuals or offices they contacted. Total federal lobbying expenditures have topped $3 billion every year since 2008. The industry that has spent the most over the past two decades (from 1998 to 2016) are pharmaceuticals and health products, with total expenditures over that period of time of $3.4 billion. Pharmaceuticals were not alone: insurance companies spent $2.3 billion; electric utilities spent $2.1 billion, electronics manufacturing and equipment companies spent $1.9 billion, the oil and gas industry spent $1.8 billion, and education organizations spent $1.5 billion.[16] Table 13.3 shows the top spenders on lobbying the federal government in 2014.

The amount spent to influence state legislatures is also substantial. For example, in 2015, lobbyists spent $300 million to influence California

---

15 According to the Center for Responsive Politics, there were 11,800 registered lobbyists in 2014 and 9,500 in 2015. See www.opensecrets.org/lobby (accessed 8/20/15).

16 "Top Industries," OpenSecrets, Center for Responsive Politics, www.opensecrets.org/lobby/top.php?showYear=a&indexType=i (accessed 9/5/16).

Table 13.3

TOP SPENDERS ON LOBBYING, 2014

LOBBYING CLIENT	TOTAL ($)
U.S. Chamber of Commerce	124,080,000
National Association of Realtors	55,057,053
Blue Cross/Blue Shield	21,888,774
American Hospital Association	20,773,146
American Medical Association	19,650,000
National Association of Broadcasters	18,440,000
National Cable & Telecommunications Association	17,460,000
Comcast Corporation	17,020,000
Google Inc.	16,830,000
Boeing Co.	16,800,000
Pharmaceutical Research & Manufacturers of America	16,640,000
United Technologies	15,738,000
General Electric	15,170,000
Business Roundtable	14,840,000
CVS Health	14,787,640
Lockheed Martin	14,581,800
Dow Chemical	14,430,000
AT&T Inc.	14,200,000
Koch Industries	13,800,000
FedEx Corp.	13,414,536

SOURCE: Center for Responsive Politics, www.opensecrets.org/lobby/top.php?indexType=s (accessed 8/23/15).

ANALYZING THE EVIDENCE

Some groups spend more on lobbying than others. What patterns are there in this list of top spenders? Why are some groups willing to spend millions of dollars on lobbying? What groups are absent from the list?

Interest Group Influence

Contributed by
Beth L. Leech
Rutgers University

Which interest groups have the most influence over political outcomes? It is generally accepted among those who study interest groups that business and economic interests predominate. Economic interests are more likely to form organized groups, are more likely to be active, and on average spend more money and more time on political issues than are noneconomic interests like citizen groups or "public interest" groups. When we look at interest groups' involvement in the policy-making process, however, the sheer number of groups or dollars may not directly equal the amount of influence that those groups have. While numbers and dollars are important indicators of which interests are represented, it would be preferable to try to measure which groups actually were influential in politics. To address this question, the political scientist Frank Baumgartner and his colleagues interviewed 315 lobbyists and government officials about 98 randomly selected policy issues. Citizen groups were more likely to be mentioned as being important in the debates than any other type of group, despite the fact that they spent less and they made up a smaller part of the overall group population.

Why were citizen groups seen as so influential despite their relative lack of resources? It may be that those groups have important ties to constituents, granting them greater legitimacy in the eyes of members of Congress, or it could be that some members of Congress already supported the policies that the citizen groups were advocating. Whatever the reason, it is clear that citizen groups have greater voice in Washington than the dollar counts might suggest.

Groups with Washington Lobbying Offices

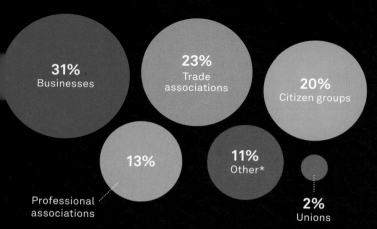

31% Businesses

23% Trade associations

20% Citizen groups

13% Professional associations

11% Other*

2% Unions

*Includes governmental groups, think tanks, universities, and hospitals.

These data from the National Survey of Governmental Relations and Lobbyists.Info show the dominance of business organizations in Washington. Businesses make up 31 percent of those with dedicated national lobbying offices. Trade associations, which represent groups of businesses, make up another 23 percent. Citizen groups, professional associations, and unions together have less than half of all lobbying offices, and it is especially striking to note that unions are only 2 percent of the total.

Average Spending on Lobbying and Campaign Contributions

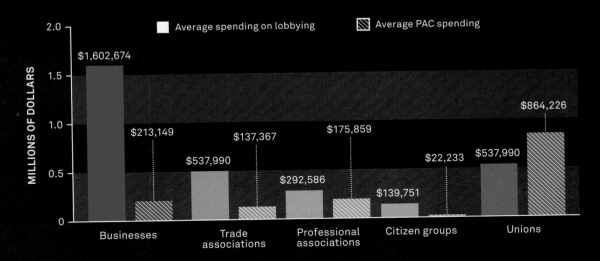

■ Average spending on lobbying   ▧ Average PAC spending

MILLIONS OF DOLLARS

- Businesses: $1,602,674 / $213,149
- Trade associations: $537,990 / $137,367
- Professional associations: $292,586 / $175,859
- Citizen groups: $139,751 / $22,233
- Unions: $537,990 / $864,226

The graph shows the average amounts spent on lobbying or campaign contributions by interest groups. Citizen groups on average spent much less on lobbying and campaign contributions than other types of groups. Unions on average spent more on campaign contributions than any other type of group, but that spending is tempered by the fact that there are fewer unions. (Note: Lobbying figures represent total reported spending in 2012; PAC campaign contributions are for the two-year election period ending with the 2012 election.)

Who Is Seen as Important in Policy Making?

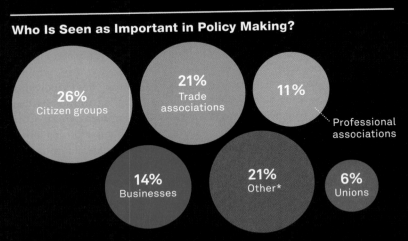

- 26% Citizen groups
- 21% Trade associations
- 11% Professional associations
- 14% Businesses
- 21% Other*
- 6% Unions

SOURCES:

Frank B. Baumgartner, Jeffrey M. Berry, Marie Hojnacki, David C. Kimball, and Beth L. Leech, *Lobbying and Policy Change: Who Wins, Who Loses, and Why* (Chicago: University of Chicago Press, 2009).

Center for Responsive Politics, www.opensecrets.org/pacs (accessed 12/2/15).

Leech, Beth L., National Survey of Governmental Relations, 2012.

Lobbyists.Info, www.lobbyists.info, (accessed 12/2/15).

*Includes coalitions, governmental associations, and think tanks.

Although the overall population of interest groups has fewer citizen groups than business groups, as seen in the figure on the facing page, not all groups are equally influential. Baumgartner and his colleagues interviewed 315 lobbyists and government officials about 98 randomly selected policy issues. Citizen groups were more likely to be mentioned as being important in the debate than any other type of group. More than a quarter of the interest groups seen as being influential were citizen groups.

lawmakers, $150 million in Texas, $230 million in New York, $240 million in Pennsylvania, and $69 million in Massachusetts.

Lobbying involves significant activity on the part of someone speaking for an interest. Lobbyists pepper legislators, administrators, and committee staff members with facts about pertinent issues and with facts or claims about public support of them.[17] Indeed, lobbyists serve a useful purpose in the legislative and administrative process by providing this kind of information.

However, within each industry, the many different individuals and organizations involved in government advocacy usually do not speak with a common voice. Rather, each advocates for its own interests, often in conflict with other firms in the same industry. What the leading organization or peak association of an industry may advocate may be undercut by the activities of individual firms. For example, the Entertainment Software Association, which spent roughly $5.6 million on lobbying in 2015, likely seeks a different set of regulations than Microsoft or Google.

Lobbying Members of Congress. Interest groups have substantial influence in setting the legislative agenda and helping craft the language of legislation (Figure 13.2). Today sophisticated lobbyists win influence by providing information about policies to busy members of Congress, who actually may refuse to see them unless they have useful information to offer. But this is only one of the many services lobbyists perform. They may also testify on their clients' behalf at congressional committee and agency hearings, help their clients identify potential allies with whom to construct coalitions, draft proposed legislation or regulations to be introduced by friendly lawmakers, and talk to reporters and organize media campaigns. Lobbyists also are important in fund-raising, directing clients' contributions to members of Congress and presidential candidates. Seeing an opportunity to harness the enthusiasm of political amateurs, lobbyists now organize comprehensive campaigns that combine simulated grassroots activity with information and campaign funding for members of Congress.[18]

Some interest groups go still further. They develop strong ties to individual politicians or policy communities within Congress by hiring former staffers, former members of Congress, or even relatives of sitting members of Congress. The frequent rotation of those in positions of power into lobbying jobs, a practice known as revolving-door politics, is driven by the continual turnover of staff, lobbyists, and even the political parties in Washington. Because lobbying firms must stay current and connected to Congress in order to offer the best

---

17 For discussions of lobbying, see Jeffrey M. Berry, *Lobbying for the People: The Political Behavior of Public Interest Groups* (Princeton, NJ: Princeton University Press, 1977); and John R. Wright, *Interest Groups and Congress: Lobbying, Contributions, and Influence* (Boston: Allyn & Bacon, 1996).

18 An excellent example is the mobilization of corporate executives in tax reform efforts in the mid-1980s. See Jeff Birnbaum and Alan S. Murray, *Showdown at Gucci Gulch: Lawmakers, Lobbyists, and the Unlikely Triumph of Tax Reform* (Westminster, MD: Random House, 1987).

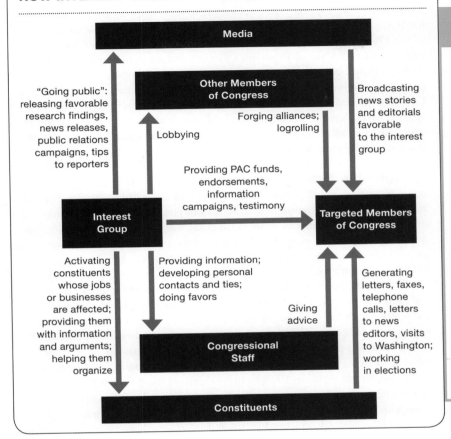

Figure 13.2
HOW INTEREST GROUPS INFLUENCE CONGRESS

Media

Other Members of Congress

"Going public": releasing favorable research findings, news releases, public relations campaigns, tips to reporters

Lobbying

Forging alliances; logrolling

Broadcasting news stories and editorials favorable to the interest group

Providing PAC funds, endorsements, information campaigns, testimony

Interest Group

Targeted Members of Congress

Activating constituents whose jobs or businesses are affected; providing them with information and arguments; helping them organize

Providing information; developing personal contacts and ties; doing favors

Giving advice

Generating letters, faxes, telephone calls, letters to news editors, visits to Washington; working in elections

Congressional Staff

Constituents

service to their clients, most large lobbying firms in Washington have strong ties to both the Democrats and the Republicans on the Hill. This revolving door has been cause for concern, and a number of states have put restrictions on how quickly former lawmakers can return as lobbyists. Seventeen states have one-year restrictions, and seven have two-year bans.[19]

Lobbying the President. All these efforts and more are needed when the target of a lobbying campaign is the president of the United States. So many individuals and groups clamor for the president's time and attention that only the most skilled and well connected can hope to influence presidential

---

19 Peggy Kerns, "Revolving Door Laws," National Conference of State Legislators, www.ncsl.org/legislatures-elections/ethicshome/legisbrief-revolving-door.aspx (accessed 3/4/13).

decisions. When running for president, Barack Obama made a bold promise to "free the executive branch from special-interest influence." No political appointee, the Obama team promised, "will be permitted to work on regulations or contracts directly and substantially related to their prior employer for two years." That promise proved exceedingly difficult to keep, as many in the Obama transition team had close ties to lobbyists or had worked for lobbying firms.[20] One of President Obama's first executive orders created an ethics standard and pledge for all executive branch appointments, and the administration imposed further restrictions on those receiving funds from the Emergency Economic Stabilization Act and the American Recovery and Reinvestment Act. Anyone wishing to receive funds from those economic stimulus bills had to show that they did not have conflicting interests and were not involved in lobbying the government.[21]

Lobbying the Executive Branch. Even when an interest group succeeds at getting its bill passed by Congress and signed by the president, full and faithful implementation of that law is not guaranteed. Often a group and its allies do not go home as soon as the president turns their lobbied-for law over to the appropriate agency. Instead, on average, 40 percent of interest group representatives continue to regularly contact legislative and executive branch organizations.[22]

In some respects, federal law actually promotes interest group access to the executive branch. The Administrative Procedure Act, enacted in 1946 and frequently amended, requires most federal agencies to provide notice and an opportunity for comment before implementing proposed rules and regulations. So-called notice-and-comment rule making gives interests an opportunity to make their views known and participate in the implementation of federal legislation that affects them. In 1990, Congress enacted the Negotiated Rulemaking Act to encourage administrative agencies to engage in direct and open negotiations with affected interests when developing new regulations. These two pieces of legislation, strongly enforced by the federal courts, have been important in opening the bureaucratic process to interest group influence. Today few federal agencies would consider implementing a new rule without consulting affected interests, which are known as "stakeholders."[23]

---

20 Chris Frates, "Daschle Lobby Ties Bump Obama Vow," *Politico*, November 30, 2008, www.politico.com/news/stories/1108/16015.html (accessed 4/7/09); and David Kirkpatrick, "In Transition, Ties to Lobbying," *New York Times*, November 15, 2008, www.nytimes.com/2008/11/15/us/politics/15transition.html (accessed 4/7/09).

21 Jacob Straus, *Lobbying the Executive Branch: Current Practices and Options for Change*, Report 7-5700, Congressional Research Service, December 6, 2010, pp. 3–4.

22 John P. Heinz, Edward O. Laumann, Robert L. Nelson, and Robert H. Salisbury, *The Hollow Core: Private Interests in National Policy Making* (Cambridge: Harvard University Press, 1993).

23 For an excellent discussion of the political origins of the Administrative Procedure Act, see Martin Shapiro, "APA: Past, Present, Future," *Virginia Law Review* 72 (1986): 447–92.

Regulation of Lobbying. As a result of the constant access to important decision makers that lobbyists seek out, stricter guidelines regulating lobbyists' actions have been adopted in recent decades. For example, as of 1993, businesses may no longer deduct from their taxes the cost of lobbying. Trade associations must report to members the proportion of their dues that goes to lobbying, and that proportion may not be reported as a business expense. Most important, the 1995 Lobbying Disclosure Act significantly broadened the definition of individuals and organizations that must register as lobbyists. According to the filings under this act, almost 12,000 lobbyists were working the halls of Congress in 2015.

Congress also restricted interest group influence by passing legislation in 1996 that limited gifts from a single source to $50 and no more than $100 annually. It also banned the practice of paying honoraria, which many special interests had paid out to supplement congressional salaries. But Congress did not limit the travel of representatives, senators, their spouses, or congressional staff members. Interest groups can pay for congressional travel as long as a trip is related to legislative business and is disclosed on congressional reports within 30 days. On these trips, meals and entertainment expenses are not limited to $50 per event and $100 annually. Congressional rules also allow members to travel on corporate jets as long as they pay an amount equal to first-class airfare.

In 2007, congressional Democrats secured the enactment of ethics rules that sought to prohibit lobbyists from paying for most meals, trips, parties, and gifts for members of Congress. Lobbyists were also required to disclose the amounts and sources of small campaign contributions "bundled" into large contributions. And interest groups were required to disclose the funds they used to rally voters for or against legislative proposals. As soon as the rules were enacted, however, lobbyists and politicians found ways to circumvent them, and the reforms have had little impact. Executive rulings and memoranda issued by President Obama in 2009 have made it much more difficult for lobbying firms to influence executive decision making either through direct lobbying or indirectly by hiring people with direct access to decision makers.

Using the Courts

Interest groups sometimes turn to the courts to augment other avenues of access. They can use the courts to affect public policy in at least three ways: (1) by bringing suit directly on behalf of the interest group, (2) by financing suits brought by individuals, and (3) by filing a companion brief as *amicus curiae* (literally, "friend of the court") to an existing court case.

Significant modern illustrations of the use of the courts for political influence are those that accompanied the sexual revolution of the 1960s and the emergence of the movement for women's rights. Beginning in the mid-1960s, a series of cases was brought into the federal courts in an effort to force the definition of a right to privacy in sexual matters. The effort began in *Griswold v. Connecticut* with a challenge to state restrictions on obtaining contraceptives for nonmedical purposes; here the Supreme Court held that states could neither prohibit the dissemination of information about nor prohibit the actual use of contraceptives by married couples. In a case that followed, the Court held that states could not prohibit the use of contraceptives by single persons any more than it could prohibit their use by married couples. One year later, in the 1973 case of *Roe v. Wade*, the Court held that states could not impose an absolute ban on voluntary abortions. Each of these cases, as well as others, were part of the Court's enunciation of a constitutional doctrine of privacy.[24]

Roe v. Wade sparked a controversy that brought conservatives to the fore on a national level. Conservative groups then made extensive use of the courts to whittle away the scope of the privacy doctrine. They obtained rulings, for example, that prohibit the use of federal funds to pay for voluntary abortions. And in 1989, right-to-life groups employed a strategy of litigation that significantly undermined the *Roe v. Wade* decision—namely, in the case of *Webster v. Reproductive Health Services*, which restored the right of states to place restrictions on abortion.[25]

Another significant use of the courts as a strategy for political influence surrounds the history of the NAACP. The most important of these cases was *Brown v. Board of Education* in 1954, in which the Supreme Court held that legal segregation of the schools was unconstitutional.[26]

Business groups are also frequent users of the courts because so many government programs apply to them, primarily in such areas as taxation, antitrust issues, interstate transportation, patents, and product quality and standardization. Often a business is brought to litigation against its will by virtue of initiatives taken against it by other businesses or by government agencies. But many major corporations and their trade associations bring suit themselves to influence policy, paying huge fees each year to prestigious Washington law firms. Some of this money is expended in gaining access, but most of it serves to keep the most experienced lawyers prepared to represent the corporations in court or before administrative agencies.

The forces of the new politics movement made significant use of the courts during the 1970s and 1980s, and judicial decisions were instrumental in advancing their goals. Facilitated by changes in the rules governing access to the courts (the rules of standing are discussed in Chapter 9), the new politics agenda was visible in decisions handed down in several key policy areas. In environmental policy, new politics groups forced federal agencies to pay attention to environmental issues even when the agencies' activities were not directly related to environmental quality. By the 2000s, the courts often were the battleground on which the new political movements waged their fights. Perhaps most dramatic were a string of lawsuits spanning 30 years (1986–2016) in which pro- and antiabortion organizations, such as Pro-Life Action Network, Operation Rescue, and the National Organization for Women, repeatedly sued state and local governments, and sometimes each other, to establish the rules governing

---

24 *Griswold v. Connecticut*, 381 U.S. 479 (1965); *Eisenstadt v. Baird*, 405 U.S. 438 (1972); and *Roe v. Wade*, 410 U.S. 113 (1973).

25 *Webster v. Reproductive Health Services*, 492 U.S. 490 (1989).

26 *Brown v. Board of Education*, 347 U.S. 483 (1954).

protests near abortion clinics. Ultimately, the U.S. Supreme Court sided with the antiabortion organizations, but not before deciding three separate cases on the matter, at extremely high cost to both sides.[27]

Mobilizing Public Opinion

Organizations try to bring pressure on politicians by mobilizing public opinion. This strategy is known as **going public**. When groups go public, they use their resources to try to persuade large numbers of people to pay attention to their concerns. They hope that greater visibility and public support will underscore the importance of such issues to those in power. Advertising campaigns, protests, and grassroots lobbying efforts are examples of going public. Increased use of this kind of strategy is traced to the rise of modern advertising at the beginning of the twentieth century. As early as the 1930s, political analysts distinguished between the "old lobby" of direct group representation before Congress and the "new lobby" of public-relations professionals addressing the public at large in order to reach Congress indirectly.[28] Going public, then, differs from other interest-group strategies to influence public policy. The new lobby techniques seek to change the way people think, rather than changing the actions of insiders.

 going public

The act of launching a media campaign to build popular support

Advertising. One way of going public is conventional advertising. For example, a casual scan of major newspapers, magazines, and websites often reveals expensive, well-designed ads by major companies and industry associations, such as those from oil and gas, automobile, and health and pharmaceutical companies. Such ads frequently highlight what the firms do for the country, not merely the products they develop. Their purpose is to create and maintain a positive association between the organization and the community at large in hopes that the community's favorable feelings can be drawn on in political controversies later.

Sometimes groups advertise expressly to shift public opinion on a question. One of the most famous such advertising campaigns was run by the Health Insurance Association of America in 1993 and 1994 in opposition to President Bill Clinton's proposed national health insurance plan. These ads featured a middle-class couple, Harry and Louise, sitting at their kitchen table disparaging the excessive bureaucratic problems they would face under Clinton's plan. These ads are widely attributed with turning public opinion against Clinton's plan, which never got off the ground in Congress. A decade later, when President Barack Obama proposed an extensive overhaul of the health insurance industry, a trade group representing drug makers brought the same actors back and remade the Harry and Louise spot—but this time

---

27 *Scheidler v. National Organization for Women,* 547 U.S. 9 (2006).

28 Pendleton Herring, *Group Representation before Congress* (1928; repr.: New York: Russell & Russell, 1967). See also Kenneth W. Kollman, *Outside Lobbying: Public Opinion and Interests Group Strategies* (Princeton, NJ: Princeton University Press, 1998).

fully supporting the administration's plan. Louise concludes the new ad by saying, "A little more cooperation, a little less politics, and we can get the job done this time."[29]

Grassroots Lobbying.

Grassroots lobbyists use many of the same organizing methods we see in political campaigns—developing lists of supporters and urging them to voice their concern with an issue and to recruit others to do so as well. It is common practice today to send direct mail that includes a draft letter that the recipient can adapt and then send to her representative in Congress, or to send e-mails urging people to contact their member of Congress regarding a particular bill or controversy. A grassroots campaign can cost anywhere from $40,000 to sway the votes of one or two crucial members of a committee or subcommittee, to millions of dollars to mount a national effort aimed at Congress as a whole. Such grassroots campaigns are often organized around controversial, prominent legislation or appointments, such as nominees to the U.S. Supreme Court.

Grassroots lobbying has become more prevalent in Washington in recent decades because congressional rules limiting gifts to members have made traditional lobbying more difficult. But has grassroots campaigning reached an extreme? One case in particular illustrates the extremes of what has come to be known as "Astroturf" lobbying (a play on the brand name of an artificial grass used on many sports fields). In 1992, 10 giant companies in the financial services, manufacturing, and high-tech industries began a grassroots campaign and spent millions of dollars to influence a decision in Congress to limit investors' ability to sue for fraud. Retaining an expensive consulting firm, these corporations paid for the use of specialized computer software to persuade Congress that there was "an outpouring of popular support for the proposal." Thousands of letters from individuals flooded Capitol Hill. Many came from people who sincerely believed that investor lawsuits are often frivolous and should be curtailed, but much of the mail was phony, generated by the Washington-based campaign consultants. More and more people are charging that these are not genuine grassroots campaigns but instead are Astroturf lobbying. Such campaigns have increased in frequency as members of Congress grow more skeptical of Washington lobbyists and far more concerned about demonstrations of support for a particular issue by their constituents. It is interesting that after the consulting firms generated thousands of letters in attempting to influence the sue-for-fraud legislation, they came to the somber conclusion that "it's more effective to have 100 letters from your district where constituents took the time to write and understand the issue," because "Congress is sophisticated enough to know the difference."[30]

29 Natasha Singer, "Harry and Louise Return, with a New Message," *New York Times,* July 16, 2009, www.nytimes.com/2009/07/17/business/media/17adco.html?_r=1&ref=media (accessed 10/3/11).

30 Jane Fritsch, "The Grass Roots, Just a Free Phone Call Away," *New York Times,* June 23, 1995, pp. A1 and A22.

Protest. Protests are the oldest means of going public. Those who lack money, contacts, and expertise, can always resort to protest as a means of making their concerns public. Indeed, the right to assembly is protected in the First Amendment. Protests may have many different consequences, depending on how they are managed. One basic consequence of a well-run protest is that it attracts attention. Peaceful demonstrations at city hall, the state legislature, Congress, the Supreme Court, or some other location typically involve people holding signs and chanting slogans. Passersby notice, and occasionally news outlets cover the event; the larger the protest, the more likely it is to attract attention. By getting on the news, the protesters hope to draw attention to their issue, possibly raise the sympathies of others, and bring them into the movement.

Organized protests also create a sense of community among those involved and raise the consciousness of people outside the protest. Civil rights protests during the 1960s brought hundreds of thousands of people to march in the nation's capital. Newspapers and television news programs nationwide carried images of Martin Luther King, Jr. and other civil rights leaders speaking to an audience that stretched from the Lincoln Memorial across the Washington Mall and surrounded the Reflecting Pool. That image wrapped the civil rights movement in the symbolism of the nation; it was not a violent confrontation between protesters and police but a peaceful plea for equal voting and civil rights. Forty years later, similar marches mobilized protesters for immigrants' rights. In spring 2006, hundreds of thousands of people, organized mainly by Hispanic and Latino groups, as well as unions and local churches, marched in Washington, D.C., and in several state capitals to protest anti-immigration policies. That movement drew attention to immigrants' concerns in an increasingly hostile political environment, and it influenced the political debate over the issue. One in four Hispanics in the United States participated in these protests.[31] More recently, the encampments organized by Occupy Wall Street were designed to promote solidarity and community among the protesters.

The nature of organized protest has changed, especially as communication and social media have changed. In July 2013, Alicia Garza wrote a Facebook post called "a love letter to black people." The post expressed her disgust at the acquittal of George Zimmerman, a neighborhood watch volunteer who shot and killed a black teenager, Trayvon Martin, but Garza also expressed her love of her community and her wish for strength and healing. "I continue to be surprised how little Black lives matter," she wrote, ending her post with, "black people. I love you. I love us. Our lives matter." Her friend Patrisse Cullors added the hashtag #BlackLivesMatter.[32] That social media post became a rallying point for a movement, slowly at first. The next summer, following the shooting of another black teenager, Michael Brown, by a police officer in Ferguson, Missouri, Black

31 Pew Hispanic Center and Pew Forum on Religion & Public Life, "Changing Faiths: Latinos and the Transformation of American Religion," 2007, http://pewhispanic.org/files/reports/75.pdf (accessed 4/7/09).

32 Jelani Cobb, "The Matter of Black Lives," *The New Yorker*, March 14, 2015, www.newyorker.com/magazine/2016/03/14/where-is-black-lives-matter-headed (accessed 9/12/16).

Lives Matter became a national call for awareness of structural racism. Similar incidents involving the deaths of black men and women around the country have resulted in both peaceful protest and civil unrest.

Finally, protests often attempt to impose costs on others by disrupting traffic or commerce, thereby forcing people to bargain with the protesters. Labor strikes are a form of political action against companies, industries, or the government. Striking workers refuse to work, costing the company the revenue it would have gained from services rendered. In the automotive industry, companies may have enough existing stock of cars and parts to continue for weeks or months of negotiations without disrupting sales. However, in an industry such as education or the airlines, once the teachers or pilots go on strike, all service stops. On rare occasions labor organizations can instigate a general strike—all workers in the entire industry, a city, or a nation stay home from work, bringing all commerce to a stop. Such strikes have a significant effect on businesses and the larger economy; they remind government and industry leaders of labor's political pull.

But unions aren't the only groups that organize protests. One impressive demonstration occurred during the winter of 1977–78, when American farmers were frustrated with federal agricultural policies and increasing failures of family farms. The farmers organized a peaceful but highly disruptive convoy of 600 tractors and other farm vehicles to Washington, D.C. Snarling traffic for weeks and tearing up the grassy mall between the Lincoln Memorial and the Capitol, the protest generated compelling news photographs and garnered extensive coverage in national media. The farmers did not get a revision of the 1977 Farm Bill, but they did get a promise from the Federal Housing Administration (FHA) temporarily to cease seizures of land and equipment of farmers who could not repay loans.[33] Farmers' protests, teachers' strikes, and other activities disrupt government and business activity in order to force negotiation of a better deal.

Of course, protests may become riots or civil conflict, or they may spur counterprotests. Companies affected by protests, as well as the government, have an interest in containing or breaking up demonstrations and strikes. However, the First Amendment is generally interpreted as protecting free expression through protests and strikes so long as they do not erupt into open rioting. For example, during George W. Bush's second inauguration in January 2005, 250 to 300 people protested the war in Iraq by marching through the streets of the Adams Morgan neighborhood in Washington, D.C. Police broke up the march with mass arrests. Some of the protesters sued to overturn their convictions and complained of alleged damages from police actions. The district court agreed, reasoning that the protesters were engaged in a peaceful demonstration, but had they been involved in riotous behavior, police actions may have been justified.[34]

33 "Furious Farmers," *Time*, December 19, 1977, www.time.com/time/magazine/article/0,9171,945836,00.html (accessed 4/7/09); and Marty Strange, *Family Farming: A New Economic Vision* (Lincoln: University of Nebraska Press, 1988).

34 *Carr et al. v. District of Columbia*, U.S. District Court of the District of Columbia, Civil Action, No. 2006-0098, July 15, 2008, https://ecf.dcd.uscourts.gov/cgi-bin/show_public_doc?2006cv0098-69 (accessed 4/7/09).

Using Electoral Politics

In addition to attempting to influence members of Congress and other government officials, interest groups use the electoral process to elect the "right" legislators in the first place and ensure that those elected will owe them a debt of gratitude for their support. To put matters into perspective, groups invest far more resources in lobbying than in electoral politics. Nevertheless, financial support and campaign activism can be important tools for organized interests.

Political Action Committees. By far, the most common electoral strategy employed by interest groups is that of giving financial support to the parties or to particular candidates. But such support can easily cross the threshold into outright bribery. Therefore, Congress has occasionally sought to regulate this strategy. For example, the Federal Election Campaign Act of 1971 (FECA; amended in 1974) limits campaign contributions and requires each candidate or campaign committee to provide comprehensive information about every person who contributes more than $100. The FECA requires that any organization wishing to contribute to a candidate must do so through a "separate and segregated fund"—a political action committee.

These provisions have been effective up to a point, considering the large number of embarrassments, indictments, resignations, and criminal convictions in the aftermath of the Watergate scandal of the 1970s. The scandal itself was triggered when Republican "dirty tricksters" were caught breaking into the office of the Democratic National Committee in the Watergate complex in Washington, D.C. An investigation revealed numerous violations of campaign finance laws, involving millions of dollars passed from corporate executives to President Nixon's reelection committee.

Reaction to Watergate produced further legislation on campaign finance, but the effect has been to restrict individual rather than interest group campaign activity. Individuals may now contribute no more than $2,700 to any candidate for federal office in any primary or general election. A political action committee, however, can contribute $5,000, provided it contributes to at least five different federal candidates each year.[35] Beyond this, the laws permit corporations, unions, and other interest groups to form PACs and pay the costs of soliciting funds from private citizens for the PACs.

Electoral spending by interest groups has increased steadily despite campaign finance reforms: total PAC contributions increased from nearly $260 million in 2000 to $470 million in the 2014 election cycle. Interest groups focus their direct contributions on Congress, especially the House. After all, given the enormous cost of running modern political campaigns (see Chapter 11), most politicians are eager to receive PAC contributions. A typical House incumbent receives half

---

35 Federal Election Commission, "Contribution Limits 2013–14," www.fec.gov/pages/brochures/contriblimits.shtml (accessed 3/4/13).

of his campaign funds from interest groups. There is little evidence that interest groups buy roll-call votes or other favors from members of Congress with their donations, but group donations do help keep those who are sympathetic to groups' interests in office.[36]

The potential influence of interest group campaign donations over the legislature has prompted frequent calls to abolish PACs or limit their activities. The challenge is how to regulate groups' participation without violating their members' rights to free speech and free association. In 1976, the Supreme Court weighed in on this matter in terms of the constitutionality of the 1974 Federal Elections Campaign Act.[37] In its decision to let the act stand, the majority on the Court ruled that donors' rights of expression are at stake, but that these must be weighed against the government's interest in limiting corruption, or the perception of corruption. The Court has repeatedly upheld the key tenets of the decision: (1) that money is a form of speech but (2) that speech rights must be weighed against concerns about corruption. The balance between free speech and protection against corruption lies at the heart of not just campaign finance law but how Americans think about the representation of interests in our government. We value both the right of people and organizations to say freely what they want government to do and the quality and integrity of representation provided through the electoral and legislative process.

Independent Expenditures. The balance between free speech and corruption has led to a system of limitations on direct campaign contributions to candidates and parties through political action committees.

As we saw in Chapter 11, Congress in 2002 imposed significant limits on independent campaign expenditures via the Bipartisan Campaign Reform Act (BCRA). BCRA restricted donations to nonfederal (for example, state party) accounts to limit corruption, and it imposed limits on the types of campaign commercials that groups could air within 60 days of an election. It also raised the limits on direct campaign contributions to compensate for the effect of inflation.

In 2010, the Supreme Court struck down the restrictions on independent advertising.[38] The case involved a political movie critical of then-senator and presidential candidate Hillary Clinton and created by an organization called Citizens United. The movie aired on cable television inside the blackout date for independent political advertising stipulated by the BCRA. A 5–4 majority on the Court ruled that such blackout dates restricted the rights to free speech of corporations and other associations. This decision firmly established the right

---

36 See Stephen Ansolabehere, John de Figueiredo, and James M. Snyder, Jr., "Why Is There So Little Money in U.S. Politics?" *Journal of Economic Perspectives* 17 (2006): 105–30.

37 *Buckley v. Valeo,* 424 U.S. 1 (1976).

38 *Citizens United v. Federal Election Commission,* 558 U.S. 310 (2010).

of business corporations and labor unions to engage in political advocacy and opened the gates to a flood of money in the political arena.

This flood was evident during the 2016 national elections, in which independent expenditures amounted to some $1.7 billion (Figure 13.3), and $785 million in the 2014 midterms. A significant portion of this money was raised by independent expenditure committees that the media dubbed "Super PACs," which are allowed to raise unlimited amounts of money from any source—individuals, businesses, or other associations. There are some restrictions, however: Super PACs must report donors to the Federal Election Commission, and they must not directly coordinate their activities with political candidates. However, they are allowed to advertise for and against candidates. In the 2016 election campaign, most Super PAC money was spent on negative advertising, but a substantial amount also went to get-out-the-vote activities.

Campaign Activism. Financial support is not the only way in which organized groups seek influence through the electoral process. Sometimes activism can be even more important than campaign contributions.

Perhaps the most notable instance of such activism occurs on behalf of Democratic Party candidates through labor unions, which regularly hold massive get-out-the-vote drives. The largest such activities come from the Service Employees International Union (SEIU), which represents workers ranging

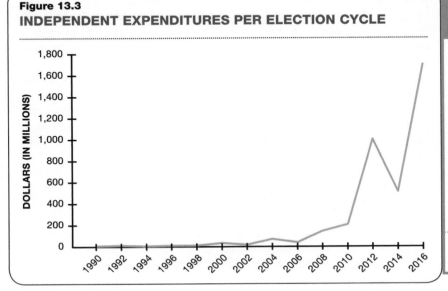

Figure 13.3
INDEPENDENT EXPENDITURES PER ELECTION CYCLE

ANALYZING THE EVIDENCE

Independent campaign expenditures on ads advocating for the election or defeat of political candidates increased significantly in 2016. What might explain this increase? What might be the impact of such an increase on future campaigns and elections?

NOTE: The years 1992, 1996, 2000, 2004, 2008, 2012, and 2016 were presidential election years.
SOURCE: Center for Responsive Politics, www.opensecrets.org/outsidespending/fes_summ.php (accessed 11/12/16).

from hotel and restaurant workers to clerical staff, and the United Auto Workers (UAW). Other sorts of groups routinely line up behind the Democratic and Republican campaigns. The National Rifle Association, for example, spent $52 million in the 2016 election cycle, and all of that money was either in support of Republicans or against Democrats.

The cumulative effect of such independent campaign activism is difficult to judge. One important research initiative seeks to measure the marginal effectiveness of campaign contact. Professors Alan Gerber and Donald Green have developed a program of field experiments in which campaigns agree to randomly assign direct campaign activity to some neighborhoods but not others. The researchers have been able to measure the marginal effect of an additional piece of mail, direct canvasser, or phone call. In a typical election context, it costs about $40 to get an additional voter to the polls. Gerber and Green further find that campaign activism initially can have a large impact, but after six or so attempted contacts the effects of campaign contact diminish dramatically. This research has given campaigns and reformers some sense of the effectiveness of campaign activism in stimulating turnout and possibly influencing elections. Especially in low-turnout elections, such as for city council or state legislature, interest groups' get-out-the-vote activities can significantly affect the outcome; but as other money enters the scene, especially candidates' own campaign expenditures, the effects of interest groups' direct campaign activities become muted.[39]

initiative ➡

A process by which citizens may petition to place a policy proposal on the ballot for public vote

The Initiative. Another political tactic sometimes used by interest groups is sponsorship of ballot initiatives at the state level. The **initiative** allows proposed laws to be placed on the general election ballot and submitted directly to voters, thus bypassing the state legislature and governor. Perhaps the most famous initiative was Proposition 13 in California, which placed a limit on property tax increases and forever changed the way that state finances education.

Ironically, most initiative campaigns today are sponsored by interest groups seeking to circumvent legislative opposition to their goals. In recent years, for example, the insurance industry, trial lawyers' associations, and tobacco companies have sponsored initiative campaigns. The role of interest groups in initiative campaigns is no surprise because such campaigns can cost millions of dollars.

Are Interest Groups Effective?

Do interest groups have an effect on government and policy? A clear answer is difficult to find among the mountains of research on this question. A survey of dozens of studies of campaign contributions and legislative decision

---

39 Donald Green and Alan Gerber, *Get Out the Vote: How to Increase Voter Turnout,* 2nd ed. (Washington DC: Brookings Institution Press, 2008).

making found that in only about 1 in 10 cases was there evidence of a correlation between contributors' interests and legislators' roll-call voting.[40]

Earmarks are a good case in point. Earmarks are expenditures on particular projects in specific districts or states, and they are usually included in a bill late in the legislative process to help secure enough votes for passage. Millions of dollars in earmarks are written into law every year. In a study of lobbyists' effectiveness in obtaining earmarks for college and university clients,[41] lobbying was found to have a limited impact. The more money schools spent on lobbying activities, the more earmarked funds they received; however, the magnitude of the effect depended greatly on institutional factors. A few cases, though, showed exceedingly high returns. Schools in states with a senator on the Senate Appropriations Committee received $18 to $29 in earmarks for every $1 spent on lobbying. Schools in congressional districts whose representative served on the House Appropriations Committee received between $49 and $55 for every $1 spent on lobbying. Having a legislator on the relevant committee, then, explains most of the observed influence.[42]

These results suggest that institutions and politics are profoundly related. Schools without access to influential members of Congress cannot gain much from lobbying. Schools with such access still need to lobby to maximize the potential that representation on congressional appropriations committees can give them. But if they do so, the potential return is substantial.

Perhaps the largest challenge to the claim that interest group politics drive American democracy arises when we consider how much political advocacy occurs. The usual argument about the influence of lobbyists and campaign contributions suggests that any dollar spent by an organization on political activity is a dollar well spent. One can turn that thinking on its head. If it is a dollar well spent, then groups should spend as much as possible on politics, and total spending should reflect the value of political action to those groups, relative to their other investments. In other words, view the political actions of any firm— and most organizations involved in politics are firms—as a business decision. What insight comes from that perspective?

Those engaged in lobbying provide a valued service for the firms they represent by helping shape legislation, influence administrative decisions, and advocate in court. There are, however, other possible investments a firm can make: buy new machines, purchase another company, hire additional employees. How do lobbying and campaign contributing compare with those sorts of bottom-line decisions?

....

40 Ansolabehere et al., "Why Is There So Little Money in U.S. Politics?"

41 John M. de Figueiredo and Brian S. Silverman, "Academic Earmarks and the Returns to Lobbying" working paper 9064, National Bureau of Economic Research, 2002; substantially rev., 2003, http://web.mit.edu/jdefig/www/papers/academic_earmarks.pdf (accessed 4/7/09).

42 John M. de Figueiredo and Brian S. Silverman, "Academic Earmarks and the Returns to Lobbying," *Journal of Law and Economics* 42 (October 2006): 597–626.

As a business and economic matter, the amount of money spent on political activity by firms is small. The value of goods purchased in a market is approximately equal to the amount of money someone is willing to pay for them. The total U.S. economy is valued at $17.9 trillion; government expenditures are about $3.8 trillion; corporate profits alone exceed $1.5 trillion. As a fraction of total government expenditures, total lobbying expenditures equal less than one-tenth of 1 percent, and lobbying is only a trace amount of firms' total expenses. This simple calculation suggests that the total influence of groups cannot be substantial.[43] If the returns on political investment were high, then we ought to see large firms like Microsoft, General Electric, and Walmart spending much more on politics.

Why isn't there more money in politics? Mancur Olson suggests that groups are simply free riding. But that still implies an opportunity for influence for those who are engaged because they should spend even more to get even greater returns. The pluralist line of thinking suggests a more compelling answer. The United States has a wide-open political system with many points of access and influence, meaning that no one group can have much influence. There is not much money in politics because the separation of powers and other features of our political system make it exceedingly difficult to have much immediate influence over the legislative and executive branches. The pluralist argument is wrong in asserting that all interests will find expression through political organization, but it is perhaps right that a system of divided political authority, such as in the United States, still allows for the expression of many different interests and makes it very hard for particular groups to dominate the political process or even to pass a law.

CONCLUSION: INTEREST GROUP INFLUENCE IN U.S. POLITICS

The institutions of American government embrace an open and democratic process to ensure that government is responsive to the public's preferences and needs. The Bill of Rights provides for the rights of free speech, freedom of the press, and freedom of assembly. The nation's laws have further cemented this commitment, providing for open meetings, citizen advisory commissions, lobbying, direct contact from constituents, contributions from interested individuals and groups, an open legal system, protests, and many other routes through which individuals and groups may advocate for their interests. These are the institutions through which people can express intensely held preferences or interests, preferences for which voting is not enough. Through these many

---

43 See Ansolabehere et al., "Why Is There So Little Money in U.S. Politics?"

points of access, representatives and government officials learn how their decisions affect the public. Politics, then, becomes the arena in which many interests compete for the attention and support of government. Indeed, tens of thousands of organizations compete in the political sphere in the United States, and countless other movements and coordinated efforts of citizens rise and fall as issues come into the public arena. This is pluralism at work, and it aligns closely with the sort of politics the Founders envisioned.

But this system of government is hardly perfect. The policies and laws the U.S. government enacts are often thought to favor those who are organized. The American interest group system creates opportunities for those who can use their resources to represent their interests before the government. People and organizations that can muster the financial resources or the manpower can best make their case before the legislature, before the administrative agencies of the executive, before the courts, and even before the electorate. Economic organizations, such as firms and unions, that exist for some other reason than to gain political influence have the least difficulty amassing such resources. Problems of collective action and free riding prevent many latent interests from developing permanent political organizations capable of pressuring the government. Businesses, unions, and professional and industry associations usually have less trouble overcoming the obstacles to organization and group maintenance than do volunteer associations. Interest group politics in Washington, D.C. and state governments, consequently, can often reflect the interests of and conflicts among those engaged in economic activity.

Although firms, unions, and other organizations can solve the collective action problem, they do not necessarily succeed in the political arena. Unlike economic activity, politics involves power derived from the ability to vote on measures, introduce legislation or rules, or block actions from happening. Interest groups are outsiders that can do none of these things directly. Nonetheless, these organizations seek support in the appropriate institutions, such as a court with a sympathetic judge or a congressional subcommittee with a sympathetic chair. Often, groups succeed not by bringing pressure but by providing expertise to the government and by learning from those in office about the impact of new rules and regulations.

Interest group politics today does not fit stereotypical notions of political power and influence clearly. There are as many lobbyists as ever, but the backroom dealings of the "old lobby" are an anachronism. Interest group politics spans all branches of government and involves myriad interests vying for attention in an increasingly crowded field. Moreover, competing interests may very well cancel out a given organization's efforts. Further, the activities of all groups constitute just one facet of legislators', judges', and executives' deliberations. Those who must ultimately make political decisions and be held accountable consider other voices as well, especially those of their constituents. Perhaps a better contemporary characterization is that the organized and disorganized interests participating in politics today are really contributing to a much broader sphere of political debate. That debate takes place inside the institutions of government—Congress, courts, executives, and elections. It also takes place in the media. That forum is the final leg of our discussion of democracy in America, and to that subject we turn in the next chapter.

For Further Reading

Abramoff, Jack. *Capitol Punishment: The Hard Truth about Washington Corruption from America's Most Notorious Lobbyist*. New York: WND Books, 2011.

Ainsworth, Scott. *Analyzing Interest Groups*. New York: Norton, 2002.

Alexander, Robert, ed. *The Classics of Interest Group Behavior*. New York: Wadsworth, 2005.

Ansolabehere, Stephen, John M. de Figueiredo, and James M. Snyder, Jr. "Why Is There So Little Money in U.S. Politics?" *Journal of Economic Perspectives* 17, no. 1 (winter 2003): 105–30.

Baumgartner, Frank, Jeffrey M. Berry, Beth L. Leech, David C. Kimball, and Marie Hojnacki. *Lobbying and Policy Change: Who Wins, Who Loses, and Why*. Chicago: University of Chicago Press, 2009.

Cigler, Allan, and Burdett A. Loomis. *Interest Group Politics*. 8th ed. Washington, DC: CQ Press, 2011.

Esterling, Kevin. *The Political Economy of Expertise*. Ann Arbor: University of Michigan Press, 2004.

Galanter, Marc. "Why the 'Haves' Come Out Ahead: Spectulations on the Limits of Legal Change." *Law and Society Review* 9, no. 1 (1974): 95–160.

Gilens, Martin. *Affluence and Influence: Economic Inequality and Political Power in America*. New York and Princeton, NJ: Russell Sage Foundation and Princeton University Press, 2012.

Harrison, Paul, Christopher Deering, and Clyde Wilcox. *Interest Groups Unleashed*. Washington, DC: CQ Press, 2012.

Lowi, Theodore J. *The End of Liberalism: The Second Republic of the United States*. 2nd ed. New York: Norton, 1979.

Nownes, Anthony. *Total Lobbying: What Lobbyists Want and How They Try to Get It*. New York: Cambridge University Press, 2006.

Olson, Mancur, Jr. *The Logic of Collective Action: Public Goods and the Theory of Groups*. 1965. Reprinted with new preface and appendix. Cambridge: Harvard University Press, 1965.

Rosenthal, Alan. *The Third House: Lobbyists and Lobbying in the States*. Washington, DC: CQ Press, 2001.

Strolovitch, Dara. *Affirmative Advocacy: Race, Class, and Gender in Interest Group Politics*. Chicago: University of Chicago Press, 2007.

Verba, Sidney, Kay Schlozman, and Henry E. Brady, *The Unheavenly Chorus*. Princeton, NJ: Princeton University Press, 2013.

14

The Media

The media constitute one of the most unusual institutions of American democracy. They are not a singular institution, such as the Congress or the presidency, but an industry that exists primarily for communication and entertainment. The main business model is simple enough. Using communication technologies such as the printing press and Internet, media firms develop and distribute content—news articles, TV shows, websites, and the like—to attract an audience. The audience pays for access to content by purchasing subscriptions; paying cover prices and access charges; and buying computers, televisions, and radios. More significant, other businesses, organizations, and individuals want access to that audience too and will pay media firms to advertise their messages. Most media revenue derives from advertising—from selling access to the audience attracted by television and radio, newspapers and magazines, and the Internet.[1] And the audience is huge. Nearly every household in the United States has at least one television; three-quarters have Internet access. The typical American adult watches three hours of television a day.[2]

Politics and public affairs are an important part of media content. People are willing to pay for this information, and politicians and organized interests are willing to pay to reach that audience through advertisements or events that attract coverage. Most major media outlets offer news coverage and analysis as a way to attract readers and listeners. The major television networks—ABC, CBS, NBC, and Fox—offer approximately six hours of news programming every day, and some media organizations are devoted exclusively to politics and public

---

1 Roughly 75 percent of newspaper revenue comes from advertising and 20 percent from subscriptions. See Laura Houston Santhanam and Tom Rosenstiel, "Why U.S. Newspapers Suffer More Than Others," *The State of the News Media, 2011,* Pew Research Center's Project for Excellence in Journalism, http://stateofthemedia .org/2011/mobile-survey/international-newspaper-economics/ (accessed 10/3/11).

2 Ben Leubsdorf, "We're Working More Hours—and Watching More TV," *The Wall Street Journal,* June 24, 2015, www.wsj.com/articles/were-working-more-hoursand-watching-more-tv-1435187603 (accessed 9/5/15).

affairs. The cost of news programs to consumers is minimal, even free, and the content is presented in a widely accessible manner. In this way, the media offer an easy—sometimes even entertaining—way to learn about the important actions of government, the state of the nation, and the choices in an election.

The media, then, address one of the most important problems of democracy—how to create an informed electorate. As we discussed in Chapters 10 and 11, democratic politics assumes some awareness among the electorate about who is in power, what problems the nation faces, and what actions and policies the government has taken. The news media make information about politics and public affairs readily and widely accessible, even entertaining. Most Americans learn about government and politics not through firsthand experience but from media sources and through the lenses of those who report the news or comment on issues and events.

The challenge for every democracy is how to foster the development of media that will allow for robust discourse and dissent. The United States, from its inception, has embraced the principle that a free press allows people to speak freely and to make reasoned electoral decisions. The First Amendment to the Constitution states that "Congress shall make no law . . . abridging the freedom of speech, or the press." Over time the Supreme Court has expanded that idea to cover all forms of communication and has interpreted that restraint to apply to all levels and branches of government, not just Congress.

A free, open, and largely unregulated media environment is the engine of American democracy. It is the great marketplace of ideas. Collectively the media

CORE OF THE ANALYSIS

 The primary objective of the American media is to make profits, which they do by charging fees to access their content and by selling advertising.

 The market for news is extremely large, as most Americans rely on the media to find out about issues, government activities, and electoral choices. This makes the private media industry into an important part of the public sphere.

 Politicians, bureaucrats, organized interests, and private citizens can shape how the media portray public issues by providing information to journalists.

 The U.S. government takes a light hand in regulating media ownership and operation, relying on the marketplace to produce a robust flow of information about politics and government affairs.

present a vast range of ideas, opinions, and information that any consumer may choose to watch, listen to, or read. Those media that do not attract consumers fail; those that offer what people want succeed. This system may not always provide the ideal outcome, but it is considered the best way to guarantee an adequately informed public.[3] The First Amendment, wrote Judge Learned Hand at the height of World War II, "presupposes that right conclusions are more likely to be gathered out of a multitude of tongues, than through any kind of authoritative selection. To many this is, and always will be, folly; but we have staked upon it our all."[4]

An alternative view holds that journalists and owners of media firms hold a privileged position in any society, and with that privilege comes responsibilities that can be ensured only through regulation. Most countries regulate political speech by limiting advertising, require a minimum amount of public affairs programming, and regulate what reporters may and may not say. Slander and libel laws apply to American journalists, as do restrictions owing to national security, but there is far less regulation of reporting in the United States than in just about every other country. Most other countries underwrite or own their main broadcast media outlets, such as the Canadian or British Broadcasting Corporations. In the United States, media firms succeed or fail as businesses based on their ability to attract audiences and revenue, not on whether they provide a public service or good.

How and how well does the marketplace of ideas work? Is there enough competition? Today, for example, very few cities are served by more than one local newspaper. Local news monopolies may give owners, editors, and journalists excessive political power in their local markets. Or is there too much competition? The Internet has cut into the profit margins of traditional media, forcing newspapers and television and radio companies to cut their more expensive staff—often the very reporters who produce the news content. Media firms, Congress, and executive agencies (especially the Federal Communications Commission [FCC]) must deal with these and other questions as new communications technologies transform the nation's media industry and the ways that people become informed about and engage in politics.

THE MEDIA AS A POLITICAL INSTITUTION

Perhaps the most salient feature of the American media, as an industry and as a political institution, is the diversity of sources, firms, and technologies. Hundreds of weekly magazines, independent television stations, and affiliates of smaller networks are devoted to national politics. Countless websites stream news from sources worldwide. These media reach every community in the United States and provide information in every language.

---

3   This idea is most elegantly expressed in the majority opinion in the Supreme Court case *New York Times v. Sullivan,* 376 U.S. 254 (1964).

4   *United States v. Associated Press,* 52 F. Supp. 362, 372 (D. C. S. D. N. Y. 1943).

Types of Media

There is some order to the apparent chaos. The American media are organized into three categories—print, broadcast, and Internet—and regulations follow these lines. Print media, such as newspapers and magazines, have long enjoyed strong First Amendment protections and provide a good example of the marketplace of ideas. The technology of printing presses and digital reproduction make it easy for new papers to enter local markets, and that fact has led the courts to stay the hand of those pushing for regulation of print media.

Broadcast and cablecast media, by contrast, have historically faced technological limits leading to restrictions on ownership, distribution, and at times content. With the advent of radio in the 1920s, the need for regulation became evident. Broadcasters would vary their signal strength and the part of the radio-frequency spectrum over which they broadcast to find audiences and squelch other broadcasters. That behavior threatened to ruin the medium because consumers could not reliably find the programming they wanted. In 1927, the first regulations of broadcast media required every broadcaster to secure a license from the U.S. government and agree to send its signal only over a narrow band of the spectrum (which would be allocated to that station within a certain region). The government could revoke that license for failure to comply. In the late 1940s, concern about use of the spectrum in emerging television technology led the government to freeze that nascent industry's development for four years while the FCC worked out a distribution and ownership plan. Regulation of the broadcast spectrum continues to dictate federal communications policy to this day. Because the spectrum is limited, broadcasting and cablecasting firms serve a public trust and bear responsibility for their actions.[5] But the spectrum is not very limited anymore. Rather, this view exhibits the history principle at work. When broadcasting and cable were developed, the technology was not as good as today's and thus limited the number of stations possible, with only some firms having access; hence the public responsibility. Today, broadcasting and cable technology permit hundreds of channels. Nonetheless the rules developed in the 1920s persist, and firms that have flourished under them fight to keep their control over the airwaves.

Since the mid-1990s a third media sector has arisen—one driven by Internet technology, which blurs the line between the other two sectors. It requires governance for the assignment of web domains but otherwise operates as perhaps the most open and competitive of the three sectors. The Internet sector is still developing a distinctive identity as a mode of communication, especially political communication. For the first two decades of its existence, traditional media dominated the Internet provision of content, as print and broadcast firms moved their content online. But since 2000 an increasingly distinctive form of

---

5   Perhaps the best account of these developments is Erik Barnouw's excellent three-volume history *A Tower in Babel: A History of Broadcasting in the United States to 1933; The Golden Web: A History of Broadcasting in the United States, 1933 to 1953;* and *The Image Empire: A History of Broadcasting in the United States from 1953* (New York: Oxford University Press, 1966, 1968, and 1970).

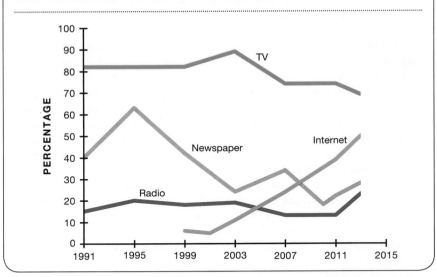

Figure 14.1

AMERICANS' MAIN SOURCE FOR NEWS

SOURCE: Pew Research Center, www.people-press.org/2013/08/08/amid-criticism-support-for-medias-watchdog-role-stands-out/ (accessed 7/15/16).

web-based political communication has emerged, including blogs and citizen journalism, which many fear is supplanting traditional media and the norms of professional journalism.[6] The 2008 election marked the Internet's arrival as one of the three pillars of the media: for the first time, more people reported obtaining news from a digital platform—including websites, social networking, and mobile devices—than from newspapers (Figure 14.1). By 2009, the Internet as a source of news surpassed radio and newspapers. Television news remained the most common source of information, but fully half of all Americans reported getting their news from Internet or social media sources.[7]

Broadcast Media. Television news reaches more Americans than any other news source. Tens of millions of individuals watch national and local news programs every day. This remains true even in the era of digital news because the most frequented sources of news online are the websites of ABC, CBS, NBC, CNN, and Fox News. Television news, however, covers relatively few topics and provides little depth of coverage. More like a series of newspaper headlines connected to pictures, television news alerts viewers to issues and events but provides little else.

6   Cass R. Sunstein, *Republic.com 2.0* (Princeton, NJ: Princeton University Press, 2007).

7   Kenneth Olmstead, Mark Jurkowitz, Amy Mitchell, and Jodi Enda, "How Americans Get TV News at Home," Pew Research Center, October 11, 2013, www.journalism.org/2013/10/11/how-americans-get-tv-news-at-home (accessed 7/1/16).

The 24-hour news stations such as CNN offer more detail and commentary than the networks' evening news shows. Cable news outlets grabbed some of their largest audiences ever with the coverage of the invasions of Iraq in 1991 and 2003. At the start of these conflicts, CNN, Fox News, and MSNBC provided 24-hour coverage, including video of bombs targeting Iraqi government buildings and military installations, on-the-scene reporting by American journalists embedded in Iraq, expert commentary, and interviews with government officials. Normally, such networks offer a steady stream of headlines and commentary. But during wars, floods, earthquakes, and other disasters the cable news networks are on the spot with continuous coverage.

Radio news is essentially a headline service without pictures. Usually devoting five minutes per hour to news, radio stations announce the day's major events with little detail. News stations such as WTOP (Washington, D.C.) and WCBS (New York City) generally repeat the same stories each hour to present them to new listeners. Recently, radio talk shows have become important sources of commentary and opinion. Numerous conservative radio hosts, such as Rush Limbaugh, have huge audiences and have helped mobilize support for conservative political causes and candidates. Liberals have had less success in talk radio and complain that biased radio coverage has hurt them in elections. Podcasts represent one of the fastest growing ways that people receive programs, including the news. From 2008 to 2016, the percentage of adults in the United States who say they have listened to a podcast in the past month grew from 8 percent to 22 percent.[8]

In recent years, much news content, especially of local news, has shifted away from politics toward "soft news," focusing on celebrities, health tips, consumer advice, and other topics more likely to entertain than enlighten. Even a lot of political coverage is soft. For example, articles about the Obamas' choice of their dog outnumbered stories about the Iraq War by three to two during April 2009.[9]

Another category of programming, sometimes called *infotainment,* purports to combine information with entertainment. *The Daily Show with Trevor Noah* (formerly with Jon Stewart) on Comedy Central calls itself America's "most trusted name in fake news," yet many people under age 35 consider it one of their main sources of political information and news. The news on *The Daily Show* offers a comedic twist on current events and on the media itself, especially CNN and Fox News.

Print Media. Newspapers remain an important source of news even though they are not most Americans' primary news source. Also important are magazines of opinion such as the *Economist*, the *New Republic*, and the *National Review*. These magazines have relatively small circulations but are read by politically influential Americans who count on them for news and analysis. Two Washington periodicals, the *Hill* and *Roll Call*, are important sources of political news for Washington insiders including members of Congress, congressional staffers, and lobbyists. The print

---

8 "State of the News Media 2016," Pew Research Center, June 15, 2016, www.journalism. org/2016/06/15/state-of-the-news-media-2016/ (accessed 9/6/16).

9 Project for Excellence in Journalism, "The Dog Days of Spring," April 22, 2009, http:// journalism.org/TheDogDaysofSpring+ (accessed 5/7/09).

media are important for at least three reasons. First, as we see later in this chapter, the broadcast media rely on leading newspapers such as the *New York Times* and the *Washington Post* to set their news agenda. The broadcast media do very little actual reporting; they primarily cover stories that have been initially reported by the print media. One can almost say that if an event is not covered in the *New York Times*, it is unlikely to appear on the *CBS Evening News*. An important exception is "breaking" news, which broadcast media can carry as it unfolds or soon after, whereas print media must catch up later. For example, on September 11, 2001, tens of millions of Americans saw dramatic real-time videos of the collapsing World Trade Center towers before the print media could publish the news the next day. Print media are also important because they provide more detailed and more complete information, offering a better context for analysis. Finally, they are the prime news source for educated and influential individuals. Indeed, the nation's economic, social, and political elites rely on print media's detailed coverage to inform their views about key public matters. The print media may have a smaller audience than their cousins in broadcasting, but they have an audience that matters.

Today, however, the newspaper industry is in serious economic trouble. Online competition has dramatically reduced newspapers' revenues from traditional advertising, such as retail, help wanted, and personal ads. Newspaper advertising revenue dropped by over 50 percent over the past decade: from $50 billion in 2006 to $20 billion in 2014.[10] Facing serious financial difficulties, some papers have closed (such as the *Rocky Mountain News* in Denver) or have adopted an online format only (such as the *Seattle Post-Intelligencer*). Closures of major newspapers serving large U.S. cities and metropolitan areas often leave many cities with one or possibly no daily print newspapers. And in 2013, the Graham family, which had owned the *Washington Post* for three generations, surprised the industry by announcing the sale of the paper to Jeffrey Bezos, founder and CEO of Amazon.com. All these changes signal a wider transformation of print media that may leave the country with few or no print newspapers—the traditional "press"—in the future. The great unknown is whether online venues, such as social media, blogs, or news apps for mobile devices, can adequately replace print newspapers, especially in providing news about local area politics and public affairs. So far, the loss of newspapers' revenues from print advertising has far surpassed the rise in their revenues from online advertising.[11]

The possible demise of major city newspapers raises important concerns. Since the beginning of the Republic, newspapers have been ingrained in the way we think about political communication. The First Amendment specifically protects a "free press," and legal doctrines and laws concerning political

---

10 Amy Mitchell and Jesse Holcomb, "State of the News Media 2015," Pew Research Center on Journalism and Media, June 15, 2016, www.journalism.org/2015/04/29/state-of-the-news-media-2015 (accessed 7/01/16). Figures on newspaper readership and revenues are from Michael Barthel, "Newspapers: Fact Sheet," Pew Research Center on Journalism and Media, April 29, 2015, www.journalism.org/2015/04/29/newspapers-fact-sheet (accessed 7/01/16).

11 24/7 Wall Street, "The 10 Most Endangered Newspapers in America," *Time*, March 9, 2009, www.time.com/time/business/article/0,8599,1883785,00.html (accessed 5/7/09). See also, Barthel, "Newspapers: Fact Sheet."

communication in the United States have evolved around the idea of a robust press serving every community. As cities now face the prospect of having no significant press, in the conventional sense, there will likely be a rethinking of the laws governing many aspects of political communication in this country—from campaign finance laws to obscenity standards to ownership guidelines. So far, the U.S. Supreme Court has not extended the same set of free press protections to broadcasters.[12] However, the tremendous changes in the media over the past decade may lead the Court to rethink the First Amendment protections afforded to online providers. The case of *Citizens United,* one of the most sensational campaign finance cases decided by the Supreme Court in recent years, turned on the fact that the lines between print and broadcast are blurred by online distribution of content. One can just as easily download a book online as view an ad, so any restrictions on online advertisers would apply to book distributors.[13]

This transformation of print media may change the extent to which people are informed about politics and public affairs. The media that replace newspapers may raise the public's overall level of information or may segment the audience further, reducing the number of people aware of public affairs. Social science research suggests that the decline of newspapers is changing our news-gathering behavior. Rather than rely on a single source—the daily paper—Americans are sampling many sources, a practice known as "grazing." And that behavior is facilitated by the Internet.[14]

The Internet. The Internet emerged as a major form of communication in the mid-1990s. As with radio in the 1920s and television in the 1950s, over a single decade the Internet grew from a curiosity into one of the dominant modes of communication. Internet news providers now constitute a significant competitor to traditional media outlets. Every day tens of millions of Americans scan one of many news sites for coverage of current events. And websites such as Craigslist have taken away one of newspapers' key sources of revenue—classified advertising.

In many ways, the Internet as a medium parallels newspapers, television, radio, and magazines. The main newspapers and television outlets—such as the *Wall Street Journal* and the *New York Times,* Reuters and the Associated Press, CNN and Fox News—are mainstays of the Internet. All have websites through which they attract audiences to their traditional media. The Internet, however, has revolutionized how content is provided and what content is accessible to audiences. It combines the depth of newspaper coverage with the timeliness of television and radio, but it goes much further as well. Look at the website of any traditional media

---

12 *Red Lion Broadcasting Company v. Federal Communications Commission,* 395 U.S. 367 (1969).

13 Michael W. McConnell, "Reconsidering Citizens' United as a Press Clause Case," *Yale Law Journal* 123 (2013): 412, heinonline.org/HOL/LandingPage?handle=hein.journals/ylr123&div=12&id=&page= (accessed 7/01/16).

14 "Key News Audience Now Blend Online and Traditional Sources," Pew Research Center for the People and the Press, August 17, 2008, http://people-press.org/report/444/news-media (accessed 5/7/09).

Where Do Americans Get News about Politics?

CHAPTER

Contributed by
Rasmus Kleis Nielsen
University of Oxford

st of political life is distant from our own personal experience and social circles. Thus when we k nething about a recent international summit, a deal made in Congress, or a war abroad, it is us cause someone covered it as news.

How people get news, however, is changing and varies across generations. Throughout the twen ntury, news media were Americans' number one source of information about politics. Traditionally, ne pers have produced the most detailed and extensive coverage, and television has reached the wi diences and was for several decades the most important source of news for many.

The development and spread of digital media from the 1990s onward has changed the news m ndscape. Newspapers have seen declining readership, make less money, and therefore invest les ws production. Television audiences have been more stable but are increasingly made up of c ople. Younger people increasingly get news online.

By 2015, 85 percent of all Americans used the Internet, and 64 percent had a smartphone.[1] Am ople who are online, digital media have now overtaken television as the most important sources of ne 2015, 43 percent of American Internet users named digital sources as their most important source ws, compared to 40 percent who named television and 5 percent who named printed newspapers.

Main Source of News by Age

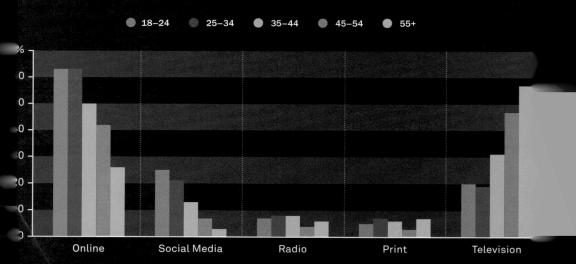

are clear generational differences in how people get news. Older Americans rely f[...] [...]onal media, such as television, than do younger people, who mostly get news online[...] [...]e, getting news online is about going directly to the websites and apps of news organizatio[...] [...]papers like the *New York Times*, broadcasters like NBC, or digital-only news sites like the[...] But for many, online news is increasingly accessed via digital intermediaries like sear[...] [...]aging apps, and social media. In 2015, 11 percent of American Internet users named social[...] [...]sources of news.

[Rela]tive Importance of News: Twitter and Facebook Compared

● I think of _____ as a useful way of getting news.   ● I mostly see news when I'm on _____ for other reasons.

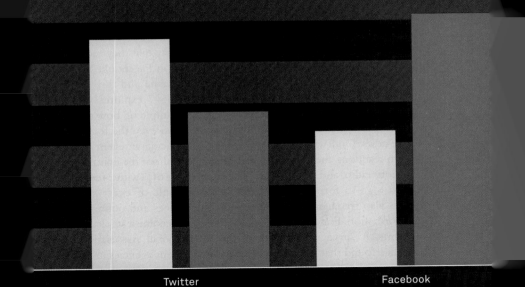

Twitter   Facebook

[...]raph above shows that some social media, such as Twitter, are often directly linked w[...] [...]ast, people mostly visit Facebook for other reasons but often stumble upon news when o[...] [...]ing media environment has sometimes been associated with the rise of "selective expos[...] [...]e seek out information that reflects their existing views. However, the rise of widely used s[...] [...]acebook seems to be associated with a resurgence in "incidental exposure," where p[...] [...]s news unintentionally.

[...]: Nic Newman, Rasmus Kleis Nielsen, and David Levy, "2015 Digital News Report," University of Oxfor[...]

outlet, such as the *New York Times* or CNN. There you will see a reproduction of the content from the newspaper or headline news from television that resembles a traditional newspaper, but there is also streaming video that resembles a television report, audio similar to a radio program, and commentary from many sources like that found in an opinion or news magazine.

Unlike a newspaper, which is wholly new every day, a website can keep important stories up for many days. Most news websites contain easily searchable archives and also function as aggregators, accumulating news on a given topic from many different sources. Perhaps the most powerful aggregator is Google, whose news service accumulates information from organizations as different as the *Wall Street Journal* and Al Jazeera, Reuters and the Associated Press, and the *Lebanon Daily Star* and *Shanghai Daily*. In addition to traditional news sites, there have emerged more specialized sites. BuzzFeed, Politico, and the Huffington Post are three of the most frequently visited sites for news online. They offer a wide range of content, including reporting, commentary, and analytics. Some sites are more focused content. Slate, for instance, specializes in commentary, and Cook Political Report offers analytics.

Increasingly, social media are transforming online provision and distribution of the news. Social media have changed how information is distributed through sharing, person to person, and how news information is generated. Facebook is a good example of how social media are changing the distribution of information. Half of all people who say that they receive news online report that they read news posted by others on Facebook. Young people are more likely than older people to get news online and through social media. (The Analyzing the Evidence unit on pp. 586–7 explores where Americans get news about politics.) Twitter is a good example of how social media have altered how news information is generated and even the form and format of the news. On Twitter, those who are experiencing an event can provide their own reactions and reports in real-time, and without the editorial filters of television, radio, and newspapers. The immediacy of Twitter feeds has made this into a go-to form of media. Twitter is a staple of every serious campaign. It is also frequently used by government offices and politicians to distribute information. For example, social media have become a staple for police departments. A survey conducted by the International Association of Chiefs of Police found that 96 percent of law enforcement agencies in the United States use social media in some capacity. Eighty-six percent of police departments use social media for crime investigations, and 73 percent use it to improve police-community relations.[15]

In many ways, the Internet most closely approximates the marketplace of ideas mentioned in this chapter's introduction. There is an unparalleled amount of information and commentary available on any one news site, let alone on one of the aggregator sites.

---

15 "2013 Social Media Survey Results," International Association of Chiefs of Police, www.berkeleyside.com/wp-content/uploads/2014/02/2013SurveyResults.pdf (accessed 9/6/16).

The Internet differs from traditional outlets in another important way: it enables people to get involved directly. Individual citizens now can more easily help create the news and interpret it, as most news sites allow commenting, through which people can offer their own opinions and share links to their own photos, videos, blogs, and social media pages. Individuals at the scene of a natural disaster or key political event can provide more (and sometimes even better) coverage of a story and more quickly than a reporter.

The ability to connect with others through the Internet—through e-mail, blogs, Facebook, Twitter, and other social media venues—makes the new media a two-way street. Traditional media firms can distribute information and citizens can contribute to journalism, and people can also connect with one another directly. The power of the new media is not lost on political organizers and campaigns. Entrepreneurs within social movements and the political parties have sought to organize online advocacy groups to raise money, communicate their positions through e-mail and letter campaigns, and provide support for politicians who accept their views. Consider MoveOn.org, founded by two liberal Silicon Valley entrepreneurs. MoveOn seeks to build electronic advocacy groups, allowing members to propose issues and strategies and then acting on behalf of those that appear to have the greatest member support. Reflecting the importance of the Internet, President Obama's Press Office developed White House Live, a service that streamed video of events live and kept an archive of past events. A typical day may have covered the president touring a natural disaster, holding a press conference, or meeting with other world leaders. The Internet was the medium of choice during the 2012 and 2016 presidential campaigns. In 2016, Hillary Clinton kicked off her presidential campaign with a YouTube video. Both she and Donald Trump made particular use of Twitter, with their campaigns often tweeting multiple times a day.

Regulation of the Broadcast and Electronic Media

In most countries, the government controls media content and owns the largest media outlets. In the United States, the government neither owns nor controls the communications networks, but it does regulate content and ownership of the broadcast media.

The print media in the United States are essentially free from government interference. The broadcast media, in contrast, are subject to federal regulation. American radio and television are regulated by the FCC, an independent agency. Radio and TV stations must renew their FCC licenses every five years. Licensing provides a mechanism for allocating radio and TV frequencies in such a way as to prevent broadcasts from interfering with one another. License renewal requests are now filed online.

Through regulations prohibiting obscenity, indecency, and profanity, the FCC has sought to prohibit radio and television stations from airing explicit sexual and excretory references between 6 A.M. and 10 P.M., the hours when children are most likely to be in the audience, though it has enforced these rules haphazardly.

For more than 60 years, the FCC also sought to regulate and promote competition in the broadcast industry, but in 1996 Congress passed the Telecommunications Act, a broad effort to eliminate most regulations in effect since 1934. The act loosened restrictions on media ownership and allowed for telephone companies, cable television providers, and broadcasters to compete for the provision of telecommunication services. Following the passage of the act, several mergers between telephone and cable companies and between different segments of the entertainment media produced an even greater concentration of media ownership.

The Telecommunications Act of 1996 also attempted to regulate the content of material transmitted via the Internet. This law, known as the Communications Decency Act, made it illegal to make "indecent" sexual material on the Internet accessible to anyone under age 18. The act was immediately denounced by civil libertarians and brought to court as an infringement of free speech. In 1997, the U.S. Supreme Court ruled that the act was an unconstitutional infringement of the First Amendment's guarantee of freedom of speech.

Although the government's ability to regulate content of the electronic media on the Internet has been questioned, the federal government has used its licensing power to impose several regulations that can affect the political content of radio and TV broadcasts. The first is the **equal time rule**, under which broadcasters must provide candidates for the same political office equal opportunities to communicate their messages to the public. If, for example, a television station sells commercial time to a state's Republican gubernatorial candidate, it may not refuse to sell time to the Democratic candidate for the same position.

The second regulation affecting broadcast content is the **right of rebuttal**, which requires that individuals be allowed to respond to personal attacks. In the 1969 case of *Red Lion Broadcasting Company v. Federal Communications Commission*, for example, the U.S. Supreme Court upheld the FCC's determination that a radio station was required to provide a liberal author with an opportunity to respond to an attack by a conservative commentator that the station had aired.[16]

For many years, a third important federal regulation was the **fairness doctrine**, under which broadcasters airing programs on controversial issues were required to provide air time for opposing views. In 1985, the FCC stopped enforcing the fairness doctrine on the grounds that there were so many radio and television stations—to say nothing of newspapers and newsmagazines— that in all likelihood many different viewpoints were being presented even without the requirement that each station present all sides of an argument. Critics of this FCC decision charge that in many media markets the number of competing viewpoints is small. Nevertheless, a congressional effort to require the FCC to enforce the fairness doctrine was blocked by President Ronald Reagan's administration in 1987, and the doctrine died.

equal time rule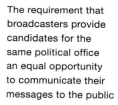

The requirement that broadcasters provide candidates for the same political office an equal opportunity to communicate their messages to the public

right of rebuttal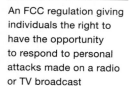

An FCC regulation giving individuals the right to have the opportunity to respond to personal attacks made on a radio or TV broadcast

fairness doctrine

1 FCC requirement that
dcasters that air
isms on controversial
opprovide time for
iews

---

16 *Red Lion Broadcasting Company v. Federal Communications Commission,* 395 U.S. 367 (1969).

The emergence of the Internet has presented two substantial regulatory challenges: (1) protecting intellectual property and (2) setting standards to create a rational system of domains and websites. The first issue concerned whether the Internet could function as a profitable means of distributing content. In *A&M Records v. Napster*, the Ninth Circuit court sided with record companies against firms that offered free Internet distribution of copyrighted content.[17] The second sort of challenge is how to organize and govern the Internet. In the 1990s, the British computer scientist Tim Berners-Lee organized researchers, firms, and government agencies involved in the development of the Internet in the international World Wide Web Consortium.[18] The consortium is a form of self-regulation by corporations and organizations that has led to the development of new concepts of intellectual property and communication wholly different from traditional print and broadcast media. The consortium's philosophy calls for much less government regulation and a much more communal flavor than the notion of competitive markets that underlies America's conception of print media. Reflecting this communal flavor, the World Wide Web Consortium alone does not run the Internet; rather, the governance of the Internet is distributed among a variety of organizations (see the Policy Principle section on p. 592).

Freedom of the Press

Unlike broadcast media, print media are not subject to federal regulation. Indeed, the great principle underlying the federal government's relationship with the press is the doctrine against **prior restraint**. Beginning with the landmark 1931 case of *Near v. Minnesota*, the U.S. Supreme Court has held that, except under the most extraordinary circumstances, the First Amendment prohibits government agencies from seeking to prevent newspapers or magazines from publishing whatever they wish.[19] Indeed, in the 1971 case of *New York Times v. United States*, the so-called Pentagon Papers case, the Supreme Court ruled that the government could not even block publication of secret Defense Department documents furnished to the *New York Times* by an opponent of the Vietnam War who had obtained the documents illegally.[20] In 1990, however, the Supreme Court upheld a lower-court order restraining CNN from broadcasting tapes of conversations between the former Panamanian leader Manuel Noriega and his lawyer, supposedly recorded by the U.S. government. The Court held that CNN could be restrained from broadcasting the tapes until the trial court in the Noriega case had heard them and decided whether their broadcast would violate Noriega's right to a fair trial. This case would seem to weaken the no-prior-restraint doctrine. But in later decisions,

 prior restraint

An effort by a government agency to block the publication of material it deems libelous or harmful in some other way: censorship. In the United States, the courts forbid prior restraint except under the most extraordinary circumstances

---

17   *A&M Records v. Napster*, 239 F.3d 104 (9th Circuit 2001).

18   Tim Berners-Lee with Mark Fischetti, *Weaving the Web: The Original Design and Ultimate Destiny of the World Wide Web by Its Inventor* (New York: HarperBusiness, 1999).

19   *Near v. Minnesota ex rel.*, 283 U.S. 697 (1931).

20   *New York Times v. United States*, 403 U.S. 713 (1971).

Who Runs the Internet?

As we saw in Chapter 1, individual self-interest can sometimes have damaging collective consequences for a community. This idea is known as the "tragedy of the commons," which posits that unregulated use of a shared resource, such as land, inevitably results in negative consequences for the common good—leading, in the classic example, to overgrazing and the demise of everyone's cattle. The tragedy of the commons is often cited as a rationale for government action. In some realms, however, relatively unregulated private activity can produce positive results for everyone. One such realm is the Internet. The Internet is unlike traditional media, such as television networks or newspapers. While television networks and newspapers are owned and run by corporations, no single company, organization, or government runs or owns the Internet. Instead, the Internet is a network of many independent networks throughout the world that are voluntarily linked together.

The U.S. government and European Commission created the networks that became the Internet. Perhaps the most important part of these was the ARPAnet, a system developed as early as the 1960s that allowed researchers for the Defense Department to communicate remotely about collaborative research. Access to ARPAnet was expanded to include other government agencies, and by the late 1980s, the commercial value of such networked communications had become increasingly obvious. At that time, Tim Berners-Lee, a researcher in the United Kingdom, developed protocols to link hypertexts, and the modern Internet was born. Making the network function, however, requires a fair amount of coordination among those who develop the computer architecture for the various networks.

The governance of the Internet is dispersed among many different voluntary organizations. The World Wide Web Consortium, for example, is a forum where corporations and individuals discuss the issues facing the system and negotiate appropriate standards for Web technologies. The Internet Society, whose mission is "to promote the open development, evolution, and use of the Internet for the benefit of all people throughout the world," is an international nonprofit organization with approximately 145 organizational and 65,000 individual members, half of whom are from the United States and half from other countries.[1]

These and similar organizations have shaped the way that the Internet has developed. The members of these organizations negotiate over the standards and other rules for the development of web technologies, including the configuration of software and hardware and website naming and numbering. These organizations also develop policies and try to influence government policies that affect the Internet, such as laws governing intellectual property and privacy.

Some critics have charged that an Internet tragedy of the commons is inevitable and point to the need for government regulation to protect such matters as users' privacy, to guard against cyber bullying, and to punish the authors of computer viruses and other malware. In the meantime, however, the wide-open Internet seems to be a boon for businesses and individuals.

---

1 Internet Society, "Who We Are," www.internetsociety.org/who-we-are (accessed 7/01/16).

the Supreme Court ruled that cable television systems were entitled to essentially the same First Amendment protections as the print media.[21]

Even though newspapers may not be restrained from publishing whatever they want, they may be subject to sanctions after the fact. Historically, newspapers have been subject to the law of libel, which provides that newspapers that print false and malicious stories can be compelled to pay damages to those they defame. Over time, however, American courts have greatly narrowed the meaning of libel and made it extremely difficult, particularly for public figures, to win a libel case against a newspaper. The most important case is the 1964 case of *New York Times v. Sullivan*, in which the Supreme Court held that to be deemed libelous, a story about a public official not only had to be untrue but also had to result from "actual malice" or "reckless disregard" for the truth.[22] In other words, the newspaper had to deliberately print false and malicious material. In practice, it is nearly impossible to prove this. Libel suits against CBS News by General William Westmoreland and against *Time* magazine by Ariel Sharon of Israel, both financed by conservative legal foundations that hoped to embarrass the media, were defeated because they failed to show actual malice. In the 1991 case of *Masson v. New Yorker Magazine*, this tradition was again affirmed by the Court's opinion that fabricated quotations attributed to a public figure were libelous only if the fabricated account "materially changed" the meaning of what the person said.[23] Essentially, the print media can publish almost anything they want about a public figure.

Organization and Ownership of the Media

The scope of the media industry in the United States is impressive: more than 2,000 television stations, approximately 1,400 daily newspapers, and more than 13,000 radio stations. There are 20 major television networks, as well as an extensive system of public television and radio stations.

The media environment since the 1980s has opened considerably, and wholly new networks devoted to news have emerged. CNN became a major news source in the late 1980s and gained a substantial market share during the first Gulf War in 1991, sometimes even providing live coverage of American bombing raids on Baghdad after the major networks' correspondents had fled to bomb shelters. In the 2000s, a competitor emerged: Fox News. By 2003, Fox had displaced CNN as the nation's primary cable news source, and by 2014 Fox News was the second highest rated weekday primetime cable channel, trailing only ESPN.[24] Throughout 2016, Fox News averaged 2.3 million viewers nightly in primetime.

21 *Cable News Network v. Noriega*, 498 U.S. 976 (1990); and *Turner Broadcasting v. Federal Communications Commission*, 512 U.S. 622 (1994).

22 *New York Times v. Sullivan*, 376 U.S. 254 (1964).

23 *Masson v. New Yorker Magazine, Inc.*, 501 U.S. 496 (1991).

24 Matt Wilstein, "2014 Cable News Ratings: CNN Beats MSNBC in Primetime Demo, Fox Still #1," Mediaite, December 30, 2014, www.mediaite.com/tv/2014-cable-news-ratings-cnn-beats-msnbc-in-primetime-demo-fox-still-1 (accessed 7/01/16).

By contrast, CNN had roughly half that audience (1.2 million) and MSNBC less than half as many viewers (970,000).[25] The rise of Fox News has had important political implications because its coverage and commentators are considerably more conservative than CNN's. Fox News also demonstrates the importance of having more and varied news sources. When there are few sources, each is likely to appeal to the same broad national audience and to maintain a middle-of-the-road stance. When there are more sources, each is likely to position itself within an ideological or partisan niche, increasing the diversity of viewpoints presented.

News Concentration. Nonetheless, there is a real concern that these trends mask considerable concentration in the industry. The problem is most evident in the wire services, which provide a steady stream of stories and images. There is just one American wire service, the Associated Press (AP). In Europe, Reuters has the dominant market position similar to AP. It is interesting that CNN may make a run at offering its own competing service, especially for graphics and images.

Concentration of ownership of media outlets raises further concerns about the robustness of the marketplace of ideas. The 1996 Telecommunications Act opened the way for additional consolidation in the industry, and a wave of mergers and consolidations has further reduced the field of independent media nationwide. Since that time, among the major news networks ABC was bought by the Walt Disney Company; CNN was bought by Time Warner; and NBC, which General Electric owned from 1986 until 2011, is now owned by Comcast. The Australian press baron Rupert Murdoch owns Fox plus a host of radio, television, and newspaper properties around the world. CBS remains a holding of the CBS Corporation. As a result of these consolidations, a relatively small number of giant corporations now control a wide swath of media holdings, including television networks, movie studios, record companies, cable channels and local cable providers, book publishers, magazines, and newspapers. This development has prompted questions about whether enough competition exists among the media to produce a diverse set of views or whether the United States has become the prisoner of media monopolies (Figure 14.2).[26]

In 2003, the FCC announced new rules that seemed to pave the way for even more concentration in the media industry. The rules mandated that the major networks could own television stations that collectively reached 45 percent of all viewers, up from 35 percent under the old rules. The new rules also permitted a single company to own the leading newspaper, as well as multiple television and radio outlets, in a single market. Major media companies, which had long lobbied for the right to expand their activities, welcomed the new rules. Critics, however, expressed concern that a narrower range of views and issues presented to the public would result. Following disagreement within Congress and a threatened

---

25 Anousha Sakoui, "At Fox News, Election Year's Big Ratings Mask Many Wrinkles," *Bloomberg Technology*, August 24, 2016, www.bloomberg.com/news/articles/2016-08-24/at-fox-news-election-year-s-big-ratings-mask-lots-of-wrinkles (accessed 9/6/16).

26 For a criticism of the increasing consolidation of the media, see the essays in Erik Barnouw, *Conglomerates and the Media* (New York: New Press, 1997).

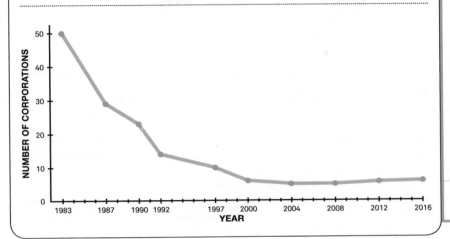

Figure 14.2

NUMBER OF CORPORATIONS THAT CONTROL THE MAJORITY OF U.S. MEDIA

ANALYZING THE EVIDENCE

After several years of mergers and acquisitions, a small number of corporations have come to dominate the print, broadcast, cable, and Internet industries. What factors precipitated this media consolidation? What effects, if any, does media consolidation have on news reporting?

NOTE: Included are newspapers, magazines, TV and radio stations, books, music, movies, videos, wire services, and photo agencies.

SOURCE: Media Reform Information Center, www.corporations.org/media; *Business Insider*, www.businessinsider.com/these-6-corporations-control-90-of-the-media-in-america-2012-6 (accessed 6/6/13); and *New York Times*, www.nytimes.com/2014/07/26/business/a-21stcentury-fox-timewarner-mergerwould-narrowalready-dwindlingcompetition.html?_r=0" (accessed 6/9/15).

presidential veto, a federal appeals court placed the new regulations on hold, and in 2007 the FCC debuted new rules to comply with the court's ruling. In 2012, a proposal to streamline the cross-ownership rules was introduced for the third time in a decade. The cross-ownership rule, however, might outlive the printed newspaper itself. The fight over the cross-ownership rule shows the power of institutions and regulations even when it comes to the flow of information in our democracy.

Distribution of news over the Internet goes against the trend of increased concentration of media ownership. From the audience's perspective, increased concentration will lead to less variety in the news and fewer voices heard. The Internet has made people less dependent on a single local newspaper to get information, however. Using websites that aggregate news from many sources, consumers can readily get many views on the same event. And people can easily search official websites to find out local information, such as meeting times of city councils and school committees.

One important question is whether increased concentration of Internet news distribution will occur as well. Google, the dominant search firm, has the power to block certain sites and thereby censor the news. This problem arose recently in China, where the government forced Google China, a subsidiary of Google, to censor many websites, especially those of dissidents. In order to maintain access to the enormous China market, Google complied, effectively blocking non-Chinese media from those users and conversely blocking Chinese media websites from others, including users in the United States. Eventually, Google directed traffic to those websites through its Hong Kong subsidiary; China eventually shutdown gmail service in the country, but the tense back-and-forth over access to the web and to the Chinese market continue between Google and the Chinese government.[27] Google was sufficiently powerful to negotiate access to censored websites, but it also had the market power to restrict access of U.S. users to China.

WHAT AFFECTS NEWS COVERAGE?

Because of the important role the media can play in national politics, it is essential to understand the factors that affect media coverage.[28] What accounts for the media's agenda of issues and topics? What explains the character of coverage? In other words, why does a politician receive good or bad press? What factors determine the interpretation, or spin, of a particular story? Although many minor factors play a role, there are three major ones: (1) journalists or producers of the news, (2) politicians or other sources of the news, and (3) consumers.

Journalists

The people who produce the news shape its character. Although a strong norm of objectivity pervades the journalism profession, it is impossible to expect that reporters, editors, and media owners will always set aside their personal perspectives, interests, and biases. What motivates those who produce the news, and how do their beliefs and interests shape what we see and hear?

The marketplace of ideas sets out a single objective for owners of media organizations: making a profit. Owners seek to maintain a successful business, and if their personal political beliefs endanger that business, then those beliefs will be pushed aside by the internal organization in the newspaper or broadcasting station. This has not always been the case. At one time, newspaper publishers exercised considerable influence over their papers' news content. Publishers such as William Randolph Hearst and Joseph Pulitzer became political powers through their manipulation of news coverage. Hearst, for example, almost single-handedly pushed the United States into war with Spain in 1898 through his papers' relentless coverage of Spain's alleged brutality in its efforts to suppress a rebellion in

---

27 Aaron Mamiit, "Gmail Service Slowly Recovering: What Really Happened?" *TechTimes*, January 2, 2015, www.techtimes.com/articles/24108/20150102/gmail-service-slowly-recovering-in-china-what-really-happened.htm (accessed 7/01/16).

28 See the discussions in Michael Parenti, *Inventing Reality: The Politics of the Mass Media* (New York: St. Martin's Press, 1986); Herbert Gans, *Deciding What's News: A Study of CBS Evening News, NBC Nightly News, Newsweek, and Time* (New York: Vintage, 1980); and W. Lance Bennett, *News: The Politics of Illusion*, 5th ed. (New York: Longman, 2002).

Cuba, then a Spanish colony. The sinking of the American battleship *Maine* in Havana Harbor under mysterious circumstances gave Hearst the ammunition he needed to force a reluctant President William McKinley to lead the nation into war. Today, few publishers have that kind of power. The business end dominates the papers' editorial content, although a few continue to impose their interests on the news.

Individual reporters and editors have far more influence today over what is presented in the news. They also pursue their own interests and professional objectives, including considerations of ratings, career success and professional prestige, and political influence. For all these reasons, journalists seek not only to report the news but also to interpret it. Their goals definitely influence what is created and reported as news.

Those who cover the news for national media generally have considerable discretion to interpret stories and, as a result, have an opportunity to interject their own views. For example, some reporters' personal friendship with and respect for Franklin Delano Roosevelt and John F. Kennedy helped generate favorable news coverage for those presidents. In contrast, many reporters' disdain for Ronald Reagan was evident in stories suggesting that he was often asleep or inattentive when important decisions were made.

Do Journalists Bias the News? From the perspective of the marketplace of ideas, perhaps most troubling is the possibility that journalism is biased heavily in favor of one party or one set of ideals. Surveys of reporters and editors at major media outlets have repeatedly found that those who produce the news are overwhelmingly liberal and Democratic. And surveys have found repeatedly that Democrats and liberals outnumber Republicans and conservatives by about two to one among journalists. One survey found that 28 percent of journalists (across all media) identify as Democrats, 7 percent identify as Republicans, and 50 percent say that they do not identify with any party. The remaining 15 percent identify with another party.[29]

Do journalists' political orientations color the news? A classic study by CBS and the *New York Times* in the 1980s suggested little evidence of political favoritism or bias.[30] Subsequent studies by the Pew Project for Excellence in Journalism echo that conclusion. Comparing press coverage of the first 100 days of the administrations of presidents Bill Clinton and George W. Bush, the Pew Project found nearly identical patterns of coverage: about half of printed stories were neutral toward the new presidents; a quarter were positive and a quarter negative. It is interesting that Barack Obama received a much different welcome from the press. Using the same methodology, the Pew Project found that Obama's coverage was considerably more positive. He received

---

29 Lars Willat and David H. Weaver, "The American Journalist in the Digital Age: Key Findings," Indiana School of Journalism, 2014, http://news.indiana.edu/releases/iu/2014/05/2013-american-journalist-key-findings.pdf (accessed 7/01/16).

30 Michael J. Robinson and Margaret A. Sheehan, *Over the Wire and on TV: CBS and UPI in Campaign '80* (New York: Russell Sage Foundation, 1983).

positive coverage in 42 percent of stories, neutral coverage in 38 percent of stories, and negative coverage in 20 percent of stories.[31] In the 2016 primary elections, many commentators pointed to the apparent biases favoring Donald Trump over other candidates. An analysis of news coverage of the candidates found that Trump received considerably more coverage than other Republican candidates, while Democratic candidates Hillary Clinton and Bernie Sanders received roughly the same amount of coverage. In the initial contests, Trump received 37 percent of coverage of the Republican primary, compared with Ted Cruz receiving 28 percent and Marco Rubio 25 percent. By Super Tuesday in March, coverage had shifted even further in Trump's favor. He was covered by 44 percent of stories, while Cruz and Rubio each received 22 percent of the coverage—half as much as Trump. In the Democratic contests, by comparison, Clinton received 54 percent of the coverage and Sanders 46 percent. The tone of the media coverage also reflected biases and shifting narratives within the media. Throughout the campaign, news stories about Clinton were equally positive and negative. Sanders, on the other hand, received very positive coverage through Super Tuesday, but afterwards the media seemed to turn against his candidacy, and more than 60 percent of the news about him became negative. On the Republican side, the news coverage was more negative than positive, and it was especially negative toward Rubio, Cruz, and Kasich.[32]

More subtle biases do exist, usually arising from the nature of the language used. A 2005 study found that reporters use ideologically loaded terms when referring to some politicians but not others. Press reports typically mention both parties in a story, but they do so with no small degree of editorializing, using words like *radical* or *extreme conservative* to describe one politician or another. Analysis of such language revealed that most major media outlets slanted their reporting to the left, with three important exceptions. The *Wall Street Journal* and Fox News leaned to the right. Only PBS—the publicly owned and licensed network—presented balanced reporting of politics, government, and current events.[33]

Editorial endorsements of papers offer further evidence of news organizations' political leanings. *Editor and Publisher*, a trade journal of the media business, tracks endorsements of newspapers across the United States. Before the 1960s, the editorial endorsements and political leanings of the editors of most newspapers were overwhelmingly Republican. Since the 1960s, however, newspaper endorsements for president, the U.S. Senate, the U.S. House, and

31 Pew Research Center's Project for Excellence in Journalism, "Obama's First 100 Days: How the President Fared in the Press vs. Clinton and Bush," April 28, 2009, http://journalism.org/files/100%20DAYS.pdf (accessed 5/7/09).

32 Thomas E. Patterson, "News Coverage of the 2016 Presidential Primaries: Horse Race reporting Has Consequences," Shorenstein Center on Media, Politics, and Public Policy, Harvard Kennedy School, July 11, 2016, www.shorensteincenter.org/news-coverage-2016-presidential-primaries/ (accessed 9/6/16).

33 Timothy Groseclose and Tom Milyo, "A Measure of Media Bias," *Quarterly Journal of Economics* 120 (2005): 1191–37.

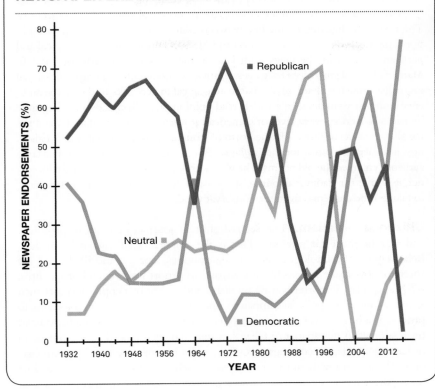

Figure 14.3
NEWSPAPER ENDORSEMENTS

NEWSPAPER ENDORSEMENTS (%)

■ Republican

Neutral ■

■ Democratic

YEAR

SOURCES: Harold W. Stanley and Richard G. Niemi, *Vital Statistics on American Politics, 2001–2002* (Washington, DC: CQ Press, 2001), pp. 194–5; 2004, 2008, 2012, and 2016 data from *Editor and Publisher*, www.editorandpuplisher.com.

statewide offices have generally balanced out between Democrats and Republicans. George W. Bush received a solid majority of endorsements in 2000; John Kerry edged Bush out in 2004; in 2008, Barack Obama received nearly 70 percent of the endorsements over John McCain; and in 2012, Mitt Romney just edged out Obama (Figure 14.3). The figures for 2016 were most stunning. Hillary Clinton received 77 percent of major newspaper endorsements, and Donald Trump got just 2 percent, with the remainder going to other candidates. To the extent that there is a partisan bias to editorials and endorsements, it is toward those already in office.[34]

Journalism, as a profession, has attempted to rise above personal motivations and biases. Most reporters adhere to strong norms of fairness and balance,

34 Stephen Ansolabehere, Rebecca Lessem, and James M. Snyder, Jr., "The Orientation of Newspaper Endorsements 1940–2002," *Quarterly Journal of Political Science* 1, no. 4 (October 2006): 393–404, http://dx.doi.org/10.1561/100.00000009 (accessed 5/8/09).

attempting to give the perspectives of all sides of a controversy. Even coverage of popular presidents still attempts to maintain balance. But the important ethos of objectivity and fairness appears to be changing.

Two shifts in journalism are eroding the professional standards of objectivity. The first is the blurring of the line between editorializing and reporting in traditional media. For example, Fox News and MSNBC present more ideological and partisan versions of the news, with Fox on the right and MSNBC on the left. Many traditional journalists have been tempted to follow suit. Among professional journalists, much is made of the battle among cable networks to divide the audience along partisan lines. In a widely read opinion piece, Tom Edsall, a long-time journalist covering every level of American government, wrote that it was time for all journalists to throw off the norm of nonpartisanship and fairness.[35] Edsall, now a regular columnist for the *Huffington Post*, argues that Fox News and its large audience changed the old norms. The gloves are off, and at least from Edsall's corner, it is time for traditional journalists, most of whom have a liberal orientation, to take on the challenge from the conservatives directly.

Citizen Journalism. The second shift in journalism is more profound and may be more far reaching. That is the emergence of citizen journalism. Relatively new technologies such as smartphones, laptops, and iPads, and the Internet now make it possible for anyone to report on events. For example, CNN's regular i-Reporter feature publishes video sent by people at events such as natural disasters, political campaigns, and protests and rebellions. Needless to say, this is a huge threat to traditional journalism, which relies on highly trained professionals. A newspaper or television station does not need a large bureau in order to get instant recordings of events, and it is expensive to keep journalists on staff and deploy them to faraway places such as China or Iraq. By the same token, these technologies have allowed journalism to flourish in countries with very little media or tight government controls on television and the press, such as those in central Africa and the Middle East.

The subtle revolution behind citizen journalism comes from the perspective of the reporter, as citizen journalism replaces the "objective reporter" with the "subjective participant." A traditional reporter from the *New York Times*, the AP, or another agency will seek different perspectives on the same event and offer an investigative report that attempts to answer the key questions (also known as the 5 Ws and 1 H) taught on day one of Journalism 101: what, who, when, where, why, and how? Citizen journalists become reporters of an event precisely because they are *in* the event. A protester who sends a video of a violent clash with police in Damascus or Tripoli or London is in the event, as are a legislative staffer who tweets about a committee meeting or a campaign worker who texts about a rally. There is no attempt to rise above and answer the 5 Ws. The texts and videos from citizens' communications are raw and in the moment; they are

---

35 Thomas Edsall, "Journalism Should Own Its Liberalism: And Then Manage It, Challenge It, and Account for It," *Columbia Journalism Review*, October 8, 2009, www.cjr.org/campaign_desk/journalism_should_own_its_libe.php?page=all (accessed 10/4/11).

some of the most compelling journalism today. This sea change in journalism will not replace the old style, which has survived many a technological revolution. Rather, citizen journalism will augment traditional journalism: it gives traditional journalists license to be more subjective.

News Sources

News Leaks. A news leak is the disclosure of confidential information to the news media. Leaks may emanate from a variety of sources, including whistle-blowers, lower-level officials who hope to publicize what they view as their bosses' improper activities. In 1971, for example, a minor Defense Department staffer named Daniel Ellsberg sought to discredit official justifications for America's involvement in Vietnam by leaking top-secret documents to the press. The *New York Times* and the *Washington Post* published these classified documents, the so-called Pentagon Papers, after the U.S. Supreme Court ruled that the government could not block their release. The social media era already has its own version of the Pentagon Papers and Daniel Ellsberg—Wikileaks founder Julian Assange and Edward Snowden. Owing to the nature of the information released and the breadth of government and corporate activities involved, however, the consequences of Wikileaks will likely be more far ranging than the Pentagon Papers. The group has release a number of high-profile confidential reports (usually from governments) that immediately grab headlines. In November 2010, Wikileaks collaborated with the UK newspaper the *Guardian*, the German newsmagazine *Der Spiegel*, and other global news organizations to release classified and highly sensitive U.S. State Department diplomatic cables and other documents related to the wars in Afghanistan and Iraq. In June 2013, Wikileaks had an even more sensational disclosure of classified documents. Edward Snowden, a computer programmer and analyst, was employed as a contractor for the National Security Agency (NSA). Working with several global news organizations, such as the *New York Times*, the *Guardian*, and *Der Spiegel*, he leaked 9,000 to 10,000 documents from the NSA, including revelations that the agency was listening to the phone calls and harvesting the e-mails, texts, and additional communications of other governments and other world leaders, even its allies. Thus Snowden exposed the extent of United States' spying on foreign governments and its till-then classified cyberwarfare program. Snowden fled the United States and, eventually, received asylum in Russia. More recently, during the 2016 presidential campaign, Wikileaks released thousands of hacked e-mails from Democratic candidate Hillary Clinton's campaign.

Most leaks, though, originate with senior government officials and prominent politicians and activists. Such individuals often cultivate long-term relationships with journalists, to whom they regularly leak confidential information, knowing that it will likely be published on a priority basis in a form acceptable to them. Their confidence is based on the fact that journalists generally regard high-level sources of confidential information as valuable assets whose favor must be retained. And the more recipients of leaked information strive to keep their sources secret, the more difficulty other journalists will have in checking the information's validity.

Through such tacit alliances with journalists, prominent figures can manipulate news coverage to serve their purposes. The Valerie Plame affair, which was ultimately the undoing of Scooter Libby, exposed the complexities of the culture of leaks in Washington, D.C. Plame was an undercover CIA analyst married to Joseph Wilson, a prominent career diplomat. Wilson had angered the Bush White House by criticizing the president's policies in Iraq. In an apparent effort to discredit Wilson, one or more administration officials informed prominent journalists that Plame had improperly used her position to help Wilson. In so doing, these officials may have violated a federal statute prohibiting the disclosure of the identities of covert intelligence operatives. The subsequent investigation revealed that the story had been leaked to several journalists, including the *Washington Post*'s Bob Woodward, who did not use it, and the *New York Times*'s Judith Miller, who did. Miller spent several months in jail for contempt of court after initially refusing to testify before a federal grand jury investigating the leak. After Miller finally testified, Libby was convicted of lying and obstruction for his role in the affair, although it later emerged that the information was actually leaked by a former State Department official. The leak in the Plame case came to light only because it might have been illegal. Thousands of other leaks each year are seamlessly incorporated into the news.

The Press Release. Also seamlessly incorporated into daily news reports each year are thousands of press releases. The press release is a story written by an advocate or publicist and distributed to the media in the hope that journalists will publish it under their own bylines with little or no revision. The inventor of the press release was a New York public relations consultant named Ivy Lee. In 1906, a train operated by one of Lee's clients, the Pennsylvania Railroad, was involved in a serious wreck. Lee wrote a story about the accident presenting the railroad in a favorable light and distributed the account to reporters. Many papers published Lee's slanted story as their own objective account of events, and the railroad's reputation for safety remained intact.

Consistent with Lee's example, today's press release presents facts and perspectives that serve an advocate's interests but is written in a way that mimics the factual news style of the paper, periodical, or television news program to which it has been sent. It is quite difficult for the audience to distinguish a well-designed press release from a news story. According to some experts, more than 50 percent of the articles in a newspaper on any given day are based on press releases. Indeed, more than 75 percent of journalists responding to a survey acknowledged using press releases for their stories.[36]

Journalists are certainly aware that the authors of press releases have their own agendas and are hardly unbiased reporters of the news. Nevertheless, the

---

36 Dennis L. Wilcox and Glen T. Cameron, *Public Relations: Strategy and Tactics*, 8th ed. (Boston: Allyn & Bacon, 2006), p. 357. See also Justin Grimmer, *Representational Style in Congress* (New York: Cambridge University Press, 2013), Chapter 8.

economics of publishing and broadcasting dictate that large numbers of stories will always be based on press releases. Newspapers and television stations are businesses, and for many the financial bottom line is more important than journalistic integrity.[37] The use of press releases allows a newspaper or a broadcast network to present more stories without paying more staff or incurring the other costs associated with investigating and writing the news. As one newspaper executive said, the public relations people who generally write news releases are our "unpaid reporters."[38]

Today, the printed press release has been joined by the video news release, designed especially for television stations. The video release is a taped report, usually about 90 seconds long, the typical length of a television news story, designed to look and sound like any other broadcast news segment. In exchange for airing material that serves the interests of some advocate, the television station is relieved of the considerable expense and bother of identifying and filming its own news story. The audience is usually unaware that the "news" it is watching is someone's canned publicity footage.

Hiring Reporters. From creating phony reporters to reading make-believe news stories, it is but a small step to hiring real reporters to present sham accounts. A number of cases have come to light in which the government or a private concern has paid journalists to write favorable accounts of its activities. In 2005, for example, the U.S. military acknowledged that contractors in its employ had regularly paid Iraqi newspapers to carry positive news about American efforts in that nation. The Washington-based Lincoln Group, a public-relations firm working under contract for the federal government, said it had placed more than 1,000 news stories in the Arab press since 2001.[39] Iraqis reading the articles would have had no way of knowing that the material was produced at the behest of American authorities.

As local newspaper budgets have shrunk, some local governments have hired reporters or paid newspapers for reporters to cover local government. The Metropolitan Government of Portland, Oregon, hires a local reporter to cover goings-on such as council meetings, events, and changes in policies and laws. The Los Angeles Kings hockey franchise, a Los Angeles County Supervisor, and a California trial lawyers group all hire journalists to follow their activities. The list goes on.

One group especially noted for paying writers and reporters for favorable coverage is the pharmaceutical industry. Indeed, many articles in popular—and even scientific—journals reporting favorably on particular drugs are written by the drug companies themselves. In some cases, the writers are actually paid by the drug companies; in other instances, the writer cited in the story's byline is

---

37 See, for example, Davis Merritt, *Knightfall: Knight Ridder and How the Erosion of Newspaper Journalism Is Putting Democracy at Risk* (New York: Amacom Books, 2005).

38 Quoted in Wilcox and Cameron, *Public Relations*, p. 357.

39 Jeff Gerth, "Military's Information War Is Vast and Often Secretive," *New York Times*, December 11, 2005, p. 1.

not the actual author. Often a ghostwriter employed by a drug company writes the story while the nominal author is paid for the use of his name.[40]

All these practices—hiring of reporters, press leaks, and planted news stories—offend our sensibilities about the news because we expect objectivity from reporters. They are our main source of information, and fair and balanced reporting helps us sort out complex issues. The media also play an important watchdog role, making noise when something is amiss. That becomes increasingly difficult if the main revenues for the news come from the firm or government agency being covered. Of course, although politicians try to use the media for their purposes, reporters often have their own agenda. Often enough, hostile or merely determined journalists will break through the smoke screens thrown up by the politicians and report annoying truths.

Consumers

The print and broadcast media are businesses that, in general, seek to show a profit. Thus, like any other business, they must cater to the preferences of consumers. Doing so has important consequences for the content and character of the news media. The long-term success of the media as a political institution depends on their ability to find a sizable audience.

Catering to the Upscale Audience.
Especially in the political realm, the print and broadcast media and the publishing industry not only are responsive to consumers' interests generally but also are particularly responsive to the interests of the audience's better-educated and more affluent segments. The preferences of these segments have a profound effect on the content and orientation of the press, radio and television programming, and books, especially in areas of news and public affairs.[41]

Affluent and well-educated consumers are the core audience of news magazines, journals of opinion, books dealing with public affairs, serious newspapers such as the *New York Times* and the *Washington Post*, broadcast news, and evening and weekend public affairs programming. Of course, other segments of the public also read newspapers and watch television news. Overall, however, level of interest in "hard news" (world events, national political issues, and the like) is closely related to level of education (Table 14.1). As a result, upscale Americans are overrepresented in the news and public affairs audience. The concentration of these strata in the audience makes news, politics, and public affairs potentially very attractive topics to advertisers, publishers, radio broadcasters, and television executives.

---

40 Anna Wilde Matthews, "At Medical Journals, Writers Paid by Industry Play Big Role," *Wall Street Journal*, December 13, 2005, p. 1.

41 See Tom Burnes, "The Organization of Public Opinion," in *Mass Communication and Society*, James Curran, Michael Gurevitch, and Janet Woollacott, eds. (Beverly Hills, CA: Sage, 1979), pp. 44–230. See also David L. Altheide, *Creating Reality: How TV News Distorts Events* (Beverly Hills, CA: Sage, 1976).

Table 14.1

EDUCATION AND ATTENTION TO THE NEWS

LEVEL OF EDUCATION	% WHO GOT NEWS ON A DAILY BASIS OR SEVERAL TIMES A WEEK	% WHO WATCHED, READ, OR HEARD IN-DEPTH STORIES IN PAST WEEK
College or graduate school	95	57
High school or some college	88	36
Not a high school graduate	83	20

SOURCE: "The Personal News Cycle: How Americans choose to get their news," American Press Institute, March 17, 2014, www.americanpressinstitute.org/publications/reports/survey-research/personal-news-cycle/single-page/ (accessed 9/6/16).

As a result, entire categories of events, issues, and phenomena of interest to lower-, middle-, and working-class Americans receive scant attention from the national print and broadcast media. For example, trade union news and events are discussed only in the context of major strikes or revelations of corruption. No network or national periodical routinely covers labor organizations. Religious and church affairs receive little coverage unless scandal is involved. The activities of veterans', fraternal, ethnic, and patriotic organizations are also generally ignored.

The rise of new media sources has not altered this picture. For example, a study by Markus Prior of the rise of cable television shows that the restructuring from three networks to a vast range of cable venues during the 1980s and 1990s actually increased the knowledge gap among different groups in the electorate. Further, Gary Jacobson's research found that viewers of different cable news channels (such as, Fox News, MSNBC, and CNN) held widely varying beliefs about basic facts concerning public affairs. Jacobson's research contrasts sharply with research from the 1970s on CBS, NBC, and ABC, which found that the three main networks tended to present the news from similar perspectives. The three networks generally provided the same information in the same way as one another and as print media.[42]

---

42 Markus Prior, *Post-Broadcast Democracy: How Media Choice Increases Inequality in Political Involvement and Polarizes Elections*, New York: Cambridge University Press. 2007; and Gary C. Jacobson, "How the Economy and Partisanship Shaped the 2012 Presidential and Congressional Elections," *Political Science Quarterly*, 128, no. 1 (spring 2013). On TV and newspaper reporting in the 1970s, see Michael J. Robinson and Margaret A. Sheehan, *Over the Wire and on TV* (New York: Russell Sage Foundation, 1983).

The Media and Conflict. Although the media respond most to the upscale audience, groups that cannot afford media consultants and issues managers can publicize their interests through protest. Frequently, the media are accused of encouraging conflict in response to the fact that their audiences mostly watch news for the entertainment value that conflict can provide. Clearly, conflict can be an important vehicle for drawing media attention to groups that lack the financial or organizational resources to broadcast their views. However, conflict and protest ultimately do not allow groups low on the social ladder to compete effectively in the media.

The chief problem with protest as a media technique is that, in general, the media have considerable discretion in reporting and interpreting the events they cover. For example, should the media focus on the conflict itself or on the issues that the conflict addresses? The answer is typically determined by the media, not by the protesters. Therefore, media interpretation of protest activities is more a reflection of the views of groups to which the media are responsive—usually segments of the upper middle class—than it is a function of the wishes of the protesters themselves. It is worth noting that civil rights protesters in the 1960s received their most favorable media coverage when a segment of the white upper middle class saw blacks as potential political allies in the Democratic Party.

Typically, upper-middle-class protesters—student demonstrators and the like—have little difficulty securing favorable publicity for their causes, being more skilled than their lower-class counterparts in the techniques of media manipulation. That is, they usually have a better sense—often as a result of formal courses on the subject—of how to package messages for media consumption. For example, it is important to know what time of day a protest should occur if it is to be carried on the evening news. Similarly, the definition of issues, the character of the rhetoric used, and so on all help determine whether a protest will receive favorable coverage, unfavorable coverage, or none at all. Moreover, upper-middle-class protesters can often produce their own coverage through "underground" newspapers, college papers, student radio and television stations, and the Internet. The same resources and skills that generally allow upper-middle-class people to publicize their ideas are usually not left behind when segments of this class engage in disruptive political action.

CONCLUSION: MEDIA POWER AND RESPONSIBILITY

The content and character of news and public affairs programming—what the media choose to present and how they present it—can have far-reaching political consequences. Media disclosures can greatly enhance or fatally damage the careers of public officials. Media coverage can rally support for or intensify opposition to national policies. The media choose what issues to cover and how and, as discussed in Chapter 10, set the national political agenda and frame political discourse.

The media have been central in shaping some of the most significant events in recent American political history. News media were critically important in the civil rights movement of the 1950s and 1960s, as television footage and photographs of marchers attacked by club-swinging police galvanized public support among northern whites and greatly increased pressure on Congress to end segregation.[43] The media were also central in the Watergate affair, which ultimately forced President Richard Nixon to resign in disgrace after investigations by the *Washington Post*, the *New York Times*, and the television networks led to the disclosure of abuses of power by those in the White House.[44]

Mass media have been central to every election of the past century. They cover the emergence and activities of the candidates, political debates and conventions, and election-night returns. They are vehicles for political advertising. They even generate their own campaign news, especially by conducting public-opinion polls and reporting who is ahead and who is behind, who is gaining momentum and who is fading.

And the media go to war along with the U.S. military. Since the time of the Civil War, news reporting and photography have brought wars home. Graphic depictions of atrocities in Vietnam and of American war dead and wounded helped turn popular sentiment against that war, which compelled the government to negotiate an end to the conflict.[45] Video of precision bombs destroying targets in Baghdad and of the rout of Saddam Hussein's army in 1991 pushed up President George H. W. Bush's popularity and solidified his reputation as commander in chief.[46] News coverage of the Iraq War in 2003 portrayed the toppling of Hussein's statue in Baghdad, and President George W. Bush's announcement of "Mission Accomplished" at the end of combat in 2003, would later be used against the president as the military struggled to restore stability in Iraq.

The tremendous power that reporters and editors sometimes wield emanates from the free hand that the press enjoys in American politics. As long as they do not overstep the bounds of libel, journalists can criticize the government openly. Given the diversity of media outlets today, it is not uncommon to find defenders and critics of government or of particular political decisions, and often those on either side of the debate argue their positions side by side. The new media has brought more voices to the fore and a broader potential debate over public policy. Wide-open debate and criticism of public officials is essential, but it sometimes exacts a social cost.

---

43 David J. Garrow, *Protest at Selma: Martin Luther King, Jr., and the Voting Rights Act of 1965* (New Haven, CT: Yale University Press, 1978).

44 Todd Gitlin, *The Whole World Is Watching: Mass Media in the Making and Unmaking of the New Left* (Berkeley: University of California Press, 2003).

45 William M. Hammond, *Reporting Vietnam: Media and Military at War* (Lawrence: University of Kansas Press, 1998).

46 Jon Krosnik and L. A. Brannon, "The Impact of the Gulf War on the Ingredients of Presidential Evaluations," *American Political Science Review* 87 (1993): 963–75.

Free media are essential to democratic government. We depend on them to investigate wrongdoing, publicize and explain governmental actions, evaluate programs and politicians, and bring to light matters that might otherwise be known only to a handful of government insiders. In short, without free and active media, popular government would be virtually impossible. Citizens would have few means of knowing or assessing the government's actions, other than the pronouncements of the government itself. Moreover, without active—indeed, aggressive—media, citizens would be hard-pressed to make informed choices among competing candidates at the polls. Often enough, the media reveal discrepancies between candidates' claims and their records and between the images that candidates project and the underlying realities.

At the same time, politicians increasingly rely on news coverage, especially favorable coverage. National political leaders and journalists have had symbiotic relationships, at least since Franklin Delano Roosevelt's presidency. Initially, politicians were the senior partners. Thus, for example, reporters did not publicize potentially embarrassing information, widely known in Washington, D.C., about the personal lives of such figures as Roosevelt and John F. Kennedy. Today, the balance has shifted. Often it seems the journalists have the upper hand. Now that individual politicians depend so heavily on media to reach their constituents, journalists no longer need fear that their access to information can be restricted in retaliation for negative coverage. It is not uncommon today to hear the White House press corps challenge the president's press liaison or even the president himself.

Freedom gives the media enormous power. The media can make or break reputations, help launch or destroy political careers, and build support for or rally opposition against programs and institutions.[47] Wherever there is so much power, there exists at least the potential for its abuse. All things considered, free media are so critically important to the maintenance of a democratic society that we may be willing to take the risk that the media will occasionally abuse their power. The forms of government control that would prevent the media from misusing their power would also pose a serious risk to our freedom.

For Further Reading

Arnold, R. Douglas. *Congress, the Press, and Political Accountability*. Princeton, NJ: Princeton University Press, 2004.

Bagdikian, Ben. *The New Media Monopoly*. Boston: Beacon Press, 2004.

Baum, Matthew, A. *Soft News Goes to War: Public Opinion and American Foreign Policy in the New Media Age*. Princeton, NJ: Princeton University Press, 2003.

---

47 See Martin Linsky, *Impact: How the Press Affects Federal Policy Making* (New York: Norton, 1991).

Cook, Timothy. *Governing with the News: The News Media as a Political Institution.* Chicago: University of Chicago Press, 1997.

Groseclose, Timothy, and Jeffrey Milyo. "A Measure of Media Bias." *Quarterly Journal of Economics* 120, no. 4 (November 2005): 1191–1237.

Hamilton, James T. *All the News That's Fit to Sell: How the Market Transforms Information into News.* Princeton, NJ: Princeton University Press, 2003.

Iyengar, Shanto. *Media Politics: A Citizen's Guide.* 2nd ed. New York: Norton, 2011.

Kellner, Douglas. *Media Spectacle and the Crisis of Democracy: Terrorism, War, and Election Battles.* Boulder, CO: Paradigm, 2005.

Merritt, Davis. *Knightfall: Knight Ridder and How the Erosion of Newspaper Journalism Is Putting Democracy at Risk.* New York: Amacom Books, 2005.

Norris, Pippa, Montague Kern, and Marion R. Just, eds. *Framing Terrorism: The News Media, the Government, and the Public.* New York: Routledge, 2003.

Schudson, Michael. "The News Media as Political Institutions." *Annual Review of Political Science* 5 (June 2002): 249–69.

Starr, Paul. *The Creation of the Media.* New York: Basic Books, 2004.

Appendix

Appendix

The Declaration of Independence

In Congress, July 4, 1776

When in the course of human events, it becomes necessary for one people to dissolve the political bands which have connected them with another, and to assume among the Powers of the earth, the separate and equal station to which the Laws of Nature and of Nature's God entitle them, a decent respect to the opinions of mankind requires that they should declare the causes which impel them to the separation.

We hold these truths to be self-evident, that all men are created equal, that they are endowed by their Creator with certain unalienable rights, that among these are Life, Liberty, and the pursuit of Happiness. That to secure these rights, Governments are instituted among Men, deriving their just powers from the consent of the governed. That whenever any Form of Government becomes destructive of these ends, it is the Right of the People to alter or to abolish it, and to institute new Government, laying its foundation on such principles and organizing its powers in such form, as to them shall seem most likely to effect their Safety and Happiness. Prudence, indeed, will dictate that Governments long established should not be changed for light and transient causes; and accordingly all experience hath shown, that mankind are more disposed to suffer, while evils are sufferable, than to right themselves by abolishing the forms to which they are accustomed. But when a long train of abuses and usurpations, pursuing invariably the same Object evinces a design to reduce them under absolute Despotism, it is their right, it is their duty, to throw off such Government, and to provide new Guards for their future security.—Such has been the patient sufferance of these Colonies; and such is now the necessity which constrains them to alter their former Systems of Government. The history of the present King of Great Britain is a history of repeated injuries and usurpations, all having in direct object the establishment of an absolute Tyranny over these States. To prove this, let Facts be submitted to a candid world.

He has refused his Assent to Laws, the most wholesome and necessary for the public good.

He has forbidden his Governors to pass Laws of immediate and pressing importance, unless suspended in their operation till his Assent should be obtained; and when so suspended, he has utterly neglected to attend to them.

He has refused to pass other Laws for the accommodation of large districts of people, unless those people would relinquish the right of Representation in the Legislature, a right inestimable to them and formidable to tyrants only.

He has called together legislative bodies at places unusual, uncomfortable, and distant from the depository of their public Records, for the sole purpose of fatiguing them into compliance with his measures.

He has dissolved Representative Houses repeatedly, for opposing with manly firmness his invasions on the rights of the people.

He has refused for a long time, after such dissolutions, to cause others to be elected; whereby the Legislative powers, incapable of Annihilation, have returned to the People at large for their exercise; the State remaining in the mean time exposed to all dangers of invasion from without, and convulsions within.

He has endeavored to prevent the population of these States; for that purpose obstructing the Laws of Naturalization of Foreigners; refusing to pass others to encourage their migrations hither, and raising the conditions of new Appropriations of Lands.

He has obstructed the Administration of Justice, by refusing his Assent to Laws for establishing Judiciary powers.

He has made Judges dependent on his Will alone, for the tenure of their offices, and the amount and payment of their salaries.

He has erected a multitude of New Offices, and sent hither swarms of Officers to harass our People, and eat out their substance.

He has kept among us, in times of peace, Standing Armies without the Consent of our legislature.

He has affected to render the Military independent of and superior to the Civil Power.

He has combined with others to subject us to a jurisdiction foreign to our constitution, and unacknowledged by our laws; giving his Assent to their Acts of pretended Legislation:

For quartering large bodies of armed troops among us:

For protecting them, by a mock Trial, from Punishment for any Murders which they should commit on the Inhabitants of these States:

For cutting off our Trade with all parts of the world:

For imposing taxes on us without our Consent:

For depriving us in many cases, of the benefits of Trial by jury:

For transporting us beyond Seas to be tried for pretended offences:

For abolishing the free System of English Laws in a neighboring Province, establishing therein an Arbitrary government, and enlarging its Boundaries so as to render it at once an example and fit instrument for introducing the same absolute rule into these Colonies:

For taking away our Charters, abolishing our most valuable Laws, and altering fundamentally the Forms of our Governments:

For suspending our own Legislatures, and declaring themselves invested with Power to legislate for us in all cases whatsoever.

He has abdicated Government here, by declaring us out of his Protection and waging War against us.

He has plundered our seas, ravaged our Coasts, burnt our towns, and destroyed the lives of our people.

He is at this time transporting large armies of foreign mercenaries to compleat the works of death, desolation, and tyranny, already begun with circumstances of Cruelty & perfidy scarcely paralleled in the most barbarous ages, and totally unworthy the Head of a civilized nation.

He has constrained our fellow Citizens taken Captive on the high Seas to bear Arms against their Country, to become the executioners of their friends and Brethren, or to fall themselves by their Hands.

He has excited domestic insurrections amongst us, and has endeavored to bring on the inhabitants of our frontiers, the merciless Indian Savages, whose known rule of warfare, is an undistinguished destruction of all ages, sexes, and conditions.

In every stage of these Oppressions We have Petitioned for Redress in the most humble terms: Our repeated Petitions have been answered only by repeated injury. A Prince, whose character is thus marked by every act which may define a Tyrant, is unfit to be the ruler of a free people.

Nor have We been wanting in attention to our British brethren. We have warned them from time to time of attempts by their legislature to extend an unwarrantable jurisdiction over us. We have reminded them of the circumstances of our emigration and settlement here. We have appealed to their native justice and magnanimity, and we have conjured them by the ties of our common kindred to disavow these usurpations, which, would inevitably interrupt our connections and correspondence. They too must have been deaf to the voice of justice and of consanguinity. We must, therefore, acquiesce in the necessity, which denounces our Separation, and hold them, as we hold the rest of mankind, Enemies in War, in Peace Friends.

WE, THEREFORE, the Representatives of the UNITED STATES OF AMERICA, in General Congress, Assembled, appealing to the Supreme Judge of the world for the rectitude of our intentions, do, in the Name, and by Authority of the good People of these Colonies, solemnly publish and declare, That these United Colonies are, and of Right ought to be FREE AND INDEPENDENT STATES; that they are Absolved from all Allegiance to the British Crown, and that all political connection between them and the State of Great Britain, is and ought to be totally dissolved; and that as Free and Independent States, they have full Power to levy War, conclude Peace, contract Alliances, establish Commerce, and to do all other Acts and Things which Independent States may of right do. And for the support of this Declaration, with a firm reliance on the Protection of Divine Providence, we mutually pledge to each other our Lives, our Fortunes, and our sacred Honor.

The foregoing Declaration was, by order of Congress, engrossed, and signed by the following members:

John Hancock

NEW HAMPSHIRE	MASSACHUSETTS BAY	RHODE ISLAND
Josiah Bartlett	Samuel Adams	Stephen Hopkins
William Whipple	John Adams	William Ellery
Matthew Thornton	Robert Treat Paine	
	Elbridge Gerry	

CONNECTICUT
Roger Sherman
Samuel Huntington
William Williams
Oliver Wolcott

NEW YORK
William Floyd
Philip Livingston
Francis Lewis
Lewis Morris

NEW JERSEY
Richard Stockton
John Witherspoon
Francis Hopkinson
John Hart
Abraham Clark

PENNSYLVANIA
Robert Morris
Benjamin Rush
Benjamin Franklin
John Morton
George Clymer
James Smith
George Taylor
James Wilson
George Ross

DELAWARE
Caesar Rodney
George Read
Thomas M'Kean

MARYLAND
Samuel Chase
William Paca
Thomas Stone
Charles Carroll,
of Carrollton

VIRGINIA
George Wythe
Richard Henry Lee
Thomas Jefferson
Benjamin Harrison
Thomas Nelson, Jr.
Francis Lightfoot Lee
Carter Braxton

NORTH CAROLINA
William Hooper
Joseph Hewes
John Penn

SOUTH CAROLINA
Edward Rutledge
Thomas Heyward, Jr.
Thomas Lynch, Jr.
Arthur Middleton

GEORGIA
Button Gwinnett
Lyman Hall
George Walton

Resolved, That copies of the Declaration be sent to the several assemblies, conventions, and committees, or councils of safety, and to the several commanding officers of the continental troops; that it be proclaimed in each of the United States, at the head of the army.

The Articles of Confederation

Agreed to by Congress November 15, 1777;
ratified and in force March 1, 1781

To all whom these Presents shall come, we the undersigned Delegates of the States affixed to our Names send greeting. Whereas the Delegates of the United States of America in Congress assembled did on the fifteenth day of November in the Year of our Lord One Thousand Seven Hundred and Seventy seven, and in the Second Year of the Independence of America agree to certain articles of Confederation and perpetual Union between the States of Newhampshire, Massachusetts-bay, Rhodeisland and Providence Plantations, Connecticut, New-York, New-Jersey, Pennsylvania, Delaware, Maryland, Virginia, North-Carolina, South-Carolina and Georgia in the Words following, viz. "Articles of Confederation and perpetual Union between the states of Newhampshire, Massachusetts-bay, Rhodeisland and Providence Plantations, Connecticut, New-York, New-Jersey, Pennsylvania, Delaware, Maryland, Virginia, North-Carolina, South-Carolina and Georgia.

Art. I. The Stile of this confederacy shall be "The United States of America."

Art. II. Each state retains its sovereignty, freedom and independence, and every Power, Jurisdiction and right, which is not by this confederation expressly delegated to the United States, in Congress assembled.

Art. III. The said states hereby severally enter into a firm league of friendship with each other, for their common defence, the security of their Liberties, and their mutual and general welfare, binding themselves to assist each other, against all force offered to, or attacks made upon them, or any of them, on account of religion, sovereignty, trade, or any other pretence whatever.

Art. IV. The better to secure and perpetuate mutual friendship and intercourse among the people of the different states in this union, the free inhabitants of each of these states, paupers, vagabonds and fugitives from Justice excepted, shall be entitled to all privileges and immunities of free citizens in the several states; and the people of each state shall have free ingress and regress to and from any other state, and shall enjoy therein all the privileges of trade and commerce, subject to the same duties, impositions and restrictions as the inhabitants thereof respectively, provided that such restriction shall not extend so far as to prevent the removal of property imported into any state, to any other state of which the Owner is an inhabitant; provided also that no imposition, duties or restriction shall be laid by any state, on the property of the united states, or either of them.

If any Person guilty of, or charged with treason, felony, or other high misdemeanor in any state, shall flee from Justice, and be found in any of the united states, he shall upon demand of the Governor or executive power, of the state from which he fled, be delivered up and removed to the state having jurisdiction of his offence.

Full faith and credit shall be given in each of these states to the records, acts and judicial proceedings of the courts and magistrates of every other state.

Art. V. For the more convenient management of the general interests of the united states, delegates shall be annually appointed in such manner as the legislature of each state shall direct, to meet in Congress on the first Monday in November, in every year, with a power reserved to each state, to recall its delegates, or any of them, at any time within the year, and to send others in their stead, for the remainder of the Year.

No state shall be represented in Congress by less than two, nor by more than seven Members; and no person shall be capable of being a delegate for more than three years in any term of six years; nor shall any person, being a delegate, be capable of holding any office under the united states, for which he, or another for his benefit receives any salary, fees or emolument of any kind.

Each state shall maintain its own delegates in a meeting of the states, and while they act as members of the committee of the states.

In determining questions in the united states, in Congress assembled, each state shall have one vote.

Freedom of speech and debate in Congress shall not be impeached or questioned in any Court, or place out of Congress, and the members of congress shall be protected in their persons from arrests and imprisonments, during the time of their going to and from, and attendance on congress, except for treason, felony, or breach of the peace.

Art. VI. No state without the Consent of the united states in congress assembled, shall send any embassy to, or receive any embassy from, or enter into any conference, agreement, or alliance or treaty with any King, prince or state; nor shall any person holding any office or profit or trust under the united states, or any of them, accept of any present, emolument, office or title of any kind whatever from any king, prince or foreign state; nor shall the united states in congress assembled, or any of them, grant any title of nobility.

No two or more states shall enter into any treaty, confederation or alliance whatever between them, without the consent of the united states in congress assembled, specifying accurately the purposes for which the same is to be entered into, and how long it shall continue.

No state shall lay any imposts or duties, which may interfere with any stipulations in treaties, entered into by the united states in congress assembled, with any king, prince or state, in pursuance of any treaties already proposed by congress, to the courts of France and Spain.

No vessels of war shall be kept up in time of peace by any state, except such number only, as shall be deemed necessary by the united states in congress assembled, for the defence of such state, or its trade; nor shall any body of forces be kept up by any state, in time of peace, except such number only, as in the judgment of the united states, in congress assembled, shall be deemed requisite to garrison the forts necessary for the defence of such state; but every state shall always keep up a well regulated and disciplined militia, sufficiently armed and accoutred, and shall provide and constantly have ready for use, in public stores, a due number of field pieces and tents, and a proper quantity of arms, ammunition and camp equipage.

No state shall engage in any war without the consent of the united states in congress assembled, unless such state be actually invaded by enemies, or shall have received certain advice of a resolution being formed by some nation of Indians to invade such state, and the danger is so imminent as not to admit of a delay, till the united states in congress asssembled can be consulted; nor shall any state grant commissions to any ships or vessels of war, nor letters of marque or reprisal, except it be after a declaration of war by the united states in congress assembled, and then only against the kingdom or state and the subjects thereof, against which war has been so declared, and under such regulations as shall be established by the united states in congress assembled, unless such state be infested by pirates; in which case vessels of war may be fitted out for that occasion, and kept so long as the danger shall continue, or until the united states in congress assembled shall determine otherwise.

Art. VII. When land-forces are raised by any state for the common defence, all officers of or under the rank of colonel, shall be appointed by the legislature of each state respectively by whom such forces shall be raised, or in such manner as such state shall direct, and all vacancies shall be filled up by the state which first made the appointment.

Art. VIII. All charges of war, and all other expences that shall be incurred for the common defence or general welfare, and allowed by the united states in congress assembled, shall be defrayed out of a common treasury, which shall be supplied by the several states, in proportion to the value of all land within each state, granted to or surveyed for any Person, as such land and the buildings and improvements thereon shall be estimated according to such mode as the united states in congress assembled, shall from time to time direct and appoint. The taxes for paying that proportion shall be laid and levied by the authority and direction of the legislatures of the several states within the time agreed upon by the united states in congress assembled.

Art. IX. The united states in congress assembled, shall have the sole and exclusive right and power of determining on peace and war, except in the cases mentioned in the sixth article—of sending and receiving ambassadors—entering into treaties and alliances, provided that no treaty of commerce shall be made whereby the legislative power of the respective states shall be restrained from imposing such imposts and duties on foreigners, as their own people are subjected to, or from prohibiting the exportation of any species of goods or commodities whatsoever—of establishing rules for deciding in all cases, what captures on land or water shall be legal, and in what manner prizes taken by land or naval forces in the service of the united states shall be divided or appropriated—of granting letters of marque and reprisal in times of peace—appointing courts for the trial of piracies and felonies committed on the high seas and establishing courts for receiving and determining finally appeals in all cases of captures, provided that no member of congress shall be appointed a judge of any of the said courts.

The united states in congress assembled shall also be the last resort on appeal in all disputes and differences now subsisting or that hereafter may arise between two or more states concerning boundary, jurisdiction or any other cause whatever; which authority shall always be exercised in the manner following. Whenever the legislative or executive authority or lawful agent of any state in controversy with another shall present a petition to congress stating the matter in question and praying for a hearing, notice thereof shall be given by order of congress to the legislative or executive authority of the other state in controversy, and a day assigned for the appearance of the parties by their lawful agents, who shall then be directed to appoint by joint consent, commissioners or judges to constitute a court for hearing and determining the matter in question: but if they cannot agree, congress shall name three persons out of each of the united states, and from the list of such persons each party shall alternately strike out one, the petitioners beginning, until the number shall be reduced to thirteen; and from that number not less than seven, nor more than nine names as congress shall direct, shall in the presence of congress be drawn out by lot, and the persons whose names shall be so drawn or any five of them, shall be commissioners or judges, to hear and finally determine the controversy, so always as a major part of the judges who shall hear the cause shall agree in the determination: and if either party shall neglect to attend at the day appointed, without shewing reasons, which congress shall judge sufficient, or being present shall refuse to strike, the congress shall proceed to nominate three persons out of each state, and the secretary of congress shall strike in behalf of such party absent or refusing; and the judgment and sentence of the court to be appointed, in the manner before prescribed, shall be final and conclusive; and if any of the parties shall refuse to submit to the authority of such court, or to appear to defend their claim or cause, the court shall nevertheless proceed to pronounce sentence, or judgment, which shall in like manner be final and decisive, the judgment or sentence and other proceedings being in either case transmitted to congress, and lodged among the acts of congress for the security of the parties concerned: provided that every commissioner, before he sits in judgment, shall take an oath to be administered by one of the judges of the supreme or superior court of the state, where the cause shall be tried, "well and truly to hear and determine the matter in question, according to the best of his judgment, without favour, affection or hope of reward:" provided also that no state shall be deprived of territory for the benefit of the united states.

All controversies concerning the private right of soil claimed under different grants of two or more states, whose jurisdictions as they may respect such lands, and the states which passed such grants are adjusted, the said grants or either of them being at the same time claimed to have originated antecedent to such settlement of jurisdiction, shall on the petition of either party to the congress of the united states, be finally determined as near as may be in the same manner as is before prescribed for deciding disputes respecting territorial jurisdiction between different states.

The united states in congress assembled shall also have the sole and exclusive right and power of regulating the alloy and value of coin struck by their own authority, or by that of the respective states—fixing the standard of weights and measures throughout the united states—regulating the trade and managing all affairs with the Indians, not members of any of the states, provided that the legislative right of any state within its own limits be not infringed or violated—establishing and regulating post-offices from one state to another, throughout all the united states, and exacting such postage on the papers passing thro' the same as may be requisite to defray the expences of the said office—appointing all officers of the land forces, in the service of the united states, except regimental officers—appointing all the officers of the united states—making rules for the government and regulation of the said land and naval forces, and directing their operations.

The united states in congress assembled shall have the authority to appoint a committee, to sit in the recess of congress, to be denominated "A Committee of the States," and to consist of one delegate from each state; and to appoint such other committees and civil officers as may be necessary for managing the general affairs of the united states under their direction—to appoint one of their number to preside, provided that no person be allowed to serve in the office of president more than one year in any term of three years; to ascertain the necessary sums of Money to be raised for the service of the united states, and to appropriate and apply the same for defraying the public expences—to borrow money, or emit bills on the credit of the united states, transmitting every half year to the respective states an account of the sums of money so borrowed or emitted,—to build and equip a navy—to agree upon the number of land forces, and to make requisitions from each state for its quota, in proportion to the number of white inhabitants in such state; which requisition shall be binding, and thereupon the legislature of each state shall appoint the regimental officers, raise the men and cloath, arm and equip them in a soldier like manner, at the expence of the united states, and the officers and men so cloathed, armed and equipped shall march to the place appointed, and within the time agreed on by the united states in congress assembled: But if the united states in congress assembled shall, on consideration of circumstances judge proper that any state should not raise men, or should raise a smaller number than its quota, and that any other state should raise a greater number of men than the quota thereof, such extra number shall be raised, officered, cloathed, armed and equipped in the same manner as the quota of such state, unless the legislature of such state shall judge that such extra number cannot be safely spared out of the same, in which case they shall raise, officer, cloath, arm and equip as many of such extra number as they judge can be safely spared. And the officers and men so cloathed, armed and equipped, shall march to the place appointed, and within the time agreed on by the united states in congress assembled.

The united states in congress assembled shall never engage in a war, nor grant letters of marque and reprisal in time of peace, nor enter into any treaties or alliances, nor coin money, nor regulate the value thereof, nor ascertain the sums and expences necessary for the defence and welfare of the united states, or any of them, nor emit bills, nor borrow money on the credit of the united states, nor appropriate money, nor agree upon the number of vessels of war, to be built or purchased, or the number of land or sea forces to be raised, nor appoint a commander in chief of the army or navy, unless nine states assent to the same: nor shall a question on any other point, except for adjourning from day to day be determined, unless by the votes of a majority of the united states in congress assembled.

The congress of the united states shall have power to adjourn to any time within the year, and to any place within the united states, so that no period of adjournment be for a longer duration than the space of six Months, and shall publish the Journal of their proceedings monthly, except such parts thereof relating to treaties, alliances or military operations as in their judgment require secrecy; and the yeas and nays of the delegates of each state on any question shall be entered on the Journal, when it is desired by any delegate; and the delegates of a state, or any of them, at his or their request shall be furnished with a transcript of the said Journal, except such parts as are above excepted to lay before the legislatures of the several states.

Art. X. The committee of the states, or any nine of them, shall be authorised to execute, in the recess of congress, such of the powers of congress as the united states in congress assembled, by the consent of nine states, shall from time to time think expedient to vest them with; provided that no power be delegated to the said committee, for the exercise of which, by the articles of confederation, the voice of nine states in the congress of the united states assembled is requisite.

Art. XI. Canada acceding to this confederation, and joining in the measures of the united states, shall be admitted into, and entitled to all the advantages of this union: but no other colony shall be admitted into the same, unless such admission be agreed to by nine states.

Art. XII. All bills of credit emitted, monies borrowed and debts contracted by, or under the authority of congress, before the assembling of the united states, in pursuance of the present confederation, shall be deemed and considered as a charge against the united states, for payment and satisfaction whereof the said united states and the public faith are hereby solemnly pledged.

Art. XIII. Every state shall abide by the determinations of the united states in congress assembled, on all questions which by this confederation are submitted to them. And the Articles of this confederation shall be inviolably observed by every state, and the union shall be perpetual; nor shall any alteration at any time hereafter be made in any of them; unless such alteration be agreed to in a congress of the united states, and be afterwards confirmed by the legislatures of every state.

AND WHEREAS it hath pleased the Great Governor of the World to incline the hearts of the legislatures we respectively represent in congress, to approve of, and to authorize us to ratify the said articles of confederation and perpetual union. KNOW YE that we the undersigned delegates, by virtue of the power and authority to us given for that purpose, do by these presents, in the name and in behalf of our respective constituents, fully and entirely ratify and confirm each and every of the said articles of confederation and perpetual union, and all and singular the matters and things therein contained: And we do further solemnly plight and engage the faith of our respective constituents, that they shall abide by the determination of the united states in congress assembled, on all questions, which by the said confederation are submitted to them. And that the articles thereof shall be inviolably observed by the states we respectively represent, and that the union shall be perpetual. In Witness whereof we have hereunto set our hands in Congress. Done at Philadelphia in the state of Pennsylvania the ninth Day of July in the Year of our Lord one Thousand seven Hundred and Seventy-eight and in the third year of the independence of America.

The Constitution of the United States of America

Annotated with references to *The Federalist Papers*

[PREAMBLE]

We the People of the United States, in Order to form a more perfect Union, establish Justice, insure domestic Tranquility, provide for the common defence, promote the general Welfare, and secure the Blessings of Liberty to ourselves and our Posterity, do ordain and establish this Constitution for the United States of America.

84 (Hamilton)

ARTICLE I

Section 1

[LEGISLATIVE POWERS]

All legislative Powers herein granted shall be vested in a Congress of the United States, which shall consist of a Senate and House of Representatives.

10, 45 (Madison)

Section 2

[HOUSE OF REPRESENTATIVES, HOW CONSTITUTED, POWER OF IMPEACHMENT]

The House of Representatives shall be composed of Members chosen every second Year by the People of the several States, and the Electors in each State shall have the Qualifications requisite for Electors of the most numerous Branch of the State Legislature.

39, 45, 52–53, 57 (Madison)

No Person shall be a Representative who shall not have attained to the Age of twenty-five Years, and been seven Years a Citizen of the United States, and who shall not, when elected, be an inhabitant of that State in which he shall be chosen.

52 (Madison)

60 (Hamilton)
54, 58 (Madison)

Representatives and *direct Taxes*[1] shall be apportioned among the several States which may be included within this Union, according to their respective Numbers, *which shall be determined by adding to the whole Number of free Persons, including those bound to Service for a Term of Years,* and excluding Indians not taxed, *three-fifths of all other Persons.*[2] The actual Enumeration shall be made within three Years after the first Meeting of the Congress of the United States, and within every subsequent Term of ten Years, in such Manner as they shall by Law direct. The Number of Representatives shall not exceed one for every thirty Thousand, but each State shall have at Least one Representative; *and until such enumeration shall be made, the State of New*

55–56 (Madison)

---

1   Modified by Sixteenth Amendment.

2   Modified by Fourteenth Amendment.

Hampshire shall be entitled to chuse three, Massachusetts eight, Rhode-Island and Providence Plantations one, Connecticut five, New-York six, New Jersey four, Pennsylvania eight, Delaware one, Maryland six, Virginia ten, North Carolina five, South Carolina five, and Georgia three.[3]

When vacancies happen in the Representation from any State, the Executive Authority thereof shall issue Writs of Election to fill such Vacancies.

79 (Hamilton)

The House of Representatives shall chuse their Speaker and other Officers; and shall have the sole Power of Impeachment.

Section 3
[THE SENATE, HOW CONSTITUTED, IMPEACHMENT TRIALS]

39, 45 (Madison)
60 (Hamilton)

The Senate of the United States shall be composed of two Senators from each State, *chosen by the Legislature thereof,*[4] for six Years; and each Senator shall have one Vote.

62–63 (Madison)
59, 68 (Hamilton)

Immediately after they shall be assembled in Consequence of the first Election, they shall be divided as equally as may be into three Classes. The Seats of the Senators of the first Class shall be vacated at the Expiration of the second Year, of the second Class at the Expiration of the fourth Year, and of the third Class at the Expiration of the sixth Year, so that one third may be chosen every second Year: *and if vacancies happen by Resignation, or otherwise, during the Recess of the Legislature of any State, the Executive thereof may make temporary Appointments until the next Meeting of the Legislature, which shall then fill such Vacancies.*[5]

62 (Madison)
64 (Jay)

No person shall be a Senator who shall not have attained to the Age of thirty Years, and been nine Years a Citizen of the United States, and who shall not, when elected, be an Inhabitant of that State for which he shall be chosen.

The Vice-President of the United States shall be President of the Senate, but shall have no Vote, unless they be equally divided.

The Senate shall chuse their other Officers, and also a President pro tempore, in the Absence of the Vice-President, or when he shall exercise the Office of President of the United States.

39 (Madison)
65–67, 79 (Hamilton)

The Senate shall have the sole Power to try all Impeachments. When sitting for that Purpose, they shall be on Oath or Affirmation. When the President of the United States is tried, the Chief Justice shall preside: And no Person shall be convicted without the Concurrence of two-thirds of the Members present.

84 (Hamilton)

Judgment in Cases of Impeachment shall not extend further than to removal from Office, and disqualification to hold and enjoy any Office of honor, Trust or Profit under the United States: but the Party convicted shall nevertheless be liable and subject to Indictment, Trial, Judgment and Punishment, according to Law.

Section 4
[ELECTION OF SENATORS AND REPRESENTATIVES]

59–61 (Hamilton)

The Times, Places and Manner of holding Elections for Senators and Representatives, shall be prescribed in each State by the Legislature thereof; but the

---

3 Temporary provision.

4 Modified by Seventeenth Amendment.

5 Modified by Seventeenth Amendment.

Congress may at any time by Law make or alter such Regulations, except as to the Places of chusing Senators.

The Congress shall assemble at least once in every Year, and such Meeting shall be on the first Monday in December, unless they shall by Law appoint a different Day.[6]

Section 5
[QUORUM, JOURNALS, MEETINGS, ADJOURNMENTS]

Each House shall be the Judge of the Elections, Returns and Qualifications of its own Members, and a Majority of each shall constitute a Quorum to do Business; but a smaller Number may adjourn from day to day, and may be authorized to compel the Attendance of absent Members, in such Manner, and under the Penalties as each House may provide.

Each House may determine the Rules of its Proceedings, punish its Members for disorderly Behavior, and, with the Concurrence of two-thirds, expel a Member.

Each House shall keep a Journal of its Proceedings, and from time to time publish the same, excepting such Parts as may in their Judgment require Secrecy; and the Yeas and Nays of the Members of either House on any questions shall, at the Desire of one-fifth of the present, be entered on the Journal.

Neither House, during the Session of Congress, shall, without the Consent of the other, adjourn for more than three days, nor to any other Place than that in which the two Houses shall be sitting.

Section 6
[COMPENSATION, PRIVILEGES, DISABILITIES]

The Senators and Representatives shall receive a Compensation for their Services, to be ascertained by Law, and paid out of the Treasury of the United States. They shall in all Cases, except Treason, Felony and Breach of the Peace, be privileged from Arrest during their Attendance at the Session of their respective Houses, and in going to and returning from the same; and for any Speech or Debate in either House, they shall not be questioned in any other Place.

No Senator or Representative shall, during the time for which he was elected, be appointed to any civil Office under the authority of the United States, which shall have been created, or the Emoluments whereof shall have been encreased during such time; and no Person holding any Office under the United States, shall be a Member of either House during his Continuance in Office.

55 (Madison)
76 (Hamilton)

Section 7
[PROCEDURE IN PASSING BILLS AND RESOLUTIONS]

All Bills for raising Revenue shall originate in the House of Representatives; but the Senate may propose or concur with Amendments as on other Bills.

66 (Hamilton)

Every Bill which shall have passed the House of Representatives and the Senate, shall, before it become a Law, be presented to the President of the United States; if he approve he shall sign it, but if not he shall return it, with his Objections to that House in which it shall have originated, who shall enter the Objections at large on their Journal, and proceed to reconsider it. If after such Reconsideration

69, 73 (Hamilton)

---

6 Modified by Twentieth Amendment.

two-thirds of that House shall agree to pass the Bill, it shall be sent, together with the Objections, to the other House, by which it shall likewise be reconsidered, and if approved by two-thirds of that House it shall become a Law. But in all such Cases the Votes of both Houses shall be determined by Yeas and Nays, and the Names of the Persons voting for and against the Bill shall be entered on the Journal of each House respectively. If any Bill shall not be returned by the President within ten Days (Sundays excepted) after it shall have been presented to him, the Same shall be a Law, in like Manner as if he had signed it, unless the Congress by their Adjournment prevent its Return, in which Case it shall not be a Law.

69, 73 (Hamilton)

Every Order, Resolution, or Vote to which the Concurrence of the Senate and House of Representatives may be necessary (except on a question of Adjournment) shall be presented to the President of the United States; and before the Same shall take Effect, shall be approved by him, or being disapproved by him, shall be repassed by two-thirds of the Senate and House of Representatives, according to the Rules and Limitations prescribed in the Case of a Bill.

Section 8
[POWERS OF CONGRESS]

The Congress shall have Power

30–36 (Hamilton)
41 (Madison)

To lay and collect Taxes, Duties, Imposts and Excises, to pay the Debts and provide for the common Defence and general Welfare of the United States; but all Duties, Imposts and excises shall be uniform throughout the United States;

56 (Madison)
42, 45, 56
(Madison)
32 (Hamilton)

To borrow Money on the Credit of the United States;

To regulate Commerce with foreign Nations, and among the several States, and with the Indian Tribes;

To establish an uniform Rule of Naturalization, and uniform Laws on the subject of Bankruptcies throughout the United States;

42 (Madison)

To coin Money, regulate the Value thereof, and of foreign Coin, and fix the Standard of Weights and Measures;

42 (Madison)

To provide for the Punishment of counterfeiting the Securities and current Coin of the United States;

42 (Madison)
42, 43 (Madison)

To establish Post Offices and post Roads;

To promote the Progress of Science and useful Arts, by securing for limited Times to Authors and Inventors the exclusive Right to their respective Writings and Discoveries;

81 (Hamilton)
42 (Madison)

To constitute Tribunals inferior to the supreme Court;

To define and Punish Piracies and Felonies committed on the high Seas, and Offences against the Law of Nations;

41 (Madison)

To declare War, grant Letters of Marque and Reprisal, and make Rules concerning Captures on Land and Water;

23, 24, 26 (Hamilton)

To raise and support Armies, but no Appropriation of Money to that Use shall be for a longer Term than two Years;

41 (Madison)

To provide and maintain a Navy;

To make Rules for the Government and Regulation of the land and naval forces;

29 (Hamilton)

To provide for calling for the Militia to execute the Laws of the Union, suppress Insurrections and repel Invasions;

To provide for organizing, arming, and disciplining, the Militia, and for governing such Part of them as may be employed in the Service of the United States, reserving to the States respectively, the Appointment of the Officers, and the Authority of training the Militia according to the discipline prescribed by Congress;

29 (Hamilton)
56 (Madison)

To exercise exclusive Legislation in all Cases whatsoever, over such District (not exceeding ten Miles square) as may, by Cession of particular States, and the Acceptance of Congress, become the Seat of the Government of the United States, and to exercise like Authority over all Places purchased by the Consent of the Legislature of the State in which the Same shall be, for the Erection of Forts, Magazines, Arsenals, dock-Yards, and other needful Buildings;—And

32 (Hamilton)
43 (Madison)

To make all Laws which shall be necessary and proper for carrying into Execution the foregoing Powers, and all other Powers vested by this Constitution in the Government of the United States, or in any Department or Officer thereof.

29, 33 (Hamilton)
44 (Madison)

Section 9
[SOME RESTRICTIONS ON FEDERAL POWER]

The Migration or Importation of such Persons as any of the States now existing shall think proper to admit, shall not be prohibited by the Congress prior to the Year one thousand eight hundred and eight, but a Tax or Duty may be imposed on such Importation, not exceeding ten dollars for each Person.[7]

42 (Madison)

The privilege of the Writ of *Habeas Corpus* shall not be suspended, unless when in Cases of Rebellion or Invasion the public Safety may require it.

83, 84 (Hamilton)

No Bill of Attainder or ex post facto Law shall be passed.

84 (Hamilton)

No Capitation, or other direct, Tax shall be laid, unless in Proportion to the Census or Enumeration herein before directed to be taken.[8]

No Tax or Duty shall be laid on Articles exported from any State.

No Preference shall be given by any Regulation of Commerce or Revenue to the Ports of one State over those of another; nor shall vessels bound to, or from, one State, be obliged to enter, clear, or pay Duties in another.

32 (Hamilton)

No Money shall be drawn from the Treasury, but in Consequence of Appropriations made by Law; and a regular Statement and Account of the Receipts and Expenditures of all public Money shall be published from time to time.

No Title of Nobility shall be granted by the United States: And no Person holding any Office of Profit or Trust under them, shall, without the Consent of the Congress, accept of any present, Emolument, Office or Title, of any kind whatever, from any King, Prince, or foreign State.

39 (Madison)
84 (Hamilton)

Section 10
[RESTRICTIONS UPON POWERS OF STATES]

No State shall enter into any Treaty, Alliance, or Confederation; grant Letters of Marque and Reprisal; coin Money; emit Bills of Credit; make any Thing but gold and silver Coin a Tender in Payment of Debts; pass any Bill of Attainder, ex post facto Law, or Law impairing the Obligation of Contracts, or grant any Title of Nobility.

33 (Hamilton)
44 (Madison)

---

7 Temporary provision.

8 Modified by Sixteenth Amendment.

32 (Hamilton)
44 (Madison)

No State shall, without the Consent of the Congress, lay any Imposts or Duties on Imports or Exports, except what may be absolutely necessary for executing its inspection Laws: and the net Produce of all Duties and Imposts, laid by any State on Imports or Exports, shall be for the Use of the Treasury of the United States; and all such Laws shall be subject to the Revision and Control of the Congress.

No State shall, without the Consent of Congress, lay any Duty of Tonnage, keep Troops, or Ships of War in time of Peace, enter into any Agreement or Compact with another State, or with a foreign Power, or engage in War, unless actually invaded, or in such imminent Danger as will not admit of Delay.

ARTICLE II

Section 1

[EXECUTIVE POWER, ELECTION, QUALIFICATIONS OF THE PRESIDENT]

39 (Madison)
70, 71, 84
(Hamilton)
68, 69, 71, 77
(Hamilton)
39, 45 (Madison)

The executive Power shall be vested in a President of the United States of America. *He shall hold his Office during the Term of four years and, together with the Vice-President, chosen for the same Term, be elected, as follows:*[9]

Each State shall appoint, in such Manner as the Legislature thereof may direct, a Number of Electors, equal to the whole Number of Senators and Representatives to which the State may be entitled in the Congress: but no Senator or Representative, or Person holding an Office of Trust or Profit under the United States, shall be appointed an Elector.

66 (Hamilton)

The electors shall meet in their respective States, and vote by ballot for two Persons, of whom one at least shall not be an Inhabitant of the same State with themselves. And they shall make a List of all the Persons voted for, and of the Number of Votes for each; which List they shall sign and certify, and transmit sealed to the Seat of the Government of the United States, directed to the President of the Senate. The President of the Senate shall, in the Presence of the Senate and House of Representatives, open all the Certificates, and the Votes shall then be counted. The Person having the greatest Number of Votes shall be the President, if such Number be a Majority of the whole Number of Electors appointed; and if there be more than one who have such Majority and have an equal Number of Votes, then the House of Representatives shall immediately chuse by Ballot one of them for President; and if no person have a Majority, then from the five highest on the List the said House shall in like Manner chuse the President. But in chusing the President, the Votes shall be taken by States, the Representation from each State having one Vote; A quorum for this Purpose shall consist of a Member or Members from two-thirds of the States, and a Majority of all the States shall be necessary to a Choice. In every Case, after the Choice of the President, the person having the greatest Number of Votes of the Electors shall be the Vice-President. But if there should remain two or more who have equal vote, the Senate shall chuse from them by Ballot the Vice-President.[10]

The Congress may determine the Time of chusing the Electors, and the Day on which they shall give their Votes; which Day shall be the same throughout the United States.

---

9 Number of terms limited to two by Twenty-Second Amendment.

10 Modified by Twelfth and Twentieth Amendments.

No Person except a natural born Citizen, or a Citizen of the United States, at the time of the Adoption of this Constitution, shall be eligible to the Office of President; neither shall any Person be eligible to that Office who shall not have attained to the Age of thirty-five Years, and been fourteen Years a Resident within the United States.

64 (Jay)

In Case of the Removal of the President from Office, or his Death, Resignation, or Inability to discharge the Powers and Duties of the said Office, the same shall devolve on the Vice-President, and the Congress may by Law provide for the Case of Removal, Death, Resignation, or Inability, both of the President and Vice-President, declaring what Officer shall then act as President, and such Officer shall act accordingly, until the Disability be removed, or a President shall be elected.

The President shall, at stated Times, receive for his Services, a Compensation, which shall neither be encreased nor diminished during the Period for which he shall have been elected, and he shall not receive within that Period any other Emolument from the United States, or any of them.

73, 79 (Hamilton)

Before he enter on the Execution of his Office, he shall take the following Oath or Affirmation:—"I do solemnly swear (or affirm) that I will faithfully execute the Office of President of the United States, and will to the best of my Ability, preserve, protect and defend the Constitution of the United States."

Section 2
[POWERS OF THE PRESIDENT]

The President shall be Commander in Chief of the Army and Navy of the United States, and of the Militia of the several States, when called into the actual Service of the United States; he may require the Opinion, in writing, of the principal Officer in each of the executive Departments, upon any Subject relating to the Duties of their respective Offices, and he shall have Power to grant Reprieves and Pardons for Offences against the United States, except in Cases of Impeachment.

69, 74 (Hamilton)

He shall have Power, by and with the Advice and Consent of the Senate, to make Treaties, provided two-thirds of the Senators present concur; and he shall nominate, and by and with the Advice and Consent of the Senate, shall appoint Ambassadors, other public Ministers and Consuls, Judges of the Supreme Court, and all other Officers of the United States, whose Appointments are not herein otherwise provided for, and which shall be established by Law: but the Congress may by Law vest the Appointment of such inferior Officers, as they think proper, in the President alone, in the Courts of Law, or in the Heads of Departments.

42 (Madison)
64 (Jay)
66, 69, 76, 77
(Hamilton)

The President shall have Power to fill up all Vacancies that may happen during the Recess of the Senate, by granting Commissions which shall expire at the End of their next Session.

67, 76
(Hamilton)

Section 3
[POWERS AND DUTIES OF THE PRESIDENT]

He shall from time to time give to the Congress Information of the State of the Union, and recommend to their Consideration such Measures as he shall judge necessary and expedient; he may, on extraordinary Occasions, convene both Houses, or either of them, and in Case of Disagreement between them, with Respect to the Time of Adjournment, he may adjourn them to such Time

69, 77, 78
(Hamilton)
42 (Madison)

as he shall think proper; he shall receive Ambassadors and other public Ministers; he shall take Care that the Laws be faithfully executed, and shall Commission all the Officers of the United States.

Section 4
[IMPEACHMENT]

39 (Madison)
69 (Hamilton)

The President, Vice-President and all civil Officers of the United States shall be removed from Office on Impeachment for, and Conviction of, Treason, Bribery, or other high Crimes and Misdemeanors.

ARTICLE III

Section 1
[JUDICIAL POWER, TENURE OF OFFICE]

65, 78, 79, 81, 82
(Hamilton)

The judicial Power of the United States, shall be vested in one supreme Court, and in such inferior Courts as the Congress may from time to time ordain and establish. The Judges, both of the supreme and inferior Courts, shall hold their Offices during good Behavior, and shall, at stated Times, receive for their Services, a Compensation, which shall not be diminished during their Continuance in Office.

Section 2
[JURISDICTION]

80 (Hamilton)

The judicial Power shall extend to all Cases, in Law and Equity, arising under this Constitution, the Laws of the United States, and Treaties made, or which shall be made, under their Authority;—to all Cases affecting Ambassadors, other public Ministers and Consuls;—to all Cases of admiralty and maritime Jurisdiction;—to Controversies to which the United States shall be a party;—to Controversies between two or more States;—*between a State and Citizens of another State;*—between Citizens of different States,—between Citizens of the same State claiming Lands under Grants of different States, *and between a State,* or the Citizens thereof, *and foreign States, Citizens or Subjects.*[11]

81 (Hamilton)

In all Cases affecting Ambassadors, other public Ministers and Consuls, and those in which a State shall be Party, the supreme Court shall have original Jurisdiction. In all the other Cases before mentioned, the supreme Court shall have appellate Jurisdiction, both as to Law and Fact, with such Exceptions, and under such Regulations as Congress shall make.

83, 84 (Hamilton)

The Trial of all Crimes, except in Cases of Impeachment, shall be by Jury; and such Trial shall be held in the State where the said Crimes shall have been committed; but when not committed within any State, the Trial shall be at such Place or Places as the Congress may by Law have directed.

---

11 Modified by Eleventh Amendment.

Section 3
[TREASON, PROOF, AND PUNISHMENT]

Treason against the United States, shall consist only in levying War against them, or in adhering to their Enemies, giving them Aid and Comfort. No Person shall be convicted of Treason unless on the Testimony of two Witnesses to the same overt Act, or on Confession in open Court.

43 (Madison)
84 (Hamilton)

The Congress shall have Power to declare the Punishment of Treason, but no Attainder of Treason shall work Corruption of Blood, or Forfeiture except during the Life of the Person attained.

43 (Madison)
84 (Hamilton)

ARTICLE IV

Section 1
[FAITH AND CREDIT AMONG STATES]

Full Faith and Credit shall be given in each State to the public Acts, Records, and judicial Proceedings of every other State. And the Congress may by general Laws prescribe the Manner in which such Acts, Records and Proceedings shall be proved, and the Effect thereof.

42 (Madison)

Section 2
[PRIVILEGES AND IMMUNITIES, FUGITIVES]

The Citizens of each State shall be entitled to all Privileges and Immunities of Citizens in the several States.

80 (Hamilton)

A person charged in any State with Treason, Felony or other Crime, who shall flee from Justice, and be found in another State, shall on Demand of the executive Authority of the State from which he fled, be delivered up to be removed to the State having Jurisdiction of the Crime.

No person held to Service or Labour in one State, under the Laws thereof, escaping into another, shall, in Consequence of any Law or Regulation therein, be discharged from such Service or Labour, but shall be delivered up on Claim of the Party to whom such Service or Labour may be due.[12]

Section 3
[ADMISSION OF NEW STATES]

New States may be admitted by the Congress into this Union; but no new State shall be formed or erected within the Jurisdiction of any other State; nor any State be formed by the Junction of two or more States, or Parts of States, without the Consent of the Legislatures of the States concerned as well as of the Congress.

43 (Madison)

The Congress shall have Power to dispose of and make all needful Rules and Regulations respecting the Territory or other Property belonging to the United States; and nothing in this Constitution shall be so construed as to Prejudice any Claims of the United States, or of any particular State.

43 (Madison)

---

12 Repealed by Thirteenth Amendment.

Section 4

[GUARANTEE OF REPUBLICAN GOVERNMENT]

39, 43
(Madison)

The United States shall guarantee to every State in this Union a Republican Form of Government, and shall protect each of them against Invasion; and on Application of the Legislature, or of the Executive (when the Legislature cannot be convened) against domestic Violence.

ARTICLE V

[AMENDMENT OF THE CONSTITUTION]

39, 43 (Madison)
85 (Hamilton)

The Congress, whenever two-thirds of both Houses shall deem it necessary, shall propose Amendments to this Constitution, or, on the Application of the Legislatures of two-thirds of the several States, shall call a Convention for proposing Amendments, which, in either Case, shall be valid to all Intents and Purposes, as Part of this Constitution, when ratified by the Legislatures of three-fourths of the several States, or by Conventions in three-fourths thereof, as the one or the other Mode of Ratification may be proposed by the Congress; *Provided that no Amendment which may be made prior to the Year One thousand eight hundred and eight shall in any Manner affect the first and fourth Clauses in the Ninth Section of the first Article;*[13] and that no State, without its Consent, shall be deprived of its equal Suffrage in the Senate.

ARTICLE VI

[DEBTS, SUPREMACY, OATH]

43 (Madison)

All Debts contracted and Engagements entered into, before the Adoption of this Constitution, shall be as valid against the United States under this Constitution, as under the Confederation.

27, 33 (Hamilton)
39, 44 (Madison)

This Constitution, and the Laws of the United States which shall be made in Pursuance thereof; and all Treaties made, or which shall be made, under the Authority of the United States, shall be the supreme Law of the Land; and the Judges in every State shall be bound thereby, any Thing in the Constitution or Laws of any State to the Contrary notwithstanding.

27 (Hamilton)
44 (Madison)

The Senators and Representatives before mentioned, and the Members of the several State Legislatures, and all executive and judicial Officers, both of the United States and of the several States, shall be bound by Oath or Affirmation, to support this Constitution; but no religious Test shall be required as a Qualification to any Office or public Trust under the United States.

ARTICLE VII

[RATIFICATION AND ESTABLISHMENT]

39, 40, 43
(Madison)

The Ratification of the Conventions of nine States, shall be sufficient for the Establishment of this Constitution between the States so ratifying the Same.[14]

---

13 Temporary provision.

14 The Constitution was submitted on September 17, 1787, by the Constitutional Convention, was ratified by the conventions of several states at various dates up to May 29, 1790, and became effective on March 4, 1789.

Done in Convention by the Unanimous Consent of the States present the Seventeenth Day of September in the Year of our Lord one thousand seven hundred and Eighty seven and of the Independence of the United States of America the Twelfth. *In Witness* whereof We have hereunto subscribed our Names,

G:^{0} WASHINGTON—
*Presidt, and Deputy
from Virginia*

NEW HAMPSHIRE
John Langdon
Nicholas Gilman

MASSACHUSETTS
Nathaniel Gorham
Rufus King

CONNECTICUT
Wm Saml Johnson
Roger Sherman

NEW YORK
Alexander Hamilton

NEW JERSEY
Wil: Livingston
David Brearley
Wm Paterson
Jona: Dayton

PENNSYLVANIA
B Franklin
Thomas Mifflin
Robt Morris
Geo. Clymer
Thos. FitzSimons
Jared Ingersoll
James Wilson
Gouv Morris

DELAWARE
Geo Read
Gunning Bedfor Jun
John Dickinson
Richard Bassett
Jaco: Broom

MARYLAND
James McHenry
Dan of St Thos Jenifer
Danl Carroll

VIRGINIA
John Blair—
James Madison Jr.

NORTH CAROLINA
Wm Blount
Richd Dobbs Spaight
Hu Williamson

SOUTH CAROLINA
J. Rutledge
Charles Cotesworth Pinckney
Charles Pinckney
Pierce Butler

GEORGIA
William Few
Abr Baldwin

Amendments to the Constitution

Amendments I–X, known as the Bill of Rights, were proposed by Congress on September 25, 1789, and ratified on December 15, 1791. *The Federalist Papers* comments, mainly in opposition to a Bill of Rights, can be found in number 84 (Hamilton).

AMENDMENT I
[FREEDOM OF RELIGION, OF SPEECH, AND OF THE PRESS]

Congress shall make no law respecting an establishment of religion, or prohibiting the free exercise thereof; or abridging the freedom of speech, or of the press; or the right of the people peaceably to assemble, and to petition the Government for a redress of grievances.

AMENDMENT II
[RIGHT TO KEEP AND BEAR ARMS]

A well regulated Militia, being necessary to the security of a free State, the right of the people to keep and bear Arms, shall not be infringed.

AMENDMENT III
[QUARTERING OF SOLDIERS]

No Soldier shall, in time of peace be quartered in any house, without the consent of the Owner, nor in time of war, but in a manner to be prescribed by law.

AMENDMENT IV
[SECURITY FROM UNWARRANTABLE SEARCH AND SEIZURE]

The right of the people to be secure in their persons, houses, papers, and effects, against unreasonable searches and seizures, shall not be violated, and no Warrants shall issue, but upon probable cause, supported by Oath or affirmation, and particularly describing the place to be searched, and the persons or things to be seized.

AMENDMENT V
[RIGHTS OF ACCUSED PERSONS IN CRIMINAL PROCEEDINGS]

No person shall be held to answer for a capital, or otherwise infamous crime, unless on a presentment or indictment of a Grand Jury, except in cases arising in the land or naval forces, or in the Militia, when in actual service in time of

War or in public danger; nor shall any person be subject for the same offence to be twice put in jeopardy of life or limb; nor shall be compelled in any Criminal Case to be a witness against himself, nor be deprived of life, liberty, or property, without due process of law; nor shall private property be taken for public use, without just compensation.

AMENDMENT VI

[RIGHT TO SPEEDY TRIAL, WITNESSES, ETC.]

In all criminal prosecutions, the accused shall enjoy the right to a speedy and public trial, by an impartial jury of the State and district wherein the crime shall have been committed, which district shall have been previously ascertained by law, and to be informed of the nature and cause of the accusation; to be confronted with the witnesses against him; to have compulsory process for obtaining Witnesses in his favor, and to have the Assistance of Counsel for his defence.

AMENDMENT VII

[TRIAL BY JURY IN CIVIL CASES]

In suits at common law, where the value in controversy shall exceed twenty dollars, the right of trial by jury shall be preserved, and no fact tried by a jury shall be otherwise re-examined in any Court of the United States, than according to the rules of the common law.

AMENDMENT VIII

[BAILS, FINES, PUNISHMENTS]

Excessive bail shall not be required, nor excessive fines imposed, nor cruel and unusual punishments inflicted.

AMENDMENT IX

[RESERVATION OF RIGHTS OF PEOPLE]

The enumeration in the Constitution, of certain rights, shall not be construed to deny or disparage others retained by the people.

AMENDMENT X

[POWERS RESERVED TO STATES OR PEOPLE]

The powers not delegated to the United States by the Constitution, nor prohibited by it to the States, are reserved to the States respectively, or to the people.

AMENDMENT XI

[Proposed by Congress on March 4, 1794; declared ratified on January 8, 1798]
[RESTRICTION OF JUDICIAL POWER]

The Judicial power of the United States shall not be construed to extend to any suit in law or equity, commenced or prosecuted against one of the United States by Citizens of another State, or by Citizens or Subjects of any Foreign State.

AMENDMENT XII

[Proposed by Congress on December 9, 1803; declared ratified on September 25, 1804.]

[ELECTION OF PRESIDENT AND VICE-PRESIDENT]

The Electors shall meet in their respective states, and vote by ballot for President and Vice-President, one of whom, at least, shall not be an inhabitant of the same state with themselves; they shall name in their ballots the person voted for as President, and in distinct ballots the person voted for as Vice-President, and they shall make distinct lists of all persons voted for as President, and of all persons voted for as Vice-President, and of the number of votes for each, which lists they shall sign and certify, and transmit sealed to the seat of the government of the United States, directed to the President of the Senate;—The President of the Senate shall, in presence of the Senate and House of Representatives, open all the certificates and the votes shall then be counted;—The person having the greatest number of votes for President, shall be the President, if such number be a majority of the whole number of Electors appointed; and if no person have such majority, then from the persons having the highest numbers not exceeding three on the list of those voted for as President, the House of Representatives shall choose immediately, by ballot, the President. But in choosing the President, the votes shall be taken by states, the representation from each state having one vote; a quorum for this purpose shall consist of a member or members from two-thirds of the states, and a majority of all states shall be necessary to a choice. And if the House of Representatives shall not choose a President whenever the right of choice shall devolve upon them, before the fourth day of March next following, then the Vice-President, shall act as President, as in the case of the death or other constitutional disability of the President. The person having the greatest number of votes as Vice-President, shall be the Vice-President, if such a number be a majority of the whole number of Electors appointed, and if no person have a majority, then from the two highest numbers on the list, the Senate shall choose the Vice-President; a quorum for the purpose shall consist of two-thirds of the whole number of Senators, and a majority of the whole number shall be necessary to a choice. But no person constitutionally ineligible to the office of President shall be eligible to that of Vice-President of the United States.

AMENDMENT XIII

[Proposed by Congress on January 31, 1865; declared ratified on December 18, 1865]

Section 1

[ABOLITION OF SLAVERY]

Neither slavery nor involuntary servitude, except as a punishment for crime whereof the party shall have been duly convicted, shall exist within the United States, or any place subject to their jurisdiction.

Section 2

[POWER TO ENFORCE THIS ARTICLE]

Congress shall have power to enforce this article by appropriate legislation.

AMENDMENT XIV

[Proposed by Congress on June 13, 1866; declared ratified on July 28, 1868]

Section 1

[CITIZENSHIP RIGHTS NOT TO BE ABRIDGED BY STATES]

All persons born or naturalized in the United States, and subject to the jurisdiction thereof, are citizens of the United States and of the State wherein they reside. No state shall make or enforce any law which shall abridge the privileges or immunities of citizens of the United States; nor shall any State deprive any person of life, liberty, or property, without due process of law; nor deny to any person within its jurisdiction the equal protection of the laws.

Section 2

[APPORTIONMENT OF REPRESENTATIVES IN CONGRESS]

Representatives shall be apportioned among the several States according to their respective numbers, counting the whole number of persons in each State, excluding Indians not taxed. But when the right to vote at any election for the choice of electors for President and Vice-President of the United States, Representatives in Congress, the Executive and Judicial officers of a State, or the members of the Legislature thereof, is denied to any of the male inhabitants of such State, being twenty-one years of age, and citizens of the United States, or in any way abridged, except for participation in rebellion, or other crime, the basis of representation therein shall be reduced in the proportion which the number of such male citizens shall bear to the whole number of male citizens twenty-one years of age in such State.

Section 3

[PERSONS DISQUALIFIED FROM HOLDING OFFICE]

No person shall be a Senator or Representative in Congress, or elector of President and Vice-President, or hold any office, civil or military, under the United States, or under any State, who, having previously taken an oath, as a member of Congress, or as an officer of the United States, or as a member of any State legislature, or as an executive or judicial officer of any State, to support the Constitution of the United States, shall have engaged in insurrection or rebellion against the same, or given aid or comfort to the enemies thereof. But Congress may by a vote of two-thirds of each House, remove such disability.

Section 4

[WHAT PUBLIC DEBTS ARE VALID]

The validity of the public debt of the United States, authorized by law, including debts incurred for payment of pensions and bounties for services in suppressing insurrection or rebellion, shall not be questioned. But neither the United States nor any State shall assume or pay any debt or obligation incurred in aid of insurrection or rebellion against the United States, or any claim for the loss or emancipation of any slave; but all such debts, obligations and claims shall be held illegal and void.

Section 5
[POWER TO ENFORCE THIS ARTICLE]

The Congress shall have power to enforce, by appropriate legislation, the provisions of this article.

AMENDMENT XV
[Proposed by Congress on February 26, 1869; declared ratified on March 30, 1870]

Section 1
[NEGRO SUFFRAGE]

The right of citizens of the United States to vote shall not be denied or abridged by the United States or by any State on account of race, color, or previous condition of servitude.

Section 2
[POWER TO ENFORCE THIS ARTICLE]

The Congress shall have power to enforce this article by appropriate legislation.

AMENDMENT XVI
[Proposed by Congress on July 12, 1909; declared ratified on February 25, 1913]
[AUTHORIZING INCOME TAXES]

The Congress shall have power to lay and collect taxes on incomes, from whatever source derived, without apportionment among the several States, and without regard to any census or enumeration.

AMENDMENT XVII
[Proposed by Congress on May 13, 1912; declared ratified on May 31, 1913]
[POPULAR ELECTION OF SENATORS]

The Senate of the United States shall be composed of two Senators from each State, elected by the people thereof, for six years; and each Senator shall have one vote. The electors in each State shall have the qualifications requisite for electors of the most numerous branch of the State Legislature.

When vacancies happen in the representation of any State in the Senate, the executive authority of such State shall issue writs of election to fill such vacancies: Provided, That the Legislature of any State may empower the executive thereof to make temporary appointment until the people fill the vacancies by election as the Legislature may direct.

This amendment shall not be so construed as to affect the election or term of any Senator chosen before it becomes valid as part of the Constitution.

AMENDMENT XVIII

[Proposed by Congress December 18, 1917; declared ratified on January 29, 1919]

Section 1
[NATIONAL LIQUOR PROHIBITION]

After one year from the ratification of this article the manufacture, sale, or transportation of intoxicating liquors within, the importation thereof into, or the exportation thereof from the United States and all territory subject to the jurisdiction thereof for beverage purposes is hereby prohibited.

Section 2
[POWER TO ENFORCE THIS ARTICLE]

The Congress and the several states shall have concurrent power to enforce this article by appropriate legislation.

Section 3
[RATIFICATION WITHIN SEVEN YEARS]

This article shall be inoperative unless it shall have been ratified as an amendment to the Constitution by the legislatures of the several states, as provided in the Constitution, within seven years from the date of the submission hereof to the states by the Congress.[15]

AMENDMENT XIX

[Proposed by Congress on June 4, 1919; declared ratified on August 26, 1920]
[WOMAN SUFFRAGE]

The right of the citizens of the United States to vote shall not be denied or abridged by the United States or by any state on account of sex.

Congress shall have power to enforce this article by appropriate legislation.

AMENDMENT XX

[Proposed by Congress on March 2, 1932; declared ratified on February 6, 1933]

Section 1
[TERMS OF OFFICE]

The terms of the President and Vice-President shall end at noon on the 20th day of January, and the terms of the Senators and Representatives at noon on the 3rd day of January, of the years in which such terms would have ended if this article had not been ratified; and the terms of their successors shall then begin.

Section 2
[TIME OF CONVENING CONGRESS]

The Congress shall assemble at least once in every year, and such meeting shall begin at noon on the 3rd day of January, unless they shall by law appoint a different day.

---

15 Repealed by Twenty-First Amendment.

Section 3

[DEATH OF PRESIDENT-ELECT]

If, at the time fixed for the beginning of the term of the President, the President-elect shall have died, the Vice-President-elect shall become President. If a President shall not have been chosen before the time fixed for the beginning of his term, or if the President-elect shall have failed to qualify, then the Vice-President-elect shall act as President until a President shall have qualified; and the Congress may by law provide for the case wherein neither a President-elect nor a Vice-President-elect shall have qualified, declaring who shall then act as President, or the manner in which one who is to act shall be selected, and such person shall act accordingly until a President or Vice President shall have qualified.

Section 4

[ELECTION OF THE PRESIDENT]

The Congress may by law provide for the case of the death of any of the persons from whom the House of Representatives may choose a President whenever the right of choice shall have devolved upon them, and for the case of the death of any of the persons from whom the Senate may choose a Vice-President whenever the right of choice shall have devolved upon them.

Section 5

[AMENDMENT TAKES EFFECT]

Sections 1 and 2 shall take effect on the 15th day of October following ratification of this article.

Section 6

[RATIFICATION WITHIN SEVEN YEARS]

This article shall be inoperative unless it shall have been ratified as an amendment to the Constitution by the legislatures of three-fourths of the several States within seven years from the date of its submission.

AMENDMENT XXI

[Proposed by Congress on February 20, 1933; declared ratified on December 5, 1933]

Section 1

[NATIONAL LIQUOR PROHIBITION REPEALED]

The eighteenth article of amendment to the Constitution of the United States is hereby repealed.

Section 2

[TRANSPORTATION OF LIQUOR INTO "DRY" STATES]

The transportation or importation into any State, Territory, or Possession of the United States for delivery or use therein of intoxicating liquors, in violation of the laws thereof, is hereby prohibited.

Section 3
[RATIFICATION WITHIN SEVEN YEARS]

This article shall be inoperative unless it shall have been ratified as an amendment to the Constitution by conventions in the several States, as provided in the Constitution, within seven years from the date of the submission hereof to the States by the Congress.

AMENDMENT XXII
[Proposed by Congress on March 21, 1947; declared ratified on February 26, 1951]

Section 1
[TENURE OF PRESIDENT LIMITED]

No person shall be elected to the office of President more than twice, and no person who has held the office of President or acted as President for more than two years of a term to which some other person was elected President shall be elected to the Office of the President more than once. But this Article shall not apply to any person holding the office of President when this Article was proposed by the Congress, and shall not prevent any person who may be holding the office of President, or acting as President, during the term within which this Article becomes operative from holding the office of President or acting as President during the remainder of such term.

Section 2
[RATIFICATION WITHIN SEVEN YEARS]

This Article shall be inoperative unless it shall have been ratified as an amendment to the Constitution by the legislatures of three-fourths of the several states within seven years from the date of its submission to the States by the Congress.

AMENDMENT XXIII
[Proposed by Congress on June 21, 1960; declared ratified on March 29, 1961]

Section 1
[ELECTORAL COLLEGE VOTES FOR THE DISTRICT OF COLUMBIA]

The District constituting the seat of Government of the United States shall appoint in such manner as the Congress may direct:

A number of electors of President and Vice-President equal to the whole number of Senators and Representatives in Congress to which the District would be entitled if it were a State, but in no event more than the least populous State; they shall be in addition to those appointed by the States, but they shall be considered, for the purposes of the election of President and Vice-President, to be electors appointed by a State; and they shall meet in the District and perform such duties as provided by the twelfth article of amendment.

Section 2
[POWER TO ENFORCE THIS ARTICLE]

The Congress shall have power to enforce this article by appropriate legislation.

AMENDMENT XXIV

[Proposed by Congress on August 27, 1963; declared ratified on January 23, 1964]

Section 1
[ANTI-POLL TAX]

The right of citizens of the United States to vote in any primary or other election for President or Vice-President, for electors for President or Vice-President, or for Senator or Representative of Congress, shall not be denied or abridged by the United States or any State by reasons of failure to pay any poll tax or other tax.

Section 2
[POWER TO ENFORCE THIS ARTICLE]

The Congress shall have power to enforce this article by appropriate legislation.

AMENDMENT XXV

[Proposed by Congress on July 7, 1965; declared ratified on February 10, 1967]

Section 1
[VICE-PRESIDENT TO BECOME PRESIDENT]

In case of the removal of the President from office or his death or resignation, the Vice-President shall become President.

Section 2
[CHOICE OF A NEW VICE-PRESIDENT]

Whenever there is a vacancy in the office of the Vice-President, the President shall nominate a Vice-President who shall take the office upon confirmation by a majority vote of both houses of Congress.

Section 3
[PRESIDENT MAY DECLARE OWN DISABILITY]

Whenever the President transmits to the President pro tempore of the Senate and the Speaker of the House of Representatives his written declaration that he is unable to discharge the powers and duties of his office, and until he transmits to them a written declaration to the contrary, such powers and duties shall be discharged by the Vice-President as Acting President.

Section 4
[ALTERNATE PROCEDURES TO DECLARE AND TO END PRESIDENTIAL DISABILITY]

Whenever the Vice-President and a majority of either the principal officers of the executive departments, or of such other body as Congress may by law provide, transmit to the President pro tempore of the Senate and the Speaker of the House of Representatives their written declaration that the President is unable to discharge the powers and duties of his office, the Vice-President shall immediately assume the powers and duties of the office as Acting President.

Thereafter, when the President transmits to the President pro tempore of the Senate and the Speaker of the House of Representatives his written declaration that no inability exists, he shall resume the powers and duties of his office unless the Vice-President and a majority of either the principal officers of the executive departments, or of such other body as Congress may by law provide, transmit within four days to the President pro tempore of the Senate and the Speaker of the House of Representatives their written declaration that the President is unable to discharge the powers and duties of his office. Thereupon Congress shall decide the issue, assembling within 48 hours for that purpose if not in session. If the Congress, within 21 days after receipt of the latter written declaration, or, if Congress is not in session, within 21 days after Congress is required to assemble, determines by two-thirds vote of both houses that the President is unable to discharge the powers and duties of his office, the Vice-President shall continue to discharge the same as Acting President; otherwise, the President shall resume the powers and duties of his office.

AMENDMENT XXVI
[Proposed by Congress on March 23, 1971; declared ratified on June 30, 1971]

Section 1
[EIGHTEEN-YEAR-OLD VOTE]

The right of citizens of the United States, who are eighteen years of age or older, to vote shall not be denied or abridged by the United States or by any State on account of age.

Section 2
[POWER TO ENFORCE THIS ARTICLE]

The Congress shall have power to enforce this article by appropriate legislation.

AMENDMENT XXVII
[Proposed by Congress on September 25, 1789; ratified on May 7, 1992]

No law varying the compensation for the services of the Senators and Representatives shall take effect until an election of Representatives shall have intervened.

NO. 10: MADISON

Among the numerous advantages promised by a well-constructed Union, none deserves to be more accurately developed than its tendency to break and control the violence of faction. The friend of popular governments never finds himself so much alarmed for their character and fate as when he contemplates their propensity to this dangerous vice. He will not fail, therefore, to set a due value on any plan which, without violating the principles to which he is attached, provides a proper cure for it. The instability, injustice, and confusion introduced into the public councils have, in truth, been the mortal diseases under which popular governments have everywhere perished, as they continue to be the favorite and fruitful topics from which the adversaries to liberty derive their most specious declamations. The valuable improvements made by the American constitutions on the popular models, both ancient and modern, cannot certainly be too much admired; but it would be an unwarrantable partiality to contend that they have as effectually obviated the danger on this side, as was wished and expected. Complaints are everywhere heard from our most considerate and virtuous citizens, equally the friends of public and private faith and of public and personal liberty, that our governments are too unstable, that the public good is disregarded in the conflicts of rival parties, and that measures are too often decided, not according to the rules of justice and the rights of the minor party, but by the superior force of an interested and overbearing majority. However anxiously we may wish that these complaints had no foundation, the evidence of known facts will not permit us to deny that they are in some degree true. It will be found, indeed, on a candid review of our situation, that some of the distresses under which we labor have been erroneously charged on the operation of our governments; but it will be found, at the same time, that other causes will not alone account for many of our heaviest misfortunes; and, particularly, for that prevailing and increasing distrust of public engagements and alarm for private rights which are echoed from one end of the continent to the other. These must be chiefly, if not wholly, effects of the unsteadiness and injustice with which a factious spirit has tainted our public administration.

By a faction I understand a number of citizens, whether amounting to a majority or minority of the whole, who are united and actuated by some common impulse of passion, or of interest, adverse to the rights of other citizens, or to the permanent and aggregate interests of the community.

There are two methods of curing the mischiefs of faction: the one, by removing its causes; the other, by controlling its effects.

There are again two methods of removing the causes of faction: the one, by destroying the liberty which is essential to its existence; the other, by giving to every citizen the same opinions, the same passions, and the same interests.

It could never be more truly said than of the first remedy that it was worse than the disease. Liberty is to faction what air is to fire, an aliment without which it instantly expires. But it could not be a less folly to abolish liberty, which is essential to political life, because it nourishes faction than it would be to wish the annihilation of air, which is essential to animal life, because it imparts to fire its destructive agency.

The second expedient is as impracticable as the first would be unwise. As long as the reason of man continues fallible, and he is at liberty to exercise it, different opinions will be formed. As long as the connection subsists between his reason and his self-love, his opinions and his passions will have a reciprocal influence on each other; and the former will be objects to which the latter will attach themselves. The diversity in the faculties of men, from which the rights of property originate, is not less an insuperable obstacle to a uniformity of interests. The protection of these faculties is the first object of government. From the protection of different and unequal faculties of acquiring property, the possession of different degrees and kinds of property immediately results; and from the influence of these on the sentiments and views of the respective proprietors ensues a division of the society into different interests and parties.

The latent causes of faction are thus sown in the nature of man; and we see them everywhere brought into different degrees of activity, according to the different circumstances of civil society. A zeal for different opinions concerning religion, concerning government, and many other points, as well of speculation as of practice; an attachment to different leaders ambitiously contending for pre-eminence and power; or to persons of other descriptions whose fortunes have been interesting to the human passions, have, in turn, divided mankind into parties, inflamed them with mutual animosity, and rendered them much more disposed to vex and oppress each other than to co-operate for their common good. So strong is this propensity of mankind to fall into mutual animosities that where no substantial occasion presents itself the most frivolous and fanciful distinctions have been sufficient to kindle their unfriendly passions and excite their most violent conflicts. But the most common and durable source of factions has been the various and unequal distribution of property. Those who hold and those who are without property have ever formed distinct interests in society. Those who are creditors, and those who are debtors, fall under a like discrimination. A landed interest, a manufacturing interest, a mercantile interest, a moneyed interest, with many lesser interests, grow up of necessity in civilized nations, and divide them into different classes, actuated by different sentiments and views. The regulation of these various and interfering interests forms the principal task of modern legislation and involves the spirit of party and faction in the necessary and ordinary operations of government.

No man is allowed to be judge in his own cause, because his interest would certainly bias his judgment and, not improbably, corrupt his integrity. With equal, nay with greater reason, a body of men are unfit to be both judges and parties at the same time; yet what are many of the most important acts of legislation but so many judicial determinations, not indeed concerning the rights of single persons, but concerning the rights of large bodies of citizens? And what are the different classes of legislators but advocates and parties to the causes which they determine? Is a law proposed concerning private debts? It is a question to which the creditors are parties on one side and the debtors on the other. Justice ought to hold the balance between them. Yet the parties are, and must be, themselves the judges; and the most numerous party, or in other words, the most powerful faction must be expected to prevail. Shall domestic manufacturers be encouraged, and in what degree, by restrictions on foreign manufacturers? are questions which would be differently decided by the landed and the manufacturing classes, and probably by neither with a sole regard to justice and the public good. The apportionment of taxes on the various descriptions of property is an act which seems to require the most exact impartiality; yet there is, perhaps, no legislative act in which greater opportunity and temptation are given to a predominant party to trample on the rules of justice. Every shilling with which they overburden the inferior number is a shilling saved to their own pockets.

It is in vain to say that enlightened statesmen will be able to adjust these clashing interests and render them all subservient to the public good. Enlightened statesmen will not always be at the helm. Nor, in many cases, can such an adjustment be made at all without taking into view indirect and remote considerations, which will rarely prevail over the immediate interest which one party may find in disregarding the rights of another or the good of the whole.

The inference to which we are brought is that the *causes* of faction cannot be removed and that relief is only to be sought in the means of controlling its *effects*.

If a faction consists of less than a majority, relief is supplied by the republican principle, which enables the majority to defeat its sinister views by regular vote. It may clog the administration, it may convulse the society; but it will be unable to execute and mask its violence under the forms of the Constitution. When a majority is included in a faction, the form of popular government, on the other hand, enables it to sacrifice to its ruling passion or interest both the public good and the rights of other citizens. To secure the public good and private rights against the danger of such a faction, and at the same time to preserve the spirit and the form of popular government, is then the great object to which our inquiries are directed. Let me add that it is the great desideratum by which alone this form of government can be rescued from the opprobrium under which it has so long labored and be recommended to the esteem and adoption of mankind.

By what means is this object attainable? Evidently by one of two only. Either the existence of the same passion or interest in a majority at the same time must be prevented, or the majority, having such coexistent passion or interest, must be rendered, by their number and local situation, unable to concert and carry into effect schemes of oppression. If the impulse and the opportunity be suffered to coincide, we well know that neither moral nor religious motives can be relied on as an adequate control. They are not found to be such on the injustice and violence of individuals, and lose their efficacy in proportion to the number combined together, that is, in proportion as their efficacy becomes needful.

From this view of the subject it may be concluded that a pure democracy, by which I mean a society consisting of a small number of citizens, who assemble and administer the government in person, can admit of no cure for the mischiefs of faction. A common passion or interest will, in almost every case, be felt by a majority of the whole; a communication and concert results from the form of government itself; and there is nothing to check the inducements to sacrifice the weaker party or an obnoxious individual. Hence it is that such democracies have ever been spectacles of turbulence and contention; have ever been found incompatible with personal security or the rights of property; and have in general been as short in their lives as they have been violent in their deaths. Theoretic politicians, who have patronized this species of government, have erroneously supposed that by reducing mankind to a perfect equality in their political rights, they would at the same time be perfectly equalized and assimilated in their possessions, their opinions, and their passions.

A republic, by which I mean a government in which the scheme of representation takes place, opens a different prospect and promises the cure for which we are seeking. Let us examine the points in which it varies from pure democracy, and we shall comprehend both the nature of the cure and the efficacy which it must derive from the Union.

The two great points of difference between a democracy and a republic are: first, the delegation of the government, in the latter, to a small number of citizens elected by the rest; secondly, the greater number of citizens and greater sphere of country over which the latter may be extended.

The effect of the first difference is, on the one hand, to refine and enlarge the public views by passing them through the medium of a chosen body of citizens, whose wisdom may best discern the true interest of their country and whose patriotism and love of justice will be least likely to sacrifice it to temporary or partial considerations. Under such a regulation it may well happen that the public voice, pronounced by the representatives of the people, will be more consonant to the public good than if pronounced by the people themselves, convened for the purpose. On the other hand, the effect may be inverted. Men of factious tempers, of local prejudices, or of sinister designs, may, by intrigue, by corruption, or by other means, first obtain the suffrages, and then betray the interests of the people. The question resulting is, whether small or extensive republics are most favorable to the election of proper guardians of the public weal; and it is clearly decided in favor of the latter by two obvious considerations.

In the first place it is to be remarked that however small the republic may be the representatives must be raised to a certain number in order to guard against the cabals of a few; and that however large it may be they must be limited to a certain number in order to guard against the confusion of a multitude. Hence, the number of representatives in the two cases not being in proportion to that of the constituents, and being proportionally greatest in the small republic, it follows that if the proportion of fit characters be not less in the large than in the small republic, the former will present a greater option, and consequently a greater probability of a fit choice.

In the next place, as each representative will be chosen by a greater number of citizens in the large than in the small republic, it will be more difficult for unworthy candidates to practise with success the vicious arts by which elections are too often carried; and the suffrages of the people being more free, will be more likely to center on men who possess the most attractive merit and the most diffusive and established characters.

It must be confessed that in this, as in most other cases, there is a mean, on both sides of which inconveniencies will be found to lie. By enlarging too much the number of electors, you render the representative too little acquainted with all their local circumstances and lesser interests; as by reducing it too much, you render him unduly attached to these, and too little fit to comprehend and pursue great and national objects. The federal Constitution forms a happy combination in this respect; the great and aggregate interests being referred to the national, the local and particular to the State legislatures.

The other point of difference is the greater number of citizens and extent of territory which may be brought within the compass of republican than of democratic government; and it is this circumstance principally which renders factious combinations less to be dreaded in the former than in the latter. The smaller the society, the fewer probably will be the distinct parties and interests composing it; the fewer the distinct parties and interests, the more frequently will a majority be found of the same party; and the smaller the number of individuals composing a majority, and the smaller the compass within which they are placed, the more easily will they concert and execute their plans of oppression. Extend the sphere and you take in a greater variety of parties and interests; you make it less probable that a majority of the whole will have a common motive to invade the rights of other citizens; or if such a common motive exists, it will be more difficult for all who feel it to discover their own strength and to act in unison with each other. Besides other impediments, it may be remarked that, where there is a consciousness of unjust or dishonorable purposes, communication is always checked by distrust in proportion to the number whose concurrence is necessary.

Hence, it clearly appears that the same advantage which a republic has over a democracy in controlling the effects of faction is enjoyed by a large over a small republic—is enjoyed by the Union over the States composing it. Does this advantage consist in the substitution of representatives whose enlightened views and virtuous sentiments render them superior to local prejudices and to schemes of injustice? It will not be denied that the representation of the Union will be most likely to possess these requisite endowments. Does it consist in the greater security afforded by a greater variety of parties, against the event of any one party being able to outnumber and oppress the rest? In an equal degree does the increased variety of parties comprised within the Union increase this security? Does it, in fine, consist in the greater obstacles opposed to the concert and accomplishment of the secret wishes of an unjust and interested majority? Here again the extent of the Union gives it the most palpable advantage.

The influence of factious leaders may kindle a flame within their particular States but will be unable to spread a general conflagration through the other

States. A religious sect may degenerate into a political faction in a part of the Confederacy; but the variety of sects dispersed over the entire face of it must secure the national councils against any danger from that source. A rage for paper money, for an abolition of debts, for an equal division of property, or for any other improper or wicked project, will be less apt to pervade the whole body of the Union than a particular member of it, in the same proportion as such a malady is more likely to taint a particular county or district than an entire State.

In the extent and proper structure of the Union, therefore, we behold a republican remedy for the diseases most incident to republican government. And according to the degree of pleasure and pride we feel in being republicans ought to be our zeal in cherishing the spirit and supporting the character of federalist.

PUBLIUS

NO. 51: MADISON

To what expedient, then, shall we finally resort, for maintaining in practice the necessary partition of power among the several departments as laid down in the Constitution? The only answer that can be given is that as all these exterior provisions are found to be inadequate the defect must be supplied, by so contriving the interior structure of the government as that its several constituent parts may, by their mutual relations, be the means of keeping each other in their proper places. Without presuming to undertake a full development of this important idea I will hazard a few general observations which may perhaps place it in a clearer light, and enable us to form a more correct judgment of the principles and structure of the government planned by the convention.

In order to lay a due foundation for that separate and distinct exercise of the different powers of government, which to a certain extent is admitted on all hands to be essential to the preservation of liberty, it is evident that each department should have a will of its own; and consequently should be so constituted that the members of each should have as little agency as possible in the appointment of the members of the others. Were this principle rigorously adhered to, it would require that all the appointments for the supreme executive, legislative, and judiciary magistracies should be drawn from the same fountain of authority, the people, through channels having no communication whatever with one another. Perhaps such a plan of constructing the several departments would be less difficult in practice than it may in contemplation appear. Some difficulties, however, and some additional expense would attend the execution of it. Some deviations, therefore, from the principle must be admitted. In the constitution of the judiciary department in particular, it might be inexpedient to insist rigorously on the principle: first, because peculiar qualifications being essential in the members, the primary consideration ought to be to select that mode of choice which best secures these qualifications; second, because the permanent tenure by which the appointments are held in that department must soon destroy all sense of dependence on the authority conferring them.

It is equally evident that the members of each department should be as little dependent as possible on those of the others for the emoluments annexed to their offices. Were the executive magistrate, or the judges, not independent of the legislature in this particular, their independence in every other would be merely nominal.

But the great security against a gradual concentration of the several powers in the same department consists in giving to those who administer each department the necessary constitutional means and personal motives to resist encroachments of the others. The provision for defense must in this, as in all other cases, be made commensurate to the danger of attack. Ambition must be made to counteract ambition. The interest of the man must be connected with the constitutional rights of the place. It may be a reflection on human nature that such devices should be necessary to control the abuses of government. But what is government itself but the greatest of all reflections on human nature? If men were angels, no government would be necessary. If angels were to govern men, neither external nor internal controls on government would be necessary. In framing a government which is to be administered by men over men, the great difficulty lies in this: you must first enable the government to control the governed; and in the next place oblige it to control itself. A dependence on the people is, no doubt, the primary control on the government; but experience has taught mankind the necessity of auxiliary precautions.

This policy of supplying, by opposite and rival interests, the defect of better motives, might be traced through the whole system of human affairs, private as well as public. We see it particularly displayed in all the subordinate distributions of power, where the constant aim is to divide and arrange the several offices in such a manner as that each may be a check on the other—that the private interest of every individual may be a sentinel over the public rights. These inventions of prudence cannot be less requisite in the distribution of the supreme powers of the State.

But it is not possible to give to each department an equal power of self-defense. In republican government, the legislative authority necessarily predominates. The remedy for this inconveniency is to divide the legislature into different branches; and to render them, by different modes of election and different principles of action, as little connected with each other as the nature of their common functions and their common dependence on the society will admit. It may even be necessary to guard against dangerous encroachments by still further precautions. As the weight of the legislative authority requires that it should be thus divided, the weakness of the executive may require, on the other hand, that it should be fortified. An absolute negative on the legislature appears, at first view, to be the natural defense with which the executive magistrate should be armed. But perhaps it would be neither altogether safe nor alone sufficient. On ordinary occasions it might not be exerted with the requisite firmness, and on extraordinary occasions it might be perfidiously abused. May not this defect of an absolute negative be supplied by some qualified connection between this weaker branch of the stronger department, by which the latter may be led to support the constitutional rights of the former, without being too much detached from the rights of its own department?

If the principles on which these observations are founded be just, as I persuade myself they are, and they be applied as a criterion to the several State constitutions, and to the federal Constitution, it will be found that if the latter does not perfectly correspond with them, the former are infinitely less able to bear such a test.

There are, moreover, two considerations particularly applicable to the federal system of America, which place that system in a very interesting point of view.

First. In a single republic, all the power surrendered by the people is submitted to the administration of a single government; and the usurpations are guarded against by a division of the government into distinct and separate departments. In the compound republic of America, the power surrendered by the people is first divided between two distinct governments, and then the portion allotted to each subdivided among distinct and separate departments. Hence a double security arises to the rights of the people. The different governments will control each other, at the same time that each will be controlled by itself.

Second. It is of great importance in a republic not only to guard the society against the oppression of its rulers, but to guard one part of the society against the injustice of the other part. Different interests necessarily exist in different classes of citizens. If a majority be united by a common interest, the rights of the minority will be insecure. There are but two methods of providing against this evil: the one by creating a will in the community independent of the majority—that is, of the society itself; the other, by comprehending in the society so many separate descriptions of citizens as will render an unjust combination of a majority of the whole very improbable, if not impracticable. The first method prevails in all governments possessing an hereditary or self-appointed authority. This, at best, is but a precarious security; because a power independent of the society may as well espouse the unjust views of the major as the rightful interests of the minor party, and may possibly be turned against both parties. The second method will be exemplified in the federal republic of the United States. Whilst all authority in it will be derived from and dependent on the society, the society itself will be broken into so many parts, interests and classes of citizens, that the rights of individuals, or of the minority, will be in little danger from interested combinations of the majority. In a free government the security for civil rights must be the same as that for religious rights. It consists in the one case in the multiplicity of interests, and in the other in the multiplicity of sects. The degree of security in both cases will depend on the number of interests and sects; and this may be presumed to depend on the extent of country and number of people comprehended under the same government. This view of the subject must particularly recommend a proper federal system to all the sincere and considerate friends of republican government, since it shows that in exact proportion as the territory of the Union may be formed into more circumscribed Confederacies, or States, oppressive combinations of a majority will be facilitated; the best security, under the republican forms, for the rights of every class of citizen, will be diminished; and consequently the stability and independence of some member of the government, the only other security, must be proportionally increased. Justice is the end of government. It is the end of civil society. It ever has been and ever will be pursued until it be obtained, or until liberty be lost in the pursuit. In a society under the forms of which the stronger faction can readily unite and oppress the weaker, anarchy may as truly be said to reign as in a state of nature, where the weaker individual is not secured against the violence of the stronger; and as, in the latter state, even the stronger individuals are prompted, by the uncertainty of their condition, to submit to a government which may protect the weak as well as themselves; so, in the former state, will the more powerful factions or parties be gradually induced, by a like motive, to wish for a government which will protect all parties, the weaker as well as the more powerful. It can be little doubted that if the State of Rhode Island was separated from the Confederacy and left to itself, the insecurity of rights under the popular form of government within such narrow limits would be displayed by such reiterated oppressions of factious majorities that some power altogether independent of the people would soon be called for by the voice of the very factions whose misrule had proved the necessity of it. In the extended republic of the United States, and among the great variety of interests, parties, and sects which it embraces, a coalition of a majority of the whole society could seldom take place on any other principles than those of justice and the general good; whilst there being thus less danger to a minor from the will of a major party, there must be less pretext, also, to provide for the security of the former, by introducing into the government a will not dependent on the latter, or, in other words, a will independent of the society itself. It is no less certain than it is important, notwithstanding the contrary opinions which have been entertained, that the larger the society, provided it lie within a practicable sphere, the more duly capable it will be of self-government. And happily for the *republican cause,* the practicable sphere may be carried to a very great extent by a judicious modification and mixture of the *federal principle.*

PUBLIUS

Glossary

administrative adjudication The application of rules and precedents to specific cases to settle disputes with regulated parties

administrative legislation Rules made by regulatory agencies and commissions

adverse selection The problem of incomplete information—of choosing alternatives without fully knowing the details of available options

affirmative action A policy or program designed to redress historic injustices committed against specific groups by making special efforts to provide members of these groups with access to educational and employment opportunities

after-the-fact authority The authority to follow up on the fate of a proposal once it has been approved by the full chamber

agency loss The difference between what a principal would like an agent to do and the agent's performance

agency representation The type of representation according to which representatives are held accountable to their constituents if they fail to represent them properly—that is, constituents have the power to hire and fire their representatives

agenda power The control over what a group will consider for discussion

agenda-setting effect The power to bring attention to particular issues and problems

amicus curiae "Friend of the court," an individual or group that is not party to a lawsuit but has an interest in securing the outcome

amnesty A pardon extended to a group of persons

appellate jurisdiction The class of cases provided in the Constitution and by legislation that may be appealed to a higher court from a lower court

Articles of Confederation and Perpetual Union America's first written constitution; adopted by the Continental Congress in 1777, they were the formal basis for America's national government until 1789, when they were superseded by the Constitution

Australian ballot An electoral format that presents the names of all the candidates for any given office on the same ballot; introduced at the end of the eighteenth century, it replaced the partisan ballot and facilitated split-ticket voting

authoritarian government A system of rule in which the government recognizes no formal limits but may nevertheless be restrained by the power of other social institutions

autocracy A form of government in which a single individual rules

bicameral legislature A legislative assembly composed of two chambers, or houses

bicameralism The division of a legislative assembly into two chambers, or houses

Bill of Rights The first 10 amendments to the U.S. Constitution, adopted in 1791; it ensures certain rights and liberties to the people

block grants Federal funds given to state governments to pay for goods, services, or programs, with relatively few restrictions on how the funds may be spent

brief A written document in which an attorney explains—using case precedents—why the Court should rule in favor of his or her client

bureaucracy The complex structure of offices, tasks, rules, and principles of organization that all large-scale institutions use to coordinate the work of their personnel

bureaucratic drift The oft-observed phenomenon of bureaucratic implementation that produces policy more to the liking of the bureaucracy than faithful to the original intention of the legislation that created it, but without triggering a political reaction from elected officials

Cabinet The secretaries, or chief administrators, of the major departments of the federal government. Cabinet secretaries are appointed by the president with the consent of the Senate

casework An effort by members of Congress to gain the trust and support of constituents by providing personal services; one important type of casework consists of helping constituents obtain favorable treatment from the federal bureaucracy

categorical grants-in-aid Funds given by Congress to states and localities that are earmarked by law for specific categories, such as education or crime prevention

checks and balances The mechanisms through which each branch of government is able to participate in and influence the activities of the other branches

chief justice The justice on the Supreme Court who presides over the Court's public sessions

civil law The branch of law that deals with disputes that do not involve criminal penalties

civil liberties The protections of citizens from improper governmental action

civil rights The legal or moral claims that citizens are entitled to make on the government

class-action suit A procedural device that permits a large number of people with common interests to join together under a representative party to bring or defend a lawsuit.

clear and present danger The criterion formerly used to determine whether speech is protected or unprotected, based on its capacity to present a clear and present danger to society

clientele agency A department or bureau of government whose mission is to promote, serve, or represent a particular interest

closed primary A primary election in which only those voters who registered with the party a specified period before the primary election day can participate

closed rule The provision by the House Rules Committee that prohibits the introduction of amendments during debate

cloture A procedure allowing a supermajority of the members of a legislative body to set a time limit on debate over a given bill

coalitional drift The prospect that enacted policy will change in the future because the composition of the enacting coalition is temporary and provisional

collective action The pooling of resources and the coordination of effort and activity by a group of people (often a large one) to achieve common goals

comity clause Article IV, Section 2 of the Constitution, which prohibits states from enacting laws that treat the citizens of other states in a discriminatory manner

commander in chief The power of the president as commander of the national military and the state national guard units (when called into service)

commerce clause The clause found in Article I, Section 8, of the Constitution that delegates to Congress the power "to regulate Commerce with foreign Nations, and among the several States, and with the Indian Tribes." This clause was interpreted by the Supreme Court to favor national power over the economy

concurrence An opinion agreeing with the decision of the majority in a Supreme Court case but not with the rationale provided in the majority opinion

concurrent powers The authority possessed by *both* state and national governments, such as the power to levy taxes

conference committee A joint committee created to work out a compromise for House and Senate versions of a piece of legislation

congressional caucus An association of members of Congress based on party, interest, or social characteristics such as gender or race

conservative Today this term refers to those who generally support the social and economic status quo and believe that a large and powerful government poses a threat to citizens' freedoms

constituency The district making up the area from which an official is elected

constitutional government A system of rule—a constitution—that specifies formal and effective limits on the powers of the government

cooperative federalism A type of federalism existing since the New Deal era, in which grants-in-aid have been used strategically to encourage states and localities to pursue nationally defined goals; also known as intergovernmental cooperation

court of appeals (or appellate court) A court that hears the appeals of trial-court decisions

criminal law The branch of law that regulates the conduct of individuals, defines crimes, and specifies punishment for proscribed conduct

de facto segregation Racial segregation that is not a direct result of law or government policy but is, instead, a reflection of residential patterns, income distributions, or other social factors

de jure segregation Racial segregation that is a direct result of law or official policy

decisiveness rules A specification of when a vote may be taken, the sequence in which votes on amendments occur, and how many supporters determine whether a motion passes or fails

delegate A representative who votes according to the preferences of his or her constituency

delegated powers Constitutional powers assigned to one branch of the government but exercised by another branch with the express permission of the first

delegation The transmission of authority to some other official or body for the latter's use (though often with the right of review and revision)

democracy A system of rule that permits citizens to play a significant part in the governmental process, usually through the selection of key public officials

deregulation The policy of reducing or eliminating regulatory restraints on the conduct of individuals or private institutions

devolution The policy of removing a program from one level of government by deregulating it or passing it down to a lower level, such as from the national government to the state and local governments

dissenting opinion A decision written by a justice who voted with the minority opinion in a particular case in which the justice fully explains the reasoning behind his or her opinion

distributive tendency The tendency of Congress to spread the benefits of a policy over a wide range of members' districts

divided government The condition in American government in which the presidency is controlled by one party while the opposing party controls one or both houses of Congress

double jeopardy The Fifth Amendment right providing that a person cannot be tried twice for the same crime

dual federalism The system of government that prevailed in the United States from 1789 to 1937 in which fundamental governmental powers were shared between the federal and state governments, with the states exercising the most important powers

due process Proceeding according to law and with adequate protection for individual rights

Duverger's Law Law of politics, formalized by Maurice Duverger, stating that plurality-rule electoral systems will tend to have two political parties

Electoral College The presidential electors from each state who meet in their respective state capitals after the popular election to cast ballots for the president and vice president

eminent domain The right of the government to take private property for public use, with reasonable compensation awarded for the property

equal protection clause The provision of the Fourteenth Amendment guaranteeing citizens "the equal protection of the laws." This clause has been the basis for the civil rights of African Americans, women, and other groups

equal time rule The requirement that broadcasters provide candidates for the same political office an equal opportunity to communicate their messages to the public

establishment clause The First Amendment clause that says, "Congress shall make no law respecting an establishment of religion." Today this phrase is generally interpreted as meaning that a wall of separation exists between church and state

exclusionary rule The requirement that courts exclude evidence obtained in violation of the Fourth Amendment

executive agreement An agreement between the president and another country that has the force of a treaty but does not require the Senate's "advice and consent"

Executive Office of the President (EOP) The permanent agencies that perform defined management tasks for the president; created in 1939, it includes the Office of Management and Budget, the Council of Economic

Advisers, the National Security Council, and other agencies

executive orders A rule or regulation issued by the president that has the effect of legislation

executive privilege The claim that confidential communications between the president and the president's close advisers should not be revealed without the consent of the president

expressed powers The powers that the Constitution explicitly grants to a branch of the federal government

fairness doctrine An FCC requirement that broadcasters that air programs on controversial issues provide time for opposing views

Federal Reserve System A system of 12 Federal Reserve banks that facilitates exchanges of cash, checks, and credit; regulates member banks; and uses monetary policy to fight inflation and deflation

federalism The system of government in which a constitution divides power between a central government and regional governments

fighting words Speech that directly incites damaging conduct

filibuster A tactic used by members of the Senate to prevent action on legislation they oppose by continuously holding the floor and speaking until the majority backs down; once given the floor, senators have unlimited time to speak, and it requires a cloture vote of three-fifths of the Senate to end a filibuster

fiscal policy Policies that regulate the economy through taxing and spending powers

formula grants Grants-in-aid in which a formula is used to determine the amount of federal funds a state or local government will receive

framing The power of the media to influence how events and issues are interpreted

free exercise clause The First Amendment clause that protects a citizen's right to believe and practice whatever religion he or she chooses

free riding Enjoying a benefit while letting others bear the costs of providing it

full faith and credit clause The provision in Article IV, Section 1, of the Constitution requiring that each state normally honors the public acts and judicial decisions that take place in another state

gatekeeping authority The right and power to decide if a change in policy will be considered

gender gap A distinctive pattern of voting behavior reflecting the differences in views between women and men

gerrymandering The apportionment of voters in districts in such a way as to give unfair advantage to one political party

going public The act of launching a media campaign to build popular support

government The institutions and procedures through which a land and its people are ruled

grand jury A jury that determines whether sufficient evidence is available to justify a trial. Grand juries do not rule on the accused's guilt or innocence

grants-in-aid A general term for funds given by Congress to state and local governments

Great Compromise An agreement reached at the Constitutional Convention of 1787 that gave each state an equal number of senators regardless of its population but linked representation in the House of Representatives to population

home rule The power delegated by the state to a local unit of government to manage its own affairs

impeachment The charging of a government official (president or otherwise) with "Treason, Bribery, or other high Crimes and Misdemeanors" and bringing him or her before Congress to determine guilt

implementation The efforts of departments and agencies to the development of rules, regulations, and bureaucratic procedures to translate laws into action

implied powers Powers derived from the necessary and proper clause (Article I, Section 8) of the Constitution; such powers are not specifically expressed but are implied through the expansive interpretation of delegated powers

incumbency Holding the political office for which one is running

inherent powers Powers claimed by a president that are not expressed in the Constitution but are said to stem from the "rights, duties, and obligations of the presidency," claimed mostly during war and national emergencies.

initiative A process by which citizens may petition to place a policy proposal on the ballot for public vote

institutions The rules and procedures that provide incentives for political behavior, thereby shaping politics

instrumental Done with purpose, sometimes with forethought, and even with calculation

interest group An organized group of individuals or organizations that makes policy-related appeals to government

intermediate scrutiny The test used by the Supreme Court in gender discrimination cases, which places the burden of proof partially on the government and partially on the challengers to show that the law in question is constitutional

issue voting An individual's propensity to select candidates or parties based on the extent to which the individual agrees with one candidate more than others on specific issues

judicial activism The judicial philosophy that posits that the Court should see beyond the text of the Constitution or a statute to consider broader societal implications for its decisions

judicial restraint The judicial philosophy whose adherents refuse to go beyond the text of the Constitution in interpreting its meaning

judicial review The power of the courts to determine whether the actions of the president, the Congress, and the state legislatures are or are not consistent with the Constitution. The Supreme Court asserted the power to review federal statutes in *Marbury v. Madison* (1803)

jurisdiction The types of cases over which a court has authority

legislative initiative The president's inherent power to bring a legislative agenda before Congress

legislative supremacy The preeminent position assigned to Congress by the Constitution

***Lemon* test** Rule articulated in *Lemon v. Kurtzman* according to which governmental action with respect to religion is permissible if it is secular in purpose, does not lead to "excessive entanglement" with religion, and neither promotes nor inhibits the practice of religion. The *Lemon* test is generally used in relation to government aid to religious schools.

libel A written statement made in "reckless disregard of the truth" and considered damaging to a victim because it is "malicious, scandalous, and defamatory"

liberal A liberal today generally supports political and social reform; government intervention in the economy; the expansion of federal social services; more vigorous efforts on behalf of the poor, minorities, and women; and greater concern for consumers and the environment

line-item veto The power of the executive to veto specific provisions (lines) of a bill passed by the legislature

lobbying An attempt by a group to influence the policy process through persuasion of government officials

logrolling A legislative practice wherein reciprocal agreements are made between legislators, usually in voting for or against a bill; in contrast to bargaining, logrolling unites parties that have nothing in common but their desire to exchange support

majority leader The elected leader of the party holding a majority of the seats in the House of Representatives or the Senate. In the House, the majority leader is subordinate in the party hierarchy to the Speaker

majority party The party that holds the majority of legislative seats in either the House or the Senate

majority rule A type of electoral system in which, to win an office seat, a candidate must receive a majority (50 percent plus one) of all the votes cast in the relevant district

measurement error The failure to identify the true distribution of opinion within a population because of errors such as ambiguous or poorly worded questions

median-voter theorem A proposition predicting that when policy options can be arrayed along a single dimension, majority rule will pick the policy most preferred by the voter whose ideal policy is to the left of half of the voters and to the right of exactly half of the voters. (See Chapter 6 for further discussion.)

minority leader The elected leader of the party holding less than a majority of the seats in the House or Senate

Miranda rule The convention derived from the Supreme Court's 1966 ruling in the case of *Miranda v. Arizona* whereby persons under arrest must be informed of their legal rights, including their right to counsel, before undergoing police interrogation

monetary policy Regulation of the economy through manipulation of the supply of money, the price of money (interest rates), and the availability of credit

money bill A bill concerned solely with taxation or government spending

mootness A criterion used by courts to avoid hearing cases that no longer require resolution

moral hazard The problem of not knowing all aspects of the actions taken by an agent (nominally on behalf of the principal but potentially at the principal's expense)

National Security Council (NSC) A presidential foreign policy advisory council composed of the president; the vice president; the secretaries of state, defense, and treasury; the attorney general; and other officials invited by the president

necessary and proper clause Article I, Section 8, of the Constitution, which enumerates the powers of Congress and provides Congress with the authority to make all laws "necessary and proper" to carry them out; also referred to as the elastic clause

nomination The process by which political parties select their candidates for election to public office

oligarchy A form of government in which a small group of landowners, military officers, or wealthy merchants controls most of the governing decisions

open primary A primary election in which voters can choose on the primary election day itself which party's primary to vote in

open rule The provision by the House Rules Committee that permits floor debate and the addition of amendments to a bill

opinion The written explanation of the Supreme Court's decision in a particular case

oral argument The stage in Supreme Court proceedings in which attorneys for both sides appear before the Court to present their positions and answer questions posed by the justices

original jurisdiction The class of cases provided in the Constitution (Article III) that may be taken directly to a federal court

oversight The effort by Congress, through hearings, investigations, and other techniques, to exercise control over the activities of executive agencies

pardon Forgiveness of a crime and cancellation of relevant penalty

party activist A partisan who contributes time and energy beyond voting to support a party and its candidates

party caucus, or party conference A normally closed meeting of a political or legislative group to select candidates or leaders, plan strategy, or make decisions regarding legislative matters

party identification An individual's attachment to a particular political party, which might be based on issues, ideology, past experience, or upbringing

party machine In the late nineteenth and early twentieth centuries, the local party organization that controlled local politics through patronage and the nomination process

party vote A roll-call vote in the House or Senate in which at least 50 percent of the members of one party take a particular position and are opposed by at least 50 percent of the members of the other party. Party votes are less common today than they were in the nineteenth century

path dependency The idea that certain possibilities are made more or less likely because of earlier decisions— because of the historical path taken

patronage The opportunities available to legislators to provide direct services and benefits to their constituents, especially making partisan appointments to offices and conferring grants, licenses, or special favors to supporters

pluralism A condition or system in which many groups, interests, or ideas co-exist in a nation and share political power

plurality rule A type of electoral system in which victory goes to the individual who gets the most votes in an election, but not necessarily a majority of the votes cast

pocket veto A veto that is effected when Congress adjourns during the time a president has to approve a bill and the president takes no action on it

police power The power reserved to the government to regulate the health, safety, and morals of its citizens

political action committee (PAC) A private group that raises and distributes funds for use in election campaigns

political caucus A normally closed meeting of a political or legislative group to select candidates, plan strategy, or make decisions regarding legislative matters

political party An organized group that attempts to influence government by electing its members to office

politics Conflict, struggle, cooperation, and collaboration over the leadership, structure, and policies of government—over who governs and who has power

pork-barrel legislation Legislative appropriations that legislators use to provide government funds for projects benefitting their home district or state

precedents Prior cases whose principles are used by judges as the bases for their decisions in present cases

priming A process of preparing the public to take a particular view of an event or a political actor

principal-agent relationship The relationship between someone with authority (the principal) and someone to whom he or she delegates the authority (the agent). This relationship may be affected by the fact that each party is motivated by self-interest, yet their interests may not align

prior restraint An effort by a government agency to block the publication of material it deems libelous or harmful in some other way:

censorship. In the United States, the courts forbid prior restraint except under the most extraordinary circumstances

privatization The act of moving all or part of a program from the public sector to the private sector

probability sampling A method used by pollsters to select a representative sample in which every individual in the population has an equal probability of being selected as a respondent

project grants Grant programs in which state and local governments submit proposals to federal agencies and for which funding is provided on a competitive basis

proportional representation (PR) A multiple-member district system that awards seats to political parties in proportion to the percentage of the vote each party won

proposal power The capacity to bring a proposal before the full legislature

prospective voting Voting based on the imagined future performance of a candidate

public good A benefit that, first, may be enjoyed by anyone if it is provided and, second, may not be denied to anyone once it has been provided

public law Cases involving the action of public agencies or officials

public opinion Citizens' attitudes about political issues, leaders, institutions, and events

public-opinion poll A scientific instrument for measuring public opinion

random digit dialing A poll in which respondents are selected at random from a list of 10-digit telephone numbers, with every effort made to avoid bias in the construction of the sample

recall The removal of a public official by popular vote

referendum A measure that is decided by the vote of the electorate for approval or rejection

regulatory agency A department, bureau, or independent agency whose primary mission is to ensure that individuals and organizations comply with the statutes under its jurisdiction

regulatory review The OMB function of reviewing all agency regulations and other rule making before they become official policy

reprieve Cancellation or postponement of a punishment

reserved powers Powers, derived from the Tenth Amendment to the Constitution, that are not specifically delegated to the national government or denied to the states; these powers are reserved to the states

retrospective voting Voting based on the past performance of a candidate

right of rebuttal An FCC regulation giving individuals the right to have the opportunity to respond to personal attacks made on a radio or TV broadcast

right to privacy The right to be left alone, which has been interpreted by the Supreme Court to entail individual access to birth control and abortions

ripeness A criterion used by courts to avoid hearing cases that depend on hypothetical future events

roll-call votes Votes in which each legislator's yes or no vote is recorded

rule making A quasi-legislative administrative process that produces regulations by government agencies

rule of four The rule that *certiorari* will be granted only if four justices vote in favor of the petition

sample A small group selected by researchers to represent the most important characteristics of an entire population

sampling error A polling error that arises on account of the small size of the sample

selection bias A polling error in which the sample is not representative of the population being studied, so that some opinions are over- or underrepresented

selective benefits Benefits that do not go to everyone but, rather, are distributed selectively—to only those who contribute to the group enterprise

senatorial courtesy The practice whereby the president, before formally nominating a person for a federal district judgeship, finds out whether the senators from the candidate's state support the nomination

seniority The priority or status ranking given to an individual on the basis of length of continuous service on a congressional committee

"separate but equal" rule The doctrine that public accommodations could be segregated by race but still be equal

separation of powers The division of governmental power among several institutions that must cooperate in decision making

signing statement An announcement made by the president when a bill is signed into law

single-member district An electoral district that elects only one representative—the typical method of representation in the United States

slander An oral statement made in "reckless disregard of the truth" and considered damaging to a victim because it is "malicious, scandalous, and defamatory"

socialization A process through which individuals assimilate community preferences and norms through social interactions

sovereignty Independent political authority. A government holding such authority is a sovereign

spatial issue An issue for which a range of possible options or policies can be ordered, say, from liberal to conservative or from most expensive to least expensive

Speaker of the House The chief presiding officer of the House of Representatives. The Speaker is elected at the beginning of every Congress on a straight party vote. He or she is the most important party and House leader

speech plus Speech accompanied by activities such as sit-ins, picketing, and demonstrations. Protection of this form of speech under the First Amendment is conditional, and restrictions imposed by state or local authorities are acceptable if properly balanced by considerations of public order

staff agencies The agencies responsible for providing Congress with independent expertise, administration, and oversight capability

standing committee A permanent legislative committee that considers legislation within its designated subject area; the basic unit of deliberation in the House and Senate

standing The right of an individual or an organization to initiate a court case

stare decisis Literally, "let the decision stand." The doctrine whereby a previous decision by a court applies as a precedent in similar cases until that decision is overruled

state sovereign immunity A legal doctrine holding that states cannot be sued for violating an act of Congress

states' rights The principle that states should oppose increases in the authority of the national government; this view was most popular before the Civil War

strict scrutiny The most stringent standard of judicial review of a government's actions in which the government must show that the law serves a "compelling state interest"

supremacy clause A clause of Article VI of the Constitution that states that all laws passed by the national government and all treaties are the supreme laws of the land and superior to all laws adopted by any state or any subdivision

supreme court The highest court in a particular state or in the United States. This court primarily serves an appellate function

third party A party that organizes to compete against the two major American political parties

Three-Fifths Compromise An agreement reached at the Constitutional Convention of 1787 stipulating that for the purposes of the apportionment of congressional seats, only three-fifths of slaves would be counted

totalitarian government A system of rule in which the government recognizes no formal limits on its power and seeks to absorb or eliminate other social institutions that might challenge it

tragedy of the commons The idea that a common-access facility, owned by no one because it is available to everyone, will be overused

transaction costs The cost of clarifying each aspect of a principal-agent relationship and monitoring it to make sure arrangements are complied with

trial court The first court to hear a criminal or civil case

trustee A representative who votes based on what he or she thinks is best for his or her constituency

tyranny Oppressive government that employs the cruel and unjust use of power and authority

unfunded mandates National standards or programs imposed on state and local governments by the federal government without accompanying funding or reimbursement

valence issue An issue or aspect of a choice for which all voters prefer a higher value, in contrast to a spatial issue—for example, voters prefer their politicians to be honest, and honesty is a valence issue

veto power The ability to defeat something even if it has made it on to the agenda of an institution

veto The president's constitutional power to turn down acts of Congress within 10 days of their passage while Congress is in session; a presidential veto may be overridden by a two-thirds vote of each house of Congress

War Powers Resolution A 1973 resolution of Congress declaring that the president can send troops into action abroad only by authorization of Congress or if U.S. troops are already under attack or seriously threatened. For the most part, presidents have ignored the resolution

whip system A party communications network in each house of Congress by which whips poll the membership to learn their intentions on specific legislative issues and convey to members the wishes and plans of the leaders

White House staff The analysts and advisers to the president, often given the title "special assistant"

writ of *certiorari* A formal request by an appellant to have the Supreme Court review a decision of a lower court; *certiorari* is from a Latin word meaning "to make more certain"

writ of *habeas corpus* A court order demanding that an individual in custody be brought into court and shown the cause for detention; *habeas corpus* is guaranteed by the Constitution and can be suspended only in cases of rebellion or invasion

Credits

Index

American Indians. *See* Native Americans

American Medical Association (AMA), 542, *557*

American National Election Studies (ANES), 25, *294,* 294–95, 457

American Party, 524–25

American Recovery and Reinvestment Act (2009), *258–59,* 259–60, 562

American Revolution, 36–37, 69
political backdrop of, 31–36

Americans with Disabilities Act (ADA; 1990), 87, 174

American Values Survey (Pew Center), 391–92

American Voter, The (Campbell, et al.), 392

America's Community Bankers, 542

Ameron, Inc. v. U.S. Army Corps of Engineers, 283n68

amicus curiae, 356, 357–58, 370, 563

amnesty, 246

A&M Records v. Napster, 591

Amtrak, 299

ANES (American National Election Studies), 25, *294,* 294–95, 457

Annapolis Convention, 39, 74

Ansolabehere, Stephen, 476–77

Antifederalists, 32, 57–62, *58,* 534
backers of, 57–58

Bill of Rights demanded by, 61, 77, 104
governmental power and, 61–62, 374
stance of, 57, 69

Antitrust Division of Justice Department, 302

antiwar movement, 547

appellate courts, 328, 333
caseload, 336–37
districts, 335
federal, 337, 339
finality of decisions, 339
geographic boundaries of, *335*
lawmaking and, 350–51

appellate jurisdiction, 334–35

Apple Corporation, 132

appointments, Congress's control over, 51, 56, 93, 183, 190n7, 221, 234–35, 265, 340–43

apportionment, 351, 372, 444

Apportionment Act (1842), 443–44

Apportionment Act (1967), 444

appropriations, Congress's control over, 56, 222–23, 314–15

appropriations bills, 193, 250–51, 252–53

Arizona, 92, 348

Arizona et al. v. Inter-Tribal Council of Arizona, Inc., 92

Arizona et al. v. United States, 348

Arizona State Legislature v. Arizona Independent Redistricting Commission, 92, *98*

Arizona v. United States, 92

Arkansas, 161, 245

ARPAnet, 592

Articles of Confederation and Perpetual Union, 37–40, 74, 444
adoption of, 37–38
amendment provisions, 55
Constitution vs., 55, 56–57, 69
flaws of, 38–39, 40, 41, 42, 47, 48, 68, 69, 243

artisans
in colonial America, 32, 33–35
post-independence, 39, 68

Asbestos Hazard Emergency Act (1986), 87

Asian Americans
civil rights of, 172–73
party identity of, 510
proposed restrictions on, 173

Asian Law Caucus, 173

Assange, Julian, 601

assembly, freedom of. *See* freedom of assembly

Associated Press (AP), 585, 588, 594, 600

association
privacy in, 112, 139
right to, 148

Astroturf lobbying, 566

atheists, 118, 512

Atkins v. Virginia, 138

Atlantic Monthly, 394

at-large elections, 443–44

AT&T Inc., *557*

attitudes, 377–78, 384, 387–88, 389, 402–4, 406–7

Australia, voting in, 433

Australian ballot, 429, 441–42, 526

authoritarian governments, 6, 72–73

poll taxes, 150, 152, 153
Pope, Jeremy, 385, 392
Populist movement, 496
Populist Party, 527, 534, 535
pork-barrel legislation, 19, 74, 193, 224, 237, 303
pornography, 123–25
Port Authority of New York and New Jersey, 79
Posadas de Puerto Rico Associates v. Tourism Company of Puerto Rico, 127
Postal Service, U.S., 305
poverty, advocacy organizations and, 166–67
poverty programs, 87
Powell, Colin, 268
Powell, Lewis, 178
precedents, in court rulings, 102–3, 330, 332, 371, 372
precincts, 518
preclearance procedure, 154
preferences, 379–80, 386–90, 488
preference stability, 400–403
preferred position, 119
presentment clause, 285
presidency, 240–88
    of 1800–1933, 261–62
    action on bills, 218, 220
    administration as power source, 270–71, 277–84
    agencies under, 245, *266,* 277, 278–79
    age restrictions, 148, 242, 498
    amnesties and, 246
    appointments by, 277, 278–79, 310, 366
    approval ratings, 253, 275–76, *276*

budget and, 182, 269–70, 271
Cabinet and, 265, *266, 267*
as commander in chief, 245, 280
Congress and, 10–11, 50, 56, 183–84, 204
congressional powers given to, 95–96, 241, 243, 253, 255–56, 264, 348–49
in Constitution, 51, 242–61
contemporary bases of power, 270–77
delegated powers, 243, 253, 255–56, 264, 348–49
as democratic institution, 287–88
diplomatic power, 246
electoral college and, 44, *44–45,* 47, 48, 56, 93, *432,* 442–43, 445
emergency power, 285–86
executive agreements, 287
Executive Office, *266,* 267–68, 274, 284, *316–17*
executive orders, 244, 260–61, 280–82, 284, 285
executive power, 247–48
executive privilege and, 96, 248, 287, 349
expressed powers of, 243, 244–53
formal resources of power by, 265–70
indirect election, 242–43
inherent powers, 243, 256–61
institutional, 2016, *266*
judicial power, 246

judicial review of power, 349–50
legislative initiative, 257–61, 263, 269–70
legislative power, 248–51
legislative success rate, 1953–2014, 271–73
limits of power, 285
lobbying of, 561–62
as manager-in-chief, 313–14
military and domestic defense powers, 245–46
myths about, 285–87
national emergencies and, 285–86, 314
national security directives, 287
New Deal and, 262–64
nominations by, 243, 247, *247,* 273
pardons and, 243, 246
partisanship and, 272–73, 286–87
party discipline and, 233
party system and, 492, 495, 496
policy and, 269–70
political party as power source, 270, 271–73, 283–84, 506
popularity struggles of, 240
popular mobilization as power source, 270, 273–74, 283–84, 288
post–New Deal power gain by, 264–65, 348
powers of, 242
press relations, 274, 412
principal-agent relationships with bureaucracy, 309–10
public appearances, *275*
public interest and, 286–87